Praise for
The Words That Made Us

"Some see history as a series of separate events. Akhil Amar knows, and demonstrates brilliantly, that history overlaps itself, that at each stage we must find (or invent) a usable past from which to shove ourselves into the featureless future. How does one present such a complex back-and-forth use of the past to escape the past? This book shows how."

—GARRY WILLS, Pulitzer Prize–winning
author of *Lincoln at Gettysburg*

"A page-turning doorstop history of how early American courts and politicians interpreted the Constitution. A Yale professor of law and political science, Amar—who points out that most historians lack training in law and most lawyers are not knowledgeable enough about history—delivers a fascinating, often jolting interpretation. . . . Brilliant insights into America's founding document."

—*Kirkus* (starred review)

THE WORDS
THAT MADE US

America's Constitutional Conversation, 1760–1840

Akhil Reed Amar

BASIC BOOKS
New York

Basic Books
Hachette Book Group
1290 Avenue of the Americas, New York, NY 10104
www.basicbooks.com

Printed in the United States of America
First Edition: May 2021

Published by Basic Books, an imprint of Perseus Books, LLC, a subsidiary of Hachette Book Group, Inc. The Basic Books name and logo is a trademark of the Hachette Book Group.

The Hachette Speakers Bureau provides a wide range of authors for speaking events. To find out more, go to www.hachettespeakersbureau.com or call (866) 376-6591.

The publisher is not responsible for websites (or their content) that are not owned by the publisher.

Library of Congress Cataloging-in-Publication Data
Names: Amar, Akhil Reed, author.
Title: The words that made us : America's constitutional conversation, 1760–1840 / Akhil Reed Amar.
Description: First edition. | New York : Basic Books, 2021. | Includes bibliographical references and index.
Identifiers: LCCN 2020046037 | ISBN 9780465096350 (hardcover) | ISBN 9780465096367 (epub)
Subjects: LCSH: Constitutional history—United States. | Constitutional law—United States.
Classification: LCC KF4541 .A878 2021 | DDC 342.7302/9—dc23
LC record available at https://lccn.loc.gov/2020046037.

ISBNs: 978-0-465-09635-0 (hardcover), 978-0-465-09636-7 (ebook)

LSC-C

Printing 1, 2021

This book is dedicated to Lin-Manuel Miranda, Vanessa Nadal, Ron Chernow, and Khizr Khan. And of course to Neal Kumar Katyal, who introduced me to each of you. Thank you all, jointly and severally, for helping me and so many others see the true meaning of America.

Contents

Preface

The First Four Score

IN THE REIGN OF GEORGE III, the king's subjects on both sides of the Atlantic began to argue furiously about the nature of government, the structure of empire, the duties of allegiance, and the rights of Englishmen. The heated quarrel eventually came to a boil. Colonial patriots forsook an unworthy ruler, formed new constitutional governments, and forged a fresh legal identity for themselves. The transatlantic Englishmen of 1760 became the Americans of 1776.

But were they Americans first, or should their primary loyalties run to their respective colonies-turned-states? This was the key constitutional question of the next period of American history as the continent's leading statesmen pondered whether to remain states' men. The federal Constitution that won widespread popular approval in 1788 proclaimed its own answer to this question, an answer reinforced yet gentled by an extraordinary series of ratification conversations and concessions that occurred that fateful year.

As the Constitution launched in 1789, urgent new constitutional questions sprang up in rapid succession and indeed continued to spring up over the next half century. North Carolina and Rhode Island initially refused to ratify. How might President George Washington, flanked by House leader James Madison, entice these states to rejoin their sisters? How should Washington, with Treasury Secretary and Acting Secretary of War Alexander Hamilton at his side, respond to a western Pennsylvania tax rebellion in the early 1790s? When France's Louisiana territory became available for purchase in 1803, would President Thomas Jefferson need to persuade his fellow citizens to amend their Constitution, or could he do the deal by treaty and statute? Should America allow slavery to spread into any or all of this vast region stretching from New Orleans to Canada? Where did Indian tribes and nontribal Indians fit into the picture? Women? Free Blacks? What about visitors from abroad and foreign-born American citizens? What role should the Constitution's then weakest branch, a federal judiciary led for more than thirty years by Chief Justice John Marshall, play in these conversations?

In each generation, history's kaleidoscope continued to turn and create new patterns of constitutional discourse. Some issues tumbled into view, others fell out of sight, and still others reemerged in vivid new configurations as public servants and private citizens at all levels of government and society participated in a boisterous and sophisticated conversation about legal and political first principles.

This book tells the story of America's constitutional conversation during its first eighty years—from its birth in 1760 until 1840, just after the last of America's early constitutional conversationalists died and bequeathed the conversation to posterity.

BUT DO WE REALLY NEED yet another American history book—and a long one at that? I think that we do, else I would not have spent much of my life on the tome that you now hold in your hands.

While history books abound, precious few are wide-angled and multigenerational treatments of the American constitutional project. In recent decades, many great American historians have turned away from institutional and political history and toward social history, exploring the daily lives of our common folk more than the deep logic of our common law or the basic features of our constitutional government. Also, many of the best works of history are period pieces that illuminate a decade or two but do not even try to trace the analytic and narrative threads across the generations. If an exceptionally ambitious modern volume does seek to sweep across three-quarters of a century or more, it typically does so not panoramically but with a tight focus on a single issue—say, chattel slavery or western expansion or sex equality or presidential power.

Consider, for example, two of the biggest bones of constitutional contention in American history: whether a state may ever nullify federal law or secede from the union. Many of the best general history books on the Founding fail even to mention these legal issues. As most professional historians periodize the American saga, these are "antebellum era" and "Civil War" topics and thus not central questions for a founding-era historian. Yet many of the right legal answers to the burning issues raised by the South Carolina Nullification Ordinance of 1832 and the secession crisis of 1860–1861 do in fact reside in the relevant legal materials of 1787–1788.

So, too, narrow historical periodization has obscured the true and complete story of Jefferson's and Madison's peculiar views on the issue of a national bank. In 1791 the two men denounced Hamilton's bank plan as unconstitutional, but in 1816 President Madison signed a bank bill into law, and did so without a peep from Jefferson. Most scholars of the 1790s highlight Jefferson's and Madison's 1791 constitutional crusade against Hamilton, but never tell readers that a Supreme Court dominated by Jefferson and Madison appointees unanimously rejected these constitutional claims as nonsensical in 1819. The later date falls outside the closing boundary of most founding-era narratives.

Many of the best history books of late have also shied away from offering anything that might resemble an emphatic authorial opinion on a once contested legal issue. This hesitation may reflect the fact that most historians lack formal training in legal analysis. If asked, many historians today would say they simply seek to understand the past on its own terms. These scholars do not wish to opine on who was legally "right" and who was legally "wrong" in days gone by, or what the "lessons" of the past are for today's law and politics. (The scare quotes around the words *right*, *wrong*, and *lessons* reflect the diffidence of the typical modern historian.)

Lawyers, judges, and lawmakers approach the past differently. Constitutional principles and judicial precedents from long ago carry weight today, even though the world has undoubtedly changed in the interim. In the case now pending, the court must give judgment— and soon—to either the plaintiff or the defendant. The president must either sign or veto—within a few days—the bill that currently sits on his desk. Today's legal decision makers thus crave a usable past to guide them in the here and now.

Yet legal scholars have failed to fill the void left by historians. Some constitutional scholars openly mock those who rely heavily on history, while most other leading lawyers and legal academics simply ignore the appropriate historical materials or offer only superficial accounts.

Meanwhile, America's constitutional conversation continues to chug along in courtrooms, classrooms, newsrooms, family rooms, and everywhere in between. As rich and robust as this discussion is, it would be better if students, scholars, journalists, judges, pundits, politicians, and indeed, citizens more generally had a handy history of the epic American constitutional conversation in its early period. Hence this book, which aims to unite history and law in a wide-angled multigenerational narrative that seeks both to understand the past and to evaluate it using proper historical and legal tools of analysis.

Of course, no single volume could hope to cover every constitutional issue that arose between 1760 and 1840. This book does aim to trace the main thread of America's constitutional conversation and to pay special attention to the nature of the conversation itself. What was the basic structure of the conversation? Who participated, how, where, and why? American newspapers and print shops, key components of the conversational system, loom particularly large in the chapters that follow.

These chapters tell a panoramic story of America itself, a story of how various widely scattered New Worlders first became *Americans* and then continued to debate and refine what being American meant, legally, politically, militarily, diplomatically, economically, socially, ideologically, institutionally, and culturally—what being American meant *constitutionally*. Uniquely in the history of the world, Americans in the late eighteenth century constituted themselves as a people and as a nation in a series of epic and self-conscious acts of democratic self-invention. In 1776, thirteen British North American colonies renounced their common parent and created what would later become the world's mightiest power. But USA 1.0 as constituted by the Declaration of Independence, the Articles of Confederation, and thirteen independent state constitutions failed to work as hoped. Revolutionaries therefore rethought the problem from the ground up, conceiving and enacting an astonishingly ambitious yet terse text, "this Constitution," laying down the "supreme law of the land" for themselves and their "posterity." In the pivotal year of 1787–1788, more common folk were invited to vote on this proposed Constitution, USA 2.0, than had ever been invited to vote on any issue in the history of humankind. Americans high and low participated not just by voting, but by speaking and listening, writing and reading—by *conversing* with each other, pro and con, up and down the continent, in newspapers and elsewhere.

The agreement of "We, the people of the United States," to ordain and establish an audacious document in the late 1780s hardly ended the constitutional conversation, for immediately thereafter the questions became whether and how to amend the new document and how to interpret and implement it. Americans repeatedly asked themselves who should lead this constitutional conversation and what should be the basic rules of conversational and constitutional engagement. The Constitution was a set of words. What did these words mean and how should they be read and made real? Would these words continue to work as the Revolutionaries who drafted and ratified them passed from the scene and gave way to a new generation of conversationalists?

OUR STORY BEGINS IN 1760, when the very phrase, "America's Constitutional Conversation," might have prompted a wag in the tradition of Voltaire to protest that the New World's basic framework was neither American nor constitutional nor conversational. The British Empire existed as a powerful legal, political, military, diplomatic, economic, social, ideological, institutional, and cultural reality. The Province of Massachusetts Bay existed as a formal juridical entity, as did the Colony of Virginia. But *America* did not exist—at least not as an official legal unit. Nor was there much occasion for colonists to converse continentally and constitutionally. Boston and Williamsburg paid far more attention to London than to each other. As yet, London had given New World inhabitants little reason to think deeply about the (unwritten) British Constitution—little reason, in particular, to think about the legal structure of empire and the legal rights and duties of Englishmen on opposite sides of the ocean.

Then, quite suddenly, everything began to change.

PART I
REVOLUTION

one

"SEEDS"

THE NEWS REACHED AMERICA ON a steed that had no legs but promised swiftness.

The merchant ship *Racehorse* landed in Boston on Saturday, December 27, 1760, after forty days on the choppy ocean that both connected and divided Old England and New England. The trader bore incontrovertible tidings from early November British newspapers, copies of which Captain Samuel Partridge immediately distributed to Boston print shops for partial republication. As passengers and crew came ashore, word also spread from mouth to mouth: the old king was dead and a young king now sat on the throne.[1]

The aged George II had passed away two months earlier—on October 25, to be precise. Officials across Great Britain promptly proclaimed the dead monarch's twenty-two-year-old grandson King George III in what seemed to the London papers a smooth transfer of power.

The transition was not seamless in colonial Massachusetts in the winter of 1760–1761. Hairline cracks emerged that would later widen into a gulf between America and Britain as vast as the Atlantic itself.

Some of the same Boston publishers who enjoyed a good working relationship with Samuel Partridge would have harsh things to say about another captain who came to town less than a decade later, Thomas Preston. Almost exactly thirteen years after Partridge's crew dropped anchor, other men would drop other things into Boston Harbor. Britain would respond by sending many more vessels—warships, not traders—into Boston and other American ports. In 1775, war would break out within earshot of the taverns and alehouses where loyal British Americans first toasted young King George III. Only a decade and a half into the reign of a ruler whose accession they hailed when they heard the news, provincials in Massachusetts and twelve other colonies would cut all ties to this man and to the British Empire that he embodied.

PROCLAMATION

The pace of the *Racehorse* and all similar, often slower, transatlantic vessels portended trouble for the empire: How could London project power over distant, populous, and fast-rising American colonies in the decades to come? Three thousand oceanic miles lay between the Old and the New World—miles (and sometimes months) of privation and isolation, with passengers and crewmembers largely cut off from the rest of humanity.

Coastal and land miles on America's eastern edge were different. Travelers could roll along a road or sail along the shore at whatever pace and in whatever size group they preferred—all the while remaining close to good food, clean water, current newspapers, fresh company, and many of the other comforts and conveniences of civilization. By 1760, countless inns, hamlets, villages, and towns, and even several fledgling cities—Boston, Providence, Newport, New Haven, New York, Philadelphia, Baltimore, and Charlestown (now Charleston)—dotted the seaboard and its tributaries. These nodes and conduits formed multiple and overlapping networks of information and refreshment strengthening the thousand-mile stretch that encompassed thirteen distinct British North American colonies, bracketed by New Hampshire and Massachusetts up north and the Carolinas and Georgia down south.[2]

Though separated from their common mother by a wide and lonely ocean, these thirteen bustling colonies thus found themselves interlinked by shorter and less lonely highways, waterways, and information channels. If ever these provinces leagued together against Britain, they would enjoy stronger supply lines and lines of communication, not to mention an enormous advantage in potential boots (and guns) on the ground. One and a quarter million provincials of European descent peopled this New World corridor, alongside some three hundred and fifty thousand Black slaves and free Blacks, combining to form a fast-rising civilization that was already beginning to measure itself against Britain's eight million souls. Boasting astonishing birthrates and robust immigration numbers that had sextupled the population in the preceding six decades, these colonies bade fair to surpass the mother country within a few generations.[3]

Had any British minister or monarch given serious thought to colonial matters in the closing days of 1760, he would have surely appreciated the strategic need to preserve and strengthen, somehow, the slender cords connecting Britain and America. But the telling details of George III's proclamation, meticulously documented in the London papers, suggest that America was at best an afterthought for the young king and his advisers.

The days immediately following the death of George II saw a profusion of pomp, pageantry, power consolidation, and legal formality in Britain. In London and other British cities and market towns, criers quickly proclaimed the old king's grandson "by the Stile & Title of GEORGE the Third, King of Great-Britain, France [*sic*] and Ireland, Defender of the Faith." Attendants medically examined George II's corpse and laid it to rest in an elaborate multitiered coffin covered with a pall of purple velvet and lined with purple silk. An Anglican clergyman preached an official sermon under the superintending eye of the Archbishop of Canterbury. The sword of state was carried to and from the Chapel Royal. Nearly a thousand London merchants offered their new monarch condolences and congratulations, and "all had the honour to kiss his Majesty's hand." George III addressed the House of Peers and, by royal proclamation, prorogued Parliament for several days. *Yet no one thought to issue a timely legal directive to the Province of Massachusetts Bay.*[4]

Official instructions would not reach the New World until mid-January—nearly three months after the old king died—when a twenty-gun British man-o'-war, HMS *Fowey*, arrived in lower Manhattan with documents under seal from the Privy Council directing New York's provincial officials to proclaim the new king.[5] Revealingly, Parliament in its 1707 Succession to the Crown Act had mandated, upon penalty of high treason, that the Privy Council "with all convenient Speed" cause Queen Anne's successor "to be openly and solemnly proclaimed in Great Britain and Ireland," but had said nothing about proclamation in America. Later Parliaments failed to fill this gap, even as America's wealth and population soared.[6]

This imperial laxness threw the Massachusetts government into a quandary. Thanks to the *Racehorse* and Partridge's distribution of London journals, Boston newspapers would soon inform their readers about all the British ceremonies. Even so, was it proper for mere provincial officials—acting on their own and without explicit imperial authorization—to proclaim a new king? The English-born royally appointed Massachusetts governor, Francis Bernard, put the question to his locally elected council, who advised him to act promptly. As Lieutenant Governor Thomas Hutchinson later recalled the prevailing sentiment, "it was probable that many weeks would pass before orders arrived, and it would have a strange appearance, if all writs, processes, and publick acts of every kind, continued, all that time, in the name of a prince known to be in his grave." Bernard did as his council urged. But Hutchinson—also a royal appointee, albeit Boston-born—had doubts: "There is great room, notwithstanding, to question the propriety of" Bernard's improvisation.[7]

Here—in microcosm, in the tiniest of legal technicalities—lay a tension that would later grow to world-changing proportions. If Britain could not be bothered to pay close attention to colonial affairs, then colonists would have to manage on their own. Once independent action became a habit, where would it end? What would happen if Britain ever tried to tighten its leash?

For the moment, few of Hutchinson's townsmen seemed to share his anxiety, however astute it might have been. At noon on Tuesday, December 30, Bernard addressed a throng from the balcony of the Boston Court House—the province's most majestic edifice, anchoring one of the city's most distinguished thoroughfares, the aptly named King Street. Above this east-facing balcony, a large wooden lion and unicorn, symbols of the monarchy, flanked the building's pediment. George III was now, the governor declared, "our only Lawful and Rightful Liege Lord" to whom "we acknowledge all Faith and constant Obedience, with all hearty and humble Affection." Bernard dutifully "beseech[ed] GOD (by whom Kings do Reign) to bless" the new monarch "with long and happy Years to Reign over us."[8]

By all appearances, Bernard embodied the sentiments of the many on this grand occasion. According to the *Boston News-Letter*, as soon as the governor ended his proclamation with the customary "GOD Save the KING," the "vast Concourse of People of all Ranks" in attendance responded with three huzzahs for the third King George. A regiment of local militiamen, who had mustered under arms on King Street, added its own approbation by way of three celebratory volleys. Later that evening, townsfolk marked the occasion with "publick Illuminations" (candles, lanterns, bonfires, and fireworks) and "a handsome Entertainment" at Faneuil Hall, where "many . . . loyal Healths were drank" to the king and his royal family. "The whole Ceremony," observed the *News-Letter*'s printer, John Draper, "was carried on and concluded with great Decency and good Decorum."[9]

Draper had strong ties to the royal government, but other printers who did not, including the *Boston Gazette*'s copublishers, Benjamin Edes and John Gill, cheerfully copied Draper's rosy depiction. In the ensuing months, the *News-Letter* and the *Gazette* would begin to offer Bostonians contrasting accounts of the policies of the young king and his ministers. By the mid-1770s, these two newspapers' opposing patrons were firing not just words but bullets at each other. Yet none of the antipathy to come surfaced in the opening hours of 1761, when the *News-Letter* and the *Gazette* sang from the same hymnal in praise of their young ruler.[10]

As THE NEW YEAR DAWNED, Britain's greatest American asset was thus intangible: devotion. The king and the empire enjoyed the freely given, widely shared, and deeply felt love and loyalty of the colonists. Over the next fifteen years, colonial support for Britain and George would dissolve and Americans would renounce their mother country and their father figure.

According to one famous and oft-quoted observer (who will soon appear onstage in our story), the "seeds" of independence were "sown" shortly after Bernard's proclamation, in a highly technical 1761 lawsuit now known to legal experts as *Paxton's Case* and generally referred to by lay folk as "the writs-of-assistance case." Ironically, the case took shape thanks to the very event that had prompted such celebration on December 30: the accession of George III.

Our famous observer was right in his largest claim. The seeds of independence do indeed reside in this complex and intricate lawsuit. The oft-quoted observer was, however, wrong on many important specifics that mattered then and still matter now. But he was wrong in ways that can nonetheless teach us a great deal about both him and his world. To see why *Paxton's Case* was indeed the opening event of the American Revolution, we will need to wade deep into the weeds and examine this complicated case with meticulous care, with a proverbial legal and historical microscope. Our care will be rewarded. By the end of our weedy and microscopic investigation, we shall emerge with nothing less than a fresh understanding of the origins of the American Revolution and a deep appreciation of several of its most notable protagonists.

WRITS

On both sides of the Atlantic, legal writs—formulaic judicial instruments instructing addressees to do this or not do that—issued in the name of the king. Each sort of writ had its own specific label, form, purpose, and tradition. For example, a writ of *mandamus* ordered a person, typically a government official, to perform a nondiscretionary affirmative act: "Do the following, as required by law." A writ of *certiorari* directed a lower court to make its record available to the writ-issuing higher court for proper appellate review. A writ of *habeas corpus,* also known as the Great Writ, ordered its addressee to produce in court the body of a person being physically confined so that the writ-issuing court could decide whether the confinement was legal.

Under British law, when one king died and another came to power, all writs expired after a grace period of precisely six months unless reauthorized in the name of the new monarch.[11] One species of colonial writ irked one prominent Massachusetts lawyer. George II's death provided this lawyer a special chance to make his case. The lawyer thus did what lawyers throughout history have done. He went to court.

Attorney James Otis Jr. streaked across the landscape of colonial Boston in the 1760s like a flaming meteor. His many admirers, including John Adams, ranked him a profound constitutional thinker and perhaps America's greatest orator—a New World blend of Sidney and Cicero. His powerful detractors, including Thomas Hutchinson, deemed him bombastic, erratic, and undisciplined. They nicknamed him "Jangle Bluster." His widely discussed 1764 pamphlet, *The Rights of British Colonies Asserted and Proved*, sounded the alarm against incipient British tyranny and proposed a philosophical and legal framework for provincial rights, foreshadowing much of the prolific pamphleteering to follow on both sides of the debate and both sides of the Atlantic. Prior to 1761, however, Otis had yet to achieve the fame he craved.[12]

In some ways, he resembled the young king whose policies he came to oppose. Both George and James were powerful political scions with powerful political sires. Each entered the family business and aimed for the family chair—the British throne for George and the Speakership of the Massachusetts Assembly for James (a seat he eventually won in 1766 but was not allowed to occupy because of gubernatorial opposition).[13] As the oldest surviving son in a large brood, each benefited from a culture of patriarchy and primogeniture. (George was the oldest male among his parents' nine children, James the first of seven children to reach adulthood.) As youngsters, each received a rigorous classical education; each could thus hold forth in both English and Latin. Most poignantly, both George and James suffered from recurring and ultimately incapacitating mental instability.

In one critical respect, George and James were truly oceans apart. Yet here, too, they resembled each other, for each epitomized his homeland's essence—Britain's rigid class hierarchy and America's upward mobility, at least for White males. Whereas George descended from a long line of royals, James sprang from a self-made man.

James Otis Sr. did not attend Harvard, as would his son. Senior had begun his career working with his hands, later taught himself law, and eventually became a leading provincial lawyer and a potent political chieftain. By 1760, he was the Speaker of the Massachusetts Assembly and could also claim distinction as a (largely honorific) militia colonel. The Colonel's powerful and highborn detractors viewed his quick climb as worthy of ridicule. They heaped upon him the same kind of smirking contempt that George III and many of his ministers and minions harbored for most colonists. Not long after the Colonel's death, loyalist insider Peter Oliver publicly described him as a "Cordwainer [who had] work'd himself into a Pettifogger [with] a certain Adroitness to captivate the Ear of Country Jurors, who were too commonly Drovers, Horse Jockeys, & of other Lower Classes in Life." As for the Colonel's high status in the Assembly, "too great an Ingredient" of this "lower House . . . consisted of Inn-keepers, Retailers, & yet more inferior Orders of Men."[14]

In late 1760, when a vacancy arose on the province's highest tribunal, the five-member Superior Court, Otis Sr. applied to join the court and enlisted Otis Jr.'s help to make the case to Governor Bernard's inner circle. At the urging of three of the four remaining judges, the royally appointed governor instead tapped his royally ap-pointed lieutenant, Thomas Hutchinson, to be the court's new chief. Hutchinson had no formal legal training and no extensive experi-ence as a practicing lawyer. But he did have a sharp mind, a Har-vard degree, an even temperament, exalted social status, and strong family connections. He was born in, and now owned, a mansion generally viewed as the finest house in town. He had a long history of distinguished public service in both elective and appointed po-sitions, having previously served as the Speaker of the Assembly, a trial judge, a provincial councillor, and, briefly, the acting governor. His brother-in-law was the wealthy and wellborn Andrew Oliver; in turn, Andrew's prosperous brother, Peter, was one of the three sitting Superior Court judges who backed Hutchinson over the "Cord-wainer" and "Pettifogger," Colonel Otis. Also, Hutchinson's father had served on the provincial council for a quarter century, and *his* father (Hutchinson's paternal grandfather) had also served on the council and as chief justice of the Court of Common Pleas. When Bernard picked the highborn lieutenant over the self-made colonel, the Otises, father and son, smoldered with rage.[15]

At almost exactly the same moment, George III became king and the legal need arose to renew all royal writs. This gave Otis Jr. a chance to kill multiple birds with one stone—to ostentatiously dis-play his legal virtuosity and classical learning; to vindicate his family's honor; to defend (his view of) American liberty; to ingratiate himself with Boston's leading merchants and the mass of provincial consum-ers (and voters!); to smite the royal insiders who had snubbed his family; and to do all this, poetically, in a case brought before the very tribunal that had blackballed his father, a tribunal now presided over by his new nemesis, Thomas Hutchinson.

THE LEGAL ISSUES AT THE crux of the complex case involved "writs of assistance"—intricate legal cogwheels that helped drive the machinery of British anti-smuggling laws that in turn implemented British revenue, trade, and defense policy. The writs had operated in Boston since the mid-1750s but would lapse on April 25, 1761, unless reissued by the Superior Court.

The writs had roots in four landmark enactments of the British Parliament: the Navigation Acts of 1660 and 1662 that established a framework for British-American trade, a 1696 Plantation Trade Act that updated the earlier statutes, and the 1702 Demise of the Crown Act that prolonged all writs for six months after a monarch's death. The latter three statutes all specifically mentioned writs of assistance, but the 1662 act, where the phrase first appeared, was not a model of clarity. The 1696 and 1702 statutes merely echoed the phrase without additional elaboration. By interpolating and improvising, British courts and Customs House officials had nevertheless made the system work tolerably well.[16]

Armed with a writ of assistance that, per the 1662 statute, issued under seal from the Court of Exchequer (which specialized in matters involving government revenue), a customs officer in Britain could enter and search, forcibly if necessary, any manner of building—including a private dwelling—to find and seize smuggled goods. In the process, the officer could demand the "assistance" of local constables, other government agents, and even private bystanders to overcome any resistance he might encounter (hence the label writ of *assistance*, sometimes spelled writ of *assistants*). If the officer found apparent contraband in the hideaway, he would return it to the Court of Exchequer for a forfeiture adjudication. If the court determined that goods were indeed smuggled, the officer (known as the "informer"—the one who had brought the relevant *information* to the court's attention) would keep a third of the proceeds for his trouble, with the rest going to the government. In the provinces, the governmental two-thirds share was typically subdivided, with half (a third of the total) going to the royal governor and half (the final third) going to the king.[17]

In the early 1750s, Massachusetts royal governor William Shirley issued writs on his own say-so. But Parliament in 1696 had said that American writs should issue from provincial equivalents of Britain's Exchequer Court. When Massachusetts customs officials realized their mistake in 1755, they hastened to the Superior Court, which, with the aid of the provincial attorney general, issued eight requested writs (one to each of eight requesting officers) between 1755 and mid-1760.[18]

Then several things happened in tight sequence that threatened to unsettle the seemingly secure provincial practice.

First, an anonymous *London Magazine* article, initially published in England in March 1760, arrived in Boston and began to circulate informally among lawyers, judges, shippers, and merchants. The article asserted that the writs were strictly limited in Britain and that British judges did not confer on customs officialdom sweeping and lifelong general authority to search, seize, break open doors, repel resistance, and command assistance (as the Massachusetts judges had done). Rather, asserted the unnamed author, the British writs for smuggled goods were *specific*, not *general.* They were, he claimed, closely akin to common-law search warrants for stolen goods. Like these common-law warrants, writs under the 1662 act were, said the author, "never . . . granted without an Information upon oath, that the person applying for it has reason to suspect that prohibited or uncustomed goods are concealed in a house or place which he desires a power to search." In other words, the writ required an *oath* from the customs officer that he had *specific* reason to suspect a *particular* place of being an illegal hideaway. A proper writ had to be issued to an officer on a case-by-case, search-by-search, place-by-place basis, not once and for all for the life of the king. If this were indeed true, the provincial Superior Court and the provincial attorney general had blundered badly.[19]

Second, George II died. Under the 1702 Demise of the Crown Act, the Superior Court would need to reissue all writs, offering the court a perfect chance to correct its earlier blunder, if blunder it was.

Third, James Otis Jr. was now on the case. Shortly after the snubbing of Otis Sr. in late 1760, Otis Jr. resigned his own official position as Admiralty Court advocate general. That position would have obliged him to defend the admiralty and customs officers seeking writ renewals. Otis now switched sides by agreeing to represent—pro bono, he loudly proclaimed—prominent Boston merchants who hated the sweeping search regime then in place. Many merchants were smugglers, much as, nowadays, many drivers are speeders, many pedestrians are jaywalkers, and many entrepreneurs are tax evaders.[20]

THE SCENE WAS NOW SET for a confrontation in the highest court in the province, meeting in late February 1761 on the second floor of the Court House, just paces away from the balcony where Governor Bernard had proclaimed the new king, and also paces away from the Assembly chamber where James Otis Sr. presided as Speaker.

Only two persons in attendance left posterity detailed firsthand accounts of the event. One memorialist was the court's presiding officer, Thomas Hutchinson, who doubled as royal lieutenant governor and tripled as an elected member of the governor's council. Hutchinson would later become—thanks to the 1765 Stamp Act crisis, the 1770 Boston Massacre, and a series of high-profile 1773 incidents (the Hutchinson-Assembly debate, the Hutchinson Letters Affair, and the Boston Tea Party)—the most prominent American-born loyalist on the continent. The other memorialist was a fledgling lawyer from nearby Braintree, John Adams. Adams would later become—alongside George Washington, Benjamin Franklin, Alexander Hamilton, Thomas Jefferson, and James Madison—one of independent America's six most important founding fathers. The 1761 hearing was Adams's first of many appearances on history's grand stage, and by his own admission, he was at this time a bit player, listening and scribbling a few notes.

Writing half a century after the fact, Adams endowed the 1761 event with epic significance: "Then and there was the first scene of the first Act of opposition to the Arbitrary claims of Great Britain. Then and there the Child Independence was born." In Adams's now famous formulation, "The seeds of Patriots & Heroes . . . were then & there sown."[21]

Adams was particularly captivated by Otis's performance as a lawyer, thinker, and orator: "Otis was a flame of fire! With a promptitude of Classical Allusions, a depth of research, a rapid summary of historical events & dates, a profusion of Legal Authorities, a prophetic glance of his eyes into futurity, and a rapid torrent of impetuous Eloquence he hurried away all before him. . . . Every Man of an immense crowded Audience appeared to me to go away, as I did, ready to take Arms against Writs of Assistants."[22]

THERE IS SOME TRUTH HERE, some confusion, and some mythmaking. We shall later try to filter fact from fiction, but for now, let us consider the elder statesman's remembrances of the room itself: "That Council Chamber was as respectable an Apartment and more so too in proportion, than the House of Lords or House of Commons in Great Britain, or that in Philadelphia in which the Declaration of Independence was signed in 1776. In this Chamber near the fire were seated five Judges with Lieutenant Governor Hutchinson at their head as Chief Justice, all in their new fresh Robes of Scarlet English cloth in their broad bands and immense Judicial Wigs." Also in this chamber, various local lawyers, including young Adams himself, were "seated at a long Table." A pair of "Portraits at more than full length of King Charles the second and King James the second, in splendid golden frames were hung up in the most conspicuous side of the apartment. . . . [T]hese were the finest Pictures I have seen. The colours of their long flowing Robes and their Royal Ermines were the most glowing, the figures the most noble & graceful, the features the most distinct & characteristic. . . . I believe they were Vandykes [*sic*]."[23]

Over the course of several days, the judges in this stately chamber heard legal arguments from three prominent lawyers, and then proceeded to deliberate confidentially.

First up was Jeremiah Gridley, representing customs officers James Cockle and Charles Paxton and customs officialdom more generally. Gridley claimed that the statutes were on his side, as was practice on both shores of the Atlantic. The 1662 act did not expressly require oaths or individualized suspicion; nor, he argued, did it envision only time-limited, case- and place-specific writs. He cited a legal practice manual indicating that, contra the claims of the *London Magazine*, Britain's Court of Exchequer had in fact issued sweeping general writs per this statute. The 1696 act said that "like Assistance" should be given in America "as is the Custom in England," and provincial law dating back to the late 1690s made the Superior Court the counterpart of the Court of Exchequer. Recent provincial practice was icing on the cake.[24]

Gridley also stressed that sound considerations of fiscal policy and imperial security supported general writs: "Public taxes" had to be "effectually and speedily collected" to "support . . . Fleets and Armies abroad, and Ministers at home[,] without which the [British] Nation could neither be preserved from the Invasions of her foes, nor the Tumults of her own Subjects." Smuggling contraband and evading customs duties, not to mention trading with enemies in wartime, were hardly victimless frolics worthy of a smile, Gridley argued.[25]

Though he did not quite close the loop on this pragmatic appeal (at least, as captured by Adams's incomplete notes), perhaps he could have added that a case-by-case and place-by-place approach would make smuggling hard to catch. By the time specifics about who and where reached the court (which at any given moment might be sitting far away on circuit), and officials then carried the writ back to the hideaway, smugglers might well have sold the hoard or secreted it elsewhere. Added delay and uncertainty would in turn discourage potential eyewitnesses from exposing lawbreakers—a perilous business under the best of circumstances, given the real risks of public disclosure and social ostracism, tarring and feathering, or worse.[26]

After Gridley came Oxenbridge Thacher, offering different legal advice to the five gentlemen judges, none of whom had formally studied law or extensively practiced law. Unlike Gridley (but like the *London Magazine*), Thacher doubted that British judges had issued general writs. Even if they had, Thacher said that the Superior Court should not follow suit. He claimed that, despite the 1690s provincial statute, the court did not in fact exercise the totality of English Exchequer jurisdiction. In certain details, the provincial Superior Court operated differently than did the mother country's Court of Exchequer. Although highly technical, Thacher's legalistic argument had radical implications, condemning all provincial writs of assistance, no matter how narrow, oath based, specific, or limited as to time and place.[27]

The last speaker, James Otis Jr., held forth for some five hours, in a hurricane of words that showed him at his best and worst. He opened with a fervid and self-absorbed account of his decision to turn coat in the case—proclaiming his own purity, virtue, and gentility in overwrought prose:

> I take this opportunity to declare, that whether under a fee or not, (for in such a cause as this I despise a fee) I will to my dying day oppose, with all the powers and faculties God has given me, all such instruments of slavery on the one hand, and villainy on the other, as this writ of assistance is. . . . I shall not think much of my pains in this cause as I engaged in it from principle. . . . I have taken more pains in this cause, than I ever will take again: Although my engaging in this and another popular cause has raised much resentment; but I think I can sincerely declare, that I cheerfully submit myself to every odious name for conscience sake; and from my soul I despise all those whose guilt, malice or folly has made my foes. Let the consequences be what they will, I am determined to proceed. The only principles of public conduct that are worthy a gentleman, or a man[,] are, to sacrifice estate, ease, health and applause, and even life itself to the sacred calls of his country. These manly sentiments in private life make the good citizen, in public life, the patriot and the hero.

Jangle Bluster indeed.[28]

At the close of this overdone opening, Otis proclaimed that the requested writ "appears to me (may it please your honours) the worst instrument of arbitrary power, the most destructive of English liberty, and the fundamental principles of the constitution, that ever was found in an English law-book. . . . If this commission is legal, a tyrant may, in a legal manner also . . . imprison or murder any one within the realm."[29]

For a lawyer seeking to win over the judges—as opposed to a politician aiming to score points with voters in the gallery—this was an edgy strategy. Otis's purple prose could hardly "please your honours," given that the Superior Court itself had so recently and so consistently issued the very instruments that Otis was now condemning in the harshest language imaginable: "slavery," "villainy," "tyran[ny]," and "murder."

When Otis finally calmed himself and got down to business, his main argument was actually narrower than Thacher's, and thus more likely to appeal to any judge seeking a graceful exit. Echoing the *London Magazine*, he conceded the propriety of carefully tailored customs writs analogous to common-law search warrants for stolen goods: "*Special warrants only are legal.*" But sweeping writs—general writs, writs not backed by specificity of rationale or time or place of search, writs that gave their holder a lifetime pass to break into people's homes and dragoon bystanders, willy-nilly—these were anathema to first principles of British liberty. Paraphrasing to good effect *Semayne's Case*, a celebrated 1604 English lawsuit immortalized by the great champion of the common law Sir Edward Coke, Otis reminded the court that "a man's house is his castle," ringed with special legal solicitude. General writs would, said Otis, "totally annihilate" homeowners' rights. Surely Parliament had never meant to authorize anything like a lifetime general writ allowing promiscuous home searches! In the absence of a crystal-clear statement from Parliament, Otis argued that the court should read the 1662 act more narrowly, so that the newfangled statutory writs for smuggled goods would closely track the old-fashioned common-law warrants for stolen goods.[30]

In another classic English decision from the early 1600s, *Bonham's Case*, the great Coke had proclaimed, in words that Otis echoed, that the animating principles of the unwritten common law would "control an act of Parliament." At a minimum, this dictum instructed judges to construe any ambiguity in Parliamentary statutes against the backdrop of common-law first principles. Given *Bonham's Case*, if the 1662 statute was unclear, common-law principles of the sanctity of the home should prevail.[31]

But suppose, Otis continued, that Gridley was right and the *London Magazine* was wrong—suppose, that is, that *general* writs had strong roots in actual English practice and that Parliament had knowingly and unequivocally blessed this practice. Here, Otis reached his shattering climax, with an argument that would prove prophetic even if it was, when uttered, unsound under English constitutional law: "Had this writ been in any book whatever it would have been illegal. ALL PRECEDENTS ARE UNDER THE CONTROUL OF THE PRINCIPLES OF LAW. . . . No Acts of Parliament can establish such a writ." Even had Parliament authorized a general writ in the clearest and most purposeful language imaginable, "it would be void, AN ACT AGAINST THE CONSTITUTION IS VOID."[32]

Heady stuff indeed—and enough to dazzle young John Adams, who in his write-up rendered Otis's most arresting claims in screaming capital letters.

But it was not likely that a provincial court of legal amateurs at the edge of the empire, whose rulings were reversible by the English Privy Council, would dare to do what no English judge had ever done—what Coke himself never did—namely, defy an express and purposeful act of Parliament. Parliament, after all, was the highest legal authority in the empire, the ultimate sovereign under orthodox mid-eighteenth-century British constitutionalism. Unlike the short, written, democratically enacted American constitutions that would emerge over the next three decades, the unwritten British Constitution circa 1761 was not a single text that clearly defined and fenced in government power. Rather, it was a mélange of institutions, customs, principles, and understandings that had evolved and shifted over the centuries. Whatever Coke might have said or wanted in the early 1600s, the intervening Glorious Revolution of 1688 had established Parliamentary preeminence as the bedrock principle of eighteenth-century English constitutionalism. Otis seemed oblivious to this fundamental legal reality.

Nor was it likely that the Superior Court would accept Thacher's technical gambit, which would have rendered all writs, even specific ones, invalid in Massachusetts. Such a ruling would have violated both the strict letter and the obvious spirit of the 1696 Plantation Trade Act aimed directly at American courts.

Otis's narrowest argument, closely tracking the *London Magazine* article—the argument that special writs were really the only writs that Britain endorsed—gave the judges pause when they met to deliberate among themselves. At Hutchinson's urging, they agreed to postpone the matter until the fall so that Hutchinson could correspond with sources in London to either confirm the accuracy or establish the inaccuracy of the anonymous *London Magazine* article.[33]

Word eventually came back from London—in the form of a June 13 missive to Hutchinson from provincial agent William Bollan, who had made proper legal inquiries—that the claims of the *London Magazine* were erroneous and that general writs did indeed issue from the English Court of Exchequer. The Superior Court then convened a rehearing in mid-November 1761—a rehearing that Adams, oddly, did not attend. Now that the *London Magazine* claim had been discredited, as had Thacher's and Otis's similar claims, the court unanimously agreed to grant the requested general writs to Paxton and Cockle, and to any future customs officer who asked.[34]

In reporting this ruling on November 23, 1761, the pro-merchant *Boston Gazette* was aghast: "The Arguments [of Otis and Thacher] were enforced with such Strength of Reason, as did great Honour to the Gentlemen concerned; and nothing could have induced one to believe that they were not conclusive, but the Judgment of the Court [was] *immediately* given in Favour of the [writs.]" This piece was likely written in consultation with Otis, perhaps by Otis himself, praising as it did his "Strength of Reason" and his "Honour" as a "Gentlem[a]n," and prone as it was to Otisian overstatement that "nothing" in his argument was less than "conclusive."

CONTRARY TO THIS *GAZETTE* PUFF piece, Otis had erred, badly. The grand orator had omitted all mention of the best argument on the other side, an argument with roots in the express language of the act of 1660 and in early eighteenth-century British case law. Later British judges would elaborate this key argument when additional writs-of-assistance cases came before them.

The pro-writs argument ran as follows: True, statutory writs of assistance for smuggled goods lacked some of the safeguards of common-law search warrants for stolen goods—oath, probable cause, specificity of place, limited duration, and so on. Also true, these statutory writs authorized intrusive searches into private dwellings (albeit only in daytime and with a local constable present). But these writs had an immensely powerful offsetting safeguard. The writs authorized only searches of hideaways where actual contraband *was in fact located*. If the search under a writ came up empty, the innocent search victim could sue the searcher in trespass, and a civil judge and jury might well mulct the unsuccessful searcher with serious damages. Knowing this, no sensible customs officer would dare to search on a mere whim, thereby putting himself at risk of ruinous civil liability. By contrast, a common-law search warrant immunized an officer *whether or not the searcher found the suspected stolen goods*. The common-law search warrant had stronger *ex ante* protections for searchees (oath, probable cause, specificity, time limits) but infinitely weaker *ex post* safeguards; vice versa for the statutory writs.[35]

Moreover, writs of assistance aimed at entrenched, organized, lucrative, and treacherous illegal activity—smuggling and trading with the enemy, backed by tarring and feathering of snitches. In this particular policy quadrant, extra-strong governmental measures were perhaps entirely justified both in England and in Massachusetts (the Gridley argument).

In the end, Otis lost unanimously on both sides of the Atlantic. Even were we to dismiss all the members of the provincial court as legal dolts or royal lackeys, we should recognize that the best British jurists (Lord Camden, Lord Mansfield, and Sir William Blackstone) and the best British friends of America (William Pitt, Edmund Burke, and, again, Camden) never opposed general writs of assistance. Much less did these eminent judges and statesmen see the writs in the kind of apocalyptic terms ("slavery," "villainy," "tyran[ny]," and "murder") that Otis did. These towering British figures had sound, albeit not incontrovertible, legal reasons for backing general writs in both Britain and America, reasons that Otis failed to identify and engage, much less convincingly refute, carried away as he was by the power of his voice, the purity of his soul, and the profundity of his mind.[36]

ADAMS, YOUNG AND OLD

Let us now return to John Adams to separate fact from falsehood.

Some of what Adams wrote as an elder statesman, more than fifty years after the event itself in a series of letters to his former law clerk William Tudor, fails to square with the evidence from the 1760s. If the young Adams and "Every Man of an immense crowded Audience" left the Court House in February 1761 "ready to take Arms against Writs of Assistants," then why was there no contemporaneous press coverage of the February hearing, and only one brief newspaper item—the *Gazette* puff piece, likely produced by Otis himself—immediately after the disappointing November ruling? Also, why did Adams not even attend the November rehearing or inquire about it?[37]

To his dying day, Adams never realized, or at least never admitted, that such a public rehearing had occurred in November and that a public ruling had issued. In his later years he insisted—preposterously, given the *Gazette* report—that after the postponement announced in February, "no Judgment was pronounced, nothing was said about Writs of Assistants, no letters from England, and nothing more ever said in Court concerning them. . . . The public never was informed, what was the Correspondence with England, what was the practice or the grounds of it there. The public never was informed of the judgement of the Court. No Judge ever gave his opinion, or discussed the question in public." Writs ultimately issued, but "clandestinely," claimed old Adams, emphatically and erroneously.[38]

This was no small mistake. It was a whopper, and like the thirteenth chime of a broken clock, it calls into question the reliability of the elder statesman more generally. Although Adams gushed about Otis's "Classical Allusions" and "impetuous Eloquence," legal cases are typically won by brute facts and cool logic, not fine talk or hot blood. Despite all his classical learning and rhetorical exertion, young lawyer Otis had failed to even engage the strongest policy arguments against him and had gotten the biggest fact—actual British writ practice—exactly wrong in early 1761. Old lawyer Adams got the related big fact—what Hutchinson's court in late 1761 actually did and why—astonishingly wrong.[39]

CAREFUL HISTORICAL RECONSTRUCTION OF THE actual events of 1761 must begin not with the aged Adams, but with his younger self—with his notes and writings from the 1760s, alongside newspapers and other contemporaneous accounts from this period. The brief notes he scribbled in the Court House did not contain much commentary on his part. In the moment, he did not write that "Otis shone brightly" or anything of the sort. But over the next several weeks, Adams did decide to revise his Court House notes into a more complete and polished "abstract" (his word). Perhaps this abstract was simply for his own use as a budding lawyer. Perhaps he hoped to share it privately as a sample of his ability. Perhaps he hoped to publish it one day as a case report of general interest. (There was no official court reporter in that era.) Whatever his motivation, the work that went into this abstract confirms that Adams in early 1761 did think the case worthy of special attention.

Otis was the star of the abstract. Whereas no trace of Otis's opening remarks appeared in Adams's contemporaneous Court House notes, the subsequent abstract purported to quote at length from the orator's chest-thumping preface. Much of the rest of the abstract put in Otis's mouth protracted passages that were not in the skimpy original notes—all now made to look as if they were direct quotations from Otis, capturing both his style and substance at the hearing itself. Gridley's argument also grew in Adams's retelling, but Otis's grew far more, and Thacher's actually shrank.

Although Adams's abstract was not published until 1773, Adams began to circulate a draft to friends and colleagues in March 1761—shortly after the hearing, when the argument was still ringing in his ears. In composing his abstract in the weeks after the hearing, Adams probably solicited help directly from Gridley and Otis, and perhaps Thacher, the better to recapture what they had said and cited.[40]

Otis and Adams in particular shared a mutual admiration that had begun before 1761 and that would endure throughout their lives. So young Adams probably did walk away from the February hearing smitten by Otis's performance.

We should not be equally smitten. Adams loved Otis at first sight, but Adams loved himself exceedingly, and in Otis he saw a reflection of himself. Each of the two young Boston-area lawyers was an ambitious, talented, and energetic—driven—first-generation Harvard man whose same-named father (Adams, too, was a Junior) had begun adulthood as a respectable shoemaker but not a gentleman of the highest rank. Young Adams and young Otis each obsessed about the purity and impurity of his soul—just what one might expect in a town teeming with Puritans and Puritans manqués. (One does not see the same intense self-scrutiny in the public or private writings of Virginians such as Thomas Jefferson and James Madison or of immigrants such as Alexander Hamilton and James Wilson.) Both Otis and Adams often tried too hard, aiming to impress with unnecessary Latin and overdone classical references. Neither was a tight, reliable legal thinker; neither had a steel-trap mind. Each was often colorful, sporadically overwrought, and at times volcanic, prone to extreme overstatement and wild mood swings. Each was also far too quick to personalize legal and political issues; at his worst, each bordered on paranoia and egomania. (According to the charming and usually judicious Benjamin Franklin, Adams "means well for his Country, is always an honest Man, often a Wise One, but sometimes and in some things, absolutely out of his Senses.") Though both Otis and Adams could turn a great phrase, both were erratic constitutional lawyers and uneven political theorists. Neither ever managed to compose a classic constitutional argument matching the originality, breadth, and rigor—the genius—of Hamilton's, Madison's, or Wilson's best work. At no point in 1761 or thereafter did Adams do the basic research or hard thinking that should have led him to the best arguments against Otis, visible in English statutory language and case law that neither advocate Otis nor publicist Adams ever squarely confronted.[41]

In his nineteenth-century embellishments to his protégé Tudor, the elderly Adams aimed to burnish the memory of his friend Otis, who died as dramatically as he lived—struck by a lightning bolt in 1783 at age fifty-eight. As Otis's fame faded, Adams, nearing the end of his own life, sought to remind his countrymen that Otis had been a patriot hero years before all others—before Adams himself, before Adams's cousin Samuel, before Patrick Henry, before George Washington, and most emphatically before Thomas Jefferson.[42]

OTIS WAS INDEED FIRST IN key ways, but not in the way old Adams told the story to Tudor—now for the third time, and at odds with his initial draft (his skimpy Court House notes) and his second draft (his more polished abstract from mid-1761). In the Tudor-letters version, the aging Adams suggested that Otis had denounced Parliament's general power to impose taxes of any sort, internal or external, on the colonies. But according to Adams's own early notes and abstract, Otis in the Court House had emphatically and repeatedly conceded that special writs were permissible, even though they aimed to stamp out smuggling that cheated the Customs House—cheating that Gridley had expressly emphasized in highlighting Britain's compelling *revenue* interests at the heart of the case. As everyone at the trial agreed, including Otis, British writs issued from

England's *revenue* court, the Court of Exchequer. The main debate was whether these revenue-enforcing writs were specific or general.[43]

Old Adams also suggested that Otis in 1761 had attacked provincial slavery laws: "Not a Quaker in Philadelphia or Mr Jefferson of Virginia ever asserted the Rights of Negroes in Stronger Terms." Nothing in Adams's 1761 drafts supports this fuzzy memory. Had Otis in the Court House actually contested slavery's lawfulness, he would have been wandering far afield of the issues in the case, and would have risked losing any judge of remotely cautious sentiment. Indeed, old Adams told Tudor that the young Adams himself had "shuddered at the [abolitionist] doctrine" that Otis had allegedly preached in open court.[44]

Some of Adams's claims in this nineteenth-century correspondence reflect simple confusion on the part of an old man, conflating events that happened more than fifty years earlier. In speeches made and a famous 1764 pamphlet published at the dawn of the Stamp Act crisis, *The Rights of British Colonies Asserted and Proved*, Otis did indeed insist that the British Parliament could not tax colonists, who were ineligible to vote for Parliament. "*Taxation without representation is tyranny!*" Otis famously thundered; and without proper representation, "external" taxes on imports and exports, he expressly argued, were just as bad as "internal" taxes on domestic goods. Also, Otis in his famous 1764 pamphlet surely did assail slavery: "The colonists are by the law of nature free born, as indeed all men are, white or black. . . . Can any logical inference in favor of slavery be drawn from a flat nose?" Old Adams was simply reading back into the 1761 Court House argument various positions that Otis articulated several years later, elsewhere, and for very different purposes.

BUT NOT ALL OF THE elderly Adams's literal falsehoods were mere confusion. Indeed, Adams dropped hints that what he was now presenting was not pure history as it happened but art and allegory—figuratively true even if literally false. Not history, quite, but hindsight of a sort, hindsight that highlighted real and deep truths

about the underappreciated origins—the real "seeds"—of the American Revolution.

In one letter, the old man offered up (what else?) a classical allusion that might explain what he himself was doing, consciously or not. "Thucidides [*sic*], Livy, [and] Sallust," wrote Adams, routinely acted as after-the-fact ghostwriters who "would make a speech" for the likes of Pericles or Caesar.[45] In other letters, Adams repeatedly offered up a revealing metaphor from the fine arts. His storytelling was like a "scene" in a great "historical paint[ing]" of the sort that "[John] Trumbull" was then creating.[46]

The key to Adams's mind, memory, and meaning can be found in Trumbull's masterwork, *The Declaration of Independence*. This famous oil purports to depict the instant on June 28, 1776, when a five-man committee of the Second Continental Congress presented its draft Declaration to the Congress's president, John Hancock.

Trumbull placed the white-stockinged Adams at center stage, alongside, albeit slightly apart from, the well-proportioned Thomas Jefferson and the long-haired Benjamin Franklin, with dozens of less notable Congressional delegates, seated farther back, looking on. The elderly Adams knew that in this magisterial illustration—decades in the making, in different versions—Trumbull was taking enormous artistic liberties. Some of the delegates whom Trumbull depicted had been absent on June 28, though they later signed the Declaration; and some of the delegates who undoubtedly were there on the 28th failed to make the cut for Trumbull. Adams himself advised Trumbull to omit various delegates who had participated on June 28 but who were unavailable to sit for Trumbull and had no good portraits for Trumbull to copy.[47]

Trumbull chose to place Adams's breast precisely in the middle of his masterpiece, where its diagonals cross. While Jefferson's hands hold the Declaration draft, it is Trumbull's Adams who is the only committee member fully visible from head to toe. It is Adams who, by the stoutness of his stance, the thrust of his chest, and the angle of his elbow, best conveys uncompromising determination. Trumbull thus reminded the viewer that it was Adams who had championed independence more notoriously and resolutely than Jefferson or Franklin or anyone else in the frame. In the run-up to the Declaration, it was Adams who, in the admiring imagery of fellow signer Richard Stockton, stood as the "Atlas" of independence.[48]

Given all this, surely the artistic opening scene of the independence drama, as old Adams looked back upon his life and times, should begin with young Adams himself prophetically in the room—in an obscure spot, perhaps, but present in a way that other future greats were not.[49] Indeed, one letter to Tudor offered detailed artistic instructions to a would-be Trumbull about how young Adams, described by his elder self in the third person, should appear on this canvas: "John . . . should be painted looking like a short thick fat Archbishop of Canterbury seated at the table, with a pen in his hand, lost in admiration, now & then minuting those despicable notes."[50]

Tudor was not the only one to whom Adams pitched his idea about capturing the Otis argument on a grand canvas in Trumbullian fashion. The elder statesman wrote a pair of letters in the same vein to friend Benjamin Waterhouse, and indeed wrote directly to Maestro Trumbull himself for advice and assistance: "Who, of your profession will undertake to paint . . . the Arguments, in the Counsel Chamber in Boston in the Month of February 1761 between Mr Gridley and Mr Otis, upon the question of Writs of Assistants? . . . The latter, as if he had been inspired with a spirit of Prophecy, laid open to the view of a crowded Audience all that has since happened in America. Here the Revolution commenced. Then and there, the Child was born."[51]

Adams's scene-setting to Tudor, Waterhouse, and Trumbull was not just about Otis, but also about Adams himself. Barely hidden in his attempted humorous self-deprecation ("short," "fat," "despicable") was Adams's burning desire to be remembered, alongside Otis, as present at the Creation. Regional pride also swelled in Adams's breast. Virginia's Jefferson may have penned much of the Declaration, and the Old Dominion's Washington may have been first in war, first in peace, and first in the hearts of his countrymen, but Adams saw Otis and himself, proud sons of Massachusetts, brothers in arms, as first in independence.[52]

THE FIRST SCENE

Trumbull never painted the heroic Court House tableau that Adams craved. Even so, in the course of construing the Fourth Amendment to the US Constitution—which limits governmental power to search houses and other places and to seize various items, including stolen and smuggled goods—more than a dozen US Supreme Court opinions over the past century have offered readers narratives in the Adams tradition. Almost all of these Fourth Amendment opinions have been authored by northeasterners—mainly Harvard men, amusingly enough. These Yankee narrators have highlighted the importance of the 1761 Otis argument and have repeatedly quoted old Adams letters about "seeds," "the child Independence," and the Boston Court House as the "first scene of the first Act" of the Revolution—the time and place when and where independence was "born." Notwithstanding all of Adams's misdirection and myth-making, these modern storytellers have been right to draw attention to what happened in Boston in 1761.[53]

Alas, these distinguished judicial narrators have missed the real lessons of the story, as have most historians and legal scholars, who have either neglected this episode entirely or misinterpreted some of its most important elements. Adams, Otis, Hutchinson, and *Paxton's Case* should live forever in American memory, but not merely because of their interesting implications for constitutional search-and-seizure law. Rather, what happened in Boston in 1761 remains of epic import because, on close inspection, the episode reveals the profound passions, the deep tensions, and the underlying forces that would eventually rip the British Empire apart in 1776. That rupture would in turn lead to an entirely new thing in the world: the American constitutional project, full stop, and not merely one interesting and important amendment dealing with search-and-seizure rules.

SOMETIMES THE OLD MAN WAS able to stick to strict historical truth while also, poetically, capturing a deeper allegorical truth about the meaning of the Revolution. Biographer David McCullough once suggested that Adams might have made a fine novelist; Harvard historian Bernard Bailyn offered similar ruminations.[54] The colorful and engaging Tudor letters support this view: the old statesman's storytelling had strong, if unsubtle, novelistic touches, replete with rich symbols and nice metaphors. For example, why, in setting the Court House scene, did Adams take pains to mention the beautifully framed portraits of Stuart monarchs? Not just because oils of Stuart kings did in fact hang in the room as the oral argument unfolded, and would have enriched any Trumbullian painting of the event, but also because that literal truth pointed to two more profound points that the artistic Adams aimed to underscore.

First, Massachusetts in 1761 was not some cultural backwater vastly inferior to the mother country. The paintings were as good as any old master's—he thought they were likely van Dycks. (They were not, but Adams probably meant to stress that he—a shoemaker-farmer's son from Braintree—had seen the real things in Europe and had the genteel taste and discernment to recognize art of the highest order.) In this same scene-setting passage, Adams likewise insisted that the council chamber was more impressive than Parliament's chambers "in proportion." Here, too, the subtext was obvious: pound for pound, the men of Massachusetts were as good as the British, even as the latter overawed and underestimated the former.

Second, the Stuart rulers in the paintings were archetypes of monarchical overreach—the same sort of overreach that would, soon enough, bring about American independence. Poetically and literally, the writs-of-assistance oral argument occurred in the shadow of James II, who along with his brother Charles II had dishonored the provincial charter of Massachusetts in the 1680s. Why were *Stuart* oils the paintings that hung in the room? Because the royally appointed governor, Francis Bernard, loved the Stuart kings even if most Bostonians did not. What mattered in 1761, Adams was implicitly telling Tudor (and through him, posterity), was not what Bostonians wanted, but what Bernard, London's man, wanted.[55]

In Adams's words—likely literally true but also rich with symbolism—the pictures were in an earlier regime "stowed away in a Garrett among rubbish" because provincial governor Thomas Pownall, Bernard's predecessor, "was no admirer of Charles' or James'." But Bernard had placed the oils "in Council for the admiration and imitation of all men, no doubt with the concurrence of Hutchinson and all the Junto."[56]

THE ELDER STATESMAN'S MOST FAMOUS lines about Otis's speech were that there and then, "Independence was born" and "the seeds of Patriots & Heroes . . . were . . . sown." Although Otis in 1761 was surely not arguing for independence or anything close, such as colonial immunity from all external or internal Parliamentary taxation, old Adams still had a point: *The opening scene of a colorful novelistic tale of the Revolution should indeed be set in Boston in the winter of 1760–1761. Until then, the three key ingredients that would ultimately combine to produce independence in 1776 had never come together into a single tight cluster. With the benefit of hindsight, we can plausibly view the February Court House hearing as the time and place where these three key ingredients—one personal, one military, and one legal—did indeed for the first time cohere to form "seeds" that could grow into something mighty.*

Consider first the human and psychological dimensions of 1776. The Revolution was a cataclysmic political event, an earthquake in law, government, public policy, geopolitics, and civic discourse. But for most Revolutionaries, both legendary leaders and their lesser-known fellows and followers, the Revolution also entailed an emotional upheaval, a redefinition of identity and inner life: *I am no longer a Briton. The British people are no longer my brethren. George III is no more my father figure. I owe him no love or loyalty despite any solemn oaths that I may have previously taken.* The Revolution was a mass divorce of sorts. It was personal.[57]

Some of the intense emotions that would ultimately fuel the Revolution did indeed erupt into public view in Otis's volcanic Court House performance. His resignation from and challenge to the provincial establishment in 1760–1761 foreshadowed the mass renunciations and resistance to come in 1765–1776. Earlier than most, Otis felt disrespected by the power structure—by the Olivers, Hutchinsons, and Bernards of the world, who in turn were backed by the British king, his ministers, and his Parliament. Here in effect was Otis's subtext: *I am **somebody**. I attended Harvard; I know Latin; I am a legal titan; my father is House Speaker; my community admires me; smart young lawyers such as John Adams respect me. Yet I am being treated as a nobody by the likes of Oliver, Hutchinson, Bernard, and their British patrons.*

Here is how Hutchinson—himself an accomplished, discerning, and usually reliable historian, author of a multivolume provincial history—later recalled the events: After the perceived rebuff of Colonel Otis, the father and son's "resentment [was] strong. . . . Both the gentlemen had [previously] been friends to government. From this time they were at the head of every measure in opposition" both to the provincial government and to "the authority of parliament," the "opposition to which first began in this colony, and was moved and conducted by one of them [Otis Jr.], both in the assembly and the town of Boston. *From so small a spark a great fire [the Revolution] seems to have been kindled.*"[58]

Because of British class hierarchy, British snobbery toward Americans in general, and brute British indifference—worsened by the sheer physical distance between Boston and the ultimate British power structure—Otis feared he had no pathway to prominence, no chance to rise to the top of a heap dominated by "shoelickers" (Otis's word). In Virginia, a brave and able young military man named George Washington likewise smoldered when the imperial system first snubbed him as a mere colonial officer and then denied him a suitable royal commission in the regular British army. While acting as an American agent in London, Pennsylvania's Benjamin Franklin—a world-famous scientist, writer, and entrepreneur—experienced a decisive turn of heart when he was publicly disgraced in the chamber (aptly named the Cockpit) of the Privy Council. These three men—Otis, Washington, and Franklin—came of age in different decades, dwelt in different climate zones, pursued different occupations, aspired to climb different social pyramids, and eventually became spokesmen for different leading colonies. They embodied entirely different personalities and biographies. Yet they all had something in common. They all felt overlooked and underappreciated; they had all met with imperial disdain and disrespect. For these men and many like them, the Revolution was not entirely political but also intensely personal.[59]

Early 1761 was not the first time that a colonist had suffered extreme mortification or stinging disappointment. But it was the first time that blame could be laid at the feet of George III, and it was this man whom American patriots would ultimately renounce, in 1776, as a result of a "long train of abuses" all directly or indirectly identified with him. The Revolution was subjective on both sides: Revolutionaries revolted against Britain after being revolted by one particular monarch and his minions.

PATRIOTS ALSO REVOLTED ONLY WHEN they could—that is, when they had fair prospects for military success. Here, too, the opening scene properly begins in 1761, as old Hutchinson understood even better than old Adams, albeit from a different angle.

Seeking to persuade Hutchinson and his judicial brethren, attorney Gridley had played the British military card with flourish. Writs would mean "revenue" and revenue would "support . . . Fleets and Armies abroad" and protect provincial subjects from "Invasion" from the empire's "foes." As Gridley spoke these words, everyone in the Court House knew that Britain was then embroiled in an epic military conflict, now known as the French and Indian War. The smuggled goods at the heart of *Paxton's Case* were not merely goods that had evaded customs duties (the revenue angle), but also goods that were altogether prohibited, contraband items in the strictest sense. Writs of assistance aimed to thwart trading with the enemy: the French Nation, which included French colonies and outposts in the West Indies and Canada.

In a missive that arrived in Boston in late 1760, British secretary of state William Pitt complained that some colonists were treacherously furnishing "Provisions, and other Necessaries" to the French, and directed Bernard to "put the most speedy and effectual Stop to such flagitious Practices." By encouraging vigorous use of writs of assistance and by appointing Hutchinson, who was apt to follow British law unflinchingly, Bernard was doing what Pitt wanted (and was also hoping to personally profit from his gubernatorial share of the contraband proceeds in any future forfeiture). Pitt would later prove himself a good friend to America, but he never supported the Otis position on American writs. If the British Empire meant anything, surely it meant that Britons on both sides of the Atlantic needed to stand as one against the French Nation—Albion's ancient nemesis (and Catholic to boot).[60]

Loyal Britons had indeed stood as one in the late summer of 1760 when the English-born general Jeffery Amherst led a joint force of British Regulars and American provincials—some from Massachusetts—to a smashing defeat of the French near the upper Saint Lawrence River, leading to the fall of French Montreal. (A year earlier, residents of Massachusetts had named a township in Amherst's honor.) Within three years of Amherst's victory, France would cede its Canadian territory to Britain at war's end—a cession that was far from foreordained in the mid-1750s, but was foreseeable in 1761. The century-old French threat to the men of Massachusetts had just evaporated, almost overnight.

Ironically for the British Empire, adding Canada would soon mean subtracting America. After France ceded Canada to Britain in 1763, the London ministry would desperately need cash to pay off the huge bills that had piled up during the war, nearly doubling the national debt. From the British point of view, who better to pay than colonists, who had been the war's beneficiaries? The war, after all, had eliminated a major threat to British America. From the colonial point of view, why should colonists pay for a British shield that they no longer needed?

Although old Adams did not quite narrate his tale this way, old Hutchinson, the only other firsthand participant to leave extensive writings on the February 1761 showdown, did expressly link budding colonial assertiveness to the new military situation created by Amherst's triumph. Hutchinson prefaced his posthumously published recollections of the writs case by noting that when reports of the fall of Montreal reached Boston on September 23, 1760, nowhere were they received with "greater joy," because "no part of the king's dominions" had benefited more. The royally appointed Bernard addressed the locally elected Assembly, lavishly praising the "blessings" the province had received from its "subjection to Great Britain." The Assembly echoed this praise, but less fulsomely, observed the eagle-eyed Hutchinson.[61]

In language akin to old Adams's, though more careful, less colorful, and differently angled, Hutchinson recalled that he detected a new spirit aborning: "Whilst the French remained upon the continent, the English [that is, British Americans] were apprehensive lest, sooner or later, they should be driven from it. But as soon as they [the French] were removed, *a new scene opened.*" After the fall of Montreal, "there was nothing to obstruct a gradual progress of [British North American] settlements, through a vast continent, from the Atlantic to the Pacific Ocean." Although these new military realities "did not, of themselves, immediately occasion any plan, or even a desire, of independency," they "produced a higher sense of grandeur and importance of the colonies. Advantages in any respect, enjoyed by the subjects in England, which were not enjoyed by the subjects in the colonies, began to be considered in an invidious light, and men were led to inquire, with greater attention than formerly, into the relation in which the colonies stood to the state from which they sprang."[62]

Old Adams, unsurprisingly, had a different spin, but he, too, saw the fall of French Canada as critical to a full understanding of the writs-of-assistance case:

> When the British Ministry received from general Amherst his dispatches announcing his conquest of Montreal, and the consequent annihilation of the French Government and Power in America in 1759 [sic—should be 1760]; they immediately Conceived the design and took the resolution of conquering the English Colonies, and Subjecting them to the unlimited Authority of Parliament. With the intention they Sent orders to the Collector of the Customs in Boston Mr Charles Paxton, to apply to the civil Authority for Writs of Assistants.[63]

BEYOND THE PERSONAL AND THE military elements visible in the foreground and background of the February 1761 Court House showdown was a third essential element: a legal argument that, while unsound and immature when made, would grow into something much stronger and sounder in the ensuing years. In words captured by Adams's contemporaneous notes and capitalized in Adams's early abstract, Otis proclaimed that "AN ACT AGAINST THE CONSTITUTION IS VOID" and suggested that ordinary judges, including provincial judges, could disregard such a Parliamentary enactment, even if the enacting Parliament had clearly considered the supposed constitutional infirmity and expressly found it unavailing.

This was surely not orthodox British constitutional law circa 1761. The Glorious Revolution of 1688 had established the sovereignty of Parliament, the legal embodiment of the English people. As William Blackstone would distill this orthodoxy in a landmark treatise in 1765, Parliament might lawfully do "every thing that is not naturally impossible" and "what they do, no authority upon earth can undo." Parliament could not make two plus two equal five (a natural impossibility), and perhaps Parliament could not violate certain basic postulates that defined the nature of law itself; but surely Parliament could tweak common-law rules about search policies, even if such tweaks meant less *ex ante* protection of private dwellings.[64]

What the elderly Adams knew in hindsight was that some of Otis's 1761 pronouncements about the existence of constitutional limits on Parliament's power gained traction over the next decade and a half, when combined with additional legal premises and logical supports. Though blurring and bungling the details, old Adams also knew that in the months and years after the Court House argument, Otis himself played an early and notable role in this deepening American constitutional conversation about Parliamentary power.

In a significant 1764 pamphlet, Otis refined his eccentric 1761 argument into a much more plausible lawyerly claim: Parliamentary acts *taxing Americans* were unconstitutional—illegitimate in the largest sense, given that colonists were not properly represented in Parliament. Taxation without representation was tyranny. In one way, this new Otis argument was infinitely more sweeping, ranging far beyond tiny technical details of Customs House search-and-seizure policy. In another way, however, the clever new legal argument was more narrow, limiting Parliament's taxation authority *in the colonies* but not *in Britain itself.* Even if Parliament did legally embody England, post-1688, and indeed all of Britain (including Scotland) post-1707, it did not embody America. By 1776, the patriots' main claim had evolved further, even though Otis, long since overcome by mental disorder, was no longer in the vanguard: Parliamentary acts governing colonists *in any way* were unconstitutional and illegitimate. Imposition without representation was tyranny. These shifting arguments against Parliament's encroachment—arguments rooted not just in legalistic claims from British precedents and British law books but also legal-philosophical claims about universal natural rights and the foundations of legitimate government authority—would ultimately find fertile ground up and down the continent.

Also, old Adams surely understood that although Otis lost legally in 1761, the fiery lawyer had won politically. Otis played to the crowd, not to the court. In the eyes of the crowd—the leading merchant smugglers, who hated the writs; the sea of consumers, who generally sided with the smugglers (who kept consumer costs low); the patrons of the *Boston Gazette*, which would soon become his political mouthpiece—attorney Otis won his case. Less than three months after, and largely because of, his hot words in the February hearing, Otis landed his first seat in the Massachusetts Assembly. (If the case was more about launching Otis's political career than anything else, then that fact might explain why young Adams skipped the post-election and politically anticlimactic November rehearing.) Once in the Assembly, Otis used his new platform to continue to agitate against London-backed insiders like Bernard and Hutchinson—agitation that would over the next several years quite naturally splay out into broader campaigns and crusades against London itself. Otis may not have followed cool legal logic in February 1761, but he had found, and touched, a political nerve.

PERSONAL, MILITARY, AND LEGAL INGREDIENTS did indeed combine to form powerful "seeds" in 1761 Boston; but the seeds would need to sprout and spread. Personally, snubbed and spurned men in other colonies would need to seethe against the king's minions as Otis had seethed. Militarily, while post-Montreal Massachusetts had less to fear from the French in the North, the Bay Province would need allies in the South—especially in Virginia—before it could take arms against the mighty British Empire. Legally (and politically), other colonies would need to join the constitutional conversation about first principles and Parliamentary power.

In theory, the writs issue was promising, because writs of assistance and the underlying Customs House system affected not merely one province or region but all mainland colonies under the relevant Parliamentary acts. In 1761, however, no newspaper in America other than the *Boston Gazette* seemed to care about the writs.[65]

The "seeds" had indeed been "sown," but they had yet to find enough rich soil to grow into something colossal. A continent-wide debate about British rules and British rule—a truly *American* constitutional conversation—had yet to dominate the scene.

When it did, Otis, Adams, and Hutchinson would all be there.

two

RESISTANCE

I N 1761, VIRTUALLY NO ONE outside the small province of Massachusetts Bay had ever heard of James Otis Jr. or John Adams. Indeed, few *inside* the province had heard of Adams. Fifteen years later, these men were world-famous and world-infamous, extolled and excoriated in a conversational quadrant spanning a million square miles—from Boston to Williamsburg to Savannah to Montreal to Edinburgh to London and myriad points in between.

For the first time in world history, countless scribblers in and out of government, up and down the social ladder, separated by hundreds and sometimes thousands of miles, inhabiting not just different cities but different continents, directly engaged each other in spirited back-and-forth discourse about contemporary civic events. The conversation was often highly legalistic, with elaborate jurisprudential thrusts and parries, lawyerly moves and countermoves, by interlocutors on all sides. Physical action abounded in these years—bullets flew, tea chests splashed, cannons roared—but words also mattered and indeed gave meaning to the action.

WAR AND SPEECH

Most history books say that the first "world war" began in 1914 with the killing of an Austrian archduke in Europe's Balkans. In fact, the first global war began in 1754 with the killing of a French Canadian officer in America's backcountry. The slaying of Joseph Coulon de Villiers de Jumonville on May 28, 1754, forty miles south of the Forks of the Ohio (modern-day Pittsburgh), occurred at the hands of colonial and Indian fighters led by a young Virginia officer named George Washington. On July 3, Washington surrendered to a superior French force and signed (perhaps without fully comprehending) a French-language document conceding fault in the Jumonville killing, giving France a colorable excuse for full war. The May killing and July surrender were among Washington's first appearances on history's stage and moments that he later viewed with mixed emotions. Trumbull quite wisely never memorialized them on canvas.

The conflagration that ensued between 1756 and 1763—referred to by Europeans as "the Seven Years War" and by Americans as "the French and Indian War"—pitted the world's two greatest military powers against each other and sucked into its maw most of the other great powers. It generated enormous death and destruction in both Old World and New World theaters, as armies clashed on multiple continents and navies battled on multiple oceans. The war culminated in a colossal redrawing of the global map. No previous conflict in history had done all these things at once. A new era of warfare was dawning.

At the same time, a new era of discourse was also dawning, featuring an intense and iterative multiyear political conversation spanning old and new continents and once again involving great world powers—both the greatest powers in the Old World, Britain and France, and the great power in embryo that was becoming the United States of America.

Some of the same trends driving the first global war likewise drove the first global constitutional conversation. Rising urbanization, industrialization, and specialization of labor not only made weapons of war more plentiful and powerful but also made printing presses more prevalent and popular. Mid-eighteenth-century warships moved troops ever more efficiently, and mid-eighteenth-century trade ships did the same for newspapers.

In previous eras, Britons on both sides of the Atlantic had written for each other and for the wider world in theoretical, scientific, theological, and philosophical works composed for the ages. Thomas Hobbes's *Leviathan* (1651), Isaac Newton's *Principia* (1687), Jonathan Edwards's *Sinners in the Hands of an Angry God* (1741), David Hume's *An Enquiry Concerning Human Understanding* (1748), and Benjamin Franklin's *Experiments and Observations on Electricity, Made at Philadelphia in America* (1751) epitomized this grand tradition. In the 1760s, by contrast, King George's subjects in the Old and New Worlds began to *converse* back and forth with each other publicly in letters, essays, pamphlets, and pronouncements composed *for rapid transatlantic or intercolonial political and legal response.*

This new politico-legal conversation often featured common persons, not towering geniuses. Many printed pieces were short and simple—not treatises or sermons, but letters to the editor, squibs, cartoons, and even doggerel. Patriots of all sorts from all strata—lawyers, merchants, shopkeepers, farmers, tradesmen, and laborers—joined the Sons of Liberty, populated committees of correspondence, organized nonimportation agreements, and took part in astonishing forms of political protests and political theater. Loyalists cleverly countered, identifying soft spots in the patriots' arguments. Across the spectrum, writers and speakers of different nationalities, religions, and educational backgrounds joined the fray.

Anonymity and pseudonymity were rampant. In a series of influential "Letters" published and widely republished in both the colonies and the mother country in 1767–1768, John Dickinson, who had spent three years studying law at London's Middle Temple, posed as a simple "Farmer."[1] (This was an interesting twist on earlier times, when farmers had tried to pose in court as country lawyers, much to the chagrin of the Peter Olivers of the world.) On Christmas Eve 1764, when a New York printer ran a letter from "Sophia

Thrifty" urging patriots to economize, readers could not know for sure that she was a she.[2] The extraordinary conversational regime that dawned in the 1760s was not email, not the Internet, not Google, not Facebook, not YouTube, not Instagram, Twitter, or Zoom. But in hindsight this regime can be seen as anticipating these later developments, and in any event it was in its own right a distinctly new and distinctly democratic phenomenon.

While news and opinions could not travel at the speed of Franklin's electricity, a cold-weather *Racehorse* had carried newspapers across the Atlantic in a matter of weeks, a pace fast enough to influence voters even where elections were frequent, as they surely were in Massachusetts. (A popular slogan proclaimed that where annual elections end, slavery begins.) Within a single year, a Boston letter-writer or newspaper essayist could exchange three or four rounds with a London counterpart, and thrice that with a Virginia interlocutor.

Here, too, the writs-of-assistance controversy was a sign of things to come. The February 1761 hearing took its shape from a short, anonymous March 1760 English magazine essay that by summertime began to circulate among leading Bostonians. Several weeks before the hearing, the *Boston Evening-Post* brought the broader public into the know by reprinting the essay.[3] (Perhaps Otis planted the piece, hoping to soften up the judges and firm up his political base.) At the hearing, the court decided to investigate the essay's claims, echoed as they were by Thacher and Otis, not to mention the *Evening-Post*. Word went out to London and word came back from London—all in time for the court's fall session. Once it became clear that the London essay had erred in its key factual claims about current British practice, the court issued its pro-writs ruling. Behold, an early example of the emerging conversational model featuring three transatlantic trips (the magazine's arrival and the Hutchinson-Bollan back-and-forth) and a democratic cast of characters: an anonymous essayist, private printers, ambitious activists, overseas correspondents, and ordinary mariners delivering commonplace items such as newsprints and letters.

TAXATION AND REPRESENTATION

The Sugar and Stamp Act controversies of 1764–1766 took the emerging phenomenon of border-and-ocean-crossing back-and-forth constitutional conversation to a higher level. Colonists north and south started reading and answering each other's recent and sometimes widely reprinted writings on major issues of British constitutional law. Multiple colonial assemblies, acting in concert, published their views on a pending Parliamentary bill of great moment. Later, representatives of most of the mainland provinces got together in a room and, for the first time ever, acted as *united* colonies telling Parliament to change course. American printers played a large role in word and deed, both articulating and embodying American resistance to British policy. Parliament initially failed to listen closely, later began to pay heed, and largely did as the Americans advised, but without yielding on any point of constitutional principle.

THE CONVERSATION BEGAN IN EARLY 1764, when British prime minister George Grenville pushed through Parliament a Sugar Act placing customs duties on foreign molasses imported by Massachusetts and other mainland colonies. Americans had come to rely on the sweetener for both local consumption and distilleries producing rum for a worldwide market. The old Molasses Act of 1733 had imposed exorbitant duties that smugglers had easily evaded by bribing customs officers. By *decreasing* the duty, Grenville and Parliament aimed to *increase* government revenue, encouraging colonial importers to pay the new tax rather than the old bribe.

Openly proclaiming its purpose to "improv[e] the revenue of this Kingdom"—an urgent need in the aftermath of a colossally expensive world war—and to do so "by raising the said revenue *in America*," the act revised other duties and added sharp enforcement teeth. Various forfeiture cases would shift from provincial judges, who were paid by provincial assemblies, into vice-admiralty courts staffed by judges on the imperial payroll and operating free from pesky colonial juries.

(Jurors tended to sympathize with smugglers, who pushed down consumer prices.) Vice-admiralty judges and their minions could also draw fees generated by the forfeitures themselves and would thus have selfish reasons to back Customs House officers to the hilt.[4]

In colonial eyes, the new tax was bad, but Grenville's underlying legal theory was worse. If Parliament could impose a small tax today, nothing would stop Parliament from imposing a large tax tomorrow.[5] In the seventeenth century, the English had fought a Civil War and staged a Glorious Revolution to confirm a basic principle of British liberty, enunciated earlier by the great legalist Coke in the 1628 Petition of Right: taxes could be imposed only by elected representatives, not unelected kings. Eighteenth-century American colonists did not vote in or for Britain's Parliament, so how could Parliament properly tax those who were not represented?

The prospect of more Parliamentary taxes to come was no paranoid delusion or abstract hypothetical. Grenville openly announced that he would likely soon sponsor a broader colonial tax law.[6] This broader tax plan, which would eventually become the Stamp Act of 1765, would require newspapers, almanacs, atlases, deeds, diplomas, court filings, and a wide range of other printed matter (even playing cards!) in the provinces to bear an imperial stamp. Proceeds from the sale of stand-alone stamps and special stamped paper would fund the British government.[7]

Rumors and reports of Grenville's plans peppered American newspapers in early 1764. In April alone, more than a dozen articles—published in New York, Philadelphia, Boston, Newport, Portsmouth, Providence, and Savannah—warned of impending stamp taxes. In one vivid and widely reprinted squib, a note from an unnamed "Gentleman in London" predicted that colonists would "soon have a parcel of Marmadonian Ravens, who will feed upon and rip up your very vitals, such as Officers of Stamp duties. The ministry are determined to make you pay for the peace which you like so well."[8]

The Sugar Act passed Parliament on April 5, 1764. By mid-June printers in most major American seaports—Boston, New York, Philadelphia, Newport, Providence—began publishing the act's complete text or detailed summaries of its leading provisions.[9]

Enter James Otis Jr., responding with blazing speed in a pamphlet prepared in late spring and released in print by the *Boston Gazette*'s publishers in early summer. In *The Rights of British Colonies Asserted and Proved*, Otis, being Otis, ranged far wider than necessary, trying too hard to impress. But in the middle of all the hay were a few sharp and steely needles. "Every British subject born on the continent of America," he wrote, "is by the law of God and nature, by the common law, and by act of parliament . . . entitled to all the natural, essential, inherent and inseparable rights of our fellow subjects in Great Britain. Among those rights are the following: . . . [Parliament] cannot take from any man any part of his property, without his consent in person, or by representation." Thus, "No parts of his Majesty's dominions can be taxed without their consent. . . . [T]he refusal of this, would seem to be a contradiction in practice to the theory of the [British] constitution."

On May 24, the townspeople of Boston met and once again elected Otis (and others, including Otis's 1761 co-counsel Oxenbridge Thacher) to the General Assembly. At that town meeting, voters instructed their assemblymen to oppose all Parliamentary taxation. In emphatic language foreshadowing Otis's not-yet-published pamphlet—language likely drafted by John Adams's second cousin, Samuel Adams, with Otis's support—Bostonians denounced imperial taxes as "annihilat[ing] our charter right to govern and tax ourselves" and also violating "our British privileges, which . . . we hold in common with our fellow subjects who are natives of Britain." Unlimited Parliamentary taxation power would reduce Bostonians "from the character of free Subjects to the miserable state of tributary slaves."[10]

The town's written instructions ended with an enormous idea and admonition that could, *pace* old John Adams, serve as an alternative opening scene of the American Revolution: "As his Majesty's other Northern American colonies are embark'd with us in this most important bottom"—a perfect nautical metaphor befitting the hub of

New England shipping—"we further desire you [our assemblymen] to use your endeavours, that their weight might be added to that of this province. . . . [B]y the united [!] application of all who are aggrieved, all may happily obtain redress." In short, Americans in the Bay Province were beginning to see that they were in the same boat—the same "bark," the same "bottom"—as Americans in other colonies.[11]

The Massachusetts Assembly met shortly thereafter, in June. Otis the younger was now a popular leader in his own right, and his father's memory as former Speaker still lingered. Acting without the concurrence of the legislative upper house—the elected council, where the ubiquitous and conservative Thomas Hutchinson sat and held sway—the Assembly endorsed a statement composed by Otis and ordered that copies be sent to the Bay Province's agent in London. The Assembly also followed up on the Boston town meeting's big idea, creating a five-man committee—including Otis, Thacher, and yet another Bostonian, Thomas Cushing—to write a circular letter to the assemblies of other colonies urging them to jump aboard the ship.[12]

In mid-October, the New York General Assembly jumped, petitioning the House of Commons in language that by now was beginning to look familiar. Under the colony's settled "civil Constitution," the Assembly's constituents were "Exempt[] from the Burthen of all Taxes not granted by themselves." Such was "the grand Principle of every free State" without which there could be "no Liberty, no Happiness, no Security; it is inseparable from the very Idea of Property, for who can call that his own, which may be taken away at the Pleasure of another?" Expressly disclaiming any "Desire of Independency," the Assembly conceded that the British Parliament might properly legislate to regulate imperial trade, but not to raise revenue. Taxes were special under British constitutional traditions, and New Yorkers could be taxed only by a body chosen by New Yorkers themselves.[13]

Also in October, the Massachusetts Assembly reconvened and initially drafted a muscular protest message, not just against the feared future Stamp Act but against the Sugar Act already on the books: "We look upon those Duties as a tax" that "ought not to be laid without the Representatives of the People affected by them"—that is, without an approving vote by the Massachusetts Assembly itself, not some faraway Parliament whose members had never stood for election in the Bay Province. However, at the urging of Lieutenant Governor Hutchinson—who was of course also the sitting chief justice, not to mention a former House Speaker himself and a sitting member of the governor's elected council, which doubled as the upper legislative chamber—the Assembly softened its tone in its final version of official protest.[14]

In December, another important mainland colony—America's oldest and biggest—joined the crusade. Virginia's House of Burgesses sent not only a "remonstrance" to the House of Commons, but also (just to be sure!) an accompanying "memorial" to the House of Lords and a "petition" to King George himself. It was "essential to British Liberty that Laws imposing Taxes on the People ought not to be made without the Consent of Representatives chosen by themselves [and] acquainted with the Circumstances of their Constituents." The proposed stamp tax was thus "an Exercise of anticonstitutional Power" to which the burgesses would "never consent."[15]

Assemblies in several other colonies—Rhode Island, Connecticut, Pennsylvania, and both Carolinas—endorsed similar statements of opposition to Parliamentary taxation. Unwittingly, the mother country was driving her boisterous brood of colonies away from herself and toward each other. The 1764 Sugar Act and the threat of more taxes to come were grabbing America's attention in a way that the technical writs issue in 1761 had not.[16]

These 1764 pronouncements bristled with legalisms. The colonists insisted that taxation was a special category in British constitutional theory, directly linked to ideas of representation and popular election. (Thus the unelected House of Lords could not originate or amend tax legislation, which had to begin life in the House of Commons.[17]) In colonial eyes, the 1688 Glorious Revolution had not established capital-P Parliamentary supremacy, but small-p parliamentary supremacy. Colonial assemblies were in effect the relevant parliaments, at least where taxes were concerned. If revenue were needed, the king's men would have to raise it by persuading colonial assemblies to originate and authorize the necessary taxes. (Otis's pamphlet suggested that the problem could be solved if colonists were represented in Britain's House of Commons, but Virginia threw cold water on the idea. Colonial representatives would be too vastly outnumbered and too far from home in any empire-wide assembly.) Americans viewed small taxes as legally no different from large ones; but all taxes were different from, say, trade-regulation laws, where Parliament might indeed continue to call the tune. On intra-imperial and external trade issues, someone in the empire had to take the lead, and custom favored Parliament. But custom did not similarly establish Parliament's right to tax for revenue purposes, the colonists claimed. And provincials needed to say so loud and clear, lest they be deemed to have waived their objection, thereby conferring additional power on London by implicit consent or adverse possession.[18]

Americans from different parts of the continent were thus beginning to talk constitutionally to each other and were trying to talk to London.

LONDON RESPONDED, BUT SEVERAL OF its responses fell short. In a 1765 pamphlet, Grenville's treasury secretary, Thomas Whately, argued that Parliament was treating the colonists just like their proverbial cousins back in Britain: "Nine Tenths of the People of Britain" were ineligible to vote for Parliament, yet Parliament could and did tax them. Like British nonvoters, the colonists were taxable because "All British Subjects are really in the same [Situation]; none are *actually*, all are *virtually* represented in Parliament." Britain's lawmakers, wrote Whately, protected all British subjects, whether in "Old Sarum" (a tiny borough that had a seat in Parliament) or "Birmingham and Manchester" (cities without seats to match their large populations). Boston and Marblehead, Whately argued, were no different from Birmingham and Manchester.[19]

This was clever claptrap, as Maryland lawyer Daniel Dulany explained in a devastating and widely read rejoinder published in October 1765—too late to prevent passage of the Stamp Act, which was by then already on the books, but a month before the stamped-paper system was scheduled to take effect in America. In Britain, the great mass of laws fell indiscriminately on different parts of the island. Any law burdening Birmingham—say, a tax on a deck of playing cards—would also burden Old Sarum. If Old Sarum voters didn't like the tax, they could vote against their local representative in Parliament; and by thus protecting themselves they would also protect their proverbial brothers in Birmingham: "The Electors, who are inseparably connected in their Interests with the Non-Electors, may justly be deemed to be the Representatives of the Non-Electors." By contrast, both Old Sarum and Birmingham might feel nothing at all—indeed might actually benefit, via lower taxes at home—if Parliament piled extra burdens on Americans and only Americans. In countless ways America's distinct demography and geography meant that colonists were not "inseparably connected" with their cousins in Old Sarum or Birmingham or any other British district: "Not a single actual Elector in England might be immediately affected by a Taxation in America." Because the Stamp Act aimed to tax Americans *differently* than British subjects at home were taxed—and because future Parliaments using Whately's theory could raise American taxes infinitely—the "virtual representation" move was a sham.[20]

Whately and other Grenvillians advanced other arguments anchored more in legal precedent and past practice than in pure principle. First, Americans had long ago waived any right to complain about taxes. The Sugar Act and proposed Stamp Act were nothing new; venerable statutes like the 1733 Molasses Act had likewise aimed to collect revenue. Not expressly and solely, Americans countered. These older laws were also trade regulations. Besides, they were often evaded, and thus carried little weight as putative evidence of long-standing American acquiescence to the alleged principle of Parliamentary taxation authority.[21]

Second, the Irish had no seats in Parliament; what made Americans different? America's answer: Parliament in fact did not tax the Irish. Also, Ireland's and America's legal roots differed dramatically. Ireland had been conquered by the British, whereas early British subjects in America were themselves brave conquerors in the service of the Crown. As John Adams (writing under the pen name Novanglus—Latin for New England) came to distill this point in the 1770s, America "never was conquered by Britain . . . and therefore the reasonings of British writers, upon the case of Ireland, are not applicable to the case of the colonies."[22]

A third British argument tried to turn tables on the colonists. If American legislatures insisted on their exclusive constitutional right to raise revenue themselves, then, fine, let them raise it! By delaying the stamp tax bill, Grenville was giving American assemblies a chance to pay their fair share on their own. Americans countered with a simple question: Exactly how much *was* each colony's fair share of the total imperial burden? If Grenville were serious, he would need to engage each province in a conversation about exactly how much he needed from that province and why. Grenville had done no such thing.[23]

A fourth and more incisive British argument was that tax laws were no different from all kinds of other laws that colonists conceded Parliament could enact. Americans countered by insisting that British constitutional theory and practice clearly had different rules for tax laws; for these laws, elected representatives of the taxed populace needed to play the lead role.

A final British argument, far harder to rebut, knocked all the technical colonial claims off the conversational table with one mighty sweep. Parliament was sovereign, and sovereignty meant indivisible, illimitable power. If Parliament could do *some things* in America—and surely *that* question had already been decided by decades, if not centuries, of practice—then Parliament could do *everything* in America. In 1765, colonists lacked a compelling rejoinder.[24]

Indeed, Otis's 1764 pamphlet seemed to concede that however unconstitutional and violative of the spirit of British liberty Parliamentary taxation of Americans might be, only the sovereign Parliament itself could undo its own laws. No other person or entity in the empire could lawfully resist Parliament, Otis wrote: "The power of parliament is uncontroulable, but by themselves, and we must obey. They only can repeal their own acts. There would be an end of all government, if one or a number of subjects or subordinate provinces should take upon them so far to judge of the justice of an act of parliament, as to refuse obedience to it." If read at face value, this looked like a retreat from his fiery 1761 Court House oration, in which he had argued that Parliamentary acts violating the ancient, albeit unwritten, British Constitution and "natural Equity" were "VOID" in all respects. On the other hand, Otis in his 1764 pamphlet also declared that "if the reasons that can be given against an act, are such as plainly demonstrate that it is against *natural* equity, the executive courts will adjudge such acts void." The relationship between Otis's two pamphlet passages that seemed to point in opposite directions was not entirely clear.[25]

Over the next decade, the colonists would need to find a good rejoinder to the Parliamentary-sovereignty argument that had tied Otis in knots. When, ultimately, the colonists did turn and face the sovereignty argument head-on, astonished Britons would discover that the very logic and force of the argument were also its undoing.

For the moment, the colonists had more urgent problems. Parliament passed the Stamp Act in March 1765.[26] Official stamps and embossed stamped paper would soon arrive from London, and the new taxes would go into effect on November 1. Shockingly, the act authorized the government to prosecute alleged violators in juryless vice-admiralty courts. The Sugar Act had done the same thing, but that 1764 act had involved imports brought to America on ships. It made some sense to apply ship-law procedures in cases of alleged molasses smuggling. (Like its cognate *admiral*, the law of *admiralty* concerned itself with ships and maritime matters.) But the Stamp Act involved transactions taking place entirely on dry land, with no ship or ocean in sight—the issuance of college diplomas, the filing of ordinary lawsuits, the printing of local newspapers, and so on. Admiralty law in these situations was entirely inappropriate, a mere ruse to deprive Englishmen in America of ancient jury trial protections that Englishmen in England took for granted as their constitutional birthright. Though the ministry failed to send prompt notification and precise directions to royal governors about how to implement the new act—another sign of neglect—colonial newspapers filled their pages with details about the law and debates about what Americans should do next.[27]

Intercolonial conversation continued to thicken. Printers in the summer of 1765 devoted more attention than ever to reports from other colonies, even as they also were quick to give readers the latest from London. Leading merchants urged a united colonial boycott: patriots should stop importing British goods (even items having nothing to do with stamps) until Parliament repealed the new taxes. Others, moving past Otis, preached open defiance: come November, patriots should continue to use ordinary unstamped paper for all purposes and dare officials to respond.[28]

Bostonians took to the streets. Newspapers reported that Andrew Oliver—Peter's brother and Hutchinson's brother-in-law—would be named official stamp distributor. In mid-August, a crowd reached him before his formal commission did. Mobbers destroyed the rumored site of his future stamp office, ransacked his house, and dangled a crude depiction of him from a tree. Genteel patriot leaders advised him to forswear his expected appointment. He did as told. Better to be hanged in effigy than in person.[29]

These colonial moves were more than merely conversational. But they were generally proportionate and, in their own way, legalistic. Parliament had not heeded the emphatic messages sent by leading colonists and leading colonial institutions north and south. So conversation alone had not worked. Nor would ballots alone work. That was the rub: Bostonians could not simply vote the British bums out because Bostonians were legally ineligible to vote for Parliament. Thus, when Parliament resorted to the force of law, patriots needed to respond, and did respond, with the counterforce of disobedience.[30]

Surely, Americans individually were within their rights to eschew British imports. True, organized boycotts put public pressure on those wanting to continue business as before; but public pressure also existed on election days in eighteenth-century America, where public voice voting was common and paper ballots were not entirely secret. Even the ugly pressure visited upon Oliver had an arguable legalistic logic and a touch of poetic justice. If royal officials did not respect the property of the colonists, why should the colonists respect the property of royal officials? Let them have a taste of their own medicine—and in a small, measured dose, targeting one pivotal official and putting no more pressure on him than necessary.[31]

Without Oliver's forced resignation, a far greater threat to property would have arisen. Had Oliver opened a stamp office and started issuing stamps and stamped paper—and had even a modest minority (say, a fifth) of Bostonians starting buying and using the stamps and paper—Grenville could have claimed that Bostonians by their actions had actually consented to the principle of plenary Parliamentary tax authority. In a British constitutional system driven largely by unwritten custom and practice, colonists needed to engage in modest self-help *illegality* precisely to preserve their *legal* claim of collective nonwaiver.

Alas, things did not stop at Oliver. On August 26, rioters vented their fury upon Thomas Hutchinson. The mob that night was, in the words of one eminent historian, "more violent than any yet seen in America, more violent indeed than any that would be seen in the entire course of the Revolution." Hutchinson barely escaped with his skin, and his Boston mansion and surrounding gardens lay in ruins. Not content to wreck the building, destroy the trees, and loot ordinary household items such as silverware, china, carpets, bedding, clothing, furniture, paintings, and ready money, the rioters also assaulted the very emblems and instruments of reason and discourse—the very tools of America's fledgling constitutional conversation—by destroying or hurling in the mud many of Hutchinson's books and papers. Among the casualties were manuscript drafts of a provincial-history series that Hutchinson was writing for posterity, along with a trove of historical documents that he had painstakingly collected for thirty years.[32]

There was nothing proportionate, poetic, or conversational in this terrifying and grotesque incident. True, Hutchinson had a long list of royal offices and preferments. True, he was a stalwart supporter of his king, his king's British ministers, his king's British Parliament, and his king's provincial government. (Hutchinson and Governor Bernard suspected that the riot was retribution for Hutchinson's 1761 writs-of-assistance rulings, which now seemed more disturbing to Bostonians in light of recent events.)[33] True, Hutchinson had not, à la Otis in 1760, resigned any of his royal posts in protest of the Stamp Act. True, Hutchinson had not publicly promised to disregard the law if future litigants attempted to file unstamped legal papers in his courtroom once the act went into effect. And it surely seemed suspicious that his brother-in-law apparently stood to profit handsomely from the act. But unbeknownst to the mob, Hutchinson had consistently opposed the act in correspondence with London.[34] Nor had he played any role in procuring the stamp commission for his in-law, who likewise had done nothing to solicit the commission. Over many years, Hutchinson had also repeatedly won elective positions—including the Speakership of the Assembly and his current seat in the council. As to him, Bostonian ballots did count; voters and elected assemblymen (who chose the council) were free to humiliate him at election time. (Indeed, assemblymen did just that in 1766.[35]) Attacking an elected representative as rioters did that day was attacking representation itself. The mob had become a tyrant.

The morning after the riot, Hutchinson appeared in open court in order to make a judicial quorum. In dramatic contrast to his scarlet-robed colleagues, he showed up in rumpled plainclothes. Josiah Quincy Jr., a young lawyer, recorded the poignant scene in his diary that evening. A close affiliate of Adams, Otis, and Thacher, and himself a future leader of the Sons of Liberty, Quincy was no friend of Hutchinson's. But the young man's heart melted at what he saw and heard. "With tears starting from his eyes, and a countenance which strongly told of the inward anguish of his soul," wrote Quincy, Hutchinson addressed the gallery:

GENTLEMEN, . . . Some apology is necessary for my dress; indeed, I had no other. Destitute of everything,—no other shirt; no other garment but what I have on; and not one in my whole family in a better situation than myself, . . . I am obliged to borrow part of *this* clothing. . . . I am innocent [and] all the charges against me are false. . . . I call God to witness . . . that I never, in New England or Old, in Great Britain or America, neither directly nor indirectly, was aiding, assisting, or supporting—in the least promoting or encouraging— what is commonly called the Stamp Act; but, on the contrary, did all in my power, and strove as much as in me lay, to prevent it. This is not declared through timidity; for I have nothing to fear. They can only take away my life. . . . I pray the eyes of the people will be opened, that they will see how easy it is for some designing, wicked man to spread false reports, to raise suspicion and jealousies in the minds of the populace, and enrage them against the innocent. . . . I pray God give us better hearts![36]

While the emotional damage inflicted on Hutchinson was incalculable—and may partially excuse some of his more egregious mistakes over the tumultuous decade that followed—he estimated his property losses at 2,500 pounds sterling. Eventually, he received more than 3,000 pounds from the province itself. This money came from the elected provincial Assembly, meeting in late 1766, after many towns registered their support for a victim-relief bill to indemnify Hutchinson and others who had suffered at the hands of the mob. The funds appropriated by the Assembly came from the public treasury, which in turn drew from taxes paid by the Assembly's constituents. Whereas the rioters' actions had embodied revolutionary fervor at its worst, the eventual provincial decision to make Hutchinson whole—based on taxation *with* representation—was patriotism at its best.[37]

Patriotism at its best also was on display in other provinces. Led by firebrand Patrick Henry, Virginia's House of Burgesses in late May 1765 assailed the stamp tax as enacted. By year's end, eight other colonial assemblies had joined the protest, each composing its own tailored set of resolutions. All opposed taxation without representation, and almost all condemned the Stamp Act's brazen expansion of vice-admiralty jurisdiction at the expense of local juries, the historic bulwarks of English common law.[38]

MOST IMPORTANT OF ALL, IN 1765 America's intercolonial constitutional conversation finally moved indoors. In October, delegates from nine colonies gathered in New York City to converse and concert. Prior to this meeting of the Stamp Act Congress, only once had British North America ever witnessed a continental conclave of any significance. In 1754, the Privy Council, correctly anticipating increased military conflict with the French and French-allied Indian tribes in America's northwestern backcountry, had directed middle and northern colonies to send delegates to meet in Albany, New York, to discuss possible responses. Seven colonies complied, and the Albany delegates proceeded to generate an ambitious plan to create a new intercolonial legal structure to improve cooperation among His Majesty's mainland provinces. But on second thought, neither the London ministers who had inspired the Albany Congress nor the provincial politicians who had sent the delegates showed much interest in implementing the proposed plan, which would have meant ceding power to a newfangled continental institution that might one day develop a mind of its own. The Albany Plan went nowhere.[39]

The two biggest architects of the 1754 Albany Plan were both Boston-born: the incomparable Benjamin Franklin, who left Boston as a young man, and the ubiquitous Thomas Hutchinson, who stayed. A decade later, Bostonians once again took the lead in proposing increased intercolonial cooperation. The invitations to the October Stamp Act Congress came from the Massachusetts Assembly, meeting in June 1765 and continuing to build on the Boston town meeting's earlier recognition that Americans were all in the same boat. Otis originated the Assembly's invitation plan and agreed to serve as one of three delegates representing Massachusetts in New York.

As the Congress began, Otis aimed for the chair. His ambition to preside was not preposterous. More than anyone else, he could claim credit as the prime mover of the gathering. Whether or not he had personally engineered the Boston town meeting instructions, he had diligently pursued the town's same-boat idea in his home assembly. In June 1764, he and other committeemen had sent a circular letter to the other colonial assemblies urging them to induce their respective London agents to "unite in the most serious Remonstrance" against Parliamentary taxation. A year later, he had followed up with a circular letter championing a slightly different united approach— this one inviting the assemblies to send delegates to New York. And of course he had also authored the first big critique of Britain's tax plans, in a pamphlet that had by now been widely read across the continent and across the Atlantic. He was thus one of America's first best-selling political journalists, and the delegates from other colonies surely knew of him, even if they did not know him personally. But Otis was erratic on the page and in the flesh. The delegates thus chose as their presiding officer another Massachusetts man, Timothy Ruggles, a more conservative lawyer with ties to Governor Bernard.[40]

If the Boston Court House was the scene where the seeds of *independence* were first sown in early 1761, it was here, in New York's City Hall, four and a half years later, that the tree of *American Union* took root. Before the outbreak of the French and Indian War, London had convened the intercolonial Albany Congress; but now, after the fall of Montreal and the cession of Canada, colonists themselves were doing the convening, thank you, and they were convening not to challenge Montreal or Paris but to challenge London itself.

When word reached England that such a conference was in the works, the Board of Trade warned the king of the "dangerous tendency" of this extralegal and royally unauthorized "general congress." By this time, delegates were already in New York—a portentous reminder of the communications advantages enjoyed by Americans among themselves. (The Massachusetts Assembly had issued invitations quietly and delayed as long as possible public announcement of the proposed Congress.)[41]

Virginia was the most prominent colony missing at the Stamp Act Congress. By refusing to convene the House of Burgesses, the Old Dominion's royal governor had prevented the colony from properly electing delegates. Some other colonial assemblies had encountered similar resistance from unelected executives, and several deputies to the conclave thus arrived with informal and extralegal credentials.

The twenty-seven delegates who gathered in New York were men of considerable distinction and varied views. At least four, including Ruggles, would profess neutrality or remain loyal to their king in 1776; three would sign the Declaration of Independence; and others would later help draft the federal Constitution.[42] John Rutledge, a South Carolina lawyer who had trained at London's Middle Temple, would go on to be his state's first chief executive, a federal Supreme Court associate justice, his state's Supreme Court chief justice, and (briefly) chief justice of the United States. Thomas McKean would likewise become both chief executive and chief justice in Pennsylvania. Other notables included New York Supreme Court justice Robert R. Livingston, future Pennsylvania president and Supreme Court justice George Bryan, and future Connecticut Superior Court chief judge Eliphalet Dyer.[43]

These twenty-seven men—almost every one a luminary in his home state—were generally strangers to each other, precisely because cooperative political and constitutional conversation across different colonies was then in its infancy. In the recent past, the nine provinces they represented had quarreled with each other over land boundaries, trade rules, Indian affairs, currency matters, and more.[44] Unsurprisingly, complete unanimity did not prevail among these diverse, strong-willed local barons in their first meeting.

Yet in less than three weeks, the Stamp Act Congress did achieve near-perfect unanimity[45] on a series of clear pronouncements reiterating the bedrock American position, the colonies' common denominator. The Congress thus made known to British subjects on both sides of the Atlantic: (1) that as Englishmen in America, the colonists were entitled to the same rights as Englishmen at home; (2) that no taxes could properly be imposed on Americans, "but with their own Consent, given personally, or by their Representatives"; (3) that "the People of these Colonies are not, and from their local Circumstance cannot be, Represented in the House of Commons in Great-Britain" (throwing more cold water on Otis's idea of Americans in Parliament); (4) that "Trial by Jury is the inherent and invaluable Right of every British Subject in these Colonies"; and (5) that Parliament should therefore "Repeal . . . Stamp Duties, and . . . any other Acts of Parliament, whereby the Jurisdiction of the Admiralty is extended."[46]

Almost none of this was new. Except this: For the first time, Americans were beginning to speak formally, juridically, legally, about Americans as such. Not about the Province of Massachusetts Bay or the Colony of Connecticut or the Province of New York, but about "*the People of these Colonies*"—all in the same boat. Only four of the thirteen colonies that would eventually revolt in 1776 had missed the Congressional boat, and three clearly signaled their agreement— Virginia by its prior actions, and Georgia and New Hampshire by formal assembly endorsements of the Congress's resolutions. Only North Carolina stayed mum; its royal governor effectively muzzled the state's Assembly by proroguing and refusing to reconvene it.[47]

The Stamp Act Congress professed sincere loyalty to Britain. The delegates' aim was not independence. Indeed, any attempted move toward independence in 1765–1766 would have been suicidal. Independence would ultimately require the thirteen established mainland colonies to hang together and to do so tightly. That would become possible only when leaders from different parts of the continent began to come together, began to know and trust one another, began to converse collectively, face to face and friend to friend. The Stamp Act Congress was a first step. Near the close of the meeting, delegate Caesar Rodney, who would later vote for and sign the Declaration of Independence, described his new acquaintances as "an assembly of the greatest ability I ever yet saw."[48]

Although the Stamp Act Congress did not inevitably portend the end of British rule in America, the conclave did mark the beginning of a new era of increasingly intense conversation and ever tighter cooperation among the mainland provinces. It was James Otis Jr. more than anyone who had made it happen, even though he failed to win the chair, and even though the Congress squarely rejected his most original idea: American representation in Parliament itself.

The elderly John Adams was thus not wrong in recognizing the catalytic role that his voluble and volatile friend had played before Otis entirely lost his mind in the late 1760s. But the year when *America* as such—a truly continental reality—began to take root and take shape was not 1761, but rather 1765; the room where it happened was not in Adams's beloved Boston but rather in New York; nor—what grated most on old Adams—was young Adams himself in the room when it began to happen.[49]

However, at the convenings of the next intercolonial Congresses, conversing in yet a third great American seaport—the First and Second Continental Congresses of 1774 and 1775 in Philadelphia—Adams would indeed be in the room, making things happen time and again.

MEANWHILE, BACK IN THE CITY streets of late 1765 and early 1766, the Stamp Act was a dead letter almost everywhere even after it was meant to go into effect. Daunted by varying combinations of street protests and social pressures—and paying close attention to events in sister colonies, thanks to newspapers from near and far—Crown favorites in every colony that would eventually unite in 1776 followed Andrew Oliver's famous example, resigning from (or refusing to accept) royal commissions to act as distributors of stamps and stamped paper.[50]

Boycotts took their toll; imports from England plummeted. After a while, ships routinely sailed in and out of colonial ports without showing properly stamped shipping documents, and port and customs officials looked the other way. Eventually, even strong believers in law and order and Parliamentary authority had little choice but to carry on without the proper paper—even in many courts—in technical defiance of the Stamp Act. Hutchinson's judicial colleagues ultimately allowed attorneys to file court documents on ordinary unstamped paper. How could they do otherwise? There were no stamps or stamped papers to be had, given Oliver's decision to decline his stamp commission and the refusal of anyone else to take his place.[51]

Most dramatically and poetically of all, colonial newspapers across the continent went about their business as usual—sometimes without any interruption, sometimes after an initial wait-and-see pause in operations—openly churning out edition after edition on unstamped paper. Most colonial newspapers continued to overflow with ink against the act; and the very pieces of paper on which this ink appeared also spoke volumes. Even though Parliament had not slyly designed the Stamp Act as a purposeful attack on the colonial press, the act had indeed burdened businesses that were based on paper itself—most notably, newspaper printers.[52]

Thus, in addition to the act's open violations of proper principles of taxation and representation (as Americans understood these principles) and its insidious assault on jury trial rights (thanks to its vice-admiralty enforcement rules), the act was an indirect imposition on freedom of the press. Suppose a future ministry refused to sell stamps or stamped paper to a given opposition newspaper. Could the Stamp Act, with modest tweaking, deteriorate into a regime of official censorship and press licensing? Of all the things in the world that Parliament might have chosen to tax—carriages, cloth, coffee, linen, liquor, lumber, tallow, tar, tea, you name it—British lawmakers had unwisely chosen to tax an item vital to discourse itself, especially discourse aiming to span significant physical distance. Colonial printers thus pushed back hard. Unwittingly, the act enabled them to mock Parliament simply by ignoring it and doing what the press had always done: print words on paper.

Although the vast majority of the colonists' rhetorical cannons in 1764–1765 aimed directly at the issues of Parliamentary taxation and constitutional jury rights, one anonymous essayist in the October 21,

1765, edition of the *Boston Gazette* offered his readers an astute, if unduly conspiratorial, aside on the broader issues of press freedom and public discourse: "It seems very manifest from the S—p A-t itself, that a design is form'd to strip us in a great measure of the means of knowledge, by loading the Press, the Colleges, and even an Almanack and a News-Paper, with restraints and duties." Perhaps inspired by this aside, a newspaper in neighboring Connecticut came out as scheduled on November 1—the Stamp Act's operative date—and did so on unstamped paper with an open editorial ode to "the press" as "the test of truth, the bulwark of public safety, [and] the guardian of freedom." The anonymous and perhaps inspirational *Gazette* essayist was none other than John Adams, then a week shy of his thirtieth birthday and readying himself to play an increasingly public role in the great scenes unfolding all around him.[53]

ON MARCH 18, 1766, LESS than a year after it enacted the ill-fated and much-hated Stamp Act, Parliament formally repealed the law.

TOWNSHEND, TROOPS, AND TEA

When news of the repeal hit their local papers, most Americans rejoiced, thinking London had listened and agreed. Actually, London had not listened particularly carefully and had not conceded any issue of constitutional principle. In turn, many Americans themselves misinterpreted what London was saying and not saying. An intercontinental constitutional conversation had begun, but each side at times heard what it wanted to hear.

Nothing in the repeal of the Stamp Act declared that the act had violated any precept of British liberty. Nowhere did Parliament say that Americans could be taxed only by Americans—only by local representatives of their own choosing. Instead, alongside its Stamp Act repeal, Parliament passed an ominous Declaratory Act claiming for itself "full power and authority to make laws and statutes . . . to bind the colonies and people of America . . . in all case whatsoever."

Read broadly, this sweeping assertion of Parliamentary sovereignty said that Americans had no rights that Parliament was bound to respect. Parliament's power was plenary, bounded only by the self-imposed limits that Parliament might adopt as a matter of sovereign grace.[54]

Less than sixteen months after this Declaration, Parliament did indeed enact another series of high-profile taxes on its American colonists. The 1767 Townshend Acts expressly aimed at raising money via new duties on a range of imported items, including glass, lead, paint, paper (again, stupidly), and tea. The better to enforce these new duties and deter smuggling, Parliament also provided for additional writs of assistance.[55]

Why did Parliament think that Americans would accept this mixed-signal message of repeal plus declaration? Why did it think that the Townshend Acts would fare any better in America than had the Stamp Act? In turn, why did Americans not immediately understand the mixed message that Parliament was sending in 1766? When confronted in 1767 by the Townshend Acts and their new writs, how did Americans react?

As BRITAIN SAW THINGS, AMERICANS in 1764 and 1765 had obviously directed far more rhetorical firepower and nullification energy at the Stamp Act than at the Sugar Act. In 1766, Parliament had thus repealed the Stamp Act while leaving the Sugar Act intact. Yet Americans seemed mollified, even joyful. Many Americans had seemed to say that they opposed all Parliamentary taxation; yet the Sugar Act had expressly avowed a revenue-raising purpose. So perhaps the Americans thought that *external* taxes—duties on imported items like foreign molasses (per the Sugar Act)—were qualitatively different from *internal* taxes on everyday items produced in the colonies themselves, such as newspapers (per the Stamp Act)?

Some in London thought the distinction made sense. Others, including Charles Townshend, the Exchequer chancellor who hatched the 1767 tax plan, thought the distinction absurd, but assumed that the colonists were dunces. In language dripping with contempt, he said the distinction was "ridiculous in everybody's opinion except the Americans."[56]

In any event, given that the Sugar Act had passed muster in America, a new set of duties on a broader range of imported items must also be acceptable, Townshend reasoned. If the Americans tried to complain, it was too late. They had already consented to the Sugar Act (and the 1733 Molasses Act before that). If their consent was based on a silly and easy-to-outflank internal-external distinction, they had only themselves to blame for their own speciousness.

Some Americans in 1764–1765 had indeed seemed to draw an internal-external line. In honey-tongued testimony before the House of Commons in early 1766, colonial agent Benjamin Franklin had suggested that many Americans did draw this line.[57] The charming Franklin succeeded in his immediate goal—Stamp Act repeal—but did so by sowing confusion. The Stamp Act Congress had made no such internal-external distinction; nor had the vast majority of colonial assembly declarations. Otis's pamphlet had explicitly rejected the distinction, which he had attributed to various leaders in London: "There is no foundation for the distinction some make in England, between an internal and an external tax on the colonies." In other words, he thought the distinction was ridiculous in everybody's opinion except the English.[58]

Many Americans drew a different line in the sand, as lawyer John Dickinson would soon explain in an influential series of "Letters from a Farmer," which appeared in more than twenty of the mainland colonies' twenty-five newspapers and also found their way into print in England, Ireland, and even France.[59] A Parliamentary enactment designed to regulate trade within the empire or between the empire and the outside world was one thing. Such a statute was a legitimate trade law, even if it incidentally raised some revenue. But a law *plainly designed* to raise revenue from unrepresented British subjects was something entirely different. Such a law was an improper Parliamentary tax. The *purpose* of the law made all the difference. As John Adams would later argue in the Boston Massacre trial, purpose often matters in law; thus, an accidental killing should not be treated the same as a cold-blooded premeditated murder. On this view, the Stamp Act clearly fell on the improper side of the line, and so did the Townshend Duties, even though the latter were "external."

As for the Sugar Act, the Massachusetts Assembly in 1764 had initially declared that "we look upon those [Sugar Act] Duties as a tax" that "ought not to be laid without the Representatives of the People affected by them." But Hutchinson had persuaded the Assembly to refrain from sending this provocative constitutional statement to London. As a result of Hutchinson's intervention, London may have been misled about the true sentiments of the men of Massachusetts (just as Franklin's later testimony would prove misleading about the more general colonial view).[60]

But why, we might ask, did Americans misunderstand Parliament's actual message in 1766, when the repeal of the Stamp Act was pointedly paired with the Declaratory Act?

Partly because Americans had only limited access to Parliamentary debates (just as Englishmen had only limited understanding of the initial Massachusetts Assembly vote on the Sugar Act). Many Parliament members themselves understood the Declaratory Act phrase "in all cases whatsoever" to include taxes as well as all sorts of other legislation; this specific issue had in fact been debated on the floor. But many Americans did not know that. Modern norms of democratic openness and transparency in government had not yet entrenched themselves. Parliamentary sessions in the 1760s were not yet routinely open to the public, and printers could not publish accounts of what was said in Commons without special permission. (In that era, to print without permission was punishable interference with Parliamentary speech and debate.)[61]

Two things that colonists did know led them to believe, or at least hope, that the Declaratory Act was not as bad as it looked. First, the act did not expressly say, but surely could easily have said, "in all cases whatsoever, *including taxation*." (In the cagey diplomatic spirit of Franklin, the ministry had purposefully omitted the T-word, which officials thought might be unduly provocative. The result, as with

Franklin's earlier fudging, was to improve immediate harmony by sowing confusion and risking future misunderstandings.)[62] Second, the text of the 1766 Declaratory Act echoed the language of Parliament's 1719 Declaratory Act asserting plenary legislative authority over Ireland; yet Parliament had in fact never taxed Ireland.[63]

The 1767 Townshend Duties generated new rounds of intercolonial and transatlantic constitutional conversation—this time with a strong sense of déjà vu. In 1768 Massachusetts initiated another circular letter to sister assemblies, and these assemblies renewed their claims that Parliament lacked authority to tax unrepresented colonists. Merchants again organized boycotts, and patriots again took to the streets to pressure loyalists and fence-sitters to honor the boycotts. In response, supporters of the ministry on both sides of the Atlantic continued to insist that taxes were no different from anything else and that Parliament was sovereign over everything.[64]

WRITS OF ASSISTANCE WERE ALSO back in the news, far more visibly than in 1761. The Townshend Duties brought renewed attention to customs officials, who were the ones charged with collecting the new duties. If enforced, these duties meant more money for London. If evaded, they meant more profit for smugglers. However, if customs officials could catch the smugglers, the officials themselves would profit from the resulting forfeiture suits in (juryless) vice-admiralty courts, as would royal governors, who were entitled to share in the forfeiture proceeds. The vice-admiralty judges and their subordinates would also profit, as more judicial business would mean more court fees.

When customs officials went to various provincial high courts (not to be confused with vice-admiralty courts) to ask for writs of assistance in the late 1760s, the officials encountered more judicial resistance than had Charles Paxton in 1761. Why? First and most obviously, the writs were now tied (as they had not been in 1761) to the most politically sensitive issues imaginable: the Townshend

Duties and the underlying constitutional controversy about Parliamentary taxation power.

Second, Parliament in the 1764 Sugar Act tweaked the prior writs regime to favor customs officials over local juries. If an official with a writ searched and came up empty, he would now be immune from damages so long as a judge after the fact decided he had acted diligently, with a factual basis—probable cause—for his unsuccessful search. Disturbingly, the jurist making this decision would now likely be a royally paid vice-admiralty judge acting without jury oversight and with a personal financial incentive to encourage customs officials to take risks.[65]

Third, courts in different colonies were now paying closer attention to each other. When various judges in the earliest post-Townshend cases adopted a cautious wait-and-see approach, judges in most other provinces noticed and followed suit. No one wanted to incur the people's wrath for being a tool of imperial taxation. Every judge in America knew what had befallen Hutchinson and Oliver in 1765. As time passed, wait and see gradually became wait, and writs generally did not issue.[66]

American judges and newspaper printers were also paying close attention to mid-1760s events in England related to searches and seizures. The main debate there involved general search warrants, which differed in key ways from writs of assistance. General warrants aimed to immunize even if a searcher who found nothing had acted utterly capriciously, without even a shred of arguable reasonable suspicion. Not so with writs of assistance, even after 1764. Because of this key difference, leading English authorities, including the great libertarian Lord Camden, invalidated general warrants but consistently upheld writs of assistance. Nevertheless, the high-profile English general-warrant controversy intensified colonial anxieties about imperial search policies.

One litigant in particular, the flamboyant journalist and Parliament member John Wilkes, proved irresistibly fascinating to Americans. In 1763, British officials ransacked Wilkes's London home and arrested him as part of a dragnet general-warrant search. The searchers hoped to find proof that Wilkes was the anonymous author featured in the incendiary *North Briton* No. 45—a newspaper edition that had denounced Grenville's predecessor, Lord Bute, and disparaged the monarch himself. Wilkes sued the oppressive searchers and won. In a cluster of landmark rulings, the chief judge of Common Pleas, Sir Charles Pratt, condemned general warrants, championed the property and privacy rights of homeowners, and threw special protections around private papers. Soon thereafter, Pratt became Lord Camden and joined the House of Peers, where he allied himself with Parliamentary statesman William Pitt. At the close of the 1760s, Wilkes starred in yet another cause célèbre when Parliament expelled him as ethically unfit despite emphatic and repeated votes of confidence from his constituents.[67]

Colonists saw Wilkes's struggles and their own travails as two halves of a unified transatlantic crusade for British constitutional liberty. As with Wilkes, many Americans loathed Bute, who in patriot eyes personified power lust and undeserved privilege. In the colonies, the number "45" and the phrase "Wilkes and Liberty" became rallying cries for freedom, not unlike modern-day hashtags. Americans believed that Wilkes was being punished for his antiministerial stance, just as they themselves were being oppressed. By excluding Wilkes from his seat, Parliament was refusing to respect the electoral sentiments of Wilkes's constituents—much as Parliament was refusing to listen to colonists and their duly elected assemblies. Parliament's mistreatment of Wilkes was a metaphor for Parliament's mistreatment of America.[68]

AMERICAN NEWSPAPERS COVERED LONDON DEVELOPMENTS concerning Wilkes, Camden, and Pitt with gusto. Colonists across the land showed their love by naming cities, towns, and counties in honor of these defenders of British liberty—Pittsfield, New Hampshire; Pittsgrove Township, New Jersey; Pittstown (now Pittston), Pennsylvania; Pittsylvania County, Virginia; Camden, New Jersey; Camden, South Carolina; Camden, Massachusetts (now Maine);

Wilkes-Barre, Pennsylvania; Wilkes County, North Carolina; Wilkes County, Georgia; and more. Reciprocally, Pitt, Camden, and Wilkes paid heed to what colonists were writing and saying.[69]

Indeed, these three ranked among the most prominent defenders of the colonial cause in London. In the House of Lords, Camden opposed the Declaratory Act and in doing so expressly endorsed colonial claims that taxes were special and that taxation without representation was wrong. In the debate over repealing the Stamp Act, Pitt likewise seemed to recite the colonists' catechism: "This kingdom has no right to lay a tax upon the colonies. . . . At the same time, I assert the authority of this kingdom over the colonies, to be sovereign and supreme, in every circumstance of government and legislation whatsoever. . . . The distinction between legislation and taxation is essentially necessary to liberty." A bit later, England's Pitt, anticipating America's Dickinson, said this: "There is a plain distinction between taxes levied for the purposes of raising a revenue, and duties imposed for the regulation of trade."[70]

Perhaps Pitt's best moment came when he showed genuine love for the colonists: "Americans are the sons, not the bastards of England." Consciously or not, he was echoing a similar phrase deployed by his ally Colonel Isaac Barré, an Irish-born, university-educated soldier who had fought valiantly in the North American theater of the recent global war. Barré entered Parliament in 1761 and played a particularly notable role defending America in early 1765, even before the Stamp Act's passage. Unlike many others in Parliament—haughty Englishmen who openly referred to Americans as "children"—Barré spoke admiringly and did so from personal experience: "I claim to know more of America than most of you, having seen and been conversant in that Country. The People there are as truly Loyal, I believe, as any Subjects the King has: But a People jealous of their Liberties, and who will vindicate them, if they should be violated." Americans, Barré declared, were "Sons of Liberty."[71]

Muscular bands of patriots in local cells across America requited Barré's love for them by taking that grand phrase and making it their own: they began calling themselves "Sons of Liberty." Thus a label made famous in London by a man born in Dublin who had spent formative world-war-related years of his life in America quickly traveled from the imperial capital back across the Atlantic thanks to public letter-writers and newspapers.[72]

In short, some in London were getting the American message, and more Americans than ever were closely following legal and political issues in London and in sister colonies. However imperfectly, northern colonists, mid-Atlantic colonists, southern colonists, and Londoners were beginning to converse together about the latest constitutional developments, drawing intellectual connections between events simultaneously unfolding thousands of miles apart.

CUSTOMS HOUSE OFFICIALS FEARED FOR their personal safety. They were the linchpins in the Townshend Acts' tax regime—much as stamp distributors had been the linchpins in the Stamp Act system. The Stamp Act had failed thanks in large part to popular intimidation of stampmen organized by the Sons of Liberty. Intimidation—widespread blacklisting, occasional tarring-and-feathering—had also been visited upon loyalist merchants and various other law-abiding colonists who leaned toward the ministry.[73] They, too, feared for their safety. How would Townshend and his allies prevent a replay of the Stamp Act debacle?

By sending troops. In late 1768, more than a thousand Regulars tramped into Boston. Earlier, New York City had also received uninvited guests in uniform, and under Parliament's Quartering Act of 1765, the cost of maintaining these soldiers fell on the host colony. From the ministry's point of view, British law needed to be enforced—and Americans needed to be taught a lesson. From the patriots' point of view, standing armies in peacetime portended tyranny.

The expense was bad enough—a vicious cycle of higher taxes to support troops who were there to enforce these very tax laws, whose underlying unpopularity would in turn require even more troops and even more taxes to pay for even more troops, endlessly. But the threat to liberty was worse. *Whom were the troops there to daunt?* Bostonians asked. Not the French Canadians—they had been vanquished, in part thanks to colonial valor. If, as some in power claimed, the troops were there to protect the frontier against Indians, then why were the soldiers stationed in major seaports with large civilian populations of lawyers, printers, preachers, schoolmasters, students, and scribblers?

The quartering of more than a thousand armed soldiers in a major colonial city was an iron-fisted move. At the height of the occupation, Redcoats accounted for more than a third of Boston's adult male population. London aimed to compel, not converse, and to compel using swords rather than writs, by deploying British-born Regulars in uniform rather than American-born magistrates in robes and American-born jurors and militiamen in plain clothes.

On March 5, 1770, professional soldiers far from home killed civilian locals on a city street. The Sons of Liberty were ready with their response—not muskets or swords (not yet!) but legal quills and artists' pencils. The patriots had lost the street skirmish but would use that loss to win the ensuing constitutional conversation.

WE CALL IT THE "BOSTON Massacre," but that label itself is a reflection of the rhetorical triumph of one side of this conversation—the self-described "patriots" or "Whigs," as opposed to the "loyalists," "Tories," or "conservatives"; the "popular party" or "country party" arrayed against "the court party"; the "Sons of Liberty" as distinguished from the "friends of government." Perhaps it might just as well be called the "Boston Melee" or the "Boston Brawl," or, more neutrally, the "Boston Incident" or the "Boston Tragedy."

John Adams, who would later defend the soldiers involved, was characteristically colorful and, also characteristically, more than a tad bigoted in his description of events. As soldiers stood guard in front of the Boston Customs House, on King Street near the Court House, they faced, in Adams's words, a "motley rabble of saucy boys, negroes and mulattoes, Irish teagues, and outlandish jack tars." The raucous crowd, some fifty strong, pelted the soldiers with snowballs, ice chunks, and other painful projectiles, jeering the men in uniform and daring them to respond. At some point, shots rang out. Eleven civilians fell; five died on the spot or soon thereafter. Colonial blood had now spilled on colonial soil. Coffins were needed, as they had not been (thanks more to luck than anything else) when a vicious mob had ruined Hutchinson's mansion in August 1765.[74]

Speaking of Hutchinson . . . it was he—the all-in-one former House Speaker, former councillor, former chief judge, former lieutenant governor, and now the acting governor—who quickly appeared on the scene after the shooting to restore law and order and credibly offer a promise of blind justice to his native Boston. At real risk to his own person, he waded into the melee, threading through inflamed Bostonians brandishing bludgeons and cutlasses until he reached the soldiers, their outthrust bayonets ready for further action. The judicious, law-revering words that he cried out to the officer in charge, Captain Thomas Preston, showed Hutchinson at his finest: "How came you to fire without orders from a civil magistrate!" Equally fine were his words to the King Street crowd from the east-facing balcony, the very same spot where Bernard had once stood to proclaim King George III: "The law shall have its course! I will live and die by the law!" After getting the crowd to disperse, Hutchinson immediately began an on-the-scene investigation that lasted into the wee hours.[75]

Hutchinson was true to his word. Regular criminal trials of Preston and eight of his men did indeed take place in late 1770. The fact that a royally appointed governor would allow the law to run its course, with the fate of British-born soldiers in the hands of overwhelmingly colonial-born jurors, showed that not all Crown supporters were tyrants, even though the Crown's underlying policy of military intimidation in Boston had tyrannical foundations.

In the end, most of the soldiers were acquitted of the most serious charges against them—murder with malice aforethought. Their lead defense attorney was not a Crown supporter and was surely no friend of Hutchinson. He was himself a Son of Liberty and kinsman to Samuel Adams, perhaps the most important leader of the Sons of Liberty. This defense attorney did not take the case to throw it. He took it to win it, and win it he did, in the main. Why would a staunch patriot do such a thing? Because, despite his pathological hatred of Hutchinson, John Adams shared Hutchinson's ultimate belief in law; because most of his clients had valid legal defenses (provocation and confusion); and because he wanted to show the world, and especially the king and the ministry, that Boston was not a lawless pit. Local juries of colonials could be trusted to do the right thing. And this was exactly why, Adams and other Sons believed, England was so wrong in its recent vice-admiralty legislation that denied Americans their basic rights as Englishmen to serve on juries and be tried by juries—juries that would do proper and impartial justice to both defendants and victims, based on the facts and the law.

OTHER MEMBERS OF THE SONS of Liberty used the Massacre to promote the patriot cause in more obvious ways. In so doing, they quite literally illustrated another notable aspect of America's rapidly thickening constitutional conversation: the remarkable power of a new conversational tool, the political cartoon.

Proverbially, a picture is worth a thousand words. But not all pictures are equally useful in a quickly unfolding back-and-forth global constitutional conversation aiming to achieve immediate legal and political effects in a self-governing society based on frequent elections. In certain situations, the conversational intervention must be lightning fast—composed quickly, easy to understand, easy to emulate swiftly on cheap coarse newsprint, and designed to immediately frame the big issues for constitutional discussion.

Trumbull's magisterial depiction of the Declaration of Independence, for example, is a magnificent piece of political art, but it does not work (nor was it meant to work) as a political cartoon. It took decades to compose. Likewise, the oils of Stuart monarchs that Adams admired aesthetically and detested politically surely were not done overnight. England's brilliant satirical artist William Hogarth is today often but undeservedly considered the father of the now common art form of the political cartoon. Hogarth's best work was, like Trumbull's, time-consuming both to compose and to appreciate. Much of Hogarth's work was not obviously political or remotely constitutional. (Hutchinson's country house in Milton featured a handsome set of Hogarth's famous etchings mocking marriages of financial convenience.) Even when Hogarth did venture into overtly political caricature—such as a nasty 1763 sketch of John Wilkes, who had previously said nasty things about Hogarth—the art does not quite do what a different kind of political image would need to do: grab the viewer by the throat, in the moment.[76]

America, not England, originated the modern-style political cartoon, reflecting and reinforcing America's more open and democratic conversational culture. Two of history's earliest and most successful political cartoons, by Son of Liberty Paul Revere, followed in the tradition of an even earlier Boston-born cartoonist named Benjamin Franklin. Revere's first Massacre imagery appeared within a week of the shooting, in the *Boston Gazette*, published by another Son of Liberty, Benjamin Edes.

The message is unsubtle and the artwork is, well, cartoonish, but Revere's arrayed coffins still pack a conversational wallop. *They are*

killing us! The image was easy to imitate, and variations of it were reprinted elsewhere.[77] Revere's implicit punchline here was every bit as forceful as the explicit slogan that Otis had popularized a few years earlier: *Taxation without representation is tyranny!*

Three weeks after the shooting, Revere began selling, directly to the public, a more detailed engraving of what he labeled *The Bloody Massacre*. Here, too, the message is powerful, whether true or not: *The soldiers shot on orders, in disciplined fashion, intentionally and unprovoked, and the victims were as faultless and unthreatening as the gentle puppy at their feet.* As John Adams would successfully argue at trial, that was probably not what actually happened. But in 1770 (and even today) Revere's depiction is what many people in America thought (and continue to think) happened.

OTHER SONS OF LIBERTY WERE artists in a different way. One of their most memorable and, in retrospect, world-changing, contributions to America's constitutional conversation occurred three and a half years after the Massacre, in a brilliant piece of political performance art now known, in a label that came into vogue in nineteenth-century America, as the Boston Tea Party.

The tempest over tea began in early April 1770, when Parliament repealed most of the Townshend Duties. Colonial boycotts had punished British manufacturing and shipping, just as they had in the Stamp Act crisis, and once again, Britain seemed to concede defeat. This time, the ministry announced that no new taxes would follow.[78]

Yet once again, British pride and British constitutional ideas about Parliamentary sovereignty prevented complete capitulation. Instead of a new Declaratory Act, Parliament simply kept in place the Townshend duty on tea to preserve the point of legal principle that it had plenary power over all colonial matters, including tax matters.

This incomplete repeal was not the pure principle that the colonists had insisted on for so long, but it was more than half a loaf from the most powerful empire in the world, and many colonists had wearied from the years of conflict with the mother country. No intercolonial Congress had gathered since 1765, and in the absence of tight agreement among all colonies, the boycott began to fall apart. Merchants who broke ranks early enjoyed commercial advantages over those who initially held firm. Eventually, many colonists openly resumed importing British items, including in some places taxed molasses and even taxed tea. Boston, however, continued to be a center of resistance, generally eschewing taxed tea, preferring to drink smuggled Dutch tea.[79]

Tea smuggling required paying bribes to corrupt officials. What if colonists could be induced to pay an honest tax rather than a dishonest bribe? (This was a repeat of the thinking that had led to the Sugar Act of 1764.) In mid-1773, the British East India Company, a government-supported monopoly, convinced Parliament to allow the company to sell its tea directly in the colonies through special brokers at a lower price than before, but with the modest Townshend tea tax still in place. Now, in addition to the old worries about taxation without representation, new worries about government-backed monopolies and favoritism among merchant-distributors gripped the patriots' imaginations. Once again, self-help remedies commended themselves to anxious Bostonians. Much as they had pressured Andrew Oliver into refusing his Stamp Act commission, so now they would pressure ship captains into taking their tea elsewhere.

For if the tea were unloaded; and if even a few Bostonians took the bribe and bought cheap tea; and if the ministry then were to say that the colonists had thus abandoned their earlier professed principles; and if a future ministry were to change course and pile new taxes on colonists; and if in the future the East India monopoly were, in addition, to boost prices, as monopolists were wont to do . . . well, if all that were to happen, then the colonists would be back where they started in 1764, but with a weaker claim of constitutional principle, because a few of them had fallen for the ruse and taken the bribe.

This elaborate line of thought was strikingly legalistic, focused as it was on the special problem of waiver/consent in the British system of unwritten constitutionalism,[80] and attentive as it was to the difficulty of drawing any suitable *legal* line between small taxes and big ones. Britain was effectively *lowering* the price of tea, and the Sons of Liberty were apoplectic! The fact that Hutchinson's adult sons were among the handful of monopoly-favored merchants authorized to sell the tea in America at low prices only intensified patriot outrage.[81]

The trick was to prevent the tea from being unloaded onto the wharf. Legally, that was the moment when the tax would attach and the precedent would be set. The dazzling performance-art solution arrived at by agitator Samuel Adams, *Gazette* publisher Benjamin Edes, and other Sons of Liberty on December 16, 1773,[82] was for the Sons to unload the tea themselves—sans tax, of course—not onto the wharf in the daylight, but into the water at night; not overtly as proud "Sons," but covertly as putative "Savages."

"Savages" is a charged word today, but one used by the Sons in their earliest public descriptions of the event. According to an anonymous "Impartial Observer" (who was hardly impartial, and likely not a mere observer—Edes, perhaps?), a "number of Persons, supposed to be the Aboriginal Natives from their complection [*sic*], . . . gave the War-Whoop. . . . The Savages repaired to the ships which contained the pestilential Teas, and . . . began their ravage."[83] A contemporaneous broadside celebrating the Tea Partiers as "YE GLORIOUS SONS OF FREEDOM" in verse featured this rhyme: "Though you were INDIANS come from distant shores, like MEN you acted—not like savage Moors." Later, we shall return to the troubling word "savages," which subsequently appeared in the Declaration of Independence, but for now let us note several critical features of the Sons' performance-art solution.

The solution was *nonviolent.* Unlike the soldiers at the Massacre, the Sons killed no one. Unlike the mob at Hutchinson's house, the Sons did not come close to killing anyone.

The solution was *proportionate.* The Sons destroyed no more property than necessary. They tossed overboard and thus ruined approximately 340 chests of East India tea, valued at about 9,700 pounds sterling. But no books or papers were disturbed or destroyed, as had happened at Hutchinson's mansion. The three tea-laden ships involved in the episode were unharmed, and their non-tea cargo was untouched. The Sons made a point of sweeping the decks. The patriots would have preferred simply to scare the ships off, but Governor Hutchinson (no longer merely acting governor as he had been at the Massacre) had forbidden the ships to leave the harbor, and for technical customs-law reasons the clock was ticking down fast.[84]

The solution was *public spirited* and *non-piratic*. The Sons dumped the tea to make a legal and political point. They did not plunder or pilfer for their own private use—again, unlike the mob at Hutchinson's mansion, where looters disgraced the patriot cause. The Sons and their allies in the press proudly stressed this fact: "A watch . . . was stationed to prevent embezzlement, and not a single ounce of Tea was suffered to be purloined by the populace."[85]

The solution was *conversation-starting* and *attention-grabbing*, designed to win publicity across America and also in London, to counter the ministry's low-tax-now gambit that threatened high taxes later. (What comes down must go up, thought the Sons.) Like Revere's eye-catching cartoons, Otis's ear-grabbing slogans, Pitt's soaring speeches, and Barré's fetching phraseology, the Sons' performance art was part of an emerging democratic culture that rewarded those able to capture the attention and woo the hearts of the many.

The solution was *playful, satiric,* and *stylish*—worthy of Hogarth himself. London snobs had treated their colonial cousins as if they were uncivilized aborigines, rather than proper New World Englishmen entitled to all the rights of proper Old World Englishmen. Well, the Sons replied, winkingly, don't blame us for the destruction of tea. Blame the Indians, against whom your soldiers are allegedly protecting us! The Sons may also have relished the performance pun that New World "Indians" were thwarting Britain's *East India* monopoly. In a note the following day to James Warren (brother-in-law of James Otis Jr.), John Adams gave the Sons' theatrical performance a rave review: "This is the grandest Event which has ever yet happened Since the Controversy with Britain opened! The Sublimity of it charms me!"

From today's perspective, the Sons' solution—facetiously disguising themselves as brown-skinned Natives—was also arguably racist in its cultural appropriations and ethnic humor. Even as American patriots demanded rights for themselves against the British, what rights were they willing to recognize for the Indians? This would become one of the central questions of America's constitutional conversation in the years and decades ahead.[86]

COERCION, COMMITTEES, AND CORRESPONDENCE

Thomas Hutchinson was smart, brave, honest, pious, industrious, tolerant, even-tempered, and public-minded. He loved his hometown and his king. Had he lived only twenty years earlier he would never have been obliged to choose between them. He was a scrupulous and accomplished historian. But like many a historian, he had mastered the past better than he understood the present, and far better than he envisioned the future. The world around him was churning furiously—giving birth to new kinds of discourse and new forms of democracy and generating new patterns of legitimacy and civic virtue. Boston was the epicenter of the earthquake, but Hutchinson could not feel the ground shifting under his feet until he was already plunging into disaster.

Although Hutchinson loved his hometown, he did not prize all its people, especially those well below him in the status hierarchy. He did not connect—instinctively, viscerally—with middling and common folk the way Isaac Barré had evidently connected while in America. The viciousness of the attack on his mansion in 1765 flowed from his lack of feeling for many Bostonians and their reciprocal lack of feeling for him. Whether fair or not—and in fact it was in many respects unfair—Otis's sustained campaign to demonize Hutchinson had worked.[87]

Hutchinson inspired fear and commanded respect, as evidenced by his ability to limit the chaos immediately after the Massacre. But as politics and communications became increasingly popular and democratic, even demagogic, in the 1760s and early 1770s, the ubiquitous Boston statesman found it impossible to maintain his political footing. In the end, Thomas Hutchinson was doomed by his too-strong sense of hierarchy and his too-weak understanding of the intense yearnings and deep emotions of the men around him—men who perhaps were his social and intellectual lessers but nonetheless his legal equals, as another notable American named Thomas would soon famously insist.[88]

Also, from a very young age, Hutchinson had shown no sense of humor.[89] With their jaw-dropping, tea-splashing coup, the Sons of Liberty had made a fool of him in a grand carnival and on a world stage. Temperamentally, this old-fashioned, straitlaced man could not quite laugh at himself and adjust, as the most adept political leaders in the New World aborning would eventually learn to do.

Hutchinson had precipitated the tea crisis by his own rigidity, refusing to allow the ships to leave port and take their toxic tea with them. He thought he had the patriots in a box, but in a maneuver worthy of wily Odysseus, the Sons had outwitted him. Had he been their equal in the new conversational style of democratic politics, he might have countered with his own *beau geste,* something like this:

My dear fellow subjects of His Majesty's Province of Massachusetts Bay: As you once indemnified me in my hour of loss, I will now indemnify you. For the moment, I pledge to pay for all the damage done to the tea out of my own pocket—some ten thousand pounds, though this promise that I now make may well ruin me and will at least undo almost all my family's fortune, hard won over many generations of honest toil. For if I do not pay out of my own pocket, I fear that His Majesty's government in London will make all of Boston pay, and this inevitable insistence will only further estrange His Majesty's government from the good people of this province and the good people of this province from His Majesty's government. This must not happen. We are one people, and we must never become estranged. We must never become enemies. But I also say this: *Those who did this foul deed are cowards.* They have not acted in the light of day and with their faces undisguised. I now say to them: Unmask yourselves! If you are proud of what you have done, step forward and own your actions! I, in turn, reserve the right to bring a civil lawsuit against each and every one of you for your trespasses; and I shall be content to let an honest jury of our fellow subjects apportion the final costs between us.[90]

But Hutchinson, being Hutchinson, did nothing of the sort. Politically, he lacked flair. Personally, his extreme acquisitiveness made it unthinkable to throw away his fortune in a flourish, even though it might astonish and inspire the masses, as the Sons themselves had astonished and inspired their audience.

In the end, Hutchinson proved unable to keep what was his anyway. Hobbled by the Tea Party crisis, he eventually found himself in exile in Britain. After independence, the new patriot government of the Commonwealth of Massachusetts seized much of his property, along with the property of other loyalist exiles, to fund the Revolutionary War effort.

Hutchinson's favorite residence was a beautiful country estate in Milton, six miles south of his once stunning but later ruined mansion in Boston proper. In the early 1780s, this elegant Milton estate came into the possession of Mercy Otis Warren, daughter of Colonel James Otis Sr. and sister of James Otis Jr.[91]

WHEN WORD OF THE TEA Party reached London in early 1774, Parliament lost all patience with its unruly children—for that is how Parliament viewed them—and resolved to teach Boston a lesson, via a series of Coercive Acts. American patriots, fast mastering the art of sloganeering, promptly relabeled these laws "Intolerable Acts."

First, the Boston Port Act closed the city's harbor (with exceptions for food and fuel shipments) until someone paid for the spoiled tea. Second, the Massachusetts Government Act eliminated some of the most democratic and distinctive features of the old provincial

charter. Colonists would now be less free to assemble and make collective pronouncements in town meetings, and the General Assembly would no longer elect the colonial council. Third, if royal soldiers,
customs officials, or various other imperial officers committed local
crimes, they might no longer need to answer to local juries, but instead could be tried back in England. Parliament labeled this law
"An Act for the Impartial Administration of Justice." Patriots called
it the Murder Act. Regardless of label, the new law trampled ancient common-law principles that crimes should be tried where they
happened—where the blood had spilled, where the witnesses lived,
and where a local jury of the vicinage could fairly hold the scales of
justice, as indeed had happened in the Massacre trials. Fourth and
most menacingly, a new Quartering Act promised that troops would
once again return to the city streets of Boston. (To ease tension after
the Massacre, Hutchinson had sensibly relocated soldiers in a harbor
fort outside the town.)[92]

As with several previous Parliamentary impositions, these initiatives provoked massive resistance. This time, the resistance would
eventually prove so deep, wide, and firm that the empire would sun-
der. The colonists would fight—not just with words and cartoons,
but with swords and cannons; not just with boycotts and blacklists,
but with bayonets and bullets; not just with feathers, face paint, and
political theater, but with muskets, militias, and a continental army.

The British did not understand what they were up against because
they were not listening carefully—in part because they simply did
not care enough, in part because they were not focusing on the wisest and most relevant interlocutors, and in part because they did not
appreciate the significance of the communications-and-conversation
revolution already under way.

For example, Massachusetts town meetings had irked London.
Boston townsmen had assembled from time to time to issue collective
pronouncements; scores of other towns had then met and responded,
often reinforcing the initial message and triggering additional press
reports and commentary.[93] The Coercive Acts aimed to stamp out
this irksome and relatively recent conversational practice. Henceforth,

declared Parliament, towns could ordinarily meet only once a year, to elect members of the General Assembly. Parliament's new pronouncement was as unavailing as if that grand imperial legislature, in its infinite wisdom and sovereignty, had commanded the tide to stop rising. Massachusetts patriots had already established a reliable chain-letter network enabling local cells to converse with each other and communicate messages of wider interest.

To be sure, these self-described "committees of correspondence" were informal and extralegal. But they were nevertheless powerful tools in the new world of constitutional conversation. (Analogously, many of the delegates to the Stamp Act Congress had arrived via unofficial channels, and the Congress as a whole had itself been informal and extralegal.) Indeed, there were real advantages to quiet communications among patriots that did not tip off loyalists, as the organizers of the Tea Party had brilliantly demonstrated. If anything, Parliament to its own detriment was driving legitimate and thoughtful conversational resistance underground. In any event, these local committees of correspondence had already spread, contagiously, far beyond the Bay Province. The cats were already out of the bag, and Parliament could not put them back.

In 1773, Americans had added a dramatic new layer of correspondence atop the rising edifice. The Virginia House of Burgesses sent a circular letter proposing the formation of a permanent network of correspondence among colonial assemblies. Under Virginia's plan, each assembly would create a standing committee to correspond with each other standing committee. These committees could converse and coordinate even if some assemblies were formally in self-imposed recess or had been dissolved or prorogued by royal governors acting on their own or under London's orders. By 1774, almost all the other colonies had accepted Virginia's invitation and were now conversing among themselves.[94]

By singling out Massachusetts as uniquely obstreperous, the Coercive Acts aimed to isolate her from her sister American colonies, but Americans refused to take the bait. Had Parliament been paying close attention, it should not have been surprised. Fully a decade earlier, the Sugar Act and the then impending Stamp Act had begun to unify the colonies, as evidenced by multiple circular letters and by the Stamp Act Congress itself. The Townshend Acts controversy had only strengthened these intercolonial ties.

True, these earlier acts had formally applied to all colonies. But when London had tried to play divide-and-conquer against Massachusetts in 1768, the clumsy effort had backfired. In that year, the Massachusetts Assembly had issued a circular letter to its sister assemblies in the spirit of its earlier circular letters of 1764 and 1765—this time to mobilize opposition to the Townshend Duties. London had responded by ordering Bernard to dissolve the General Assembly, and had directed other colonial assemblies to treat the Massachusetts missive "with the contempt it deserves." Instead, most of the other assemblies had approved or echoed the Massachusetts message, showing London the contempt *it* deserved.[95]

As in the Stamp Act Congress, intercolonial communication had portentously proved faster than transatlantic discourse. By the time royal governors had received word from London to prevent their assemblies from embracing the 1768 circular letter—by dissolving assemblies if need be—many assemblies had already acted. And then, in 1769, after the Virginia royal governor did dissolve the Virginia House of Burgesses, the burgesses simply met extralegally and sent their own circular letter to sister assemblies criticizing yet another recent Parliamentary excess—this one involving fair trial rights for colonists critical of the Crown. Even before the Coercive Acts, it thus should have been clear to Parliament that its efforts to single out Massachusetts had made the Bay Province a model for emulation—especially by the Virginians.[96]

By 1774, even without frequent town meetings in Massachusetts, at least five interrelated and overlapping networks were thus operating that had not existed a decade earlier: standing committees of correspondence among the assemblies, intracolonial local committees, local chapters of the Sons of Liberty, merchant groups organizing boycotts, and interlinked local newspapers copying each other's copy (a colonial ancestor of retweeting). With or without interconnected official town meetings, colonists were increasingly in conversation with each other and in the process were increasingly becoming Americans.[97]

Rather than joining the widening and deepening conversation, London unwisely tried to squelch it and in the process further isolated itself.

SOVEREIGNTY AND MONARCHY

The Coercive Acts aimed to end the burgeoning American constitutional conversation by brute force—by using warships to shut down a bustling port; by unilaterally abrogating a colonial charter; by muzzling townships; by trampling ancient jury-trial principles; and, worst of all, by reintroducing an imperial standing army onto city streets in peacetime. Britain's highborn prime minister, Lord North, and other British leaders did not try to hide the empire's iron fist. Instead, they proudly embraced the "Coercive" label. These coercive measures failed to end the conversation in America, but they did force the Americans to embrace an entirely new set of constitutional arguments.

For a decade, Americans had insisted that taxes were distinct from ordinary legislation. Colonists claimed immunity from Parliamentary taxation but conceded that in many other areas, Parliament could legislate over them for the benefit of the empire. Parliament's most cogent reply was that it was sovereign. If it could do one thing, it could do everything. Relatedly, Parliament's defenders argued that the line between taxation and legislation was not particularly sensible, even if it was not ridiculous (as was, for many, the line between internal and external taxes). If Parliamentary taxation without representation was tyranny, then why was general Parliamentary legislation without representation so different? "I know of no line that can be drawn," Governor Hutchinson asserted in a widely publicized January 1773 address to the Massachusetts Assembly.[98]

The most farsighted patriots worried about this point this early on, even as they also beat the drum about taxation (both internal and external). As early as 1765, colonists in most assemblies and in the Stamp Act Congress had objected to vice-admiralty rules that undermined Americans' historic birthrights as Englishmen to jury trials. These objections went beyond taxes as such. In 1765 the Virginia House of Burgesses had likewise claimed exclusive authority not just over all matters of "taxation" but also over Virginia's "internal polity."[99]

In 1774, the Coercive Acts proved beyond all doubt that Parliament could indeed tyrannize without taxing. Parliament could tyrannize by abolishing colonial governments altogether. (If Parliament could abrogate some aspects of the Massachusetts charter, why not all aspects, and why not any other colony's charter?) Parliament could tyrannize by shutting down at whim a humming hub of commercial activity and a beating heart of political discourse. (Without trade ships, colonial Boston, connected to the mainland by the thinnest of necks, was almost cut off from the wider world.) Parliament could tyrannize by quartering troops anywhere. (Today it was Boston and New York City; tomorrow it could be Philadelphia or Newport or New Haven or Charlestown.) Parliament could tyrannize by allowing troops to murder with impunity. (If Parliament could create sham trials, why not drop the charade and let soldiers kill at will?)

Put another way, if Whately had lost and Dulany had won round one—if Parliament really did not represent colonists—then why should colonists trust Parliament in any area involving sensitive liberty or property concerns? Taxation was one sensitive area, but hardly the only one. If unelected Parliaments could not tax Americans because unelected kings in England could not unilaterally tax, then, by the same logic, unelected Parliaments could not do other things in America that unelected English kings could not unilaterally do at home—suspend habeas corpus, raise an unwanted standing army, quarter troops in peacetime, abrogate jury trials, and so on.

Why, then, had the colonists not said this all along? Why had they failed to offer any compelling and early counterargument to the assertions of indivisible Parliamentary sovereignty?

Perhaps the colonists had simply misframed the debate. Although they had spilled much ink on the tax issue, perhaps their better argument was rooted in tradition more generally. Essentially, they yearned to preserve the basic system that had been in place for most of the previous century. Deep down, many Americans wanted to codify the status quo ante bellum—a world, prior to the French and Indian War, in which Parliament did not intrude much into colonial life, except for some underenforced trade laws such as the old Navigation and Molasses Acts. Given that the British Constitution was an unwritten mélange of institutions, laws, customs, and principles, colonists should have placed primary emphasis on *custom* (Parliament should continue to leave us alone, mostly) rather than *principle* (taxes are categorically different).

Granted, the colonists' nostalgic desire to return in all respects to the good old days of benign imperial prewar neglect failed to confront the harsh new reality that the empire had massive postwar revenue needs. But the colonists' emphatic insistence on tax autonomy could have been a starting point for good-faith transatlantic negotiation and conversation. A wise and responsive ministry could have seriously engaged each colony and specified its proper share of the overall revenue burden, leaving it up to each colonial assembly to determine how to raise the money. (If a colony failed to meet its requisitioned amount, imperial taxes could have been a fallback enforcement device about which the delinquent colony could not justly complain.)

The most likely explanation for colonists' initial unwillingness to carry the logical implications of their anti-Whately arguments to their logical conclusion is that those arguments could too quickly lead to complete colonial independence, and in 1765 the colonists were not emotionally ready to cut the umbilical cord to their mother country. The Coercive Acts changed everything. Parliament had shown its true colors. It did not care about or for Americans and thus could not be trusted. It was now passing laws—contra Whately—that would be utterly unthinkable at home, laws that English voters would never have allowed to stand if applied against Englishmen in England. The voters in Old Sarum were not protecting their cousins in New England.

If the ultimate 1766 Declaratory Act logic of sovereignty was that no line limiting Parliament made sense—that sovereignty was all or nothing—then the visceral colonial answer after the Coercive Acts was: *All right, then. Nothing. Parliament has no legitimate authority over us at all.* The very power of the sovereignty argument was its undoing. It was too powerful. It proved too much. It demanded that colonists place blind trust in a Parliament that, as the Coercive Acts proved beyond doubt, was not structured to deserve absolute colonial deference. "When you drive him hard," Edmund Burke warned his fellow Parliament members, "the boar will surely turn upon the hunters. If that sovereignty and their freedom cannot be reconciled, which will they take? They will cast your sovereignty in your face. Nobody will be argued into slavery."[100]

As they began to contemplate complete independence from Parliament, colonists came to see that such independence need not entail cutting ties to all things British. Led by John Adams and Pennsylvania lawyer James Wilson, creative colonial theorists increasingly championed an imperial structure that later scholars would call the "dominion" model.[101] In this model, each colonial assembly would be its own small-p parliament; no parliament, not even Britain's, would lord over any other parliament, but all would share a common king, much as England and Scotland had operated as separate realms with a common crown for most of the seventeenth century. True, the colonies and Britain were not contiguous, as were England and Scotland. But the German electorate of Hanover was likewise noncontiguous with Britain, and George III was monarch of both. Britain's Parliament did not properly legislate over Hanover, nor did any Hanoverian body properly legislate over Britain; the two were connected in a merely personal union via their shared monarch.[102]

In his famous 1773 address to the Massachusetts Assembly proclaiming that "no line" could be drawn between "the supreme authority of Parliament and the total independence" of the colonies, Governor Hutchinson conceded that formally independent colonials and Britons back home could in theory share a common king. But then, he warned, Massachusetts and Britain would be "two governments as distinct as the kingdoms of England and Scotland before the union," and his beloved homeland could no longer formally claim in all circumstances Britain's military shield against "the Spanish, French, or Dutch." Tiny Massachusetts would then cease to enjoy the absolute and invariable protection of the British nation, the British Parliament, the British fleet, the British army, the British population, the British economy, and so forth. Massachusetts would be no more secure against the slings and arrows of a cruel world than the paltry electorate of Hanover (which would indeed eventually be gobbled up by Prussia in the nineteenth century as Britain watched). Even if George III continued as its nominal and faraway monarch, a stand-alone Massachusetts would, Hutchinson feared, quickly become "the prey" of "one or the other Powers of Europe, such as should first seize upon us."[103]

Aided by John Adams as its outside legal adviser and draftsman, the Massachusetts Assembly offered a formal response to Governor Hutchinson in a high-level constitutional debate covered by newspapers far and wide.[104] The governor's nightmare scenario, Adams and the Assembly argued, was actually rather dreamy: "Being united in one Head and common Sovereign"—that is, having the same monarch—Massachusetts and Britain "may live happily in that Connection and mutually support and protect each other."[105]

Wilson's and Adams's position, foreshadowed by Benjamin Franklin's private musings in the late 1760s and echoed by Thomas Jefferson's and Alexander Hamilton's public pamphlets in the mid-1770s, was farsighted. At a certain point—already on the conceptual horizon, given America's explosive population growth, rising economic power, and rapid cultural maturation—it would make no sense for the voters and assembly of a smaller and less populous old island to lord over the voters and assemblies of a larger and more populous new continent. Or, at least, it would make no sense if the unwritten British Constitution was, as its admirers claimed, a system of liberty and freedom (as distinct from, say, French absolutism or Russian despotism).[106]

Some colonial writers (including Adams) tried to make the case for the dominion schema purely as a matter of hoary history, claiming that when the first English émigrés founded various New World settlements, they had been tied only to the king and not to Parliament. Given the long tradition of Parliamentary regulation of America—the 1660s Navigation Acts, the 1696 Plantation Trade Act, the 1702 Demise of the Crown Act, the 1733 Molasses Act, and so on, reinforced by repeated and emphatic colonial admissions of Parliamentary trade-regulation authority in the mid-1760s—the founding-history argument was more than a tad tendentious. Yet the argument did fit within a recognizable style of British constitutional discourse. Jurists sometimes packaged sensible reform suggestions as imperfect but cute historical claims. Instead of openly advocating for an avowed innovation, common-law lawyers at times invoked a mythic past, asserting that they were merely bringing to light genuine fossils, freshly unearthed.[107]

The best and most candid argument for the dominion model blended law, history, philosophy, geography, economics, and demography in the spirit of British living constitutionalism. The historic British Constitution had worked well for the island in the past, but would not work well going forward for the empire as a whole as that empire was now unfolding. An *Imperial* Constitution (as distinct from the good old British Constitution for the island itself) now needed to be created *ex nihilo*, or at least renegotiated. In keeping with the spirit of English liberty and British constitutionalism at its best, a proper imperial structure would need to do justice to the legitimate yearnings and expectations of Britons in the colonies. This structure would also need to reflect the relatively recent and fundamental fact that the colonies were fast approaching demographic, economic, and cultural parity with the mother country—parity that should now be officially recognized and reflected in a new-modeled imperial system.

Instead, blindered Britons in the 1770s scoffed at the seventeenth-century Scottish analogy and the contemporaneous Hanoverian analogy. Trapped in (their view of) the past and unwilling to think imaginatively about the future, British officialdom dismissed the generative colonial ideas put forth by Wilson (himself a Scottish émigré), Adams, Franklin, Jefferson, Hamilton, and others. Eventually Britain would fully embrace a version of these very ideas, but only after yet another transformative global war—World War II (itself a continuation of World War I)—and thanks in part to pressure and encouragement from the now mightier United States. Today, the United Kingdom, Canada, Australia, New Zealand, and Jamaica (along with about a dozen other, smaller nations) each has its own parliament; no parliament lords over any other; and all share a common monarch, much as leading Americans proposed in the 1770s. Here as elsewhere, the American colonists were far ahead of their time, envisioning the future far more impressively than their supposed betters in London.[108]

IN LESS THAN FIFTEEN YEARS, the colonists had gone from being proud Britons in America, toasting their new king and rejoicing in their empire's triumphs over the French, to being severe critics of *British rules* and then skeptics of *British rule*. Emotionally, one cord remained—the personal cord connecting each colonist to King George III.

Almost every colonist had been born under the protection of a British king, whether the current king or one of his Georgian namesakes. In premodern times, the bond between king and subject was lifelong and virtually unbreakable. Just as a person was born to a specific mother and father, so he was born owing allegiance to his king. In the late medieval era, a man by his own volition and unilateral action could no more change that birth-bond than he could erase his parents, alter his blood, trade his liver, or reverse his sex.

The English Civil War, the Glorious Revolution, and the writings of John Locke and other Whig thinkers had softened this premodern ideological framework. Allegiance and protection became more truly reciprocal. If a king ceased to offer any protection to his subjects, if he made war against them rather than protecting them from war, if he tyrannized over them rather than protecting them from foreign tyrants—well, then, his misconduct would shatter the birth contract and subjects en masse could justifiably shed their allegiance. But as late as mid-April 1775—that is, even a year after the first Coercive Acts—the thought of cutting ties with their king seemed unnatural to many colonists who would do just that in July 1776.

What, then, changed so many minds so quickly? Two things— war and Paine.

First, war. Perhaps the 1770 Massacre had been mostly unintentional. But the matter was different at Lexington, some dozen miles west of Boston, on the morning of April 19, 1775. Once again, professional British-born soldiers killed and maimed local American civilians. True, the fallen were militiamen who had arrayed in arms on the town green to make a symbolic statement as Regulars were marching by. But the colonials had not blocked the soldiers' path or menaced the marchers. Rather, the soldiers had turned from their path to confront the locals. Regardless of who shot first and whether the first shots had been intentional, the colonists had not returned fire in any effective military way. Only one Redcoat suffered any wounds, and slight ones at that. Eight colonists—not professional killers but civilians within minutes of their homes and wives and children—lay dead, and at least eight more were wounded. What did the British-born professional soldiers then do? Did they weep that things had come to this and that their colonial cousins now lay dead and injured at their hands? No. They cheered, and did so with the formal blessing of their British-born officers. The king's men were not here to protect colonists; they were here to cow and kill colonists. If that did not justify renouncing the king in whose name they cowed and killed and cheered, nothing would.[109]

Over the next few hours, hundreds and eventually thousands of other American civilians from the surrounding area poured out of their homes, joined the fight, and made the Redcoats pay. In Lexington's neighboring town of Concord, the first British Regulars fell at the hands of colonists. When the dust had settled after many hours of fighting along a twenty-mile stretch, more than a hundred men lay dead, most of them Regulars. Over the ensuing weeks, open clashes and siege warfare ensued in and around Boston, culminating in a ferocious battle just north of the city, near Bunker Hill, in June. More than a thousand died or suffered serious injury, mostly on the British side. Fully a year before the Declaration of Independence, a shooting war had begun, and patriots were giving as good as they got. Fence-sitting colonists everywhere would soon have to choose sides.

Then came Thomas Paine, who took the global constitutional conversation to an entirely new level. The publication of Paine's pamphlet *Common Sense* in Philadelphia in early 1776 was like nothing the world had seen. Originally published anonymously ("Written by an ENGLISHMAN," hinted the second edition), Paine's tract sold tens of thousands of copies within weeks—proportionately more, perhaps, than any American political publication before or since. In a matter of months it was reprinted across the English-speaking world, from Lancaster to London; from New York, Newport, and Newburyport to Newcastle; from Boston, Providence, Salem, Norwich, and Hartford to Dublin and Edinburgh.

Common Sense was written in strong prose aimed at middling folk. Its title promised *common* sense for the common man. Its style was more tart than that of any previous constitutional tract, including the works of Otis, Whately, Dulany, and Dickinson, not to mention less famous essays by the likes of Wilson, Adams, Jefferson, and Hamilton, among others.

Paine's substance was also transformative. Monarchy itself was wrong. It ran counter to the Bible, rightly read. (Paine personally was not a conventional Christian but in the pamphlet he hid that fact.) The English monarchy in particular was rooted in crime and superstition. William the Conqueror was "a French bastard landing with an armed banditti, and establishing himself king of England against the consent of the natives." More generally, no one was born to rule or to be ruled. In America, the law should be king, not a "royal brute" named George. In addition, "there is something very absurd in supposing a continent to be perpetually governed by an island. In no instance hath nature made the satellite larger than its primary planet."

In addition to arresting prose, Paine had good timing. Just as his pamphlet was hitting the streets of America, so were transcripts of a smug and stupid October 27 speech that George had delivered to Parliament. In this royal address, George praised the Coercive Acts and showed no comprehension of the colonists' underlying grievances. Had he read *anything* that Americans had been saying and writing over the past decade? Maybe Paine was right. Highborn kings really could be fools and dullards shrouded in a self-created fog of ignorance and privilege.[110]

Paine himself was an English-born craftsman with no university education and a history of business and personal failures. He arrived in the New World in late 1774 with little more than a letter of introduction from Benjamin Franklin. A year and a half later—once he threw down his initial mask of anonymity—Thomas Paine was one of the most famous and best-selling political authors in world history, a household name on both sides of the Atlantic. Almost overnight, he upended colonists' emotions about their king and revolutionized their attitudes about kingship in general. Only in America and only after 1760—when a new American and transatlantic conversational infrastructure began to emerge—could such a thing have happened.

THE PERSONAL AND LEGAL PRECONDITIONS for revolution were rapidly snapping into place after 1774. But one key element—the military element—remained doubtful. The patriots would need to prevail by force of arms against the world's mightiest empire at the peak of its power.

How could two and a half million Americans possibly hope to defeat nine million Britons?[111]

three

INDEPENDENCE

"HIS MAJESTY'S OTHER NORTHERN AMERICAN colonies are embark'd with us in this most important bottom. . . . [B]y the united application of all who are aggrieved, all may happily obtain redress." So the town meeting of Boston had declared in 1764. Back then, Bostonians had urged their provincial assembly to reach out to other colonies to protest Parliamentary taxation. A decade later, as patriots began to contemplate armed resistance against the empire, they yet again felt the need—this time more urgently and indeed existentially—to achieve "united application of all who are aggrieved."[1]

Accomplishing this "united application" would be challenging. Founded at different times by different types of settlers for different purposes, British colonies in North America had long functioned as separate legal entities. Virginia was more than a century older than Georgia. Each colony had its own charter or other governing instrument; each had its own unique political history and legal institutions. Perhaps no two neighboring colonies had ever enjoyed perfectly harmonious relations. Several "landed" colonies had legal claims stretching far westward, and these claims sometimes clashed. Even "landless" colonies squabbled over boundaries. Religious traditions and practices varied considerably across the colonies, as did dominant economic patterns and interests. And then, of course, there was slavery, which was becoming anathema to some in the North but remained part of everything—law, culture, social structure, the economy, even religion—in much of the Deep South.

Given the geography and demography of America, with most of its population and infrastructure unfurling in a wide ribbon along the Atlantic coast from Portsmouth to Savannah, the defection of any province in this stretch would be devastating. If war came, Britain could use land bases in any cooperative colony in this ribbon to ravage neighboring colonies.[2]

To prevail against the British Empire, thirteen previously separate colonies would thus need to unite militarily. They would also need to fashion a common set of reasons justifying their united revolt—explaining themselves to each other, to their British kinsmen, to the wider world, and ultimately to us, their posterity.

In the tumultuous months between the dumping of British tea in Boston and the declaring of American independence in Philadelphia, patriots squarely confronted and impressively surmounted these daunting and interrelated challenges—with one large exception. They failed to squarely confront, much less impressively surmount, the problem of slavery in their midst, and indeed at their root.

FRANKLIN'S SNAKE

In signing the Declaration of Independence, Benjamin Franklin is reputed to have quipped to fellow signer John Hancock that "we must indeed all hang together or we shall assuredly hang separately." Whether or not he actually said this about his own neck and the noose that awaited all traitors if caught by His Majesty's government, Franklin had long insisted that the *colonies* had to hang together or die.

When Franklin first made the point, he did so in reference to the backcountry French and Indian threat in 1754, weeks before he and the ubiquitous Hutchinson hatched their unsuccessful Albany Plan for tighter intercolonial coordination. And he did so via a political cartoon that in effect invented and epitomized the genre, a cartoon destined to be repeatedly revived by the colonists in the 1760s and 1770s. The revivals came with a dramatic serpentine twist: after 1763, the main threat to America was no longer French or Indian, but British.

Franklin's cartoon initially appeared in his own newspaper, the *Pennsylvania Gazette*, on May 9, 1754, sandwiched between two short essays. The first essay told readers about a young Virginia officer, George Washington, who on orders had ventured into western Virginia and Pennsylvania to inform French agents infiltrating the region that these lands belonged to His Majesty George II. The French aimed to control the Forks of the Ohio (modern-day Pittsburgh), with the help of allied Indians willing to scalp British frontier folk—"our Farmers, with their Wives and Children." The "disunited" condition of the various distinct British colonies, argued the essay, gave the French "the very great Advantage of being under one Direction, with one Council, and one Purse." The second essay discussed the upcoming Albany Congress, to which various Indian leaders had been invited in the hopes of (at a minimum) wooing them away from any alliances they may have formed with

the French, and (ideally) inducing them to affirmatively back the British in the war on the horizon. (Over the next two months, Washington's men would first kill a small band of French Canadians and then surrender to a superior French force. Full-blown war eventually followed.) In between these two brief essays lay the illustration of a sinuous snake divided into eight sections.

Each section was labeled with initials, making clear that the snake represented the mainland British colonies from New England ("N.E.") to the Carolinas, North and South ("N.C." and "S.C."), connected by New York, New Jersey, Pennsylvania,

Maryland, and Virginia ("N.Y.," "N.J.," "P.," "M.," and "V."). These contiguous colonies, the cartoon argued, would survive only if they held together. Franklin here offered a clear message and a catchy slogan—"JOIN, or DIE"—well adapted to the democratic culture aborning in midcentury Philadelphia. The simple image was easy to imitate precisely because it was not high art. On May 13, only four days after the birth of Franklin's snake, it was reborn in Manhattan, when the *New-York Mercury* reprinted Franklin's two essays and sandwiched in its own version of the cartoon.[3]

On May 21, the snake found yet another nesting place and also found its voice—this time in New England, as the *Boston Gazette* reprinted Franklin's essays-and-image sandwich with yet another variant of the cartoon. Not to be outdone, the *Boston News-Letter* on May 23 served up its own variation, featuring a rather more anxious, round-eyed snake. In both graphics, the snake urged colonists to "unite and conquer."

OVER THE NEXT TWO DECADES, Franklin's snake would experience repeated rebirths. As the serpent's popularity grew, the fact that its toothed end faced east, toward London (right, on a conventional map), and not west, toward the French-and-Indian backcountry, would take on a significance that the initially Anglophilic Franklin had not originally intended.[4]

On September 21, 1765, when a pseudonymous New Jersey scribbler, "Andrew Marvel," issued an impassioned handbill urging united colonial resistance to the Stamp Act, he splashed across

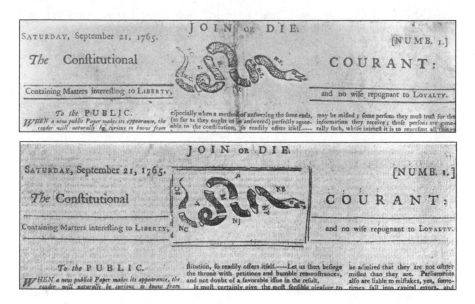

the masthead his own rendition of Franklin's snake and slogan. The handbill appeared in several incarnations, with one version (top) closely tracking Franklin's original image and another (bottom) evidently patterned on the round-eyed 1754 *Boston News-Letter* serpent.

On October 7, the *Boston Evening-Post* quoted excerpts from Marvel's handbill and printed an incarnation of the snake and slogan that mirrored the handbill's round-eyed image with remarkable fidelity—clues suggesting that perhaps the *Evening-Post* itself was the printer of this version of the handbill. (In this version, the tail tip curves to the right.)

Simultaneously, the mighty and immortal snake sailed across the ocean. On November 9, the *London Gazette* told its readers about a handbill received from "yesterday's North American packet." The *Gazette* did not imitate the cartoon but did paint a picture with words. Marvel's handbill, reported the London paper, featured "an emblematical Head-Piece of a Snake or Serpent cut into several pieces, on each of which are the initial letters of the several Colonies; and over it are the Words *Join or Die*, in large Letters." And then, to complete its transatlantic tour, the snake sailed back to America, with the London essay reprinted in full in the *Boston News-Letter* on January 16, 1766, in the *Boston Post-Boy* and Hartford's *Connecticut Courant* on January 20, and in Portsmouth's *New Hampshire Gazette* four days after that.

In modern parlance, Franklin's meme had gone viral. With three words and a crude woodcut, he had managed to bring hundreds of thousands of persons, whether highly educated or semiliterate, whether in Britain or America, into a single political conversation.

But the meaning of his meme had begun to shift. It was now being used *against* the British Empire, as Hutchinson in Boston mournfully wrote to Franklin in London in late 1765: "The riots at N York have given fresh spirits to the rioters here. An uniformity of measures it is said will be effectual and join or die is the motto. When you and I were at Albany ten years ago we did not Propose an union for such Purposes as these."[5]

THE JOURNALISTIC REVIVAL OF THE "Join or Die" slogan in the fall of 1765 was of course accompanied by an actual joining of sorts, as delegates from nine colonies came together in the Stamp Act Congress at that very moment. The next great colonial joining—the First Continental Congress—took place in September and October 1774, this time in Philadelphia, the city that had birthed the immortal snake. Once again, as if on cue, Franklin's snake arose from its hibernation.

First, in a running Manhattan masthead beginning in late June, young Georgia made its initial appearance at the tail. The word JOIN gave way to the word UNITE, which had featured in the snake's vocal 1754 Boston appearances ("unite and conquer") and had also loomed

large, along with its cognate, "united," in the 1764 Boston town meeting and ensuing provincial circular letter.[6]

Then, in a more elongated headpiece of Boston printer Isaiah Thomas's *Massachusetts Spy* in early July—a headpiece designed by none other than Paul Revere—the serpent's east-facing mouth, New England, directly confronted the British dragon.[7]

Finally, thanks to the *Pennsylvania Journal*'s new masthead, obviously patterned on its Manhattan precursor, Franklin's creature returned home to its Philadelphia birthplace in late July. There it would remain for many months to welcome and encourage the Continental Congress that would build on the 1754 Albany Congress that had inspired the snake and the 1765 Stamp Act Congress that had revived it.[8]

MASSACHUSETTS MEETS VIRGINIA

The First Continental Congress met to fashion a *united*—as in "unite or die"—American response to the Coercive Acts. More than fifty delegates representing twelve mainland colonies (all except Georgia) participated in the conclave. Most delegates had been chosen, extralegally, either by ad hoc patriot groups or by rump assemblies meeting informally—assemblies now routinely conversing and coordinating across colonies via standing committees of correspondence.[9] This network of standing committees had been the brainchild of the

Virginia House of Burgesses in a 1773 plan spearheaded by Peyton Randolph, Richard Henry Lee, Patrick Henry, Richard Bland, Benjamin Harrison, Edmund Pendleton, and Thomas Jefferson, among others.[10]

In September 1774, six of these seven Virginia luminaries came to the Philadelphia conclave. Jefferson did not attend; instead, Virginia sent a respected planter with serious military experience, George Washington. (After some early military mistakes in 1754, the esteemed Colonel over the next several years had won wide acclaim for his bravery and skill in the French and Indian War.[11])

Other colonies sent similarly distinguished representatives. Nine alumni of the Stamp Act Congress reunited, as did two venerable alumni of the Albany Congress. (New York's Philip Livingston had actually attended both previous continental conclaves.) Rhode Island sent two former governors, Stephen Hopkins and Samuel Ward, who had also served as chief justices. (Unlike most colonies, which were saddled with royally selected governors, Rhode Island elected its chief executive.) More than fifteen of the delegates would go on to become state chief executives in independent America, and seven would return to Philadelphia to draft the US Constitution in 1787. New York delegate John Jay and South Carolina delegate John Rutledge would later be selected by Virginia delegate George Washington to serve as America's first two chief justices.[12]

The Massachusetts delegation represented the province that was in the bull's-eye of Parliament's Coercive Acts. Otis was no longer in public life; his mind was gone. At his peak, he had combined the technical talents of a lawyer with the rabble-rousing instincts of an agitator. At Philadelphia, those two roles would be divided between two cousins, lawyer John Adams and provocateur Samuel Adams. The 1770 Massacre trial, the 1773 dominion debate between Thomas Hutchinson and John Adams, and the ensuing Hutchinson Letters Affair and Boston Tea Party had brought the Adams kinsmen onto a continental stage. They would now need to play their parts alongside great men from other colonies who knew them only by reputation.

Joining them in representing the Bay Province were Robert Treat
Paine and Thomas Cushing.

The Massachusetts delegates knew they would need strong Congressional support from the other colonies to save the Bay Province
from ruin. Hutchinson was now out, and a new man was in: British-
born and battle-tested General Thomas Gage. Under the command
of this new military governor, hundreds of armed imperial soldiers
now roamed the streets of Boston. Thousands more would likely
soon arrive. Open confrontation between imperial soldiers and local
militiamen had yet to occur—the Battles of Lexington and Concord
still lay half a year in the future—but the British seemed bent on
teaching the Bostonians a lesson, by military force if need be. "Join
or Die," indeed.

The mortal threat to Boston patriots was the talk of the town—
actually, the talk of many towns. Loyalists everywhere were embold-
ened, some even gleeful. On August 25, 1774, as the earliest delegates
approached Philadelphia, the feisty *Rivington's New-York Gazetteer*
ran a provocative poem that was blasted in the September 1 edition
of the patriot *New-York Journal*. But it was cheerfully reprinted in the
September 8 edition of the loyalist *Boston News-Letter*:

> On the SNAKE, depicted on the Head of some American NEWS
> PAPERS
>> Ye Sons of Sedition, how comes it to pass,
>> That America's typed by a SNAKE—in the grass?
>> Don't you think 'tis a scandalous, saucy reflection,
>> That merits the soundest, severest Correction?
>> NEW-ENGLAND's the Head too;—NEW-ENGLAND's abused;
>> For the *Head of the Serpent* we know *should be* BRUISED.

How would the Congress respond to the existential threat posed
by Gage and the troops, and by the Coercive Acts more generally?
Ideally, by presenting a *united* front, one led not just by the Bay Province, but also by the Old Dominion.

VIRGINIA WAS AMERICA'S OLDEST, WEALTHIEST, and most populous mainland colony. In 1774, it included all of present-day Kentucky and West Virginia and claimed land rights all the way to the Pacific. Virginia had not sent delegates to either the Albany Congress or the Stamp Act Congress. In Philadelphia, the leaders of America's two most significant colonies, Massachusetts and Virginia, would at last come together.

Love at first sight between these two proud and powerful colonies was not inevitable. In its earliest days, Massachusetts attracted Puritans seeking religious independence; Virginia, Anglicans seeking profit. In the English Civil War, Roundheads went to Massachusetts, Cavaliers to Virginia. Though each colony could claim a great center of learning—Harvard and William & Mary, respectively—Massachusetts boasted several bustling commercial hubs while Virginia's embryonic cities lagged behind. The diversified Massachusetts economy revolved around family farms, fishing, shipping, trade, and a rising manufacturing sector anchored by shipbuilding. Its maturing economic system increasingly replicated and rivaled England's. The Navigation Acts, based on British mercantile policies discouraging colonial manufacturing, pinched Massachusetts sharply, and Bostonians had responded by creating a culture of smuggling and evasion. Virginia, by contrast, was more emphatically agrarian, focused on mass production of cash and staple crops, especially tobacco.

Virginia's economy was essentially plantation based, more akin to the economy of the British West Indies than to that of Massachusetts. In referring to America, Parliament and the ministry sometimes spoke of "provinces," sometimes of "colonies," but also, often, of Britain's New World "plantations"—a word that fit Virginia well but not Massachusetts.

There was another obvious difference that the word *plantation* immediately calls to mind today, and called to mind even in 1774: slavery. Virginia did not vastly exceed Massachusetts in its White population but had exponentially more slaves. Slaves accounted for 40 percent of Virginia's total population, compared to less than 4 percent in Massachusetts.* To reduce these provincial differences to a pointed personal comparison: John Adams was a gentleman *farmer* and George Washington was a gentleman *planter*. In the months and years to come these two ambitious and rising local heroes, whom the world was beginning to notice thanks to the global communications revolution under way, would need to work together, for they were now truly in the same political boat.

THE MASSACHUSETTS DELEGATES PLAYED THEIR roles well at the 1774 conclave thanks to careful preparation, especially on the part of John Adams.

When Adams left home for Philadelphia at the age of thirty-nine, he embarked on a journey that began his transformation from a provincial into an American—a self-conscious political identity felt by only a tiny fraction of New World inhabitants in 1774. America had started to take note of him, but he knew little of America, save what he had read in books, pamphlets, and newspapers. True, he was a voracious reader—that was one of several things that he and the Virginian Jefferson would have in common when they eventually met. But Adams had never savored with his own senses neighboring Connecticut, much less New York, New Jersey, or Pennsylvania. Despite a deep Massachusetts bias that he never entirely overcame, Adams was psychologically open to becoming an American, both because

---

*Slavery was lawful in the Bay Province, despite Otis's denunciation of the practice in his widely read 1764 pamphlet. The *Boston Gazette* often ran ads offering or seeking slaves for sale, or promising rewards for the recapture of runaways, in proximity to pieces challenging Parliamentary oppression. See, e.g., *BG*, 6-11-1764, 4 ("WANTED, A Healthy Negro Girl, between 14 and 20 years old . . . us'd to Country Work. . . . Also, a likely Negro Boy, of the same age, for a Gentleman's Servant. Enquire of Edes and Gill") (same issue as early reports of the Sugar Act); *BG*, 7-2-1764, 4 ("To be sold at a very reasonable Price, a Negro Woman, about 38 years old, . . . washes and cooks very well. . . . Enquire of Edes and Gill") (same issue advertising the forthcoming Otis pamphlet); *BG*, 12-20-1773, 6 ("TO BE SOLD: A hearty, healthy NEGRO-MAN, about 24 Years of Age. Inquire of Edes and Gill") (same issue as first report of the Tea Party).

he relished new experiences, and because Americanness was in his interest and in the interest of the province he would represent at Philadelphia.

Before setting out, Adams felt the heavy weight of history on his shoulders and, Puritan manqué that he was, fretted that he was unworthy: "This will be an assembly of the wisest Men upon the Continent. . . . I feel myself unequal to this Business. A more extensive Knowledge of the Realm, the Colonies, and of Commerce, as well as of Law and Policy, is necessary, than I am Master of." He resolved to "keep an exact Diary, of my Journey, as well as a Journal of the Proceedings of the Congress." Even before leaving, Adams evidently understood that the "Journey" itself would help him to begin to acquire the "more extensive Knowledge of . . . the Colonies" that he craved.[13]

Adams's diary entries between August 10, when he and his fellow delegates left Boston, and August 29, when he arrived in Philadelphia, were not designed for immediate publication. But they do reflect another aspect of America's deepening constitutional conversation: more and lengthier face-to-face discussions than ever, over good food and good wine and good coffee (not tea!), between Americans from different colonies, sizing each other up personally, and gaining more penetrating insights into their respective colonies' similarities and differences. The Massachusetts delegates took longer than necessary to reach Philadelphia because they scheduled extra stops and breaks. All along the route, they acquired intelligence and met for the first time people who had arranged to host them, often thanks to local committees of correspondence and Sons of Liberty pipelines. In today's lingo, the Massachusetts delegates were networking.

Shortly before Adams left for Philadelphia, Hutchinson had sailed to London to brief the ministry. Hutchinson's marine voyage itself was just so much time wasted—surveying a monotonous ocean day after day and trying unsuccessfully to avoid seasickness. When not nauseated, he could read and write on ship. But while on board, he learned nothing about England that he could not have learned more easily back in Boston. Adams's journey, by contrast, was time well spent. He was discovering America.[14]

At least three sets of questions were of special interest to Adams on this fraught but also fun road trip. First, what did inhabitants of other provinces think of Massachusetts? Would they stand by her, even at risk to themselves? Second, and related, how did they view the unprecedented intercolonial conclave that was about to meet? Did they see this Congress as legitimate or seditious? Third, what could he learn in advance about other delegates, either by meeting with them en route or by talking to hosts or others who knew them personally? What were their political views, their personal biographies, their familial connections, their temperaments and tendencies? What did they think about Massachusetts in particular? Would they likely be allies or adversaries at Philadelphia?

Adams was particularly touched by the reception the delegation received in Connecticut. In 1749, Connecticut had bickered with the Bay Province over boundary lines in a dispute whose legal settlement had involved—who else?—the ubiquitous Hutchinson.[15] Now, all was forgiven:

> As We came into the Town all the Bells in Town were set to ringing, and the People, Men, Women and Children, were crowding at the Doors and Windows as if it was to see a Coronation. At Nine O Clock the Cannon were fired, about a Dozen Guns I think. These Expressions of Respect to Us, are intended as Demonstrations of the Sympathy of this People with the Massachusetts Bay and its Capital, and to shew their Expectations from the Congress and their Determination to carry into Execution whatever shall be agreed on. No Governor of a Province, nor General of an Army was ever treated with so much Ceremony and Assiduity, as We have been, throughout the whole Colony of Connecticutt [*sic*], hitherto, but especially all the Way from Hartford to N. Haven, inclusively.

As for some of the delegates themselves: Upon meeting Roger Sherman in Sherman's hometown of New Haven, Adams deemed him "a solid sensible Man." The two discussed Otis's 1764 pamphlet, now a decade old, which Sherman thought had conceded too much power to Parliament. New Yorker John Jay, Adams was told, was a rising young lawyer, a "hard Student and a good Speaker." Adams was rather less impressed by Jay's uncle-in-law Philip Livingston: "There is no holding any Conversation with him. He blusters away."

Adams was especially interested, as was his cousin and colleague Samuel, in any intelligence he could acquire about the Virginia delegation. In late July, Samuel had written directly to Virginia's Richard Henry Lee on the questions (and the Adamses' hoped-for answers) that would decide the fate of all:

> Will the people of America consider [the Coercive Acts] as an attack on the Constitution of an individual Province, in which the rest are not interested, or will they view the model of government prepared for us as a system for the whole continent? Will they, as unconcerned spectators, look on it to be designed only to lop off the exuberant branches of democracy in the Constitution of this Province, or as part of a plan to reduce them all to slavery? These are questions, in my opinion, of great importance, which I trust will be thoroughly weighed in a general Congress. May God inspire that intended body with wisdom and fortitude, and unite and prosper their counsels.

At a Manhattan coffeehouse (probably Merchants) in mid-August, John read a newspaper containing some of the Virginia Assembly's recent anti-Parliamentary resolutions, which he promptly pronounced "really grand." Several days later, in southern New Jersey, Adams was told that some of these Virginians orated as well as they wrote: those who had heard them in person "speak in Raptures about Richard Henry Lee and Patrick Henry—one the Cicero and the other the Demosthenes of the Age."

These episodes were emblematic of the new American constitutional conversation afoot. A *Massachusetts* lawyer-politician was (for the first time) in *New York* and *New Jersey*, where he read a *newspaper* in a public *coffeehouse*, and *talked* about the *constitutional views* and *communication styles* of *Virginia's* leading statesmen, whom he would soon enough meet (for the first time) in *Pennsylvania.*

Beyond topics immediately and directly related to the upcoming conclave, Adams, being Adams, was endlessly curious about all the new things he was seeing, hearing, touching, smelling, tasting. All the members of his delegation were Harvard alumni, and he made a point of visiting Yale in New Haven, King's College (modern-day Columbia) in Manhattan, and the College of New Jersey (modern-day Princeton). Perhaps these campus tours were merely frolics. Or perhaps Adams had already intuited that, just as his alma mater had produced countless political leaders in his own province, many of independent America's other early leaders would likely come from the learning centers he was now visiting.

At Princeton, Adams spent a Sunday with college president John Witherspoon, whom he pronounced a "clear, sensible, Preacher." Witherspoon was not a delegate in 1774. But this good preacher would end up serving as a delegate in the Second Continental Congress, arriving in late June 1776—just in time to join Adams in voting for, and later signing, the Declaration.[16]

While on the good preacher's campus, Adams was also mesmerized by "a most beautiful Machine" designed by inventor David Rittenhouse—a planetarium that "exhibits almost every Motion in the astronomical World. The Motions of the Sun and all the Planets with all their Satellites. The Eclipses of the Sun and Moon &c." Three years later, this brilliant inventor would begin a long stint as the treasurer of independent Pennsylvania, and in 1792 he would accept George Washington's appointment as the first director of the US Mint.

Some of Adams's diary entries had no obvious connection to the upcoming Congress, but did reflect his boundless curiosity, trademark pungency, and residual Boston bias. After religious services at Princeton, he wrote that the "Scholars sing as badly as the Presbyterians at New York." Choral inadequacy was not Adams's only complaint about New Yorkers. While he greatly admired the orderliness of lower Manhattan's layout and the grandeur of its best buildings, he found its inhabitants overbearing: "With all the Opulence and Splendor of this City, there is . . . no Conversation that is agreeable. There is no Modesty—No Attention to one another. They talk very loud, very fast, and all together. If they ask you a Question, before you can utter 3 Words of your Answer, they will break out upon you, again—and talk away." Nearly two and a half centuries after Adams wrote these words, some would say that Manhattan continues to bear some resemblance to this colorful portrait.

UNLIKE OTIS AND RUGGLES IN October 1765, the members of the Massachusetts delegation did not aim for the chair in September 1774. They were content to lead from behind, and the Congress picked Virginia's Peyton Randolph to preside. In 1765, a Massachusetts man had presided because the Bay Province had in effect called the meeting. In 1774, Virginia was leaning forward in coordinating intercolonial conversation and thus deserved presiding honors.

The immediate task was to generate a united front against the Coercive Acts. The colonies needed to prove to Britain and to each other that they were capable of standing as one. Join or die. By the end of the conclave, which lasted less than eight weeks, the delegates announced to the world that the Coercive Acts and various related statutes were "infringements and violations of the rights of the colonists; and that the repeal of them is essentially necessary, in order to restore harmony between Great-Britain and the American colonies." The Congress further agreed that unless Parliament repealed these laws, their respective colonies would unite in boycotting British goods—America's tactic of choice. Finally and perhaps most importantly, the Congress agreed to keep the intercolonial conversation going and to preserve an indoor, in-person component. Thus, the delegates decided that unless Britain did as requested, the colonies would meet again in Philadelphia, in a Second Continental Congress, on May 10, 1775.[17]

The delegates sent private letters inviting Georgia and several other New World British colonies (East Florida, West Florida, St.

John's, and Nova Scotia) to join the 1775 gathering, and Congress made a public appeal to the new British colony of Quebec to do the same. Support from these peripheral colonies would be nice, but not essential, with the exception of Georgia, which guarded the Carolinas' southern flank. (The Carolinas, in turn, guarded Virginia's southern flank.)[18]

The Congress also narrowly defeated an attempt by Pennsylvania delegate Joseph Galloway, an old friend of Franklin's, to revive a version of the Franklin-Hutchinson Albany Plan. Galloway envisioned a new intercolonial American Parliament capable of legislating for America and vetoing the British Parliament's legislation concerning America. Like the Albany Plan itself, this scheme threatened to drain power from individual colonial assemblies. Most of the 1774 delegates had been chosen by these very assemblies, formally or informally. Even though each colonial delegation was beginning to get to know and trust delegations from other colonies in this extraordinary conclave in the City of Brotherly Love, the breathtakingly continental aspects of the Galloway Plan gave leading delegates pause.[19]

Plus, there was a catch. Galloway's new intercolonial American Parliament would work alongside a royally appointed president-general, who would wield an absolute veto. In Britain, the monarch had not negatived any major legislation for several generations. If a new imperial Constitution were to be negotiated on terms of the pure equality of Britons everywhere, the Galloway Plan fell short, offering Britons in America a weaker parliament than enjoyed by Britons in the mother country.

In addition to publishing to the world and sending to Parliament a set of formal Declarations and Resolves, the delegates composed a private petition to George III. The king had not merely accepted, but had enthusiastically supported, the Coercive Acts and other objectionable statutes that Parliament had enacted in his reign. Even without attempting to revive the royal negative, George had ways to influence Parliament. For example, he retained broad powers to dissolve and prorogue Parliaments, to favor pet ministers, and to bribe uncooperative members with sinecures and other plums.

The delegates humbly beseeched George to use his many and mighty powers on their behalf rather than to their detriment. To modern ears, Congress's tone in this private petition seems self-abasing in the extreme—exactly the sort of cringing and fawning that Paine would later excoriate in his biting attack on monarchy. The petition began as follows: "*To the King's Most Excellent Majesty:* Most gracious Sovereign: We, your Majesty's faithful subjects . . . by this our humble Petition, beg leave to lay our grievances before the throne." After itemizing American objections to the Coercive Acts and other disastrous Parliamentary policies, the petition closed, as it had begun, in courtly fashion: "We therefore most earnestly beseech your Majesty, that your royal authority and interposition may be used for our relief; and that a gracious answer may be given to this petition. That your Majesty may enjoy every felicity through a long and glorious reign, over loyal and happy subjects, and that your descendants may inherit your prosperity and dominions 'til time shall be no more, is and always will be our sincere and fervent prayer."[20]

King George III never did his American subjects the courtesy of responding to this exceedingly polite petition. The colonists' manners were better than the king's.

THE AMERICANIZATION OF FRANKLIN, WASHINGTON, AND ADAMS

On May 10, 1775, only half a year after they left Philadelphia, colonial delegations returned and reconvened with many of the same delegates as before. Now the stakes were infinitely higher. "Join or Die" was no longer a purely theoretical principle or a merely arresting woodcut. Death was at hand. Scores of American militiamen and scores of British Regulars had already fallen just weeks before in the Battles of Lexington and Concord. In the aftermath, Massachusetts was now mobilizing over ten thousand soldiers and requesting aid from its sisters.

The celebrated originator of the "Join or Die" motto was also, providentially, at hand. Benjamin Franklin had returned just days earlier to his adopted city, the birthplace of his immortal snake, after more than a decade in London advocating for colonists.

In his final months in the imperial capital, America's most accomplished man had been ridiculed—and thereby radicalized—by some of King George's leading counselors and courtiers in a high-profile fracas that grew out of a series of transatlantic epistles involving the ubiquitous Hutchinson. Along with his in-law Andrew Oliver, Hutchinson had carried on a robust correspondence with various influential Londoners, including Whately, in the late 1760s. Several of the letters somehow fell into Franklin's hands in 1772. Franklin sent the bundle back across the Atlantic to Boston, where the missives came before Samuel Adams, John Adams, and other Hutchinson haters. Sidestepping Franklin's instructions to keep the correspondence confidential, patriot leaders published the letters via the *Boston Gazette*'s print shop in June 1773. The haters read key passages as proof that Hutchinson had betrayed his native province by encouraging London to abridge various privileges of Englishmen in America. This was not the most charitable interpretation of the correspondence, but Hutchinson's Boston enemies always chose the path of uncharity where he was concerned. A provincial uproar ensued, undermining Hutchinson's credibility as royal governor. By a mid-June vote of 80 to 11, the Massachusetts Assembly called for the ouster of Governor Hutchinson and Lieutenant Governor Oliver. Other printers on both sides of the Atlantic quickly leaped into the fray. The pamphlet of purloined (?) letters went through at least ten printings in America and England, and newspapers in virtually every colony ran excerpts and commentaries highlighting various aspects of the widening controversy. Meanwhile, Hutchinson somehow procured a copy of a letter that Franklin had sent to Boston, and sent *that* letter back to London authorities so that Franklin could be exposed and punished for undermining duly constituted authority in the province. Franklin himself appeared before the Privy Council—in the Cockpit—where he was publicly denounced as a thief, a scoundrel, and a turncoat.[21]

The timing was particularly awkward for Franklin: the council hearing took place in late January 1774, days after reports of the

Tea Party reached London and in the wake of the London publication of anonymous but recognizable Franklin essays lampooning Britain's imperial overreach. Immediately after the Cockpit spectacle, His Majesty's government heaped further dishonor upon Franklin by unceremoniously removing him from his position as deputy postmaster for America.

In multiple ways, this complex and consequential episode reflected the new world of intercontinental constitutional conversation. It had begun with transatlantic missives back and forth discussing weighty issues of imperial and colonial law and policy. Then, prompted by Samuel Adams and other members and affiliates of the Sons of Liberty, the *Gazette*'s printers and various republishers jumped onstage. All this aroused intense attention in Boston to events and persons in London and vice versa, heightened by the Adams-and-Sons-and-*Gazette*-led Tea Party, which created a political and communicative splash three thousand miles from where the tea splashed. At the center of it all, of course, was a New World postmaster and former printer who had long been, and would continue to be, a brilliant practitioner of short, anonymous, satirical essays for public consumption.[22]

WITHIN HOURS OF FRANKLIN'S ARRIVAL in Philadelphia, the Pennsylvania Assembly unanimously invited the great man to join the host colony's delegation to the Second Congress. Along with the Adams cousins from the North and leading Virginia burgesses from the South—especially Washington, Jefferson, and Lee—Franklin from the Middle would play a critical role in the months ahead.[23]

Events were now rushing forward at a furious pace. Congress had to react quickly, but not rashly, and it had to act with unity. It had to meet the military threat at hand while allowing a continental consensus to develop. No colony could sensibly declare formal independence from Britain without the support of her sisters. "America . . . is like a large Fleet sailing under Convoy," explained John Adams in a June 1775 letter to his wife, Abigail. "The fleetest Sailors must wait for the dullest and slowest. Like a Coach and six—the swiftest Horses must be slackened and the slowest quickened, that all may keep an even Pace." The head of the snake—New England—would have to mind its mid-Atlantic midsection and its southern tail.[24]

The Congress opened with abundant evidence that the partnership between Massachusetts and Virginia remained strong. On May 24, delegates chose Boston's John Hancock to replace Williamsburg's Peyton Randolph as presiding officer. In mid-June, Braintree's farmer-lawyer Adams backed Mount Vernon's planter-soldier Washington to serve as the head of a newly formed Continental Army. The delegates then unanimously selected the upright Virginian, who within days left to take command of colonial forces near Boston. In his letter to Abigail, John elaborated both the personal and political reasons that made the decision easy. Washington was "modest and virtuous, . . . amiable, generous, and brave." His "Appointment will have a great Effect, in cementing and securing the Union of these Colonies." Franklin couldn't have said it better.[25]

As Washington prepared to depart Philadelphia, fierce fighting broke out above Boston around Bunker Hill and Breed's Hill, leaving more than a thousand dead and wounded. Washington assumed formal command of some seventeen thousand men outside Boston in early July. Adams was now farther south than he had ever been and Washington farther north than Adams's beloved Braintree. For the next year, Washington would work intimately with Bostonians while Adams would work alongside many Virginians. The Americanization of the two men, who would soon become independent America's most visible icons, along with Franklin, was now beginning in earnest.

Meanwhile, the Philadelphia delegates made one last desperate appeal to their king, sending him yet another polite petition to take their grievances seriously. America's leaders pleaded that they were seeking redress and rights-protection, not independence. It was still not too late, they declared, for both sides to pull back from the brink and reconcile. Once again, His Majesty declined to converse, this time refusing even to allow the petition to be read to him.[26]

In late August, George declared the colonies—all of them, evidently—to be in open rebellion. Massachusetts was no longer alone. The king himself was now putting all colonists "within *any* of our Colonies and Plantations in North America" in the same boat. Again, Franklin couldn't have said it better.[27]

George evidently had no interest in conversing, but Georgia (named in honor of the monarch's grandfather George II) now did. On July 20, Congress received word from Savannah that a delegation would soon arrive. By the middle of September, distinguished statesmen from all thirteen mainland colonies, for the first time in history, sat in the same room. Adams's metaphoric convoy could now tighten its formation.[28]

Over the next several months, armed conflict spread far and wide. British forces burned Falmouth (present-day Portland, Maine). Open war erupted in Virginia and North Carolina. Quebec became a ferocious battleground. Congress commissioned a Continental Navy and appointed a secret committee to begin informal correspondence with potential European allies.[29]

As formal royal government collapsed in most colonies, informal patriot organizations across the land increasingly assumed governmental functions. In October, George III opened Parliament by declaring that rebellious Americans were "manifestly" aiming to establish an "independent empire." In December, the king agreed to a Prohibitory Act effectively placing American ships out of the protection of British law. Specifically, the act closed all American ports and proclaimed that American trading ships and cargo violating the blockade "shall become forfeited to his Majesty, as if the same were the ships and effects of open enemies."[30]

On May 10 and 15, 1776, Congress adopted a two-part resolution, championed by John Adams, that was tantamount to independence. "Whereas His Britannic Majesty, in conjunction with the lords and commons of Great Britain," had effectively declared war on America, the people of each colony should "totally suppress[]" "every kind of authority" under the Crown and form a new government that would "best conduce to the happiness and safety" of the colony "in particular, and America in general."[31]

And then, on July 2, Congress officially declared independence, formally and unanimously (voting by colony) adopting a motion that had been introduced on June 7 by Richard Henry Lee of Virginia and seconded by John Adams of Massachusetts: "*Resolved, That these United Colonies are, and of right ought to be, free and independent States; that they are absolved from all allegiance to the British Crown, and that all political connection between them and the State of Great Britain is, and ought to be, totally dissolved.*"[32]

DECLARATION

"The Second Day of July 1776," exulted John to Abigail in a letter penned on the Third, "will be the most memorable Epocha, in the History of America.—I am apt to believe that it will be celebrated, by succeeding Generations, as the great anniversary Festival. . . . It ought to be solemnized with Pomp and Parade, with Shews, Games, Sports, Guns, Bells, Bonfires and Illuminations from one End of this Continent to the other from this Time forward forever more."

Adams here foresaw everything about subsequent Independence Day celebrations—the annual observance, the fireworks, the parades, the picnics, the hoopla—except, of course, the date. Why did Americans come to treat the Fourth with the revelry and reverence that Adams initially thought would belong to the Second?

Part of the answer lies in the partisan politics of the late 1790s. When Washington stepped off the political stage after two decades of service as America's leading man, the two remaining statesmen most closely associated with American independence, John Adams and Thomas Jefferson, became presidential rivals. (Franklin was by then long gone, having died in 1790.) As one of many members of the 1776 Continental Congress, Jefferson had voted on the Second. But he had starred on the Fourth, when Congress approved a document—the Declaration of Independence—whose first draft he had largely composed. Adams, too, had served on the five-man drafting committee, as Trumbull would famously remind posterity. But in committee, Jefferson's pen had predominated, as Trumbull also dramatized. Thus, when Jefferson ran against Adams twice, first in 1796 and then in 1800, the Virginian's partisans loved to highlight a piece of music where their man had stood out as first violinist and Adams had played second fiddle.

But even before the 1790s, the Fourth emerged as the proper day of celebration and remembrance—an annual tradition that began with the first anniversary in 1777. Several Philadelphia newspapers carried nearly identical accounts of the secular holiday in a report that soon made its way into newspapers in Baltimore, Williamsburg, Boston, and elsewhere: "Last Friday the 4th of July, being the Anniversary of the Independence of the United States of America, was celebrated in this city with celebrations of joy and festivity." After ceremonial cannon fire from ships and galleys in the early afternoon and a sumptuous dinner featuring members of Congress (including Adams himself), the evening "closed with the ringing of bells, and at night there was a grand exhibition of fire-works (which began and concluded with thirteen rockets) on the Commons, and the city was beautifully illuminated. Every thing was conducted with the greatest order and decorum, and the face of joy and gladness was universal. Thus, may the fourth of July, that glorious and ever memorable day, be celebrated through America, by the sons of freedom, from age to age till time shall be no more."[33]

Although merrymakers did not typically read the Declaration aloud at early annual celebrations, the date to remember and revere was nevertheless the Fourth, the date of the Declaration, not the date of formal independence—which, to repeat, and despite what all the 1777 newspapers erroneously said, was July 2, 1776. (Indeed, Adams himself seems to have forgotten the point. A note of July 5, 1777, to his daughter began as follows: "Yesterday, being the anniversary of American Independence, was celebrated here with a festivity and ceremony becoming the occasion.")

In his jubilant July 3, 1776, letter to his lady, Adams also under-estimated the importance of length. The July 2 resolution was perfect for its moment in 1776. Indeed, it was the punchline performative sentence of the July 4 Declaration itself—the only sentence, that is, that did not just say something but did something, and something rather important at that. But the payoff sentence standing alone was too short to anchor an annual day of remembrance and celebration, especially over the centuries, long after independence was won. Generations unborn in 1776 would want to know not just what happened in July 1776—independence!—but why.

Sometimes, short is exactly what is needed for a certain kind of democratic communication. "Join or Die." "Taxation without representation is tyranny!" "Americans are Sons of Liberty." "Wilkes and Liberty!" "Nobody will be argued into slavery." "In America the law is king." "I have grown gray in your service and now find myself growing blind." All of these were extraordinary rallying cries. But a proper day of remembrance calls for a proper oration, not a snippet. Not five hours—not Otis in 1761—but also not five seconds. Even Lincoln needed two minutes. The Declaration—some 1,300 words—took about ten minutes to read. This was (and still is) long enough to actually say something, but not so long as to lose the audience.

THE DECLARATION FIT WELL WITH the democratic communication revolution that gave it birth. In 1776, the document was designed to be, and it was immediately, printed in newspapers and in broadsides. It first appeared in full in the July 6 edition of the *Pennsylvania Evening Post*. Over the next few weeks, the complete text appeared in more than thirty other newspapers in cities and towns throughout the land, including Philadelphia, Baltimore, New York, New London, Providence, Norwich, Hartford, Salem, New Haven, Worcester, Boston, Newport, Newburyport, Portsmouth, Williamsburg, and Watertown.[34]

Of course, not all Americans read newspapers, and the Declaration aimed at collectives as well as individuals. The document was designed to be, and it was immediately, publicly proclaimed—declared!—to large crowds gathered in public squares, much as George III had been proclaimed king in the winter of 1760–1761, but this time with public reasons. Particularly large or otherwise notable proclamations of the Declaration in the summer of 1776 occurred in Philadelphia, Trenton, New York, Boston, Providence, Baltimore, Williamsburg, and Savannah. Hundreds if not thousands of public proclamations took place elsewhere.[35]

The document was also designed to be, and it was immediately, read aloud to the Revolutionary troops, to boost morale and explain to them what they were fighting for. Unlike Old World Hessian mercenaries who were (as Americans saw things) fighting for nothing but pay, would-be New World American soldiers would need substantive justifications for taking up arms. The first important reading of the Declaration to American troops occurred in New York on July 9, on orders of General Washington.[36]

The Declaration worked as a rhetorical text as well as a reasoned one. (We shall return to the reasons shortly.) At its best, its prose sang, soared, and stung, sometimes all at once, with flicking jabs worthy of another Thomas—Franklin's friend Thomas Paine. Because common language and prose styles have changed over the intervening two centuries, modern Americans often miss the sting and style of the language. Here are a few illustrative modern translations and paraphrases: Americans, the document proclaims, have "a decent respect for the opinions of mankind" and are willing to submit "facts to a candid world." (Unlike George III, we Americans care about what others think of us.) The king has "sent hither swarms of officers to harass our people, and eat out their substance." (They are like locusts.) The king has "plundered our seas, ravaged our coasts, burnt our towns, & destroyed the lives of our people." (War is already upon us; the king is the aggressor; we are simply defending ourselves.) The king is "at this time transporting large armies of foreign mercenaries to compleat the works of death, desolation & tyranny, already begun."

(The time for talk is over—if Americans do not act, we will soon be dead. George's gunmen are paid, foreign, amoral, professional killers, whereas we patriots are fighting for our homes and lives.) "We mutually pledge to each other our lives, our fortunes, and our sacred honor." (This is life or death for us patriots of wealth and repute; it is not just a poor man's fight. If America loses this contest, we the undersigned will hang by the neck, and our children will eat dirt. There is no going back.)

And then there was the most soaring line of all, whose contested meaning has structured much of America's constitutional conversation ever since, and to which we shall thus repeatedly return in later chapters: "All men are created equal" and are endowed with "unalienable rights" to "life, liberty, and the pursuit of happiness."

RHETORIC INTERTWINED WITH REASON IN the July 4 document. The Declaration aimed to "declare the causes" for what Americans were doing—justifications for America's break with Britain that were critical in 1776 and have become even more important in the intervening centuries, as Americans in every generation have asked themselves what propositions animate America. Before we can assess these reasons, we must understand the Declaration's multiple purposes and audiences and its technical legal significance.

In its narrowest but deepest sense, the document was exactly what it called itself: a declaration of independence. The document was not simply a justification for fighting; Congress had actually adopted a text of that sort (a "Declaration of the Causes and Necessity of Taking of Arms") almost exactly a year before—on July 6, 1775, shortly after armed conflict had broken out at Lexington and Concord and in the greater Boston area. Nor was the Declaration of Independence just a statement of grievances or a catalog of Americans' rights as humans and as Englishmen. Texts of that sort had emerged countless times in America, often drafted by local bodies, formal and informal.[37] No, a formal declaration of independence meant that Americans were now declaring themselves a legal nation-state on the world stage, a member of a relatively small group of post-Westphalian entities that were, juridically, sovereign, that were not dependencies or subsets of any other proper Westphalian sovereign.[38]

In particular, the thirteen former colonies no longer formed part of the British Empire and owed no allegiance to George III. All connection to it and to him was "totally dissolved." The key words that said all this appear in a sentence that most Americans and even many scholars today entirely overlook—the Lee-Adams sentence from July 2: "We therefore [the document is giving us its punchline] . . . do [right now, hereby, with this performative word and sentence] . . . declare, that these united colonies are and of right ought to be free and independent states." How? Because we just declared it! Declaring it makes it so—or at least will make it so if we Americans can back up these bold and brave words with the ability to make them stick. (Analogously, saying "I do" in the right way makes a marriage; and saying "I hereby accept" in the right way makes a contract.) In the earliest printed newspaper editions, the only words in the Declaration consistently rendered in full capital letters (or sometimes in italics) were "UNITED STATES OF AMERICA," "GENERAL CONGRESS," and "FREE AND INDEPENDENT STATES."

Why was formal independence—Westphalian sovereignty—so important? Because without it, the war could not be won. America would need help from abroad. True, a three-thousand-mile-wide moat lay between America and Britain, providing some protection; but water alone would not win the war against nine million Britons with His Majesty's royal fleet and troops at their disposal. America would likely need lots of French naval support and lots of European loans. To secure this help and these loans—to play the diplomatic balance-of-power game of grand strategy on a world stage—Americans would have to stop being mere domestic rebels, as they had been, in a strict international-law sense, ever since Lexington and Concord. They would need to win international-law recognition from established Westphalian sovereigns such as France; they would need to enter into formal treaties. They would need to prove to any European power inclined to support them that they would not jilt their new suitors if Britain in three months wanted them back. (A family-law analogy might be that one must formally divorce—that is, declare independence from—one's spouse before one can properly cavort with someone else.) They would need to offer Europeans inducements that only a sovereign nation could offer: if you help us in our hour of need, we can, via treaties, provide you attractive trading privileges. As John vented to Abigail in his July 3, 1776, letter, "Had a Declaration of Independency been made seven Months ago, it would have been attended with many great and glorious Effects. . . . We might before this Hour, have formed Alliances with foreign States.—We should have mastered Quebec and been in Possession of Canada."[39]

Although the July 2 resolution did declare independence, the July 4 text elaborated the legal significance of this: "*As free and independent states, [the new United States now] have full power to levy war, conclude peace, contract alliances, establish commerce, & to do all other things which independent states may of right do.*" With these words, America announced that it had joined the club of nation-states and was open for international business.[40]

Thus, one obvious audience for the July 4 text consisted of European princes and diplomats. This key fact helps solve one of many modern debates about the meaning of the Declaration's phrase "all men are created equal." Did the Declaration oppose hereditary monarchy as such? If all are truly created equal, then, it has been argued, surely no one can be born a king and no one is born a mere subject. And indeed, Paine so believed. But Thomas Jefferson was not in this particular sentence trying to channel Thomas Paine. Context is all. A document aimed at winning over King Louis XVI of France and other European princes would hardly have attacked the very idea of hereditary princes or invited violent revolution against such princes everywhere.

Also, such a reading of this key sentence would render most of the Declaration's specific charges against George III oddly beside the point. It would have been enough for the Declaration to have said that George was born an heir to the throne—a fact nowhere even mentioned in the document—and that the very idea of hereditary rule was revolting and a basis for revolt. That was not the theory of the Declaration.

Rather, the Declaration recognized that a society might permissibly consent to a hereditary monarch. Such a monarch would be safe from the Declaration's theory of revolution so long as he respected rights and did not tyrannize. The Declaration's long list of complaints against George aimed to establish "a long Train of Abuses and Usurpations" evincing a desire to establish "absolute Despotism" and "absolute Tyranny." This long train, not mere hereditary kingship, triggered a right to revolt under the Declaration's Lockean vision.

Although the Declaration surely had foreign regimes in mind, had these regimes been the Declaration's only audience, the July 2 sentence alone (or an ever so slightly expanded version of the July 2 sentence) would have sufficed. Winning the war—and winning it on terms that would make it worth winning—would require more than mere foreign backing. Winning the war and doing so deservedly would require, first and foremost, winning the hearts and minds of most Americans—the very thing that a man such as, say, Thomas Hutchinson could not do in the end, despite all his talents, virtues, offices, and advantages.

Thus, we cannot consider the July 4 text as a mere international-law instrument and nothing more. While it undoubtedly was a tool to win the war—an instrument in one sense no different from a musket or a ship—it was in the most profound sense entirely different from a musket or a ship. It aimed to win a war by winning men's minds—by reason and rhetoric, by persuasion, by conversation of a certain sort. Muskets and ships cannot do this. A cannon can roar but it cannot speak. It cannot truly persuade. It cannot converse. In his 1766 Parliamentary testimony on the Stamp Act, Benjamin Franklin put the point well: "No power, how great soever, can force men to change their opinions."[41]

THE DISTINGUISHED HISTORIAN PAULINE MAIER powerfully documented that much of the Declaration was not particularly original.

Its substance and even much of its prose borrowed from and built upon earlier colonial essays, pamphlets, and pronouncements. Jefferson did not try to compose an original argument. Rather, he aimed to distill what Americans had already said, what Americans already believed. He did not begin a conversation with America; he powerfully summarized an intense American conversation that had been unfolding for more than a dozen years. He restated, with a few of his own rhetorical flourishes, the common sense of common people.[42] Then Congress as a whole carefully edited his draft precisely to sand off its most original and personal edges.

So who really wrote the Declaration? Let us consider several possible answers:

A. Congress did. This is a good answer. The document technically came from Congress, and Congress did significantly edit the committee draft—especially by eliminating some idiosyncratic (and, as we shall see, idiotic) things that Jefferson had written about moral culpability for colonial slavery. This answer has the added advantage of being a democratic answer. The final text was effectively crowd-sourced by several dozen impressive statesmen who had in turn been selected by an even broader democratic base back in their home colonies.[43]

B. The five-man drafting committee did. This is also a good answer. It has the virtue of showcasing Benjamin Franklin, not just because he himself was on the committee, but also because the committee was the embodiment of his snake, uniting as it did New England (Adams from Massachusetts and Sherman from Connecticut), New York (Robert R. Livingston—son and namesake of the Stamp Act congressman), Pennsylvania (Franklin), and Virginia (Jefferson). This answer also draws strength from the fact that committee members gave Jefferson preliminary suggestions and at least two members reviewed his initial draft before it came before the Congress.[44]

C. Jefferson did.[45] This, too, is a good answer for certain purposes. It is the most common answer today; it is the answer that Jefferson's partisans gave in the late 1790s and thereafter; and it is the answer that Jefferson himself ultimately gave to posterity. The inscription on his gravesite obelisk, pursuant to his strict instructions, described him as "Author of the American Declaration of Independence." But the elder Jefferson gave his younger self too much credit (much as the elder Adams did for his own younger self and for his friend Otis in his important but flawed remembrances of 1761). The obelisk answer also emphasized style over substance. Style, as we have seen, is important. And the man could write! Indeed, Adams would later recall that he urged Jefferson to take the lead on the drafting committee because "you can write ten times better than I can."[46]

But surely substance is also important, and much of the Declaration's substance was hardly unique to Jefferson. So the best answer of all is . . .

D. America did. America in effect slowly refined and purified the precious metal of the Declaration in an extraordinarily wide and deep conversation between 1763 and 1776. Jefferson was a stylish note-taker—not a transcriptionist recording every word verbatim, but a good student summarizing and organizing the key points—much as young Adams had done in composing his initial notes and abstract of the writs-of-assistance argument. At his more modest moments, this is indeed how Jefferson described the document and his role: "The object of the Declaration [was] not to find out new principles, or new arguments, never before thought of, not merely to say things which had never been said before; but to place before mankind the common sense of the subject. . . . [I]t was intended to be an expression of the American mind . . . harmonising sentiments of the day, whether expressed in conversations, in letters, [or in] printed essays."[47]

WE CAN NOW SEE THE Declaration with fresh eyes.

The document aimed to declare independence from the king and not from Parliament because the colonists had long argued that they were never properly subject to Parliament, save as each colony chose to allow Parliament to manage certain imperial affairs for the common benefit of all concerned. The Declaration's punchline proclaimed that Americans were absolved of "all Allegiance to the British Crown." Americans never owed any "Allegiance" to Parliament or to the British nation. They were never, formally, dependent on Parliament even if they were "connected" (the Declaration's word) to Great Britain through a common monarch.[48]

In leading up to this punchline, the document targeted King George—"the present king of Great Britain"—and itemized his many wrongs: "He" has done this. "He" has done that. But its references to Parliament as such were dismissive and oblique: "He has combined with others to subject us to a jurisdiction foreign to our constitutions and unacknowledged by our laws, giving his assent to their acts of pretended [!] legislation."

This "dominion" theory was not the consistent and universally held patriot position, but it was the view put forth in earlier writings by Jefferson and Adams (both on the drafting committee), and earliest of all by Franklin (also on the committee) and James Wilson (another Pennsylvania delegate and signer). The Declaration also alluded to the hoary historical claims underlying this dominion theory when, in speaking of the British people more generally, it said that "we have warned" our "British brethren from time to time of attempts by their [not our!] legislature to extend an unwarrantable jurisdiction over us. We have reminded them of the circumstances of our emigration and settlement here."

The justification for severing all allegiance to the king was a standard Lockean justification with two prongs. First, George had ruled as a tyrant who had inflicted on his American subjects "a long train of abuses"—a phrase lifted directly from John Locke's 1689 publication *Two Treatises of Government*.[49] Some of the abuses itemized in the Declaration were the king's alone, whereas many others occurred in a conspiracy with Parliament. On this view, George had an obligation to thwart his British Parliament in order to properly protect his American parliaments and subjects. He had tyrannized by "giving his assent to" Parliament rather than vetoing, or at least scolding, Parliament.

Acting alone or with others, the king had wronged his American subjects by, among other things, imposing taxation without representation; violating jury trial rights (both the rights of defendants and the rights of jurors themselves to govern their communities); foisting a servile judiciary and corrupt bureaucracy upon America; abrogating colonial charters; inflicting standing armies in peacetime without colonial consent; quartering troops to overawe civilians; preventing colonial assemblies from properly meeting; and shutting down American ports. If the Declaration was a mass divorce of sorts, the first prong of the divorce suit was domestic cruelty.

The second prong was abandonment. Americans were not leaving George; he had already left them. He was no longer protecting them; he was waging war on them. He had himself thus dissolved the basic social contract in which he promised protection to his subjects, who in return owed him allegiance. In effect, he had abdicated—much as James II had fled the throne in 1688.[50]

And then, the Declaration, building to a crashing crescendo, identified the master sin that encapsulated all of King George's other misdeeds and rendered Americans without any choice but to leave. George had not listened to Americans; he had not even heard their petitions; he had refused to respond. He had failed to converse: "In every stage of these oppressions we have petitioned for redress in the most humble terms; our repeated petitions have been answered only by repeated injury. A prince, whose character is thus marked by every act which may define a tyrant, is unfit to be the ruler of a free people."[51]

THESE WERE LEGALISTIC ARGUMENTS OF a certain sort—arguments about law and about the foundations of law, captured by law-related words like "legitimacy." Were the Declaration's legal claims valid, when judged by legal standards of the time?

In the narrowest sense, no. Under the British Constitution of 1776—an unwritten hodgepodge of institutions, practices, and principles that had accreted and evolved over the centuries—the most basic principle and institutional practice of all was Parliamentary sovereignty. After the Glorious Revolution of 1688, Parliament was the supreme lawmaker and also the supreme judge.[52] In 1776, Parliament did not find Jefferson and company persuasive. Hence a long and brutal war—indeed, another world war—ensued, continuing through the 1781 Battle of Yorktown until the 1783 Treaty of Paris.

But Parliamentary fiat cannot be the sole test of legitimacy. If British law said (as in fact it did, in 1776) that Britain had a right to rule France, surely it might matter what the French thought about this claim. For law to be truly law—to be true to its own inner logic, to be more than mere force, to be fully legitimate and law-full—legal authorities had to pay at least some attention to the views of those whom law purported to rule, to the "consent of the governed," to borrow a phrase. Jefferson and company were not really trying to persuade Parliament. Rather, they were trying to persuade colonists to reject Parliament and British rule altogether.

Not all Americans were persuaded. Many remained loyal to king and Parliament. Some loyalists stayed; others left for Canada, Britain, the West Indies, and elsewhere. Many other Americans tried to avoid choosing sides. But an overwhelming number of Americans in the 1770s did affirmatively choose to side with the Declaration. Modern scholars have estimated that loyalists likely accounted for 20 percent or less of America's free population.[53]

Among America's top political leaders, loyalist ranks seem remarkably thin. The American-born loyalist of greatest ability and accomplishment was without doubt Thomas Hutchinson. Pennsylvania's Joseph Galloway, a friend of Franklin's who unsuccessfully tried to revive a version of the intercolonial Albany Plan at the First Continental Congress, also chose the path of loyalty in 1776. So did Timothy Ruggles of Massachusetts, former president of the Stamp Act Congress, and Stamp Act pamphleteer Daniel Dulany, a long-serving member of Maryland's appointed council. Another American-born loyalist of note was New Jersey's William Franklin—a colonial governor who broke with his famous father, Benjamin, but never came close to matching his father's achievements or to winning the love of his fellow colonials as did his father. William, after all, was a royally appointed governor; only in Rhode Island and Connecticut did colonists themselves elect governors. By contrast, although Hutchinson did hold many royal appointments over the course of his long career, he had also won electoral triumphs time and again in his native province in the decades preceding the Stamp Act crisis. Galloway in Pennsylvania had likewise won election repeatedly. Indeed, Galloway, uniquely among the most impressive loyalists, had done so well into the 1770s.

The Declaration succeeded in its main mission. It won the hearts and minds of the lion's share of America's genuine leaders, from Franklin and Washington on down.[54] The patriot leadership list included both established notables and newer, fast-rising public figures. It included both those who were in Congress and those who stayed back, men from many walks of life who were admired by their communities—opinion leaders in a modern sense, leaders who were followed by a vast number of Americans who were by definition less notable.

From north to south, this galaxy of leaders included the Adams cousins in Massachusetts, flanked by wealthy merchants such as John Hancock and Elbridge Gerry, respected artisans such as Paul Revere, and politically active printers such as Benjamin Edes and Isaiah Thomas; Rhode Island's distinguished Stephen Hopkins, a former governor and chief justice with more than a decade of service in these two top offices; Connecticut's Roger Sherman (a self-made cobbler-politician), Jonathan Trumbull (the long-standing governor and father of the famous patriot painter), Chief Justice Matthew Griswold, and prominent associate justice Samuel Huntington; New York's smooth young lawyer John Jay and various illustrious Livingstons, who sat atop the colony's social order; New Jersey's preacher-scholar John Witherspoon and ingenious inventor David Rittenhouse; Pennsylvania's lawyer-scholar (and Scottish émigré) James Wilson, radical scribbler (and English émigré) Thomas Paine, and civic leader Benjamin Rush; Delaware's leading lawyer-politician, Thomas McKean; Virginia's revered legal scholar George Wythe, lawyer-orator Patrick

Henry, polymath planter Thomas Jefferson, various notable Lees, and the highly respected lawyer Edmund Pendleton; and South Carolina's preeminent politico, John Rutledge.

To this list we should add various ambitious and adept younger men who flocked to the patriot cause and would later achieve fame in independent America, but who would likely have languished in obscurity had the king remained in charge, because these men, despite their talents, were not closely enough connected to the aristocrats and authorities in London who mattered. Lowborn genius Alexander Hamilton, a New Yorker originally from the West Indies, surely belongs at the top of this list, alongside Virginia's James Madison and John Marshall. An even younger Revolutionary was South Carolina's Andrew Jackson, who would later move west. Other young men whose careers were catapulted by the Revolution include Massachusetts's Henry Knox (who would serve as Washington's first secretary of war), Pennsylvania's Thomas Mifflin (who would serve for eleven years as Pennsylvania's chief executive), and Maryland's James McHenry (an Irish émigré who would serve as Washington's third secretary of war).

On the other side of the ledger, Benedict Arnold probably ranks as the most recognizable loyalist name in the twenty-first century. It might seem a cheap shot to mention Arnold, but his famous defection/loyalism (depending on how one looks at it) contains a profound lesson. Patriots pointedly and publicly dishonored the turncoat Arnold and mobilized broad support for their stance. On September 30, 1780, thousands of Philadelphians high and low—what Continental Congressman Benjamin Huntington described as "the Greatest Concourse of People I ever Saw"—paraded through the streets and then burned an elaborate two-faced effigy of Arnold designed by the great artist Charles Willson Peale. A devil mannequin, holding a money-purse in his left hand and a pitchfork in his right, stood behind Arnold's image. A contemporaneous Philadelphia broadside captured the moment, combining performance art in the spirit of Samuel Adams and the Tea Party with an easy-to-understand public cartoon/engraving in the spirit of Franklin and Revere.[55]

And how was Arnold thought of and publicly depicted by his loyalist and British friends? Revealingly, although Britain was willing to bribe Arnold handsomely for his services, Britons did not in the Revolutionary era—and do not now—honor Arnold the way Americans of all social strata have always honored leading patriots. One big reason is that, contrary to what Whately said, Revolutionary-era Britain didn't think much of, or think much about, *any* Americans. British neglect and disdain were part of what triggered the Revolution.

Jefferson stylishly captured the point in one of the Declaration's most poignant and personal passages:

> Nor have we been wanting in our attentions to our British brethren. . . . We have appealed to their native justice and magnanimity; and we have conjured them, by the ties of our common kindred, to disavow these usurpations which would inevitably interrupt our connections and correspondence. They too have been deaf to the voice of justice and of consanguinity. We must, therefore, acquiesce in the necessity which denounces our separation, and hold them as we hold the rest of mankind, enemies in war, in peace friends.[56]

WHICH TAKES US BACK TO our initial analysis of the legality of the Declaration as judged by British constitutional standards of 1776.

Not only did the Declaration persuade most Americans, but many of its principles were proper British principles, if one focuses not merely on post-1688 Parliamentary sovereignty but also on the spirit of British liberty claimed by British jurists themselves to infuse British constitutionalism. John Locke was British, and the Americans had the better reading of him. Almost no high-level elected American leader, other than Hutchinson and Galloway, stood by the king; but several of Britain's leading statesmen did on key points, even if not on ultimate independence, side with the colonists: William Pitt, Edmund Burke, and Lord Camden most preeminently, but also former royal Massachusetts governor Thomas Pownall and the impressive Irish-born war hero Isaac Barré. (It is probably not a coincidence that two of the leading British figures with the most visceral and sympathetic understanding of what the colonists were trying to say—Burke and Barré—came from Ireland.[57])

The British system of 1776 allowed the king to pick favorites. King George III chose to listen to lesser men—arrogant, ignorant, petty, and belligerent grandees who were more geographically and socially proximate to him than were his talented American subjects who were humbly bending their knees and seeking his ear. The king and his inner circle, trapped as they were in an Old World set of institutions and understandings, did not appreciate the democratic revolution exploding in the New World, with audacious newspapers, edgy cartoons, essays by anonymous authors, extralegal and self-selected assemblages everywhere, massive civil disobedience, and grand-scale performance art. The king heard Hutchinson, but humiliated Franklin. Indeed, the monarch met Hutchinson within hours of the governor's 1774 arrival in London, but never bothered to meet Franklin even once during Franklin's ten-plus years in the imperial city, when Franklin was widely recognized as one of the world's great men and the New World's greatest man. George never tried to converse or correspond with either of the talented Adams cousins or with James Wilson or with any of the leading Virginia burgesses. He evidently did not read American newspapers. And the king was in a position to matter, hugely, because England was an Old World hereditary monarchy. When James Otis became unsound, his neigh-bors stopped voting for him. When George III evinced instability, his subjects kept bowing to him.[58]

Put differently, it was the Americans, not the British, who better foresaw the long-term future of the British Constitution itself as that Constitution worked itself pure. In that future, an evolving set of British constitutional norms and rules would follow American ideas and practices by (1) clipping the military and patronage powers of monarchs; (2) expanding the sphere of action available to informal peaceful gatherings and democratic assemblies; (3) abandoning im-perialistic Parliamentary claims to rule foreign lands; (4) embracing a version of the dominion model; (5) improving the actual represen-tativeness of Commons; and (6) rewarding British politicians able to master modern techniques of democratic communication and con-versation—especially those future British politicians able to converse well with Americans and attend to American public opinion.

BUT IF LAW, TO BE truly law-full and legitimate, must take some account of the views of those whom it seeks to rule, what about American women in 1776? What about indigenous peoples, referred to by the Declaration as "merciless savages"? What about American slaves and American slavery?

The status of women, Indians, and slaves would structure much of America's constitutional conversation in the decades to come; we shall thus return to these questions in future chapters. For now, as we focus especially on the moment of decision in 1776, we should note that on none of these issues were the British better than the Ameri-cans. Moreover, Americans had strong answers—unhypocritical an-swers, answers that were genuinely defensible, given the world they inherited and sought to remake—on women and Native Americans. On slavery, however, the Declaration hypocritically sacrificed justice and truth—self-evident truth at that—on the altar of self-interest, unity, and military expediency.

Women. Women did not vote, yet they were taxed by colonial assemblies and would continue to be taxed by the new state governments in independent America. Many other legal impositions would also be heaped upon these nonvoters. How could this be squared with the Declaration's principles?

Because Whately was right in some ways. Sometimes virtual representation could indeed protect nonvoters, as Dulany and others had conceded. In 1776, American male voters plausibly saw themselves as virtual representatives of the women in their lives—their wives, daughters, sisters, and mothers.

American women themselves were not—not yet!—claiming otherwise. They were not petitioning American men the way colonists had petitioned the king and Parliament. They were not writing woman-suffrage essays, convening feminist or feminine assemblies, organizing all-female committees of correspondence, engaging in female civil disobedience, boycotting men, or doing any of the things that patriots were doing to dramatize and explain their sense of aggrievement toward Britain. (This apparent quiescence would not last. Mid-nineteenth-century American women would indeed proliferate petitions for women's equality, pen and print suffragist books and essays, convene pro-women assemblies, organize feminist boycotts, and do much, much more. And when they did, they would in fact brilliantly echo and adapt the very language of the Declaration of Independence itself in iconic statements such as the Seneca Falls Declaration of 1848.)[59]

Women in the 1760s and 1770s were of course participants in the great debate between Britain and America. Patriot "Daughters of Liberty" made homespun and brewed indigenous teas to support boycotts. Loyalist women tried to stiffen the spines of their spouses. Once war broke out, women on both sides of the contest often "manned" their households, freeing up men to fight on battlefields.[60] That said, many Revolutionary-era women, from patriot Betsy Ross (who sewed a flag) to loyalist Peggy Shippen Arnold (who whispered sweet things to her husband Benedict and bamboozled Washington and Hamilton with fake hysteria[61]), played highly gendered roles. The major pamphlets, essays, orations, and the like in this era came from men as men, either openly or under pen names at first, with men later admitting authorship.

The most pointed discussion of the rights of women came from the era's shrewdest political spouse, and it came, notably, in a private letter to her husband. The letter is now famous, but it was not published until the mid-nineteenth century. On March 31, 1776, Abigail Adams wrote to John that "I long to hear that you have declared an independency." Then she pivoted:

> And by the way in the new Code of Laws which I suppose it will be necessary for you to make I desire you would Remember the Ladies, and be more generous and favourable to them than your ancestors. Do not put such unlimited power into the hands of the Husbands. Remember all Men would be tyrants if they could. If particular care and attention is not paid to the Ladies we are determined to foment a Rebellion, and will not hold ourselves bound by any Laws in which we have no voice, or Representation.

Abigail began here by reminding John that she wholeheartedly supported his crusade for American independence. They were in this together—John could never have left home for Philadelphia without Abigail's unwavering support. With good reason did John think that he virtually represented Abigail. We have already seen that John loved talking politics with Abigail, as evidenced by his July 3 letter in which he began to explain and explore the international-law, diplomatic, military, and geostrategic implications of formal independence. John thus conversed with Abigail far better than the king and various ministers did with colonial dependents.

What, specifically, was Abigail asking John to do in this letter? Not to support women's suffrage, or even equal rights for women to own property, make contracts, publish newspapers, or do anything of the sort. Rather, Abigail was arguing that independent America should reform marriage laws to eliminate ancient English common-law powers of husbands to physically discipline their spouses—what the common law referred to as a husband's power of "domestic chastisement" and "moderate correction," and what Americans today would describe as spouse abuse.[62] In her words:

> That your Sex are Naturally Tyrannical is a Truth so thoroughly established as to admit of no dispute, but such of you as wish to be happy willingly give up the harsh title of Master for the more tender and endearing one of Friend. Why then, not put it out of the power of the vicious and the Lawless to use us with cruelty and indignity with impunity. Men of Sense in all Ages abhor those customs which treat us only as the vassals of your Sex. Regard us then as Beings placed by providence under your protection and in imitation of the Supreme Being make use of that power only for our happiness.

In his epistolary response to Abigail, John missed the force of Abigail's point. He was not always a gifted listener. She countered, briefly, but based on the tenor of the hundreds of extant letters between John and Abigail, one suspects that she may well have communicated her more detailed views to him in person on some later occasion. She was not one to hold back, and he genuinely loved conversing with his extraordinarily clever and articulate spouse, who in much of their back-and-forth wore the affectionate nickname Portia.[63]

Indians. High on the list of the king's atrocities itemized in the Declaration was his effort to enlist certain Indian tribes in the war already under way: "He has . . . endeavored to bring on the inhabitants of our frontiers the merciless Indian savages, whose known rule of warfare is an undistinguished destruction of all ages, sexes, and conditions."

The Declaration did not condemn all Indians—just the ones allied with King George. Americans would happily ally with any tribes who would aid their cause—just as they would happily work with the French. As colonists, Americans such as Washington had fought against both the French and various hostile tribes in a war that took its very name from that fact. It was *the French and Indian War*. The Declaration was quite frank about the realpolitik of international affairs: free and independent states "levy war, conclude peace, [and] contract alliances." The British people would no longer be Americans' "brethren," and thus Americans would be obliged to "hold them as we hold the rest of mankind, enemies in war, in peace friends." (The belligerent order in both formulations—war before peace—is worth noting.)

On matters of Indian affairs, Americans were essentially no better and no worse than the British: both would use Indian tribes for their own purposes, and in truth, Indian tribes in turn had tried, and would continue to try, to play European "tribes" off against each other— French against British in 1754–1763, and British against Americans after 1775.

In 1776, the threat to Indian tribes from the Americans was generally greater because Americans had vastly more boots, guns, shovels, axes, plows, horses, and oxen on the ground and were indeed aiming to oust Indian tribes.[64] Had the British prevailed in the Revolutionary War, they would doubtless have done much the same on their own schedule, and in fact they later did dispossess most indigenous tribes in Canada.

Americans, especially leading Virginians, were particularly frustrated by a 1763 royal proclamation that prohibited colonists from settling west of the Appalachian crest. Much of this pristine land seemed ripe for the taking. Indigenous peoples only thinly inhabited this region. Over the preceding centuries, European diseases such as smallpox, influenza, and measles had ripped through Native tribes and caused massive depopulation. By 1776, European Americans east of the Appalachians outnumbered aboriginal folk between the mountains and the Mississippi by a ratio of roughly twenty to one.[65]

The massive displacement of Native peoples would become an especially important issue in future decades (as shall be seen in later chapters). One way to begin to understand the issue is to note that British American notions of land and property differed dramatically from Native American concepts. British Americans in 1776 were Lockean not just in their embrace of a right of legitimate revolution against tyranny but also in their ideas of land use and ownership. For Locke and his followers, the first person on a virgin continent was not entitled to claim legal title to all that his eye could see and more. He could own only what he used in a certain way, only real estate that he cultivated and improved, only land with which he mixed his own labor.

On this view, although Indians were using large swaths of land as areas for hunting and gathering, this use alone, especially if sporadic or nomadic, did not entitle the Natives to perfect ownership of, and the absolute right to exclude others from, the entire region. Indians intensively cultivated only a small percentage of the land. In general, northeastern Native tribes lived in very different ways from, say, the Aztecs who confronted Spanish conquistadors in the early sixteenth century. Northeastern Indians did not build elaborate permanent structures on the land, lay major roads through it, significantly improve its waterways, build notable bridges or dams across its streams and rivers, harness its wind or water with mills, clear or plant large portions of its acreage, measure it, bound it, register title to it, or commodify it so that it could eventually come into hands that would use it most efficiently. As between Lockean understandings and tribal understandings there was a massive cultural impasse and no easy conversational mechanism for resolving the confrontation.[66]

More generally, Indian tribes were not active and effective participants in the emerging system of constitutional discourse that British Americans were developing. Whatever British elites might think, the colonists were themselves not "savages." On the contrary, colonials were fast approaching conversational parity with their English cousins. They had mastered the common law; Otis and Adams here were exemplary. Many colonial opinion leaders lived in bustling cities featuring grand multistory brick structures, such as the Boston Court House and the Pennsylvania State House, today known as Independence Hall. Colonists wrote, read, sent, and received private letters at an astonishing rate, sustaining a strong and ever-expanding postal system headed at times by Benjamin Franklin.

American-made trade ships plied the oceans on a par or nearly so with British-made trade ships, and British America boasted world-class scientists and inventors, led by Franklin and Rittenhouse. Good, if small, colonial institutions of higher learning abounded—Harvard, William & Mary, Yale, the College of New Jersey (modern-day Princeton), King's College (now Columbia), the College of Philadelphia (now Penn), the College of Rhode Island (now Brown), Queen's College (now Rutgers), and Dartmouth. The colonies had great political artisans and rising political artists, such as Revere, Peale, and Trumbull. Prizing literacy, mainland colonists printed and read books, pamphlets, newspapers, and broadsides prodigiously. Indeed, America's newspaper density and readership per capita would soon surpass Britain's, if they had not already done so. Even common folk such as Paine and his wide readership who lacked advanced degrees knew Newton's laws of planetary motion. (Smaller moons revolve around bigger planets—so why, Paine had asked, should America forever revolve around Britain?)

Colonists were thus conversing with other colonists from elsewhere on the continent and trying to converse with London on equal terms. Indian tribes in the region were simply not part of that elaborate conversational system. Most tribes did not yet have a written language, did not use inked paper, and lacked many other elements of the colonial conversational infrastructure.

One eighteenth-century English word describing the cultural and conversational chasm between European colonists and various indigenous tribes was "savage." On this view, individual Indians who wanted to join the Anglo-European conversation would eventually have to leave their tribes and assimilate. They would ultimately have to join the economy, read books and newspapers, learn about Newton and Locke, and become Americans.*

---

*On learning: Dartmouth College was founded in 1769 with a special focus on the education of Indians. On assimilation: The first man to fall at the 1770 Boston Massacre was Crispus Attucks—"C.A." in the far right coffin in Revere's throat-grabbing image on page 76. Often described as a "mulatto" (a word sometimes denoting complexion)

Slaves. If all men were truly created equal, how could some men own other men—and own their yet unborn progeny unto the last generation? If life and liberty were unalienable rights, how could slavery be law-full or legitimate in the deepest sense of these words?

There were no principled answers to these obvious questions, which laid bare the basic contradiction at the core of the Declaration and of Thomas Jefferson's convoluted contortions.

Masters did not virtually represent the best interests of slaves the way John genuinely and plausibly understood himself to virtually represent Abigail. Slaves thirsted for freedom and ached to win it whenever and however possible. Newspapers teemed with ads offering rewards for the capture of runaways. Colonists themselves obviously understood all this and more when they referred routinely to objectionable British policies as tantamount to "slavery."

Nor did slaves constitute some different sovereign or quasi-sovereign entity like, say, the Mohawk or the Oneida or the Seneca. Slaves spoke the same language and lived in the same cities, towns, and counties—in the same buildings, sometimes—as their masters. They were part of the same civilization and they surely were in daily conversation with masters and the agents of masters.

---

by Adams and other contemporaries, Attucks was widely seen in 1770 as having strong "Indian" heritage—most likely, Wampanoag, according to modern scholars. By most accounts, Attucks was a fully assimilated colonial seaman. Revere and other Sons of Liberty placed him indiscriminately (*le mot juste*) alongside the Whites who fell, and he is buried (with a suitably dignified tombstone) alongside the others in truly hallowed ground within steps of the gravesites of Samuel Adams, James Otis Jr., John Hancock, and many other White heroes. On the "merciless" and "savage" Indian mode of "warfare" condemned in the Declaration: Conflicts between western settlers and Native Americans at times involved indiscriminate butchery, even of noncombatants, on both sides. For example, many tribes scalped enemies, even civilians, as Franklin took pains to highlight in his 1754 essay flanking his "Join or Die" cartoon. This was a theme Franklin continued to emphasize long after 1754. See, e.g., his July 7, 1775, letter to a British friend, the distinguished clergyman Jonathan Shipley: "Dr. Johnson, a Court Pensioner, in his *Taxation No Tyranny* adopts and recommends . . . hiring the Indian savages to assassinate our Planters in the Back-Settlements. They are the poorest and most innocent of all People; and the Indian manner is to murder and scalp Men Women and Children."

The explanation for the beam in the Declaration's eye was geo-strategic. To defeat the British would require the unity of all thirteen mainland colonies. The snake could not be divided. Unity meant agreement from South Carolina, in particular. And the South Carolinians were so wedded to slavery as the basis of their society that they were not even willing to discuss the institution in the 1776 Congress. "If it is debated, whether . . . slaves are [our] property," declared South Carolina delegate Thomas Lynch Jr., "there is an end of the confederation." Franklin's serpent had quite a sting in its tail, as it turned out.[67]

Thus was born a basic contradiction between what Americans professed at their best and what they practiced at their worst. As finally adopted, the Declaration's text muted the contradiction. The document assailed King George for "excit[ing] domestic Insurrections amongst us"—slave revolts—but said no more. In an earlier draft, Jefferson had passionately condemned the international and domestic slave trade—though not, quite, slavery itself—and had tried to blame the British for introducing and imposing the slave trade on America:

> He [the king] has waged cruel war against human nature itself, violating it's most sacred rights of life & liberty in the persons of a distant people who never offended him, captivating & carrying them into slavery in another hemisphere, or to incur miserable death in their transportation thither. This piratical warfare, the opprobrium of *infidel* powers, is the warfare of the CHRISTIAN king of Great Britain. Determined to keep open a market where MEN should be bought & sold, he has prostituted his negative for suppressing every legislative attempt to prohibit or to restrain this execrable commerce: And that this assemblage of horrors might want no fact of distinguished die, he is now exciting those very people to rise in arms among us, and to purchase that liberty of which he has deprived them, & murdering the people upon whom he also obtruded them; thus paying off former crimes committed against the *liberties* of one people, with crimes which he urges them to commit against the *lives* of another.

But the king and Parliament had not generally prevented masters from freeing their own slaves; the masters' own greed had prevented that. Nor had the king and Parliament mandated that Americans buy and sell slaves domestically. If Americans could voluntarily refrain from buying black tea, why not Black slaves? Jefferson's effort to shift blame away from himself and other masters was clumsy and confused, and Congress wisely excised the entire passage.

British critics sneered at the hypocrisy of American patriots in the 1770s. The classic line came from a 1775 pamphlet, *Taxation No Tyranny*, by the ever-quotable Samuel Johnson: "How is it that we hear the loudest yelps for liberty among the drivers of negroes?" It was a great put-down—a brilliant proto-tweet from a distinguished Englishman whose opposition to slavery was sincere and abiding. But in the end, the last laugh was on Johnson himself, who in this reactionary pamphlet obtusely defended the Coercive Acts, and much more, openly embraced Whately's discredited account of America's virtual representation in Parliament. Johnson notwithstanding, the British Empire in 1776 was every bit as steeped in slavery as were the mainland colonies. The West Indies were even worse than South Carolina.

True, in November 1775 Virginia's royal governor, Lord Dunmore, promised freedom to certain runaway slaves—the specific gravamen of the Declaration's grievance about royal incitement of "domestic Insurrections." But the cynicism of Dunmore's gambit was obvious on close inspection. Only slaves of rebels (not of loyalists) would be freed, and only if they served His Majesty's armed forces—fleeing from one servitude to another.[68]

More generally, we must distinguish between freeing individual slaves—even many of them—and ending slavery as a system. *Emancipation*, also described as *manumission*, was not the same as *abolition*. Dunmore never proposed abolition. Nor had any other British official or entity. (In a landmark 1772 lawsuit, *Somerset v. Stuart*, Lord Mansfield ruled that slavery did not operate on British soil proper, but recognized slavery's legality in vast parts of the British Empire governed by Britain's Parliament and Crown.) Most contemporaneous and previous regimes in world history had allowed slavery of some sort; few governments had ever adopted a sweeping and enduring ban on all forms of unfreedom. No major British organization prior to 1775 had advocated for complete abolition.

But in 1775 there arose a remarkable civic society that aimed to end slavery itself. The society was formed not by Johnson, nor in Johnson's vaunted London, nor indeed anywhere in Britain proper, but rather in Philadelphia, the host city of the Continental Congress. Two of the society's early leaders were Benjamin Franklin and Benjamin Rush, who both, in the summer of 1776, added their names to the American Declaration of Independence.

The Society for the Relief of Free Negroes Unlawfully Held in Bondage was founded in Philadelphia in April 1775. The outbreak of war interrupted its activities. In 1780, thanks in part to its members, Revolutionary Pennsylvania enacted a legal plan of partial emancipation and complete albeit gradual abolition. In 1787, the organization renamed itself "The Pennsylvania Society for Promoting the Abolition of Slavery and the Relief of Free Negroes Unlawfully Held in Bondage, and for Improving the Condition of the African Race." Franklin became its president, Rush its secretary.[69]

COURT HOUSE

Let us now return to the scene of the "seeds"—to the precise spot where, some say, the Revolution truly began, when Otis argued before Hutchinson, and young Adams looked on, spellbound.

By July 4, 1777—the first anniversary of the Declaration—the old Court House had a new name, function, look, and address. It was now the State House, home to a new provisional government stripped of all vestiges of royal authority. The elegant paintings of Stuart monarchs that Adams loved aesthetically and loathed politically no longer adorned the council chamber, having come down in 1768 at the insistence of the elected council and to the chagrin of Lieutenant Governor Hutchinson. After independence, the grand thoroughfare facing the elegant edifice, previously named King Street, became State Street. Thomas Paine approved.[70]

Also, the large wooden unicorn and lion—ornate symbols of the Crown that had loomed above Bernard's shoulders when he proclaimed the young king back in 1760—were no more. On July 18, 1776, shortly after a copy of the Declaration of Independence reached Boston and was publicly proclaimed, a patriot crowd pulled down the statues and burned them. With a poignancy worthy of their Tea Party predecessors, Boston patriots that night staged a powerfully symbolic anti-Georgian bonfire precisely repudiating the pro-Georgian bonfires the night of the king's proclamation. Poignant, too, was the fact that the Declaration was proclaimed from the very balcony where Bernard had stood in 1760 to bless the king, and where Hutchinson had stood in 1770 to quell the crowd.[71]

As for Hutchinson himself . . . he too was no more, politically and legally. At the time of Otis's oral argument, the ubiquitous Hutchinson had indeed been everywhere—presiding over the Superior Court, anchoring the council, and serving as the lieutenant governor. In June 1774, in the wake of the Hutchinson-Assembly debate, the Hutchinson Letters Affair, and the Tea Party, a new governor, Thomas Gage, arrived in Boston to restore order. Hutchinson then left his native city to travel to London and explain himself to his king and his king's ministry. He thought the trip would be temporary. On January 11, 1775, he wrote to a friend, "I had rather die in a little country farm house in New England, than in the best Nobleman's seat in Old England; and have therefore given no ear to any proposal of settling here. I think the controversy must be settled this summer." But the events of 1775 did not unfold the way Hutchinson predicted. Far from settling the controversy between his king and his province, the Battles of Lexington, Concord, and Bunker Hill triggered a wider conflict that made it impossible for America's leading loyalist to return to his beloved New England. In June 1780—the month that a new Massachusetts constitution, drafted in part by John Adams, commenced operation—Hutchinson would die in Old England, far from his native land but close to his king.[72]

By July 4, 1777, Thomas Hutchinson's life of public service was thus over, and James Otis had likewise left history's grand stage. John Adams's constitutional adventures were just beginning.

PART II

CONSTITUTION

— four —

WE

AMERICANS WERE NOW ON THEIR own in the world, facing a future both terrifying and exhilarating. In mid-August 1776, the British amassed more than thirty thousand soldiers, including nearly ten thousand German mercenaries, near New York City. If these professional troops could smash General Washington's raw and ragtag army in the vicinity, the war might end almost before it could start in earnest. As European powers received word of Congress's July 4 Declaration, none seemed in any great hurry to recognize the self-proclaimed United States of America, much less send the massive military and financial support that Washington and Congress so desperately needed. Most likely, Americans would have to continue to prove themselves on battlefields before major European investors and governments would be willing to bet big on the Revolutionaries. It seemed an almost insoluble paradox: to win, America would need aid, but to get aid, America would need to win.

Alongside the overwhelming military and diplomatic challenges at hand, Americans would have to forge new constitutions or constitution-equivalents, locally and continentally, to replace the old provincial and imperial legal order they had just cast off. Unless these new legal systems made life significantly better than it had been under Britain, all the patriots' foreseeable sacrifices of blood and treasure would be for naught.

For all their anxiety, Americans also thrilled at the prospect before them. "We have every opportunity," wrote Thomas Paine in his stirring closing passage of *Common Sense*, "to form the noblest, purest constitution on the face of the earth. We have it in our power to begin the world over again. A situation, similar to the present, hath not happened since the days of Noah."

John Adams, usually far less utopian than Paine, also waxed rhapsodic. "You and I," he wrote to a friend in a meditation that soon became a widely read pamphlet, "have been sent into life, at a time when the greatest law-givers of antiquity would have wished to have lived. How few of the human race have ever enjoyed an opportunity of making an election of government . . . for themselves or their children. When! Before the present epocha, had three millions of people full power and a fair opportunity to form and establish the wisest and happiest government that human wisdom can contrive?"[1]

The situation was indeed utterly unprecedented, both locally and continentally. Locally, now that each free and independent state—colony no more—could govern itself, what form of government should it adopt, and how should it go about adopting it? At the continental level, how should these thirteen states, now united as never before, operate? In exactly what manner were they in fact "united"? In what ways were they a unit, and in what ways a plural? How would their new-modeled united continental structure interact with new state constitutions simultaneously taking shape?

THE STATES' FIRST DRAFTS

On May 17, 1776, John wrote Abigail. He had just successfully championed a two-part resolution urging each colony to form its own government entirely free from any political or legal connection to George III or Britain. This resolution, he explained with a mixture of pride and awe, was tantamount to "absolute Independence." In his view, "Confederation among ourselves, or Alliances with foreign Nations are not [logically] necessary, to a perfect Separation from Britain." Confederations and alliances were, at this exhilarating and terrifying moment, tactical means to the ultimate end, the true prize. While "Confederation will be necessary for our internal Concord, and Alliances may be so for our external Defence," the real reward would be the freedom of Massachusetts, and every other former mainland colony, to choose its own state government and then to govern itself. A "whole Government of our own Choice, managed by Persons whom We love, revere, and can confide in, has charms in it for which Men will fight."

To find the true meaning of American independence circa 1776, we must thus look beyond the Continental Congress. We will not find all the answers to the meaning of 1776 in documents that fully emerged only years later: the Articles of Confederation (1781), the Northwest Ordinance (1787), and the ultimate federal Constitution (1787–1788). No, if we are to understand what all the shouting was about in 1776—what the main point of the conversation was—we must first ponder the state constitutions that sprouted like so many daffodils up and down the continent in the springtime of the New World.

The essence of these early constitutions did not reside in minute details or even in larger patterns on specific day-to-day substantive issues.[2] The key to 1776 was not that most of the state constitutions born that year prescribed annual elections, lacked a regular system of census and reapportionment, featured chief executives who had no veto power and were selected by legislatures, specified religious qualifications for public service, and omitted an explicit right of free speech for ordinary citizens. Although all of these things were true of most 1776 state constitutions, and none of these things is generally true of state constitutions today, these modern documents nevertheless descend emphatically and directly from 1776. Nor was the essence of 1776 state constitutionalism fully captured by certain day-to-day governmental features that have largely continued over the centuries: bicameral elected legislatures with good-sized assemblies and short fixed terms, flanked by executive and judicial branches staffed by persons lacking seats in the legislature itself.

Rather, the most remarkable features of these first state constitutions were certain overarching elements that are now so commonplace that we forget how truly revolutionary they were in 1776: writtenness, concision, replicability, rights declaration, democratic pedigree, republican structure, and amendability. Never before in history had this particular combination of features come together. After 1776, this cluster would sweep across the continent and, eventually, across much of the modern world.

The history of the world before 1776 was a history of "accident and force."[3] Most people in most places were ruled by brute power or by old customs that the populace had never formally consented to in any self-conscious moment of collective choice. Very few advanced societies in or before 1776 could be described as self-governing. The history of the world was a history of emperors, kings, princes, dukes, czars, sultans, mogul lords, tribal chieftains, and the like. Among advanced civilizations, even those few societies that were moderately self-governing never had anything like a 1776-style written constitution.

In many places—including eighteenth-century Britain—the fundamental rules and norms governing the system had never been reduced to a single comprehensive text, much less a relatively short and readable one that had been democratically approved in some manner and made generally available to members of society. Mastering the vaunted British Constitution required long years of close study of many sources, including a slew of important judicial opinions in scattered reports, a library of learned treatises, a host of statutory enactments, and a plethora of administrative and procedural arcana. Many of the individual items in this hodgepodge were written in thick and ponderous English, if written in English at all (as distinct from Latin or law-French). Much of this unwritten Constitution had deep roots in hereditary political powers of kings and noblemen.

Ancient democracies at times claimed written constitutions, Athens most famously. But the best-known version of the ancient Athenian Constitution was written by one man (Solon, the lawgiver), was never voted upon after its announcement, and was proclaimed (by the lawgiver) to be unamendable for a hundred years. In ancient Sparta, the lawgiver Lycurgus had contrived to make his constitution permanently unamendable.

IN 1776, STATE AFTER STATE, building on each other in self-conscious conversational fashion, introduced the world to an entirely different constitutional model. Representatives, plausibly claiming democratic authority based on at least one actual if imperfect set of elections, composed and promulgated a short composite set of basic rules, expressed in ordinary language, easily publishable in the state's newspapers, and easily republishable elsewhere for edification and emulation. This document, an American-style constitution, would typically identify fundamental rights and map out the basic schema of governmental power. The schema might well privilege property, including property in slaves, and might also exalt native White men over all others, but did not in any other way confer political authority based on hereditary birth status. Property qualifications for voting were remarkably low compared to rules then in place in Britain and previously in place in colonial America; given the widespread availability of land and other ways of amassing property, most free men in most states comfortably met the thresholds specified in early state constitutions. Whether or not these short documents explicitly said so, and even if they seemed to say otherwise, these texts quickly came to be understood as generally amendable at any time by a broad popular majority.[4]

Building on the Great Debate of 1763 to 1776, America's first generation of state constitutions was designed for newspapers and for those who read them—not just lawyers and not just locals. State constitutions themselves became yet another kind of intercolonial network, a standing body (now of texts, not humans) that could inform Americans in one part of the continent about key legal ideas and developments in other parts of the continent—much like newspapers, pamphlets, and circular letters in the run-up to the Revolution.

VIRGINIA TOOK THE LEAD IN 1776, issuing a new and influential constitution at the end of June. The newborn state began with a "Declaration of Rights" that were, textually if not necessarily philosophically, prior to the rules creating government institutions. Even before the Declaration of Rights was finalized, Americans were talking about it, and not just in Virginia.

On June 1, the *Virginia Gazette* in Williamsburg published a committee draft of the document, which had been spearheaded by planter George Mason. Here is how it opened: "All men are born equally free and independent, and have certain inherent natural rights, . . . among which are the enjoyment of life and liberty, with the means of acquiring and possessing property, and pursuing and obtaining happiness and safety."[5]

Over the next week and a half, this draft made its way to Philadelphia, where it appeared in at least four newspapers—the *Pennsylvania Evening Post*, the *Pennsylvania Ledger*, the *Pennsylvania Journal*, and the *Pennsylvania Gazette*. The draft's opening language thus came to the attention of congressmen working on an early version of the Declaration of Independence. Echoes of Mason's draft reverberated in what is today the Declaration's most memorable line: "All Men are created equal [and] are endowed by their Creator with certain unalienable Rights, . . . among [which] are Life, Liberty, and the pursuit of Happiness."[6]

Mason's Virginia draft also made an appearance in the June 12 issue of Baltimore's *Maryland Journal*. By June 20, Bostonians could read the draft in their own hometown *New-England Chronicle*, or hear it read aloud in coffeehouses and taverns, which often subscribed to a wide assortment of non-Boston papers. July saw additional republication elsewhere in New England.[7]

In late summer, the state constitutional story took a dramatic new turn. Pennsylvania was now in the process of producing its own new state constitution and Declaration of Rights. On August 20, the *Pennsylvania Evening Post* published its home state's new Declaration in full. Here is how it opened: "All men are born equally free and independent, and have certain natural, inherent and unalienable rights, amongst which are, the enjoying and defending life and liberty, acquiring, possessing and protecting property, and pursuing and obtaining happiness and safety." Additional republication in Philadelphia quickly ensued; and in less than two weeks, multiple New England papers were giving their readers the full text of the Pennsylvania constitutional document.[8]

The Delaware and Maryland Declarations of Rights generated an analogous diffusion pattern. On September 11, the Delaware Convention promulgated a Declaration of Rights whose full text appeared in the September 24 issue of the *Pennsylvania Packet* and then in the October 2 issue of another Philadelphia newspaper, the *Pennsylvania Gazette*. The Delaware Declaration began as follows: "All government of right originates from the people, is founded in compact only, and instituted solely for the good of the whole." On November 11, neighboring Maryland promulgated its own Declaration of Rights. It began as follows: "All government of right originates from the people, is founded in compact only, and instituted solely for the good of the whole." The Maryland text was published in full by *Dunlap's Maryland Gazette* on November 19 and by Philadelphia's *Pennsylvania Gazette* the following day. By early January 1777, the Boston press was offering its readers full access to the Maryland constitutional pronouncement.[9]

Nor was the pattern of short documents aimed at common readers and designed for newspaper distribution both within and across states limited to the rights-declaring portions of state constitutions in 1776. The main body of the Virginia Constitution, which spelled out the powers of and the selection rules for each governmental branch, was immediately published in full in the July 6 issue of the *Virginia Gazette* and then quickly and widely republished in other states, most notably Maryland, Pennsylvania, New York, and Massachusetts. The July 17 issue of the *Pennsylvania Gazette* served up for its readers a veritable interstate constitutional buffet, giving them the full text of New Jersey's new constitution on page one and the main body of Virginia's constitution on page two.[10]

ALTHOUGH VIRGINIA LED IN 1776, later in the decade Massachusetts introduced a dramatic procedural improvement in the emerging state constitutional system.

Virginia's constitution came from the existing legislature, which promulgated the document immediately. Although the situation in June 1776 was indeed urgent, Jefferson and other critics worried that the procedures Virginia had followed were democratically deficient. The electorate had been given no chance to vote directly on the state constitution. Nor had the document's start date been delayed to allow for a new legislative election that might operate as an indirect test of the document's popularity. Nor, in the preceding election, had the voters even been on notice that legislators would try to turn themselves midsession into a special body of Solons empowered to promulgate a constitution defining the parameters of their own legislative powers.[11]

If the constitution had simply come from an ordinary legislature elected in an ordinary way, critics asked, what made the so-called constitution any different from an ordinary statute? Why couldn't a later legislature elected in the ordinary way repeal the constitution at will and substitute something else?

In 1778, the men of Massachusetts aimed to improve upon the Virginia procedure. The legislature drafted a new constitution, and, seeking to avoid Virginia's mistake, submitted their draft text for a special ratification vote in statewide town meetings. At these town meetings, ordinary property qualifications were waived. All adult free male citizens could vote on the new proposed constitution. This special ratification procedure would distinguish the constitution from a mere statute and would also cure the Virginia self-dealing problem. Unlike what the Virginians had done, the Massachusetts legislature acting alone would not be defining its own powers and limits.[12]

The voters were not impressed. They rejected the 1778 proposal by an overwhelming margin. In 1779, the Massachusetts legislature went back to the drawing board and devised a new and even more democratically impressive protocol. First, voters in town meetings were asked whether they wished to authorize an election for a special ad hoc convention that would meet "for the sole Purpose" of drafting a new constitution. Voters said yes. A special election was then called to choose convention members—men elected with an express electoral mandate to act as so many Solons, men who were formally and emphatically distinct from the ordinary legislature whose power, tenure, and structure (along with other government powers, tenures, and structures) would be defined by the constitution itself. John Adams, freshly returned from a diplomatic stint in Paris, was elected to the convention, as was his cousin Samuel. At the convention itself, which commenced in late 1779, John ended up serving as the main legal draftsman. In 1780, the convention's draft constitution was submitted for popular ratification by township, and ordinary property rules were once again suspended to allow extra-wide participation in the ratification process.[13]

This time, the constitution went through.[14] In 1784, neighboring New Hampshire successfully adopted a new state constitution using a variant of the 1779–1780 Massachusetts protocol, rather than the 1776 Virginia procedure.

On both substance and procedure, the new states were thus conversing with and learning from each other's constitutional triumphs, trials, and errors.

MASSACHUSETTS IMPROVED ON VIRGINIA IN one other especially notable way. Mason's draft declaration had opened with a sweeping affirmation of *birth equality*: "All men are born equally free and independent, and have certain inherent natural rights, . . . among which are the enjoyment of life and liberty." Read at face value, these words swept broadly. They could just as easily have come from the pen of Thomas Paine. If Britons in America were born the equals of Britons in the mother country, were Blacks born the equals of Whites? Was a slave baby born the equal of a free baby? If so, and if "life and liberty" were "inherent natural rights," how could slavery ever be lawful?

Concerned about just these implications, the Virginia Convention had tweaked the language of Mason's committee draft. In the final version of the Virginia Declaration of Rights, the word "born" disappeared. Instead, the final version declared that all men are "by nature" equally free, and that their rights become effectively unalienable only "when they enter into a state of society" with other men.

These were legal weasel words. Pro-slavery lawyers could tell themselves that "natural" law could be displaced by "positive law"— by statutes or custom. Even though slavery was "unnatural," positive law in Virginia and elsewhere allowed it. (In the famous 1772 *Somerset* case, Britain's Lord Mansfield had treated slavery as unnatural but had not denied its lawfulness in many parts of the British Empire; nor had he denied that Parliament could choose to authorize slavery in England itself. He had merely held that Parliament had not done so, and until it did, natural law operated as the background presumption, the default norm.) Also, many Virginia Whites denied that they were in the same "society" as Black slaves—despite the obvious facts that they lived in the same place, spoke the same language, and were part of the same culture and economy. Slaves were not like tribal Indians, even though some White Virginians wanted to pretend otherwise. In any event, no matter what Virginia's Declaration said or did not say, the deep questions of slavery's legitimacy—of its lawfulness in the most profound sense—remained.

The Massachusetts Convention declined to follow the Virginians down the tortuous rabbit hole of equality for me but not for thee. The Bay State's constitution opened with a "Declaration of Rights" whose first words were as follows: "ARTICLE I. All men are born free and equal, and have certain natural, essential, and unalienable rights;

among which may be reckoned the right of enjoying and defending their lives and liberties; that of acquiring, possessing, and protecting property; in fine, that of seeking and obtaining their safety and happiness."

These words, partly borrowed though they were from two Virginia slave masters (Mason and Jefferson), also resonated with the spirit of Revolutionary Massachusetts. James Otis Jr. had probably not attacked slavery itself in his 1761 oral argument to Thomas Hutchinson and the other Superior Court judges (as old Adams misremembered), but Otis that day had hyperbolically described writs of assistance as akin to "slavery." By 1764, the conflict with England had moved Otis to think seriously about the rights of colonists as Englishmen and as humans; and this in turn evidently prompted him to seriously reflect on the rights of Blacks. In his widely read 1764 pamphlet, he discussed the issue with passion, logic, and wit: "The Colonists are by the law of nature free born, as indeed all men are, white or black. . . . Does it follow that tis right to enslave a man because he is black? Will short curl'd hair like wool, instead of Christian hair, as tis called by those, whose hearts are as hard as the nether millstone, help the argument? Can any logical inference in favour of slavery, be drawn from a flat nose, a long or a short face[?]"[15]

Similar logic, wit, and moral principle rose to the surface of the ratification process of the failed 1778 Massachusetts Constitution, which had proposed a racial test for voting rights. Opposition to this provision ranked high among the most commonly mentioned reasons in town meetings for rejecting the document. The residents of Georgetown, Massachusetts, expressed their contempt in a particularly witty way reminiscent of Otis: "Rejected . . . Because . . . a Man being born in Africa [or] India or ancient American, or even being much Sun burnt deprived him of having a Vote for Representative."[16]

Adams and the other draftsmen in 1779 got the message, omitted race tests, and opened their proposed constitution with a sentence featuring a key word that had united Otis, Mason, and the plainspoken Georgetown farmers. All men were "born" equal—born equal, presumably, whether born Black or White, whether born first or fifth in a family, whether born in or out of wedlock, and whether born to a slave mother or a free mother.

Over the next several years, judges and juries used the 1780 constitution's opening sentence affirming birth freedom and birth equality to abolish slavery in the Bay State. When America's first census was taken in 1790, no slaves were recorded in Massachusetts.

Somewhere, the spirit of James Otis was smiling.

AMERICA'S FIRST DRAFT

Members of the Continental Congress began work on a continental governing document even before they declared independence. Progress was agonizingly slow. Urgent military, diplomatic, administrative, and financial matters competed for the congressmen's attention. Although the states were united against Britain, they were sharply divided on many other issues. How should voting power in interstate affairs be allocated, and how should tax and defense burdens be apportioned? How should western land issues be resolved? Could other would-be states eventually join the union, and if so, on what terms? Were free Blacks entitled to protection if they traveled in or moved to another state? Would free states be obliged to return escaping slaves?[17]

Eventually, in November 1777, Congress endorsed a governing document labeled "Articles of Confederation." By its own terms and logic, the document could not go into effect until approved by every state's home government. That did not happen until early 1781. In the interim, the makeshift Continental Congress continued to sit and coordinate war and diplomacy, often using the unratified Articles as a template for its actions.

Meanwhile, America's armies and militias avoided catastrophic defeat and even scored some significant moral and morale-boosting victories against the vaunted British troops and their foreign mercenaries, who were operating far from home and with less inspiration than Americans fighting for their families and freedom. A crucial geostrategic turning point occurred in 1778 when the French monarchy—impressed by the military tenacity of the Americans, charmed by the amiable diplomacy of Benjamin Franklin, and hoping to avenge France's humiliating defeat in the Seven Years War—formally recognized the United States and entered a treaty of alliance with America against the British. In population, Britain was more than thrice the size of America; but in turn, France was thrice the size of Britain. In 1779, Spain, hoping to wrest Gibraltar back from Britain (which had controlled the strategic promontory since 1704), allied with France, but not directly with the fledgling United States. Then, in 1780, the British declared war on the Dutch for supplying the French. Thus embroiled in yet another world war, Britain had to keep half its fleet at home to repel any possible invasion from its European foes while also straining to defend far-flung colonies and outposts in Africa, Asia, the West Indies, and elsewhere.[18]

In late 1781, only months after the Articles of Confederation formally commenced operation, French and American forces on land and sea combined in the Yorktown peninsula to capture Britain's best army, led by Lord Charles Cornwallis. After years of refusing to converse with their American cousins, Britain would now have to do so, and the chief subject of the conversation would be when and how Britain would remove its residual troops and recognize American independence. Ironically, both the lead British negotiator in this conversation (the Earl of Shelburne) and Cornwallis himself had been among the handful of farsighted Peers who had joined Camden in opposing the Declaratory Act of 1766, which had passed by a lopsided vote of 125 to 5.

The Articles of Confederation and the interim Congressional improvisations inspired by the Articles (most importantly, the 1778 treaty with France) thus achieved America's most pressing purpose—victory and real independence—almost immediately after the document's ratification. But could this document actually work as a blueprint for the indefinite future?

THE QUESTION OF "SOVEREIGNTY" LOOMED large in conversations about the Articles, much as it had in the conversations during the imperial crisis. From 1766 to 1776, while Parliament had insisted on its absolute sovereignty, patriots had other ideas. And the war came. The ensuing Articles made emphatically clear that each of the thirteen states was sovereign: "Each state retains its sovereignty, freedom and independence." The newly minted "Congress" that would henceforth superintend the thirteen states—in effect filling the shoes of George III and Parliament—was merely the embodiment of a "league," an avowed "confederation" designed mainly to resolve interstate squabbles and realize "common defense." The latter phrase appeared three times in the text of the Articles.

Under orthodox legal theory as elaborated by influential seventeenth- and eighteenth-century treatise writers (Locke, Vattel, Blackstone, and others), leagues and confederations were treaties of a certain sort. Because each state was sovereign as of July 2, 1776—because each state was "free and independent," independent even vis-à-vis each other state, save as states chose to concert their actions—no state could speak for any other in forming the Articles. Thus, the Articles would not bind any state unless that state itself consented; hence the requirement of initial unanimity before the Articles could formally operate. Even after the thirteen colonies-turned-states had joined together to declare their independence from Britain, it was generally acknowledged that any of the newly independent states could in theory legally secede from the Continental Congress.[19]

But such action would have been militarily suicidal and morally perfidious. The Confederation held firm as the war progressed, and the United States as a whole, via Congress, spoke for each of its member states when dealing with the outside world. Thus, France in 1778 could and did make a treaty with "the United States," knowing that each member state would be bound by that treaty so long as it remained in the fledgling league.

The Articles optimistically referred to the alliance as a "perpetual" union—but in 1787–1788, eleven states would peacefully and lawfully secede from the Articles to form a new, more perfect union called the United States Constitution. (The two laggards—North Carolina and Rhode Island—would later choose to rejoin the others.) This mass secession drew legal support from the Articles' own deep theoretical structure. A sovereign state inherently retained the right to withdraw from a treaty in order to safeguard its own sovereign existence and vital interests. Also, if a treaty were substantially breached—and eventually the Articles would be routinely breached—that, too, would trigger a legal right of a sovereign state to exit under traditional principles of international law.[20] One of the Confederation's greatest moments would come when a strong majority of states took necessary Congressional action that used the Articles' formal procedures to violate the Articles' substantive terms. Poetically, the Constitution's majoritarian state dissolution of the Articles in 1787–1788 would closely track key practices and landmark precedents under the Articles themselves.

EVEN THOUGH THE ARTICLES OF Confederation collapsed less than a decade after the regime formally commenced, the document had many virtues, especially once we recall that Americans were making things up as they went along, improvising by necessity because history offered few genuinely apt guideposts. For all its flaws and ultimate failures, the document was an earnest first draft of an entirely novel and extremely challenging legal project—the "United States of America."

USA 1.0 avoided many of the worst features of the British Empire while pioneering several admirable principles and introducing several clever practices. The system was strong enough, barely, to win key diplomatic recognitions and thus to win the war, and weak enough, happily, to collapse thereafter. Unwittingly, the Articles paved the way for a vastly superior successor—a second draft of the "United States of America" that pointedly described itself not as a "Confederation" but as a "Constitution." Ironically and luckily, the major weaknesses of the Confederation canceled out and thus became strengths. Precisely because the Articles of Confederation were so weak, they nicely imploded when something far better—the Constitution—became available.

The Articles were entirely republican and true to some of the best ideas underlying the Revolution. Evidently, leading Americans had listened to other leading Americans (as King George and Parliament had not) in the Great Constitutional Conversation of 1760 to 1776. The document did not replace an Old World king with a New World king, nor a house of British lords with a house of American lords. Although the Confederation imposed relatively few restrictions on individual states on matters of internal governance—in general, each sovereign, free, and independent state could choose for itself how to structure its affairs—no state could grant any "title of nobility" to any person, whether native or foreign-born. Nor could Congress. While the best-selling journalist Thomas Paine played no formal role in drafting the Articles, *Common Sense* prevailed on these key points.

A relatively egalitarian vision also informed what the document said and did not say about race and slavery. True, the document did not oblige states to free slaves or even to take any steps in that direction. Here, the iron limits of America's emerging system of constitutional conversation were painfully evident. In late July 1776, South Carolina delegate Thomas Lynch Jr. seemed to say that merely *discussing* the issue of slavery would prompt his state to secede: "If it is debated, whether . . . slaves are [our] property, there is an end of the confederation." Perhaps he was exaggerating or posturing, but his remarks foreshadowed much of the rest of the next century, in which the Deep South, led by South Carolina, would repeatedly threaten both unionism and free speech in defense of slavery and racial oppression.

Happily for slavery's critics, such as Benjamin Franklin, silence did not always and invariably benefit slave masters. For example, the fact that the document said nothing about interstate fugitive slaves favored the cause of freedom. Under background principles of international and common law (as elaborated by Britain's Lord Mansfield in the famed 1772 *Somerset* case), anti-slavery states could choose to enforce their own free-soil laws on their own turf and thus reject any

claims by masters that slave law operated outside the boundaries of slave states.

The Articles also omitted any racial test in defining the rights that citizens of each state could expect in sister states. In setting the quota of soldiers each state should provide, the Articles did use the word "white," but the document pointedly omitted that limiting word when telling each state to handle non-indigent citizens of other states as gently as the state handled its own citizens. Thus, Virginia could treat an Englishman as an alien, but had to treat a citizen of Massachusetts as a Virginian for most purposes. When South Carolina proposed restricting this guarantee to "whites," Congress refused.[21] It did so knowing that free Blacks had fought nobly alongside White Americans. In January 1776, Congress, at Washington's urging, had explicitly authorized the reenlistment of "the free negroes who have served faithfully in the army at Cambridge."[22] Several months earlier, eyewitness accounts and newspapers across the continent had reported that Blacks had participated in the Battles of Lexington, Concord, and Bunker Hill—a fact later memorialized by Trumbull on the far right side of his famous depiction of the latter battle.[23]

By the end of 1776, free Blacks and soon-to-be freed Blacks constituted roughly a tenth of the Continental Army.[24]

The Articles, in their own way, also tried to embody revolutionary ideology regarding taxation and representation. States and only states were formally represented in the Confederation Congress—as with the earlier Continental Congress, each state legislature chose a delegation to represent the state. Thus, states and only states were subject to Congressional taxation. Congress would simply tell each state what its fair share of the total union burden was, just as Grenville should have done but did not do in the Stamp Act crisis.

Perhaps the most striking feature of the Articles of Confederation was its strong commitment to equality of states: each state, qua state, in the Confederation Congress would have one vote, regardless of population. On the one hand, this could be seen as replicating one of Parliament's worst features—the overrepresentation of tiny "rotten boroughs" such as Old Sarum at the expense of large and growing population centers such as Birmingham and Manchester. On the other hand, the Articles' structure could instead be seen as an attempt to adjust the Revolutionaries' "dominion" model of the British Empire to a New World operating without monarchs.

In the dominion model, George III was the monarch of both Britain and Hanover, but the British Parliament could not lord over Hanover, even though Britain was obviously much more populous. In post-Paine America, hereditary monarchs were out. The law would be king, and a Confederation Congress would in effect play the unifying role that monarchs played in the dominion model. But if Congress itself were structured to give big states like Virginia, Massachusetts, and Pennsylvania far more voting power than small states like Delaware and Rhode Island, then wouldn't this be akin to big Britain lording over tiny Hanover? If each state was free, sovereign, and independent—the animating premise of the Articles—then didn't pure equality of these sovereigns in any common council logically (or at least plausibly) follow?

The state-equality approach had certain other advantages for pragmatic draftsmen. It sidestepped the explosive slavery issue. A state got one vote whether it had slaves or not, and no state would get more voting power by adding more slaves. Any alternative arrangement based on population would have forced the draftsmen to decide how to count slaves. To count them at zero would have risked incurring the wrath of South Carolina, and perhaps other states in the Deep South. But any non-zero weight would have rewarded the South for buying and breeding slaves, risking disaffection in the North.

The state-equality approach also avoided giving a state more clout because it was wealthier or older. Under Article XI of the document, Canada was preapproved for membership, should it at some point seek to join the club. The strong implication was that Canada would be treated just like the original thirteen states even though it would be entering later: "Canada acceding to this confederation, and adjoining in the measures of the United States, shall be admitted into, and entitled to all the advantages of this Union." Here lay the seeds of an important anti-imperial ethos, later made clearer still in the most significant postwar achievement of the Confederation Congress, the Northwest Ordinance of 1787.

BEFORE WE TURN TO THAT singular accomplishment, let us catalog the biggest flaws of the Confederation, flaws that Americans identified soon after the regime began operation and that would eventually lead to the regime's collapse. First, the system failed to solve the fundamental problems that had led to Revolution and the problems created by the Revolution itself, problems of tax apportionment, military power, international respectability, western lands, and law enforcement. Second, and more fatally, the Articles of Confederation failed to create an effective amendment procedure to fix the Confederation's other flaws.

On taxes: Beginning with the Stamp Act crisis, colonial assemblies had insisted on the right to tax themselves, because Parliament did not represent them. Under the Articles, Congress likewise lacked the power to tax Americans as such. Congress, for example, could not tax imports, exports, property, sales, heads, income, or estates.

Perhaps this was because Congress was seen as the dominion substitute for the monarch, and kings could not tax in England.[25] True, unlike a hereditary monarch, Congress would be indirectly electorally accountable—chosen by state legislatures whose members were in turn chosen by voters. But on a strict understanding of the taxation-representation linkage, Congress represented states, so Congress could tax only states. Local assemblymen in each state would, in theory, know best how to raise the money requisitioned by Congress. In one state, perhaps a sales tax ("excise") would be most acceptable to the citizenry; in another state, a land tax might be best; in a third, a per capita or per household "head tax" might be best adapted to local norms and enforcement systems.

The Articles thus established a revenue requisition system. Congress would tell each state what it owed, based on the value of the state's land and buildings, and the state would then decide how to raise the money. But state delegations in Congress squabbled over how to measure property value. Worse, many state governments simply failed to pay their assessed amount. In late 1787, Virginia congressman James Madison reported, in a letter to his friend and mentor Thomas Jefferson, who was off in Paris, that "it may well be doubted whether the present Government can be kept alive thro' the ensuing year."[26]

Without money, a desperate Congress had no way to repay European creditors who had funded the war or American veterans who had waged and won it. If the union was not good for its existing debts, who would ever loan money or sign up to fight in the next national security crisis that would inevitably arise? What if, in the dangerous and fluid world of European power politics, France at some future point turned against America, or Britain decided to try its luck again?

What was Congress to do?

On the military: America in the 1760s and 1770s had been victimized by a professional standing army imposed from above by Britain. Americans responded by limiting the ability of Congress to raise its own Continental Army. Rather, Congress would tell each state to provide its proper quota (as with taxes, though based on a different formula). Under proper Revolutionary ideology, states were represented, so states could be taxed and requisitioned for soldiers. But states often failed to provide the men as promised, preferring to keep their forces close to home for emergency use and to avoid the expense of protecting other parts of the union. The old problem of unwanted standing armies had been solved, but only by creating real problems getting wanted armies to materialize when and where needed. If, in some future conflict, states failed to send men as promised, what was Congress to do?

On international respectability: The Articles empowered Congress to wage war, secure peace, and make treaties of every sort on behalf of all America, and promised the world that states would abide by these treaties. (Here, too, the Articles in effect put Congress into the old monarch's shoes; in Britain, the Crown played a large role in matters of war, peace, and treaty.) But strictly honoring American treaties was not always in each state's short-term interest, even if it was in the union's long-term interest. For example, in the 1783 Treaty of Paris ending the Revolutionary War, Britain promised to abandon its military outposts in America's northwestern backcountry. In exchange, America promised to limit state confiscation of loyalist property. Despite the treaty, various states kept confiscating to fill their treasuries, and Britain used these treaty violations to justify keeping its forts. This hurt some states more than others. In a closely related collective-action conundrum, some states resisted honoring the treaty unless all other states did likewise; without complete compliance, Britain would still have an excuse to hold on to its outposts.

These British garrisons, in turn, encouraged local Indian warriors to fight American settlers and trappers seeking farms and furs.[27] In the southern backcountry, Georgia waged unauthorized war against local tribes, usurping Congress's authority to make and maintain proper Indian treaties, to decide continentally on matters of war and peace, and to "manag[e] all affairs with the Indians." When a single state flouted a federal Indian treaty or initiated improper armed conflict against a tribe, it put its sister states at risk of tribal reprisal.

When rogue states undermined continental policy and American honor vis-à-vis European and Indian nations, what was Congress to do?

On western lands: In 1763, King George had proclaimed that colonists could not settle west of the Appalachian crest. Americans, especially Virginians, chafed at this restriction.[28] The Articles of Confederation said nothing about the issue, in part because it generated discord among the states. Various "landed" states claimed ancient charter grants into the Far West, but these claims (often based on faulty maps) at times conflicted. Also, recent British policies (the 1763 proclamation and the 1774 Quebec Act) arguably abrogated some of these older claims. More generally, if all post-Declaration Americans were fighting in unison against Britain, why should "landed" states get a special reward at war's end? The "landless" state of Maryland thus declined to join the Articles until its "landed" neighbor Virginia promised to cede its western claims to the union.[29]

But how should the union respond to this and other cessions? The Articles gave no explicit power to Congress to regulate these lands, and the document went on to forbid Congress from exercising any power not "expressly delegated." Done right, Congressional regulation of the West might solve many of the Confederation's financial woes. With proper land surveys and sensible land policies, the West was a veritable gold mine. But with no "expressly delegated" authority to act in the West, what was Congress to do?

On law enforcement: The imperial crisis between 1763 and 1776 had made Americans fearful of central power and hostile to judges imposed by the center on the periphery. Parliament had claimed that as sovereign it could do anything it wanted in America. High-level judges in almost all the colonies were royally appointed and often deeply loyal to Britain. In ten of the eleven colonies where London chose the top judges, the colonial chief justices in 1776 had chosen George III over George Washington. (Former chief judge Thomas Hutchinson was emblematic here, as was his in-law successor Peter Oliver.)[30]

In response, the Articles created a system that avoided central tyranny, but only by substituting a rope of sand. Structurally, Congress, unlike Parliament, could be trusted because Congress was indeed representative, albeit indirectly. But the Articles of Confederation did not quite see it that way. Still in the grip of traditional sovereignty thinking, the first generation of draftsmen in independent America could not quite conceive of a central legislature that could properly legislate over some matters but not others. How could a proper system in, say, New York have two distinct legislatures—the legislature of New York and also a continental legislature called Congress?[31]

Under the Articles' traditionalist approach, the Confederation Congress was not a legislature, strictly speaking. It was thus qualitatively different from the body called "Congress" in the United States Constitution that had not yet appeared on the scene. Rather, the Confederation "Congress"—like the Albany Congress of 1754, the Stamp Act Congress of 1765, the First and Second Continental Congresses, and the later European Congress of Vienna—was more akin to an international assemblage of ambassadors. In matters of day-to-day governance, it was more an executive body than a legislative one. It would, in effect, stand in the shoes of a proper dominion monarch—making treaties, superintending military matters, and asking local parliaments for money (but not directly raising money itself).[32] Thus the Articles did not describe themselves as "law." Nor did they describe Congressional actions as "law." Nor did they ever describe Congress itself as a "legislature" or as a body wielding "legislative" power. By contrast, the document did repeatedly allude to state "legislatures" wielding "legislative" powers. Under the Articles, states were sovereign, and under traditional sovereignty ideology, two sovereign legislatures in a single system seemed impossible.

On paper, "Every State shall abide by the determination of the United States in Congress assembled, on all questions which by this confederation are submitted to them. And the Articles of this Confederation shall be inviolably observed by every State." In practice, this piety was not fully legalized. Local judges did not take oaths to Congress or to the Confederation—just as American judges today do not take oaths to international law or to the North Atlantic Treaty Organization or to the United Nations.[33] Here, too, the Articles thus solved the old problem of too much central power, but only by creating a new problem of too little central power. State legislatures and state executives routinely violated the provisions of the Articles and the pronouncements of Congress. State judges, bound by oaths to state governments and state law, followed their local oaths and local law at the expense of the union.

Here, too, what was Congress to do?

On amendment: The obvious solution to all these problems was to amend the Articles. None of the flaws in USA 1.0 was in itself fatal, nor were they fatal collectively. The truly fatal flaw was that none of the nonlethal flaws could be formally repaired without resort to the Confederation's amendment procedures, and these procedures were themselves irreparably broken. Amendments failed to materialize even when the vast majority of the continent's leaders and followers agreed on sensible amendment proposals addressing serious problems. The most important piece of the Confederation's intricate machinery—its safety valve—was frozen shut.

In the mid-1780s, amendments were proposed to substitute a tighter tax apportionment formula for the flabby one in the Articles, and to give Congress power to impose import duties to make up for state failures to pay as promised. But given the state-sovereignty, treaty-based logic of the Articles, both the letter and the spirit of the document required unanimous agreement among all thirteen states. Securing unanimity had been a Herculean achievement even in the existential crisis of 1776. At war's end, when the existential threat subsided—or at least seemed to subside, to some who were not paying close attention—unanimity proved impossible to achieve. There was always at least one state that balked, and it was not always the same state. (New York and Rhode Island were the worst offenders; their well-positioned seaports enabled them to siphon substantial revenue from goods produced by or destined for residents of sister states.)

Nor would the problem get better over time. It would get worse if and when America expanded westward and new states joined the club. Getting thirteen out of thirteen states to say yes to any necessary amendment had proved impossible, despite the dire situation in the mid-1780s of a nearly bankrupt and defenseless Confederation in a dangerous world. How much harder would it be in the future to get, say, thirty out of thirty states to say yes to some future necessary amendment?

Here is another telling detail, reflecting the 1777 draftsmen's failure to imagine the distant future, desperately focused as they were on solving immediate problems: in two key clauses, the document required "nine" state delegations to agree to various important Congressional measures. How would this fixed number make any sense in a future Confederation of, say, thirty states?

So what was Congress to do?

THE CONGRESSIONAL IMPROVISATION IN 1787 was brilliant in its boldness and jujitsu logic: given that the Articles were not being enforced as agreed upon, then Congress should simply disregard the Articles and do what needed to be done—but do so *unitedly*. Paradoxically, the very weakness of the Articles was their ultimate strength. In the imperial crisis of 1763 to 1776, the Parliamentary sovereignty argument was so strong that it failed. As Burke predicted, nobody could be argued into slavery. Now in 1787, the Articles were so weak that they succeeded—succeeded, that is, in persuading Congress, meeting in New York and acting by a vote of eight states to zero (many of the states simply weren't showing up as promised), to regulate western lands even though the Articles gave it absolutely no power to do so. Two wrongs made a right: state governments were not doing as promised back home, so state delegations in Congress would fill the vacuum, even though filling it was also a violation of the Articles' strict letter.

This Congressional action—the adoption of the Northwest Ordinance of 1787—would also, serendipitously, provide a powerful precedent for another group meeting in another conclave in 1787.[34] Under the logic of state sovereignty, the massive and repeated violations of the Articles by virtually all the states—which were flagrantly

failing to do what they had promised to do—could have legally justified any single state in repudiating the Articles, if it so chose. The
1787 Philadelphia delegates decided that it would be far better—
and in keeping with the unionism of the Articles themselves—for
a strong majority of consenting states to repudiate the Articles en
masse. America could then reunite as USA 2.0, in a document that
fixed the major flaws of USA 1.0 and simply cut the Gordian knot
of unanimity by dispensing with it. With luck, straggler states that
declined to embark on the new ship *Constitution* as it left port could
board the vessel at some later point, and eventually all the states
would be back in one boat—and a far sturdier one at that.

THE WEST'S FIRST DRAFT

We shall soon turn to Philadelphia in 1787, but let us first consider
more carefully what happened in New York that same summer, when
the improvisers in Congress adopted the Northwest Ordinance.

The "Ordinance" (recall that Congress had no explicit power to
make "laws" as such) created a template for governance—a proto-
constitution, of sorts—for lands northwest of the Ohio River, south
of the Great Lakes, and east of the Mississippi. The region was vast,
encompassing all or part of modern-day Ohio, Michigan, Indiana,
Illinois, Wisconsin, and Minnesota.

Much of this region had been claimed by Britain (and by certain
British "landed" colonies such as Virginia and Massachusetts) for
more than a century, but France had initially contested the matter.
In the Treaty of Paris of 1763, which formally ended the French and
Indian War, France renounced its own claims and ceded all contested
areas to Britain. Twenty years later, Britain, in turn, renounced all entitlement to this domain and ceded it to America in the 1783 Treaty
of Paris that brought a formal end to the Revolutionary War. As a
result of these two Paris accords exactly twenty years apart, Britain
in effect won Canada and lost America. America first helped Britain
best France, and in turn France helped America best Britain. And
then, at the bargaining table, America further exploited the Brit-

ish-French rivalry to get both Great Powers to recognize America's expansive western land claims. In only two short decades, Britain's most stunning feat had brought about its most startling defeat.

Americans relished the irony and resolved to learn from it. Britain had allowed its distant American colonies to drift away, at first emotionally and ultimately legally. The Confederation must not let something similar happen to the new union. Although the Northwest was not an ocean away, it was over the mountains. Few good roads spanned the spine of the northern Appalachians. Easterners flocking west to make new lives for themselves needed to know they were still Americans, and would be treated as such, with all the rights of Americans—including, when the time was right, the right to form new states that would join the old states as new sisters and not as permanent children.

That is precisely what Congress promised—technically without proper authority, but brilliantly nonetheless—in New York on July 13, 1787. Western settlers were offered a basic bill of rights "as articles of compact between the original States and the people and States in the said territory" that would be "forever . . . unalterable, unless by common consent." This rights catalog expressly included the free exercise of religion, trial by jury, habeas corpus, due process, a common-law judicial system, just compensation for takings of private property, a ban on immoderate fines and improper punishments, broad access to bail, protections against contractual impairments, a promise of properly apportioned local assemblies, and more. The Ordinance also embraced egalitarian inheritance rules (restricting Old World primogeniture) and provided for a system of public education.

Many of these provisions broke sharply with the principles underlying Parliament's 1774 Quebec Act, which had outraged colonists, especially Virginians, almost as much as had the contemporaneous Coercive Acts. Parliament had proposed to govern the lands won from France—including the very lands covered by the Ordinance—without jury trials or other common-law guarantees, and without local assemblies.

In emphatic contrast, the Ordinance contemplated that the Northwest would be divided into several distinct fledgling states. Within each fledgling state, once the population reached certain benchmarks, settlers, organized into New England–style townships, would begin to vote for representatives to a well-apportioned territorial assembly. Ultimately, each baby state would join the Confederation on equal terms—as early as possible, promised the Ordinance.

Specifically, "whenever any of the said States shall have sixty thousand free inhabitants therein, such State shall be admitted, by its delegates, into the Congress of the United States, on an equal footing with the original States in all respects whatever, and shall be at liberty to form a permanent constitution and State government." There was a proviso, but unlike a typical legal proviso, this one gave more than it took: "*Provided*, the constitution and government so to be formed, shall be republican, and in conformity to the principles contained in these articles; and, so far as it can be consistent with the general interest of the confederacy, such admission shall be allowed at an earlier period, and when there may be a less number of free inhabitants in the State than sixty thousand."

On paper, the Ordinance even seemed to protect certain Indian rights: "The utmost good faith shall always be observed towards the Indians; their lands and property shall never be taken from them without their consent; and, in their property, rights, and liberty, they shall never be invaded or disturbed, unless in just and lawful wars authorized by Congress; but laws founded in justice and humanity, shall from time to time be made for preventing wrongs being done to them, and for preserving peace and friendship with them."

The Ordinance also said this: "There shall be neither slavery nor involuntary servitude in the said territory, otherwise than in the punishment of crimes whereof the party shall have been duly convicted." Some thirty years later, a lad who would grow up to be history's most famous northwesterner would move with his family into this region. The family was drawn to this region, in part, by the free-soil vision of the Ordinance. When this lad, Abraham Lincoln, became a man, he would spearhead an amendment to the US Constitution that would take the Ordinance's anti-slavery words, virtually verbatim, and make them the supreme law of the land—for all America, not just for the lands north and west of the Ohio.

IN PROCLAIMING GEORGE III KING from the Court House balcony in the waning hours of 1760, the English-born and royally appointed governor, Francis Bernard, aptly enough, had faced east—toward London and toward the past. Most of his American-born audience, doubtless unaware of the poetic portent of their stance, had faced west. Toward Lexington and Concord. Toward the future. Toward the vast continent that stretched out before them, and toward unborn states that would, one day, join the first thirteen as full and equal siblings.

In the 1760s and early 1770s, arrogant Londoners had treated their western cousins in the colonies like children. In the Confederation Congress's single most impressive postwar accomplishment, its members renounced all pretension to lord over their own western cousins.

But the problem of the West was only one of an interlocking set of problems that young America needed to solve. How would the Revolutionaries solve the remaining existential issues of USA 1.0, and where would the key solutions come from?

— five —

AMERICA

I F AMERICA, MORE THAN THOMAS Jefferson, truly wrote the Declaration of Independence, did America, more than James Madison, truly write the Constitution?

Imagine, for a moment, that lightning had struck Virginian James Madison as he made his way toward Philadelphia in early May 1787. In the preceding months, Madison and several dozen other notables who ranked among America's most distinguished statesmen had been tapped by their home state governments, with the blessing of the Confederation Congress, to meet in a grand constitutional convention to propose modification of the failing Articles of Confederation. The delegates' charge was to devise a legal blueprint that would render the continental governance structure adequate to its basic purposes. Had Madison—or for that matter, had any single American Solon other than the indispensable George Washington—missed the Philadelphia Convention, would Americans nonetheless have ended up with something similar to the Constitution that in fact materialized?

AMERICA'S SECOND DRAFT

Proper analysis begins by considering the broad outlines of the draft document that emerged from the Philadelphia Convention in September 1787 and thereafter received a sufficient number of state ratifications to go into effect by its own terms in late 1788.

The document described itself as a "Constitution" and not as a "confederation" or "league" or "treaty." Nowhere did the new document proclaim, as had the old Articles, that each state would remain "sovereign"—a notable and pointed omission. Like its state constitutional precursors, the document was compact, written in plain English, and designed for easy newspaper publication and republication in full. It opened with a single sentence, promising that the document's legal force and legitimacy would come from the citizenry themselves via a special series of exceptionally democratic votes. "We, the People," not ordinary legislatures, would "ordain and establish" this new "Constitution for the United States of America."

This Preamble did not detail how this would happen; but the Constitution closed with a one-sentence coda, Article VII, that stylistically counterbalanced and substantively clarified the Preamble's one-sentence intro. The coda specified that the people would do the Preamble-promised "establishment" via special ratifying conventions. Each state would hold an ad hoc convention, which would ideally receive its mandate from a particularly inclusive electorate, Massachusetts-style. No state convention would bind any other, and nine state convention approvals would suffice to "establish" the Constitution among the ratifying states. The Preamble also set forth the basic purposes of the new Constitution, which promised a "more perfect union" than the evidently imperfect one then in place under the Articles of Confederation, and linked that more perfect union to strengthening the "common defence"—the Articles' thrice-mentioned raison d'être.

After the Preamble came Article I, introducing a very new kind of "Congress." Unlike the unicameral and quasi-executive Confederation Congress, the Constitution's new bicameral Congress would operate as a true legislature, modeled on standard state legislatures and explicitly vested with "legislative Powers" to make real "Laws." A lower house would be directly elected by voters every other year and would be apportioned based on population, with each slave counted as three-fifths of a free person. A smaller upper house, the "Senate," retained vestiges of the Confederation Congress: its members would be picked by state legislatures and each state would count equally. Unlike members of the old Congress, however, members of this new Senate would vote per capita rather than by state delegation, would serve for long (six-year) terms, would be immune from state recall, would draw payment from the central government, and would be free to seek unlimited reelection.

The powers of this new Congress were sweeping. Inheriting almost all the old Congress's specific powers, the new body would also have power to impose a wide range of taxes on individual Americans—import duties, sales excises, land assessments, head taxes, and more. Rather than relying on states to provide requisitioned troops, as had the Congress under the Articles of Confederation, the new Congress could create, regulate, and fund a new national army in both wartime and peacetime. This new Congress would moreover have power to regulate trade and other interactions with Indian tribes and foreign nations, as well as between Americans in different states. More generally, Congress 2.0 would not be limited to powers "expressly" conferred; the new national legislature could in addition claim powers fairly implied from the document as a whole. The new Congress would also have broad powers to regulate and monitor two new branches—a distinct federal executive and federal judiciary—that the Constitution summoned into existence.

In contrast to the Articles, whose collective Congress performed a range of war-directing and other executive functions, the Constitution created a separate executive branch headed by a single and muscular new officer. Described in Article II as the "President of the United States," this officer would negotiate treaties, command armies and navies, supervise executive underlings, and perform a wide range of other functions, not all of them itemized in detail. He would wield a powerful veto pen and a sturdy pardon pen. He would not be directly elected by American voters, but would have an electoral base independent of Congress and could seek reelection every four years, without limit.

Article III mapped out a new standing federal judiciary, which likewise was given considerable independence from Congress—life tenure and guaranteed salary. The new judges would rule on federal law, including the law of the Constitution itself, and enjoy appellate authority over state courts that could hear federal-law cases in the first instance, but would not be the last word.

Article IV echoed and clarified the interstate provisions of the Articles of Confederation, detailing how each state would treat sister states and their citizens fairly. As with the Articles, these rules applied indiscriminately to free Whites and free Blacks alike. But free-soil states such as Massachusetts would now be required to return escaping slaves to slave-soil states such as Virginia. Article IV of the Constitution also filled a glaring gap in the Articles of Confederation by giving Congress explicit power to regulate federal territory. Congress under the Articles of Confederation had enacted a landmark ordinance to govern the union's Northwest Territory, but had done so without any proper express textual authority. The Constitution's Article IV closed with new and arresting language promising that the federal government would ensure that each state maintained a "Republican Form of Government."

Article V laid down procedures for amending the Constitution. Unlike the Confederation, which was a mere treaty among sovereign states, and therefore required unanimous state approval of any treaty modification, Article V made plain that future constitutional amendments could operate everywhere even if a few states said no. Nevertheless, future Article V amendments would need to clear a high democratic bar, requiring much broader democratic support than necessary for enacting ordinary statutes. In contrast to the Virginia Constitution, which had issued from the standing legislature acting by simple majority, every future federal constitutional amendment could claim—as could the original text of the federal Constitution—a democratic pedigree superior to that of any mere statute. Legally and democratically, the federal Constitution and its future amendments would outrank all other laws—even federal statutes and state constitutions, none of which could claim a comparably emphatic continental democratic mandate.

Hammering these points home and breaking decisively with the Articles of Confederation, Article VI made clear that the new Constitution would stand as the "supreme Law of the Land," binding and uniting all Americans. Even state officials would pledge allegiance to the federal Constitution above all. State and federal officials would also pledge to obey all proper federal statutes, which would trump state statutes and even state constitutions.

WE CAN NOW RETURN TO our question: If a different set of delegates had convened at Philadelphia, how much would their solution have differed from the document that in fact emerged from the conclave? John Adams was not in the room, nor was Thomas Jefferson. If we substitute them for, say, James Madison and Elbridge Gerry, would the result have changed dramatically? What if Samuel Adams or Patrick Henry had attended?

Of course, history happened as it happened, once and complexly. We cannot run a laboratory experiment to test and conclusively prove whether it would have happened differently and by how much, had this person never been born or had that person never entered the room or had yet another person showed up instead or in addition. Still, if we take seriously the American constitutional conversation from 1764 to 1787, we can see that most of the Constitution that emerged simply followed from the logic of that previous conversation. A set of grave—indeed, existential—concerns existed in 1787, as did a set of available legal and intellectual tools generated by the conversation. The challenge confronting the delegates was akin to an intricate but solvable math problem in the tradition of Euclid and early expositors of algebra. Certain constants, equations, axioms, and postulates were already locked in place. Given all these, the delegates were asked to "solve for x." More precisely, their charge could be paraphrased as follows: "The Confederation is broken. Please propose something that will actually work to achieve the Confederation's basic goals."

Let us now methodically try to work through the problem as it existed in 1787.

Massachusetts and Virginia had only recently met, metaphorically. They had come together, along with other states that had only recently met, to stage a Revolution and win a war against the world's mightiest empire. In this war, the states, for certain limited purposes, had to join or die. Massachusetts wanted to govern itself, and Virginia likewise sought self-rule. The same was true for the other former colonies that became free and independent states in 1776. The state constitutions of 1776–1784 were exuberant expressions of self-governance and also illustrations of how states were following and learning from sister states as part of a genuinely continental and fast-unfolding American constitutional conversation.

But no state could have any self-governance whatsoever if the British were to return and reconquer America. Or if the French were to turn against their recent American allies and crush them. Or if the French and the British were to form a cynical alliance and partition America between the two empires, as Europe's great powers had recently partitioned Poland. Or if Spain were to strengthen its position and successfully ally with other powers against America.[1]

Old World monarchies and aristocracies commanded vastly more wealth and much larger populations than did the budding United States. France alone had more than eight times as many inhabitants, nearly thirty million in all. These Old Powers had acted ruthlessly to expand their empires over the past century. Alliances had at times shifted dramatically in the balance-of-power game. Prior to the Seven Years War, Prussia had historically allied with France; Austria, with Britain. But then, as if dancing a quadrille, the Great Powers switched partners in an instant: Austria paired up with France and Prussia with Britain. In the 1750s, George Washington fought under the British against the French. A quarter century later, he was fighting alongside the French against the British. Who could guarantee that all the geopolitical spinning and shifting had now stopped?

Britain refused to evacuate its northwestern forts as promised, and of course retained Canada. With British backing, several northern Indian tribes impeded access to the fur trade and vexed settlers. British and French trade barriers had closed certain European and West Indian ports to various American goods and American ships. Spain, which controlled vast tracts on the Confederation's southern and western flanks, had shut the Port of New Orleans to American farmers, hoping thereby to dislodge large chunks of America's backcountry and pull them into Madrid's orbit. (Without access to and through the mouth of the Mississippi, how would trans-Appalachian folk supply themselves or get their goods to market?) Barbary pirates plundered American ships that tried to ply the Mediterranean and even enslaved American sailors. To thrive, America would need to pry all these boxes open, by extreme force if necessary.[2]

Washington more than anyone knew just how precarious America's geostrategic situation truly was. The survival of his army at Brooklyn in 1776 was a miracle. So was his jaw-dropping, war-winning 1781 adventure at Yorktown, where friendly French soldiers and sailors had outnumbered American ground troops more than two to one. Thousands of American soldiers had reached the battle site via French transport ships. The siege succeeded only because the French navy had arrived in the nick of time to pound Cornwallis from the sea and thwart the British fleet's efforts to rescue the Redcoats. Washington believed that the hand of Providence had intervened, but it was best not to tempt fate going forward. The Lord would help those who helped themselves.

In a future crisis, America had to be capable of fielding an army, equipping a navy, and borrowing money from abroad if needed. The central government would have to pay future troops and to repay future war loans. The union had not paid American veterans or American creditors as promised for the last war. This was a stain on American honor and might doom efforts to raise money and troops the next time around. Washington knew there would be a next time, even if it was not clear how, where, when, and against whom.

In theory, the Articles had empowered the Confederation Congress to raise troops and money by requisitioning states. In practice, states had not complied as promised. The obvious solution—"solve for x"—was to empower Congress to raise money and troops directly. Almost all the states had in fact agreed to Confederation amendments authorizing a direct federal impost on imported items, but the system had repeatedly failed to reach the requisite unanimity.

So unanimity itself would need to be abandoned. The Confederation Congress in New York had itself showed how this could be done—by a strong majority of states acting together and doing what needed to be done, the Articles be damned! (When the Confederation Congress enacted the Northwest Ordinance in mid-July 1787, only eight states were in the room, but all eight said yes. Likewise, at Philadelphia that same summer, not all states came as invited. Rhode Island boycotted, and New Hampshire arrived midway, about the time the New York delegation quit, leaving Alexander Hamilton alone to speak, but not to vote, on behalf of his state.)

If the new Congress were allowed to raise troops directly and tax individual Americans, it would be a true legislature. To have proper Revolutionary legitimacy, Congress would need to derive its authority from direct popular election. Given that individuals themselves were to be taxed, individuals themselves should be represented in a new House of *Representatives* that would be America's House of Commons. Indeed, America's new Commons would need to look something like Otis's proposed British Commons, with elected representatives of all parts of the far-flung regime in the same room.

If the new Congress became a real legislature directly regulating individuals, it could be given other express legislative competences that were obviously necessary but withheld by the Articles because draftsmen in the late 1770s were trapped in a theory denying that Congress was truly a legislature. This shift—recognizing that Congress was a genuine legislature—would require rethinking traditional sovereignty theory. By September 1787, America had already crossed that bridge, de facto. Failed amendments to the Articles had tried to give the Confederation Congress the ultimate legislative power— power to lay taxes on individuals—and at various times almost all the states in Congress and in their home capitals had approved. Likewise, the Northwest Ordinance had effectively legislated for the West, because America urgently needed true legislation.

The other necessary legislative competences would include the ability to regulate foreign trade and foreign affairs more generally beyond making treaties. America could treat on more favorable terms if Congress had sweeping power to block access to all American ports unless other nations opened their own ports to American goods and American ships. Congress should also have express and sweeping legislative power to regulate the West. Done right—done the way the extant Congress was already doing, albeit without proper authorization—western regulation would rectify innumerable problems. It would bring money from land sales, push the British out of their forts with an irresistible flood of new western settlers, and lure countless immigrants from Europe seeking freedom and prosperity. In the next war or crisis, every new immigrant would be one more body for America and one less for the Old World monarchies.

If Congress did not regulate the West, states might be inclined to jump in and would likely clash, as they had when they were colonies. The possibility of state conflict was not limited to the West, so the new Congress would also need sweeping legislative power to regulate all matters that genuinely spilled across state lines. No state should be allowed unilaterally to impose costs or other burdens on sister states or their citizens. Such impositions would be akin to taxation without representation, in violation of Revolutionary principles. Matters that spilled across state lines should be decided in a true continental legislature in which all states and citizens would be properly represented.[3]

If Congress were to be a real legislature, it should look like one. Indeed, it should look like the legislatures of the several states. Just as each state was already paying attention to constitutional ideas and institutions in sister states in an extraordinary continental constitutional conversation, so the new federal Constitution should learn from the state constitutional experience. On detail after detail, and as a whole, the new Constitution should follow the best practices that had emerged among the several states. Almost all the states had bicameral legislatures (as did Britain); America's Constitution should emulate this best state practice. Each branch of the legislature could check and balance the other and keep the system honest. Also, if each branch had a different size, electoral base, and reelection timetable, the overall system might better represent the complexity of shifting public opinion over time.

The state with the most democratically authorized constitution of all—Massachusetts—also had the strongest independent executive. This was not a coincidence. In 1776, the sitting Virginia legislators had turned themselves midsession into Solons and promulgated a state constitution in which the legislative branch dominated. Under that constitution, the legislature picked the chief executive, who in turn had no veto pen or unilateral pardon power. By contrast, the Massachusetts Constitution had come from a single-purpose body directly approved by the electorate and separate from the standing legislature. That document had created a strong governor who was independently elected and endowed with a formidable veto pen. A sensible federal Constitution should emulate Massachusetts on these points. A powerful Congress that was a true legislature should be checked by a powerful and independent executive. A strong executive would also be invaluable in foreign affairs and war-making, as well as in enforcing law domestically without the need to rely on inconstant states. Executive power should obviously be centered in one person—that was the practice of every state except Pennsylvania. Acting as a collective executive, the Confederation Congress had tried to run the Revolutionary War, but administration by committee had not worked well.

Every state government had a judicial branch that was to some extent distinct from the legislature. The best state constitutions, such as the one in Massachusetts, had strengthened judicial independence, and the new federal Constitution should follow suit. Precisely because a continental legislature with true legislative power could threaten freedom if unchecked (as Parliament had seemed unchecked between 1764 and 1776, and as some state legislatures had seemed after 1776), a strong federal judiciary should be created as a counterbalance. Such a judiciary should also have sweeping power to review and reverse any state court ruling on matters of federal law in order to ensure that state judges would not ignore the new federal Constitution and federal statutes and treaties in the way that these jurists had often ignored the Articles of Confederation.

So X ENTAILED Y AND z.[4] What else? The new system would fix the main problems of the Articles of Confederation, but would drain considerable power from state legislatures. These legislatures, filled with small-minded and shortsighted leaders who did not understand the larger geostrategic threats—many of these men had never been more than a hundred miles from home—might initially resist a bold new plan for USA 2.0. But ordinary Americans might well approve of the new system as long as it realistically promised to work and was backed by George Washington and enough other respectable notables up and down the continent.

Article XIII of the Articles of Confederation said that no amendment to the Articles could take effect unless every single state legislature said yes. That would never happen. Unanimity was unrealistic—history had already proved that. (The two most recalcitrant states were Rhode Island and New York, whose superb seaports enabled them to drain money from neighboring states.) In the Northwest Ordinance, the Confederation Congress was boldly sidestepping state legislative unanimity. The Congress was not proposing an amendment to the Articles authorizing western regulation and requiring every state legislature to say yes. Instead, the Congress was simply doing what needed doing, backed by a majority of state delegations.

The Constitution should take this contemporaneous development and improve on it dramatically, and should do so by wedding it to the best state constitutional practice of all—the strikingly democratic protocol that Massachusetts had pioneered for adopting its constitution in 1780, a protocol also embraced and enacted by its neighbor New Hampshire. A new union system would earn legitimacy to outrank all other law only if it was true to the ideals of the Revolution and the best state constitutional practices and principles. The new Constitution would thus have to come, Massachusetts-style, from the people themselves—not merely from the people of one state, but from the people of every state that would be part of USA 2.0.

No state could be bound absent its consent. Each state was properly free, sovereign, and independent in 1787. But precisely because each state was sovereign, and precisely because a strong union was necessary if states were to survive and thrive, a strong majority of these sovereign states should be free to reunite in a different way. Rather than creating another rope of sand—another mere treaty or league or confederation—the states should combine to form a new continental people under a new continental Constitution.

In that new Constitution, each state could no longer be fully "sovereign," as it had been between 1776 and 1787. The consenting states would need to merge into a new, larger, Westphalian nation-state, much as the separate kingdoms of Scotland and England had merged eighty years earlier to form—this was the key phrase in 1707—"an entire and perfect union."[5] Scotland and England had entered this merger for geostrategic reasons: the British snake would be easier to defend if not divided in two. Four score years later, America would need to do something similar for similar reasons.

If fewer than thirteen states agreed to the merger, there would doubtless be initial complications. But so long as a strong majority of strong states merged, the laggard states would likely join up later, because—as Hutchinson had argued back in 1773—no tiny New World entity could survive as a stand-alone sovereign in the brutal world of international diplomacy and power politics. Ironically, the best way to get to thirteen would be to set the initial bar at eight or nine or ten, thereby preventing one or two or even three obstreperous states—say, New York, Rhode Island, and one other misguided member—from holding the other states hostage. Perhaps nine might be the best number; the Articles of Confederation themselves had specified that at least nine states had to concur in certain particularly momentous matters, such as wars, treaties, and appropriations.

The imperative of popular ratification of a special and extraordinary sort to launch USA 2.0 would in turn create still more entailments. George Washington would need to support the plan. Washington was indispensable because, as America's commander in chief, he had served as the singular embodiment of the union in the fight for independence. He had unrivaled credibility as the man who had bested Britain and then dissolved his army, resigned his commission, and returned home, to his proverbial vine and fig tree. He would also likely need to serve as the first president—the new, civilian commander in chief—of the new regime. Beyond Washington, most of America's best minds and statesmen would need to support the plan, though no single one of them was indispensable.

In order to gain popular support, the document would need to have democratic bona fides beyond the ratification procedure itself. In order to win one crucial set of continental ratification elections in 1787 and 1788, the document would need to promise ongoing democracy for myriad future elections ad infinitum. The House would thus need to be more representative than the Congress under the Articles of Confederation, in which state delegates were typically not chosen by direct popular vote. Property qualifications for voting and public service would need to be low or nonexistent. USA 2.0 would also need to promise fair rules of apportionment and reapportionment—as the Confederation Congress was contemporaneously promising fair apportionment for local western assemblies in the Northwest Ordinance, and as New York and Pennsylvania had promised in their state constitutions. On each of these issues and many others, USA 2.0 would need to follow the best state practices in order to be credible in the ratification election.

IN BROAD OUTLINE, THEN, ALL this was the abstract answer—the most logical answer—to the problem that the Philadelphia framers were asked to solve. This abstract solution does indeed closely re-semble the plan that emerged from the conclave. The Constitution was not a complete hodgepodge or a mere jumble of compromises at every level, as has sometimes been thought—although there were compromises aplenty, not all of them morally attractive. As human instruments go, the Constitution had an impressive inner logic, co-herence, and systematicity to it, growing as it did out of a rich and mature continent-wide constitutional conversation that had occurred between 1776 and 1787.

Of course, the matter is infinitely clearer in hindsight. Humans trapped within a maze cannot see the structure of the maze itself from above; the passage of time gives us perspectives that the par-ticipants did not enjoy. Certain answers that seem self-evident to us—of course x and y would lead to z!—were not always clear to all participants in the moment.

To say that America, more than, say, James Madison, wrote the Constitution is to speak metaphorically. What does this metaphor aim to capture?

First, the metaphor highlights that the Philadelphia plan as ul-timately hammered out built on the best state practices that had emerged between 1776 and 1787. Whether or not the Philadelphia delegates were conscious of this fact at every single moment, they were less authors than editors, compilers, sifters, and digesters of America's prodigious state-level constitutional work product between 1776 and 1787. Both in the drafting and in the ratification stage, participants routinely compared the proposed federal Constitution to extant state constitutions.

To be sure, state constitutions were themselves in flux in 1787. Just as the federal Constitution built on best state practices, later state constitutions adjusted to better resemble the best features of the America-approved federal model. Immediately after the fed-eral plan won popular votes of confidence across the land, many a state started to embrace—and today almost every state embraces—a strong independently elected chief executive armed with a veto pen, the elimination of property qualifications for public service, salaries for lawmakers (thus opening seats to persons of modest means), fair and regular reapportionment of lower houses, an end to religious tests for office-holding, and more.

Most literally, the metaphor aims to capture the fact that the document that emerged from Philadelphia in 1787 did not closely track the preferred plan of any individual delegate (other than Washington) or small group of delegates, even the most dazzling delegates in the room.

In this respect, 1787 resembled 1776 and 1780. Thomas Jefferson was a powerful penman, but the most genuinely original passage of his draft Declaration—a convoluted aside on culpability for the international slave trade—was wisely excised by the Continental Congress. That same year, John Adams composed his *Thoughts on Government*, brimming with specific ideas about the ideal state constitution. Several of his signature proposals—term limits for all public servants, an absolute executive veto, legislative election of governors—did not make their way into the Massachusetts Constitution of 1780 even though Adams himself was the chief draftsman. Conversely, Adams in 1776 failed to anticipate and endorse *any* of the 1780 Constitution's most dramatic and generative features—composition by a single-purpose elected convention, popular ratification by a uniquely broad (and unpropertied) electorate, a distinct and robust declaration of rights, abolition of slavery (via an emphatic affirmation of birth equality), a directly elected governorship, and a veto power subject to supermajoritarian legislative override.[6]

Likewise, the delegates of 1787, gathering in the very same Philadelphia building where Jefferson, Adams, and others had crafted the Declaration, rejected many an innovative idea proposed by this or that clever delegate. The draft Constitution was genuinely a collective project, hammered out within the broad outlines of the logical solution to the problems at hand. The delegates had come from across the continent, and their proposed plan truly did reflect America more than it did any one person's vision, with the exception of Washington.

THE DELEGATES AND THE DOCUMENT

Many of Madison's darlings died in the summer of 1787. He argued relentlessly for a Senate that, like the House, would be apportioned by population. He lost. He advocated tirelessly for a Congressional negative over state law. He lost again. He wanted the president to be joined with leading judges in wielding the veto power. Here, too, he lost. He pleaded for broad federal power to tax exports. Yet again he lost.

The proposed Constitution that emerged from Philadelphia also contained signature features that Madison had not pondered prior to the Convention. For example, Article II created a muscular executive branch centered in one person, independently elected, perpetually reeligible, and vested with sweeping powers. In a letter to Washington a few weeks before the start of the Convention, Madison confessed that although "a national Executive must also be provided[,] I have scarcely ventured as yet to form my own opinion either of the manner in which it ought to be constituted or of the authorities with which it ought to be cloathed."[7]

Madison did win on one idea that he championed with particular passion, even though the idea was not unique to him. (Had it been unique, he would have likely lost on it, too; that is how conclaves work.) The Constitution as a whole focused almost entirely on the problems of the Confederation, especially as these problems involved foreign relations or conflicts between states. Madison believed that each state was internally unstable, even in ways that did not spill over across state lines or affect Confederation policy. Within each state, majorities sometimes tyrannized over local minorities, especially religious minorities and economic minorities. (Madison felt special sympathy for creditors victimized by what he viewed as unjust debtor relief and paper money laws.) Prior to 1776, royal governors and the

Privy Council had at times stabilized the colonial system, thanks to their power to negative unjust colonial bills and (in the case of the Privy Council) reverse unjust colonial court rulings.

Madison's most original successful idea at Philadelphia was that the federal government could stand in the shoes of the Privy Council by thwarting injustice within a state. Madison lost in his most sweeping versions of this idea—a general Congressional negative on every state law, or (Madison's fallback) on every state law that Congress deemed unconstitutional. He did, however, succeed in expanding the category of prohibitions on each state vis-à-vis its own citizens. No state would be allowed to issue a title of nobility, a provision borrowed from the Articles of Confederation. In addition—and thanks largely to Madison—no state could enact an ex post facto criminal law (making an action that was innocent when done retroactively criminal), or pass a bill of attainder (legislatively naming and punishing specific individuals as criminals), or impair the obligation of contract by retroactively cheating creditors in favor of the larger debtor class, or adopt inflationary paper-money schemes likewise unfair to creditors who had been promised repayment in hard currency. Ultimately, these prohibitions would be enforced not directly by Congress—which was itself barred from enacting titles of nobility, ex post facto laws, and bills of attainder—or by the federal executive branch, but by federal courts acting as a continental Privy Council in appellate review of local rulings.[8]

Madison was not alone in his bitter disappointment about Senate apportionment. If states were indeed sovereign, as they were under the Articles of Confederation, then state equality followed naturally, even if not as a matter of necessary legal logic. Once states were no longer sovereign, surely apportionment by population was democratically superior, thought Madison and his big-state allies. Treating tiny Delaware as the equal of mighty Virginia, Pennsylvania, or Massachusetts seemed absurd—an American version of the Old Sarum rotten-borough system in Parliament.

But there were countervailing considerations. True, now that states were no longer sovereign, there was no strict need for state equality; but nothing in the logic of the situation prohibited the equal treatment of states as such in certain parts of the system. Several sturdy and interlocking structures successfully resisted the powerful republican arguments of Madison and his accomplices.

A VERSION OF THIS ISSUE initially arose in 1765, when, for the first time ever, American colonies met on their own initiative to coordinate strategy. By what voting rule would the delegates vote at the Stamp Act Congress itself? Some suggested per capita voting—one delegate, one vote. But Delaware's Thomas McKean (who would later relocate to Pennsylvania) successfully thwarted this idea in favor of an equal vote for each colonial delegation. The gathering was a meeting of colonies—it was akin to a meeting of ambassadors—and each colony entered as the formal equal of each other colony. Also, it seemed arbitrary to allow a colony that was closer to the meeting spot, or that for any other reason had sent a larger delegation, to have more clout than any other colony. Perhaps the idea that each colony was equal to each other colony was also arbitrary in a way, but such was the long history of the continent—with each colony conceiving itself as a distinct jurisdiction not bound to any other colony, save through their common parent. This long history created a powerful inertial bias in favor of colonial equality.

In 1774, a similar issue perplexed John Adams and his fellow delegates in their very first hours at the First Continental Congress. Voting by delegate seemed problematic (as it had in 1765). But why shouldn't each colonial delegation's vote be weighted by population? Surely Massachusetts should count for more than, say, tiny Rhode Island at the Congress.

But how much more? No census existed yet. And how, if at all, would slaves count for this purpose? (Virginia's Patrick Henry was willing to count only free persons; South Carolina's Thomas Lynch Sr., unsurprisingly, disagreed, and argued for factoring in "property," by which he doubtless meant slaves.) In modern game-theoretic terms, provincial equality had strong advantages as an easy focal point for coordination.[9]

Also, by what initial jump-starting voting rule would the Congress even decide by what rule it would generally vote? Here was a nearly intractable infinite-regress problem, solvable only by a strong focal point of some sort, either delegate equality or colonial equality: in the initial vote about how Congress would generally vote, either each delegate or each colony would need to vote equally. The latter jump-starting procedure would likely result in recapitulation: any conclave that began by giving each colony an equal vote in determining the conclave's basic ground rules would likely end with equal colonial voting, at least for the conclave itself, and perhaps for any permanent system endorsed by the conclave. (Analogously, it was not a coincidence in 1776 that the Virginia Solons in the state legislature had created such a strongly pro-legislature constitution.)

After several hours of conversation, the First Continental Congress somehow resolved—the records are not entirely clear how—that "in determining questions in this Congress, each Colony or Province shall have one Vote[, the] Congress not being possess'd of, or at present able to procure proper materials for ascertaining the importance of each Colony."[10] That is also how the Second Continental Congress opened and operated. And it is how the vote on the Declaration of Independence was tallied and described—it was a unanimous vote of the colonies, not a unanimous vote of the delegates. That document itself described each state as "free and independent." In the drafting of the Articles of Confederation, each state continued to have one vote; and each state ratified the Articles for itself on a plane of perfect formal equality with each other state. The Articles themselves expressly provided that "in determining questions in the United States in Congress assembled, each State shall have one vote." That is how the Confederation Congress operated (when it operated) day after day, year after year. The inertial bias was by this point growing very strong.

Prior to the formal opening of the 1787 Philadelphia Convention, Madison and several other big-state delegates huddled together to strategize, but (just as in 1774) the large states could not overcome the inertia bias, the no-census problem, the slave-count complexity, the focal-point challenge, and the infinite-regress problem.[11] The Convention began on day one voting by state. Ultimately, proposals for proportional representation in the Senate failed at Philadelphia, but they "failed" because of the Convention's voting rule.[12] Most big states supported a proportionate Senate; most small states supported a Senate based on state equality. The Convention itself weighted these unequally populous states equally. Had the Convention instead somehow weighted its own voting by population, proposals for a proportionate Senate would have passed. (This was one example of the recapitulation problem.)

Given all the interlocking structural forces resisting any move away from state equality, perhaps the more interesting theoretical question is not why the new Senate looked so much like the old Congress, but why the new House looked so different.

One reason was that deep principles and the logic of America's constitutional conversation since 1760 genuinely did matter, up to a point. If individuals were to be taxed, then individuals should be represented. At least one house of the new bicameral legislature should thus be based on population, and it should be better than Commons with its corrupt Old Sarums. It should be as good as the best state assemblies—New York and Pennsylvania—which promised regular censuses and reapportionments.

Relatedly, Madison and his allies genuinely persuaded some fence-sitters by pointing out that formal equality under the Articles coexisted with informal influence wielded by bigger states. Because requisitions did not really bind as promised, big states had extra leverage when they threatened to withhold their required contributions. Under the Constitution, this leverage would disappear, because Congress would rely on taxing individuals. As a matter of Revolutionary first principles, a new-modeled Congress taxing individuals and legislating on individuals should have at least one house reflecting the actual distribution of individuals.

These arguments carried real weight. Impressively, Madison and his allies succeeded in overcoming, for the first time in colonial or independent America, all the forces favoring colonial/state equality.

It would have been better still, thought Madison and his allies, that the Senate likewise give big states more seats, but small-state delegates were unyielding, and often unprincipled, on the point. A small-state plan at Philadelphia championed by New Jersey's William Paterson was a particularly egregious example. Some credulous scholars have treated this plan, which purported to work within the Articles' iron frame of continued state sovereignty, as a serious proposal, but it was not. It came nowhere close to sensibly solving the problems that the delegates had been asked to solve; it was merely a stalking horse for state equality within at least one branch of the new national legislature that most of the delegates understood needed to be created. One critic of Paterson's plan (South Carolina's Charles Pinckney) was particularly blunt in laying bare the plan's true purpose: "Give N. Jersey an equal vote, and she will dismiss her scruples, and concur in the Natl. system."[13]

Despite all this, Madison and his allies were not uniquely on the side of the angels. The House that they supported counted slaves, albeit at a discount. This meant that a slave state would get more seats by buying more enchained humans from Africa in the horrendous slave trade. A Senate based on state equality had certain vicious features, but not this one.

One other large factor helped Madison and his allies win a proportional House. The Constitution's ratification would dispense with unanimity. The need for strong unanimity in years past had given tiny states extra leverage. Now, they would have less leverage, a smaller threat advantage. If they wanted to say no to the new-modeled USA 2.0, they were free to do so, but the other and bigger states would leave port without them. Soon the naysayers would likely seek readmission, because the threat advantage and leverage would favor the new union over the tiny laggards, unable to stand alone in a cruel world of European power politics filled with monarchs seeking to expand their reach.

THE CONSTITUTION THUS OMITTED MANY items that Madison most wanted and included many important features that he either sharply opposed or had never carefully considered prior to the Convention. Why, then, is Madison widely viewed as "the father of the Constitution"?

Here is the case for Madison:[14]

He was instrumental in precipitating the Philadelphia Convention and persuading Washington to emerge from retirement to attend and preside. Madison's home state of Virginia in effect called the Convention, and Madison was the chief architect of the "Virginia Plan" that defined the Convention's conversational agenda. He prepared for this conclave more carefully than did anyone else. At the Convention itself, he was one of a handful of delegates with a perfect attendance record, and he vigorously participated in most of the major debates. He also kept the most extensive set of notes of the proceedings, a veritable treasure trove for historians.

After the Convention, he worked tirelessly for ratification. He orchestrated the successful defense of the Constitution in all-important Virginia. He also brilliantly collaborated with Alexander Hamilton and John Jay under the pen name Publius to produce eighty-plus essays comprehensively analyzing and defending the Constitution. Most of Publius's essays first appeared in newspapers beginning in late 1787; the entire package appeared in mid-1788 as a two-volume book, *The Federalist.* These essays were the most impressive and comprehensive analysis of the Constitution available to Americans deciding whether to vote yes or no. Centuries later, *The Federalist* remains the first thing that any thoughtful American who wants to understand the Constitution in historical context should read.*

---

*While Madison's Publian collaborators, Hamilton and Jay, played crucial roles in the ratification process, Jay was not a delegate at Philadelphia, and Hamilton was stymied by his fellow New Yorkers, John Lansing and Robert Yates, who quit the Convention midway, leaving Hamilton free to speak but not to vote. The final version of the Philadelphia plan fell far short of Hamilton's ideal. In addition to favoring a population-apportioned Senate, Hamilton wanted presidents and senators to serve for life and federally appointed state governors to have an absolute veto on all state laws. Essentially, Hamilton's plan was a republicanized version of the British imperial system circa 1775. *Farrand's Records*, 1:282–311 (June 18), 3:617–30.

After ratification, Madison went on to champion a series of amendments to the Constitution—a bill of rights—that improved the Constitution's substance and helped win over initial doubters and opponents. When the freedom of speech and of the press, enshrined in the First Amendment, came under assault in the late 1790s, Madison, who had sponsored the amendment in 1789, powerfully and successfully championed these fundamental freedoms—freedoms at the very bedrock of a proper system of constitutional conversation. Still later, he served as secretary of state, and then for eight years as America's fourth president. One of his biggest, best, and earliest sets of constitutional ideas—about the need for strong federal oversight of individual states to protect in-state minorities—would eventually become a new constitutional cornerstone when the Constitution was reconstructed after the Civil War. Throughout his long career of public service, he was a rare combination—a powerful thinker and a powerful doer. The Constitution was central to much of what he thought about and much of what he did.

Here is the case against Madison:

Despite all of Madison's constitutional service before, during, and after Philadelphia, the stubborn fact remains that the final Philadelphia plan reflected few of his most original and distinctive ideas. Before the Convention, Jay, Henry Knox, and Madison (in that order) had all sent Washington outlines proposing that a new federal Constitution broadly resemble tripartite and bicameral state constitutions. This basic structure was not distinctly Madisonian (or Adamsonian, for that matter). It was distinctly American. In mid-1783, when Washington had barely heard of Madison and had yet to correspond with him on any issue of constitutional substance, the general had privately told a friendly clergyman that, for reasons of national security, America needed to call "a Convention of the People" to invest the central government with more power. Similar continentalist themes prominently appeared in Washington's famous 1783 circular letter to state governors on the occasion of the general's anticipated retirement. Thus, the Constitution's most notable elements—a bicameral and tripartite continental regime, authorized by the people, rooted in national-defense considerations, conferring more power on central officials, and summoning into existence a robust central executive—were Washington's darlings before they were Madison's.[15]

Nor did Madison's most creative contributions to *The Federalist* reach or sway large numbers of undecideds in the ratification process. In the moment, Hamilton's and Jay's *Federalist* essays were far more important and influential. Madison may have been one of the Constitution's best friends and guardians, but he was not its father.[16]

Although the surviving accounts of the Philadelphia Convention attest to Madison's active—almost superhuman—involvement and his powerful advocacy from start to finish, much of what we know about what happened behind closed doors at Philadelphia comes from Madison himself, who published his account after everyone else in the room had died. Like Adams and like Jefferson, he lived past many others, and in his old age, he told the tale from his perspective. Just as the elderly Adams skewed his story of the writs, and just as Jefferson's obelisk offered one—rather self-aggrandizing—version of the Declaration's authorship, so, too, perhaps, the elderly Madison nipped and tucked just a bit to suit his own purposes.[17]

Madison was more scrupulous than most politicians of his era, but he was no saint, especially on the issue of slavery. Unlike Washington and several other great Virginia contemporaries, Madison, like Jefferson, never freed his slaves, and he sold some when he felt the need. During the ratification process, Madison's worst moment occurred in *The Federalist* No. 54. Using the power of pseudonymity to pose as an anti-slavery New Yorker, he disingenuously defended counting slaves at the rate of three-fifths of free folk in apportioning the House of Representatives. Horses, cows, other farm animals, and other types of property were not counted, but slaves would be (at a discount), reflecting, Madison/Publius suggested, the slave's status "as a moral person." On this (il)logic, counting slaves at five-fifths would have been even better.[18]

Madison here was a sophist. The issue was not whether slaves would be allowed to vote, but rather how much extra clout each slave state would get thanks to the existence of slaves within that state. Surely Madison knew—because the issue had been extensively discussed at Philadelphia, as captured by his own notes—that no actual slave, had he or she been asked "as a moral person," would ever have wanted any slave state to have any extra clout in the federal government whenever its slave masters bought extra slaves. Five-fifths would have been worse than three-fifths; Madison in No. 54 was turning everything upside down and he knew it. Later in this essay, his guilt peeked through when he confessed that his defense of three-fifths "may appear to be a little strained in some points." He had a conscience, but it had not stopped him from telling a whopper (or from owning slaves and selling them and never freeing them).[19]

Under the Articles, the key issue had been taxation, not representation. Each state had one vote in the old Confederation, regardless of population, free or slave. In that old system, each state was to be taxed based on wealth. State population was a rough proxy for state wealth; and anti-slavery forces in the early 1780s had argued that slaves should be taxed fully, at the same rate as others—five-fifths—for taxation purposes. But under the Constitution, the key issue would not be state taxation, because the requisition system was being scrapped in favor of federal taxation of individuals at the Customs House and elsewhere. The big debate about how to count slaves was now about representation, not taxation;[20] and the obvious anti-slavery position was that slaves should never be counted. Counting slaves in any way—one-fifth, three-fifths, or five-fifths—would create vicious incentives for South Carolina and other slave-importing states to increase their power in the House (and in the Electoral College, whose apportionment was largely based on House seats). Madison understood all this perfectly, but used the pen name Publius to bamboozle—to make it seem as if counting slaves was actually a mark of respect for the slaves themselves as "moral persons."

Madison/Publius also alluded to the fact that various nonvoters, such as women and children, would count for apportionment purposes. Why not slaves? The obvious answer, as we saw earlier, was that a male voter (such as John Adams) could with a straight face claim to virtually represent the interests of nonvoters (such as Abigail or the couple's minor children). Masters could not plausibly claim to virtually represent the best interests of their slaves. Rather, masters claimed the right to maim and sell slaves at will, and to doom their posterity to perpetual bondage. If this could count as virtual representation, anything could, and Whately was right. The Revolution and Declaration had rightly rejected Whately's nonsense. But if Parliament could not plausibly claim to represent Americans, surely masters could not plausibly claim to represent slaves. If George III and his Parliamentary enablers had no right to speak for Americans after seeking to deny colonists their "unalienable Rights" of "Life, Liberty, and the Pursuit of Happiness," so as to "reduce them under absolute Despotism," surely slaveholders had no right to speak for their slaves.

Madison's *Federalist* No. 54 was a shabby performance, reminiscent of Jefferson's moral obtuseness in his draft Declaration passage on the slave trade. The dishonesty of Jefferson and Madison on the slavery issue—dishonesty to others and ultimately of each man to himself—would reverberate far and wide in the antebellum republic, when this political duo became America's third and fourth presidents and the founders of a pro-slavery political dynasty that would reign until the election of Abraham Lincoln.

IF THERE WAS A SINGLE thinker who did contribute a large, original, and possibly indispensable idea to the Philadelphia Convention, arguably it was the conclave's other leading James—James Wilson. An immigrant from Scotland, Wilson had served in the Continental Congress and later in the Confederation Congress as a Pennsylvania delegate. He had voted for and signed the Declaration, and some viewed him as America's best lawyer and legal scholar. During the imperial crisis with Britain, Wilson had put forth, early and elegantly, the dominion theory of empire that the Declaration had followed: Britain and each American colony (and Hanover!) shared the same king, but nothing more. Wilson's theory had cut the Gordian knot of the Declaratory Act and Parliamentary sovereignty theory by deny-

ing that Parliament had ever rightfully possessed any ounce of sovereignty or authority over America.[21]

Now, in 1787, Wilson began to develop a different way to cut the
knot. The Articles of Confederation seemed trapped in an iron cage
of sovereignty theory. Sovereignty was indivisible and illimitable. It
admitted of no gradations. It was all or nothing. "Imperium in imperio" was a "solecism." No place could have two sovereigns—two legislatures ruling over it and dividing authority between them.[22] Thus, the
Articles had vested sovereignty in states, recognized state legislative
actions as law, denied that the Confederation Congress was truly a
legislature, and treated the old Congress simply as if it were a Crown
substitute, in a republican variant of Wilson's own dominion model.

But suppose, Wilson explained in the 1780s and thereafter—first
behind closed doors at Philadelphia, then publicly in a powerful defense of the proposed Constitution in the ratification period, and still
later in a dazzling series of scholarly lectures—that no government as
such, no legislature as such, was ever sovereign in a proper republic.
Only the people were sovereign. In establishing a government, the people did not ever give up their sovereignty, or permanently vest it in any
government or government body, or even (à la Locke and the Declaration) provisionally vest it in government subject to repossession
if (and only if) government tyrannized. Rather, the people parceled
out portions of limited government power as they saw fit, retaining
always the sovereign authority to reallocate at will these limited portions of power. Legislatures were no more sovereign than executives.
Indeed, there was nothing particularly special about legislative power
as such; it was merely one kind of power that the people could parcel
out. The people could ladle out some power to a lower house, other
power to an upper house, some to an executive, some to a judiciary.
And if all that were so, then surely, Wilson argued, the people could
give some power to central officials and other power to local officials.
Two legislatures could operate in, say, Pennsylvania, because neither
one—neither a new Congress as a true legislature nor the old Pennsylvania Assembly as another true legislature—was, strictly speaking,

sovereign. Only the people were sovereign, and they never divested themselves of their supreme, absolute, indivisible power.[23]

Click, click, click. Implications of Wilson's popular sovereignty theory snapped into place and made perfect sense of what Americans had already been doing. Americans had embraced state bills of rights, implying that American legislatures did not have illimitable Parliament-style Declaratory Act sovereignty. American legislatures could not properly legislate "in all cases whatsoever." Massachusetts had been right to put its constitution to a special popular vote, because a proper constitution came from the people as sovereign. It was right for constitutions to be short and written and published widely in newspapers, so that the sovereign people themselves could understand what powers they were giving to whom, and what things they were withholding from all government agents and agencies. Government was not the source of all law; the people were the source of all law, and governments existed under law and under the people. It was right for states to understand that their constitutions could be amended at all times and for any reason—not just when government tyrannized—because the people in America retained their sovereign right to alter and abolish existing rules, just as in Britain the (allegedly) sovereign Parliament had claimed a right to modify rules as it saw fit.

ON MANY ISSUES, JAMES WILSON and James Madison saw eye to eye at Philadelphia, and indeed they often worked as a team—backing each other's points and seconding each other's motions. Both favored (and succeeded in getting) a strong national government with sweeping policy authority that rested on the broad foundations of a popularly ratified Constitution and a national legislature whose proportionate lower house would answer directly to voters. Both favored (and failed in securing) a Senate proportioned by population. Both (unsuccessfully) backed a council of revision uniting judges with the chief executive in the veto process. Both (successfully) backed "liberal" eligibility rules for federal public service that would encourage "foreigners of merit & republican principles" to immigrate to America. Both argued passionately (and victoriously) for fair constitutional treatment of Americans residing in western territories.[24]

At Philadelphia, Wilson and Madison diverged on the critical issue of presidential selection. The egalitarian Pennsylvanian favored national election—one person, one vote. This was the best state gubernatorial practice (although it was not Pennsylvania's). Madison purported to agree, but then shared with the secret conclave a mathematical insight that politically doomed Wilson's idea: although direct national election might benefit Pennsylvania, where slavery was tiny and becoming tinier by the day, a directelection system would hurt Virginia and other states with large and growing slave populations. Slaves would obviously not vote in any direct-election system; only free voters would vote. By contrast, a system of indirect presidential election—here, Madison hinted at what would later become the Convention's Electoral College compromise—would enable slave states to count their slaves in some way.[25]

Ultimately, the Convention endorsed a scheme in which Virginia and every other state would receive House seats based on free population plus three-fifths of slave population. This extra clout in the House—giving slave states credit for their slaves, albeit only three-fifths credit—would carry over into the system of presidential election. In the Electoral College that would in the first instance choose the president, each state would have the same number of seats as it had in the House, plus two (to match its two US Senate seats).

In the 1790 census, Wilson's home state of Pennsylvania had almost the same number of White persons as Madison's home state of Virginia. Pennsylvania in fact had more eligible voters (thanks to lower property qualifications) than did Virginia, but Virginia got far more electoral votes because of its slaves, who accounted for roughly 40 percent of its population (compared to less than 1 percent of Pennsylvania's). Madison likely knew exactly what he was doing when, while purporting to back Wilson's direct-election idea, he signaled to the other slave-state delegates that they should block this idea at all costs.

Here is the case for Wilson as the father of the Constitution:

Earlier and better than anyone else, Wilson publicly articulated the dominion theory of empire that eventually undergirded the Declaration of Independence. A republican adaptation of that theory—with Congress substituting for King George and providing a common executive hub for states leagued together—animated USA 1.0 in the Articles of Confederation. When it became clear that the Articles were failing, Wilson theorized a brilliant new approach—popular sovereignty—that underpinned and unified the Constitution crafted at Philadelphia. At that drafting Convention, Wilson participated vigorously, contributing from start to finish and present every day or nearly so. Better than anyone, he systematically demonstrated to his fellow draftsmen the basic inadequacy of any approach that did not approximate the quasi-mathematical Euclidian solution to the problems at hand.[26]

After the Convention, Wilson led the Federalist forces to an early and important victory in the key state of Pennsylvania. His widely reprinted arguments carried special weight, both in that state and in other states, because he did not act anonymously (unlike, say, Publius). He spoke with special credibility as a draftsman of the proposal being decided. In 1790 he played the lead role in remodeling his home state's constitution to better resemble the new federal Constitution. That same year, Wilson delivered a magisterial series of public law lectures in Philadelphia. President Washington, Vice President Adams, members of both houses of Congress, and a galaxy of state dignitaries attended the opening lecture to hear America's counterpart to the British scholar-judge William Blackstone hold forth and show the world what America's legal thinkers could produce. These lectures foreshadowed the founding of the University of Pennsylvania Law School and helped lay the groundwork for a strong constitutional culture in the fledgling nation. Not long after taking his seat as one of Washington's first batch of nominees to the United States Supreme Court, Wilson delivered the single most ambitious constitutional opinion to issue from any American jurist prior to the arrival of John Marshall. (The case involved whether states were "sovereign" in a strong sense; Wilson, as we shall see in more detail later, said no.)[27]

As an immigrant rising from modest origins, James Wilson epitomized the promise of America's open system—not as dramatically as the even lower-born Alexander Hamilton, but surely more than southern aristocratic planters such as Madison and Jefferson. More than any other founder, James Wilson foresaw the Constitution's future, championing fairness for the West, a muscular presidency, direct election of senators, and the eventual abolition of slavery. More than most of his contemporaries, he publicly celebrated women. If, in future decades or centuries, America adopts a system of direct presidential election or a Senate proportioned to population, Wilson will deserve even more credit as a prophet.[28]

Here is the case against Wilson:

Like Madison, Wilson did not get everything or nearly everything he wanted at Philadelphia. He theorized the Constitution but cannot be credited or blamed for several of its most significant features: state legislative selection of senators, equality of states in the Senate, the contours of the veto process (in which judges play no role), and the rejection of direct presidential election. Wilson was the spiritual adviser, not the father, of the Constitution.

In addition, Wilson did not live long enough to shape this child's upbringing and help it reach maturity. He died less than a decade after ratification, and held a position in the then weakest branch of government. By contrast, Washington would set the tone for the entire regime as America's president for the first eight years of the new system. Madison would first lead the legislative branch, as the political chieftain of the House, and later preside over the executive branch for eight years. In both positions, Madison wielded far more power than Wilson to adjust the complex constitutional engine that they had both helped design in 1787.

Madison also survived Wilson by nearly four decades. He spent his final years carefully curating the story of his own constitutional contributions. Adams and Jefferson likewise had many years to take care in crafting their own constitutional obituaries. Wilson, by contrast, died relatively young, in debt, disgrace, and disarray. Nor did Wilson have a close friend to tell his tale. Otis had Adams; Jefferson had Madison.

THE FATHER OF OUR COUNTRY has the strongest claim to be the father of its Constitution. Indeed, the two concepts—Constitution and country—form one system. The Constitution is the country's legal spine; without the former, the latter would have an entirely different shape.

Here is the case for Washington:

No one else came into the Convention with anything like Washington's stature. Common folk across the continent had never heard of James Madison or James Wilson, or any other delegate except Franklin. At best, a typical delegate was known to political elites and perhaps to ordinary voters in his home state. Every American knew of George Washington.

At the Convention itself, Washington presided by acclamation and signed the parchment before all others. Uniquely, he got everything he wanted—in part because he wanted fewer things than did some of his more theoretically minded fellow delegates.[29]

Unlike Madison, who came to the Convention with no clear vision of executive power, Washington cared deeply about creating a strong unitary president to lead the nation domestically and internationally. (He knew, as indeed all America knew, that if the Convention's reforms prevailed, he would likely be summoned as America's first leader under the new plan.) On key issues of executive structure and authority, he got what he wanted—a presidency far more muscular than any state counterpart, with an independent electoral base, a substantial (four-year) term of office, unlimited reeligibility, a powerful pair of veto and pardon pens, broad appointment and removal power, military and diplomatic heft, personal control over executive-department heads, and more.[30]

Indeed, the federal Constitution's single most distinctive feature—its biggest and most obvious break with all thirteen state regimes then in place—was its breathtakingly strong chief executive, by American Revolutionary standards. This distinctive feature owed more to Washington alone than to all the other delegates combined.

Washington also cared passionately about empowering the national government as a whole so it could win the next war (or at least not lose it), and also win the love and loyalty of ordinary Americans. Here, too, his wish came true.

Other than that, he did not sweat the details. The Senate could be directly or indirectly elected, proportionate to population or not. The president should be able to win and hold office independently of Congress, but both direct election and an Electoral College could work. (Crucially, both would tend to frustrate foreign intrigue in presidential selection. Both would involve decisions made by a large number of voters and/or electors scattered across a continent, who would be hard to find and bribe.) A president should have a hefty veto pen, but its precise shape did not obsess Washington at Philadelphia.

Put differently, Washington cared passionately about fixing the geostrategic problem with some blueprint closely approximating the Euclidian solution. Indeed, Washington epitomized the geostrategic problem to be solved: America would need a Constitution that would enable Washington personally, and all who would afterward stand in his shoes, to stymie the British again, if necessary, and to do so with or without the French. (Or, if necessary, to stymie the French, with or without the British.) The Constitution that emerged from Philadelphia gave him what he wanted and needed for himself and for his country.

The copious notes that James Madison and others took can easily mislead. Washington's voice almost never appears. He did not speak because he did not need to. On the biggest issues, the men in the room knew what Washington wanted, and they obliged him. Most of the delegates had borne arms in the war; a third were veterans of the Continental Army; and five of them, one from each of five distinct states, had personally served as aides-de-camp to Washington himself: New York's Alexander Hamilton, Pennsylvania's Thomas

Mifflin, Maryland's James McHenry, Virginia's Edmund Randolph, and South Carolina's Charles Cotesworth Pinckney. On smaller issues, Washington did not engage, because it made little sense to put his prestige on the line in this skirmish or that one. He reserved his power for the major battles. Unlike his experience in the Revolutionary War, he won all the big battles at Philadelphia.[31]

In the ratification process, his name alone counted for more than all the elegant arguments of Publius and Wilson put together times two. Indeed, his five-paragraph explanatory letter to Congress accompanying the proposed Constitution was reprinted alongside the text of the Constitution itself in tens of thousands of copies of the document that circulated among the citizenry in 1787–1788.[32] Washington was a succinct, charismatic, easy-to-grasp, and three-dimensional personification of the Join or Die meme—a meme that was the strongest argument for the new Constitution, a meme that had been born more than thirty years earlier in a newspaper woodcut appearing alongside an account of young George Washington's military and diplomatic service in America's backcountry. The fact that Washington put his name on the Constitution, and the hope that he would, when summoned, return to public service to launch the new system, sufficed to persuade many a fence-sitter and skeptic. His unanimous election and unanimous reelection in America's first two presidential contests attest to his unique stature in that era, and indeed, in all of American history.

As America's first president, he succeeded in making the Constitution succeed. Others succeeded because of him. Wilson sat on the Supreme Court because Washington put him there. Wilson's opening law lecture, a grand event in the development of a mature and independent American jurisprudence, was immeasurably ennobled by Washington's attendance. Madison succeeded early on in the House because he worked to shape and implement Washington's agenda. When he later turned against Washington, his political fortunes plummeted. (They would rebound after Washington's death.)

From his selection as commander in chief in 1775 to his final retirement from public service in 1797, Washington held the public stage as America's leading man, even during his first attempted retirement in the mid-1780s.[33] No other leading man in American history has held center stage so long.*

Here is the case against Washington:

Washington indeed personified the Philadelphia plan. Its virtues were his virtues, but so were its vices. The Constitution's Article IV Fugitive Slave Clause, for example, bolstered slavery; it went beyond the Articles of Confederation and the background rules of law as laid down by England's *Somerset* case. Far more importantly, the Constitution rewarded slavery in the Three-Fifths Clause that governed both House and Electoral College apportionment.

Some accommodation of slavery was necessary to get the Carolinians on board—and without the Carolinas, Virginia's southern flank would be dangerously exposed. But a more farsighted plan would have used time more cleverly.

The document gave Congress power to end the international slave trade, but not slavery itself, in 1808. South Carolina had insisted on

---

*Benjamin Franklin, another leading man of sorts, was also present at the Philadelphia Convention, but unlike Washington he did not get all that he wanted. His home state featured a unicameral Assembly and a weak plural executive. He would have preferred a similarly unicameral Congress and had deep doubts about the strong— Washingtonian!—unitary federal executive created at the Convention. He believed that slavery should be abolished in the long run. The Constitution fell far short of this ideal. Still, he got much of what he wanted: a continental union updating his Albany Plan, shielding against both European monarchs and western Indians, and (slavery aside) a union that was truly republican. Franklin's name ranked next to, but after, Washington's in the American pantheon of 1787. The Pennsylvanian was old and ailing; he could not lead the new nation forward as could the younger Virginian. Had Franklin opposed ratification, he would have dealt a serious blow to the document's prospects. Such opposition, however, was not in his nature; he respected the deliberations that led to the final plan and thus urged unanimity at the Convention's end. His endorsement of the plan was less indispensable than was Washington's. Had lightning struck Franklin before the conclave, a result similar to what actually happened would still have been possible. Without Washington, by contrast, there would have been no Constitution closely akin to what actually materialized.

a twenty-year window before any ban could operate. As Madison explained in the Virginia ratification debates, "the [Deep] Southern States would not have entered into the Union of America without the temporary permission of that trade; and if they were excluded from the Union, the consequences might be dreadful to them and to us. . . . Great as the evil [of the international slave trade] is, a dismemberment of the Union would be worse. If those states should disunite from the other states for not indulging them in the temporary continuance of this traffic, they might solicit and obtain aid from foreign powers." Connecticut's Oliver Ellsworth had expressed similar concerns at Philadelphia. Without this clause, "he was afraid we should lose two States, with such others as may be disposed to stand aloof," with the result that America might "fly into a variety of shapes & directions, and most probably into several confederations and not without bloodshed."[34]

A better document that nonetheless would have fit within the needed geostrategic solution would have used 1808 (or any other date—say, 1818 or 1828, or 1858 or 1876, for that matter) to phase out slavery more generally. The Constitution could have specified that after 1808 (or any other date), the international slave trade *must* (not merely *might*) end, and slavery in the West must end, and the Three-Fifths Clause must end in favor of zero fifths, and so on. Several states, including the Convention's host state of Pennsylvania, had already adopted various time-delayed laws to abolish slavery gradually. This was indeed the best state practice on this devilish topic.

The Philadelphia Constitution's failure to put slavery on a path of ultimate extinction would ultimately imperil the entire federal constitutional project and lead to the very sort of internecine warfare between Americans that the document was aimed to prevent. The Philadelphia Constitution's failures in this regard were Washington's failures, and vice versa. In 1787, Washington had not yet become the man he would be later in life, a man who in his last will and testament would provide for the freeing of his own slaves.

Had Washington in 1787 been that man, the Constitution might have been different, as might have all the rest of American history. More than anyone else at Philadelphia, Washington did have some power, personally, to bend history. But he bent it only so much.*

INSIDE THE ROOM

The process that would end with a Massachusetts-style ratification had begun with a Virginia invitation that in turn built on a Massachusetts precedent. In 1765, the Otis-led Massachusetts Assembly had issued a circular letter to sister colonies to meet in a room to coordinate against the Stamp Act. Virginia missed that Congress but later emulated Massachusetts by sending its own circular letters that helped trigger the First Continental Congress in 1774. In the mid-1780s, Virginia did it again; the Confederation system was dying, and Virginia took the lead in suggesting that the states meet once more in a grand conclave.

Of course, by the mid-1780s, a regular meeting arrangement already existed—the Confederation Congress. By calling for an extraordinary ad hoc Convention with a special reform mandate, Virginia was hoping, as in 1774, to bring together the continent's greatest men, men a cut above the less-than-dazzling figures in the Confederation Congress. Lest this invitation seem seditious or disrespectful to Congress itself, Virginia got the Congress to endorse the call for a grand Convention to consider how to fix the failing Confederation.[35]

For Virginia's plan to work, Virginia's greatest man—America's greatest man—would need to be coaxed out of retirement. This would not be easy. Washington had thrilled the world at war's end in 1783. Rather than making himself America's next King George,

---

*The careful reader will have noted that this is not so much a claim against Washington's paternity of the Constitution as it is a claim that both father and child shared the same congenital defect.

he had publicly promised to return forever to private life and had surrendered his military commission to the Confederation Congress.

The moment would later be memorialized by John Trumbull, yet another of Washington's aides-de-camp. Here, as elsewhere, Trumbull took artistic liberties. The chair behind the general, draped with a maroon cloak, symbolized the royal throne and robe Washington was spurning in this epic moment of republican humility and deference to civilian supremacy. The swooning audience behind the chair and in the gallery represented an awestruck and inspired world and various absent loved ones and acolytes beyond persons actually in the chamber. Trumbull placed Madison against the far wall, even though the short, balding Virginian had in fact left Congress the previous month. The artist also took care to highlight Jefferson, who was indeed in the room where it happened, by seating the young redhead precisely in the center of the Congressional semicircle facing the virtuous general.

Persuading the general in 1787 to risk his good name and all the accolades he had earned for his professedly permanent 1783 resignation was thus no simple task, but Madison, Hamilton, and others succeeded in their appeals to Washington's ultimate patriotism. It would be wrong, they argued, for Washington to put his own reputation above his country's urgent needs. When Washington agreed, once more, to leave his vine and fig tree to answer the call of duty, all America knew that the Philadelphia Convention was credible.

In the opening hours of the Convention, the delegates, in secret, voted (recapitulatingly) to stay secret—to keep the Convention's doors and curtains closed, and to ban any unauthorized disclosures of the Convention's deliberations while the body was still in session. According to the rules agreed upon on May 29, 1787, "nothing spoken in the [Convention] may be printed, or otherwise published, or communicated without leave" of the Convention itself.[36]

This decision aimed to be *conversation-promoting*. Delegates would be more candid with each other in the moment, and more free to revise their initial positions after hearing other viewpoints, if sheltered from the ongoing daily glare of a gallery.[37] The goal was to create the best plan possible. Once that plan was publicly released, a broader public conversation would ensue. *In that post-drafting phase, the code of silence would lapse. Any delegate could publicly endorse or oppose the plan and report what he had said or what others had said behind closed doors. Although no member openly breached secrecy during the Convention, delegates spoke and wrote with abandon immediately thereafter about what had happened in the closed room.* (These points are italicized because many eminent historians have misunderstood and misstated the basic rules of democratic and conversational engagement that operated in 1787–1788.)[38]

The delegates understood that in the short run this initial secrecy would prompt public speculation and anxiety, and no small amount of suspicion, about what was or was not quietly transpiring. Two midsummer disclosures, perhaps informally blessed by Washington or the publicity-savvy Franklin, appeared in the local press to buy the delegates time to do their work. On July 19, the *Pennsylvania Packet* shared a tiny (untrue) tidbit with its readers: "So great is the unanimity, we hear, that prevails in the Convention, upon all great federal subjects, that it has been proposed to call the room in which they assemble—Unanimity Hall." On August 22, the *Pennsylvania Journal* published a less fluffy and more truthful scrap of inside information: "We are informed, that many letters have been written to the members of the fœderal convention from different quarters, respecting the reports idly circulating, that it is intended to establish a monarchical government. . . . [T]o which it has been uniformly answered, tho' we cannot, affirmatively, tell you what we are doing, we can, negatively, tell you what we are not doing—we never once thought of a king."

BETWEEN LATE MAY AND MID-SEPTEMBER, ordinary Americans may have been shut out of the closed room, but the spirit of America as a whole loomed over the entire conclave and drove the key decisions. Delegates brought into the room ideas drawn from the actual constitutional practices of their respective home states. When these ideas predictably conflicted in granular ways on issue after issue, the specific idea that prevailed was often the idea that, among the set of plausible good-government alternatives, would be more likely to be approved by the populace during the ratification process. The delegates were not trying to fashion the best imaginable Constitution in principle for some Utopia. They did not see themselves as so many Platos or Thomas Mores. *They were trying to fashion the best Constitution that America would approve in the wide-open popular ratification process to come, a process that the delegates knew would teem with continental conversation at every level.*[39]

This point, along with merely temporary secrecy and equal voting within the Convention itself, was clear from the Convention's opening moments. On May 29, the delegation of the Old Dominion—the state that had spearheaded the call for the Convention (and, of course, the home state of the Convention's presiding officer, George Washington)—dramatically unveiled its package of proposed reforms. This Virginia plan ended with an extraordinary Massachusetts-style proposal: "The amendments which shall be offered to the Confederation by the Convention ought at a proper time, or times, after the approbation of Congress, to be submitted to an assembly or assemblies of

Representatives, recommended by the several Legislatures *to be expressly chosen by the people, to consider & decide thereon.*"[40]

Here, too, Madison's notes can easily mislead, if not read with great care. Madison wrote down (some of) what (he said) delegates actually said (as he paraphrased them) in the room.[41] Of course, Madison did not record some booming heavenly voice from above—*America!*—literally proclaiming, "This is my idea, in which I am well pleased." Subjectively and psychologically, it probably felt to Madison as if the delegates were speaking for America, rather than America speaking through the delegates, himself included. But if we read Madison's and other delegates' notes with care, we can indeed see and hear America in the room.

On August 7, when some elitist delegates, including Madison and Pennsylvania's urbane lawyer Gouverneur Morris, had kind words to say about property qualifications for federal elections, other more egalitarian delegates, led by Wilson and Franklin, opposed these restrictions on principle. Had the delegates seen themselves as Platos, perhaps the elitists might have prevailed. But Madison's notes record his fellow Princetonian Oliver Ellsworth (who would later become America's third chief justice) offering a decisive rebuttal: "The right of suffrage was a tender point, and strongly guarded by most of the State Constitutions. The people will not readily subscribe to the Natl. Constitution, if it should subject them to be disfranchised."[42]

In the end, the Philadelphia Constitution eschewed property qualifications for those seeking federal election, and declined to add any property qualifications for federal voters beyond what state constitutional law required for state assembly elections. Only one state had a package that was comparably democratic—Wilson and Franklin's home state of Pennsylvania.

Pennsylvania's constitution, uniquely among states, also promised to pay lawmakers for their services, a democratic reform enabling middling men lacking great estates to serve in government. Once again, the Philadelphia Convention ended up endorsing the Pennsylvania model—on this issue, the best and most egalitarian state practice. Here, no specific smoking-gun quotation à la Ellsworth appears in Madison's notes. But on this question, and every other question that came before the Convention, every delegate in the room surely understood the most basic fact of all: the Constitution would need to be ratified by the people, Massachusetts-style, and democratic sweeteners would likely help.

Beyond ratification of the document itself, many delegates hoped to be summoned by their fellow citizens to serve in the effective new government they aimed to create. Their desires to be honored by their countrymen with additional public service, or, at a minimum, to continue to enjoy widespread public respect—repute, fame, glory—gave the Philadelphia delegates additional reasons to constantly consider, even though they did not invariably bow to, likely popular opinion.[43]

Only once during the Convention did Washington himself speak substantively, and what he said confirms that he in particular had his eyes on the popular ratification process that loomed on the horizon; the acclaimed general was already aiming for high ground in the big battles to come. Over the course of its three and a half months of deliberation, the Convention had agreed that the House should be quite small, by American standards—sixty-five members at first, and then a maximum of one member for every forty thousand constituents after the first census. These numbers threatened to make the House seem too elitist—not only vulnerable to bribery, but also far removed from the concerns of ordinary voters and beyond the realistic reach of most local politicians dreaming of moving up within the political system. Having maintained an official silence on every issue that had arisen in the conclave, Washington dramatically chose the Convention's final minutes—on Monday, September 17, just as the delegates were set to add their names to the engrossed parchment now ready for their signatures—to voice his views. He urged his colleagues to reconsider the issue of House size. "It was," he said, "much to be desired that the objections to the plan recommended might be made as few as possible—The smallness of the proportion of Representatives had been considered by many members of the Convention, an insufficient security for the rights & interests of the people."[44]

Despite the obvious irregularity and untimeliness of Washington's intervention, the delegates obliged their august presider by immediately and unanimously voting to rewrite the troublesome clause. The smudge is still visible on the ceremonial parchment on display at the National Archives. As modified in this final Philadelphia moment of high drama, Article I's public and published text provided for a maximum of one representative for every thirty thousand constituents instead of every forty thousand, as had initially been decided and inked. This modification would enable Congress to grow more quickly after the first census.

Washington's political ear was nearly pitch-perfect. Even after his extraordinary intercession, the issue of Congressional size would indeed become one of the two biggest popular objections to the Philadelphia plan in the contentious ratification process that lay ahead.

six

PEOPLE

T HE YEARLONG DEBATE OVER THE Philadelphia Convention's proposal took the rising system of America's constitutional conversation to its highest level yet. More participants than
ever before in world history tightly focused on a clearly defined constitutional question (Do We ordain and establish or don't We?) and
directly engaged each other in multiple and intersecting ways—in
newspapers, in coffeehouses and taverns, in face-to-face public ratification debates, in correspondence, and elsewhere, with words and
pictures both simple and complex.

The composite facts and figures are astonishing, and they are worth
summarizing and savoring before we examine the process close up.

First, on the number of elections: The Philadelphia proposal aimed
to come before an entire continent for a two-step vote in each of thirteen states—twenty-six proposed contests in all. In the initial step,
voters in each state would select delegates to a special single-purpose
ratifying convention, with full foreknowledge of the specific plan on
the continental agenda. In the next step, delegates in each convention
would discuss the plan in detail—face to face, issue by issue, in full

public view, with newspapermen in attendance—before saying yea or nay.

Second, on the breadth of voter and delegate eligibility: In eight of the thirteen states, ordinary property qualifications were lowered or eliminated for this special Massachusetts-style ratification process—allowing more persons than usual to vote, or more persons than usual to seek election, or both. For example, New York waived its standard voting rules and for the first time in history allowed all adult free male citizens to vote—no race tests, no property tests, no religious tests, and no literacy tests. Two other states followed standing voting rules that routinely allowed virtually all taxpaying adult male citizens to vote. No state followed stricter suffrage rules than usual—rules that allowed free Blacks to vote in most states, even most slave states. Never in American history—never in world history—had so many persons enjoyed the right to vote on any single question, much less the question of how they and their posterity would be governed.[1]

Third, on the breadth and depth of conversation: When the Philadelphia Convention released the document on September 17, 1787, nearly every newspaper in America rushed to print in full the proposal's 4,500 words. At least six print shops in Philadelphia alone published the complete text within the first few days. Over the next several weeks, republication in full occurred in dozens of other cities and towns, including (in chronological order of initial publication) New York, Baltimore, Boston, New Haven, Elizabeth, Carlisle, Frederick, Providence, Richmond, Alexandria, Annapolis, Worcester, Norwich, New London, Norfolk, Portsmouth, Hartford, Middletown, Litchfield, Bennington, Charleston, Salem, Poughkeepsie, Northampton, Newburyport, New Bern, Portland, Pittsburgh, Newport, Fredericksburg, and Windsor.[2]

Over the ensuing year, Americans along a one-thousand-mile stretch directly conversed with each other as never before, and did so because it mattered. Newspaper essayists jousted with each other conversationally, with repeated rounds back and forth in tight temporal sequence. Delegates in ratifying conventions likewise conversed on countless points large and small, and did so in public. Many actually listened as well as spoke. Some openly changed their minds and their votes during these conversations.

In astonishing contrast to prior violent episodes—the Hutchinson riot, the Boston Massacre, the multiple instances of colonial-era tarring and feathering, the general intimidation of loyalists (many of whom ultimately fled America), and of course the unspeakable carnage of the Revolutionary War itself—almost no one was killed or maimed in political struggle during the fateful year of constitutional ratification. Even as tempers flared and passions raged—because the stakes were enormous—Americans *conversed* but did not *combat*. The losers in this conversation were not bullied into submission or forced into exile. Rather, Anti-Federalists (the name given the naysayers) were listened to. Some of their smartest concerns found their way into the Constitution's first round of amendments; and some of their smartest leaders eventually found their way into the Constitution's highest posts, from the presidency on down.[3]

Appeals ranged from the extremely erudite to the stunningly simple. Two sites of conversation, newspapers and conventions, framed the debate, and the dynamic interaction between these sites defined a truly New World model of American-style constitutionalism.

PUBLIUS

More than two centuries after its composition, *The Federalist* continues to stand as the single greatest commentary on the United States Constitution.

Modern Americans experience *The Federalist* as a book, rather like Thomas Hobbes's *Leviathan* or John Locke's *Two Treatises of Government*. *The Federalist* was indeed published in two bound volumes in mid-1788, but it did not begin its career as a book. Unlike *Leviathan*, *Two Treatises*, and all previous great works of political philosophy, *The Federalist* originated as a series of newspaper essays. Although it speaks to the ages, it was written for the moment, written by a trio of authors sharing a pen name (because the clock was ticking fast, and one man could do only so much on deadline), and written in brisk and pointed response and rejoinder, back and forth, to other newspaper essays of the moment.

The first essay, by Hamilton/Publius (though his early readers did not know the Hamilton part, only the Publius part), begins in extraordinary *conversational* fashion. It is in express dialogue with the reader: "you." But that reader, that "you," was not a college student in a Political Science 101 class in the twenty-first century. The reader was a New York newspaper reader in late October 1787 who would soon decide how to vote in the upcoming election for state convention delegates. (When the essay was reprinted as part of the book in March 1788, "you" might also have been a prospective convention delegate with a still-open mind.)

Recalling the opening three words of the Constitution's Preamble ("We the People"), Publius starts with a properly populist but nononsense salutation "To the People of the State of New-York." Then comes a subordinate clause reminding the reader that the Confederation is a mess—"After an unequivocal experience of the inefficiency of the subsisting Federal Government . . ."—followed by a direct and republican conversational appeal: ". . . you are called upon to deliberate on a new Constitution for the United States of America."

What was at stake, Publius explains in the next three remarkable sentences, was nothing less than the fate of the earth, perhaps forever, or at least for an epoch (*Not to put any pressure on "you," but . . .*):

The subject speaks its own importance; comprehending in its consequences nothing less than the existence of the UNION, the safety and welfare of the parts of which it is composed, the fate of an empire in many respects the most interesting in the world. It has been frequently remarked that it seems to have been reserved to the people of this country, by their conduct and example, to decide the important question, whether societies of men are really capable or not of establishing good government from reflection and choice, or whether they are forever destined to depend for their political constitutions on accident and force. If there be any truth in the remark, the crisis at which we are arrived may with propriety be regarded as the era in which that decision is to be made; and a wrong election of the part we shall act may, in this view, deserve to be considered as the general misfortune of mankind.

IN THIS ESSAY AND THE seven that followed, Hamilton and Publian collaborator John Jay (author of *The Federalist* Nos. 2–5) powerfully presented the geostrategic argument for the Constitution's more perfect and indissoluble union. As Jay/Publius explained in *The Federalist* No. 5, this union was expressly modeled on the indissoluble geostrategic "entire and perfect union" of Scotland and England fourscore years earlier. Britain was free and strong, Hamilton/Publius explained in the climactic *Federalist* No. 8, because it was a defensible island protected by the English Channel. By uniting indissolubly, America could likewise be free and strong, protected by the Atlantic Ocean. Land borders between continental European nation-states had led to standing armies, military dictators, and horrific bloodshed on the continent itself. International land borders between thirteen sovereign American states would ultimately lead to the same fate in the New World. The states thus needed to merge into one continental nation-state, as Scotland and England in 1707 had merged to form the mighty British nation.

Building on ideas that Hamilton had first published in a prescient set of "Continentalist" essays in the early 1780s, this was the main argument that persuaded open-minded fence-sitting readers—"you"—in 1787–1788. It was an argument that a farmer or tradesman could understand in response to his obvious questions: *Why do we need to go beyond sovereign states and try to create a continental republic the likes of which have never been seen in human history? Given that most of history's successful republics have been small—given that, until now, our sovereign state has never been indissolubly linked to any other sovereign state—why must we become continental?*[4]

Madison/Publius had his own answer to these questions in *The Federalist* No. 10—the masked Virginian's first contribution to the collaborative project. This answer was not geostrategic. It did not fit within the main outlines of the Hamilton-Jay solution to the Confederation crisis, but rather aimed to offer a different reason to vote yes on the proposed Constitution. Madison's essay built on the most original ideas that he had pitched at Philadelphia, and in college courses today this essay is widely taught for its intriguing claims about democracy, demography, representation, majority rule, minority rights, and governmental economies of scale. Arguing that the new federal government would likely protect minority rights better than would individual states—because majority tyranny would be harder to pull off in a large democracy, and because continental lawmakers would likely be men of greater wisdom than would state legislators—the essay foreshadowed much of post–Civil War American history.

In 1787–1788, almost no one paid any attention to Madison's masterpiece, except perhaps to notice that Publius here referred to friends of the Constitution as proud and self-described "Federalists" as distinct from "Nationalists"—a less attractive banner at that moment. The early geostrategic *Federalist* essays were widely reprinted; *The Federalist* No. 10 was not. Unlike the main ideas of *The Federalist* Nos. 1–8, Madison's concepts in *The Federalist* No. 10 were not echoed in other newspaper pieces by other authors or by speakers in ratifying conventions. The essay failed to make a deep impression in American coffeehouses and taverns where patrons read both local and out-of-town newspapers aloud and discussed them.[5] (If Publius had a great answer to the farmer-tradesman's basic question—*Why a truly continental nation-state?*—the best place to give that answer in a newspaper would be in the first few essays, not the tenth.) The only Madison essay that was widely reprinted in 1787–1788, *The Federalist* No. 14, opened with a nice recapitulation of the geostrategic argument, an argument that Madison plainly endorsed even though he had some other, more original ideas that he had to get off his chest.

The Federalist No. 14 closed out the opening series of essays. (Its last words signaled rhetorical closure by echoing the opening sentence of No. 1: The Confederation "is the work which has been new modelled by the act of your convention, and it is that act on which you are now to deliberate and to decide.") Some seventy more essays followed, elaborating virtually every article of the proposed Constitution in impressive detail, often comparing and contrasting the Philadelphia plan to the best and worst aspects of America's state constitutions.

These essays worked brilliantly on two levels. First, essay by essay, argumentative brick by brick, Publius responded directly, quickly, and powerfully to competing newspaper essays by the critics of the Constitution. Then, when Publius mortared all the bricks together, these once separate essays fit tightly to constitute an extraordinary expositional edifice, a grand intellectual structure offering the most comprehensive analysis of the Constitution that emerged in the extraordinary year when Americans, according to Publius, decided the fate of the earth.[6]

THE FEDERAL EDIFICE

Speaking of edifices, that fateful year witnessed a powerful set of simple cartoons using the metaphor of a "federal edifice" abuilding. These modest newspaper woodcuts, which appeared over several months in the *Massachusetts Centinel*, a Boston-based and fiercely Federalist newspaper, illustrated a different style of conversation on display in 1788. The cartoons in this enchanting series were deceptively simple, charting the state-by-state ratifications of the Philadelphia plan as the erection of so many pillars combining to form a hoped-for "GRAND FEDERAL EDIFICE." The cartoons were the brainchild of publisher Benjamin Russell, a self-made artisan with strong ties to Boston's mechanics (that is, tradesmen of various sorts: blacksmiths, coopers, printers, shipwrights, masons, and so on).

First came a trio of cartoons focusing on ratification by the home-state Massachusetts Convention—a ratification hoped for on January 16 and again on January 30 (not pictured) and accomplished, with help from the cloud-shrouded hand of Providence, on February 7, as

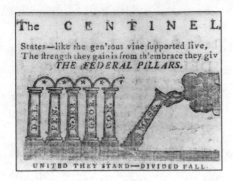

depicted two days later in print. A catchy caption summarized Russell's views: "UNITED THEY STAND—DIVIDED FALL."

Later in February, the *Centinel* optimistically but erroneously predicted, in a pair of cartoons on February 13 (not pictured) and February 27, that neighboring New Hampshire would be the next (seventh) pillar of the "The GLORIOUS FABRICK": "It WILL yet rise."

On April 12, Russell published a poem from "A FEDERALIST" who added his own touch of whimsy to the conversation. In one stanza, the pseudonymous New Hampshire author paid homage to the cartoons:

> *When the* PILLAR *we raise, the New-Hampshire huzzas*
> *Will be heard in each part of the State,*
> *Though the* Shaysites *and* Tories, *with terrible stories,*
> *Some weak minds may intimidate*

The word "huzzas" here should be pronounced *huzzās* (long A) to best complete this rhyme scheme (raise/huzzas—the New Hampshire accent has always been distinctive). The reference to "*Shaysites*" also merits mention. Most modern scholars have focused on the class issues raised by Shays' Rebellion, a 1786 uprising in western Massachusetts. On this view, Federalists favored wealthy eastern creditors at the expense of desperate western debtors sympathetic to agitator Daniel Shays. Many Federalists instead saw Shays' Rebellion through a national-security lens, believing that Canadian-British forces were secretly supporting this backcountry revolt to weaken America. In keeping with this perspective, the New Hampshire Federalist poet explicitly linked "*Shaysites* and *Tories.*"

On April 23, Russell reported (with his trademark capital letters) that accounts from "a gentleman" from Annapolis "give us lively hopes, that within the course of a few weeks we shall have the pleasure of announcing the erection of a SEVENTH PILLAR of the great FEDERAL SUPERSTRUCTURE." The ensuing weeks did indeed bring the expected news of Maryland's ratification (at the Annapolis Convention on April 28), leading to a May 7 cartoon ("SEVENTH PILLAR UP," not pictured) in which Russell yet again predicted that

"It [the not-yet-erect New Hampshire pillar] will yet rise." On June 11, the *Centinel* celebrated a yes vote in South Carolina (at the Charleston Convention on May 23) with a bit of Latin, "*REDEUNT SATURNIA REGNA*" (The Kingdom of Saturn Returns). Virginia was now depicted as the next state most likely to join the colonnade, but New Hampshire remained promising: "It will rise."

And then, at last, on June 25, Russell showed his readers that he had been right all along to focus on New Hampshire, which on June 21 had become the "NINTH and the SUFFICIENT

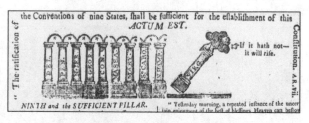

PILLAR" to be erected, thus ensuring that the Constitution would go into effect.

To remind his readers of the epic significance of this event, he added another touch of Latin, "ACTUM EST" (It is done) and wrapped the cartoon with the key words from the Constitution's closing sentence: "The ratification of the Conventions of nine States, shall be sufficient for the establishment of this Constitution."

Actually, he also hedged his bets: it was possible that Virginia had ratified even earlier, but that word had not yet reached Boston. The Old Dominion pillar was thus depicted as rising, with the explanation that "If it hath not—it will rise." In fact, New Hampshire had truly erected the ninth and sufficient pillar; Virginia ratified as the tenth state (before news from New Hampshire reached Richmond) on June 25. When word of Virginia got back to Russell, he of course ran a cartoon (on July 5), which he entitled "The Tenth PILLAR erected," with Virginia placed after (to the right of) New Hampshire.

On August 2, Russell ran yet another cartoon in his series to celebrate New York's ratification, which, he reminded readers, added an "Eleventh PILLAR of the great National DOME" that would soon sit atop the colonnade. North Carolina and Rhode Island had not yet joined the edifice, but Russell thought there was still hope for them.

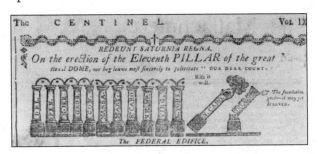

Print shops near and far copied Russell's motifs in both pictures and prose. Boston's *Independent Chronicle* actually beat Russell to the punch in celebrating Massachusetts's ratification in its February 7 edition (left) and echoed Russell (right) when word arrived in late June that New Hampshire had erected its decisive pillar. Not to be outdone by Russell's classical grace notes, *The Chronicle* added its own allusions to the glory of ancient Rome, quoting Virgil's announcement of a golden age to come: "INCIPIENT MAGNI PROCEDERE MENSES" (The great months begin).

In New Hampshire itself, the local *Spy* (left) and *Gazette* (right) likewise echoed Russell's words and themes—not just his pillars and his early motto ("United We Stand—Divided We Fall"), but also, in the *Spy*'s case, his exuberant Latin, "SOLI DEO GLORIA" (Glory to God alone), and in the *Gazette*'s case, his pointed quotation of Article VII.

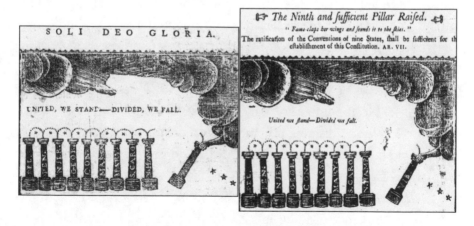

All told, the *Centinel*'s motifs appeared in dozens of editions of other newspapers spanning at least eight states, from New Hampshire up north to both Carolinas down south.[7]

WE MUST NOT UNDERESTIMATE BENJAMIN Russell's democratic genius in these simple cartoons, which in their own way made a powerful constitutional argument not so different from Publius's ultra-sophisticated analysis as modern readers might at first think.

Several visual and verbal metaphors interlocked in Russell's series. One involved language and imagery of *founding* and *foundations*. Let's recall in particular Russell's observation in his August 2 cartoon that even for Rhode Island, "the foundation is good—it may yet be SAVED."

We call those who crafted and launched the Constitution "founders" and they called themselves that. They sought to found a new continental republic, and they obsessed about laying the proper *foundations*—foundations that needed to be deep and wide and strong, because these founders were seeking to build something big. These men had a grand vision of national greatness.

Russell obviously had no access to Madison's notes from Philadelphia, which would not be published until 1840, but the printer's cartoons harmonized remarkably well with what both Wilson and Madison said at the outset of the secret drafting Convention. Alluding more directly to ancient Egyptian pyramids than to the Greco-Roman columns and domes that Russell would deploy, Wilson "contended strenuously for drawing the most numerous branch of the Legislature immediately from the people. He was for raising the federal pyramid to a considerable altitude, and for that reason wished to give it as broad a bas[e] as possible." Madison here echoed Wilson, as he often did at Philadelphia (just as Wilson often echoed Madison): "He thought too that the great fabric to be raised would be more stable and durable if it should rest on the solid foundation of the people themselves, than if it should stand merely on the pillars of the [state] Legislatures."[8]

In *The Federalist* No. 22, first published in New York on December 14, 1787—in time to make its way to Boston before Russell's cartoons began—Hamilton/Publius used similar imagery: "The foundations of our national government [must lie] deeper than in the mere sanction of delegated authority. The fabric of American empire ought to rest on the solid bas[e] of the consent of the people." Madison/ Publius, at the end of the earlier *Federalist* No. 14, had likewise used imagery—especially the imagery of a "fabric," meaning a building— that would recur in Russell. (Russell, however, spelled it "fabrick.") American Revolutionaries "reared the fabrics of governments which have no model on the face of the globe. They formed the design of a great Confederacy, which it is incumbent on their successors to improve and perpetuate [and] new model[]."[9]

In Russell's series, as for Wilson, Madison, and Hamilton, the broad base beneath the pillars, their deep and wide and strong foundation, is the American people themselves. This foundational imagery came naturally to Russell. His father had been a stonemason. But Russell had also been reminded of this imagery by reading Federalists (including, of course, *The Federalist*) and by hearing Federalists daily at the Massachusetts Ratifying Convention, which met in public from January 9 to February 7, 1788. Russell regularly attended these deliberations and published detailed accounts of the delegates' speeches and votes so that his readers could experience in print what he was seeing and hearing in person. Here we see one of the many powerful kinetic interactions between the two New World insitutions of rising significance, conventions and newspapers.

Beyond foundations, the image of distinct and formally equal state pillars also featured prominently in Russell's artwork. Behind closed doors, Madison, Wilson, and many of their big-state allies had hated the idea of state equality in certain contexts, such as Senate apportionment; but in the ratification process friends of the Constitution tried to present the continued existence of states and the Constitution's various recognitions of state equality as selling points, in order to assuage those who were worried that states would disappear in the new federal edifice. Hamilton/Publius, in *The Federalist* No. 9 (first published in New York on November 21, 1787), had taken the lead in emphasizing that any system that preserved states as such was, strictly speaking, a *federal* system. Madison/Publius in No. 10 had likewise insisted that friends of the Constitution were "Federalists," not "Nationalists." Madison/Publius also played up the significance of states in *The Federalist* No. 39 and even managed, through gritted teeth, to say some nice things about Senate equality in No. 62. Here, too, Russell was on message.

Russell stressed that state convention ratifications would support a great national dome. The tops of the pillars were connected in his image—that is in part what "united" them, so that they would not "fall." At a minimum, this imagery reinforced Federalist insistence that states, once in the new system, would be fixed in place. A dome does not work if pillars are removed haphazardly. More expansively, the dome imagery harmonized with Madison's idea that the federal government could help stabilize each state pillar from above. Beneath his triumphalist eleventh-pillar cartoon, Russell composed a verse for the dome to come: "Soon o'er the whole, shall swell the beauteous DOME, / COLUMBIA's boast—and FREEDOM's hallow'd home."

Finally, and most simply of all, Russell's themes were progress, momentum, erection, and building. *We Federalists*, he pictorially said, in effect, week after week, month after month, *are doing something. We are moving forward and making progress, adding new pillars. We have a plan, a blueprint, and it is materializing. What is the plan of our critics?* On this big but laughably simple point, Russell was right, as was Madison/Publius when he made a similar point in *The Federalist* No. 38, and as was Hamilton/Publius when he closed on this note in the final essay, *The Federalist* No. 85. In the end, the Anti-Federalists deserved to lose, because they were Anti. They had gripes but no plan. They were not erecting anything useful as a credible alternative to the glorious federal edifice abuilding.

THE HIBERNATING SNAKE

Even as they illuminate, good metaphors, analogies, and motifs can also mislead.

For example, was it really true that Delaware and Pennsylvania were equal constitutional pillars in all respects? Surely not in the

House or the Electoral College. But in the ratification process itself—the main subject of Russell's series—each state did count for one and only one, Pennsylania no more than Delaware. Also, no pillar would join the expanding colonnade unless it erected itself. These basic aspects of Article VII, quoted in part in Russell's "NINTH and the SUFFICIENT PILLAR" cartoon, were captured every bit as powerfully, and more charmingly, by Russell than by Madison/Publius. (*The Federalist* Nos. 39 and 62 patiently but at times tediously elaborated how states under the Constitution would be equal in some ways, including Article VII, and unequal in others.) Despite his brevity, Russell actually captured a key feature of Article VII that Publius did not, anywhere. The states could ratify in any order—perhaps New Hampshire before Virginia or perhaps the reverse.[10]

For all the imperfections of the edifice/foundation/pillar/dome motif, Russell chose images and words that were analytically and politically stronger than the obvious imaginable alternative—a widespread revival of Franklin's snake. Recall that this serpentine creature, born in 1754, had reawakened in 1765 and again in 1774. All three times it had slithered its way up to Boston, with various inky appearances in the *Boston Gazette*, the *Boston News-Letter*, the *Boston Evening-Post*, the *Boston Post-Boy*, and the *Massachusetts Spy*. But in the epochal year that, according to Publius, might decide the fate of the world, the snake slept. Almost no one revived it.[11]

Why didn't Russell reawaken it? Perhaps because the snake was the wrong metaphor for the moment, at least compared to the edifice. The snake projected the strong theme of geostrategic union—"Join or Die" grabs the viewer by the throat—but reptilian revival would have played into Anti-Federalist fears. Franklin's snake did not take states seriously. It did not treat them as the separate and equal— sovereign!—structures/pillars that they were in early 1787 and would continue to be unless they chose to join. In Franklin's snake, no section is truly more than a part of a larger organic whole. Even as pillars form an ensemble, each pillar quite literally also stands alone.

Franklin's meme, unlike Russell's, also seemed to require complete unanimity, immediately. How could South Carolina and Georgia at the tail end join the same snake as Virginia, and states farther north, if North Carolina was not part of the lower midsection? A colonnade of pillars, by contrast, could work. Any nine pillars would do. Russell's edifice ignored size and geography, as did Article VII itself, formally. Russell thus ended his 1788 series with two pillars—including North Carolina—not yet erect even though Russell obviously hoped that these two would soon be raised to join the others.[12]

Each meme/cartoon had the virtues of its vices. Franklin's snake called attention to geography, and the fundamental argument for union was indeed geographic and geostrategic. Russell's decision to ignore geography altogether was faithful to the part of the Constitution that he was highlighting: the text of Article VII paid no heed to geography. In theory, the smallest nine states could have ratified and left behind Massachusetts, New York, Pennsylvania, and Virginia. The ratifying nine would have been sufficient formal pillars under Article VII and in Russell's cartoons. But absent the four most vital states, the system would likely have been wholly unworkable. The snake would have had too many holes in it, and large ones at that. Each metaphor, snake and stone, thus captured aspects of the Constitution blurred by the competing metaphor.

Russell did not begin his cartoons until after Pennsylvania had said yes, and when the situation in Massachusetts looked hopeful. Once Massachusetts erected its pillar, that erection would build momentum in other states, which would then make ratification in Virginia and New York more likely. That was part of Russell's political genius, to craft a series of illustrations highlighting—and by highlighting, reinforcing—the exhilarating momentum of the moment.

Franklin had crafted his cartoon at a very different moment and for very different purposes. A second look at his meme, as it had first appeared in Philadelphia and Boston, should remind us of how much things had changed, and how much they had not, between 1754 and 1787.

Franklin did not take sovereign states seriously because sovereign states did not exist in 1754. Colonies existed as contiguous parts of the British Empire, an empire to which Franklin was thoroughly loyal in 1754. Boundaries between colonies were not carved in stone. Indeed, Britain had changed colonial boundaries within living memory.

Franklin likely chose to depict New England ("N.E.") as a unit because that was artistically easier. But as a native Bostonian, he surely knew that for one brief moment in the 1680s, the Crown had merged all the New England colonies into a single administrative unit. Indeed, Franklin's own parents had married just as this short-lived Dominion of New England was lapsing. Franklin's snake did not treat Delaware with extreme tenderness; the tiny colony was depicted merely as part of Pennsylvania ("P." between "N.J." and "M."—New Jersey and Maryland). For Franklin's purposes, geography mattered but sovereignty did not.

The basic geography, of course, remained the same in 1787—Delaware did not move and neither did Pennsylvania. But in 1787, Delaware was emphatically distinct from Pennsylvania, and was its own sovereign state. That sovereignty, strictly speaking, would end if Delaware and at least eight other states ratified; but the ongoing integrity of Delaware's territorial borders, and of every other state's territorial borders, was emphatically guaranteed by the new Constitution's Article IV. Unlike the British Empire in 1754, the new Congress under the new Constitution would have no power to redraw the lines of its constituent parts at random. Madison/Publius highlighted this point in *The Federalist* No. 43, as did Russell, more subtly, via his motif of separate and distinct pillars. In Russell's series, the boundaries between states were literally carved in stone.

Franklin's snake would have been a much scarier image for any moderate Anti-Federalist worried that the Philadelphia Convention's plan would swallow up the states entirely. There were good reasons for Russell and other Federalists to let sleeping snakes lie.

CONVENTIONS

Modern critics of the Constitution's evident democratic pretensions ("We, the People . . .") never tire of reminding us that the Constitution did not emerge from a direct popular vote in the fashion of a modern California or Swiss referendum. These critics sometimes forget that in 1787 modern California did not yet exist, and the Swiss had yet to stage any direct referendum. But Massachusetts and New Hampshire did exist in 1787, and only a few years earlier they had put their state constitutions to more direct votes than the protocol provided for by the Philadelphia plan's Article VII. The reason for this difference can be captured by one word: *conversation.*

Although the proposed Constitution was, by world historical standards, remarkably short, it nonetheless had many intricate parts, which meshed in subtle and complex ways to create larger systems of power, purpose, and meaning. The text needed to be publicly discussed, at length, before it could properly earn the right to displace all other law in America—to become the law of law and the king of kings, as Paine would say. In short, the proposed Constitution required collective deliberation—conversation among persons scattered across a vast territory.

Ordinary eighteenth-century elections did not elect laws, much less basic laws designed to endure for the ages. Ordinary elections elected persons, who in turn passed laws in bodies—legislatures—that conversed about proposed laws before enacting them. Not for nothing was Britain's legislature known as *Parliament*—a place for speech of a certain sort, a parley place, derived from the French verb for speech, *parler.*

The Massachusetts Constitution of 1780 had not broken with this central idea of speaking and listening before enacting. Going back to colonial days, Massachusetts had a system of town meetings. Every person was assigned to a town, and elections at town meetings did indeed involve quite a lot of talking and listening—collective deliberation, conversation—before voting. Other New England states, including New Hampshire, had town-meeting structures as well, but states outside New England did not.

Thus, the Philadelphia Convention proposed a sensible way of blending the desire for democracy with the need for serious and extended conversation. Initially, ordinary voters everywhere could read the would-be Constitution in newspapers at their leisure; talk about it at length in their homes, neighborhoods, churches, local taverns, nearby coffeehouses, and elsewhere; and then vote. In this vote, they would not vote directly on the document. Rather, they would vote for men whom they knew to be honest and intelligent and whom they trusted to think generally like themselves on the single issue at hand—the proposed Constitution. These specially chosen delegates would then attend a statewide convention that would discuss that proposed Constitution, and nothing else, in vastly greater detail—listening to other men from other neighborhoods, who might have something useful to contribute to the collective conversation. In any state with a large slice of skeptics, these conversations would not likely conclude in an hour, a day, or even a week. That indeed was why a convention was needed; it would take time to converse constitutionally, and it would not be realistic to demand that all voters abandon their livelihoods for weeks on end. Rather, extended constitutional conversation would occur among a special ad hoc group with a unique mandate and a single charge, a group of men who would of course deliberate and vote publicly, with newspapers and other members of the broader electorate watching—intently—to keep everyone honest. (Here we see another aspect of the newspaper-convention interplay: while Russell and his readers would learn from the delegates, the presence of newspapers would incentivize delegates to act properly.)

As Americans were meeting and conversing in ways that no one on earth had yet done—as part of a truly continental conversation that could culminate in enacting a written continental Constitution—they sometimes paused to reflect, self-consciously, about what they were doing. At times they thus talked about the fact that they were talking. They constitutionally conversed about constitutional conversation itself.

America's leading scholar-lawyer put it best and connected this theme to larger ideas about popular sovereignty, American-style. "In our governments," James Wilson told his fellow delegates at the Pennsylvania Ratifying Convention, meeting in late November and early December 1787, "supreme, absolute, and uncontrollable power remains in the people, [who] possess over our constitutions control in act as well as right. . . . These important truths, sir, are far from being merely speculative. *We, at this moment, speak and deliberate under their immediate and benign influence.*" In America, he explained a few days later, sovereignty "continues, resides, and remains, with the body of the people. *Under the practical influence of this great truth, we are now sitting and deliberating*, and under its operation, we can sit as calmly and deliberate as coolly, in order to change a constitution, as a legislature can sit and deliberate under the power of a constitution, in order to alter or amend a law."[13]

Alas, Wilson and his Keystone State allies talked a better game than they played. In late September 1787 they had used aggressive, albeit legal, parliamentary tactics in the Pennsylvania Assembly to trigger a quick convening of the ratifying conclave. These tactics left Anti-Federalists feeling bruised. The state's Federalists won the ratification convention vote (on December 12, by a final tally of 46 to 23), but in the process they lost winnable hearts and minds.[14]

Pennsylvania was the only early state where the Federalists faced serious convention opposition. The document sailed through ratifying conventions in various small states and slave states that knew a good deal when they saw one; Senate equality and the Three-Fifths Clause were, for these states, good deals. In addition to Pennsylvania, pre-Russell pillars went up in Delaware on December 7 by a vote of 30 to 0, in New Jersey on December 18 (39–0), in Georgia on January 2 (26–0), and in Connecticut on January 9 (128–40).

THE MASSACHUSETTS RATIFYING CONVENTION VOTE promised to be much closer. Indeed, at the outset, most delegates inclined against the plan, largely because Massachusetts apportionment rules gave populous Federalist-leaning coastal districts less than their proportionate share of delegates while overrepresenting the Anti-Federalist backcountry. It was here and now that the men of Massachusetts, led by Governor John Hancock doubling as the Convention's presiding officer, improvised yet another improvement in the emerging American constitutional system and thereby killed five birds with one stone.

Bird one: The Federalists needed to persuade their skeptics. They did not enter the room with the votes plainly in hand, as had the Federalists in Pennsylvania and every previous state. Massachusetts Federalists would actually have to talk and listen rather than talk about talk and pretend to listen. Bird two: Precisely because the men in the room were a convention rather than an electorate—a manageable-size group of specially chosen representatives deliberating together over several weeks, rather than ordinary voters showing up on a single election day—delegates could do more than simply vote yes or no. They could vote *yes, but*. They could talk among themselves about what future amendments to the Constitution might be sensible, post-ratification. Bird three: This strategy—vote yes, but propose nonbinding amendment ideas for the future—would highlight for skeptics and initial naysayers the most fundamental and irreparable problem of the Articles of Confederation, namely, the impossibility of amending the Articles within their own terms. If Massachusetts voted down the Constitution and it failed, there would be no way to amend the Articles, given the unanimity problem. Because Article V of the new Constitution required less than unanimity going forward,

Anti-Federalists should vote yes, and Federalists could agree to consider future amendments that did indeed have a chance of passing. Bird four: This yes-but strategy would help bring the Anti-Federalists on board. They could begin to be early framers of USA 2.1 and the process could begin even before USA 2.0 commenced operation. Since the delegates were all in the same room for a few weeks, meeting for the sole purpose of conversing constitutionally with each other, Convention members could use their time together to deepen and extend the constitutional conversation. That is, they could talk and listen to each other not just about the constitutional proposal on the table, but also about closely related ideas that some delegates might have to offer, even if those delegates happened to have entered the room leaning Anti. Bird five: Even if various Anti-Federalists in the Convention persisted in voting no, the Federalists' willingness to hear amendment proposals might soften the intensity of opposition. The Massachusetts Federalists needed not just to win, but to win in a way that would not generate Pennsylvania-style sore losers.

The Massachusetts yes-but ratification approach would not have been possible had the Philadelphia Convention somehow proposed a system of direct popular ratification. The modern criticism of Article VII gets it backward, or at least sideways. The model of convention ratification had genuine advantages—democratic advantages, conversational advantages, deliberative advantages, anti-polarization advantages—over its plausible alternatives in 1787. Article VII, in modern parlance, enabled sensible crowd-sourcing of the proposed Constitution and possible future reforms.

On February 6 and 7, the Massachusetts Convention said yes, but by a vote of 187 to 168, becoming Russell's sixth pillar. Alongside its yes vote, the convention endorsed a series of proposed amendments for Americans in the Bay State and elsewhere to consider. None of the first five pillar states had done this; most of the states thereafter would follow the Bay State's crowd-sourcing approach, saying yes while tossing amendment ideas into the hopper. Once again, as they had done so often since 1760, the men of Massachusetts showed the way forward.

AMAZINGLY, DELEGATES IN THE BAY State's convention did not just talk past each other but actually listened to each other, actually *conversed*. Minds were opened and minds were changed. Men in the room taught each other and learned from each other. Gallery observers, such as the *Centinel*'s Benjamin Russell, quickly published these seminars for a general readership. More than fifty print shops in sister states then republished the proceedings, giving Americans everywhere a far more profound understanding of the relevant issues than could have been generated by any mere referendum. (Here was yet another aspect of the interactive newspaper-convention dynamic driving and reflecting the emerging American constitutional system.)[15]

The convention got off to a great start when the men of Massachusetts, on January 14, 1788, promised to take their time and to consider the plan before them collectively and with care—to have the sort of fulsome constitutional conversation that simply would not have been possible in any mere one-day popular vote. Deliberation, the delegates agreed, would begin with a detailed, paragraph-by-paragraph examination of the Philadelphia plan: "This Convention, sensible how important it is that the great subject submitted to their determination should be discussed and considered with moderation, candor, and deliberation, will enter into a free conversation on the several parts thereof, by paragraphs, until every member shall have had an opportunity to express his sentiments on the same; after which the Convention will consider and debate at large the question whether this Convention will adopt and ratify the proposed Constitution."[16]

Over the next day and a half, substantive conversation began in earnest. Delegate Samuel Adams asked a question: Why had the Philadelphia framers abandoned traditional American annual elections in favor of biannual ones?[17] It was a fair question, all the more important because Samuel Adams might well be the key to the state, and the state might well be the key to the nation. Adams was a leader—many other delegates might follow his lead—and he had not entered the convention as an avowed Federalist. Indeed, in a December 3 letter to Virginia Anti-Federalist Richard Henry Lee, Adams had confessed that the strong continentalism of the Preamble—its evident repudiation of state sovereignty—gave him great pause: "As I enter the Building, I stumble at the Threshold. I meet with a National Government instead of a Federal Union of Sovereign States."*

Led by Nathaniel Gorham, Caleb Strong, Theodore Sedgwick, and Fisher Ames, Adams's fellow delegates responded with care to his query about biannual elections. Gorham and Strong had been in the room at Philadelphia; Sedgwick and Ames had not. These delegates explained to Adams—and to the hundreds of other delegates and audience members in the chamber—that it would take time for congressmen under the new Constitution to brief themselves on conditions in other states and other countries. State lawmakers might well be personally familiar with the different parts of their state; but congressmen would need to learn about all of America— indeed, about much of the world—before they could sensibly legislate at a continental level. That learning could not occur overnight, and thus longer terms of service for federal lawmakers made good sense. "It is admitted that annual elections may be highly fit for the state legislature," conceded Ames. "Every citizen grows up with a knowledge of the local circumstances of the state. But the business of the federal government will be very different. . . . At least two years in office will be necessary to enable a man to judge of the trade and interests of the state which he never saw."[18]

---

*Note the obvious edifice motif here: the Constitution was for Adams the "Building" and its Preamble was its "Threshold." Russell and Adams traveled in similar circles; both were well connected to Boston's tradesmen and mechanics, including, of course, those who constructed and repaired buildings—masons, carpenters, and the like. Note also that two old Revolutionaries, Adams and Lee, a Massachusetts-Virginia tag team, were once again corresponding to consider possible coordinated opposition to a perceived central threat to local liberty. Shades of 1774! Cf. page 110. Note, finally, Adams's clear understanding that, whereas the Articles of Confederation were indeed a union of sovereign states, states would no longer be fully sovereign under "the more perfect union" proposed by the Philadelphia plan.

In response, Adams told the convention, and thus the gallery, that he was now fully persuaded—at least on this issue: "He only made the inquiry for information, and . . . he had heard sufficient to satisfy himself of its [the biannual election rule's] propriety."[19]

We may never know all the particular reasons why Samuel Adams publicly pronounced himself persuaded on this issue. Perhaps specific thoughts crossed Samuel's mind when he heard Ames say that "it is not by riding post to and from Congress that a man can acquire a just knowledge of the true interests of the Union." Perhaps Samuel at that moment flashed back to his first journey to Philadelphia with his cousin John in 1774, when he and John had begun to discover America. John and Samuel had doubtless learned things about the union when they rode—not "post" (or "express," as we might say today), but in a more leisurely fashion—to the First Continental Congress in Philadelphia. The cousins had traveled through only a few states on that trip. Surely he and John had learned a great deal more once they reached Congress and spent time listening to and learning from men from all the other states. So perhaps this specific line from Ames did indeed move Samuel Adams. Or perhaps it was something else that Ames or another delegate said that Adams found compelling.

What we can know with confidence is that in this specific instance the conversational structure of the convention had allowed a fruitful back-and-forth exchange between thoughtful delegates on an intricate yet important question of constitutional architecture. In 1776, John Adams had written, in his widely circulated *Thoughts on Government* pamphlet, that there was not "in the whole circle of the sciences, a maxim more infallible than this, 'Where annual elections end, there slavery begins.'" The Philadelphia framers evidently thought otherwise, and had good reasons for so thinking, as elaborated by the Massachusetts Federalists on January 14 and 15. (Here, as elsewhere, Samuel's second cousin John had quite overstated things; John was prone to exaggeration.) The conversational format of the ratifying convention had allowed this fine-grained question—two years or not two years?—to be nicely ventilated, in a public conversation republished in exquisite detail by Russell and at least two dozen other contemporaneous printers spanning at least six states.[20]

There were scores of similarly significant questions that needed to be pondered before the men of Massachusetts were willing to say yes. Over the next three weeks, countless back-and-forth exchanges took place in Boston as delegates conversed about constitutional issues at every level of generality and specificity. Meanwhile, men like Russell looked on from the gallery, copiously and contemporaneously printing these extraordinary conversations for their readers.

At convention's end, Samuel Adams voted yes. Many others who, like him, had entered the room as skeptics or opponents followed his lead. Among those who switched sides and provided the Constitution its narrow margin of victory (187 to 168), Nathaniel Barrell from York County (present-day Maine) offered the most detailed and persuasive public explanation.

Barrell had arrived in Boston an avowed Anti-Federalist, in line with the leanings of his community. He had bridled at the haste that had marred Pennsylvania's ratification: "Sir, I could wish the Constitution had not been, in some parts of the continent, hurried on, like the driving of Jehu, very furiously; for such important transactions should be without force, and with cool deliberation." In "the course of these debates," he continued, some of his initial objections "have been removed . . . by the ingenious reasonings of the speakers. . . . [T]he arguments which have been used in the debates . . . have eased my mind." Nevertheless, some of his concerns "yet remain[] on my mind." Why, then, vote yes? "I am possessed with an assurance that the proposed amendments will take place [and] I dread the fatal effects of anarchy [and] I am convinced that the Confederation is essentially deficient, and that it will be more difficult to amend that than to reform this; and . . . I think this Constitution, with all its imperfections, is excellent, compared with that, and that it is the best constitution we can now obtain."[21]

AS DRAMATIC AS BARRELL'S CONVENTION conversation conversion experience was, no less dramatic were the post-vote speeches of those who had voted no—those who had lost. Unlike Pennsylvania's Anti-Federalists, the Massachusetts naysayers were not sore losers. They took pains to express appreciation for the process in which they had participated, a process that had allowed them to speak their piece and make their case.

William Widgery declared that "he should return to his constituents, and inform them that he had opposed the adoption of this Constitution; but that he had been overruled, and that it had been carried by a majority of wise and understanding men" who were "as full a representation of the people as can be convened." Thus he would "endeavor to sow the seeds of union and peace among the people he represented." Major Benjamin Swain announced that, despite his no vote, "many of the doubts which lay on his mind had been removed" by the deliberations and he would "support the Constitution as cheerfully and heartily as though he had voted on the other side of the question."[22]

Even Anti-Federalists who did not say that they had been persuaded on individual issues made clear that the Massachusetts process had been a good one and had therefore earned the right to bind naysayers. Daniel Cooley declared that "as it [the Constitution] had been agreed to by a majority, he should endeavor to convince his constituents of the propriety of its adoption." Doctor John Taylor said that although he had "uniformly opposed the Constitution . . . he found himself fairly beaten, and expressed his determination to go home and infuse a spirit of harmony and love among the people." Benjamin Randall announced that he would "sit down contented," hoping that various recommended amendments "will take place" and that "we may all live in peace." Joshua Whitney promised that "though he had opposed the Constitution, he should support it as much as if he had voted for it." Major Samuel Nasson "intimated his determination to support the Constitution, and to exert himself to influence his constituents to do the same." Alexander White said much the same thing. He would "use his utmost exertions to induce his constituents to live in peace under and cheerfully submit to" the plan he had just voted against.[23]

ONCE MASSACHUSETTS'S PILLAR WENT UP, the next crucial battleground state was America's other oldest and proudest jurisdiction, which had over the previous quarter century time and again combined with Massachusetts to produce and redeem the American Revolution. Would this pattern recur once more, with yet another Massachusetts-Virginia partnership?

Virginia's most conspicuous citizen, America's leading man, had personally endorsed the Philadelphia plan out of the gate, not just by signing his name above the names of thirty-eight other delegates but also by submitting a short accompanying letter to the Confederation Congress on behalf of the drafters. Washington opened his letter of September 17, 1787—reprinted everywhere alongside the proposed Constitution itself[24]—by summarizing the military, diplomatic, economic, and legal problems to be solved and the resulting need for a radical restructuring of governmental power: abandoning a unicameral all-purpose Confederation Congress in favor of a bicameral legislature flanked by independent executive and judicial branches. "The friends of our country have long seen and desired, that the power of making war, peace and treaties, that of levying money and regulating commerce, and the correspondent executive and judicial authorities should be fully and effectually vested in the general government of the Union," he wrote. "The impropriety of delegating such extensive trust to one body of men is evident—Hence results the necessity of a different organization." This new institutional system, the letter continued, also compelled a rethinking of the "independent sovereignty" of each state in order to effectuate a "consolidation of our Union, in which is involved our prosperity, felicity, safety, perhaps our national existence."[25]

Washington intended to say no more than this publicly until the American people rendered their final judgment. Throughout the ratification period, he confined himself to his Mount Vernon home, from which he closely followed unfolding events via prolific private correspondence and voracious consumption of newspapers and pamphlets, but he himself wrote no pamphlets or essays and issued no other public pronouncements.[26] One unintentional exception occurred when Washington wrote what he thought was a private letter to an acquaintance, Charles Carter, filled with copious farming advice about "Barley, . . . Jerusalem Artichokes, . . . Irish Potatoes, Carrots, Turnips, [and] yard dung." In closing, Washington let slip a few candid thoughts about a non-farming topic that was surely on his mind at all times: "There is no alternative between the adoption of [the proposed Constitution] and anarchy. . . . General Government is now suspended by a thread[.] I might go farther and say it is really at an end." The Philadelphia proposal, he concluded, "is the best that can be obtained at this day and . . . *it* or disunion is before us," adding that when "the defects of it are experienced a Constitutional door is open for amendments." Without Washington's approval, and to his chagrin, Carter shared this December 14 letter with publishers who widely reprinted Washington's blunt language.[27]

In keeping with his efforts to model modesty and embody republican restraint, Washington declined to participate in the Virginia Ratifying Convention. At the Richmond conclave, the general's surrogates thus took the lead in defending the Philadelphia plan, spearheaded by two former Philadelphia delegates and supported by a promising newcomer to the conversation.

The state's sitting governor (and former Washington aide-de-camp) Edmund Randolph now publicly supported the Constitution, even though he had pointedly refused to sign the parchment at the end of the Philadelphia Convention. James Madison ably reinforced Randolph at every turn, offering several dozen careful speeches in defense of this clause or that one, while prepping allies by feeding them copies of *The Federalist* to use as their debaters' handbook.[28]

The promising newcomer playing a supporting role in the constitutional conversation was a young lawyer and Revolutionary War veteran named John Marshall. Marshall was clever, charismatic, and well-spoken. He, too, had served under General Washington, and had done so, among other places, at Valley Forge. Those who survived that brutal winter encampment knew firsthand—felt in their very bones—that patriot soldiers had suffered horribly and died pointlessly because the old Congress had failed them in their hour of need and sacrifice. Marshall also had a popular touch. His Richmond speeches stressed the Constitution's abiding commitment to popular self-government: "Supporters of the Constitution claim the side of being firm friends of the liberty and the rights of mankind. [We] consider it as the best means of protecting liberty. *We, sir, idolize democracy.* . . . We prefer this system to any monarchy, because we are convinced that it has a greater tendency to secure our liberty and promote our happiness. We admire it, because we think it a well-regulated democracy. . . . We contend for a well-regulated democracy."[29]

LED BY VIRGINIA'S BRILLIANT BUT erratic orator Patrick Henry— the James Otis of the Old Dominion—Richmond Anti-Federalists seized on Randolph's recent reversal. Was Randolph weak-minded, or had someone bought him off after he said no at Philadelphia? The Richmond Convention proceedings were of course conducted in public, and Randolph repelled this open attack on his character with a powerful combination of Publian geostrategy, Russellian pillar mathematics, and the Massachusetts third way (yes-but).

First, on June 6, Randolph made the basic geostrategic case for indivisible union on the model of Scotland and England: "Call to mind the history of every part of the world, where nations bordered on one another, and consider the consequences of our separation from the Union. . . . A numerous standing army, that dangerous expedient, would be necessary. . . . If you wish to know the extent of such a scene, look at the history of Scotland and England before the union; you will see their borderers continually committing depredations and cruelties of the most calamitous and deplorable nature, on one another."[30]

This was an argument lifted straight from *The Federalist*, especially Jay/Publius's *Federalist* No. 5 and Hamilton/Publius's *Federalist* No. 8. Here was dramatic evidence of a truly American constitutional conversation, driven by the interplay of newspapers and conventions. Thanks to Publius and other essayists, newspapers informed conventions, which, in turn, thanks to Russell and other publishers, generated additional newsprint for readers near and far.

The next day, Randolph elaborated:

> I allude to the Scotch union. If gentlemen cast their eyes to that period, they will find there an instructive similitude between our circumstances and the situation of those people. The advocates for a union with England declared that it would be a foundation of lasting peace, remove all jealousies between them, increase their strength and riches, and enable them to resist more effectually [foreign invasions]. These were irresistible arguments . . . and the predictions of the advocates for that union have been fully verified. The arguments used on that occasion apply with more cogency to our situation.[31]

But if all this was so, why had Randolph not signed the Constitution in Philadelphia? Why was he now switching sides? Here, Randolph explained Russellian mathematics and the appeal of the Massachusetts approach to ratification (yes-but). In Philadelphia back in September 1787, he had hoped for amendments that could be added to the Philadelphia plan *before* ratification. But now, in June 1788, that was no longer realistic. Eight other states had ratified. Russell's pillars had gone up, and these erections were generating a momentum that could not be ignored. (Post-Massachusetts, both Maryland and South Carolina had ratified by lopsided votes—Maryland, Russell's seventh pillar, on April 28 by a vote of 63–11, and South Carolina, Russell's eighth pillar, on May 23 by a vote of 149–73.)

Word had yet to reach Virginia from New Hampshire. If New Hampshire said yes as Russell's ninth pillar, the Constitution could go into effect without Virginia, but with neighboring Pennsylvania and Maryland. This would be catastrophic for Virginia. Marylanders did not always love Virginians. Plus, Massachusetts had shown the way forward: Virginia could say yes, but by putting sensible amendment ideas into circulation and relying confidently on the Article V amendment process to make the adjustments that Randolph had favored all along.

In Randolph's words, in direct conversation with Henry:

We are next informed [by Henry] that there is no danger from the borders of Maryland and Pennsylvania, and that my observations upon the frontiers of England and Scotland are inapplicable. He distinguishes republican from monarchial borderers, and ascribes pacific meekness to the former, and barbarous ferocity to the latter. There is as much danger, sir, from republican borderers as from any other. History will show that as much barbarity and cruelty have been committed upon one another by republican borderers as by any other. We are borderers upon three states, *two of which are ratifying states.*[32]

Several weeks later, Randolph put forth his closing argument, powerfully blending Russell with Publius and endorsing the yes-but Massachusetts model of post-ratification amendment:

Many other states have adopted it [the Constitution], who wish for many amendments. I ask you if it be not better to adopt, and run the chance of amending it hereafter, than run the risk of endangering the Union. The Confederation is gone; it has no authority. If, in this situation, we reject the Constitution, the Union will be dissolved, the dogs of war will break loose, and anarchy and discord will complete the ruin of this country. [Immediate] adoption will prevent these deplorable mischiefs. The union of sentiments with us in the adopting states will render subsequent amendments easy.[33]

By convention's end, the vigorous back-and-forth had nicely clarified Governor Randolph's position. His argument was essentially three-pronged: Publius plus Russell plus Massachusetts. Disunion would be disaster (Publian geostrategy); the edifice was almost up and would likely be sufficient with or without Virginia (Russell's math); and the yes-but approach made the most sense (Massachusetts). Combined with Madison's detailed defenses of specific constitutional provisions, and Marshall's infusion of democratic enthusiasm—with Washington's spirit hovering over everything, of course[34]—Randolph's concluding argument carried the day. On June 25, after New Hampshire had indeed become the ninth pillar (on June 21, by a vote of 57–47), but before word from New England reached Richmond, the Virginia Convention ratified by a vote of 89–79.

The federal edifice was now sufficient. *Actum Est.*

But New York, home state of the two remaining Publians, Jay and Hamilton, had yet to join. Even though the Constitution would now formally take effect, could the geostrategic system work without the mighty Hudson River and the magnificent seaport of New York City? Could Franklin's snake live without its midsection?[35]

MODERN CRITICS WHO ANACHRONISTICALLY ATTACK Article VII for being insufficiently Californian or Swiss love to point out that many New Yorkers voted for Anti-Federalist delegates only to watch a large number of these delegates turn coat at the Poughkeepsie Convention and vote yes. These critics often fail to stress that two critical—indeed, world-changing—months intervened between these two votes.

When New York voters chose delegates in late April, no one knew whether the federal edifice would in fact rise. Russell thought it would, but others were betting against him. Even if nine pillars went up, the system could not really work without Virginia. Who could say what would happen there? But by mid-July, ten pillars were up. Virginia had said yes. And the same logic that impelled Randolph to move off the fence and into the Federalist camp operated even more powerfully in New York after Randolph had prevailed.

If we substitute New York for Virginia and New Jersey for Maryland, the cases were remarkably similar in midspring. Just as it made sense for Virginia to join a union that envious Maryland had already agreed to enter, so, too, with New York, given that rivalrous New Jersey had already said yes. John Jay thus played the Jersey card with flourish in a pamphlet published on April 15, *Address to the People of New York*. Here Jay wrote not as Publius but as "A Citizen of New-York." (In *The Federalist* No. 85, Hamilton/Publius had some kind words for the almost-Publius pamphlet, kind words that might today be seen as akin to sock-puppetry: "The reasons assigned in an excellent little pamphlet recently published in this city are unanswerable.") Jay's analysis was in effect the same argument as Randolph's—or, to be more precise, Randolph's analysis was in fact Jay's. Jay/Citizen in April was merely elaborating what Jay/Publius had said back in October and November in *The Federalist* Nos. 2–5, and Randolph surely had both at hand in June.

The old Confederation, Jay/Citizen argued, was in the process of falling apart:

> Then every State would be a little nation, jealous of its neighbour, and anxious to strengthen itself, by foreign alliances, against its former friends. Then farewell to fraternal affection, unsuspecting intercourse, and mutual participation in commerce, navigation, and citizenship. Then would rise mutual restrictions and fears, mutual garrisons and standing armies, and all those dreadful evils which for so many ages plagued England, Scotland, Wales, and Ireland, while they continued disunited, and were played off against each other. . . . You know the geography of your State, and the consequences of your local position. Jersey and Connecticut, to whom your impost laws have been unkind . . . have adopted the present plan and expect much good from it. . . . They cannot, they will not, love you; they border upon you and are your neighbours, but you will soon cease to regard their neighbourhood as a blessing.

In mid-April, Jay was merely predicting the geopolitical chaos that might ensue if the Constitution failed to win nine state ratifications, or (in more guarded prose) if nine or more states, including envious bordering states, said yes while New York stayed out. By July, four more states—Maryland, South Carolina, New Hampshire, and Virginia—had all said yes. The Constitution would now undoubtedly launch, with at least ten states—and strong states at that.

Did New Yorkers really want to go it alone or somehow league up with pathetic Rhode Island?

"*IN TOTO*, AND *FOR EVER*"

On July 2, 1788, exactly twelve years to the day after twelve states meeting in Philadelphia had agreed to declare themselves free and independent, word reached the Poughkeepsie Convention that Virginia had said yes to the Constitution. Back in 1776, New York's Philadelphia delegation had not been authorized to say yes on July 2, and the colony had belatedly joined her twelve sisters on July 9. Now, history seemed to be repeating itself. New York's sisters were leaving port, with or without her. Would she, once again, quickly board the good ship *Union*?

Word of New Hampshire's June 21 ratification, which reached Poughkeepsie on June 24, had not seemed to faze the New York Anti-Federalists. Virginia's ratification was different. Now, America's three largest states—Virginia, Massachusetts, and Pennsylvania—were all aboard the ship. Now, there was no doubt that George Washington would lead the new United States of America. (Had Washington's home state of Virginia said no, perhaps, some thought, he might choose home over union.)

On July 4, Philadelphians staged a joyous celebration and parade that attracted some twenty thousand merrymakers—the largest such gathering ever in post-independence America—and featured a grand constitutional oration by James Wilson, one of six men to have signed both the Declaration and the Constitution. Pennsylvania was of course already in the new union, and Philadelphia hoped to be America's new capital—fittingly, thought many Philadelphians, given that the Constitution had originated in their hometown. Manhattanites had other ideas. On July 23, as the Poughkeepsie Convention neared its climax some eighty miles upstate, New York City Federalists staged their own massive celebration of the Constitution. Ten proud horses drew a twenty-seven-foot frigate named *Hamilton* (in honor of Alexander) through the cheering streets in a procession that stretched for a mile and a half.[36]

The stage was now set for a compromise. New York's Anti-Federalists would need to say yes, but they hoped for some concession from Federalists to show the voters back home that they had not simply turned tail. Their initial offers tempted Hamilton and his fellow Federalists, who were not at all sure where the votes were in the room, but ultimately the Federalists stood firm.

First, the Anti-Federalists offered to ratify the Constitution "upon condition" that the new Congress take steps to initiate new amendments. The Federalists said no. The Constitution could be ratified with the hope and expectation of future amendments—"in full confidence" that the new Congress would make way for sensible constitutional revisions—but a formally conditional ratification was improper. The Federalists then beat back another Anti-Federalist motion: "that there should be reserved to the state of New York a right to withdraw herself from the Union after a certain number of years, unless" Congress acted on various amendment proposals.[37]

At the risk of losing everything—and with all of America watching, breathlessly—the Federalists thus insisted that New York say yes or no, cleanly. She could say "yes, but" as had Massachusetts and most post-Massachusetts states. But the "but" was not legally enforceable. Formally, ratifying conventions in Massachusetts and elsewhere were simply putting amendment ideas onto an agenda for future good-faith continental deliberation and decision. Yes, various Federalist delegates in Massachusetts and elsewhere were personally and publicly promising that they would support various sensible amendments down the road. But Hamilton and his fellow Federalists insisted that, formally, ratification had to be unconditional. Any unilateral effort by a state to secede post-ratification would be unconstitutional, and any attempt to reserve such a right in the process of ratifying the Constitution was invalid.

In a July 20 letter to Hamilton, Confederation Congress member Madison (now back in New York City after his labors in Richmond) emphasized that "the Constitution requires an adoption *in toto*, and *for ever.* It has been so adopted by the other States" (including Madison's Virginia). On July 24, Hamilton read the letter aloud to the Poughkeepsie Convention and then invoked the Article VI Oath Clause obliging every state and federal public servant to follow the supreme law of the Constitution. That oath, Hamilton explained, "stands in the way" of any conditional ratification or purported reservation of a right of unilateral secession.[38]

Printers and the public across the continent were watching the Poughkeepsie Convention's climax with rapt attention. According to timely accounts published in more than a dozen newspapers circulating in virtually every state (including, notably, Virginia and both Carolinas), both Hamilton and his fellow delegate John Jay insisted that "a reservation of a right to withdraw . . . was inconsistent with the Constitution, and was *no ratification*."[39]

Thus, the only compromise the Federalists offered in late July was, strictly speaking, an informal one. New York could ratify on the Massachusetts yes-but model, and Anti-Federalist delegates could show their constituents all the amendment ideas that the convention had put into circulation, and could further point out that many Federalist delegates had supported these ideas.

The decisive showdown took place on July 26. As that day dawned, no one knew for sure what the final vote count would be. Hamilton, Jay, Madison, and their allies had placed everything at risk—not just in New York, but, as a practical matter more generally—by insisting that no secession right whatsoever could be recognized and that no other formal condition of any sort could be attached. Had the Federalists, by taking this strict position, impaled themselves?

When the final tally was announced, the New York Federalists won by a single vote.[40]

WERE THE FEDERALISTS RIGHT IN insisting that no state, having ratified, could unilaterally withdraw after the ninth pillar went up and the Constitution commenced operation? Abraham Lincoln thought so in 1861; Jefferson Davis thought otherwise.

This question is ultimately a legal one. The Constitution is law. Indeed, it calls itself the supreme law of the land. Legally, either it permits unilateral secession, or it prohibits unilateral secession, or it is simply indeterminate. So who was right, legally, in the 1860s?

Lincoln, by a wide margin.

True, some of Lincoln's claims were not quite right, and he missed some of the best arguments for his conclusion.[41] But the Great Constitutional conversation of 1787–1788 had not been indeterminate on this question. Nor had the conversation supported a secession right.

Nowhere, ever, in the entire year of intense continental conversation, did any leading Federalist try to woo skeptics and fence-sitters by suggesting that a right of secession would exist, and that if any state were dissatisfied, it could leave at will. Given how close the contest was in so many states, surely, if such a right had existed, Federalists would have emphasized it. It would have made Anti-Federalists infinitely more willing to give the plan a trial run. Instead, the Federalists repeatedly said that the union they were proposing would be strict and indissoluble on the model of Scotland and England. This indivisibility was central to the geostrategic argument for union. If any state at any time could take its land and waters and ally with some foreign European power, the Constitution's entire system—promising the permanent elimination of international borders from Georgia to Maine—would make no sense. Anti-Federalists in every key state grasped this point and loudly warned their fellow citizens that a state's decision to join would be irreversible.[42] Everyone in 1787–1788 understood what the deal was. Indeed, at the risk of losing everything, and with all America and the world looking on, the Federalists in New York at the end of the process reaffirmed what had been clear from the beginning: ratification would be "*in toto, and for ever.*"[43]

America's constitutional conversation did not begin in 1787. It was already in full swing in 1776, and the 1787 document must thus be understood as a continuation of a long conversation that Americans had been conducting among themselves. Understanding what the Constitution said requires understanding what the Constitution did not say. It did not call itself a "Confederation" or a "league" or a "treaty." These were pregnant omissions, because all these words did prominently appear in the Articles of Confederation in describing USA 1.0. The Constitution did not say that states would remain "sovereign." This, too, was a pointed omission, and every leading Anti-Federalist got the point.

Now turn to what the document did say, from start to finish. It called itself a "Constitution"—on the model of state constitutions that embodied Americans' deepest aspirations for self-government in 1776. It proudly promised a "more perfect union" openly patterned on the indissoluble 1707 union of Scotland and England, as Federalists emphasized at every turn, in many states, in both speech and print, from the beginning to the end of the ratification process.[44] It described itself as "supreme law" even over state constitutions. No state, merely by purporting to modify its own constitution, could change the supreme legal status of the federal Constitution. Only a proper federal amendment could change the federal Constitution itself, and Article V's amendment rules required the approval of many states, not just one. Article V also made clear that future amendments could indeed go into effect in all states even if some states said no to these amendments. Article V thus decisively broke from the state-sovereignty model of the Articles of Confederation, in which no state could be bound to any constitutional change absent its own consent.

Article VII took preexisting state sovereignty seriously. Rhode Island and North Carolina would not be bound unless they themselves agreed—and in 1788, these two jurisdictions in fact did not agree. But once a sovereign state did agree to ratify the Constitution, and once eight or more other sovereign states did the same, each merging state would no longer be fully sovereign, post-merger. The federal Constitution would be the supreme law. Everything would change, because it had to change if America was to meet the geostrategic challenge posed by Britain, France, Spain, and the like. Washington's letter to the Confederation Congress—a letter reprinted everywhere, often directly alongside the proposed constitutional text itself—minced no words in explaining what was happening and why. The "independent sovereignty" of each state would need to yield so Americans could experience a *"consolidation of our Union, in which is involved our prosperity, felicity, safety, perhaps our national existence."*[45]

And if all that were not enough, the Constitution explicitly defined the post-ratification status of any American who took up arms against the United States, for any reason, even if that American had the backing of persons claiming to represent his home state government. Any American who did that, said Article III, would thereby be committing "Treason."

Although many South Carolinians in 1861 would in fact commit treason, South Carolinians in 1788 surely understood what the Constitution said and meant. Indeed, on August 11, 1788, Charleston's leading newspaper, the *City Gazette*, treated its readers to a detailed account of Hamilton's and Jay's Poughkeepsie Convention speeches

ELEVENTH PILLAR!

rejecting a state's right to "withdraw," post-ratification, and the convention's subsequent decision to unconditionally take the Federalists' take-it-or-leave-it deal. The *Gazette* flanked this dramatic account with a joyous Russell-inspired cartoon, *Eleventh Pillar!*, that powerfully illustrated Hamilton's and Jay's point. No pillar, once up, could be unilaterally removed, lest the great federal dome supported by and in turn supporting the ensemble of pillars tumble to the ground—and with it, liberty itself, capping the grand federal edifice.

Unlike Russell, who arrayed his pillars chronologically by order of ratification, the *City Gazette*, exquisitely attentive to dome-ish geometry and sound architectural engineering, arranged its pillars geographically from south (left) to north (right) à la Franklin's snake.

The two pillars yet to be erected, as the cartoon elegantly illustrated, were geographically symmetric: the third most southerly (North Carolina) and the third most northerly (Rhode Island).

PROMISES MADE

The Philadelphia framers won the great constitutional debate of 1787–1788 and won it on their terms. But they blundered badly on two critical issues, Congressional size and citizens' rights. On both issues, the continental constitutional conversation exposed the magnitude of these blunders.

The Article VII convention process generated priceless information—specific reasons why men were skeptical or opposed—in ways that no mere referendum could have done. The convention process also enabled informal solution of the problems identified by the process itself. Leading Federalists could agree with their leading critics that the Philadelphia delegates had blundered, and could informally commit to working with the Constitution's critics, post-ratification, to repair these blunders.

America had been in the room at Philadelphia, but on the key issue of Congressional size, the delegates had failed to listen carefully. The Philadelphia Convention proposed a House of Representatives of sixty-five persons to legislate for an entire continent, less than one-twentieth of the fifteen hundred aggregate assemblymen who legislated for the thirteen separate states. Only two states, and tiny ones at that, had lower houses with fewer than sixty-five members. A tiny lower house was not the best state practice.[46]

Madison and Hamilton had both argued behind closed doors that the proposed House of Representatives was far too small. Washington himself had dramatically weighed in on their side in the Convention's closing moments, but his proposed last-minute erasure and rewrite was too little too late.[47]

Anti-Federalists pounced on this little number early and often.[48] Congress was simply too small to be genuinely trustworthy. The smaller the group, the easier it would be for a grandee or a foreign tyrant to bribe a majority. Corruption aside, a typical congressman representing an unduly large district would be unfamiliar with the lives and concerns of his constituents. There would be insufficient sympathy between voters and their representatives. These were issues with deep roots, tracing back to the writings of Whately and Otis and many others in the 1760s.

In the ensuing ratification convention conversations, Federalists scrambled. Sixty-five, they said, was merely a placeholder until the first census. In Massachusetts, Philadelphia delegate Caleb Strong assured his colleagues that Congress would expand "very soon." Virginia's George Nicholas parroted Publius verbatim—the orator likely had a copy of *The Federalist* No. 55 in hand, thanks to fellow delegate Madison—when he promised his audience that after the first census the House would swell: "I take it for granted that the number . . . will be increased . . . to one hundred representatives . . . [and] that the number of representatives will be proportioned to the highest number we are entitled to." Hamilton said the same thing in New York: "One representative for every thirty thousand inhabitants is fixed as the standard of increase." In "three years," Hamilton asserted, the House "would exceed one hundred."[49]

But the Constitution's text said nothing of the sort. It set out a *maximum* House size of one representative for every thirty thousand but nowhere guaranteed that Congress would meet that benchmark. Indeed, it failed to guarantee that after the first census Congress would not shrink *below* sixty-five. In Virginia, Patrick Henry rightly ridiculed what the text in fact said: "In the clause under consideration, there is the strangest language that I can conceive. . . . 'The number shall not exceed one for every thirty thousand.' This may be satisfied by one representative from each state. Let our [population] be ever so great, this immense continent may, by this artful expression, be reduced to have but thirteen representatives."[50] The House could in theory end up even smaller than the Senate, resulting in state equality in both branches. If the House ended up with thirteen members, seven would be a quorum, and four would be a majority of the quorum!

The Philadelphia framers here had goofed, but the Article VII process provided the solution. Nicholas, Strong, Hamilton, and other leading Federalists assured prominent skeptics that the maximum would also be the minimum. Once the decennial census process began, the House would have one member for every thirty thousand for the foreseeable future. We promise.

In effect, the text of the Constitution here was informally renegotiated in the ratification process because the crowd-sourcing had indeed identified a bug.

The Philadelphia framers had also plainly missed the voice of America in the room when they neglected to include a bill of rights. Such bills had been standard features of state constitutions beginning with Virginia's Declaration of Rights, which had been drafted by George Mason even before the Declaration of Independence. These state declarations had been widely printed by both in-state and out-of-state newspapers and had been quickly copied by sister states.

Why, then, did the framers omit a federal bill of rights? George Mason himself was a Philadelphia delegate. Toward the end of the Convention, Mason called attention to the omission and offered to help fill it. The delegates turned him down. The simplest explanation is the most human one. The delegates were tired and homesick. The end was in sight, and they rushed to the finish line. Mason had said that he could craft something quickly, but Mason could be cranky. Who knew how much time it would actually take to fashion a proper bill?[51]

Here, too, Anti-Federalist critics attacked relentlessly in the ratification process. Americans had become accustomed to written bills of rights. They were the state of the art, the best state practice. Indeed, the Declaration of Independence had ringingly proclaimed that governments were instituted among men *to secure basic rights*. The Philadelphia plan's omission was a glaring one.

Some Federalists—Wilson in Pennsylvania, Hamilton/Publius in *The Federalist* No. 84, Madison at first—tried to defend the omission with fancy (and at times contradictory) theoretical arguments: bills of rights were unnecessary and indeed downright dangerous;

and besides, the proposed Constitution already contained a functional bill of rights.[52] As the ratification process progressed and the rights objections continued, and even intensified, the Federalists listened, learned, and pivoted. The Massachusetts yes-but approach provided a graceful exit strategy and a basis for compromise. If Anti-Federalists would vote yes, but, Federalists would promise to consider seriously the addition of a bill of rights, post-ratification. Better still, this promise would allow Anti-Federalists to feel some ownership of the federal constitutional project. They were the originators of this idea, and the Constitution would be theirs as well as the Federalists'.

THE CONVERSATIONAL STRUCTURE OF ARTICLE VII thus deepened the nature of the consent generated in the course of this extraordinary year. If, as Federalists said time and again, America was teetering on the edge of anarchy or collapse—if civil war or European reconquest loomed just over the horizon—then sensible people would vote for just about anything, even a Hobbesian Leviathan. But if so, it might be argued that the people did not consent in any profound way to any of the specifics of the Philadelphia plan. The people in effect were saying yes with a gun to their heads. Perhaps the Constitution was not an act of technical extortion, because Washington and company had not themselves created the geostrategic crisis, nor had they acted with improper force (slavery aside). But did the Federalists win genuine, deep, and resounding consent to their plan in 1788?[53]

Yes, in at least two important ways. First, as has just been seen, the Constitution that they proposed was subtly renegotiated during the ratification process, via informal promises of future policies (a larger House, post-census) and even future amendments (a bill of rights, at a minimum).

Second, the Philadelphia delegates sought not just a yes vote on their plan, but also a yes vote on themselves. Leading Federalists intended to accept, and in some cases even openly seek, elective and appointed positions under the new Constitution, in order to make their system actually work as they hoped it would and to fulfill the personal promises they made in the ratification process.

Concretely, the Federalists envisioned a small House of large men. Not just the Senate but even the House would attract the truly great men of the continent—men of enlightened vision and undeniable achievement—men like, well, the Philadelphia delegates themselves. Even if the House grew at the maximum rate, as promised during the yes-but ratification process, it would still be a select body, compared to state lower houses. The mighty state of Virginia would initially send only ten men to the federal House, as compared to the nearly four hundred lawmakers selected annually for the state Assembly. Gentlemen of wide repute—the social and political elite—might well have the inside track in federal House elections, compared to the more common folk who dominated state legislatures. A given tavern owner, shopkeeper, silversmith, farmer, cobbler, or weaver might be popular enough in his local neighborhood, and knowledgeable enough about local issues (roads, mills, jails, wolves, crops, and so on), to win a state assembly race in a tiny state assembly district. But such a man, who perhaps knew little about the world beyond his own home county, would face an uphill climb in a Congressional election conducted either in a large electoral district or (better still, thought many Federalists) in a statewide at-large contest. For every twenty lawmakers in a given state assembly, only one or two could serve in the federal House—the best one or two, hoped the Federalists. A similar merit-favoring (or elitist, depending on one's perspective) dynamic would guard the gate to the smaller federal Senate and to high-level executive and judicial officialdom.

Thus the Constitution's proposed system might well incline toward the Philadelphia delegates themselves and men like them— cosmopolitans with a better sense of the continent and the world, genteel folk with some combination of personal wealth, social standing, commercial repute, college learning, lawyerly expertise, and military glory. Anti-Federalists took note and took offense. In the pivotal Massachusetts Ratifying Convention, Anti-Federalist Amos Singletary, a self-taught backcountry gristmill operator, spoke bluntly:

"These lawyers, and men of learning, and moneyed men, that talk so finely, and gloss over matters so smoothly, to make us poor illiterate people swallow down the pill, *expect to get into Congress themselves; they expect to be the managers of this Constitution, and get all the power and all the money into their own hands*, and then they will swallow up all us little folks, like the great Leviathan . . . yes, just as the whale swallowed up Jonah. This is what I am afraid of."[54]

In fact, the fix was not in. Led by Federalist Russell himself, more than a dozen publishers across the continent reprinted Singletary's tart critique. Several of these print shops operated in states that had yet to decide—New Hampshire, New York, and Rhode Island. Americans in 1788 understood what they were voting for.[55]

Even if many ordinary voters and state convention delegates in 1788 felt compelled by circumstance to support the Constitution—because the alternative was anarchy, civil war, or European reconquest—every voter in the first set of elections and appointments under the new Constitution was free to support whichever candidates he truly preferred. *In that critical era of formal constitutional ratification and functional re-ratification, American voters, state lawmakers, and other public opinion leaders elected*—le mot juste—*to support those who had drafted and/or strongly backed the new plan.* Philadelphia Convention alums alone made up fully half of the first Senate and soon constituted half of the inaugural Supreme Court and more than half of the first cabinet. American voters also rewarded prominent Federalists with seats in the first House—a galaxy that included James Madison, Roger Sherman, George Clymer, Daniel Carroll, Abraham Baldwin, Thomas Fitzsimons, Nicholas Gilman, Hugh Williamson, Fisher Ames, Theodore Sedgwick, Alexander White, John Laurance, Egbert Benson, Jeremiah Wadsworth, and Samuel Livermore.

MOST IMPORTANT OF ALL, AMERICANS rewarded George Washington with the presidency. Indeed, the Electoral College unanimously backed Washington in 1789; every single elector who participated cast a vote for America's George. By installing Washington by acclamation, Americans in effect consented yet again—truly, deeply—to the Constitution that was now inextricably intertwined with Washington himself. Though he had maintained a dignified low profile for most of the ratification process, he had at the outset vouched for the Constitution in the most dramatic way imaginable. He had come out of retirement not just to participate in the Philadelphia Convention, but to preside over it. He had signed the Constitution above and before all others and had relayed it to the Confederation Congress with a cogent and widely reprinted cover letter signed by him alone. When he put his name on the plan, he put himself on the line.

While quietly occupying center stage in the ensuing national ratification conversation of 1787–1788, he had been more prop than player—a human statue of liberty. Now that eleven states had erected their pillars, he would need to act and speak in new ways—to act as a civilian commander in chief and to speak officially for a new nation under a new, untried Constitution. He would need to coax the two states that had yet to say yes, North Carolina and Rhode Island, to erect their pillars and rejoin the snake.

How would he fare in this new and difficult role? How would the new Constitution fare under him?

PART III
CONSOLIDATION

— seven —

WASHINGTON

ANERICA HAD GIVEN ITSELF A republic, if it could keep it. Having won convention votes in even more than the nine states that sufficed under Article VII, the Federalists had cleared the high legitimation bar they had erected for themselves. But as 1789 dawned, the friends of the Constitution still had promises to keep and miles to go before the republic could soundly sleep.[1]

The supposedly perpetual union of 1781 had shattered. Only eleven of the original thirteen states had said "yes, We do." The other two states were now foreign soil.

Within the new, shrunken, United States of America, there remained large pools of honorable and capable men who had strongly opposed the Constitution. Unlike the loyalists of the previous generation, many of whom had fled America and few of whom had local political muscle after 1775, Anti-Federalists were all staying put, and many of them enjoyed strong civic support in their home districts. They could spell trouble for the new regime. Other American patriots had reluctantly endorsed the Constitution, but expected to see a proper bill of rights, and perhaps other constitutional amendments, posthaste.

Nor could the new regime take for granted those who had unreservedly supported the Constitution. Some had said yes only because they expected Washington and company to work miracles. Among the most talented and determined Federalists, many aspired to serve in the new government, animated by complex mixtures of pure patriotism and personal ambition. Some of these personal ambitions would surely clash, as would honest opinions about the best path forward for the new nation.

Presiding, quite literally, over the entire scene would be an utterly new constitutional officer—a "President of the United States," with powers far less than those of King George but far more than those of any state governor. Exactly how much less and how much more remained to be seen.

A daunting constitutional agenda confronted the first occupant of this new-modeled office. He would need to handle foreign relations—not just with the Old Powers of Europe and with Indian tribes but also with the two sovereign republics on his flanks, North Carolina and Rhode Island. He would need to work with the new legislative branch of the federal government; handpick and oversee officers, both military and civilian, within his own executive branch; and select jurists to populate an embryonic judicial branch. He would also need to manage affairs with eleven strong-minded state governments and with fledgling regimes in western lands. And in doing all this, he would need to maintain the goodwill of Americans who supported the new constitutional order while wooing its skeptics and opponents.

As he pondered these daunting challenges, George Washington could take some comfort in the wide and deep support of his countrymen. Then again, in 1760 another George had begun his time in power with similarly wide and deep American support, and had managed to lose it all.

LAUNCHING THE SHIP

Historians have hindsight. Hindsight can help us today see things that historical actors in the moment did not, and perhaps could not, see.

In 1761, no one outside the Bay Province paid much attention to young James Otis, much less to the even younger John Adams. But historians now know that Otis did seethe after his 1761 oral arguments, that he did turn the town of Boston against Thomas Hutchinson (even though we can now see that Hutchinson's 1761 rulings on the writs were legally solid), and that a Boston mob did in 1765 destroy Hutchinson's mansion. In addition, we now know that the Revolution did begin in Boston, via the 1770 Massacre (involving Hutchinson and Adams), the 1773 Hutchinson-Adams debate, the 1773 Tea Party (involving Hutchinson and Adams's kinsman Samuel), the 1773–1774 Hutchinson Letters Affair (again featuring Hutchinson, and radicalizing Franklin), the 1774 Coercive Acts (targeting Boston), and the 1775 battles that followed in Boston's environs. We today also know that Otis more than anyone else prompted the Stamp Act Congress, which foreshadowed the Continental Congress, which declared independence, which in turn led to state constitutions, the Articles of Confederation, the Northwest Ordinance, and the US Constitution. We know that Hutchinson more than anyone else epitomized the best of American loyalism on the eve of the Revolution. We know that Adams more than anyone else championed American independence in 1775–1776, penned a widely read essay in 1776 championing the bicameral and tripartite systems that came to dominate American state constitutionalism, and later helped midwife the Massachusetts Constitution of 1780—a constitution that ultimately provided key precedents and protocols for the US Constitution.

Because we today know all this, modern-day historians can trace certain threads backward even though history happens forward. It thus makes historical sense for today's storytellers to examine—with more care than did contemporaries—the first episode in which Otis, Hutchinson, and Adams were in a room together, to see if we can detect, with the benefit of hindsight, seeds of what was to come.

Yet hindsight can also hinder. If it sometimes prods us to see what contemporaries missed, it can also prompt us to miss what contemporaries saw—alternative histories that did not materialize but that might have materialized, or at least that contemporaries thought might well materialize. We today know that after New York said yes, but as the eleventh state to ratify the Constitution, North Carolina and Rhode Island did not stay out of the union for any dangerously long time period. We know that Anti-Federalists in the 1790s did not seethe and mobilize and intensify their challenge to central authority to the same extent that Otis and Adams and other patriots had seethed and mobilized and intensified in the 1760s and 1770s. We know that Indian tribes did not prevail in preventing White Americans from streaming into the Northwest in the Constitution's first decade. We know that Spain did not succeed in its schemes to break off Kentucky and Tennessee. We know that England and France did not immediately wage war against USA 2.0 in the hopes of regaining lost ground and lost glory. We know that the new American regime in the 1790s did not end in an orgy of blood, as did the new French regime in the same decade. We know that America's George did not use his military power and military prowess in the same way as did France's Napoleon.

Because we know all these things—because we often take for granted all these things—we are at risk of missing some of what happened and did not happen, and why, in the first few years under America's new Constitution.

What happened, briefly, is that America's Constitution stabilized itself and succeeded. Why? Not merely because it was a sensible system, but also because George Washington was at the helm to steady and steer the new ship of state.

THE BRANCHES OF THE CONSTITUTION's new central government materialized sequentially, in textual order.

First, the Congress created by Article I gathered in New York City, achieved House and Senate quorums in early April 1789, and commenced operation. Most of the new Congress's members were self-described "Federalists" or "friends of the Constitution"—men who had publicly supported the document in the preceding year.

Eight House members had served as constitutional draftsmen at Philadelphia, as had eleven senators. Anti-Federalists, some more outspoken than others, made up roughly a fifth of the total.[2]

The most momentous order of business for the fledgling Congress was to determine and declare the identity of America's new president under the rules of Article II. In the course of dissolving itself and making way for the new regime, the old Confederation Congress had provided that members of the Electoral College should meet separately in their home states on February 4. Sixty-nine presidential electors had participated and each participating elector had cast two equal votes—one for each of his two top choices. On April 6, Congress unsealed and counted the ballots. Acting as Senate president pro tempore, Senator John Langdon of New Hampshire announced the result: George Washington had received 69 electoral votes. In other words, every single elector had cast a vote for the Philadelphia Convention's presiding officer.[3]

In theory, because no elector could formally differentiate his two votes, Washington might have been every elector's distant second choice and no elector's true and easy first choice. Everyone in America knew otherwise. Washington won by acclamation, and was likely almost every elector's emphatic top pick. No other leader—it would be anachronistic to call anyone a *candidate*, since no one was openly running for this office—was named by even half of the 69 electors. John Adams received 34 votes—all or virtually all second-choice votes, though there was no formal way to designate this fact under the Constitution's rules. This respectable showing gave Adams the vice presidency. (Article II provided that the person who came in second in the presidential count would become vice president.) After Adams, no other American statesman received even double digits. John Jay was closest, with nine. No one gave a thought, or a vote, to Thomas Jefferson, Virginia's former governor who was now serving as an American diplomat in Paris. The only open opponent of the Constitution's ratification to receive any presidential support was New York's governor, George Clinton, who got three electoral votes.

On April 30, the new president took his prescribed oath of office, as set forth verbatim in Article II. The oath was administered on the balcony of New York's old City Hall—newly christened "Federal Hall"—by New York chancellor Robert R. Livingston. In 1765, Livingston's father (also Robert R.) had hosted the Stamp Act Congress in this same Manhattan edifice. The new president opted to swear his oath of office on a Bible, which was held in place by a ministerial employee of the Senate, Samuel Allyne Otis, younger brother of James Otis Jr.

Several months later, the Article III judicial branch took shape. On September 21 Congress enacted and on September 24 the president signed the Judiciary Act of 1789, specifying the number of Supreme Court and lower federal court positions to be filled. The Constitution had left these important numbers to be decided by statute. The act provided for a six-justice Supreme Court and thirteen lower federal court positions—one for each of the eleven states, plus one for Virginia's western district of Kentucky and another for Massachusetts's northern district of Maine. Later on the 24th, Washington, who had already done his prep work, nominated jurists to fill these posts. Over the next several days, the Senate voted to confirm the entire judicial slate. With only one exception (a district judgeship for Virginia's strongly Anti-Federalist Kentucky region), all the judges nominated by Washington and confirmed by the Senate were drawn from Federalist ranks. Led by Chief Justice John Jay and Associate Justice James Wilson, every member of the first Supreme Court had been a highly visible Federalist during the continental ratification conversation, as had most lower-court judges. No member of America's initial federal bench had voted against the Constitution in state convention.[4]

UNANIMOUS

After a year of intense continental conversation and fierce contestation, the unanimity of support for Washington in early 1789 was both welcome and stunning. Americans highlighted it at every turn, in conversations both private and public.

Senator Langdon's official letter of April 6 to Washington was short and to the point: "I have the honor to transmit to your Excellency the information of your unanimous election to the Office of President of the United States of America. Suffer me, Sir, to indulge the hope, that so auspicious a mark of public confidence will meet your approbation, and be considered as a sure pledge of the affection and support you are to expect from a free and an enlightened people." As a delegate to the 1787 Philadelphia Convention, Langdon had signed the Constitution alongside Washington, and his official letter to his Excellency was accompanied by a personal note from another former Philadelphia delegate and signer, Robert Morris, one of Pennsylvania's two inaugural senators. Morris had hosted Washington during the Philadelphia Convention and now offered his Philadelphia mansion as a resting spot for Washington on the president-elect's anticipated voyage from Mount Vernon to Manhattan: "I conclude that the unanimous voice of America is irresistible and that you will soon set out on your journey for this City."

Writing to Washington separately that same day, New Jersey senator Elias Boudinot also emphasized unanimity, viewing it as a sign from above: "I do most sincerely & affectionately congratulate my Country, on the unanimous election of your Excellency to the Presidency of the united States. The importance of this transaction, is so great in my estimation that I consider it, under Providence, as the key-Stone to our political Fabrick [*sic*—Russell would doubtless have approved of Boudinot's imagery and spelling]. . . . You have no choice in this great Business—Providence & your Country call, and there is no place for a refusal." A similar theme appeared in the oral remarks of Confederation secretary Charles Thompson, the messenger tasked with hand-delivering the official tidings to Washington: "You are called not only by the unanimous votes of the Electors but by the voice of America."[5]

Newspapers likewise underscored unanimity. "Yesterday . . . General WASHINGTON was found to have been unanimously chosen President, and John Adams, Esq. Vice President, by a plurality," reported the *New-York Daily Gazette*. Some printers gleefully stressed the point in capital letters. "His Excellency George Washington . . . was UNANIMOUSLY elected," sang the *New-York Weekly Museum*. Washington's election, trumpeted Russell's *Massachusetts Centinel*, was "UNANIMOUS in all the States."[6]

Secretary Thompson reached Washington's Mount Vernon estate with the news on April 14. Characteristically, Washington had prepared for this moment and indeed had already composed a draft inaugural address and laid plans for lodging in New York.[7] But perhaps he had not quite dared to envision so decisive a victory.[8] He declared to Thompson on the spot that "the unanimous suffrages" of his fellow citizens left him no choice but to say yes. Two days later, Washington bade adieu to his neighbors in Alexandria and shared with them his reasons for, once again, leaving their neighborhood. "The unanimity in the choice" reflected not only the support of the friends of the Constitution but also the "apparent wish" of its skeptics and open opponents—"those, who were not altogether satisfied with the Constitution in its' present form." If he, personally, was America's common denominator—the one thing Federalists and Antis could agree upon—perhaps he could be "instrumental in conciliating the good will of my countrymen towards each other."[9]

As he made his way up to New York City, feted by locals at every stop, Americans showered him with accolades and well wishes. Toasts abounded, many of them florid and, to modern ears, extravagant. One of the most astute and least gaseous salutes occurred in Baltimore on April 17: "We behold too, an extraordinary thing in the annals of mankind, a free and enlightened People chusing by a free election, without one dissenting voice, the late Commander in chief of their Armies, to watch over and guard their civil rights and privileges." Several days later, the scholars at Princeton saluted him in similar terms. Washington responded by reiterating what he had first told Thompson at Mount Vernon: "Upon perceiving the unanimous voice of my countrymen had called me to occupy the first office in confederated America, I could not hesitate to determine that it was my duty to obey that call."[10]

WHY WASHINGTON?

Literally and figuratively, George Washington towered above all alternatives in 1789. As his fellow citizens understood, he was an *energetic, experienced, geostrategic American republican* without equal. As they may or may not have appreciated—but as we today can now appreciate with the benefit of hindsight—Washington was also, to use a modern expression, media-savvy. He was himself both the product of America's emerging newspaper culture and a connoisseur of it.

CONSIDER FIRST THE ISSUES OF *energy* and *geostrategic experience*. America's constitutional commander in chief would need considerable vigor to launch an ambitious new legal regime and defend America's vital interests. The fifty-seven-year-old Washington still had some good years ahead of him. By contrast, octogenarian Benjamin Franklin was simply too ancient; born in 1706, Franklin would die less than a year after Washington's inauguration. Various younger leaders had vigor, but nothing close to Washington's blend of executive, military, and diplomatic experience. Jefferson and Jay, for example, were more than a decade junior to Washington. In 1789, these men were rather green.

Jefferson's detractors also thought him rather yellow. He had been an unsteady wartime governor, who had failed to fortify Virginia and mobilize its militia when the enemy approached, and then fled the capital in haste, allowing the British to capture weapons, ammunition, supplies, documents, and other valuables that should have been evacuated. Later he bolted from his Monticello estate and left the state leaderless for more than a week at a particularly parlous time. After his governorship, he went off to Paris as an American diplomat, but could not claim credit for much there. Franklin, Adams, and Jay had negotiated and signed the Treaty of Paris long before Jefferson's arrival.

Jay had no military or gubernatorial experience, and what diplomatic experience he could claim under the Confederation was mixed. The Treaty of Paris was a stunning triumph, but it was more Franklin's triumph as senior strategist. When negotiating on his own with Spain in 1786, Jay had been gulled into giving up American claims to use the Mississippi River for a quarter century in exchange for immediate trade concessions that would benefit New England fishermen. The Confederation Congress predictably and sensibly declined to ratify Jay's deal, but the Spanish in the process had given southwestern Americans reason to doubt the trustworthiness of northeasterners—all part of Spain's long-term strategy of prying loose America's backcountry.

In fairness, Jefferson's disgrace stemmed in part from larger flaws in the structure of executive power under Virginia's constitution, much as Jay's debacle reflected the weaknesses of American power under the Confederation. Washington, too, had suffered multiple military embarrassments because of American impotence. But Washington had responded with extraordinary physical courage, organizational discipline, republican rectitude, stoic perseverance, military cunning, tactical cleverness, and strategic vision. These gifts had enabled him to avoid annihilation in New York, boost morale at Trenton and Princeton, endure Valley Forge, rally his men at Monmouth, and ultimately triumph at Yorktown.

More generally, Washington was a far abler and more experienced diplomatist than the likes of Jefferson and Jay. Jefferson leaned too far toward the French, Jay toward the English. Washington by 1789 understood that America needed to avoid dependence on any nation, howsoever friendly that nation might seem at any given moment. From his earliest days, he had seen most of America's military rivals up close and with a keen eye. Starting in his early twenties, he had fought alongside various Indian tribes and against them, alongside the British and against them, against the French and alongside them. True, he had made diplomatic blunders. (His first one, at age twenty-two, was a doozy—it had triggered a world war.) But he had learned from his own mistakes and from others' mistakes, and by 1789 he had become a master of international affairs and related military matters. If the first job of America's president was to protect America from European reconquest—and that was, indeed, the president's first job in 1789—Washington was obviously the right man for that job. No one else came close.[11]

John Adams, born in 1735, was proximate in age to Washington, but nowhere near him in the mix of capabilities he could offer. Adams lacked military experience. He had no deep familiarity with Indian tribes. He had never served as a state governor. (Neither had Washington, but he had shown impressive managerial skill in running his bustling plantation and far-flung investment properties and in serving as the administrative head of a vast army.) Adams had worked hard as a diplomat, was fiercely loyal to America, and was far less vulnerable to diplomatic blandishment than Jefferson or Jay. But Adams was also flawed as a diplomat; his biggest problem was that he was so thoroughly . . . undiplomatic. He lacked both self-mastery and tact. Washington, by contrast, was the embodiment of public self-control, official decorum, and civic politesse.

In an early 1783 letter, written in cipher to confidant James Madison, Jefferson—then still a friend of Adams, before the two men fell out in the 1790s—put the point tartly: "The newspapers must be wrong when they say that Mr. Adams, had taken up his [French] abode with Dr. Franklin. I am nearly at a loss to judge how he will act in the negotiation. He hates Franklin, he hates Jay, he hates the French, he hates the English. To whom will he adhere?"[12]

The answer, of course, was that Adams would always adhere to America. But so would Washington, and Washington had much more to offer.

CONSIDER NEXT THE WAYS IN which Washington stood as an *American republican* without peer.

Republicanism American-style wove together several threads. At a minimum, Revolutionary republicans opposed military, autocratic, aristocratic, and dynastic rule. More affirmatively, they embraced popular self-government, civilian supremacy, rights protection, the rule of law, birth equality, impartial meritocracy, civic sacrifice, and patriotic virtue.

The seventeenth-century English philosopher Thomas Hobbes had famously argued that anarchy was the worst human condition imaginable—a war of all against all in which human life was "solitary, poor, nasty, brutish, and short." Compared to that, even a domineering and arbitrary hereditary monarch was better, so long as he maintained basic order internally and kept his subjects safe from external attack.[13]

American Revolutionaries rejected this bleak vision. They sampled from a sumptuous smorgasbord of theorists: John Locke; Algernon Sidney; James Harrington; English levelers led by John Lilburne; commonwealth pamphleteers such as John Trenchard and Thomas Gordon; Scottish Enlightenment figures including David Hume, Adam Smith, Thomas Reid, and Francis Hutcheson; and many more. Revolutionaries also built on more than a century and a half of de facto self-rule in the New World. In homegrown assemblies, juries, militias, town meetings, and other local democratic structures, Americans had made countless day-to-day, life-and-death decisions over many years without strong supervision from faraway London. This New World history inspired Revolutionaries to believe that ordinary folk were indeed capable of governing themselves without dynastic monarchs and hereditary lords directing their every move. Patriots thus wanted a leader who could protect them against King George without himself becoming a King George.

On this issue, even conservative American Revolutionaries stood with Thomas Paine. Slavery aside, no state embraced hereditary rule, and many state constitutions explicitly condemned the idea.[14] The Massachusetts Constitution of 1780 put the point pugnaciously, thanks, perhaps, to the pen of John Adams: "Title being in nature neither hereditary nor transmissible to children or descendants or relations by blood; the idea of a man born a magistrate, lawgiver, or judge is absurd and unnatural." The Confederation had imposed almost no limits on internal matters of governance within each then sovereign state, with one notable exception: no state could award hereditary titles of nobility. The Constitution repeated this ban and deepened it by requiring that each state government maintain its "republican form"—language that perfectly intermeshed with the contemporaneously drafted Northwest Ordinance, which required that all fledgling states in this vast backcountry quadrant "shall be republican." So, too, the Constitution prohibited the federal government from creating a hereditary nobility.

Many unrepublican Old World monarchs and militaries ruled by force, fear, and greed. In the worst of such regimes, unelected autocrats pursued their own self-interest and personal profit, saddled the populace with heavy taxes that had never been democratically authorized, maintained power via standing armies of paid (and perhaps foreign) mercenaries and corrupt civilian networks of bribery and patronage, and then handed off power to their offspring. Soldiers killed and cowed civilians, while civil officials fleeced the populace and lined their own pockets. Law did not matter, or if it did, it was routinely bent to favor rich and powerful insiders. Judges were merely puppets and lackeys of the unelected autocrats in charge.

Proper republics, by contrast, depended on widespread civic virtue, citizen participation, and patriotism. In the best of such regimes, common folk informed themselves about politics, especially by reading newspapers; deliberated in good faith with their fellow citizens; voted in free and fair elections, with the aim of choosing the most able and virtuous; willingly obeyed democratically enacted laws, including tax laws; participated in juries and militias when summoned; and staffed elective and appointed positions of public service when called to do so by their fellow citizens.

George Washington's entire life showed that he embraced and honored republican principles. In 1775, he had left the comforts of home to risk everything for the Revolution and had accepted no payment for his services—only reimbursement for actual expenses.[15] During the war, he had scrupulously honored Congress's commands, even when Congress had been foolish and feckless. As a true republican, he understood that to do otherwise would be to lose the war even were he to win every battle. The war was a crusade for republicanism, and winning meant that republican principles must triumph. Proper republicans believed in civilian supremacy, democratic legitimacy, and free elections—in the force of law and not the law of force.

Not only did General Washington never try to stage a military coup himself, but he successfully suppressed other officers' incipient efforts to use the army to intimidate civilian authorities. He understood, both intellectually and viscerally, that the men who served in arms with him had legitimate grievances. They had not been paid as promised, and they were not receiving the support they needed to defend America. Still, the proper republican recourse was to petition Congress or the courts, not to march on lawmakers with loaded guns and veiled threats.[16]

When the war ended and he commanded the only effective army on the continent, Washington had not named himself King (as had William the Conqueror) or Lord Protector (as had Oliver Cromwell) or Emperor (as had Augustus Caesar and as would Napoleon). Rather, in the tradition of the acclaimed Roman patrician Lucius Quinctius Cincinnatus, Washington had dismissed his troops, resigned his military commission, and returned home to resume private life. Such a man, Americans believed, could be trusted with the presidency.[17]

Some of the language in the April 1789 conversation between George Washington and his well-wishers—the repeated invocations of "a free and an enlightened people," the multiple references to his obligation to accept the "call" of service (even if he preferred a comfortable retirement), and the emphatic assurances that he could expect "the affection and support" of those who had summoned him to serve—might seem stilted to modern readers. These were standard republican refrains circa 1789.

Washington thus had what all others, even the second-place Adams, lacked: an unparalleled record of patriotic sacrifice and republican self-restraint. He also lacked what some others, especially the second-place Adams, had: a son and namesake who might yearn for the chair he would now occupy.

Tellingly, only one of the first nine presidential elections crowned a man with a (legitimate, openly acknowledged) son. The only exception, John Adams, is the only man who won but a single term. That man's son and namesake, John Quincy Adams, did indeed yearn for, and ultimately win, the chair his father once occupied. Apart from John Adams, no early president had a son or even a younger brother who went on to hold high office. Washington was a perfect fit to become father of his country because he was not a father of any children of his own, children who might tempt him to stray from the narrow path of republican rectitude and impartiality.*

In keeping with the themes of patriotism, duty, and sacrifice that he repeatedly and publicly sounded during his two-week journey from Mount Vernon to Manhattan in April 1789, Washington's Inaugural Address had originally included a pointedly personal republican reference to fatherhood and the fatherland—to paternity and patriotism. He could be trusted, he wrote, because he would not play favorites. He was politically uninterested in a throne, he explained, because he was personally disinterested; he had no one to give it to when he was gone. Elias Boudinot and Charles Thompson had told him that America's unanimity was providential. So, too, Washington mused, was his own personal family situation: "Divine Providence hath not seen fit, that my blood should be transmitted or my name perpetuated by the endearing, though sometimes seducing channel of immediate offspring. I have no child for whom I could wish to make a provision—no family to build in greatness upon my Country's

---

*On the other hand, Jefferson had a son-in-law who became Virginia's governor, and another son-in-law who served in both House and Senate; Adams, too, had a son-in-law who served in Congress. Dynastic forces also pulsed through many of the original thirteen states prior to 1825. In a typical state, at least four governors were strong sires with one or more sons, younger brothers, and/or sons-in-law who went on to hold high political positions. For the eye-opening names and numbers, see this chapter's addendum, pp. 323–326.

On a related front: When some chapters of the Society of the Cincinnati, an honorific association formed by Revolutionary War officers, persisted in maintaining their fraternity on a hereditary footing, Washington distanced himself from the organization.

ruins. . . . [No] earthly consideration beyond the hope of rendering some little service to our parent Country . . . could have persuaded me to accept this appointment."[18]

Washington was a reserved and disciplined man—a classical stoic in many ways—and he ultimately decided to omit this highly emotional and personal passage. Perhaps it was just as well. His fellow citizens did not really need this reminder. In the great constitutional conversation of 1787–1788, closely related dynastic issues had in fact been publicly ventilated.

The Anti-Federalist essayist "Federal Farmer" worried that "when a man shall get the chair, who may be re-elected, from time to time, for life, his greatest object will be to keep it; to gain friends and votes, at any rate [i.e., price]; to associate some favourite son with himself, to take the office after him: whenever he shall have any prospect of continuing the office in himself and family, he will spare no artifice, no address, and no exertions."[19]

Countering this concern about "favourite son[s]" and presidential reeligibility under Article II, Federalists emphasized another aspect of Article II—its requirement that a president be at least thirty-five years old. In language reminiscent of Paine's *Common Sense*, one Federalist essayist reminded readers that Britain's king "is hereditary, and may be an idiot, a knave, or a tyrant by nature." By contrast, America's president "cannot be an idiot, [and] probably not a knave or tyrant, for those whom nature makes so discover [i.e., reveal] it before the age of thirty-five, until which period he cannot be elected." In other words, the Constitution prevented Americans in a passing moment of weakness from crowning some untested youngster who was the apple of his presidential father's eye. Only middle-aged leaders with republican track records of their own successes and failures would be eligible for the presidency.[20]

EDWARD SAVAGE'S FAMOUS PAINTING OF the First Family circa 1790 nicely captured these republican themes.

In this painting, Washington, long and still strong, appears in dress uniform. A consummate horseman—perhaps America's best, in his prime[21]—he presents himself to us wearing riding boots and spurs. But he is not astride a rearing horse. He is not waving a sword or rallying his troops. He is a republican general at home, at peace, beside his vine and fig tree.

Geostrategic themes subtly present themselves. A globe is at hand. The flooring suggests a chessboard, perhaps reminding viewers of strategic concerns that could never be far from Washington's active mind, even when he might seem to be at rest.

A map of the new federal city in the works—what we today call "Washington, DC"—unfurls on the center table and spills over the edge. America is literally building new federal edifices in a way that Russell had foreshadowed.

George's wife, Martha, gentles the portrait with her domestic elegance, counterbalancing the military and political motifs. Washington's adopted step-grandchildren—Eleanor Parke Custis and George

Washington Parke Custis—further domesticate the scene. They bear the last name and the blood of Martha's late first husband, Daniel Parke Custis, whose early death had made her a young widow in 1757. A year and a half later, she married George, who adopted her two young children. Although both Custis children died young— one in 1773, the other in 1781—grandchildren remain to brighten life, and the youngest two surely brighten the portrait.

But there is something missing in this stiff depiction of the Washington family, in which no one makes eye contact. The missing something is both sad and inspiring. There is no true son in this picture, no true heir in the room. At the glorious center there is the rising sun (not son) and the open air (not heir) of America's expansive future. Behold, says the artist: here is a portrait of a man with no son, a truly republican man, father of none and thus father of all, a man whose personal future is, providentially, America's future.*

THERE IS ALSO A LIVERIED slave in the room—probably William Lee, later freed. Was he, too, part of the Washington family? What should we make of him? What would he think of us, and of the other persons in the portrait?

We shall return to these questions later—to the story of Lee's enslavement and eventual emancipation, and to larger issues of American slavery—but for now let us explore one closely related aspect of the case for George Washington in 1789. Washington was a Virginian, and that was important. Even more important, he was an American, far more than anyone else.

---

*Madison's notes of the Philadelphia Convention closed with an elegant anecdote: "Whilst the last members were signing it [the parchment] Doctr. Franklin looking towards the President's Chair, at the back of which a rising sun happened to be painted, observed to a few members near him, that Painters had found it difficult to distinguish in their art a rising from a setting sun. 'I have,' said he, 'often and often in the course of the Session, and the vicissitudes of my hopes and fears as to its issue, looked at that behind the President without being able to tell whether it was rising or setting. But now at length I have the happiness to know that it is a rising and not a setting Sun.'" *Farrand's Records*, 2:648 (Sept. 17).

In 1789, Virginia saw itself as the quintessential American state, the center of American gravity. So it was in many ways. To see this clearly, we must overcome certain modern hindsight biases. No one in 1789 could know (what we now know) that in 1861, Virginia would ultimately and treasonously side with the extremist pro-slavery South—one mere section of the union, and the losing section at that, in a civil war that pitted most of the North and the West against Virginia and its truly reactionary southern sisters. Even though Virginia would position itself out of the republican mainstream in 1861, it was within the mainstream—indeed, in many ways it *was* the mainstream—in 1789.

Yes, Virginia was a slave state in 1789, but so was New York. So was New Jersey. Slaves accounted for about 14 percent of New York's population, and roughly 8 percent of New Jersey's. Maryland and Delaware also had substantial slave populations in 1789, and indeed, both would remain slave states at the outbreak of the Civil War; but both would choose to adhere to the loyal free states to their north rather than join the treasonous slave states to their south. Virginia for much of its history was not entirely different.

Following the pre-1789 lead of Massachusetts and Pennsylvania and several other states north of the Mason-Dixon line, New York and New Jersey would begin to phase out slavery in the 1790s and early 1800s. In 1789, many were betting that Virginia would eventually do the same. Virginia in 1789 differed sharply from South Carolina. While the Deep South's leaders openly crusaded for slavery, Virginia's greatest statesmen criticized human bondage both publicly and privately. In 1782, the commonwealth enacted legislation to ease private manumission, and in the mid-1780s Virginia's Congressional delegates championed free-soil rules for the Northwest Territory. Two years after Washington's inauguration, the College of William & Mary, following in the footsteps of Harvard and Brown, conferred an honorary degree on the famed British abolitionist Granville Sharp.[22]

Founding-era Virginians were, metaphorically, lifelong smokers who wanted to quit. Indeed, they almost did. As late as the 1830s, Virginia would see notable efforts—which generated serious legislative and newspaper debate but ultimately failed—to begin an abolition process.[23] Even in 1861, Virginia would hesitate before plunging into folly, joining the Confederacy well after its Deep South sisters.

We must also remember that in 1789, Virginia included modern-day Kentucky and West Virginia, both of which would remain loyal to the Union throughout the Civil War. In short, we must remember that Virginia in 1789 was indeed precisely in America's middle—the state where North met South met West. Virginia's backcountry spiked northwest of neighboring Pittsburgh, and the tip of its needle came close to touching Lake Erie. Prior to Virginia's cession in the 1780s, modern-day Ohio was, in Virginia's eyes, northwestern Virginia.

Virginians had led the American Revolution alongside the men of Massachusetts. Unlike Virginia, Massachusetts did not see itself in 1789, nor was it seen by its sisters, as the modal state even if it was in many respects the model state. Massachusetts was too northern, too eastern. It was the head of the snake, perhaps, not its midsection. No one at the Founding could seriously think that the North met the South somewhere between Springfield and Hartford or that the New York–bordering portion of Massachusetts was the quintessential West.

Indeed, the *westernmost* point of the Bay State lay more than a hundred miles east of the Old Dominion's *easternmost* tip. The entities that we today call the "northern states" were at the Founding more commonly designated the "eastern states."[24] In Franklin's original incarnation and in all its various copies, the snake's New England head was depicted as due east, not north, of its Virginia midsection and its Carolinian tail. America's West at the time of Washington's election was ultimately all about Indians, Spain, the Mississippi, and New Orleans. Virginia and its Kentucky district were the keys to the continent, not Massachusetts and its Maine district.

The significance of the West went beyond the obvious and enormous fact that new western states would soon join the union on an equal footing with their eastern sisters, thanks to the Northwest Ordinance and to southwestern spin-off states (with Kentucky breaking off from Virginia in 1792 and Tennessee from North Carolina in 1796). Within most of the thirteen original states, power was also flowing west, fast. Revolutionary-era apportionment systems in state after state gave more seats to growing western and backcountry districts than had their colonial predecessors. The shifting locations of state capitals also reflected Americans' westward population flow. Between 1785 and 1800, Pennsylvanians moved their state seat from Philadelphia to Lancaster, North Carolinians from New Bern to Raleigh, South Carolinians from Charlestown to Columbia, and Georgians from Savannah to Louisville. Notably, Virginia itself was the trendsetter, having relocated its capital from Williamsburg to Richmond, some forty miles west, in 1780.[25]

Post–Stamp Act Virginians had talked a good game about being Americans first and Virginians second. Sometimes it was just talk. Patrick Henry was Exhibit A. Like James Otis Jr., Henry was an orator, a rhetorician. But he was not a deep thinker, not a man of truly global vision. At his best, he was entertaining and inspirational; at his worst, demagogic. In the opening hours of the First Continental Congress in 1774, Henry had grandly proclaimed that "the Distinctions between Virginians, Pennsylvanians, New Yorkers and New Englanders, are no more. I am not a Virginian, but an American." But he had made this majestic announcement in a self-serving cause, arguing that Virginia should have more votes than other colonies at that conclave: "It would be great Injustice, if a little Colony should have the same Weight in the Councils of America, as a great one." He had a good point, but precedent weighed against him: the Stamp Act Congress had operated on the principle of one colony, one vote. Henry oddly declared that "this was the first general Congress which had ever happened." Perhaps he meant that the Stamp Act Congress didn't count as a proper precedent because Virginia wasn't in the room at that conclave. But was he saying this as an American or as a Virginian?[26]

In 1788, Henry had the chance to choose, and he chose Virginia, fighting the proposed Constitution tooth and nail precisely because, in his words at the Richmond Convention, the envisioned "government is not a Virginian, but an American government." This was the exact antithesis of what he had said in 1774. Both times, he had played to the crowd, but he had blown hot and cold—as blowhards are wont to do.[27]

Henry was hugely popular in Virginia, but there was at least one Virginian every bit as popular, and that Virginian, unlike Henry, had unwaveringly been an American first, and not just selectively, self-servingly, and rhetorically. That Virginian was of course George Washington. He personally was an embodiment of all regions. He, singularly, was where North met South met West. In that respect he was the truest Virginian and truest American of all, once we clear away our hindsight bias that sees 1789 Virginia merely as southern.

Washington had spent more time in America's rough western backcountry, and from his earliest days as an adult, than had any other leading statesman on the continent. He could see eye to eye with a man like Daniel Boone. (The two had met in the run-up to the French and Indian War. Back then, the strapping Washington was even more rugged and physically impressive than the not-yet-legendary Boone.) In the mid-1780s, Washington had spent considerable time and money investigating ways of interlinking East and West with a canal system that, ideally, would connect Mount Vernon, via the Potomac, to the Ohio and Great Kanawha river basins, where he owned vast tracts of raw land. By contrast, most leading eastern statesmen had not even once crossed the Appalachians. What did, say, John Adams or John Jay truly know about the Forks of the Ohio or the bluegrass of Kentucky? Even Jefferson, a Virginian who spent much of his time looking west both literally and figuratively, never ventured beyond the Shenandoah Valley.[28]

Washington had also spent far more time in the North than had any other leading southerner. Indeed, he had saved the North and liberated Boston in the early days of the Revolution. On his arrival in Cambridge in the summer of 1775, his initial reaction to the locals had been harsh and provincial. In a letter to a kinsman, he referred to the mass of northern men now under his command as "an exceeding dirty & nasty people."[29] But as he came to work closely with impressive northerners—men like New Englander Henry Knox, a former bookseller whose Yankee ingenuity brilliantly got cannons all the way from Ticonderoga to Dorchester Heights, where Washington put them to good use—the Virginia general grew to respect, admire, and even love northern men and their region. Jefferson, by contrast, had lived in Paris, but in 1789 knew rather little firsthand of New York and New England.[30]

Washington had also spent time far south of Virginia. As a young man he had sailed to the West Indies. Neither Adams nor Jay—nor Jefferson for that matter—had done the same.

Again, we must remember that even though Virginia chose to side with the Carolinas and Georgia in 1861, Virginia in 1789 often saw itself more as a middle state than a southern state.[31] The regions south of Virginia were quite different from Virginia itself. South Carolina and the West Indies, in particular, were entirely different, and much more deadly for laborers. Upper South tobacco farming did not kill and waste slaves at the prodigious rate that sugar, rice, and indigo production did in the brutish, snake-infested, and disease-ridden Deep South.[32]

In the Richmond Convention, Madison's discussion of the international slave trade positioned Virginia as a middle state. When he spoke of "southern states" at this ratification conclave, he meant states south of Virginia.[33] On slavery itself, Virginia in the mid-1780s often allied with states to its south, but on banning slave imports, it sided with states to its north, for reasons of both principle and protectionism. Morally, the international slave trade was particularly heinous, involving as it did the brutal murder and enslavement of peaceful freeborn folk in Africa and the hellish transportation of these helpless captives to the New World in putrid and pestilential transatlantic death-ships. Economically, Virginia's less lethal version of slavery produced more slaves than the Old Dominion could use. Virginia masters in effect bred slaves and sold the surplus to states farther south. International slave imports lowered the price Virginians could command in this domestic interstate market.

America, in short, was a vast land, and Washington understood the lay of that land, and the various local dispositions of its inhabitants, far better than other leaders. He understood America's land as a military strategist must, because he was indeed such a strategist. (In 1777 he warned Brigadier General Thomas Nelson Jr. against stationing American troops near Yorktown. Because of the "narrow neck of land" in that peninsula, he said, soldiers positioned there "would be in danger of being cut off." In 1781, Washington and the French put British troops into the very trap he himself had avoided years earlier.) But he also understood land as a farmer might, for he was himself a farmer, or as a land speculator might, for he was that, too—and before that, a professional surveyor. In Lockean terms, Washington had mixed his labor with the American land in many different ways and many different places.[34]

He had also intertwined his life with the most truly continental entity that had ever existed. That entity was not, despite its label, the Continental Congress, or its successor, the Confederation Congress. These Congresses were akin to international assemblies of ambassadors, controlled by their home governments parochially pursuing local interests. Nor were America's colleges the dominant institutions of national assimilation that they would one day become. Harvard and Yale did not draw strongly from all regions, nor did any other school, except perhaps the College of New Jersey at Princeton, closer as it was to America's middle and closer to Virginia in particular. In any event, these academic mixing bowls were minute. A typical college graduating class consisted of two dozen students, if that.[35] The most truly continental entity was the Continental Army, and the most truly continental person was that army's commander in chief.

AFTER THE WAR, THIS RETIRED commander in chief became America's correspondent in chief, carrying on a more robust and geographically dispersed series of conversations, by letter, than anyone else, with the possible exception of Jefferson. Washington's epistolary correspondents were akin to twenty-first-century newspaper and television correspondents. They were Washington's eyes and ears beyond Mount Vernon, offering him intelligence about goings-on across the land. They summarized local news and often attached clippings or pamphlets. When Washington pumped them for more information, they obliged, much as military scouts might when doing good reconnaissance.[36]

George III and his minions had lost America in part because they lacked intelligence, in multiple senses of the word. They did not read or heed American newspapers.[37] Washington did, and did long before he became president. He was a prodigious reader of and subscriber to newspapers from all points on the map and all points on the ideological spectrum.

He was personally connected to—invested in, in various ways—many localities. For example, events in the West would affect the value of his vast backcountry landholdings. He thus had financial as well as political reasons for following western news with care.

Having saved Massachusetts in the war, Washington also took a personal interest in its fate. In 1786 and 1787, he closely followed reports about Shays' Rebellion in the western part of the Bay State. Modern historians have often stressed this unrest as a major catalyst of the Philadelphia Convention, but most narrators have missed important nuances. Washington was a strong and public nationalist long before 1786, as were most of the men who prevailed at Philadelphia. They did not need Shays' revolt to persuade them of the need for a stronger central system. If we insist on finding a last straw somewhere in the year 1786, we should attend to New York as well as Massachusetts, as did proto-Federalists at the time. In mid-1786, New York lawmakers rejected a desperately needed impost amendment to the Articles and thereby proved beyond doubt that the Confederation could never work, given its impossible requirement of unanimity for any amendment.[38] (Thanks to its exceptional Manhattan seaport, New York in the mid-1780s siphoned off significant revenue from European imports ultimately destined for New Jersey and Connecticut residents. New Yorkers selfishly resisted sharing the wealth with Congress, even though Congress was of course responsible for defending New York and all other states against European, Canadian, and Indian adversaries.*)

When we do turn our gaze to western Massachusetts, we should try to see it through Washington's eyes. Creditors' rights were surely part of the picture, but Washington saw the matter more holistically, through a more republican and geostrategic lens. The upheaval suggested that American republicanism was failing, that mobbers were now trying to shut down courts that, *unlike the courts of the 1760s and early 1770s, operated with judges chosen democratically, pursuant to the Massachusetts Constitution of 1780.* Contrary to republican principles, Shaysites were not earnestly seeking to obey laws that the people themselves had authorized. (Samuel Adams, as emphatic a Revolutionary Republican as ever lived, sharply condemned Shays' uprising. In the words of a leading Adams biographer, the old firebrand of the 1760s and 1770s saw the new disturbance as "a Tory effort to undermine the Revolution."[39])

Most ominously of all, perhaps the uprising was backed by British-Canadian forces seeking to destabilize America. Even if Britain was not behind it, wouldn't the rebellion encourage British geostrategic designs? Why should Britain give up its northwestern fortifications if America's northwestern backcountry was in tumult and turmoil?

In a November 1786 letter to Madison, Washington passed along alarming intelligence from Knox suggesting that Shays' rebels sought to "annihilate all debts public & private" via a scheme of "unfunded paper money." If the Shaysites prevailed, creditors who had lent out hard currency and bargained for repayment in the same coin would

---

*The dramatic contrast between New York's 1786 rejection of a small augmentation of central power and its ultimate 1788 acceptance (by a single vote) of the Constitution's much larger augmentation illustrates the cleverness of Article VII and Article V, compared to the Confederation's unanimity rule. Article VII pushed New York away from obstructionism and toward constructive engagement, because the Constitution would go into effect with or without the state; and Article V softened the blow by reassuring New Yorkers that sensible amendments could be added later, if New York ratified in a yes-but Massachusetts manner.

instead be forced to accept worthless paper—a prospect that offended Washington's sense of justice and fair dealing.[40]

But Washington had larger concerns: "No Morn ever dawned more favourable than ours did—and no day was ever more clouded than the present! . . . Without some alteration in our political creed, the superstructure we have been seven years raising at the expence of much blood and treasure, must fall. We are fast verging to anarchy & confusion!" Washington then repeated to Madison the gloomy estimates he had received from Knox: "The numbers of these people [rebels] amount in Massachusetts to about one fifth part of several populous Counties, and to them may be collected, people of similar sentiments from the States of Rhode Island, Connecticut, & New Hampshire so as to constitute a body of twelve or fifteen thousand desperate, and unprincipled men. They are chiefly of the young & active part of the Community." A description like this surely alarmed a military man such as Washington, who knew firsthand what fifteen thousand "desperate, and unprincipled . . . young & active" men could do, if mobilized in arms and well led.[41]

"How melancholy is the reflection that in so short a space," Washington lamented to Madison, "we should have made such large strides towards fulfilling the prediction of our transatlantic foes!—'leave them to themselves, and their government will soon dissolve.'" Meanwhile, a financially strapped Congress could offer no military assistance to the beleaguered Massachusetts government, even though British Canada would likely exploit the situation: "Thirteen Sovereignties pulling against each other, and all tugging at the fœderal head, will soon bring ruin on the whole; whereas a liberal, and energetic Constitution, well guarded & closely watched, to prevent incroachments, might restore us to that degree of respectability & consequence, to which we had a fair claim, & the brightest prospect of attaining."[42]

In a letter sent to Knox in late December, Washington elaborated his larger geostrategic concerns:

That G.B. [Great Britain] will be an unconcerned spectator of the present [Shaysite] insurrections (if they continue) is not to be expected. That she is at this moment sowing the Seeds of jealousy & discontent among the various tribes of Indians on our frontier admits of no doubt, in my mind. And that she will improve every opportunity to foment the spirit of turbulence within the bowels of the United States, with a view of distracting our governments, & promoting divisions, is, with me, not less certain. Her first Manœuvres will, no doubt, be covert, and may remain so till the period shall arrive when a decided line of conduct may avail her. Charges of violating the treaty, & other pretexts, will not then be wanting to colour overt acts, tending to effect the great objects of which she has long been in labour.[43]

AMERICA'S CONSTITUTIONAL CONVERSATION TOOK MANY forms in the 1770s and 1780s—grand oratory and public declamation, Patrick Henry–style; less florid public discourse, as in the Massachusetts Ratifying Convention; high-stakes debates and horse trades behind closed doors, as at Philadelphia; informal mealtime conversations, as when John Adams began to discover America; terse state constitutions in direct discourse with each other; elite newspaper essays; elaborate pamphlets; short squibs; cartoons; poems; performance art; public toasts; and much more. In most of these arenas, Washington did not truly stand out. He was not a rousing orator. (Late in life, he may have worried that if he opened his mouth too wide, his dentures might pop out.) He said little in public debate, and he did not routinely pen long and influential tracts like *Common Sense* or *The Federalist*. He was not a clever cartoonist or a brilliant performance artist.

Washington was, however, a conversationalist *par excellence* in his correspondence—one on one, with men he could trust, scattered widely across the continent (and across the Atlantic, thanks to pen pals such as the Marquis de Lafayette and the Comte de Rochambeau). While he often said more in these private letters than he would say publicly, much of his genius was that he was an outstanding *listener*.

He absorbed information well. It takes two to converse—a speaker and a listener. Adams loved to talk, but often failed to listen. Jefferson wore ideological blinders, and routinely took in only what he wanted to take in. Washington excelled at soliciting and processing advice and information from a broad range of sources. At the Philadelphia Convention, he was indeed the listener in chief.[44]

He was also a genius at press relations. He instinctively grasped the importance of newspapers and publicity long before many of his contemporaries—though not, of course, before Franklin. (Franklin saw most things before others did.) As a teenager, Franklin was already getting his own pieces published in his brother's newspaper, by hook or by crook. Similarly, Washington at the age of twenty-two was composing and, with official encouragement, making public his own accounts of his western adventures. (Here, too—as a backwoods chronicler—he surpassed Boone, a contemporary who did not publish his frontier exploits until after the Revolutionary War.) In mid-1754, readers in Boston, New York, and Philadelphia were all reading, simultaneously, about this intrepid young Virginian. More than fifty newspaper items by or about Washington appeared that year, in at least seven distinct publications outside his home state: the *Pennsylvania Journal*, the *Boston News-Letter*, Franklin's *Pennsylvania Gazette*, the *New-York Mercury*, the *Boston Gazette*, the *Boston Post-Boy*, and the *Boston Evening-Post*.[45] Indeed, one of these accounts appeared exactly in conjunction with the first appearances of Franklin's snake in May 1754. Press coverage about the young Virginian continued over the next several years, as the world war in America's backcountry dragged on. Prior to 1760, few if any other young Americans succeeded in getting their names mentioned and their deeds discussed so often in newspapers across the continent.

As John Adams aged, the Braintree lawyer found it hard to lag so far behind the world hero—especially when Adams recalled that he himself had helped launch Washington. (In the wake of Concord and Lexington, Adams quite rightly had backed Washington over John Hancock and all others for command of the Continental

Army.) Adams himself was an exceedingly ambitious Yankee who had read countless more books about law, history, government, politics, and philosophy than had Washington. But Washington towered over Adams in 1789, and not merely because George was a tall, opulent Virginian and John was a dumpy New Englander of more middling means.

At a particularly cranky moment in 1814, Adams asked, "Would Washington have ever been Commander of The Revolutionary Army, or President of The United States, if he had not married the rich Widow of Mr Custis?"[46] We cannot know the answer to this envy-drenched counterfactual, but we can say this: young Washington came to the attention of the rich and good-natured Martha Custis because, while still in his twenties, he had come to the attention of all America. He had done so not because of any especially famous birth name or vast inherited wealth. The Washingtons did not occupy the very highest rung of the infinitely graduated Virginia hierarchy. George was not by blood a Randolph, Lee, Carter, Byrd, or Fairfax.[47] Washington had come to national prominence by dint of his own merits—his muscular courage, his military prowess, and also his media savvy. Otis had craved the world's attention in the 1761 writs case, but no one outside Boston was watching. Adams himself was a proverbial fly on the wall at age twenty-five. But in his early twenties Washington had already shown flashes of brilliance, and that brilliance included a gift for self-presentation and subtle self-promotion. (Trumbull and Washington would later make a nice pair in this respect, forming a symbiotic relationship in which the painter made the hero look good and the hero made the painter look good.)

WITH THE BENEFIT OF HINDSIGHT, we can see that all the great founding fathers were early sires and children of America's emerging newspaper culture. By modern consensus, history's "Big Six" founders are America's first four presidents—Washington, Adams, Jefferson, and Madison—plus Franklin and Hamilton.

Franklin was a self-made printer and popular writer who amassed a fortune before age forty by creating what we would today call a media empire—a string of affiliated print shops and paper mills across the continent.[48] Hamilton published his first notable newspaper piece, a compelling description of a tropical hurricane, while a mere lad in the West Indies. This was his first big break in life—the vivid piece of prose brought him to the attention of patrons who financed his emigration to the mainland. While still a college student, he then published precocious patriot pamphlets and newspaper essays that eventually helped bring him alongside Washington as the general's scribe and right hand.[49] Thereafter he went on to become a newspaperman extraordinaire, as exemplified by his brilliant performance as Publius and in scores of other essays before and after, published under a dizzying array of pen names: Continentalist, Phocion, H.G., T.L., An American, Civis, Amicus, Fact, Catullus, Metullus, Plain Honest Man, Pacificus, Philo Pacificus, No Jacobin, Americanus, Tully, Camillus, Philo Camillus, Horatius, Americus, Titus Manlius, Lucius Crassus, Pericles, and perhaps more. In his mid-thirties Madison teamed up with Hamilton in newspapers, and in his early forties Madison turned against Hamilton in newspapers. In one six-month period in 1791–1792, the Virginia politico produced some fifteen short pseudonymous essays for a single newspaper, Philip Freneau's *National Gazette*.[50] Before his debut on the national stage, Madison had brilliantly championed religious freedom in his home state via a punchy and anonymous printed circular, his acclaimed "Memorial and Remonstrance."[51] After returning from France, Jefferson quietly created a partisan newspaper network of his own, partly financed with other people's money—a masterstroke. Long before that, in his early thirties, Jefferson had published an important 1774 pamphlet articulating the dominion theory of empire. Writing as "Novanglus," Adams published similar newspaper pieces making similar arguments at about the same time, building on prior newspaper submissions stretching back to the mid-1760s, when the Braintree lawyer was still in his late twenties.[52] Jefferson, Adams, and Franklin of course also crafted the Declaration as a poetic and punchy piece for newspaper distribution. To sum up: five of the big six were newspaper scribblers, early and often.

Although not members of history's Big Six, the early judiciary's two brightest stars, John Jay and James Wilson, were likewise popular penmen and newspaper darlings. Jay formed one-third of the Publius trio and made particularly important contributions to the opening set of essays, which were generally more influential than the essays that followed. He also published an important pamphlet of his own during the ratification process. In 1774, Wilson, then in his early thirties, published the leading colonial essay on the dominion theory of empire. (Jefferson and Adams later followed suit.) In 1787–1788, Wilson's arguments in support of the Constitution were widely recirculated by print shops everywhere—more so, even, than the essays of Publius—both in newspapers and in pamphlet form.[53]

Washington might at first seem the odd man out, because he did not write nearly so much for public consumption about the great constitutional issues of his era after the onset of the imperial crisis in the early 1760s. He was not a printer (like Franklin), a lawyer (like Adams, Jefferson, Hamilton, Jay, and Wilson), or an amateur scholar (like all of the above, plus Madison). Rather, Washington was a gentleman surveyor-planter-entrepreneur-investor-soldier-administrator. In 1775–1776, he could not devote himself to legal and political theorizing because he was attending to other matters of some importance. In 1788, he maintained an official silence and let his chief lieutenants, whom he quietly encouraged and abetted—Hamilton, Madison, Wilson, Randolph, and Marshall—make the public case for the document that reflected his vision more than anyone else's.[54]

On closer inspection, Washington was in fact as much a newspaperman as the others—probably a more prodigious newspaper reader, though doubtless a less prolific newspaper writer. Throughout his career, he proved himself exquisitely attentive, as he had been since 1754—when Adams was an unknown, Jefferson a mere schoolboy, Madison a toddler, and Hamilton perhaps a fetus—to his public image in America's increasingly continental press.

PROMISES KEPT

Immediately after taking his oath of office, Washington spoke. He kept his remarks short—in part, it is fair to surmise, so that these remarks could be widely and fully reprinted in newspapers. In the 1790s, America boasted more newspapers per capita than any other country in the world, and several leading printers were now issuing editions daily. Federalist-era Americans noticed this remarkable fact about themselves and swelled with pride. In launching a New York daily in 1793, *The American Minerva*, devoted to "Peace, Commerce, and the Liberal Arts," Noah Webster positively beamed. "In no country on earth, not even in Great Britain, are Newspapers so generally circulated among the body of the people."[55]

Washington's inaugural remarks were indeed quickly published in more than three dozen American print shops from New Hampshire to Georgia. Washington's initial draft had run to some seventy-three manuscript pages. Although it would not have worked as well as a newspaper item, it did contain a remarkable aside about Washington's relationship to newspapers: "During and since the Session of the Convention, I have attentively heard and read every oral & printed information on both sides of the question that could be procured." In private correspondence several months earlier, Washington had said the same thing to Hamilton: "I have read every performance which has been printed on one side and the other of the great question lately agitated (so far as I have been able to obtain them)."[56]

Unlike England's George, America's George was listening to America, reading as much as he could, scouring "every [!]" piece of "printed information" he could find, and, tellingly, pondering speeches and writings "on both sides of the [ratification] question." Washington himself had been emphatically on one side—the yes side—but he understood there was another side, and further understood that there were many honorable people and many honorable arguments on that side.

Yet people on both sides had evidently voted for him. When bidding farewell to his Alexandria neighbors, he had hinted that because those "who were not altogether satisfied with the Constitution in its' present form" had apparently cast their ballots for him, perhaps he might be "instrumental in conciliating the good will of my country-men towards each other." Washington's Inaugural Address was his first official step toward that hoped-for conciliation.

Much of the address was what one would expect from a classic republican of stoic sensibility. Despite his own "anxieties" about his "inferior" abilities, especially in his "declining years," and his lack of experience in "civil administration," he was now reporting for "duty," having once again been "summoned by my Country, whose voice I can never hear but with veneration and love." Washington proceeded to thank the Almighty; to offer to serve without salary;[57] to praise the new Congress as men of "rectitude" and "patriotism"; and to remind his audience of the epic significance of the moment at hand, in which "the American people" might well determine "the destiny of the Republican model of Government" for all the world.

In the middle of the address, Washington began conversing with the gathered members of Congress about one particular part of the Constitution that, fittingly, was itself all about presidential-Congressional conversation: "By the article establishing the Executive Department, it is made the duty of the President 'to recommend to your consideration, such measures as he shall judge necessary and expedient.'" In Washington's long initial draft, he had included his ideas about various pieces of legislation that Congress should consider, much as presidents do today in their grab-bag State of the Union addresses. He ultimately decided to stay mum on the great mass of laws that had to be passed. He simply referred his Congressional audience to "the Great Constitutional Charter under which you are assembled; and which, in defining your powers, designates the objects to which your attention is to be given."

Then came the edgiest passage, in which Washington urged Congress to consider adopting a bill of rights by way of constitutional amendment. This exhortation—the most substantive part of the address and the only blockbuster news item—has posed a puzzle for some modern readers. Whereas Article I provides that every ordinary piece of Congressional legislation must cross the president's desk for signature or veto, Article V gives the president no similar role in the constitutional amendment process. Proposed constitutional amendments in effect go directly from Congress to the states for ratification; two-thirds of each house of Congress must say yes, as must three-quarters of the states, but the president has no say. Puzzlingly, Washington said virtually nothing about ordinary laws, where he did have a formal role to play, via the veto, yet spoke out on the topic of constitutional amendments, where he had no formal veto role.

On closer examination, Washington's seemingly odd detour was not at all odd, nor was it truly a detour. Washington grasped that his most important role under the Constitution's letter and spirit was to keep the union together. Proper and properly timed amendments might do just that—keep America together by showing skeptics and critics that their voices had indeed been heard, that the promises made in ratification conventions (whose proceedings Washington had carefully followed) would be redeemed, not ignored.

In offering his thoughts on the matter, Washington took care not to overstep. Surely, even though he had no formal role under Article V, he had a right to have an opinion. Surely, just as everyone else in America (or so it seemed) had weighed in over the previous year, so might he now do so, having kept quiet until this inaugural moment of high drama (much as he had kept quiet until the dramatic finale at Philadelphia). Surely, the Constitution's Recommendation Clause technically permitted him to opine on virtually any public topic— after all, his words were mere recommendations, nothing more. In effect, Washington saw his role here as conversation-facilitator in chief and conciliator in chief, in keeping with his musings at Alexandria.

Washington began the key passage with a deferential bow to both Congress and the voice of America that he had heard in the preceding year:

Besides the ordinary objects submitted to your care, it will remain with your judgment to decide, how far an exercise of the occasional [amendment] power delegated by the Fifth article of the Constitution is rendered expedient at the present juncture by the nature of objections which have been urged against the System, or by the degree of inquietude which has given birth to them. Instead of undertaking particular recommendations on this subject, in which I could be guided by no lights derived from official opportunities, I shall again give way to my entire confidence in your discernment and pursuit of the public good.

In short, Washington was not proposing "particular" provisions. As at Philadelphia, he would leave the details to others. Rather, he was defining a national agenda of conversation, putting amendments at the top of that agenda, and explaining why he was putting them there. During the ratification process, "objections . . . [had] been urged against the System," and these objections had given rise to a "degree of inquietude." A prudent Congress should not ignore these objections and that inquietude. Hutchinson had ignored objections and inquietude; so had George III; so had the British Parliament. Things had not ended well for them. Congress, Washington quietly suggested, might profit from their example.

Washington concluded this section by hinting at what might be the sweet spot for national reconciliation, a compromise that would preserve the Federalists' big ideas while assuaging the most reasonable Anti-Federalist concerns. Congress should allow the basic framework of the new plan, including the federal legislature's broad tax powers and the federal judiciary's strong powers to oversee disobedient states, to operate without modification. But Congress should propose a bill of rights, à la state bills setting forth the "characteristic rights of freemen," and any other provisions that might promote harmony without undermining federal supremacy and efficacy: "I assure myself that whilst you carefully avoid every alteration which might endanger the benefits of an United and effective Government, or which ought to await the future lessons of experience; a reverence for the characteristic rights of freemen, and a regard for the public harmony, will sufficiently influence your deliberations on the question how far the former can be more impregnably fortified, or the latter be safely and advantageously promoted." This proposed compromise had taken shape in Washington's mind over many months, as evidenced by the fragments that remain of his earliest draft address.[58]

Over the next couple of years, the amendment process unfolded in a manner that followed Washington's broad outline. On June 8, Congressman James Madison introduced a series of proposed amendments, new texts that Madison proposed be interwoven into various different Articles of the original Constitution. After digesting these proposals, a House committee reported to the full House in late July. In late August, the House agreed to seventeen proposed amendments. Rather than weaving these new rules into the original document, as Madison had suggested, the House proposed to append these amendments to the end of the Philadelphia document as a series of sequential postscripts. The Senate rejected some provisions and reorganized others. On September 25, 1789, Congress, acting by the requisite two-thirds of each house, agreed to send twelve proposed amendments to the states for ratification. On December 15, 1791, Virginia became the eleventh state to ratify proposed Amendments III–XII, thereby making these the first ten amendments to the US Constitution. (Congress's first proposed amendment never received sufficient state support, and its second proposed amendment only received enough yes votes much later in American history.)

At the time of Virginia's ratification, the union had fourteen states—the eleven that were in USA 2.0 when Washington gave his address, plus three new states that joined in the interim: North Carolina, Rhode Island, and Vermont. All the new states said yes to proposed Amendments III–XII. Today, these first ten amendments are widely known as America's "Bill of Rights," even though that phrase does not formally appear anywhere in the constitutional text as proposed and ratified.

IF AMERICA, MORE THAN THOMAS Jefferson, wrote the Declaration of Independence, and if America, more than Madison, wrote the Constitution, then did America, more than Madison, write the Bill of Rights?

Yes. The Bill of Rights was not Madison's brainchild, nor was it even Washington's, originally—though both men eventually came to see the light. Madison, Washington, and almost all the other Philadelphia signers had squarely rejected George Mason's proposal to include a bill of rights in their plan. This was an enormous political blunder. Americans everywhere had grown to esteem state bills of rights, which had emerged organically from a fertile national conversation at the dawn of the Revolution. These state bills of rights were emblematic features of pre-1787 state constitutions, ranking high among the best and most popular state practices. When the Philadelphia delegates unveiled their proposed Constitution after a long summer of secrecy, the absence of a proper bill of rights quickly became one of the Anti-Federalists' two best talking points. (The other large and incisive Anti-Federalist complaint was that the House of Representatives was far too small—too small to begin with, and not guaranteed to grow quickly.)

A written bill of rights as an integral part of a written constitution was thus *America's* baby, born in 1776 and baptized in 1788. In that baptismal year, the Philadelphia plan had squeaked through several states only thanks to a yes-but ratification process in which various Federalists had smartly swiveled and signaled a willingness to consider reasonable amendments. Then, in early 1789, Madison himself won election to Congress only by promising his constituents, in open letters (two of which prominently appeared in the local press), that he would champion a bill of rights. Had he broken this promise in the First Congress, his constituents might not have been forgiving. In all this, we once again see at work the spirit of America more than the singular genius of James Madison.[59]

Madison was hardly unique. All House members in 1789 would face reelection soon enough, precisely because the Constitution itself was fundamentally democratic—more so than the Articles, which did not require direct election of Congress members. We should re-call that the Constitution's direct-election rules had themselves been written by the spirit of America at Philadelphia. Without its prom-ised direct election of House members, the Constitution would never have stood a chance of winning ratification, and every draftsman at Philadelphia had understood that. The spirit of America hovering over the Philadelphia conclave had also obliged the delegates to in-clude an Article V option to bypass Congress in the amendment pro-cess. Members of the First Congress understood that if they failed to propose a plausible set of amendments, states under Article V could call for a new amendment-proposing convention that would fill the void, and Congress would lose control over the matter.[60]

Washington's Inaugural Address made it harder still for Con-gress to avoid the issue of a bill of rights. Amendments were now on America's conversational agenda and at any moment, Washington could issue yet another "recommendation" reminding Congress of this issue and, in effect, appealing to American public opinion.

Geostrategically, Washington aimed not just to ease disquiet among Anti-Federalists already in the union, but also to woo Anti-Federalists now outside the union to rejoin the United States. Without Rhode Island and North Carolina, the new United States had gaping flanks that made the new nation vulnerable to potential European attack, should either flanking jurisdiction, especially North Carolina, embrace an Old World patron. Short of this worst-case sce-nario, one way for the new Congress to pry open foreign markets for American goods and American ships would be to close all American ports to discriminatory foreign regimes. Here, tiny Rhode Island actu-ally loomed large. A sweeping port-blocking strategy might collapse if European goods flooded into Newport or Providence and from there illegally flowed into New York or Boston.

A sensible package of amendments would be an olive branch to holdout states—a sign that their concerns had found receptive ears, that there was room in the tent for them, even though they were entering late. Without regard to the substance of the amendments themselves, the very fact of proposed amendments would enable

Anti-Federalists in North Carolina and Rhode Island who had opposed ratification in 1788 to about-face while saving face. Tellingly, in September 1789, Congress sent out thirteen copies of its proposed amendments, taking care to include North Carolina and Rhode Island, even though these regimes were, strictly speaking, outside the union. The amendments were an engraved re-invitation.

The re-invitation worked. In August 1788, a North Carolina Convention meeting in Hillsborough had withheld its assent from the original proposed Constitution by a lopsided vote of 184–84. (Back then, Russell chose not to run any cartoon marking this disappointment.) Less than sixteen months later, on November 21, 1789, a North Carolina Ratifying Convention meeting in Fayetteville accepted the olive branch by an even more lopsided vote, 194–77. A month later, the state legislature approved all twelve proposed Congressional amendments. In the spring of 1790, Rhode Island's convention narrowly ratified the Constitution, 34–32, and the state legislature then endorsed all except Congress's initial second amendment. The following year, Vermont joined the union as America's fourteenth state and agreed to all of Congress's proposed amendments.

In the end, events proved Russell, Publius, Franklin, and Washington right. Thanks to a solid foundation of American popular sovereignty, all thirteen of Russell's pillars (and indeed, a fourteenth) did indeed rise. Franklin's snake was now complete. Unanimity ultimately prevailed—but not via Article XIII of the Articles of Confederation, which had in effect demanded the impossible. Rather, unanimity came about via the kinetic interaction of no less than four of the Constitution's seven Articles. The Constitution's system worked beautifully, and indeed worked as a Publian system. First, in 1787–1788, Article VII enabled the ship to launch with any nine states, and its companion Article V facilitated a yes-but ratification process. This clever combination got the first eleven states on board. The following year, Article II encouraged Washington to make sensible recommendations based on the voice of the American people and Publian geostrategy, while Article I wonderfully concentrated the minds of members of Congress who would have to answer to their constituents at the next election. (The prospect of an Article V amendment-proposing convention that could grab the ship's wheel if Congress dawdled provided additional mind-concentration.) This clever combination got the straggler states on board.

A QUICK SURVEY OF THE substance of these amendments confirms their American authorship and paternity. Most of their provisions—affirming rights of expression, religion, privacy, property, and procedure—had previously appeared in embryo in state constitutions and/or in the amendment ideas voiced by popularly elected state ratification conventions in 1788: yes, but. As in 1787, when the delegates in Philadelphia had drafted the Constitution by sorting, digesting, considering, and compiling best state practices among existing state constitutions, so now, in 1789, the congressmen in New York sifted more than originated.[61]

The locution that appeared more than any other in the first ten amendments was "the people"—a nice example of the recapitulation phenomenon, in which the *process* by which a legal idea springs to life often influences the *substantive* shape of the resultant ideas. The Bill of Rights in effect was conceived in the 1788 ratification process by the American people themselves—the Preamble's vaunted "We the People." In that process, special conventions of the people had unsurprisingly echoed state constitutions with popular roots, especially the Massachusetts Constitution of 1780, but also precursor state constitutions that had aimed in 1776 to mobilize popular support for revolutionary new state governments.

In the federal Bill of Rights, the First Amendment explicitly affirmed a right of "the people" to assemble, much as the people had indeed assembled in state conventions to put various amendment ideas into circulation. The Ninth and Tenth Amendments spoke of rights "retained" by and "reserved" to "the people"—including, paradigmatically, the right of the people to alter governments by adding new amendments, like the Ninth and Tenth Amendments themselves. The Second Amendment celebrated the right of "the people" to participate in civic militias representative of the citizenry, and the Fourth obliquely hinted at the role of citizen juries representing "the people." (Such juries in civil cases would help decide which sorts of government searches and seizures would be deemed reasonable and thus constitutional.) These broad ideas came not from the mind of one man or from the minds of a small group of men in the First Congress, but from the entire American conversation as it had been ripening since the accession of George III. (The Fourth Amendment's rules about searches, seizures, and civil juries had particularly notable roots in the debates in the early 1760s about writs of assistance in America and Wilkesite general warrants in England.)

Madison did try to sneak in a big original idea of his own, an amendment that would have limited *state and local* interference with basic rights of religion, expression, and jury trial. No state ratifying convention had proposed a federal amendment limiting states or localities. Madison's darling amendment predictably failed, even though he deemed it "the most valuable" on his list.[62] It fit perfectly with his own farsighted ideas in *The Federalist* No. 10 that minority rights required careful protection and that small jurisdictions, such as states, posed a greater risk to such rights than did large jurisdictions, such as the federal government. In effect, the proposal was a slimmed-down version of his failed Philadelphia idea—yet again, he sought to stabilize state governments from above, this time by giving the federal courts a Privy Council–like veto over certain specified types of state law. But he was swimming against the tide. Amendment ideas in the 1788 ratification process had largely come from Anti-Federalists concerned about the federal government as a distinct threat to liberty. All the amendments as proposed in 1789 and adopted in 1791 limited the federal government and only the federal government. (That would change later in American history, but only after a civil war occasioned by state misconduct.)

Madison also lost on an intriguing stylistic question. He had wanted to thread amendments into the Constitution's original text.

Other leading members of Congress insisted on a different style—tacking on amendments as seriatim postscripts—and Madison reluctantly relented. Just as Jefferson had been seriously edited by fellow members of Congress in 1776, so now Madison. Neither man loved the editing process—few authors do—but both times the collective editors were arguably wiser than the individual penmen. Jefferson's draft Declaration contained confused ideas about slavery and moral culpability, and Madison's draft amendment package was arguably less powerful than the final version. By gathering all the amendments in the same textual neighborhood, rather than scattering them throughout the document, and by putting them all in a place of particular prominence—immediately after the original text—the First Congress in effect did more than add rights to the Constitution. Congress added a *Bill* of Rights, a conspicuous and coherent cluster that more closely tracked the bundled configurations of state constitutional bills of rights, which in turn had distilled the voice of America herself.

The initial ordering of the proposed amendments that emerged from the First Congress had little to do with their intrinsic importance or relative rank. Rather, because Madison originally aimed to weave amendments into the Constitution's main text, he sequenced his proposed textual changes to track the textual order of the original Constitution; and that sequence survived even after the weaving strategy was rejected. Thus a (failed) amendment modifying Congressional size came first simply because that issue appeared first in the original Constitution—in Article I, section 2, to be specific. Then came a proposed amendment (also not ratified in the 1790s) modifying the rules of Congressional salary, a topic addressed in Article I, section 6. Next came a series of amendments (beginning with the famous opening line of the first amendment to be ratified—*our* First Amendment—that "Congress shall make no law . . .") limiting Congressional powers (modifying Article I, sections 8 and 9). After that (beginning with our Fifth Amendment) came provisions concerning the general operations of the federal judiciary (modifying Article III). Finally, Congress added a pair of concluding proposals at the very end of the list (our

Ninth and Tenth Amendments) setting forth some global rules of interpretation applicable to the entire constitutional text.[63]

IF MADISON DID NOT GET all or even most of what he wanted, he was not alone. The Anti-Federalists likewise did not get all or even most of what they were hoping for—major revisions of federal power to tax individuals and to oversee state courts. The amendments that emerged fell in Washington's sweet spot, amendments that both Federalists and Anti-Federalists could live with, amendments in effect designed to *consolidate* and *clarify* the Constitution while *conciliating* its most reasonable critics.

In keeping with Anti-Federalist ideology, several amendments did sound in states' rights—but softly, in ways that Federalists could cheerfully accept. The Tenth Amendment reminded Americans that certain powers not given federal officials were "reserved to the states." This amendment openly borrowed both words and themes of Article II of the Articles of Confederation, while avoiding that Article's two big embarrassments: nowhere did the amendment say that states were fully "sovereign," and nowhere did it insist that Congress was limited to "express" powers.* Powers that were not expressly enumerated but were nevertheless fairly implied by the Constitution as a whole were legitimate. Here was the sweet spot: Anti-Federalist states' rights blended with Federalist implied powers. States would continue to play a special role, but were no longer sovereign in the strictest sense.

The First Amendment (which had initially been third on the proposed list) likewise affirmed states' rights. Congress could "make no law respecting" certain religious matters. Article I had given Congress power to "make all laws" on certain topics, but not on the topic

---

*Article II of the Confederation read as follows: "Each state retains its sovereignty, freedom, and independence, and every power, jurisdiction, and right, which is not by this Confederation expressly delegated to the United States, in Congress assembled." The Tenth Amendment, by contrast, provided that "the powers not delegated to the United States by the Constitution, nor prohibited by it to the States, are reserved to the States respectively, or to the people."

of religion, a domain largely left to states. By invoking and inverting Article I's "make all laws" language with its "make no law" phraseology, the First Amendment clarified that Congress simply had no Article I express or implied power to make law "respecting" religious practices as such—no power to regulate religion for religious reasons. (Secular laws regulating conduct for secular reasons were entirely different, even if such laws might incidentally affect religious practice. As John Dickinson's "Federal Farmer" essays had made clear years before, legislative purpose mattered. For example, a Congressional revenue law taxing all imported alcoholic beverages in order to fatten the treasury would be valid even if it had the incidental and unintended effect of raising the price of sacramental wine.)

Several other amendments also sounded in federalism and states' rights, alongside citizens' rights. The Second Amendment celebrated local militias as republican bulwarks, and several other amendments likewise safeguarded the militia's cousin, the jury. Juries and militias were both *local* institutions of republican participation—militia service and jury service were twin rights and duties of virtuous citizens, organized at a town and county level. The Fifth Amendment championed criminal grand juries; the Sixth Amendment, criminal trial juries; the Seventh Amendment, civil trial juries. Civil juries also played a key role in the Fourth Amendment. When citizens brought tort suits against Customs House officials and other federal actors for alleged abuses, local civil juries would help judges decide what governmental searches and seizures were unreasonable and thus unconstitutional. (Although Otis had misstated the law in his 1761 oral argument— local juries back then could sanction any Customs House official who searched on a whim and came up empty—Parliament in later years had troublingly revised its customs laws to limit jury involvement.)

THE BILL OF RIGHTS CAME from the people and spoke of the people. So, too, it had bubbled up from a great constitutional *conversation*, and much of its substance recapitulatingly reinforced various aspects of the right of constitutional conversation itself. Not all its provisions did so. There was nothing particularly conversational about the Fifth Amendment's right to receive just compensation when private property was taken for government use, or the Eighth Amendment's right to be free from excessive fines. But many other provisions were indeed all about constitutional conversation.

The First Amendment affirmed core conversational rights of speech, press, petition, and assembly. The Fourth Amendment's letter and spirit offered special safeguards against searches aimed at "papers" as distinct from other items. Personal papers surely fell into this category, but so did political newspapers like the *North Briton* No. 45, which had been the object of the infamous dragnet search in Britain's Wilkes litigation. Multiple provisions protecting juries aimed to preserve these institutions as special arenas of citizen conversation and deliberation. For example, grand juries had inherent authority to issue public reports and "presentments" condemning errant government officials or any other miscreants. Much like speeches on the floor of Congress, these words issuing from grand juries would be entirely free from the threat of libel suits. Civil and criminal trial juries were likewise themselves important sites of citizen conversation, and these institutions in turn had at times protected conversational rights of publishers—most notably in a 1730s New York seditious libel case involving the anti-government printer John Peter Zenger. The criminal jury in that case had refused to convict the printer, thus striking a blow for free expression. Grand juries had also at times famously shielded printers by refusing to approve seditious-libel indictments. The most celebrated recent examples involved the ubiquitous Hutchinson, who in the early 1770s had tried to use seditious libel law to suppress scurrilous criticism of his administration, only to be met with grand-jury defiance.[64]

Even the Second Amendment had a conversational angle. Militias, like juries, were venues of republican engagement among presumptively equal citizens. Whereas unthinking, unblinking army soldiers (who might indeed not even be citizens) were expected to simply follow orders from on high, citizen militiamen elected their leaders, who were typically local politicians. Any militia officer who abused his authority would likely pay a political price when the fighting was over. Whereas typical professional soldiers might serve in the army for life, temporary amateur militiamen came from civil society and would soon return to civil society. The conversational norms of republican equality in civil society recurred within a militia more so than in the army. In celebrating the role of militias, the Second Amendment was thus celebrating a conversational social structure.

ENACTING THE BILL OF RIGHTS redeemed one of the two biggest vows that Federalists had made in the yes-but ratification process. Under Washington's watchful eye, the fledgling government also kept the Federalists' other big ratification promise: to grow the House as fast as possible. On September 25, 1789, Congress proposed a constitutional amendment—the very first one on the list of a dozen amendments submitted for state ratification—textualizing the Federalists' 1788 commitment of one House member for every thirty thousand constituents for the near future. Although the amendment fell short in the ratification process, Congress had shown its good faith by proposing it, and even without a formal amendment in place, the Congress under Washington essentially did as pledged. In April 1792, after the results of the 1790 census became available, Congress enacted, and Washington signed, a bill that increased the House size to more than a hundred members, just as Caleb Strong, George Nicholas, Alexander Hamilton, and many other Federalists in 1788 had guaranteed.[65]

After that, there was no going back in the early republic. Even without a formal amendment, Congress continued to vote for House increases after each decennial census. Any diminution in House size would have created a musical-chairs game guaranteeing the defeat of one or more incumbents. As a matter of both public relations and political self-interest, it was far better for the early Congress to add seats, fast. Thus the House after the 1800 census swelled to 141 members, and after the 1810 census it ballooned to 181 members—more than thrice the size of the House on its opening day in

1789. Although nothing in the Constitution's naked text compelled these dramatic expansions, the promises made during the ratification period powerfully supplemented the text and helped drive America toward a federal lower house that more closely resembled its state counterparts.[66]

BEYOND THE ORAL ASSURANCES OFFERED by the Federalists in 1788, the text of the Philadelphia plan itself made sweeping promises: of a "more perfect union" that would better secure the old Confederation's main goal of "common defence," and that would additionally promote "liberty," "justice," "tranquility," and the "general welfare." No one man, howsoever heroic—not even the great George Washington—could hope to redeem all these promises by himself.

Washington chose an extraordinarily talented group of Revolutionary characters to populate the new government—John Jay and James Wilson to lead the judiciary, plus Thomas Jefferson, Alexander Hamilton, Henry Knox, and Edmund Randolph to fill the most important executive-branch posts. Washington also relied on James Madison to lead the House, while Vice President John Adams chaired the Senate. When these eight spirited stallions pulled together, as they did at the outset, Washington enjoyed the carriage ride.

But not for long. As Washington aged and those around him began to imagine what America would and should look like post-Washington, the scene changed. The judiciary took steps to assert formal independence from the executive branch. Jefferson and Hamilton feuded with rising ferocity. Madison, attentive to his political base in Virginia, allied with Jefferson and increasingly opposed Washington's and Hamilton's proposals and policies.

Washington was Virginia's and America's past and present, but might Jefferson be the future? Where would this leave Adams and Hamilton, who surely had ambitions of their own? In short, what would happen to America's Constitution as its leading man and alter ego started to drift toward his inevitable exit, and the new nation's other most lustrous founding statesmen started to drift apart?

ADDENDUM: GUBERNATORIAL DYNASTS IN THE THIRTEEN ORIGINAL STATES PRIOR TO 1825

General criteria: Compiled from multiple sources, this tally lists politically high-rising sons, "younger" brothers, and sons-in-law of state chief executives from north to south. Asterisks indicate state dynasts who left their state chief executive chairs before the commencement of America's presidency.

New Hampshire: President John Sullivan's younger brother James became governor of neighboring Massachusetts, and his son George served in Congress. Governor Josiah Bartlett's son and namesake likewise served in Congress. Governor John Taylor Gilman's younger brother Nicholas served in both houses of Congress. Governor Jeremiah Smith's younger brother Samuel served in Congress. Governor William Plumer's son and namesake likewise served in Congress. Governor Samuel Bell's brother John served as governor—though John was chronologically older, he was politically younger, serving as governor several years after Samuel—and Samuel's son James served as senator. Governor Levi Woodbury's son-in-law Montgomery Blair served as President's Lincoln's postmaster general. *Total: seven dynasts, nine direct political heirs.*

Massachusetts: Governor Levi Lincoln's son and namesake served as governor and in other high positions, and his son Enoch served as a member of Congress from Massachusetts and Maine (formerly a district of Massachusetts) and as governor of Maine. *Total: one dynast, two direct political heirs.*

Rhode Island: Governor William Greene Jr.* (himself the son of colonial governor William Greene Sr.) had a son, Ray, who served as senator. Governor Arthur Fenner's son James served as senator and governor. *Total: two dynasts, two direct political heirs.*

Connecticut: Governor Jonathan Trumbull's* son and namesake (not to be confused with his brother John, the painter) served in both houses of Congress and as governor. Governor Matthew Griswold's* son Roger served in Congress and as governor. Governor Samuel Huntington's nephew and adopted son Samuel H. served as Ohio governor (whose Western Reserve region was once part of Connecticut). Governor Oliver Wolcott (himself the son of colonial governor Roger Wolcott) had a son and namesake who served as treasury secretary and governor. *Total: four dynasts, four direct political heirs.*

New York: Governor Daniel Tompkins's younger brother Caleb served in Congress. Governor DeWitt Clinton (himself the nephew of Governor George Clinton) had a younger brother, George Jr., and a much younger half brother, James Graham, both of whom served in Congress. *Total: two dynasts, three direct political heirs.*

New Jersey: Governor William Livingston (himself the younger brother of Declaration-signer Philip Livingston) had a son, H. Brockholst, who served on the US Supreme Court, and a son-in-law, John Jay, who served as US chief justice and governor of neighboring New York. Governor William Sanford Pennington's son William served as governor and Speaker of the US House of Representatives. Governor Mahlon Dickerson's much younger brother, Philemon, served in Congress and as governor and in other high posts. *Total: three dynasts, four direct political heirs.*

Pennsylvania: President John Dickinson* (himself the son-in-law of Assembly Speaker Isaac Norris) had a younger brother, Philemon, who served as a senator from neighboring New Jersey. President Benjamin Franklin's* acknowledged son William had previously served as royal governor of colonial New Jersey. Governor Thomas McKean appointed his son Joseph state attorney general. Governor William Findlay's chronologically older but politically younger brother John served in Congress after his governorship; his younger brother James served as a congressman from neighboring Ohio; and his son-in-law Francis R. Shunk served as governor. *Total: four dynasts, six direct political heirs.*

Delaware: President John Dickinson* (himself the son-in-law of Assembly Speaker Isaac Norris) had a younger brother, Philemon, who served as a senator from neighboring New Jersey. President Nicholas Van Dyke's* son and namesake served as state attorney general and in both houses of Congress. Ditto for Governor Joshua Clayton's son Thomas. Governor Daniel Rodney's younger brother Caleb served as governor, and his son George served in Congress. *Total: four dynasts, five direct political heirs.*

Maryland: Governor Thomas Sim Lee's son John served in Congress. Governor John Eager Howard's son George served as governor, and another son, Benjamin Chew, served in Congress. Governor George Plater's son Thomas served in Congress. Governor Charles Carnan Ridgely's son-in-law George Howard served as governor. *Total: four dynasts, five direct political heirs.*

Virginia: Governor Patrick Henry's* son-in-law Spencer Roane served as a justice on the Virginia Supreme Court. Governor Thomas Jefferson's* son-in-law Thomas Mann Randolph Jr. served in Congress and as governor; another son-in-law (and nephew), John Wayles Eppes, served in both houses of Congress. Governor Thomas Nelson Jr.* (himself the son of William, who had served briefly as colonial governor) had a son, Hugh, who served in Congress. Governor Benjamin Harrison V's* son William Henry served in the House and Senate, as territorial governor of Indiana, and as president, and another son, Carter Bassett, served in Congress. Governor Henry ("Light Horse Harry") Lee's son Robert E. Lee served as the Confederacy's leading general; Henry's younger brother Charles served as US attorney general and secretary of state; and another younger brother, Richard Bland, served in Congress. Governor William H. Cabell's son Edward Carrington served in Congress. Governor John Tyler's son and namesake served as governor, House member, senator, vice president, and president. Governor James Barbour's younger brother Philip Pendleton served as US Speaker of the House and on the US Supreme Court. Governor Wilson Cary Nicholas's younger brother John served in Congress. Governor James Patton Preston's son William served in Congress and as secretary of the navy and later as Confederate senator. Governor Thomas Mann Randolph Jr. (himself Jefferson's son-in-law) had a son, George Wythe, who served as Confederate secretary of war. *Total: eleven dynasts, fifteen direct political heirs.*

North Carolina: Governor Richard Dobbs Spaight's son and namesake served in Congress and as governor. Governor Samuel Ashe's son John Baptista served in Congress and was elected governor but did not serve. Governor James Turner's son Daniel served in Congress. Governor Jesse Franklin's younger brother Meshack served in Congress. *Total: four dynasts, four direct political heirs.*

South Carolina: President/Governor John Rutledge's* younger brother Edward served as governor, and John's son and namesake served in Congress. President Rawlins Lowndes's* sons Thomas and William served in Congress. Governor Charles Pinckney's son Henry served in Congress, and his son-in-law Robert Hayne served as senator and governor. Governor Andrew Pickens's son Francis Wilkinson served in Congress and as governor. Governor Thomas Bennett's adopted son Christopher Gustavus Memminger served as Confederate treasury secretary. Governor Richard Irvin Manning's son John Laurance served as governor. *Total: six dynasts, nine direct political heirs.*

Georgia: President Archibald Bulloch's* son William Bellinger served in the Senate. Governor Edward Telfair's son Thomas served in Congress. Governor James Jackson's son Jabez Young served in Congress. *Total: three dynasts, three direct political heirs.*

— eight —

HAMILTON

BETWEEN 1760 AND 1776, AMERICA'S constitutional conversation revolved around unwritten constitutional rules and
principles of the British Empire. Over the next decade and a half,
the conversation moved to a different level: What should American constitutions—state, territorial, and federal—say and do? After
the enactment of the federal Constitution and its initial round of
ratification-inspired amendments, the fundamental nature of the
conversation shifted yet again.

The main issue was no longer (as in Part I of this book) what *Britain's unwritten Constitution could be construed or revised to say*; nor was
it (as in Part II) what *America's written constitutions should be drafted
to say*. The main issue, from this point until the Civil War, was what
America's Constitution did in fact say on this topic or that one. The
new conversation focused tightly, as the old conversation had not, on
interpreting the letter and spirit of a terse, recent, homegrown, and
popularly enacted continental text.

It would be impossible to trace all the significant constitutional
discourse that took place in the Constitution's first half century. We

shall thus pay particular attention to those specific American constitutional conversations that most directly implicated the very idea of American constitutional conversation itself and that touched upon the most basic questions about that conversation. Specifically, *who* participated in the interpretive conversation? *How* did participants do interpretation? *Where* was this conversation geographically centered? And *what* were the looming threats imperiling the very existence and integrity of the ongoing constitutional conversation?

The answers that emerged during and shortly after the Washington administration shaped the American constitutional experience for the entire antebellum era. Many institutions and individuals joined the conversation: all three departments of the federal government; both branches of the federal legislature; cabinet members among themselves and with the president within the executive branch; juries alongside judges within the judiciary; circuit jurists in the hinterlands as well as Supreme Court justices in the capital; state governments, too; and the American citizenry more generally on the pages of newspapers, in public galleries, at the ballot box, and elsewhere. Leading framers—those who had played an outsized role in the drafting and ratification process—loomed especially large in the new regime's opening years. Interpretation by these framers and others who joined them in conversation and contestation typically and properly centered on the enacted text and overall structure of the written Constitution—on what We the People had in fact agreed to when saying yes, but to the Philadelphia plan in 1787–1788 and yes, please to ten amendments in 1789–1791. By century's end, the center of gravity of these conversations had moved to a new national capital city named after Washington himself. Flanking Mount Vernon, the new conversation center was also geographically central—close to where the North met the South along the Atlantic seaboard, at a longitude about halfway between eastern Maine and western Tennessee.

Several existential threats jeopardized the entire project of American constitutionalism. The first existential threat—Europe—was external, familiar, and slowly receding. America had to survive as a sovereign juridical entity, strong enough at every moment to repel Old World Powers still hoping to control the New World and, if necessary, divide and conquer the young United States. A second existential threat—slavery—was internal, subtler, and insidiously increasing. Human bondage, if not placed on a path of ultimate extinction, threatened to destroy the soul of the American republic. A closely related threat was regional polarization. As time passed, slavery shrank in the North and metastasized in the South. This divergence made it harder for the two regions to converse with each other, as the South increasingly came under the grip of pro-slavery extremists who disdained discourse and democracy and who would ultimately take up arms against both the Constitution and the American union that it embodied.

AT THE OUTSET OF THIS new post-1789 constitutional conversation, no conversationalist loomed larger than America's greatest immigrant, Alexander Hamilton, who cleverly crafted and constitutionally defended a set of interlocking institutions and structures of national power to secure the new constitutional system from external attack and internal implosion. In the process, Hamilton also repeatedly showed by example how to do holistic and purposeful constitutional interpretation.

Hamilton's bold plan for federal assumption of state war debts did justice to existing creditors and ensured that in any future military crisis or diplomatic crunch, the new nation could borrow money as needed. Enacted by the first Congress and signed into law by Washington, Hamilton's plan funded the national debt via dedicated customs duties and excise taxes. The plan particularly irked Virginia politicians; as a sweetener, Hamilton helped broker a Congressional deal to locate the permanent national capital in or near northern Virginia. Hamilton also brilliantly defended a later set of Congressional taxes on luxury items, inspiring a noteworthy Supreme Court decision properly and unanimously upholding sweeping federal tax power.

Hamilton's related system of national currency knit states together economically, as did federal promissory notes of various sorts, which operated as money in the many places where hard currency was scarce. Hamilton also designed and defended a national bank to further lubricate peacetime economic activity and facilitate wartime borrowing. With branches situated across the continent, this bank would enable the fledgling federal government to get money and matériel quickly to armies in the field wherever the troops might be deployed and the suppliers might be located.

More powerfully and prolifically than anyone else, Hamilton also explained to his fellow citizens in American newspapers why President Washington was both constitutionally authorized and consummately wise to keep America at arm's length from a new round of warfare that erupted between England and France in the aftermath of the French Revolution. When backcountry farmers staged a Shays-like rebellion against Hamilton's domestic whiskey tax, Hamilton again positioned himself alongside America's First Man, helping Washington suppress the rebellion with a judicious constitutional blend of military might and executive mercy. As Washington exited the presidency in 1797, Hamilton once more stood by his side, ghost-writing a renowned Farewell Address stressing unionism, national security, American independence from Europe, and sacred respect for a written Constitution authored, approved, amended, and additionally amendable by the American people themselves.

HAMILTON'S "LEAST DANGEROUS BRANCH"

Over the course of his lifetime of public service, Hamilton worked as both a legislator and an executive officer, but never as a judge. Still, he had high hopes for the federal judiciary, which he famously described in his celebrated *Federalist* No. 78 as the Constitution's "least dangerous branch," driven by neither "force nor will" and ideally motivated simply by "judgment." Before turning directly to Hamilton's executive-branch service under Washington, let us consider this judgment-driven branch, with special attention to the single most important—if today, largely forgotten—lawsuit decided by the judiciary in the Washington era. Unsurprisingly, this key case, *Hylton v. United States*, was argued and won by a man with an uncanny knack for being near the center of the action at all times: Alexander Hamilton.

IN THE COMPACT TEXT CRAFTED at Philadelphia in 1787, numbers often mattered even more than words. Washington's most memorable Convention moment targeted a specific number, "forty thousand." Despite his last-minute heroics, the document's faulty numbers concerning House size almost doomed ratification. In the ensuing decades, another faulty number, three-fifths, would structure much of the constitutional conversation and ultimately endanger the very project of American constitutionalism. The importance of numbers gives rise to a puzzle. Article I plainly took pains to define, with precise numbers, the size and shape of Congress, allocating power between large and small states and between free and slave states. Article II likewise meticulously specified the size and shape of the Electoral College that would select America's chief executive. Yet Article III said next to nothing about the size and shape of the federal judiciary. Where were the numbers?

The numbers went missing because many founders failed to anticipate the rise of a muscular federal judiciary that in later generations would come to act not merely as a faithful servant of Congress but also, quite often, as the equal partner and even the master of Congress. This modest founding image, which envisioned jurists as primarily servants of Congress, had roots in the British Empire. The British Privy Council and Board of Trade had kept colonies in line by reversing colonial court rulings and rejecting colonial statutes that violated Parliament's policies. In much the same manner, thought many founders, the new federal judiciary would generally spend its energy monitoring state officials and ensuring that states obeyed valid Congressional laws. Given this modest vision of federal judges, the Constitution did not need to specify much about the size and shape of the federal government's third branch. Congress could fill in the blanks and pick the numbers as it saw fit to sculpt an institution that would largely do Congress's bidding. Much as the Constitution gave Congress wide power to structure other federal organs—the federal customs office, the federal postal department, the federal mint, and the like—so the Constitution gave Congress wide power to structure the federal judiciary, determining how many justices would sit at the apex of the judicial pyramid, which states they would come from, and so on.

But unlike many other federal agents and agencies established by Congress, life-tenured federal judges would eventually come to play a distinctive role in invalidating various laws enacted by Congress, doing so in the name of the higher law of the Constitution itself. Had every founder focused on this distinctive judicial role and fully grasped its enormous significance, especially when combined with federal judges' life tenure and non-diminishable salary, the document might well have specified how big and small states, slave and free states, and so on, would factor into the judiciary's apportionment.

In any event, the judiciary almost never challenged Congress's enactments in the founding era. Not once, prior to 1850, did the Supreme Court thwart any major Congressional measure. In an early lawsuit that today stands for the proposition that "the Supreme Court is the ultimate interpreter of the Constitution"—the famous 1803 case of *Marbury v. Madison*—the Court in fact said no such thing and did just as Congress wanted. (We shall consider this case in more detail later in our story.)

In its landmark 1789 Judiciary Act, Congress set the Supreme Court's size at six. To modern eyes, this even number looks . . . odd. What would happen if the justices divided three against three? Modern Americans focus overwhelmingly on the Supreme Court as America's highest appellate tribunal, laying down national precepts for all Americans everywhere, and doing so via written opinions of the Court, each opinion typically representing the collective judgment of at least a majority of the justices.

But much of this modern practice took root only in the nine-teenth century. In the Court's earliest years, justices typically issued opinions seriatim, each man for himself, often orally. The Court did not yet routinely declare the law within any given case with one of-ficial written pronouncement, ex cathedra, available for immediate publication and republication. A tie vote among six jurists might not settle the law for all time, but it would suffice to decide the case at hand. In a three-three split, the lower court judgment would stand. If the Supreme Court were sitting as a trial bench, a tie would sim-ply mean that the plaintiff would lose.

For most of the year, the Court's members would not sit together in the capital as an appellate tribunal, but would instead scatter across the country to preside, sometimes in pairs, over far-flung trials in their respective home regions. America was a vast land, and the new government aimed to bring justice to the people—to every man's door, proverbially. Justices "riding circuit" would spare litigants the burden of dragging every important dispute to the national capital. The circuit system would also facilitate vigorous participation by local juries, who had been slighted by British vice-admiralty practice. The 1789 act thus carved America into three distinct circuits—northern, middle, and southern. A six-man Supreme Court divided nicely by three, entitling each geographic circuit to two justices.

The seemingly odd even number of six suggests that in 1789 per-haps the most important function of the Supreme Court was not, as it is today in the minds of many citizens, to provide a timely and definitive answer to virtually every legal and constitutional question. Rather, the key role, or at least one key role, of the early justices was to fan out and spend time in cities and counties across the land, lis-tening to—literally hearing the cases of—local folk. The high and haughty British ministers of the 1760s and 1770s had shown little interest in conversing with their far-flung cousins; this failure of the center to hear the periphery had destroyed the empire. The Judiciary Act aimed to ensure that America's Privy Council substitute would not make the same mistake. Just as senators and House members would periodically return to their home states and districts, lest they forget whence they came, so, too, with the early Supreme Court.

Juries in this era were not potted plants. Far more than is true today, jurors at the Founding participated vigorously in legal and constitutional conversation. In federal trials, the 1789 act provided that two judges could in some cases team up as presiding officers. If the pair disagreed in their legal advice to the jury, individual jurors could follow whichever jurist they preferred, or, indeed, follow their own understandings of the law in certain situations—in particular, when rendering a "general verdict" involving blended issues of law and fact.[1] In one 1794 case in which the Supreme Court, en banc, presided over a civil jury trial, Chief Justice Jay expressly conceded in his instructions to the "gentlemen" of the jury that "you have . . . a right to take upon yourselves to judge of both . . . the law as well as the fact in controversy." To modern eyes, this case, *Georgia v. Brailsford*, seems utterly fantastical, involving as it did (1) the Supreme Court presiding over an actual trial in which (2) multiple trial judges (the justices) interacted with a single jury, and (3) the bench treated the jurors almost as equal partners in the enterprise. "On this, and on every other occasion," instructed Jay, "we [the justices] have no doubt, you [the jurors] will pay the respect which is due to the opinion of the court. For, as on the one hand, it is presumed that juries are the best judges of facts, it is, on the other hand, presumable that the court are the best judges of law. *But still both objects* [that is, both law and fact, in this general-verdict case] *are lawfully within your power of decision.*"[2]

THE MOST SIGNIFICANT CONSTITUTIONAL EPISODES involving the Supreme Court during the Washington-Hamilton era paint a picture of a genuinely independent but rather decentralized and weak institution compared to its modern incarnation.

In *Hayburn's Case*, various jurists—more than a decade before *Marbury v. Madison*—engaged in what is now called "judicial review." That is, several federal judges in 1792 declined to enforce as written a Congressional statute that they deemed unconstitutional—not "in pursuance of" the Constitution within the meaning of the Article VI Supremacy Clause. But the judges acted not as an en banc Supreme Court tribunal speaking with one voice in a grand opinion for the ages, but as scattered circuit court jurists issuing three distinct and mercifully short (and today largely unknown) circuit pronouncements. As the Supreme Court readied itself to tackle the issue as an en banc tribunal, Congress revised the law in question and rendered the case moot.

On its face, *Hayburn's Case* did not involve any grand issue of human rights—say, Zenger-style freedom of the press, or the right of homeowners to be free from arbitrary governmental searches à la Otis and Wilkes. Nor did the case implicate first principles of legislative authority, such as the scope of the central government's tax power—the crux of the Stamp Act crisis and an issue that would indeed prominently resurface later in the Washington-Hamilton era. Rather, *Hayburn's Case* concerned the constitutional law of the judiciary itself. Congress by statute had directed circuit judges to help enforce a program offering government pensions to disabled Revolutionary War veterans.[3] Circuit judges would assess the extent of claimants' disabilities and make appropriate factual findings. The constitutional rub was that circuit judges' findings in favor of disabled claimants would not be entirely final. The secretary of war would cross-check court-approved claimants' names against War Department records to confirm that the claimants were indeed legally eligible veterans.

The system made consummately good geographic, budgetary, and practical sense. The judges on circuit would examine the wounds and then the War Department in the capital would examine the files. Apart from federal courts and the federal postal system, no significant federal civil bureaucracy operated in the hinterlands. (Customs officials clustered along the coastline.) The federal government was paying judges decent salaries to bring justice to every man's door. What could be more just than helping disabled veterans get their due without having to hobble across the continent to the capital? The pension statute directed judges to perform a fact-finding task easily within their ken.

But the skittish circuit jurists worried that the system threatened their judicial independence by effectively treating them as executive-branch bureaucrats rather than as officials of a separate, distinct, and co-equal branch. If the secretary of war could in essence overrule a jurist's determination under this statute, perhaps executive officials might feel free to disregard judicial rulings in other, less benign, contexts—say, habeas corpus suits against soldiers arbitrarily imprisoning civilians, or damage suits against customs officers invading private homes. In Pennsylvania, Associate Justices James Wilson and John Blair, joined by District Judge Richard Peters, declared that "the business directed by this act is not of a judicial nature" subject as it was to "revision and controul . . . inconsistent with the independence of that judicial power which is vested in the courts." Chief Justice John Jay and Associate Justice William Cushing, along with District Judge William Duane, expressed similar concerns in New York, as did Associate Justice James Iredell and District Judge John Sitgreaves in North Carolina. The duties imposed by the act, these jurists fretted, were not "properly judicial," insofar as the judges' decisions were "not made final," but instead subject to executive-branch "suspension" and "revision."[4] In response to these judicial status anxieties, Congress in 1793 devised a different way to help veterans.[5]

THAT SAME YEAR, THE SUPREME Court en banc finally had occasion to rule on a juicy constitutional-law issue—and promptly got reversed by Congress and the American people.

A South Carolinian, Alexander Chisholm, sued Georgia, which saw itself as "sovereign" and thus immune from private suit. Chisholm claimed that Georgia had not paid what it owed under a contract made during the war. In a written submission—Georgia did not even send a lawyer to appear in person before the Court—the state asserted its "sovereign" immunity. Even if the state had indeed broken its prior promise to pay the contractor, Georgia officials believed that the state itself could not be sued and held liable without its express consent within the litigation itself. Sovereignty meant never having to say it was sorry.

In separate seriatim statements, four of the five sitting justices (the sixth was absent) disagreed. The four declared that the Court could properly assert jurisdiction over Georgia and also seemed to say that Georgia would have to pay what it owed.

Chief Justice John Jay bridled at the idea that Georgia—or indeed, any American government—was, in the strictest sense, "sovereign." In Europe, Jay explained, "sovereignty is generally ascribed to the Prince; here it rests with the people; there, the sovereign actually administers the Government; here, never in a single instance; our Governors are the agents of the people, and at most stand in the same relation to their sovereign, in which regents in Europe stand to their sovereigns." In America, because the people, not their agents in government, were sovereign, it was no insult or "degrad[ation]" to any state government to be obliged to appear as a litigant opposite a mere private individual. A proper American court would simply hold the scales of justice evenly between an American citizen on one balance pan and government servants on the other: "Justice is the same whether due from one man or a million." The Constitution's "great and glorious principle, that the people are the sovereign of this country," wrote Jay, "places all our citizens on an equal footing, and enables each and every of them to obtain justice without any danger of being overborne by the weight and number of their opponents."

Associate Justice James Wilson, America's great popular sovereignty theorist, agreed wholeheartedly and fairly burst with intellectual enthusiasm. Here was "a case of uncommon magnitude" giving the schoolmarmish Scottish émigré—who as a young man had studied at St. Andrews, Glasgow, and Edinburgh—a perfect opportunity to instruct his fellow Americans on basic constitutional first principles, and indeed his own favorite principle: popular sovereignty. "To the Constitution of the United States," explained Wilson, "the term SOVEREIGN, is totally unknown. There is but one place where it could have been used with propriety. But, even in that place it would not, perhaps, have comported with the delicacy of those, who ordained and established that Constitution. They might have announced themselves [in the Preamble] 'SOVEREIGN' people of the United States: But serenely conscious of the fact, they avoided the ostentatious declaration."

On this point, Wilson surely knew his stuff. Unbeknownst to the average reader, he himself had composed the first draft of the Preamble, with its majestic opening words, "We the People."[6] Ever since that Philadelphia moment, in a wide range of venues, Wilson had elaborated the deep implications of the American theory of popular sovereignty that truly was embedded in those words, and indeed that ramified throughout the Constitution.

But Wilson and Jay and the two other justices supporting them in *Chisholm v. Georgia* overreached elsewhere in the case. The lawsuit concerned a contract made during the war—when Georgia surely was "sovereign" in a strong sense, given the Declaration of Independence and the Articles of Confederation. Even if Revolution-era sovereignty, strictly speaking, resided in the *people* of Georgia as distinct from the *government* of Georgia, the plaintiff was a South Carolinian who pointed to no statement from the Georgian people that they wanted their government to pay money to outsiders—money that presumably would require more taxes on or fewer benefits for Georgians themselves. True, reneging on contractual obligations was not very nice—but background legal principles when the contract was made *allowed* governments to weasel out of paying damages, and that weasel-right was factored into the price when the deal was made. Revolution-era contractors who did not like this background weasel-right were free to avoid making deals with a state, or to demand a higher interest rate or some special collateral to protect themselves. To give the plaintiff a new entitlement in 1793 to receive full damages in court was in effect to rewrite the contract—to give creditors not what they actually bargained for during the war, but more.

Nothing in federal statutes and nothing in the Constitution strongly supported this judicial rewrite. The suit was in federal court not because substantive federal law was at issue, but simply because the lawsuit implicated multiple states: Georgia on one side and South Carolina (Chisholm's home state) on the other. In situations involving two or more diverse states, the Constitution empowered federal courts to step in to ensure that substantive state laws were applied honestly rather than slyly bent by state judges to favor in-state litigants over outsiders. In *Chisholm*, no bending problem existed. Had plaintiff Chisholm himself been a *Georgia* state resident, he would have lost in Georgia state court on the very same claim. He deserved no windfall in federal court just because he was not Georgian. Indeed, had South Carolinian Chisholm sued in his own state court, he would have lost there, too. Virtually every state court at that time refused to hold its own state's government or sister state governments liable for mere breach of contract.

On the legal merits of the lawsuit, as distinct from certain technical jurisdictional issues, the "sovereignty" issue was beside the point. Married women were not sovereign; minor children were not sovereign; yet they, too, were generally immune from lawsuits against them seeking damages for breach of contract. States were no different; they simply were not liable in damages as a matter of basic contract law. On the merits, the real question was not sovereignty, but contract law at the time the contract was made—state law, strictly speaking, which the *Chisholm* justices blithely disregarded.

States were not amused. *Chisholm* threatened to bleed the treasuries of many states that were not flush enough to satisfy all contractual creditors at full value without a massive tax increase. Some creditors were *British* merchants. Why should American courts treat such litigants with extreme favor unless substantive federal law expressly required that result? On November 21, 1793, the Georgia House of Representatives passed a bill that never became law, but did evidence the passions that the Court had stirred. Any federal marshal or other person attempting to enforce the *Chisholm* ruling, said the bill, should be declared "guilty of felony and shall suffer death . . . by being hanged"—without "benefit of clergy," the bill hastened to add.[7]

In 1794, senators and House members—who of course electorally answered to state legislators and state voters, respectively—responded

aggressively to *Chisholm* by proposing a new constitutional amendment that in early 1795 won ratification by the requisite three-
quarters of state legislatures. This amendment, the first since the Bill
of Rights and the eleventh overall, stripped federal courts of jurisdiction in lawsuits closely akin to Chisholm's—that is, suits brought
by outsiders against state governments and implicating only state
substantive law, such as contract law.[8]

By itself, the main issue in *Chisholm* was narrow and technical: the
applicability of non-statutory state contract-law principles in federal
court. (Today, lawyers would recognize this issue as an "*Erie*" question,
framed by a landmark twentieth-century case, *Erie v. Thompkins*.[9])
The larger lesson for all to see in the 1790s was that the Supreme
Court had no monopoly over constitutional discourse. *Chisholm* was
the first important constitutional issue to reach the Supreme Court
as a court, en banc, and the Congress and states had immediately
rushed in to overrule the justices.

NOT LONG AFTER *CHISHOLM*, THE Court faced an even bigger constitutional test. This time it aced the exam, thanks to Hamilton.

The case involved taxes—as explosive an issue as existed in late
eighteenth-century America. Taxes had triggered the first continent-
wide clash between Britain and America—the Stamp Act crisis—
and ultimately the British Empire had failed in no small part because
London and the colonies had continued to tilt over taxes. Parliament
persisted in claiming unlimited tax power, and Americans persisted
in believing that taxation without representation was tyranny. The
Articles of Confederation had also failed because of taxes. The old
Congress had legitimately represented and taxed states, but states
had failed to pay. Without tax revenue for armies and navies, Washington and others had worried that independent America would not
survive; one way or another, the Old Powers of Europe would gob-
ble it up. The Constitution promised an elegant solution. Congress
would both represent and tax individuals, who could more easily be
pressured to pay than could states as such. But the Constitution's de-

tails were less than limpid, obliging the justices in 1796 to confront one crucial ambiguity.

Chastened by the public's fierce response to *Chisholm*, the Constitution's third branch (the Judiciary) wisely deferred to its first branch (Congress) in this important tax case. Congress in turn had wisely deferred to the general vision of America's greatest constitutional expert on taxation, Alexander Hamilton, who also served as a private lawyer in 1796 advising the justices on what to do and say. To their credit, the justices unanimously did as advised in the case, *Hylton v. United States.*[10]

The case arose in response to the military and fiscal events of 1794. The Washington administration desperately needed additional revenue to finance defense measures against an increasingly aggressive Britain (which had yet to let go of a string of some twenty forts in America's northwestern backcountry) and various hostile northwestern Indian tribes allied to Britain. Congress responded with several measures, one of which laid a tax on the annual use of specified carriages. This was a luxury tax, a tax on the sort of high-status conveyances favored and flaunted by wealthy and genteel folk—chariots, phaetons, coaches, and other kinds of fancy voitures that Jane Austen would soon make famous in works such as *Sense and Sensibility*, *Pride and Prejudice*, *Mansfield Park*, and *Emma*. Congress expressly exempted farmers' carts, drays, and wagons hauling crops and other everyday stuff: "Nothing herein . . . shall be construed to charge with a duty, any carriage usually and chiefly employed in husbandry, or for the transporting or carrying of goods, wares, merchandise, produce or commodities."[11]

In late 1794, a carriage-owning Virginian, Daniel Hylton, refused to pay. Led by the staunch states' rightist John Taylor of Caroline—a tedious anti-administration Virginia ex-senator backed on this issue by the increasingly oppositional James Madison—Hylton's legal team claimed that the act violated the Constitution. The law, argued Hylton's lawyers, was a direct tax that failed to comply with the Constitution's strict rules about direct taxation. At Washington's urging, Hamilton, now practicing law in New York after having served some five years as treasury secretary, agreed to come to Philadelphia (the temporary capital since late 1790) to defend the law's constitutionality before the Supreme Court. In fact, Congress had adopted this very law and Washington had signed it in reliance upon Hamilton's own earlier writings and official reports to Congress.[12]

In a letter to his wife written shortly after the February 1796 oral argument, Justice James Iredell made no mention of Hamilton's co-counsel, Attorney General Charles Lee, but marveled at Hamilton's virtuoso performance: "Mr. Hamilton spoke in our Court, attended by the most crowded audience I ever saw there, both Houses of Congress being almost deserted on the occasion. Though he was in very ill health, he spoke with astonishing ability, and in a most pleasing manner, and was listened to with the profoundest attention. His speech lasted about three hours. . . . In one part of it he affected me extremely." Federalist newspapers also swooned. (To his many fans in those days, Hamilton was an eighteenth-century superstar, akin today to, well, Lin-Manuel Miranda.) In Philadelphia itself, John Fenno's *Gazette of the United States* showered praise upon the "most eloquent speech" of "this great orator and statesman" offering up a "clear, impressive, and classical" analysis. Like Iredell, Fenno noted that the audience was "very numerous" and added that it included not just a galaxy of congressmen but also "many foreigners of distinction." Newspapers in New York, Connecticut, Massachusetts, and New Hampshire reprinted Fenno's squib, and other favorable reviews surfaced elsewhere. According to Benjamin Russell's Boston-based *Centinel*, Hamilton's "eloquence, candor, and law knowledge, has drawn applause from many who had been in the habit of reviling him."[13]

Several constitutional clauses framed the great constitutional debate in *Hylton*. The longest section of the Constitution's first and longest Article—Article I, section 8, cataloging Congressional powers—opened as follows: "The Congress shall have power to lay and collect Taxes, Duties, Imposts, and Excises." With not one, not two, not three, but four distinct nouns, the Constitution thus proclaimed that the new Congress would have sweeping power to reach into constituents' pockets. Less than a dozen years after staging an anti-tax revolution in July 1776, Americans had quite evidently drafted and ratified an avowedly pro-tax Constitution.

Law commands but rarely explains. In a few places, however, the Constitution did say why. The Preamble was one of those places, and the Tax Clause was another. Indeed, textually, the two clauses were tightly intertwined. Congress needed sweeping taxation power, explained section 8, in order to "Pay the Debts, and provide for the common Defence and general Welfare of the United States." With this obvious echo not just of the Preamble's overall purposivism, but also of the Preamble's overarching purposes—common defense and general welfare—the section 8 clause further highlighted the importance of taxation to the Constitution's entire project.

But what, exactly, were the differences among the four key nouns? Did it matter? The clause implied it did, because it further provided that "all Duties, Imposts, and Excises" would need to be "uniform throughout the United States." By strong negative implication, taxes more generally, apparently, would not always need to be uniform. Indeed, at least one kind of tax, seemingly, would emphatically need to be *non-uniform*, namely, a "direct tax." Such a tax would have to be apportioned among the states to correspond to the number of seats each state would hold in the lower house: "Representatives and *direct Taxes* shall be apportioned among the several States . . . according to their respective Numbers" (emphasis added). This fixed ratio would in fact oblige the federal government to vary the direct tax, state by state—to make the tax non-uniform—in order to meet the required apportionment ratio.

The carriage tax offered a clean illustration of all this. If a tax on the annual use of a carriage was properly characterized as a "duty," the duty per carriage would need to be identical—uniform—in every state. That is precisely what the 1794 Carriage Act provided—a uniform duty that applied identically in all states and territories. But suppose instead that the carriage tax was best viewed as a "direct tax." Given that Virginia, under the 1790 census, had nineteen seats in the House of Representatives, and Massachusetts had fourteen, any federal "direct tax" on carriages would have to rake in nineteen dollars from all Virginians for every fourteen from all Massachusetts men. Carriage use per capita would doubtless differ from state to state. Thus, to meet the requisite nineteen-to-fourteen ratio, the tax per carriage could not be uniform; the government would need to jigger it state by state. And not just between Virginia and Massachusetts, but in each and every state. For every nineteen carriage-tax dollars flowing into the federal treasury from Virginia and fourteen from Massachusetts, exactly thirteen carriage-tax dollars would need to flow from Pennsylvania, ten from New York, and so on.

If the direct-tax category were construed broadly, its requirement of equal ratios across more than a dozen states would be an administrative nightmare. If, among two equal-size states, one state had one hundred carriages in use and another had eight hundred, the tax per carriage would need to be eight times as high in the former (likely poorer!) state to equalize carriage-tax revenue and thus satisfy the required ratio for direct taxes. Suppose, in one particularly abstemious state, no one used carriages. No revenue would come from that state, so no revenue could legally flow from any other state. One ascetic state would nullify the federal tax altogether in all other states!

In his oral argument, Hamilton nicely highlighted these mathematical absurdities. A facile and overbroad reading of the direct-tax category could easily lead to "ruinous" tax rates in low-carriage states, or would simply "defeat the power of laying" the tax altogether. "This is a consequence," Hamilton sensibly warned, "that ought not result from construction" if a more practical and moderately plausible alternative reading were available: "No construction ought to prevail calculated to defeat the express and necessary authority of the government. It would be contrary to reason and to every rule of sound construction, to adopt a principle for regulating the exercise of a clear constitutional power which would defeat the exercise of the power."[14]

But what was the proper line to draw and why? At one point behind closed doors at Philadelphia, Massachusetts delegate Rufus King had asked a seemingly simple question: "What was the precise meaning of *direct* taxation?" No one answered.[15] Some delegates perhaps blushed with shame at that moment, for they knew that the Direct Tax Clause was in part a fig leaf to distract popular attention from the pro-slavery bias of the Three-Fifths Clause. The actual main purpose of the fractional clause was to give the South extra credit in the House and the Electoral College. Slaves would count, albeit at a discount, even though slaves could not vote and were not in any plausible way virtually represented by those in their state who did vote (and who would get extra clout thanks to the fractional clause). To disguise this ugly fact in the impending ratification process, the delegates drafted fig-leaf language that linked the three-fifths rule not just to representation but also to taxation: "Representatives and *direct Taxes* shall be apportioned . . ." (emphasis added). The fig leaf did fool some northern ratifiers who seemed unaware that "direct taxes" were a very narrow and technical category indeed.[16] Most tax money would come from Customs House imposts and other revenue measures that would not be covered by the generally unworkable direct-tax formula.

The Constitution's text, however, did expressly identify one narrow type of tax that would be a classic direct tax. Here, too, there were reasons for some Philadelphia delegates to blush at the shameful backstory. Article I, section 9 provided that "no Capitation, or other direct Tax, shall be laid, unless in proportion to the Census." Thus the Constitution itself made clear that at least one kind of tax—a head tax, a "capitation"—was indeed a direct tax that would require state apportionment rather than national one-rate uniformity. Why did the Philadelphia delegates adopt this special rule for head taxes? In a word, slavery. If the only tax rule were the simple and general rule for duties, imposts, and excises—the rule that all such levies had to be uniform across state lines—then Congress would be free to impose a high and uniform tax on, say, playing cards in all states. Likewise, Congress could impose a high and uniform tax on whiskey or tea or cattle or carriages in all states. But if so, Congress could also impose a prohibitively high and uniform tax on slaves in all states and thereby effect abolition. That last theoretical possibility was a deal-breaker for delegates from the Deep South at Philadelphia. So human head taxes had to be limited. Slave heads could not be taxed in the same way as could heads of cattle or heads of lettuce or hogsheads of tobacco or other commodities.[17]

What else? Article I, section 9 spoke of "other direct Tax[es]" beyond "Capitation." Hamilton at oral argument suggested that land taxes could also sensibly fall within the category of "direct taxes." Historically, the old Congress under the Articles of Confederation had linked land assessments with head counts and had linked both with properly apportioned state-by-state taxes.[18] Unlike fleeting and consumable items such as carriages, cattle, whiskey, lettuce, tobacco, and playing cards, land was fixed and permanent. It was possible to imagine a state with zero carriages or zero cattle (and zero would ruin everything in an apportionment system), but it was not possible to imagine a state with zero land.

A definition of direct taxes as subsuming head taxes and land taxes, and virtually nothing else, was not merely functional and holistic but also highly plausible as a pure textual matter. A *direct* tax could be thought of as a tax that was impossible to escape, or at least very hard to escape without extreme hardship. A carriage tax was easy to escape: just don't use a carriage! But a human head tax could be escaped only by death itself, and a land tax could impose extreme hardship on the many struggling Americans in the 1790s who were land-rich but cash-poor. In the illiquid economy that was early America—a nation short on specie and banks—many a young farmer who inherited his family homestead would lack ready money to pay a substantial land tax. But a transactional duty on an item being sold—an ounce of tea, a deck of cards, a barrel of whiskey, a head of cattle—could be paid for as part of the cash involved in the sale itself. By this test, the 1794 carriage tax was much more like a standard sales tax (with no apportionment needed) than like a head tax or a land tax. True, the act technically taxed not the *sale* of a carriage—a cash-soaked transaction—but rather the *annual use* of a carriage, the yearly implicit rental value of the vehicle. No matter. Carriages were easy enough to sell or otherwise dispose of without hardship if one wanted to avoid the tax. It was not at all, functionally, like being obliged to sell one's ancient family farm to pay the taxman.

Hamilton himself made this very point—and indeed, this was the point that Iredell found particularly affecting: "Having occasion to observe, how proper a subject it [a carriage] was for taxation, since it was a mere article of *luxury*, which a man might either use, or not, as was convenient to him, he [Hamilton] added, 'It so happens, that I once had a carriage myself, and found it convenient to dispense with it. But my happiness is not in the least diminished.'"[19]

Just as Wilson knew his stuff on popular sovereignty going all the way back to Philadelphia, so, too, with Hamilton on taxes. Indeed, at the 1787 conclave, Hamilton had drafted his own constitutional plan that defined direct taxes almost exactly the way he did nine years later in *Hylton*: "Taxes on lands, houses and other real estate, and capitation taxes shall be proportioned in each State by the whole number of free persons, except Indians not taxed and by three fifths of all other persons."[20] And just as Wilson had elaborated his popular sovereignty theories at length during the ratification process, so Hamilton (as Publius) had publicly laid out his various tax theories for all would-be ratifiers to peruse and ponder. His views on the absolutely critical need for, and the technical details of, a workable federal revenue system filled no fewer than seven *Federalist* essays. In the final essay in this series, *The Federalist* No. 36, he expressly discussed "DIRECT" and "INDIRECT" taxes. "INDIRECT" taxes, he explained, "must be understood [as] duties and excises on articles of consumption," whereas the "DIRECT" taxes beyond capitation meant taxes on "real property or . . . houses and lands."

In ruling unanimously in support of the tax, of the Congress, and, indeed, of Washington himself, who had signed the law and strongly backed it, the justices not only embraced Hamilton's result, but also echoed Hamilton's reasoning. Samuel Chase opened by saying that if he thought the issue a close one—"if the case was doubtful"—he would defer to "the deliberate decision of the National Legislature." Ultimately, no deference was needed to uphold the law. On the merits, Chase thought, Congress, Washington, and Hamilton were right.

In particular, Chase reiterated Hamilton's textual, holistic, and functional argument that the category of "direct" taxes should include only those taxes that meshed with a workable census-apportionment rule:

> The Constitution evidently contemplated no taxes as direct taxes, but only such as Congress could lay in proportion to the census. The rule of apportionment is only to be adopted in such cases where it can reasonably apply; and the subject taxed, must ever determine the application of the rule. If it is proposed to tax any specific article by the rule of apportionment, and it would evidently create great inequality and injustice, it is unreasonable to say, that the Constitution intended such tax should be laid by that rule.

Chase then illustrated the point by copying Hamilton's math: if two states had equal populations but vastly unequal carriage use, carriage users in the poorer state would face ridiculously high carriage taxes. Happily, it required no stretching of words to reach a sensible result; the carriage charge was a "duty" pure and simple. "Duties," after all, had long been understood to encompass purely internal levies. (The Stamp Act crisis provided compelling support for Chase on this point: colonists in the 1760s had indiscriminately labeled stamp fees "taxes" and "duties.") Chase concluded by backing Hamilton's view that "direct taxes contemplated by the Constitution, are only two, to wit, a capitation . . . and a tax on LAND."

Justice William Paterson, who had been Hamilton's fellow delegate at Philadelphia, likewise argued for a narrow reading of the direct-tax category: "The provision was made [by the Philadelphia drafters] in favor of the southern States [who] possessed a large number of slaves," and thus should not be broadly applied in other contexts. Hamilton's math made sense and Hylton's did not: "In some states there are many carriages, and in others but few. Shall the whole sum fall on one or two individuals in a state, who may happen to own and possess carriages? The thing would be absurd, and inequitable." Apportionment was exceedingly cumbersome, and that basic Hamiltonian fact argued for a narrow definition of direct taxation in any doubtful case: "Uniformity is an instant operation on individuals . . . and is at once easy, certain, and efficacious. All taxes on expences or consumption are indirect taxes. A tax on carriages is of this kind, and of course is not a direct tax."

The admiring Iredell also expressly embraced Hamilton's holistic functionalism: "As all direct taxes must be apportioned, it is evident that the Constitution contemplated none as direct but such as could be apportioned. If this cannot be apportioned, it is, therefore, not a direct tax in the sense of the Constitution." And, indeed, a carriage tax could not sensibly be apportioned because of . . . math, just as Hamilton had insisted: "If any state had no carriages, there could be no apportionment at all. This mode is too manifestly absurd to be supported."

In the most important case decided by the Supreme Court in the eighteenth century, the justices thus unanimously backed a sweeping, sensible, and national-security-justified tax law that had been inspired by Hamilton himself—and the justices did so for expressly Hamiltonian reasons, acting publicly under Hamilton's personal tutelage in open court for all to see.[21]

FIRST MEN—WASHINGTON, MADISON, AND HAMILTON

At first, the first man in the first branch in the Constitution's first years was a strong supporter of America's First Man and that First Man's first cabinet minister. But over time James Madison came to oppose George Washington and Alexander Hamilton, and indeed to disavow his own previous positions. Ironically, Madison, Washington, and Hamilton were yanked in different directions by divergent political incentives and conversational structures implicit in the very Constitution they themselves had jointly created and, initially, jointly consolidated.

Even as these titans tugged against each other—or, to be more precise, even as Madison tugged against the other two—the three men continued to share a common constitutional grammar and culture, as did the broader American society surrounding them. Early

Americans generally played by the same basic ground rules of interpretation, placing the Constitution itself on a deservedly high pedestal and attending closely to the document's text, structure, purpose, and enactment history. On many but not all issues, Hamilton simply played the interpretive game better. That is, his arguments meshed more tightly with the Constitution's letter and spirit, and with what he and other Federalists had said and written in explaining and selling the document to the American people in the ratification process. When Hamilton's interpretive arguments were strong, as they often were, Washington and America generally sided with him. But in certain constitutional contests where Madison and his allies played the interpretive game better—where their arguments excelled on the merits, especially where basic rights were at stake—America would dramatically side with them, as we shall see in the next chapter. In a system ultimately driven by common folk with only limited constitutional knowledge, vision, and attention span, America not only somehow managed to pick truly great men and put them in the right slots at the right time, but also somehow managed to outperform them all in sensibly applying the Constitution's letter and spirit.

IF HIS EXCELLENCY GEORGE WASHINGTON was America's monarch-equivalent, who was America's prime minister? In Britain, the prime minister sat in and led the House of Commons as its political chieftain. In America, James Madison initially played that shepherd's role in the House of Representatives.[22] But Britain's prime minister was chosen by, and served at the pleasure of, the monarch. (That would change later, especially after reforms in the 1830s.) Thanks to the Constitution's separation of powers, Madison did not serve at Washington's pleasure. Indeed, he held no official executive-branch post whatsoever. The Constitution's Article I, section 6, Incompatibility Clause strictly prohibited sitting lawmakers from simultaneously serving in the administration: "No person holding any [executive or judicial] office under the United States, shall be a member of either

House during his continuance in office." Britain had no such prohibition. Ministers from the prime minister on down held seats in Parliament at the same time that they ran government departments with the Crown's blessing. Unlike contemporaneous British prime ministers, who typically came from safe constituencies, Madison could not take his House seat for granted given the sentiments of his home district, sentiments that ultimately pulled him away from the president whose pet he had once been.

Britain's prime minister was also, while holding the office, the statesman of highest standing in the government. Second only to the Crown, he stood for the regime. So perhaps America's true prime minister was Thomas Jefferson?

Unlike Madison, Jefferson had been chosen by Washington himself and did indeed serve at His Excellency's pleasure. Formally, Jefferson had no competing constituency to placate. As a matter of protocol, his position as secretary of state arguably entitled him to top honor. Internationally, he spoke for the president and the nation. Congress had created his position first, many days before the secretary of war's and more than a month before the secretary of the treasury's. Coming into his position, he outranked all, politically and socially (excepting perhaps his old friend from 1776, John Adams). Born into the Randolph clan, one of America's oldest and most distinguished families, he had served as the two-term governor of Virginia, America's largest and proudest state, and then as the multiyear minister plenipotentiary to France, America's closest and most powerful ally. He came to view himself, and would increasingly be hailed by others, as the author of the Declaration of Independence. Madison, eight years younger, had begun as his protégé and over time had become his political partner, but only his junior partner, as both men understood. As for Alexander Hamilton, Jefferson knew of him by reputation, but prior to the Washington administration he had never even met the young, haughty, lowborn *arriviste*.

On the other hand—and it was a big other hand—Britain's prime minister was intimately connected to Commons. Jefferson's only links to the House were through Madison and other friends.

That left Hamilton. (We shall consider Adams in more detail in the next chapter.) In many ways, Hamilton was in fact a closer match to the British prime minister than either of his initial colleagues and eventual rivals. His treasury-secretary salary was actually identical to Jefferson's and higher than anyone else's in government, save the president, the vice president, and the chief justice. (This was a point of public honor in a political culture obsessed by honor.) He had won confirmation weeks before Jefferson had even been nominated, and months before Jefferson had actually joined the government. Most recent British PMs had served as first lord of the treasury. Because of America's desperate need for revenue, which spawned a veritable army of federal tax collectors, customs officers, accountants, clerks, and other civil servants, Hamilton headed a bureaucracy that was many dozens the size of the State Department.[23] This gave him patronage power that even the early British prime minister Robert Walpole, notorious for his use of spoils, might have envied. Intensely jealous of its tax-related power of the purse, Congress saw the treasury secretary, uniquely, as a quasi-Congressional (yet also fully executive!) official. By statute, Congress directed the treasury secretary, but not the secretary of state, to periodically report to the legislature, even as both secretaries also of course answered directly to the president under Article II of the Constitution.[24] If one main function of a proper prime minister was to personally interlink the legislature and the administration, Alexander Hamilton, uniquely, was founding America's interpersonal link. (In one revealing letter, he referred repeatedly to "my administration."*) He served as the equivalent of the modern House Ways and Means Committee, a committee that permanently geared up only after he left office.[25]

---

*"When I accepted the Office, I now hold, it was under a full persuasion, that from similarity of thinking, conspiring with personal goodwill, I should have the firm support of Mr. Madison, in the general course of my administration. . . . Mr. Madison cooperating with Mr. Jefferson is at the head of a faction decidedly hostile to me and my administration. . . . As to the point of opposition to me and my administration[,] Mr. Jefferson with very little reserve manifests his dislike of the funding system generally." Letter to Edward Carrington, May 26, 1792 (emphasis deleted).

He also was Washington's boy, not literally (as some silly conspiratorialists whispered), but perhaps at an equally deep level. Hamilton had no reliable father and Washington had no son. The two men had bonded in complicated ways during the war, when Hamilton had served as His Excellency's scribal aide-de-camp—Washington's right and writing hand. Having together suffered years of hardship and then having experienced ultimate vindication, Washington and Hamilton had forged an ineffable bond of shared valor and sacrifice—something perhaps akin to what Henry V and his men had at Agincourt, a connection that civilians Madison and Jefferson (and John Adams, for that matter) could only envy and curse from afar. The underlying loyalties between the two men who had endured Valley Forge and taken Yorktown became increasingly symmetric and even affectionate as Washington aged and Hamilton aided.

Most fundamentally, Hamilton and Washington were much closer in their political, constitutional, and geostrategic outlook. Hamilton had lived for so long inside Washington's head that the two had almost become one on some things. For many good reasons, Washington came to rely on Hamilton implicitly in multiple domains. One especially good reason was that Hamilton had competences—financial wizardry, legal genius—that Washington lacked. Washington did not need Jefferson as his top diplomatic thinker; Washington himself was a much abler grand strategist. But Washington simply could not do without Hamilton, his true right-hand man, his de facto prime minister.

IRONICALLY, THE MAN WHO EFFECTIVELY made Hamilton premier, unwittingly, was none other than James Madison. The deed happened in the first year of the Washington administration, at a moment when Madison himself was at the peak of his eighteenth-century power. At that moment—June 1789—Madison was America's premier of sorts, working in close partnership with Washington on the Bill of Rights project and other parts of the Washington agenda and exerting political mastery over the House. In June, the positions of treasury secretary and secretary of state had yet to be created, much less filled with the likes of Hamilton and Jefferson.

The question of the hour was precisely how to structure these and other high-level executive-branch positions. This was a constitutional question—seemingly technical, as with so many constitutional questions, but no less important for all that. Virtually everyone understood that the Constitution, thanks to its Article I Necessary and Proper Clause, gave Congress broad power to enact statutes sculpting the executive departments that would operate under the president's supervision: "The Congress shall have Power . . . To make all laws which shall be necessary and proper for carrying into execution the foregoing powers, and all other powers vested by this Constitution in the government of the United States, *or in any department or officer thereof*" (emphasis added). Thus, Congress could decide by statute whether one man would control both the post office and the treasury, or whether these two outfits should operate separately, headed by different department chiefs. But what should the tenure of office be for these department heads? Was this, too, completely within Congress's discretion?

The Constitution's Article II spoke clearly about *appointments* to top executive positions: "He [the president] shall nominate, and by and with the advice and consent of the Senate, shall appoint, Ambassadors, Judges of the Supreme Court, and all other [principal] Officers of the United States [including] the Heads of Departments." But Article II was less clear about *dis-appointments*, so to speak— removals from office. Four main conceptual constitutional possibilities existed. Each had adherents in the First Congress, which debated the constitutional issue with gusto in the spring of 1789.

South Carolina representative William Loughton Smith floated one possibility: no officer, executive or judicial, could be removed except upon "an impeachment before the Senate. . . . [O]nce in office, he must remain there until convicted upon impeachment."[26] Smith's House colleagues quickly poked holes in this idea and sank it. It effectively gave every federal officer life tenure, even though the text expressly designated that status for Article III judges and by pointed contrast said nothing of the sort about executive officialdom. Surely a high executive official in a sensitive position of power should be immediately sacked if, say, he was convicted of bribery in an ordinary court, even if the House and Senate were not then in session to follow up with impeachment proceedings.[27] Even prior to criminal conviction, should a high-level official continue in power if the president had hard evidence of the official's corruption? What if an officer was not corrupt in an impeachable way, but grossly incompetent? Surely the Constitution should not be read, unless its words admitted no other plausible interpretation, to keep nincompoops in power for life.

A second position was that dis-appointments were perfectly symmetric to appointments. Just as the president would need the concurrence of the Senate to make, say, Alexander Hamilton treasury secretary, so the president would need Senate concurrence to cashier Hamilton. Amusingly enough, Hamilton himself had said just this as Publius in *The Federalist* No. 77 in 1788: "The consent of that body [the Senate] would be necessary to displace as well as to appoint." By the spring of 1789 Hamilton had changed his mind and shared his epiphany with friends in Congress.[28] Nevertheless, some Congressmen continued to find Hamilton's initial position persuasive. Virginia's Theodorick Bland opined that, as a matter of symmetry, "the power which appointed should remove."[29] Georgia's James Jackson and Virginia's Alexander White agreed virtually verbatim.[30] Massachusetts representative Elbridge Gerry, a Philadelphia delegate who had voted no at the end of the Convention, also took this view: removal power "vests with the President, by and with the advice and consent of the Senate."[31]

The Bland position was problematic. In its pure form—the Senate must play a role in every firing, by symmetry with appointments—this position has never had any traction in America over the centuries. By negative implication, the Constitution's text seems to say the opposite: the Senate does play a role in appointments, but pointedly does not in dis-appointments. Firing an executive official for, say, insubordination or incompetence seems to be a classically executive decision, and the text does not give the Senate any general or residual executive power. Technically, as the famous case of *Marbury v. Madison* would later make clear, even after the Senate has approved a given nominee, the president unilaterally *makes* the nominee an *officer* by issuing a *commission*. Thus, even after the Senate has said yes, the president may unilaterally say no. (Strictly speaking, the Senate has merely offered its *advice*.) By pure symmetry, the president should have unilateral power to decommission, mirroring his unilateral power to commission.[32]

Nor does the Bland positon make much sense as an absolute and sweeping rule (which it needs to be, if justified by pure symmetry to the Appointments Clause). What if a president catches a department head in a corrupt act—or indeed, what if a department head is convicted of bribery—but the Senate is in a multimonth recess? Would the president be obliged to call senators back from all across the land into special session just for this? Would the same be true for every midlevel official—say, an assistant deputy minister?[33] The Constitution allows presidents to make interim appointments during Senate recesses. Had the Constitution meant for the Senate to involve itself symmetrically in firings, why didn't it provide for similar exceptions for firings during recess? The fact that no such provision exists suggests that firings are simply no part of the Senate portfolio, except, of course, in impeachment situations as textually specified.[34]

A third position in the spring of 1789 was that Congress had broad choice. New York congressman John Laurance declared that because the Constitution was "silent with respect to" the issue, "Congress should define the tenure of office." The "will of the Legislature" should determine "the conditions upon which [a given executive official] shall enjoy the office."[35] Thus, Congress could, by statute, give an officer job security for a certain number of years, either absolutely (no firing, ever) or more softly (no firing except for incompetence or insubordination, or no firing unless the Senate agrees, or no firing apart from [fill in the blank]). Or Congress could instead, by statute, choose to say that department secretaries would serve at the pleasure of the president, full stop. By statute, Congress could surely empower the president at any time and for any good-faith reason to fire any department head in whom he had lost confidence.

The fourth position—the position that ultimately prevailed in the spring of 1789, and that has continued to prevail to this day in court and in our culture—was that the Constitution itself made the president the master of his own house. All department heads would serve at his pleasure, not because Congress might well choose to say so in a statute, but because, when carefully considered, the Constitution already said so in its text and structure.

In 1789, no one had thought more about presidential power than had Washington himself, and this fourth position was evidently his position: "The impossibility that one man should be able to perform all the great business of the State, I take to have been the reason for instituting the great Departments, and appointing officers therein, to *assist* the supreme Magistrate in discharging the duties of *his* trust."[36] Given that Washington was personally responsible to the American people for the entire executive branch, surely he had a right to monitor everyone under him and remove anyone who displeased him— just as he had a right at Mount Vernon to oversee and fire at will the managers of his fields or the butlers at his table.[37]

Some in 1789 might have been inclined to discount Washington's constitutional position as self-aggrandizing. Nevertheless, this was His Excellency's considered view on a matter that he understood well and cared deeply about, and it behooved James Madison, as Washington's premier, to do as Washington wished. Madison knew that he himself had not thought carefully about executive power prior to the Philadelphia Convention. Washington had. Madison had dragged a reluctant Washington out of a comfortable retirement to attend the Philadelphia Convention—and then to preside over the delegates, and then to preside over America. Surely Madison owed His Excellency the benefit of the doubt and had seen up close that Washington was not a grasping sort. So Madison had strong incentives to make the case in Congress for Washington's views. It also helped, enormously, that Washington was in fact right on the merits. The Constitution's letter and spirit, when examined carefully, supported Washington.

On June 16, 1789, Madison made the Washingtonian case succinctly and compellingly.[38] Here is what Madison said, with a bit of modern annotation in italics: "It is evidently the intention of the constitution, that the first Magistrate should be responsible for the executive department." *Indeed. This captures the Constitution's basic structure and what most ordinary Americans thought they were getting in 1788–1789 when they voted first for the document and then for His Excellency.* "The constitution affirms, that the executive power shall be vested in the President." *Exactly so. This is a direct quote from the opening sentence of Article II—the article all about the president and executive power.* "Are there exceptions to this proposition? Yes, there are. The constitution says, that in appointing to office, the Senate shall be associated with the President. . . . Have we a right to extend this exception? I believe not." *No symmetry nonsense, thank you. The Senate does not, thanks to symmetry, play a role in every firing. Rather, it plays no role; that is the true meaning by negative implication of the text's pointed omissions and silences.* "If the constitution has invested all executive power in the President . . . the Legislature has no right to diminish or modify his executive authority." *Contra Laurance, Congress has no discretion here. The Constitution itself provides the rule, thanks to the clause vesting the president and the president alone with executive power.* "The question now resolves itself into this, Is the power of displacing [removing], an executive power? I conceive that if any power whatsoever is in its nature executive, it is the power of appointing, overseeing, and controlling those who execute the laws." *Aren't syllogisms lovely? To recap: All executive power, unless otherwise specified, is vested in the president. (Major premise, undeniable as a textual matter.) Overseeing executive underlings—those who execute the law—and sacking executive slackers is surely executive power. It is surely not legislative power or judicial power. (Minor premise, functionally irrefutable or nearly so.) Therefore, the power to sack executive-branch slackers is vested in the president. QED.*

Behind closed doors, the Senate in mid-July carried the conversation forward, in debates contemporaneously summarized in Pennsylvania senator William Maclay's diary. Two Philadelphia framers, Oliver Ellsworth and William Paterson, who would both later sit on the Supreme Court (Ellsworth as chief justice), took the lead in explaining that the opening sentence of Article II vested the president with executive power, and that such power, unless elsewhere qualified by the document (as it was with appointments), comfortably covered executive-branch removals. Ellsworth especially shone, beginning with a lawyerly parsing of the text and then driving home his point with a homespun example: "The President was the executive officer. He was interfered with in the appointment, it is true, but not in the removal. The Constitution had taken one, but not the other, from him. Therefore, removal remained to him entire. . . . I buy a square acre of land. I buy the trees, water, and everything belonging to it. The executive power belongs to the President. The removing of officers is a tree on this acre. The power of removing is, therefore, his. It is in him. It is nowhere else."[39]

When the dust had settled, Congress enacted a series of statutes that embodied the Washington-Madison position—that all top executive officials, including the secretary of state and treasury secretary, would serve at the president's pleasure per the Constitution itself.[40] Lawyers and judges today refer to this series of statutes and the Washingtonian constitutional position they codified as "the Decision of 1789." Although the Decision was far from unanimous—twice, Vice President John Adams had to cast a tie-breaking Senate vote— these landmark statutes were expected to carry strong precedential weight in any future constitutional conversation on this topic.[41]

MADISON'S FATEFUL DECISION TO STAND by his man in 1789 unwittingly ended his own premiership. The Decision of 1789 codified a conversational divide that would put Hamilton into, and would leave Madison out of, Washington's inner circle. Hamilton and other department heads would serve the president and only the president under the Constitution and laws. Department chairs could not keep their positions by allying with strong senators able to shield them from the presidential axe. A president could thus trust his ministers more than he could trust, say, senators or representatives who answered to different masters—state legislators and state voters.

Thanks to the Decision of 1789, presidents could hope to have a cadre of strictly faithful and entirely subordinate advisers within the executive branch itself—a handpicked and tight-lipped executive cabinet (a word nowhere in the Constitution). This cabinet, not the Senate or the House, would become Washington's main sounding board post-1789. Hamilton would position himself near the center of that circle, with undivided loyalty to the man who picked him and could fire him in an instant. Madison would remain outside that circle. The ones who picked Madison, and who could sack him—not in an instant, but at any future election—were the voters back in his home district. Increasingly he would need to converse with them while Washington increasingly conversed with Hamilton. Unfortunately for Madison's ambitions for continued premiership, his constituents back home sharply opposed major initiatives being pursued by Washington and Washington's new right-hand man.

HAMILTON'S RISE, MADISON'S FALL

After taking office in September 1789, Hamilton readied an elaborate set of legislative proposals designed to ensure American national security by shoring up America's economy and creditworthiness.

Wars are expensive, and so are the armies, navies, and other infrastructural elements and investments sometimes necessary to deter wars. This basic fact explains much of world history on both sides of the Atlantic in this era. The massive British debt created by the French and Indian War had obliged London to milk colonial America, but the colonists had refused to be milked without their consent. Later, France found itself in a similar bind. The American War of Independence—part of a broader worldwide military conflict, yet again, between France and England—effectively bankrupted the French and precipitated the French Revolution. Hamilton aimed both to pay for the last war and to prepare America for the next war, whenever and against whomever that might be.

Assumption formed the broad and ambitious foundation of Hamilton's grand federal financial edifice—a plan that passed Congress and that President Washington unhesitatingly signed into law in mid-1790. The federal government promised not just to pay back all federal war debts, but also to *assume*—to take onto its own shoulders—various debts that individual states had incurred in fighting the War of Independence. By replacing state promissory notes with new tax-funded federal bonds promising near-full payment of the old state debt, Hamilton would give American creditors—a powerful political constituency—strong reasons to support the fledgling federal regime. Foreign investors would also be more likely to lend money in a future war if America paid what it owed for its past war. Foreigners might not always distinguish between the creditworthiness of deadbeat states and honorable ones, or between states and the United States more generally. By promising broad federal repayment, Hamilton aimed to improve the creditworthiness of all America and thereby lower the interest rate at which America could get future loans, which could in turn help it refinance its existing loan burden.

Most Virginians hated the plan. Their state had less war debt per capita than its sisters, having already paid down much of what it had owed. Why, Virginia grumbled, should its citizens—via the federal government—now pay again to bail out less responsible sister states? Ripping a page from the 1760s and early 1770s, rabble-rousing Virginia lawmaker Patrick Henry in December 1790 pushed through his state Assembly and Senate a series of Resolutions denouncing the Congressional-Hamiltonian plan as not merely unfair but also unconstitutional: "We find no clause in the constitution authorizing Congress to assume the debts of the states! . . . [T]his injudicious act . . . deserves the censure of the General Assembly, because it is not warranted by the constitution of the United States."

This was demagogic nonsense and legal gibberish, but nonsense and gibberish with portentous implications for future constitutional disputes between the United States and its single most powerful member state. The Constitution surely did have clauses allowing Congress to spend and borrow—to make appropriations and draw money from the treasury to pay federal judges, erect lighthouses, fund post offices, procure army uniforms, build navy ships, and do countless other things. Of course, federal moneys could constitution-ally flow only into proper federal projects, but Hamiltonian assump-tion was surely proper, driven as it was by the Constitution's most basic and professed purposes, the biggest and most obvious reasons why Americans had knowingly ratified the terse text in 1788: com-mon defense, national security, and international respectability. Also, Hamilton's plan replaced a bewildering welter of state IOUs circu-lating at dizzyingly different discount rates with a uniform system of transferrable federal promissory notes, providing a far more work-able and dependable currency that would facilitate interstate buy-ing, selling, borrowing, lending, and investment. This was a sensible "regulation of commerce between the states" per Article I, section 8, if ever there was one.

Writing confidentially on November 13 to his friend and fellow Publian John Jay, now chief justice (in what today might be seen as an improper *ex parte* communication regarding an issue that might one day come before Jay as a judge), Hamilton responded with pre-scient concern to an early version of Virginia's Resolution: "This is the first symptom of a spirit which must either be killed or will kill the constitution of the United States."

Constitutionality aside, critics of Hamilton's plan complained about its inequality and extravagance. Why should the current bond-holders be paid in full (or nearly so) rather than rewarding the initial holders of the IOUs and war bonds—the many virtuous farmers and brave veterans who, to make ends meet in the lean years, had sold their notes to speculators and moneymen at pennies on the dollar? Administrability was one answer. How would the initial holders be located, and how would payment properly be apportioned between the first holder and the current holder? Also, the old bonds had not been stolen, but bought and sold on free markets. Those who had scooped up the notes were themselves patriots of sorts, betting on America's future and paying farmers and veterans at various times when these original holders wanted to sell. In the process, bond-buyers had in fact propped up the value of these sundry IOUs, thus increasing the wealth of farmers and veterans who held on to their paper. Most important of all, near-full Hamiltonian payment would send the right message to future investors, by maintaining the highest level of commercial honor, lowering America's future borrowing costs, rendering federal paper more liquid to the benefit of all, and putting working capital in the hands of those likely to reinvest in future capital projects and new business ventures.[42]

Congressman Madison in particular disliked the seeming inequity of it all; but Madison had never administered anything in his life, much less a grand system on a gargantuan scale. Later, he would ignore similarly huge issues of administrability when he unwisely sided with Hylton and Taylor's implausible constitutional objections to the carriage tax—this time without any of the mitigating class-justice and Robin Hood elements of his initial 1790 skepticism about Hamilton's assumption plan. Indeed, by 1794 Madison was railing against a federal luxury tax precisely because it might lead to other federal tax schemes to soak the rich.[43]

In 1790–1791, Hamilton was backing an assumption scheme that seemed to favor the rich, buttressed as it was by a raft of taxes and excises, some of which, including a tax on whiskey, burdened the lower orders—hardscrabble backcountry folk who worked with their hands and had little to spare. (The taxes were a key part of the assumption plan. By earmarking certain taxes for a sinking fund to pay off the federal bonds, Hamilton assured investors that these new pieces of paper would hold their value and thus be worth more than the proverbial paper they were printed on.) In 1796, as we have seen, Hamilton was riding to the rescue to save a luxury tax on the wealthy. But there was no inconsistency; Hamilton had not changed his stripes in the slightest in the intervening years. He had always supported luxury taxes—including, concretely, carriage taxes. Indeed, he had done so even before the Constitution had gone into effect, and he reiterated these very ideas in his 1790 Report to Congress on how, ideally, assumption should be funded.[44]

Hamilton knew that rich moneymen might benefit from his assumption plan, but that was a side effect, not a sinister end in itself. The scheme was surely not designed to benefit himself or his friends. On issues of corruption, he was as honest a public servant as America has ever seen. Unlike, say, Aaron Burr, Hamilton sought out public service for honor and glory—for himself and his adopted country— but never for personal gain.[45]

Despite his strong misgivings, Madison in 1790 ultimately agreed to allow Hamilton's ambitious assumption program to pass Congress. In exchange for his forbearance, Madison won financial sweeteners for Virginia;[46] more importantly for the future of the republic, he won an agreement to locate the permanent national capital in or near northern Virginia, along its Potomac border with Maryland. One particularly notable moment in the complex negotiations apparently occurred at a June 1790 private dinner party—in the room where, some say, "it happened"—attended by Madison and Hamilton and hosted by Jefferson, newly arrived from France and now Washington's secretary of state. For the moment, all the president's oarsmen were rowing in the same direction.[47]

In 1791, Hamilton readied another bill in the same vein, and this time Madison jumped ship, as did his mentor and fellow Virginian Jefferson.

The new bill proposed to create a federally chartered bank of the United States, with branches located across the land. Like assumption, the bank would help Americans in scattered states buy and borrow from, sell and lend to, and invest in, each other. With a unified bank system spanning the vast country, economic actors could move money with more ease and use banknotes as a more convenient currency than, say, hogsheads of tobacco or barrels of whiskey,

which had often been used locally to offset America's chronic short-
age of hard currency. Most important of all, Hamilton understood
that Britain's national bank had been critical to its military success
in the previous century. Britain in recent decades had punched far
above its weight, besting a French nation three times its size in
the French and Indian War. To survive and thrive as a puny, albeit
promising nation, America needed to emulate Britain's formulas for
success—by ordaining and maintaining an indivisible union on the
model of Scotland and England, by creating a tax-funded national
debt to grease commerce, and by establishing a strong national bank
and a complementary regime of robust tax collection to complete
the system. As in England, a central bank could take in government
revenue (which in America would flow not just from taxes but also
land sales), lend money to encourage private initiative, stabilize a
national money supply, funnel vast amounts for governmental use in
wartime and in other crises, disperse funds whenever and wherever
needed, and facilitate trade across long distances.

Madison objected and headed toward his Rubicon. In 1789 and
1790, he had been Washington's premier on the leading elements of
the Washington agenda. Thus he had helped His Excellency craft
the Inaugural Address, pushed through the Bill of Rights, crusaded
to woo Rhode Island and North Carolina back into the union, spearheaded the Decision of 1789, aided in the creation of a national
court system, and then (with more reluctance) brokered the assump-
tion-national-capital deal. But now, in 1791, be began to move into a
new role as the leader of the increasingly organized opposition.

MADISON TOOK A STRONG DISLIKE to Hamilton's bank plan, partly
because Madison did not understand war, armies, navies, shipping,
commerce, banks, finance, and law with anything approximating
Hamilton's astonishing comprehension of each of these things and
their systematic interrelationships. (Madison had never been a warrior, trader, banker, or lawyer; Hamilton was all four, and more.)[48] But
more important than what Madison did not understand was what

he did understand: Virginia. The new central bank would likely be centered in Philadelphia, America's financial hub and provisional seat of government. A strong Philadelphia bank might enable clever congressmen to reopen the question of where to place the permanent national capital. If the bank and the treasury would need to work closely together, and if the bank needed to be in Philadelphia, well, then, perhaps so should the treasury. And if so, well, then, perhaps so should the rest of the federal government, given the gargantuan size of the treasury compared to all the other executive departments. But where would that leave Virginia?[49]

Much as Patrick Henry in 1790 had borrowed from his own and Otis's rabble-rousing in the 1760s, so now Madison borrowed from Henry, dressing up what were at root local pork-barrel concerns as cute but ultimately implausible constitutional arguments. Several intersecting and reinforcing clusters of evidence, taken together, support this harsh assessment of Madison.

First, members of Congress in both houses and from different regions saw and said that much of the opposition to the bank was rooted in national-capital concerns. Pennsylvania senator Maclay was characteristically blunt in his diary on January 19, two days before the bank bill passed the Senate: "The Potomac interest seem to regard it [the bank] as a machine which, in the hands of the Philadelphians, might retard the removal of Congress. The destruction of it, of course, was their object." Massachusetts House member Fisher Ames said the same thing in private correspondence that month. Friends of the Potomac capital site worried that the bank would instead "anchor the Gov't" in Philadelphia.[50]

Second, Virginia senator James Monroe, joined by a North Carolinian, two South Carolinians, two Georgians, and no one else, tried unsuccessfully to amend the bank's life so that it would expire in 1801—the exact date of the scheduled capital move to the Potomac, the preferred southern venue.[51]

Third, despite Madison's spirited efforts to rally opposition to the bank as beyond the scope of proper Congressional power, Hamilton's bank bill passed the House overwhelmingly, 39 to 20. All but one opposition vote came from south of the Mason-Dixon line, and most came from Virginia and Maryland, the two states closest to the agreed-upon site for the national capital. If Madison's constitutional arguments were truly valid and principled states' rights arguments, rather than mere cleverly packaged Henry-like nonsense, why was Madison so spectacularly unsuccessful in getting principled states-rightists from New England and the mid-Atlantic to join his constitutional crusade?[52]

Fourth, if Madison's constitutional arguments were sound, why would he later support a bank as president? The most parsimonious answer is that Madison was not a pure and principled constitutional thinker, as he is often misdescribed today. James Madison was also a subtle and wily politician not unlike later politicos such as Martin Van Buren, Mark Hanna, Franklin Roosevelt, Lyndon Johnson, Newt Gingrich, and Mitch McConnell. In the 1790s Madison had to tack hard toward states' rights ideology to appease his constituents—his base, to use a modern political term—in Henry-dominated Virginia. He did what he had to do.[53] (He doubtless persuaded himself that he was principled and virtuous in doing so. That hardly means that he should persuade us today.) Later, as president, Madison operated in a different political context—where his job was to protect America as a whole—and he then did what he thought was right for the country, which was, of course, what Hamilton had urged all along. In 1791, Hamilton, we must remember, needed only to stay in Washington's good graces; he did not face any pressure from demagogues like Henry or from irate local constituents. (To the extent his local affiliation may have mattered at the margins, Hamilton was a New Yorker. Manhattanites had always understood commerce and liked banks more than did Virginians.)

Fifth, Madison's constitutional arguments against the bank were superficially plausible but deeply flawed on close analysis.

IN A HOUSE SPEECH ON February 2, 1791, Madison began by invoking his own authority as a leading draftsman of the very Constitution he was now expounding.[54] He "well recollected that a power to grant charters of incorporation had been proposed in the general convention and rejected." So what? Some delegates may have voted no because they thought the power was already implied for the scenarios they most cared about (including a national bank), and viewed the proposed clause as unnecessary and possibly confusing. Many may have worried that the proposed clause seemed to treat corporation-creating power as some sort of freestanding end in itself rather than a mere means to effectuate the Constitution's other and express powers, such as its powers over national defense, interstate commercial regulation, and federal fiscal operations.

Madison then treated the House to a tedious exercise in logic chopping. The bank itself "laid no tax whatever." The bank bill "does not borrow a shilling." Again, so what? Surely the bank was genuinely connected to the taxing and borrowing capacities that had been explicitly and prominently given to Congress by the people in the Constitution. To say that x does not itself do y is to say nothing about whether x is truly, practically, and closely connected to accomplishing y. It was thus a whopper when Madison went on to say that a central bank was "wholly foreign" to the federal tax system. Or, if it was not a whopper, it was an ignorant statement from someone with no real understanding of banks and taxes; in actual fact, a national bank would be a very helpful fiscal instrument to implement the federal powers over taxing, spending, and borrowing.[55] Nor did Madison show any comprehension of how Britain's central bank and related revenue systems had been the backbone of its military superiority. Nowhere did Madison's speech carefully attend to issues of common defense.

Madison said that if Congress could pass this bill, Congress could pass any bill: "If implications, thus remote and thus multiplied, can be linked together, a chain may be formed that will reach every object." This was a classic slippery-slope argument: the Hamilton bill would, claimed Madison, lead to infinite future federal power. This, too, was an absurd claim. The bank bill *truly* and *tightly* connected to the *core* purposes of the federal government. Many future proposed laws would not do the same. Indeed, American constitutional law has for more than two centuries sided with Hamilton on the bank question—Madison himself would side with Hamilton in the 1810s!—yet even today Congressional power remains finite, not infinite as Madison feared.

Nevertheless, Madison's anxiety about slippery slopes and infinite power is deeply revealing. At Philadelphia, Madison had initially backed plenary or near-plenary federal legislative power. What had changed his mind? Not any concern about the need for a bill of rights, where Madison had indeed evolved since Philadelphia. Neither he nor anyone else claimed that a national bank would somehow violate individual rights such as freedom of conscience or freedom of speech. States could and did charter banks; the only debate was whether Congress could do the same. The bank issue was a question of federalism, not of rights.

But Virginians back home and Deep Southerners were indeed concerned about the slippery-slope infinity problem. If Congress could do *x*, and if Congress could do *y*, then could Congress . . . abolish slavery? The slavery issue lurked deep in the cracks and crevices of many early debates—even debates, as we have seen, about something so seemingly unslavery-ish as taxes on carriages. (If Congress could tax carriages as such, could it tax slaves as such, and thereby effect abolition?) Thanks to a petition backed by the venerable Benjamin Franklin, then near death, Congress in 1790 had begun discussing whether the federal government had authority over slavery, despite Madison's general desire to keep slavery off the conversational agenda. (In our final chapter, we shall return to this important episode.) Even though America's most intense abolition debates lay far in the future, the infinity trope was already beginning to operate as a southern dog whistle.

When the Hamilton bank bill reached his desk, Washington hesitated. The bill had originated from his trusted aide, Hamilton, but now faced fierce opposition from another trusted aide, Madison, who had generally worked closely with the administration. Madison not only opposed the bill, but did so on constitutional grounds. If the bill was indeed plainly unconstitutional, Washington presumably had a duty to veto it. Anything less would be faithless to his sworn inaugural oath to "preserve, protect, and defend the Constitution."

As the former presiding officer at Philadelphia, Washington himself knew a thing or two about the Constitution, to put it mildly. True, he was no lawyer. He was, however, always an advice seeker—a gifted reader and listener. And the text of the Constitution pointedly invited him to seek the opinions in writing of executive department heads—men whom he had handpicked and, thanks in no small part to Madison himself, men whom he could expect to be uncompromisingly loyal to him and his long-term best interests as a chief executive seeking to do the right thing. Washington thus asked his cabinet heads to weigh in on the bill.

In their written opinions to Washington, Attorney General Edmund Randolph and his kinsman secretary of state, Thomas Jefferson, both sided with Madison. Jefferson was particularly emphatic in reinforcing his protégé Madison's slippery-slope argument: "To take a single step beyond the boundaries thus specifically drawn around the powers of Congress [by the Constitution itself] is to take possession of a boundless field of power, no longer susceptible of any definition." (*Can you spell abolition?*) This surely heightened Washington's concern. On the other hand, Madison, Randolph, and Jefferson were all Virginians, and Virginia had beclowned itself with its Henry-esque antics in late 1790. Before signing the bill into law or vetoing it on constitutional grounds—each a truly momentous step, not to be taken lightly—Washington directed the bill's real father, Hamilton, to reanalyze the issue and respond to the various constitutional objections raised by Madison, Jefferson, and Randolph.

HAMILTON ROSE TO THE CHALLENGE in spectacular fashion. He labored under intense time pressure. The Constitution gave Washington only ten working days to make up his mind, and two days had already elapsed thanks to Randolph and Jefferson. Benefiting from his many years of writing newspaper pieces and wartime missives on tight deadlines, Hamilton within a week produced a thirteen-thousand-word document that remains one of the greatest constitutional expositions ever produced in America. Many of the best passages of legendary chief justice John Marshall's best opinion came directly from Hamilton's report to Washington. (Later, we shall examine in more detail Marshall's exposition in this 1819 case, *McCulloch v. Maryland*.)

The issue, Hamilton understood, was not merely the bank, but how to construe—how to understand and how to converse about—the Constitution more generally. Jefferson, like Madison, had played the logic-chopping game and suggested that Congress could pursue only things *mathematically necessary* to implement express powers. This might have sounded good to someone of Jefferson's background and sensibilities—a gentleman planter who had dabbled in law as a young man but entirely missed the great American constitutional conversation of 1788. Jefferson loved words, and the document did indeed use the word "necessary" in its famous Necessary and Proper Clause. But to Hamilton, a virtuoso lawyer with razor-sharp legal instincts and a leading architect of the new Constitution, the Jeffersonian idea was inane. Though Hamilton did not quite put the point this way, it should be noted that if the Constitution said x and there were, say, only two ways of doing x—$x(a)$ and $x(b)$—neither way was logically necessary. No matter which option Congress picked, a critic could say that Congress should have picked the other. Both options—the only two possible options—would flunk the inane Jefferson test.

Himself no slouch where language was concerned, Hamilton argued that in both the "grammatical" and "popular sense of the term," the word *necessary* "often means no more than *needful,* . . . *incidental, useful,* or *conducive to.*" Hamilton's invocation of the word *needful* as a synonym was a brilliant touch. Reading the Constitution holistically, Hamilton reminded Washington that Congress had already created, with Washington's blessing, a corporation of sorts to govern the territories. Indeed, Congress had done so in a statute based on the Northwest Ordinance that in an earlier version had been Jefferson's own brainchild! And Congress had created this corporation under a clause in Article IV that empowered Congress to "make all needful rules and regulations" for the territories. If a corporation was *needful* under Article IV, wrote Hamilton, surely a corporation could likewise be seen as *necessary* under Article I.

The proposed bank, Hamilton explained, genuinely connected to Congress's core powers, with an honest, not a winking, "relation . . . to the power of collecting taxes; to that of borrowing money; to that of regulating trade between the states; and to those of raising, supporting & maintaining fleets & armies." In short, a bank was truly conducive to many if not most of the biggest things the Constitution empowered the federal government to do.

Writing as one ex-soldier to another, Hamilton underscored the national security angle:

> [Suppose the] nation is threatened with a war. Large sums are wanted, on a sudden, to make the requisite preparations. Taxes are laid for the purpose, but it requires time to obtain the benefit of them. Anticipation is indispensable. If there be a bank, the supply can at once be had; if there be none, loans from individuals must be sought. The progress of these is often too slow for the exigency: in some situations they are not practicable at all. Frequently when they are, it is of great consequence to be able to anticipate the product of them by advances from a bank. The essentiality of such an institution as an instrument of loans is exemplified at this very moment. An Indian expedition is to be prosecuted. The only fund out of which the money can arise consistently with the public engagements is a tax, which will only begin to be collected in July next. The preparations, however, are instantly to be made. The money must therefore be borrowed. And of whom could it be borrowed, if there were no public banks?[56]

The real slippery slope ran the other way. If a bank was somehow invalid, then so were countless federal laws already on the books. Hamilton singled out an "act concerning light houses, beacons,

buoys, and public piers"—an act that flunked the strict mathematical necessity test but that everyone at the time of its enactment and
ever since had conceded was constitutional. Indeed, if the bank were
unconstitutional, *much* of what the Congress had already done and
would sensibly want to do in the future was and would be unconstitutional. Surely the previous year's assumption bill flunked the
Madison-Jefferson test in its strictest version. The Henryites had
said just that. But sober people had not said that. Madison, Jefferson, and Washington had all treated assumption as constitutional.
Thus, "the practice of the government is against the rule of construction advocated by the Secretary of State." Looking forward rather
than backward, "principles of construction like those established by
the Secretary of State and the Attorney General would be fatal to
the just & indispensible authority of the United States."

After reading Hamilton's tour de force and consulting further
with him in person, Washington signed the bank bill into law and
never regretted it. In the years ahead he would rely increasingly on
Hamilton and decreasingly on Madison.

MADISON'S FALL FROM GRACE OVER the next several years was a
spectacular reversal of political fortune, matched only by his later
return to power after Washington left the stage. Over the previous
four years, if Madison was not the man (as we say now), he was surely
the man's man. He had coaxed the great Washington back into public
life. He had played as big a role as anyone other than Washington at
Philadelphia, even if he had gotten much less than he hoped. He had
spearheaded ratification in the decisive state of Virginia, and then
he had served as Washington's Congressional sherpa as the two, together, conquered one epic summit after another.

Then came the bank bill. In that episode he had embraced an
extreme constitutional position that Congress overwhelmingly rejected, that Washington squarely repudiated, and that the Supreme
Court would one day unanimously spurn—indeed, mock—in one of
the most important decisions of all time. Virtually no justice since

then has openly taken Madison's 1791 position, and Madison himself wisely abandoned it as president. Andrew Jackson later killed the bank, but he never said that Congress had lacked power to create it. Rather, Jackson attacked specific details, such as the bank's special immunity from state taxation and the role of foreign investors in the system.

Nor was Madison's extreme position on the bank an isolated lapse in this deep valley of his career. As has been noted, Madison also blasted the 1794 carriage tax as unconstitutional—once again staking out a position emphatically rejected by Congress and Washington and later ridiculed by a unanimous Supreme Court. (Happily for Madison's general reputation today, but unhappily for those who value proper legal and historical understanding, almost no one now remembers *Hylton*, and his biographers have generally chosen to make no mention of it.)[57]

Egged on by Jefferson, Madison in that same period took to the newspapers, under a pseudonym, to attack Washington's Neutrality Proclamation of April 1793. Hamilton, also writing pseudonymously, had penned a characteristically muscular defense of Washington in particular and executive diplomatic power in general. Madison's strained efforts to attack Washington's sensible efforts to maintain the peace generally fell flat. (We shall revisit this issue later in our story.)

In 1796, Madison, yet again goaded by Jefferson, jousted afresh with Hamilton and Washington, this time over Jay's Treaty. The treaty aimed to improve military and trade relations with England. Although its provisions were less than generous to America, it would buy America time to grow stronger. Britain would at long last evacuate its forts in America's Northwest, opening up the Ohio Valley to American settlers and fur traders and forcing nettlesome tribes to moderate. Increased trade with Britain and the Caribbean would reopen vital markets for American producers, fatten federal coffers with increased import duties, and bolster American shipping. America's détente with England would encourage the British lion to feast on the French rather than feed on the Americans. As if on cue, Hamilton penned a powerful series of newspaper essays—this time, with

Fisher Ames under the pseudonym Camillus—defending the treaty against its critics, many of whom clustered in Virginia. (Virginians fumed about the treaty's failure to insist that Britain compensate Americans for having liberated slaves in the Revolutionary War, and about Jay's concession that Americans, including Virginia's many deeply indebted planters, had to pay what they owed to British creditors. On the eve of the Revolution, Virginians owed almost as much to British creditors as did all other colonists combined.[58]) As these essays unfolded, Washington again sided with Hamilton, opting to put the treaty into operation. When Madison in early 1796 openly and unsuccessfully opposed Washington's stern request to the House to fund the treaty without prying into the details of diplomatic discussions long since concluded, the break between the president and his former Congressional premier was complete and final.

At the peak of their collaboration, from November 1786 through June 1792, Washington exchanged over one hundred letters with Madison, a rate of nearly twenty per year, back and forth. In his last letter in this batch, the president told Madison that he aimed to retire at the end of his constitutionally allotted four years and requested Madison's assistance in composing a valedictory address to be delivered later in 1792. The request was particularly fitting, as Madison in 1789 had helped him on his inaugural remarks. But as events unfolded, Washington reluctantly agreed to serve a second term, and as we have seen, Madison in these years was generally either useless or oppositional to Washington.

In 1793, the president sent only one letter to Madison, late in the year, seeking counsel on an urgent matter: How should he respond to a deadly yellow-fever outbreak in the temporary capital city, Philadelphia, where Congress was set to convene later in the year? Washington wondered whether as president he could name another meeting spot, and on this delicate constitutional question, he sensibly sought the advice of a man who might apprise him of likely Congressional reactions.

Thereafter, Washington's correspondence with Madison dried to a trickle, mainly a few cursory notes about trivial official business. In

Washington's final retirement—a period in which he traded thousands of missives with others—His Excellency never exchanged even a single letter with Madison, or with Jefferson for that matter. Washington's most prolific correspondents in these final years at Mount Vernon, 1797 through 1799, were two men who had both been his aides-de-camp in the war, had both served as delegates at Philadelphia, and had then both served him as trusted cabinet secretaries: James McHenry and Alexander Hamilton.

CONVERSATIONAL CIRCLES, EXISTENTIAL THREATS, AND GRAND STRATEGIES

Not everyone can talk and listen to everyone else about everything all the time. In the 1790s, what conscious and unconscious factors drove the choices of leading actors about whom to converse with and what to converse about? Two analytic concepts—conversational circles and existential threats—can help us better understand the emerging and evolving shape and structure of America's constitutional conversation during these early years.

We have already begun to glimpse certain aspects of the conversational circles at work in the Washington presidency. Reinforced by landmark laws like the 1789 Judiciary Act and the Decision of 1789 statutes, the Constitution nudged senators to deliberate with senators; House members likewise to talk among themselves; justices to converse with local judges, juries, and lawyers while on circuit and with each other and oral advocates while en banc; and presidents to confer with department heads. Over time, House members and senators increasingly understood the need to converse with their constituents, indirectly and directly.

Indirectly, Congress members speechified and played to the gallery in the hopes that newspapers in the capital would take note and their hometown newspapers would reprint favorable (they hoped) copy.[59] Although not himself a congressman seeking this sort of publicity, Hamilton exemplified the larger phenomenon of capital-city rhetorical performance in his acclaimed oral argument in *Hylton*.

The Senate initially met behind closed doors, but by late 1795 it had moved into the sunshine, following the lead of the House, which had always allowed public galleries to observe suitable parts of its proceedings.

Directly, House members and senators needed to return periodically to their home districts to report to and hear from their constituents. Like the justices, they would in effect ride circuit. Despite the Senate's initial hesitation in the Decision of 1789, senators benefited from the Decision in one key respect: presidents would not need to summon them from their home districts back to the capital every time some executive official, high or low, needed the boot.

Even as the development of conversational circles between lawmakers and constituents encouraged the emergence of certain other circles (such as the presidential-cabinet circle, especially when congressmen went home), it discouraged the emergence of still other kinds of robust conversation. The complicated relationship between the Senate and the president offers a nice illustration. In the summer of 1789, Washington personally entered the Senate chamber to seek preapproval of negotiation instructions in a forthcoming parley with Indian tribes, but his well-intentioned overture did not work well. Senators felt flustered and overawed by the great man's looming presence in the room, and Senate traditions of open debate and speechifying did not mesh with Washington's executive instincts to run a tight meeting. Senator Maclay worried in his diary that senatorial haste would set a dangerous precedent. He feared that if he did not speak up about the need for debate, "these advices and consents [would be] ravished, in a degree from us. . . . I saw no chance of fair investigation of subjects while the President of the United States sat there . . . to support his opinions and overawe the timid and neutral part of the Senate." When Washington realized he would need to return on another day because it would take time for the matter at hand to be concluded, he blurted out, "This defeats every purpose of my coming here!" At one point as he left the chamber he muttered that he "would be damned if he ever went there again." After his two-visit adventure, he never did.[60]

Washington's initial instincts in this overture were commendable. As a good listener, he valued advice; the Constitution twice used the phrase "advice and consent" linking the president and the Senate; and state and colonial upper houses had long doubled as gubernatorial councils, as when Francis Bernard sought his council's advice about whether to proclaim George III king in December 1760. Besides, in mid-1789 Washington did not yet have his own department heads to consult. But the Senate was not well structured to act as an executive sounding board. It was already large for that purpose and would only grow larger. As with House member Madison, Senate members were neither picked by the president nor removable by him. (By contrast, colonial governors had typically handpicked their counselors or at least played a role in their selection; revolutionary state constitutions had typically restricted these gubernatorial powers.)

Confidentiality was also a concern. Thanks to the Decision of 1789, the president could sack any loose-lipped executive head in an instant; but Washington could only fume in 1795 when Senator Stevens Thomas Mason of Virginia (again Virginia![61]) violated Senate rules by giving the press the official and secret copy of the Jay Treaty. In theory, the Senate could have censured Mason, but ultimately it opted not to act against one of its own.

Washington also invited justices into an informal conversational circle, but, as with his Senate initiative, the Constitution's text and structure worked against this overture. Unlike cabinet heads, judges were not part of the executive branch; nor were they unilaterally removable by the chief executive; nor did they answer personally to the president under the express language of the Article II Opinions Clause. Rather, judges were supposed to be independent of the executive, unlike the system in Britain, where judges served on the monarch's Privy Council. In the summer of 1793, justices of the Supreme Court interpreted the Constitution in exactly this way when they wrote a private letter to President Washington declining to furnish him *ex parte* advice even though he had requested their views about various legal issues precipitated by the French Revolution. In rejecting Washington's request, the justices noted that "the Lines of Separation drawn by the Constitution between the three Departments of government" and the fact that the branches were "in certain Respects checks on each other" were "strong arguments" against closed-door judicial conversations with the executive: "The Power given by the Constitution to the President, of calling on the Heads of Departments for opinions, seems to have been *purposely* as well as expressly united to the *executive* Departments" as pointedly distinct from the judiciary. Notwithstanding this letter, justices individually—but not en banc— did occasionally communicate off the record with high executive officials, as when Hamilton corresponded with Jay. Early chief justices also accepted temporary assignments as overseas diplomats.[62]

THE MOST IMPORTANT CONVERSATIONAL IMPERATIVE in the early republic was the simple existential requirement that the Constitution that nurtured and structured the conversation survive. George Washington did not take survival for granted, nor should we if we seek to understand Washington, Hamilton, and the earliest years of our constitutional republic.

During the war, there had been many moments when Washington had feared the worst. On December 18, 1776—a week before his risky recrossing of the Delaware—the general wrote his brother Samuel that "if every nerve is not strained to recruit the New Army with all possible Expedition I think the game is pretty near up." America's army had been saved that season, Washington later wrote, only by "the infatuation of the enemy." For "the greatest part of the War," his troops had been "inferior to the enemy, indebted for our safety to their [the enemy's] inactivity" and their "want of enterprize." Ever the realist, he understood that even after France joined the fight on America's side, the odds did not decisively favor the Revolutionaries. "We ought not to deceive ourselves," he wrote to a confidant in mid-1780. "The maritime resources of Great Britain are more substantial and real than those of France & Spain united."[63]

Later in the letter came the critical insight that explains much of the Washington-Hamilton administration that would eventually emerge: "In modern wars the longest purse must chiefly determine the event. . . . [The British] nation is rich and their riches afford a fund which will not be easily exhausted. Besides, their system of public credit [that is, their banking and tax system] is such that it is capable of greater exertions than that of any other nation."[64]

Americans who had not been with Washington in camp and in the field (Americans such as Madison and Jefferson) did not understand America's vulnerabilities as Washington and Hamilton did—viscerally, deeply, painfully, personally. As one eminent historian wisely observed, Washington "did not dare to advertise the weakness of his force, when the only thing between him and defeat was the fact that his enemy did not realize how weak he was."[65]

Armed with this insight, we can now see how Washington and Hamilton's policies systematically cohered—much as the Constitution itself had a national-security coherence. The biggest threat remained England, but Spain too was a worry, lest its control over the Mississippi tempt western Americans to break away from their eastern cousins. The key to ousting the British from their forts was to dislodge their Indian allies, and the keys to that, in turn, were money and a strong system of public credit—beating the British at their own game. In his 1791 opinion to Washington, Hamilton had expressly linked the bank to the need to raise quick money for military operations against Indians; the 1794 carriage tax was also linked to Indian relations, and so were Washington's treaty overtures much earlier—the subject of his ill-starred trips to the Senate. (Paying Indians, if they were amenable, would be far superior to fighting them, thought Washington, who had long experience fighting both alongside and against various backcountry Indians.) In short, the grand-strategy key to the East (Britain) was the West (Indians); the potential enemy across the Atlantic had to be thwarted by initiatives over the mountains.

The year 1791 ended disastrously for Washington's grand strategy. Led by Miami chieftain Little Turtle, Shawnee war chief Blue Jacket, and Lenape warrior Buckongahelas, roughly 1,000 Indians from allied tribes killed over 600 Americans and wounded more than 250 others near the Wabash River in modern-day Ohio on November 4. In a moment of performance art of their own—a Boston Tea Party in reverse?—the victors filled the dead White men's mouths with dirt to mock America's lust for land. It was the most smashing victory that Indians would ever experience against the US Army. Congress immediately opened a broad investigation into the debacle.[66]

Indians did not pose any kind of long-term existential threat to America, but Britain surely did. What would the British think of American military (in)competence? worried Washington. Thanks in large measure to the national bank, excise taxes, carriage duties, and other Hamiltonian systems backed by Congress, Washington spent lavishly to win big in the West, culminating in a decisive victory on August 20, 1794, near modern-day Toledo. Relatively few—less than a hundred men combined—died at the seventy-minute Battle of Fallen Timbers. But the confrontation and its aftermath achieved Washington's true strategic goal by shattering the Indians' trust in their British allies. Without Indian support, Britain could not maintain its chain of northwestern garrisons much longer. Thus, Washington sent John Jay east, across the Atlantic, to cut a deal in London. In late 1794—after news of Fallen Timbers had reached British shores—Britain signed a treaty giving up the forts and broadening the peace with its former colonists. The Senate approved Jay's Treaty in June 1795, and Washington decided to effectuate the détente treaty in mid-August. Meanwhile, American treaty negotiators in the West pointedly informed Indians that Britain had once again abandoned its aboriginal allies at the bargaining table (as had also happened in the 1783 Paris treaty). Yielding to this new strategic reality, the tribes agreed to the Treaty of Greenville in early August 1795. Under the terms of the treaty, Indians would cease hostilities and yield most of modern-day Ohio to American settlers. America, in turn, would make annual payments to the Indians (payments of course funded by Hamiltonian tax dollars).[67]

American settlers could now surge into the Ohio Valley, relatively free from the threat of Indian attacks and encouraged by the Northwest Ordinance, which had been reenacted, with a few tweaks, by the first federal Congress in 1789. Americans were also continuing to flow into the Southwest, thanks in part to Washingtonian diplomacy with southern Indian tribes. Spain now realized that it could not hold back the swelling tide of American frontier folk who needed access to and through New Orleans and would soon be positioned to use force if necessary, especially now that America had pacified its northwestern frontier and brokered a deeper peace with Britain. In late 1795 America and Spain signed, and in early 1796 the two countries ratified, the Treaty of San Lorenzo, also known as Pinckney's Treaty, which guaranteed Americans navigation rights on the Mississippi River down to the Gulf of Mexico, including "deposit" rights to transfer goods without charge between vessels in the great harbor city of New Orleans.

These were brilliant diplomatic and geostrategic achievements, and they were ultimately made possible by the Hamiltonian system that many of the Virginians, other than Washington himself, failed to understand.

ONE MORE WASHINGTONIAN-HAMILTONIAN INITIATIVE ALSO fit into this larger grand strategy. Federal whiskey taxes outraged backcountry folk, who resisted by brutalizing and terrorizing federal tax collectors and their local supporters with tar and feathers, torches, whips, guns, and more. The rural mobbing in western Pennsylvania called to Washington's mind the earlier uprising in rural Massachusetts, Shays' Rebellion. This time, Washington had the muscle to show the world that a republic could in fact enforce its duly and democratically enacted laws.

In the fall of 1794, Washington, armed with a judicial court order from Justice James Wilson approving the use of military might, amassed an overwhelming force of some thirteen thousand militiamen from neighboring states. With Acting Secretary of War Hamilton at his side—two soldiers, reunited in arms—Washington saddled up and rode at the head of this awesome military force into central Pennsylvania, where he reviewed his arrayed troops. Satisfied with what he saw, he left the scene and turned the field command over to Henry "Lighthorse Harry" Lee. Terrified by the overwhelming show of force and promised amnesty for their past misbehavior, most of the armed tax resisters in the region quickly surrendered and dispersed. The few who did not were rounded up, and two leaders were later convicted of treason and sentenced to be hanged. Washington then pardoned them.

Critics of this overwhelming response to the so-called Whiskey Rebellion saw Washington and Hamilton as having grotesquely overreacted to a relatively minor provocation. Rural folk had understandable reasons for their discontent; the unruly participants were not truly aiming to topple the American government; here was no grand treasonous conspiracy or regime-threatening rebellion. Unrest was simply an aspect of Americans' fierce devotion to freedom, their strong sense of liberty, and their inborn gumption, apologists argued. Goaded by Hamilton, Washington was engaging in colossal excess—overkill, in modern parlance. Or so critics claimed, publicly and privately.

But "overkill" is precisely the wrong word, because almost no one was killed—far fewer than at Fallen Timbers, which itself had been tame in the grand scheme of backcountry warfare and savagery on both sides. Washington used overwhelming force in Pennsylvania precisely to avoid bloodshed. He aimed to awe and subdue, not kill and maim. And then, from a position of supreme strength, he showed supreme mercy with his amnesty offers and his pardon pen, closely following a script—quick and massive force combined with well-timed acts of mercy—that had in fact been outlined years before in *The Federalist* No. 71, authored by Hamilton/Publius.

Washington did all this to make two points. First, and domestically, he needed to show that whiskey taxes in the 1790s were utterly unlike stamp taxes in the 1760s. America was now a proper self-governing republic, and taxation *with* representation was wholly legitimate. Indeed, although backcountry folk might not have grasped all the subtleties of his grand strategy, federal tax money was in fact funding operations that would benefit backcountry folk themselves—Indian pacification, British evacuation, western settlement,

and Mississippi navigation. If the tax critics did not like the whiskey tax, they could vote, serve on juries, speak up, sue, and petition. They could not tar and feather, beat, maim, torture, or kill.

Second, and internationally, Washington aimed to send a strong message to Britain. *The Wabash River debacle was a fluke. America is strong and united. We can raise massive force in the backcountry if ever we need to. Leave the forts—now!* A painting attributed to Frederick Kemmelmeyer, likely done in the late 1790s, nicely captured these themes. The image of America's civilian commander in chief re-uniformed and leading troops in the field is surely arresting—the one and only time such a thing has happened in America. But on closer inspection, the scene seems not altogether terrifying or Napoleonic. This is not a battle scene but a review of the troops, a ceremonial event. The locals in the bottom left corner seem more pleased than alarmed. That said, the soldiers in the background look impressive— arrayed, well-regulated, artilleried, vast. Any European or aboriginal power behind the western mountains in the background looking to thwart the United States should surely think twice.

In a remarkably comprehensive letter in early 1795 to an old Virginia friend, Washington displayed an impressive grasp of how the various pieces of his policy fit together.[68] He was continuing to pay close attention to newspapers ("Gazettes") and displayed noteworthy awareness of the disadvantages that tribes suffered simply because they had no newspapers to tell their story in what was becoming an increasingly newspaper-saturated New World. If we make due historical allowances for his repeated use of now offensive words like "savages" and "ignorant," the letter actually suggests that Washington truly did sympathize with some of the legitimate grievances of Indians. He appreciated the need for fair treatment of tribes that had in fact been ill served by their supposed British friends, and also ill treated by greedy White Americans. The long letter is worth reading with care, evincing as it does the candor that was more possible in private correspondence than in public pronouncements:

> I hope, and believe, that the spirit of anarchy in the western counties of this State (to quell which the force of the Union was called for) is *entirely* subdued; and altho' to effect it, the community has been saddled with a considerable expence, yet I trust no money could have been more advantageously expended; both as it respects the internal peace & welfare of *this* country, and the impression it will make on *others.* The spirit with which the Militia turned out, in support of the Constitution, and the laws of our country—at the same time that it does them immortal honor—is the most conclusive refutation that could have been given to the assertions of Lord Sheffield, and the predictions of others of his cast—that without the protection of G. Britain, we should be unable to govern ourselves; and would soon be involved in anarchy & confusion. They will see that republicanism is not the phantom of a deluded imagination: on the contrary, that under no form of government, will laws be better supported—liberty and property better secured—or happiness be more effectually dispensed to mankind.

> The successes of our Army to the westward has, already, been productive of good consequences. They have dispelled a cloud which lowered very heavily in the northern hemisphere

(six [Iroquois] nations)—and . . . there is reason to believe
that the Indians with whom we are, or were, at war in that
quarter—together with their abetters—begin to see things
in a different point of view; but what effect these favorable
changes may have on the Southern Indians, is not easy, at
this moment, to decide.

I accord fully in opinion with you, that the plan of annual
presents in an abstract view, unaccompanied with other
measures, is not the best mode of treating ignorant Savages,
from whose hostile conduct we experience much distress; but
it is not to be overlooked, that they, in turn, are not without
serious causes of complaint, from the encroachments which are
made on their lands by our people; who are not to be restrained
by any law now in being, or likely to be enacted. They, poor
wretches, have no Press thro' which their grievances are related;
and it is well known, that when one side only of a Story is
heard, and often repeated, the human mind becomes impressed
with it, insensibly—The annual presents however, which you
allude to, are not given so much with a view to purchase
peace, as by way of retribution for injuries, not otherwise to be
redressed. These people are very much irritated by the continual
pressure of land Speculators & settlers on one hand; & by the
impositions of unauthorised, & unprincipled traders (who rob
them in a manner of their hunting) on the other. Nothing but
the strong arm of the Union—or in other words—energetic
laws, can correct these abuses—but here! jealousies, &
prejudices (from which I apprehend more fatal consequences
to this government than from any other source) aided by local
situations—& perhaps by interested considerations, always
oppose themselves to efficient measures.

My communications to Congress at the last and present
Session, have proceeded upon similar ideas with those
expressed in your letter—namely—to make *fair* treaties with
the Savage tribes—(by this I mean that they shall *perfectly*
understand every article & clause of them from correct &
repeated interpretations)—that these treaties shall be held

sacred, & the infractors on either side punished exemplarily; and to furnish them plentifully with goods under wholesome regulations, without aiming at higher prices than is adequate to cover the cost, & charges. If measures like these were adopted, we might hope to live in peace & amity with these borderers; but not whilst our citizens, in violation of law and justice, are guilty of the offences I have mentioned, & are carrying on unauthorised expeditions against them—and when, for the most atrocious murders, even of those of whom we have the least cause of complaint, a Jury on the frontiers, can hardly be got to listen to a charge, much less to convict a culprit.

The madness of European powers, and the calamitous situation into which all of them are thrown by the present ruinous War, ought to be a serious warning to us, to avoid a similar catastrophe as long as we can with honor & justice to our national character. What will be the result of Mr Jay's mission, is more than I am able, at this moment, to disclose. Charged as he has been with *all* matters in dispute between the two countries (not, as has been insinuated in some of the Gazettes, *merely* to that of spoliation) it may easily be conceived that there would be a large field of discussion.[69]

WHY HAMILTON?

Washington could not have done all that he did without great men at his side. None was greater than Hamilton, and Washington had remarkable skill in harnessing Hamilton's greatness.

The harnessing metaphor is apt. Washington was a gifted horse-man, not just as a rider but as a trainer. At Mount Vernon, he personally broke in his horses, and he knew how to steady high-spirited creatures.[70] Hamilton was as high spirited as they come and he greatly benefited from Washington's firm guidance. When Washington was not around, Hamilton repeatedly got himself into scrapes of all sorts—he was too clever for his own good. (Hamiltonian excesses included using the army as a political pawn, dreaming up wild military adventures posing more risk than reward, engaging in intense personal confrontations and altercations—including dueling—and philandering.) Conversely, when Hamilton was not around, Washington lost half his power—a knight without his steed. Together they made an astounding team, each completing the other. When Hamilton left the Philadelphia Convention for a while midsummer, he received a touching note from His Excellency: "I am sorry you went away. I wish you were back."[71]

Hamilton's distinctive gifts suited him best for the executive branch. As he himself had explained as Publius in *The Federalist* No. 70, "energy" was a leading feature of executive power. That he had in spades. John Adams once crudely attributed Hamilton's remarkable energy to a "superabundance of secretions"—too much testosterone, we might say today.[72] In a less crude moment, Adams hilariously reported to a friend that "Washington once said to me, that Hamilton was 'a proud Spirited little Animal, as ever existed.'"[73]

That spirit, that pride, that drive, when combined as it was with supreme talent and low birth, was bound to invite envy. In the 1791 bank debate, Washington had followed Hamilton over Jefferson and Madison, and that surely must have smarted. In 1792, Trumbull depicted Hamilton at high noon—a dapper man staring deep into the future, a man who could indeed see farther than could others, but who also might attract enmity for that very reason.

Trumbull also draws our eye to Hamilton's ungloved right hand, the source of his power, resting lightly on a writing desk, with paper, quill, ink, and blotter at the ready. Hamilton's astonishing expositional skill and speed made him a true prodigy both in print and in oral expression. Surely, he was near the center of more conversational circles than anyone else—with his massive reports to Congress[74] and the legislation he drafted or inspired; his one-on-one interactions with Washington via official written opinions, oral communications, and prolific correspondence; his feisty domination of collective cabinet meetings (much to Jefferson's vexation); his skills as a courtroom lawyer, both with juries at trial and with judges at every level, as exemplified by his compelling performance in *Hylton*, the eighteenth

century's most consequential case; and his incomparable ability to take his case directly to his fellow citizens in newspaper essays of all kinds. If anyone in independent America was even more ubiquitous than Hutchinson had been before the Revolution, it was Hamilton. (This is all the more true when we add in Hamilton's wartime record: he managed to place himself alongside Washington early on and ultimately secured a battlefield command of high risk and high honor at Yorktown.)

A few final attributes merit mention. First, Hamilton was an amazing administrator, which is precisely what the early republic needed. He knew how to get things done. Other men fancied themselves doers of various kinds, but few excelled as he did at the actual art of administration. His early years as a clerk and aide served him particularly well in this regard.

Second, he had systematic constitutional vision. He saw connections between economic, military, political, diplomatic, and legal issues. Legislators pass laws one at a time, and judges likewise hear one case at a time. A president must administer all the laws at once and fathom how policies over here affect other policies over there. Washington had this systematic vision, as we have just seen, and so did Washington's right-hand man, his true prime minister.

Third, Hamilton had genuine foresight. More clearly than most he saw all three of the biggest existential threats to the early republic—the European threat, the slavery threat, and the disunion threat. We shall consider all three in more detail later in our story; and we shall also consider the threat of discourse suppression, where Hamilton's judgment failed him.

Finally, above all, Hamilton was an American, a nationalist, a continentalist. Born and raised outside what later became the United States, he harbored no state or regional bias, unlike Braintree's Adams, or Virginia's tag team of Jefferson and Madison. After the Constitution went into operation, Hamilton did not need to placate a local base, as did Madison most obviously. The treasury secretary's power base—"an Aegis very essential to me," he later eulogized—was Washington himself. Hamilton could succeed—on the bank, on carriage taxes, on anything—only by persuading Washington.[75] This had a wonderful chastening effect on him. Like blinders on a horse, it kept him focused in just the right direction. Given that Washington himself was in many respects the embodiment of the Constitution, Hamilton's need to keep Washington astride kept the secretary on track.[76]

FAREWELLS

In late 1796, President Washington announced that he would not serve yet another term and he thus bade a fond republican adieu to his countrymen. It was not his first grand goodbye, but rather a powerful echo and reenactment of his initial effort to leave public life at the end of the war. This time Hamilton was at his side and once again in his head.

IN 1783, AMERICANS ANXIOUSLY AWAITED news from Paris of a treaty that would formally end the war and mark Britain's acknowledgment of America's independence. Washington, who loved the theater, began to ponder his grand exit from the public stage—an act of republican retirement dissolving his army and resigning his commission, combined with words of avuncular advice to his fellow citizens.

Though the war had been won, Washington knew that the Confederation's frame was deeply defective. But for its rickety continental political and fiscal system, America might have prevailed much earlier with much less total loss of blood and treasure.[77] The point went far beyond money. The new nation had suffered some twenty-five thousand military deaths—nearly 1 percent of its population, more than in any future military conflict except for the Civil War, when Americans would die in horrific numbers on both sides.[78]

In March 1783, Washington unbosomed himself to his protégé Hamilton, now a lawyer in private practice:

> No man in the United States is, or can be more deeply impressed with the necessity of a reform in our present Confederation than myself. No man perhaps has felt the bad effects of it more sensibly; for to the defects thereof, & want of Powers in Congress may justly be ascribed the prolongation of the War, & consequently the Expences occasioned by it. More than half the perplexities I have experienced in the course of my command, and almost the whole of the difficulties & distress of the Army, have their origin here.[79]

Washington was preaching to the choir, for Hamilton himself had said the same thing in a series of prescient "Continentalist" essays published in the summer of 1781 bemoaning the "WANT OF POWER IN CONGRESS" as America's central "defect." In contrast to the views that Madison/Publius would later expound in 1787–1788, Hamilton/Continentalist did not see state constitutions as particularly worrisome. "Notwithstanding their imperfections," they sufficed; and thanks to their amendability, "they seem to have, in themselves, and in the progress of society among us, the seeds of improvement." Nor were America's woes due to "a GENERAL DIS-AFFECTION of the PEOPLE," who had rallied to the glorious cause with astonishing acts of patriotism and sacrifice. Rather, the problem was one of continental legal structure. America needed to re-constitute its federal system: "We ought without delay, to ENLARGE THE POWERS OF CONGRESS. Every plan of which, this is not the foundation, will be illusory. The separate exertions of the states will never suffice. Nothing but a well-proportioned exertion of the resources of the whole, under the direction of a Common Council, with power sufficient to give efficacy to their resolutions, can pre-serve us from being a CONQUERED PEOPLE now, or can make us a HAPPY PEOPLE hereafter."[80]

This, indeed, was the theme that His Excellency himself evoked in a circular letter sent to state governors on June 8, 1783. Wash-ington's intended dramatic finale—a letter reprinted (as planned) by newspapers across the country and across the Atlantic—opened by publicly proclaiming his "determination" to eschew "any share in public business hereafter" so that he might "pass the remainder of life, in a state of undisturbed repose." Having thus freed himself from suspicion that he was arguing for more central power merely to wield it himself, Washington urged his audience to seize the day to restruc-ture America's central government:

This is the favorable moment to give such a tone to our fœderal Government, as will enable it to answer the ends of its institution—or this may be the ill-fated moment for relaxing the powers of the Union, annihilating the cement of the Confederation and exposing us to become the sport of European Politicks, which may play one State against another, to prevent their growing importance and to serve their own interested purposes; for according to the System of Policy the States shall adopt at this moment, they will stand or fall, and by their confirmation or lapse, it is yet to be decided whether the Revolution must ultimately be considered as a blessing or a curse:

a blessing or a curse, not to the present Age alone, for with our fate will the destiny of unborn Millions be involved.

First on the list of elements that Washington deemed "essential to the well-being, I may even venture to say to the existence, of the United States as an independent Power" was "an indissoluble Union of the States under one federal Head." He also reiterated the fiscal points that he had privately shared with Hamilton (among countless others), and that Hamilton himself had publicly stressed as the Continentalist: "The ability of the Country to discharge the debts which have been incurred in its defence, is not to be doubted. . . . In less time & with much less expence than has been incurred, the War might have been brought to the same happy, conclusion if the resources of the Continent could have been properly drawn forth."

Then he said goodbye: "I now bid adieu . . . at the same time I bid a last farewell to the cares of Office and all the employments of public life."

THE RAVE REVIEWS GENERATED BY this beau geste and accompanying personal surrender of his military commission to Congress—the dramatic moment captured by Trumbull—made Washington reluctant to attend the Philadelphia Convention when invited in 1787. Such attendance, he worried, could be seen as a violation of his vow—a vow that he knew (for he was always intensely media-savvy) had reached Everyman, thanks to the press: "The act [of going to Philadelphia] will, I apprehend, be considered as inconsistent with my public declaration delivered in a solemn manner at an interesting Æra of my life, never more to intermeddle in public matters. This declaration not only stands on the files of Congress, but is I believe registered in almost all the Gazettes and magazines that are published."[81]

Washington's reluctant return to public life in 1787 ultimately resulted from the same republicanism that had prompted his unreluctant retirement. He was being summoned by his state, as other prominent leaders were being summoned by theirs, to make the very kinds of continental legal changes he himself had so famously urged. In 1789, when summoned by his country—now a truly indissoluble and indivisible America, per his own advice—to serve as the Constitution's first First Man, he again agreed, but only so that he could thereafter retire and once again exemplify true republicanism. As he told Hamilton in late 1788, he "hope[d] that at a convenient and an early period, my services might be dispensed with, and that I might be permitted once more to retire—to pass an unclouded evening, after the stormy day of life, in the bosom of domestic tranquility."[82]

He initially dreamed that he might exit after a single term, but the pieces of his grand strategy for true American independence—Indian pacification, British evacuation, Spanish concession, Mississippi navigation, western integration and settlement, militia regularization—had yet to fall into place and interlock. Also, European ideological politics, pitting traditionalist England against revolutionary France, had begun to polarize America. As in 1789, he seemed to be the only person that all Americans could agree upon in 1792. Thus, he allowed himself to be unanimously reelected that year, but inwardly resolved to leave as soon as possible.

WASHINGTON'S FINAL FAREWELL SYNTHESIZED THE themes of his public life. In 1792, in contemplation of retirement after a single term, he had asked Madison to compose a draft valedictory. Madison promptly complied. However, the published version four years later was almost all Hamilton—an apt example of the shift from Madison to Hamilton as Washington's main man as events unfolded. As Washington had done throughout his public career, beginning at age twenty-two, he paid careful attention to the press. He gave an exclusive to the *American Daily Advertiser*, with specific instructions to Philadelphia printer David Claypoole about how the address should appear on the newspaper's printed page.[83] He dated the farewell letter September 17, even though the *Advertiser* published it on September 19.

This was a perfect echo of 1787. That year, the Philadelphia Convention over which he had presided had released and dated its proposed Constitution and his own accompanying letter to the Confederation Congress September 17; and both were first printed on September 19 by the *Pennsylvania Packet*, which had now become the *Advertiser*. Symbol and substance here merged: Washington's 1797 text urged all Americans to hold fast to the Constitution, his two-dimensional counterpart and his greatest legacy.

The address did not name itself, though it soon came to be named, Washington's "Farewell Address." In the spirit of both Publius and the Preamble, the text directed itself "To the PEOPLE of the UNITED STATES." It then proceeded in tender republican fashion: "FRIENDS and FELLOW-CITIZENS, . . . I should now apprise you of the resolution I have formed, to decline being considered" for re-reelection. Once more freed from any suspicion of drawing additional power to himself, Washington yet again offered earnest advice.

As with his earlier grand-strategy letter, this letter merits extensive quotation and careful examination. To understand it is to understand Washington and the constitutional system he sired, with Hamilton's help above all others:

> The unity of Government which constitutes you one people,
> is . . . a main pillar in the edifice of your real independence,
> the support of your tranquility at home, your peace abroad;
> of your safety; of your prosperity; of that very Liberty which
> you so highly prize. But as it is easy to foresee, that from
> different causes and from different quarters, much pains will
> be taken, many artifices employed, to weaken in your minds
> the conviction of this truth; as this is the point in your political
> fortress against which the batteries of internal and external
> enemies will be most constantly and actively (though often
> covertly and insidiously) directed, it is of infinite moment,
> that you should properly estimate the immense value of your
> national Union, to your collective and individual happiness;
> that you should cherish a cordial, habitual and unmoveable
> attachment to it; accustoming yourselves to think and

speak of it as of the Palladium of your political safety and
prosperity; watching for its preservation with jealous anxiety;
discountenancing whatever may suggest even a suspicion that
it can in any event be abandoned; and indignantly frowning
upon the first dawning of every attempt to alienate any portion
of our country from the rest, or to enfeeble the sacred ties
which now link together the various parts. . . .

You have in a common cause fought and triumphed together;
the Independence and Liberty you possess are the work of
joint councils, and joint efforts, of common dangers, sufferings
and successes. . . . [E]very portion of our country finds
the most commanding motives for carefully guarding and
preserving the Union of the whole. . . . While then every part
of our country thus feels an immediate and particular interest
in Union, all the parts combined cannot fail to find in the
united mass of means and efforts greater strength, greater
resource, proportionably greater security from external danger,
a less frequent interruption of their peace by foreign nations;—
and what is of inestimable value! they must derive from Union
an exemption from those broils and wars between themselves,
which so frequently afflict neighbouring countries, not tied
together by the same government; which their own rivalships
alone would be sufficient to produce, but which opposite
foreign alliances, attachments and intrigues would stimulate
and imbitter.—Hence likewise they will avoid the necessity
of those overgrown military establishments, which under any
form of government are inauspicious to liberty, and which are
to be regarded as particularly hostile to Republican Liberty;
In this sense it is, that your Union ought to be considered as
a main prop of your liberty, and that the love of the one ought
to endear to you the preservation of the other. . . .

The inhabitants of our western country have lately had a
useful lesson on this head: they have seen, in the negotiation
by the Executive, and in the unanimous ratification by
the Senate, of the treaty with Spain, and in the universal
satisfaction at that event, throughout the United States, a

decisive proof how unfounded were the suspicions propagated among them of a policy in the General Government and in the Atlantic States unfriendly to their interests in regard to the MISSISSIPPI; they have been witnesses to the formation of two treaties, that with Great Britain and that with Spain, which secure to them every thing they could desire, in respect to our foreign relations, towards confirming their prosperity. Will it not be their wisdom to rely for the preservation of these advantages on the UNION by which they were procured? Will they not henceforth be deaf to those advisers, if such there are, who would sever them from their Brethren and connect them with aliens?

To the efficacy and permanency of your Union, a Government for the whole is indispensable—No alliances, however strict, between the parts can be an adequate substitute; they must inevitably experience the infractions and interruptions which all alliances in all times have experienced. Sensible of this momentous truth, you have improved upon your first essay, by the adoption of a Constitution of Government better calculated than your former for an intimate Union, and for the efficacious management of your common concerns. This Government, the offspring of our own choice, uninfluenced and unawed, adopted upon full investigation and mature deliberation, completely free in its principles, in the distribution of its powers, uniting security with energy, and containing within itself a provision for its own amendment, has a just claim to your confidence and your support. Respect for its authority, compliance with its laws, acquiescence in its measures, are duties enjoined by the fundamental maxims of true Liberty. The basis of our political systems is the right of the people to make and to alter their Constitutions of Government—But, the Constitution which at any time exists, 'till changed by an explicit and authentic act of the whole people, is sacredly obligatory upon all. The very idea of the power and the right of the people to establish Government presupposes the duty of every individual to obey the established Government. . . .

The great rule of conduct for us, in regard to foreign nations, is in extending our commercial relations, to have with them as little *political* connection as possible. . . . Europe has a set of primary interests, which to us have none, or a very remote relation. Hence she must be engaged in frequent controversies, the causes of which are essentially . . . foreign to our concerns. Hence, therefore, it must be unwise in us to implicate ourselves, by artificial ties, in the ordinary vicissitudes of her politics, or the ordinary combinations and collisions of her friendships, or enmities. Our detached and distant situation invites and enables us to pursue a different course. If we remain one people, under an efficient government, the period is not far off, when we may defy material injury from external annoyance.

HISTORIANS HAVE RIGHTLY DESCRIBED GEORGE Washington as the indispensable man of the American Revolution. Whether or not he was logically necessary (in the Jeffersonian sense) to winning the war militarily, Washington was indeed critical to winning the war *on emphatically republican terms*. And then, as has been seen, he was truly indispensable in fashioning, ratifying, launching, and solidifying America's Constitution from 1787 to 1797. Was Washington also indispensable to the very survival of the Constitution and its intertwined project of proper constitutional conversation— robust, free, and wide-open discourse within and among multiple and overlapping conversational circles? As he relinquished the captain's wheel, was the good ship *Constitution* safely out of harbor and truly on the open sea, or were there hidden shoals ahead on which she might still founder?

In the event, many of Washington's erstwhile allies, including Hamilton, veered off course after Washington left the captain's deck. Unsteady John Adams, who succeeded His Excellency, was no George Washington. When Adams and others fell into temptation and began criminalizing the writings and speeches of their political opponents, Americans would glimpse yet another possible existential threat to their fledgling system: suppression of free political discourse, faintly reminiscent of the 1774 Coercive Acts.

Adams's former friend and now bitter rival Thomas Jefferson would respond vigorously to this new threat to freedom, much as he had in 1776, though this time more furtively. At his side, as usual, was James Madison, now bidding to make a dramatic comeback every bit as steeply angled as had been his rise and fall under Washington.

— nine —

ADAMS-JEFFERSON-MADISON

A MERICA'S FOUNDING STATESMEN DID NOT rule by dint of birth. Rather, young America nurtured (White) men of various sorts, sifted them, and often put them in just the right places—slotted them, at least in the most important instances, for positions that best fit their talent, temperament, and training.

The vaunted English Constitution did not do this, at least at the top. George III was born to rule. As king, he proved to be a blockhead who empowered other blockheads, who in turn overlooked those born far below and far away. The king and his men exalted Lord Bute and Lord North, disregarded Burke and Barré, humiliated Franklin, snubbed American Congresses, ignored American newspapers, and thus lost America. Yet the king remained king, as was his birthright.

Consider, by contrast, America's three greatest founders, in order of seniority: Franklin, Washington, and Hamilton. None was his father's firstborn, in-wedlock son. (Franklin was his father's tenth son, by way of a second wife. Washington, too, was the product of a sire's second marriage, with two older half brothers initially ahead of him in inheritance and social standing. Hamilton was technically a bastard; his mother never perfected her divorce from her first husband. Her subsequent informal mate, James Hamilton, later abandoned the family, and leading biographers have doubted whether James was Alexander's begetter.) Franklin and Washington never went to college, and Hamilton did not complete his studies. Neither Franklin, whose father was a candlemaker, nor Hamilton, whose origins were even humbler, was born or raised a gentleman. Rather, each acquired genteel status—gentled his condition, in the language of Shakespeare's Henry V—through a combination of spectacular brains and drive. All three men started out with deep loyalty to king and empire. Yet all ultimately renounced their allegiance because Britain failed to recognize their extraordinary potential and match it with sufficient opportunity for public service, the highest path to honor and glory.

The seeds of this contrast between Britain and America were visible even in 1760, in the backstory to the writs-of-assistance controversy. The Otis family, it will be recalled, raged because father and son saw the British patronage system as rigged, with no fair opportunity for them to float like cream to the top. In fact, the Otises' seething resentments may not have been justified. In Thomas Hutchinson, the Crown had picked a man impressive in his own right and enormously admired (at the time) by his local community. Still, the meteoric lives of Franklin, Washington, and Hamilton do suggest that America was somehow able to identify talent that Britain missed.

Revolutionary America not only managed to find these three men and place them on the highest pedestals of power and honor, but also identified the perfect niche for each. As one of the most savvy and charming diplomats in history, Franklin got the French to do much of the fighting and paying while somehow ensuring that America ended up with almost all the land. Likewise, Washington triumphed as a republican general holding his army together against long odds, and Hamilton dazzled as a fiscal wizard putting the new nation on a sound foundation. No one else on the horizon would have been a better French minister, supreme general and first president, and initial treasury secretary than Franklin, Washington, and Hamilton, respectively.

Yet none of these three would have excelled in either of the other top slots. Concretely, in 1776, no positions were more important to America's very survival than supreme commander and French minister. Without the right men in these two places and near-perfect partnership among them, the war was all but lost and many patriots would soon be dead. Obviously, twenty-something Hamilton was far too young and green for either position; Franklin could not have led troops in battle; and Washington in 1776 could not have enchanted the French. (How awkward would Paris have been for an unphilosophical non-French-speaking planter-warrior best known, at least in French eyes, for having culpably killed a French-Canadian diplomat in 1754! Vice versa, the image of Franklin, a gout-ridden septuagenarian, astride a blazing charger rallying troops at Trenton, Princeton, or Monmouth, seems quite ridiculous.) If Hamilton was far too young to merit a top spot in 1776, Franklin and Washington were far too old in 1789 to create a national fiscal system from scratch, even if they knew how—which they did not, quite. Only Hamilton did. And no one—surely not the ailing Franklin or the untested Hamilton—came remotely close to His Excellency as presidential timber in 1789.

The American system also managed, impressively, to ease each of these three titans out when his time came. Franklin was past his intellectual peak at the grand Convention, where he was scrupulously honored but not invariably followed. With good reason, he was not brought into the new government. (He died less than a year after Washington's inauguration.) Washington felt himself fading in his second term and died before the end of what would have been his third term. The American system sensibly encouraged him to reassess his own condition every four years, as the British system did not do then (and does not do today) for its monarch. Hamilton did not regain power after leaving the treasury, and this, too, was for the best. Without Washington to steady his high spirits, Hamilton was a Napoleonic risk.[1]

OF THE THREE MEN WHO occupied Washington's chair in the two decades that followed—Adams, Jefferson, and Madison—the latter two also fit the nation's needs fairly well when it summoned them into its highest office. Even Adams was perhaps America's best option in 1797, *faute de mieux.*

Arguably, John Jay would have provided a steadier hand on the tiller. In mid-1794, Adams—ever alert to possible competition—reminded Abigail that Jay was a strong contender.[2] But the treaty that Jay negotiated with Britain in late 1794 initially provoked widespread outrage, even though the pact made long-term strategic sense and indeed would soon help bring about the popular 1795–1796 Pinckney Treaty with Spain, opening up the Mississippi. Many Americans did not fathom just how precarious America's general military and financial situation remained compared to Britain's. Given the cards he had been dealt, Jay played them well enough, but this would become clear only in retrospect. Also, backcountry folk still remembered and resented Jay's Confederation-era willingness to barter away Mississippi navigation rights; detractors also detested his circuit court efforts to quell whiskey rebels. In May 1794, before Jay even reached London, a Kentucky mob guillotined and burned an elaborate effigy of the diplomat, who was also America's chief justice. Jay's likeness suffered similar indignities several months later in Carlisle, Pennsylvania. Shortly after the Senate ratified the then secret Jay Treaty in June 1795, Philadelphia's *Aurora General Advertiser* published a leaked version, and almost simultaneously, the administration released the official text. On July 4, a date increasingly linked in the popular mind to Jefferson as "he who penned the declaration of independence," Democratic-Republican mobbers in Philadelphia supplemented the day's standard fireworks by burning Jay in effigy and torching a replica of his treaty. In mid-July a New York mob stoned Hamilton when he tried to defend the treaty in public. One angry insomniac in Boston chalked an emphatic message on the fence enclosing the estate of Robert Treat Paine, a distinguished Federalist judge and Declaration signer: "Damn John Jay! damn every one that won't damn John Jay!!

damn every one that won't put lights in his windows and sit up all night damning John Jay!!!"[3]

With Jay largely out of the picture, Americans in 1796 opted for Adams to lead the nation. But Adams was mismatched for the presidency, as became clear once he assumed power. Thus the American people with good reason dismissed him from service when he stood for reelection. (The only other president to suffer this ignominy in the Constitution's first half century was also named John _____ Adams.) Though neither Jefferson nor Madison came close to filling Washington's shoes, by the turn of the century both middle-aged Virginians were better suited to lead America than was Adams, especially because the Virginians had paired up in ways that often brought out the best in each other. The key point is that the nation summoned them when the time was right for men of their skills and dispositions.

Concretely, Jefferson and Madison did not understand armies, navies, shipping, manufacturing, investment, banks, trade, taxation, money, and much more. They would have been bad presidents in the early 1790s when America desperately needed to create these instruments and engines to survive and thrive. But precisely because Washington and Hamilton built the system so well, it was safe for the Jefferson-Madison team. And they were indeed a team, every bit as much as Washington and Hamilton.

With American security against external attack largely achieved thanks to Washington and Hamilton, the greater threat to the American Constitution by the end of the 1790s was an internal threat to freedom—to freedom of speech and of the press, in particular. Freedom was a theme that harmonized well with what Jefferson and Madison had long preached, and freedom was, indeed, what they offered and delivered to America at the turn of the century.

Alas, these embarrassed but emphatic slaveholders, neither of whom would follow Washington's deathbed example of freeing his slaves, vigorously championed freedom only for White Americans. Indeed, as a result of the impressive political empire built by these

Virginia teammates—for they, in their own way, were system builders every bit as much as Washington and Hamilton before them—no president would openly challenge slavery, the ultimate threat to freedom, until Abraham Lincoln.

THE RETURN OF JOHN ADAMS

Before we turn directly to assess Jefferson and Madison in detail, we must consider—not for the first time and not for the last—the curious career of the curious man who unsuccessfully succeeded Washington and whose conversational failures and constitutional missteps brought the Virginia pair to power.

JOHN ADAMS PEAKED EARLY. IT was both his good fortune and his sad fate that he skyrocketed from utter obscurity in 1761 to the apex of glory in 1776, only to spend the rest of his life falling back to earth, frustrated and confused.

The imperial crisis had drawn forth his substantial gifts of intellect and character. As a lawyer who loved history—the more obscure, the better—he sparred effectively with Thomas Hutchinson and other loyalists in the early 1770s over the legal history of New England's founding, the juridical histories of Scotland and Ireland, and the constitutional status of ancient Greek and Roman colonies.[4] By the mid-1770s, he, not Hutchinson, was ubiquitous. In June 1775, he successfully backed George Washington to lead the new Continental Army. The following May, he steered through Congress a two-pronged resolution that was tantamount to independence, encouraging individual colonies to adopt new state constitutions shorn of all ties to Britain. On July 2, the Continental Congress formally proclaimed American independence, adopting a motion he had seconded. Two days later came the Declaration, revising the draft of a five-man committee on which he had served. Wherever there was Congressional work to do, he was there to do it, fueled by manic energy and fierce devotion to the patriot cause.

As state constitutions sprouted throughout the year, Adams had additional reason to beam. Most of these documents matched the basic template that he had sketched in a widely published pamphlet, *Thoughts on Government.* In that essay, which had originated as a missive to a friend, Adams argued that bicameral legislatures, with power balanced between a popular lower house and a more elitist upper house, would serve Americans better than would the simplistic unicameral legislatures that Thomas Paine and Benjamin Franklin favored. Bicameralism plus an independent executive and an independent judiciary would be the Adams prescription for the rest of his days in myriad works, short and long.

Despite these triumphs, Adams in the imperial crisis was not truly driving events or laying foundations for future and further constitutional greatness. In his newspaper debates with Hutchinson and other loyalists, he descended deep into feudal law, canon law, and ancient trivia. With his pedantic and pettifogging antiquarianism and instinct for the capillaries, Adams focused too much on the past and not enough on the present and the future. Given the importance of winning public opinion, the most candid and persuasive constitutional case for America was a line of argument closer to Paine's *Common Sense.* Regardless of who said what in the 1620s when the Pilgrims had landed, or how the early Roman and Greek colonies had originated some two thousand years earlier, the unwritten imperial system of the 1770s required adjustment to reflect increasing demographic and cultural parity between Americans and Britons. It made no sense for a small island to rule forever over a distant and destined-to-become-larger continent—or at least it made no sense if the British system was rooted in liberty and self-government, as its advocates repeatedly claimed.

Pure Adams-style historical argument—an early version of what would later come to be called constitutional "originalism"—would indeed make sense for many American constitutionalists post-1789 appealing to the "original meaning" of the federal Constitution. But *American* originalism focusing on the *American* founding has drawn strength from basic facts unique to America's founding document.

In a truly pivotal year in world history, Americans carefully crafted a written text that was then widely debated and voted on in an extraordinary continental conversation—a text that could be amended at pleasure and thus perhaps did not need willfully creative reinterpretation to remain vital. Nothing of this sort was true of an unwritten and partly mythic British Constitution that had evolved over the centuries and was continuing to evolve without formal amendment procedures. Its "original meaning," if any such thing existed, was irretrievably lost in the mists of time and the forests of yore. Important intervening events, such as the English Civil War and the Glorious Revolution, had surely changed its basic shape; why shouldn't more recent events likewise warrant additional modification?

Despite Adams's preoccupation with centuries-old British legal arcana and with ancient Mediterranean history, the details of legal practices from long ago and far away were not the keys to 1776. His 1776 *Thoughts on Government* pamphlet won acclaim precisely because it better captured the spirit of its own time and place. Historians have noted that most early state constitutions tracked Adams more than Paine on the unicameral-bicameral debate, but they have given Adams undue credit as the inspiration. The simplest explanation is that preexisting colonial legislatures were themselves generally bicameral, as was Britain's legislature. New state constitutions were not emulating Adams but exemplifying inertia. (Pennsylvania adopted a unicameral legislature, but again inertia offers the easiest explanation: the colonial Pennsylvania legislature was unicameral.) America was not Adamsonian in 1776. Adams was American.

At his best moments, Adams said just this, noting in a 1775 diary entry that he favored a "Plan as nearly resembling the Governments under which we were born and have lived as the circumstances of the Country will admit. Kings we never had among us, Nobles we never had. Nothing hereditary ever existed in the Country: Nor will the Country require or admit of any such thing: but Governors, and Councils we have always had as well as Representatives. A Legislature in three branches ought to be preserved, and independent Judges."[5]

Alas, the events of the following decade conspired to push Adams further away from the main lines of American constitutional development. Congress sent him abroad on diplomatic missions for almost an entire decade, from 1778 to 1788 (with a brief interlude back home in late 1779). A dutiful republican public servant, he obeyed this summons, but in the process he missed much of America's epic constitutional conversation in 1787–1788 and the events that underlay and preceded it. As an American agent in Paris, Holland, and London, he did gain insight into Europe that ultimately helped him as president avoid a needless war with France in the late 1790s. But consider what he missed. He developed no real firsthand sense of the military's debility. He learned almost nothing of western frontier folk, the Indians, or the Spanish along the Mississippi. He never experienced any part of America south of the Mason-Dixon line. He missed the grand Philadelphia Convention and the great constitutional debate in his own home state. Metaphorically, he was a constitutional Rip Van Winkle who had slept through many of the most important events and conversations that a sound constitutionalist needed to understand.

A less quirky and less self-absorbed statesman than Adams might have tried to make up for lost time by voraciously consulting newspapers and the like, in Washingtonian fashion. But instead of rediscovering America upon his return to the United States in mid-1788, Adams spent much of his spare time continuing his plodding investigations of ancient and early-modern Europe, pursuing other tangents, and nursing assorted real and imagined grievances. Notably, Adams did not tour America, as did Washington himself between 1789 and 1791, and as Adams himself had sensibly begun to do in 1774 when journeying to the First Continental Congress. The middle-aged statesman was not aging well—not maturing, not growing, but rather festering and brooding, haunted by bouts of depression, envy, paranoia, egomania, and rage.

Adams also showed little interest in pondering extraordinary ratification-year works such as *The Federalist*. In his later years, old Adams crowed that his own writings had strongly influenced Publius.

Publius, however, nowhere cited Adams directly. Perhaps, then, old Adams was seeing what he wanted to see—his own influence, everywhere.[6]

In Adams's mind, he, Otis, and a handful of other heroes had been first on the American scene. The upstart Publians, Hamilton and Madison, were not among the great men of 1776, as Adams himself had been, so he dismissed these young newcomers to the conversation as derivative.[7] (He was gentler to Jay, whom he knew from Paris.) Never mind that Publians Hamilton and Madison were expounding a specific document—the Constitution—that they had helped to draft and bring to life, whereas many of Adams's own writings were much further afield.

Throughout his life, Adams misjudged and maligned Hamilton in particular. His rantings about Hamilton ranged from the unbecoming to the grotesque. (Hamilton's mixed assessments of Adams, by contrast, were far more measured and discerning, acknowledging Adams's genuine virtues as a man and as a public servant.) Adams's enmity began when he learned that Hamilton in 1789 had worked behind the scenes to ensure that Washington would win America's first Electoral College vote by a wide margin. (Hamilton had worried that although almost no elector truly thought Adams a nearby second to Washington, the quirks of the system might create the misimpression of a close contest, or might even crown Adams, unless some electors strategically diverted their second-choice ballots away from the Braintree lawyer.)[8] It surely did not help matters that Adams, like Jefferson and Madison, did not understand banking institutions in the slightest; indeed, Adams saw banks as inherently fraudulent unless they kept all deposits on reserve at all times—a practice not followed by any sound bank, then or now.[9]

By both personal inclination and institutional design, Adams soon found himself generally outside many of the conversational circles forming under the new Constitution. Personally, he prided himself on his fierce independence of thought and of action even as many around him congealed into two emerging national parties— Federalists tied to Washington and Hamilton (and broadly skeptical of Revolutionary France), and Democratic-Republicans faithful to Jefferson and Madison (and generally pro-French). Over time, events pushed Adams toward the Federalists and the Federalists toward Adams, but neither side was ever comfortable in this relationship. Institutionally, although Adams presided over the Senate as America's first vice president, he was not himself a senator. He showed insufficient sensitivity to the egos and political needs of the men over whom he presided, who for their part wanted to shine in debate to do themselves and their constituents proud. Overflowing with a combination of enthusiasm, narcissism, stubbornness, and petulance, Adams could not restrain his own burning need to be the star of the show. Of course, the senators had in no way selected him as their presiding officer or political chieftain (unlike House members, who chose a Speaker and other leaders for themselves). "I am nothing, but I may be everything," he told the Senate in one self-absorbed moment. Privately, he grumbled to Abigail that "my Country has in its Wisdom contrived for me, the most insignificant Office that ever the Invention of Man contrived or his Imagination conceived."[10]

As Senate chair, Adams cast a record number of critical tie-breaking votes,[11] none more important than the two times when he backed the Washington position in the Decision of 1789. Sadly, this stance, though commendable and correct, further isolated him.

To see why, we must recall the structure of the original vice presidency prior to its transformation under the Twelfth Amendment—a transformation that, as we shall later see, occurred thanks to events in which Adams himself would play a starring role. Adams was Washington's vice president, but not because Washington handpicked him. They were not running mates, as is usually the relationship today between a president and vice president. Rather, as runner-up in the presidential vote in 1789 and again in 1792, Adams won the consolation prize of the vice presidency.

For understandable reasons, Washington did not bring Adams into his inner conversational circle.[12] Although the Braintree lawyer had enthusiastically backed the Virginia planter for the top command slot in 1775, Adams did not remain an unwavering supporter thereafter. Rather, Adams was on the fringes of the 1777–1778 "Conway Cabal" that aimed to cabin and perhaps displace General Washington. If Washington had somehow stumbled as president, his most likely replacement would have been the statesman who had come in second: Adams. Washington unsurprisingly did not confide completely in a man whom he had not picked, who had not always been loyal to him, whom he could not fire at will, who obviously had ambitions of his own, and who was the most likely person to topple him, if ever, improbably, he were toppled.

In turn, any vice president—especially one as prickly and envious as John Adams—was apt to have decidedly mixed emotions about the only officer who outranked him. Behind closed doors at Philadelphia, delegate Elbridge Gerry had worried that putting the vice president in charge of the Senate would give too much power to the president himself because of the "close intimacy that must subsist between the President & vice-president." Urbane lawyer Gouverneur Morris offered a witty rebuttal that better described this inherently fraught relationship: "The vice president then will be the first heir apparent that ever loved his father."[13]

Thanks to his tie-breaking votes on the Decision of 1789, Adams, like Madison before him, in effect encouraged Washington to confide in and confer with his handpicked and dismissible department heads over all others. Hamilton thus moved to the center of Washington's circle, while Madison continued to converse with his House colleagues and his constituents back home and also deepened his political partnership with Jefferson. Meanwhile, Adams continued to stand alone—not quite in either the inner executive circle or the inner Senate circle, a man without a branch and without a party. It was lonely at the almost-top.

WASHINGTON BADE FAREWELL IN 1796, and in the ensuing election, Americans pushed the two most notable remaining icons of 1776, John Adams and Thomas Jefferson, in that order, into the presidency and vice presidency. Neither man in 1796 chose the other as his political teammate. On the contrary.

Federalists encouraged Adams to team up with South Carolinian Thomas Pinckney, who had won the West—or at least, western navigation of the Mississippi—in the popular 1795–1796 Pinckney Treaty. Republican darling Jefferson, in turn, partnered with New Yorker Aaron Burr. Neither of the two fledgling parties got its wish. America in effect split the difference, giving Adams the most electoral votes and Jefferson the second most. As a result, Adams's main and closely matched rival ended up as his vice president, creating a far more fraught dynamic than when he himself had played distant and loyal second fiddle to Washington.

In an effort to rekindle the spirit of 1776, Adams tried to extend an olive branch to Jefferson, praising him to those who would likely forward the compliments to their intended recipient.[14] At first, Jefferson was tempted to reciprocate. In late 1796, he drafted a buttery letter to Adams that ended with the wish "that your administration may be filled with glory and happiness to yourself and advantage to us [America]." Acknowledging that "tho', in the course of our voyage thro' life, various little incidents have happened or been contrived to separate us," Jefferson proclaimed that he (referring to himself in the third person) "retains still for you the solid esteem of the moments when we [back to first person] were working for our independance, and sentiments of respect and affectionate attachment." This smooth playing of the 1776 card reflected Jefferson at his most gracious and clever. Nostalgic references to the high point of Adams's own life were always the most direct way to Adams's heart. Jefferson's letter also contained a snide aside about Hamilton, whom Jefferson loathed and whom, he believed, Adams likewise distrusted: "It is possible that you may be cheated of your succession by a trick worthy the subtlety of your archfriend of New York [a sarcastic reference to Hamilton], who has been able to make of your real friends tools to defeat their and your just wishes."[15] Translation: *We have a mutual enemy. Let's reunite?*

Specifically, Jefferson was tipping off Adams that Hamilton had been secretly angling to elect Pinckney over Adams, just as Hamilton in 1789 had encouraged strategic balloting at Adams's expense. Whether or not Hamilton was in fact trying to deceive pro-Adams Federalist electors in the process—frustrating their true and "just wishes," as Jefferson claimed—Jefferson wanted Adams to believe that this was so, and to trust Jefferson as a loyal informer.

Jefferson sent the letter to Madison, his informal campaign manager, to be forwarded to Adams at Madison's discretion. In a fateful decision that may have sharply bent the course of history, Madison opted to pocket the letter, offering Jefferson several reasons. He was unsure how the prickly Adams might respond to several particular passages, including the warning about Hamiltonian machination. Madison also wanted to preserve Jefferson's freedom to distance himself should Adams err as president, as Madison thought likely, and half hoped for: "Considering the probability that Mr. A's course of administration may force an opposition to it from the Republican quarter, & the general uncertainty of the posture which our affairs may take, there may be real embarrassments from giving written possession to him, of the degree of compliment & confidence which your personal delicacy & friendship have suggested."[16]

As events would unfold, Madison would get his wish. President Adams's "course of administration" did indeed "force an opposition to it from the Republican quarter" in 1798–1801, an opposition that would codify profound principles of American free expression and sweep the leaders of the "Republican quarter"—Jefferson and Madison themselves—into the presidency for the ensuing sixteen years.

WHY JEFFERSON? WHY MADISON?

People lie; politicians lie more than most; and Thomas Jefferson lied more than most politicians. He lied to his friends. He lied to his constituents. He lied to Washington. And he lied to himself.[17]

Thomas Jefferson was also, undeniably, one of America's most important founders. At his best he championed principles of freedom at the very foundation of America's constitutional conversation. As president, he achieved one of America's greatest diplomatic and geostrategic triumphs, the Louisiana Purchase. Flanked by James Madison, he also created an extraordinary conversational machine—a national political party backed by a national newspaper network—that dominated American politics for six decades.

JEFFERSON'S TENDENCY TO DISSEMBLE HAD deep roots. In personal conversation, he valued politeness above all—he considered it an Enlightenment virtue.[18] He avoided unpleasant confrontation and face-to-face disagreement, and thus often left listeners believing that he agreed with them when in fact he did not.[19] Adams, by contrast, cherished and embodied candor and honesty above all. Hamilton, too, was far more direct in head-on encounters. Hamilton's blunt and brusque manner surely rubbed Jefferson the wrong way—all the more so as it became increasingly clear after 1790 that Hamilton had Washington's ear and Washington had Hamilton's back.

Jefferson was also a shy and private man. At several junctures he appeared to retire from public life only to be dragged back in, seemingly reluctantly (à la Washington), by his protégé Madison, a younger, more forward-leaning, more openly political operative. Jefferson's estate, Monticello, was a notoriously private enclave—a mountaintop plantation retreat far removed from the wider world of commerce and politics. He conducted a good deal of his most interesting correspondence—especially with Madison—in cipher, lest missives somehow come into the wrong hands (a fate that had notoriously befallen another politically prominent Thomas in the Hutchinson Letters Affair).

We now know that Jefferson was a private man who had much to be private about. It seems plausible that the fact that he lied and dissembled and hid and encrypted was in some way or other connected to the fact that there was an enormous lie at the heart of his heart. The point is not merely that he had a slave mistress who bore him at least six slave children, four of whom survived into adulthood. Similar things were true of other great southern gentlemen. No, the thing to be kept private above all was much deeper and more shameful (or was it?) than that, and it surely created a jumbled welter of emotions and ratiocinations that he tried hard to prevent anyone on the outside from seeing. His mistress and the mother of several of his children, Sally Hemings, was his deceased wife Martha's younger half sister, the daughter of his father-in-law, John Wayles, by way of Wayles's half-White slave mistress, Elizabeth Hemings. Thus, Jefferson's unacknowledged slave children (the Hemingses) were related to his openly acknowledged free children (the Jeffersons) on both sides; the two sets of children were not merely half siblings, through him, but more—also half cousins, through their half sister mothers. His own slave sons and slave daughters were also his half nephews and half nieces by marriage. All this and more was true, and none of this could be said openly.[20]

Here, too, the contrast with Hamilton is notable. Both men occasioned salacious newspaper gossip about their extramarital amours. Hamilton candidly responded with a long and embarrassingly detailed tell-all pamphlet. Yes, he wrote, he had been weak as a private man, but not corrupt as a public servant. Jefferson, by contrast, said nothing in public about the many rumors about Sally and lied to his friends in private correspondence.

But perhaps Jefferson's correspondents knew that the denials were pro forma? Perhaps he knew that they knew? Perhaps they knew that he knew that they knew?

The person who did know Thomas Jefferson best, personally and politically, was James Madison. Over the course of half a century—from mid-1776 to July 4, 1826, when Jefferson's death did them part—the two men engaged in an intense and wide-ranging conversation about all manner of things. Often, when they were geographically proximate, they simply conversed in person, leaving us no clear transcript of the words that passed between them. But more than a thousand letters—with some parts originally in cipher—remain for us to sift and ponder. At the very center of their fascinating correspondence was a conversation—occasionally playful, sometimes profound, often political—about constitutional first principles.

SHARED CONSTITUTIONAL PRINCIPLES HAD DRAWN the two men together in political partnership early on. In April 1776, Madison, only weeks after celebrating his twenty-fifth birthday, managed to get himself elected to the Virginia Provincial Convention, which promised to operate as the colony's freestanding legislature now that royal authority had collapsed. Encouraged by the two-pronged May resolution that Adams pushed through the Continental Congress, the legislature-convention turned itself midsession into a constitutional convention. At the very moment that Adams, Jefferson, and others in Philadelphia were announcing America's independence to the world, Madison and others in Williamsburg were showing the world what that independence meant, promulgating a Declaration of Rights (on June 12) and a state constitution (on June 29) founded on the sovereign right of Virginia to govern itself free from British authority.

George Mason's initial draft of the Virginia Declaration of Rights said that "all men are equally free," with "inherent" rights of "life and liberty" and the right of "pursuing . . . happiness"— dramatic language that, as we saw earlier, caught the eye of Jefferson and his fellow congressmen at Philadelphia. Other language caught Madison's eye back in Williamsburg. Mason's draft declared that "all Men shou'd enjoy the fullest Toleration in the Exercise of Religion, according to the Dictates of Conscience." Young Madison thought this formulation too tepid, and proposed a more emphatic alternative: "All men are equally entitled to the free exercise of religion, according to the dictates of conscience." In Madison's rewrite, religious freedom asserted itself as a firm entitlement, linked to the deep idea of equality, and not a matter of mere "Toleration" that "shou'd" (but need not always?) be afforded. Madison's substitute passed. At a remarkably young age, he had achieved his first of many constitutional victories—prophetically, a notable blow for freedom and equality (at least for Whites).

The following year, Jefferson began working on a bill that aimed to build on Madison's foundation by declaring an even more sweeping vision of religious freedom and equality. Over the ensuing decade, the pair worked together closely on this pet project but encountered strong resistance from Patrick Henry, a religious traditionalist who wanted to recognize the special legal status of Virginia's Episcopal Church. In an encrypted 1784 missive to Madison, Jefferson, now in Paris, expressed his frustration about Henry: "What we have to do I think is devoutly to pray for his death. . . . I am glad the Episcopalians have again shewn their teeth and fangs. The dissenters had almost forgotten them."[21] Though Jefferson was joking, the letter's informality evidenced the strong bond that he and Madison had forged between themselves. The super-secretive Jefferson had found someone whom he trusted implicitly to keep his secrets secret.

In 1786, while Jefferson was still in Paris, his protégé finally succeeded in securing enactment of the religious-freedom bill. Among other things, it proclaimed that "no man shall be compelled to frequent or support any religious worship, place, or ministry whatsoever." Nor could any man be made to "suffer on account of his religious opinions or belief." The statute went on to affirm "that all men shall be free to profess, and by argument to maintain, their opinions in matters of Religion, and that the same shall in no wise diminish, enlarge or affect their civil capacities." In an exultant letter to his friend and mentor, Madison expressed his hope that the new law would "extinguish[] for ever the ambitious hope of making laws for the human mind."[22] For his part, Jefferson considered the matter so significant that he listed his authorship of this Virginia Statute for Religious Freedom on his gravesite obelisk as one of his three proudest accomplishments, alongside his (self-proclaimed) authorship of the Declaration of Independence and his paternity of the University of Virginia.

BEYOND THEIR SUCCESS IN CHAMPIONING religious freedom and equality, Jefferson and Madison together explored several other profound issues of Enlightenment constitutionalism prior to Jefferson's return from Paris in 1790. Two topics have remained perennial favorites for later generations of constitutionalists and thus merit special attention.

On September 6, 1789—the seventh anniversary of his wife's demise—Jefferson turned his thoughts to first principles of life, death, and democracy. Did "one generation of men" ever have "a right to bind another?" he wondered. He wrote Madison a sprawling, speculative, and now famous letter musing out loud. Echoing his 1776 self, he began his inquiry with a truth that he deemed "to be self evident," namely, *"that the earth belongs in usufruct to the living"* (his emphasis). How then, he asked Madison, could one generation properly saddle a later generation with debt?

Jefferson plainly had in mind the excesses of the French monarchy and aristocracy all around him—spending lavishly on themselves and throwing the burden on Frenchmen yet unborn:

> Suppose Louis XV [1710–1774] and his contemporary generation had said to the money-lenders of Genoa, give us money that we may eat, drink, and be merry in our day; and on condition you will demand no interest till the end of 19 years, you shall then for ever after receive an annual interest of 12 ⅝ per cent. The money is lent on these conditions, is divided among the living, eaten, drank, and squandered. Would the present generation be obliged to apply the produce of the earth and of their labour to replace their dissipations? Not at all.

From this not implausible starting point about intergenerational justice, Jefferson carried his argument to absurd conclusions. Using actuarial tables from a French *philosophe*, le Comte de Buffon, Jefferson estimated a generation, for his analytic purposes, to be approximately nineteen years. Jefferson's root premise was that "one generation is to another as one independant nation to another." Thus, he reasoned,

> no society can make a perpetual constitution, or even a perpetual law. The earth belongs always to the living generation. They may manage it then, and what proceeds from it, as they please, during their usufruct. They are masters too of their own persons, and consequently may govern them as they please. But persons and property make the sum of the objects of government. The constitution and the laws of their predecessors extinguished then in their natural course with those who gave them being. . . . *Every constitution then, and every law, naturally expires at the end of 19 years.* [Emphasis added.]

This was daft. Generations are not like nations in every respect. Nation-states have fixed borders. At any moment, a given person— say, Jefferson himself—might be in France or in the United States, but not in both. By contrast, generations overlap in infinite gradations and slide seamlessly into one another. (There has never been a system anywhere, at any time, in which national borders continuously and at every instant slip and slide, like so many grains of sand in an hourglass.)

Perhaps all patents should expire every nineteen years. Should all marriages? All property lines? (Jefferson's own dominion over Monticello?) All legal wills and trust instruments? All legal bonds between parents and children? All boundaries between jurisdictions—between the United States and Canada, and between Virginia and Maryland? What would it *mean* for a constitution simply to "naturally expire" the way, say, a patent might expire, or an old loan might lapse? What would be the legal status quo at the instant after constitutional expiration? A Hobbesian free-for-all state of nature? Every nineteen years, everywhere? Simultaneously? How could anyone plan anything the day before such expiration? Or a month or a year or a decade before, for that matter? How, indeed, could a new constitution even get off the ground without inertial and jump-starting rules that were themselves inescapably rooted in the dead hand of the past? (Who would vote, when, where, and how? Who would count and tally? With what procedures on what day? Who would resolve disputes? Within what borders? By what pre-voting rules would the voting rules themselves be established? By what pre-pre-voting rules would the pre-voting rules be valid? And so on, infinitely.) A proper republican constitution could of course be altered or abolished at any time—within any given generation or by any later generation—but until such a constitution was revised or replaced by a successor system, it needed to remain in place, just as ordinary laws remain in place until properly repealed.

In his epistolary response to Jefferson, Madison gently raised several of these objections and other obvious ones. Inwardly, he was probably horrified. Jefferson, for better and worse, was a dreamer, and Madison was generally a hardheaded, grounded, practical realist. (Precisely because of this striking contrast, the two men made a strong pair, with offsetting strengths, much as an alloy often outperforms a pure metal.) In *The Federalist* Nos. 49–50, published more than a year before Jefferson's Parisian flight of fancy, Madison had already pushed back against far less kooky but related constitutional-duration ideas that had appeared in Jefferson's book (the only one he ever published), *Notes on the State of Virginia*, and elsewhere. But even when writing as the pseudonymous Publius (and in contrast to Hamilton/Publius's more combative style), Madison pushed back with Enlightenment politesse, fulsomely praising "the author of the *Notes*" for his "original, comprehensive, . . . [and] enlightened" general "turn of thinking."

Beyond the intellectual merits of Jefferson's and Madison's ideas about constitutional duration, their correspondence on this issue can help us better understand several crucial points about both men and the significance of their lifelong constitutional conversation.

First, the privacy of the conversation was taken for granted and served them well. Jefferson floated a balloon, Madison politely popped it, and the two men continued as friends and conversationalists, just as before. A similar dynamic had at times operated at Philadelphia. In the moment, secrecy freed delegates to speculate boldly and then retreat if their balloons were popped, with no immediate publicity or embarrassment. Ironically, Jefferson himself did not understand the value of the Philadelphia rules at the time: in a midsummer 1787 letter from Paris to his then friend and fellow diplomat Adams, he praised the Convention as "an assembly of demigods," but blasted as "abominable" the "tying up the tongues of their members."[23]

Second, Jefferson never entirely gave up on his root idea and later tried to soften it. In an 1813 letter to his son-in-law and nephew (both—his daughter Martha married one of her White cousins), Jefferson abandoned the daft thought that all constitutions and all laws generally should poof into thin air every generation. But he continued to think that national debts should lapse every nineteen years or so. The same root premises that had first appeared in his musings to Madison now reappeared in his letter to John Wayles Eppes: "The earth belongs to the living, not to the dead. . . . [W]e may consider each generation as a distinct nation with a right, by the will of it's majority, to bind themselves, but none to bind the succeeding generation, more than the inhabitants of another country." Jefferson thought that his proposed rule—no national debts beyond a single generation—would be a "salutary curb on the spirit of war and indebtment which, since the modern theory of the perpetuation of debt, has drenched the earth with blood, and crushed it's inhabitants under burthens ever accumulating."[24]

Here, too, he went too far. What about a war of existential necessity, a war whose benefits might redound to millions unborn, and for much longer than twenty years into the future? In other words, what about the Revolutionary War itself? For want of an expensive nail at a critical hour, must the nation be lost? In his February 4, 1790, response to Jefferson's initial flight of fancy, Madison himself had made just this point: "Debts may be incurred for purposes which interest the unborn, as well as the living: such are debts for repelling a conquest, the evils of which descend through many generations. Debts may even be incurred principally for the benefit of posterity: such perhaps is the present debt of the U. States, which far exceeds any burdens which the present generation could well apprehend for itself. The term of 19 years might not be sufficient for discharging the debts in either of these cases."

Astonishingly, Jefferson seemed to show no appreciation of basic economic facts and principles—of the essential difference between current expenses and capital expenses, and the different amortization rates that sensibly applied to different types of expenditures. If assets (like national existence itself, or a nice private building—say, Monticello) lasted for more than twenty years, why shouldn't long-term borrowing occur so that intergenerational benefits and burdens were matched up and spread out sensibly? This is of course one of many reasons that banks and lenders exist—to finance long-term assets and projects—but Jefferson never understood the basics of banks or finance. Or war and its sinews.

The ironies here are rich, because Jefferson died poor. That is, he himself was a veritable Louis XV, spending ridiculous amounts on wine, women, and song—everyday expenses, not capital investments—while saddling his own heirs with massive debt, all the while humming catchy tunes of intergenerational justice. Every day of his life, he made notations in his account books about various personal transactions—buying this case of wine, selling that hogshead of tobacco. *But, astonishingly, never in his life did this classic spendthrift tote up the numbers and take stock of his overall net worth.*[25] When Jefferson died, his estate owed more than it owned, and slave families were torn apart—sold on auction blocks—to pay his creditors.[26]

Third, for all his eccentricity, Jefferson in the end did not do as he said—thanks, perhaps, to Madison. Jefferson had many vices, but some of his worst ones, happily, offset each other. Quite a few of his grand ideas were silly. But he was also a hypocrite and chose not to apply various ideas against himself when he found it inconvenient to do so. These two vices—utopian eccentricity and hypocrisy—perfectly canceled out. Nineteen years after the Constitution was launched, he himself was president, and there was that year no public talk from him about poofing or expiring.

Or, to recast this last set of points—that is, to approach the matter more politely, the way Jefferson and Madison themselves operated, at their Enlightenment best—the two Virginians made a powerful conversational pair in which Jefferson pulled back precisely because Madison helped balance him. Conversation done right works exactly that way when it generates more light than heat. On the issue of constitutional expiration, Jefferson yielded to the better set of arguments, advanced by Madison.

On another classic question of constitutional first principles—to Bill or not to Bill?—Jefferson plainly had the better view, and, thanks to their conversation, Madison yielded.

Several weeks after the Constitution went public, Madison, now free from the ban of secrecy, sent a long letter to Jefferson in Paris confiding to his mentor in great detail about how the final Philadelphia plan had failed to meet his own highest hopes. In his response, written in late December 1787, Jefferson was gentle. He began, politely, by outlining many of the virtues of the proposed Constitution. He opened three consecutive sentences with "I like," used the phrase a fourth time in another nearby sentence, and identified other elements of the Philadelphia plan that he was "captivated by" and "much pleased . . . with." He concluded this polite opening section with a catchall compliment to cheer up his depressed protégé: "There are other good things of less moment."[27]

Then he pivoted, identifying a glaring flaw that Madison had scarcely mentioned in his own initial catalog of complaints: "I will now add what I do not like. First the omission of a bill of rights providing clearly & without the aid of sophisms for freedom of religion, freedom of the press, protection against standing armies, restriction against monopolies, the eternal & unremitting force of the habeas corpus laws, and trials by jury in all matters of fact. . . . [A] bill of rights is what the people are entitled to against every government on earth, general or particular, & what no just government should refuse or rest on inference." Following up in early February 1788, Jefferson added a prescient aside: "I am glad to hear that the new constitution is received with favor. I sincerely wish that the 9 first conventions may receive, & the 4 last reject it. The former will secure it finally; while the latter will oblige them to offer a declaration of rights in order to complete the union. We shall thus have all it's good, and cure it's principal defect."[28]

Although Madison did not engage Jefferson immediately on this topic, the man in Paris refused to let the issue drop. In late July, he shot off another missive:

> I sincerely rejoice at the acceptance of our new constitution by nine states. It is a good canvas, on which some strokes only want retouching. What these are, I think are sufficiently manifested by the general voice from North to South, which calls for a bill of rights. It seems pretty generally understood that this should go to Juries, Habeas corpus, Standing armies, Printing, Religion & Monopolies. . . . I hope therefore a bill of rights will be formed to guard the people against the federal government, as they are already guarded against their state governments in most instances.[29]

Faced with this barrage of epistolary provocation, Madison at last began to engage his mentor and did so with characteristic thoughtfulness, even as he was still slow to admit the full magnitude of his earlier blunders. He and his fellow delegates had simply goofed at Philadelphia. Now, in light of all the pushback from Anti-Federalists in state after state and from Jefferson in letter after letter, Madison pivoted. In mid-October 1788—a full year after Philadelphia—he wrote Jefferson that he had "never thought the omission a material defect" but his "own opinion has always been in favor of a bill of rights." (*Really? Then why had he not backed Mason in Philadelphia?*) He worried that if it were poorly phrased a bill of rights might actually imply that the government had powers it did not. For example, why say that Congress cannot abridge the freedom of the press if Congress lacked enumerated power over this topic in the first place?

Alas, this initial thought was confused and confusing—the sort of thing someone says to avoid simply saying "oops." After all, the Constitution already had a proto–bill of rights, in Article I, section 10, that raised the same problem. Hence the rhetorical failure of many Federalists on this issue in the ratification debates, when they twisted themselves into human pretzels: *A bill of rights is dangerous, and besides, Article I already has one!*

Madison also confided to his senior partner in the crusade for religious liberty that the likely language of any bill of rights that could pass might be too tepid (just as Madison had found Mason's language too tepid in 1776): "There is great reason to fear that a positive declaration of some of the most essential rights could not be obtained in the requisite latitude. I am sure that the rights of Conscience in particular, if submitted to public definition would be narrowed." Plus, he worried that such a bill might merely be a parchment barrier, ineffective against the real threats to liberty, which were more likely to come from irresistible popular forces than from government officials pursuing their own personal agendas.

Still, he ended up conceding to Jefferson that a properly drafted bill might make sense for several reasons. It was "anxiously desired by others" and would be a nice olive branch to Anti-Federalists. In the long run, it might serve to educate popular opinion: "The political truths declared in that solemn manner acquire by degrees the character of fundamental maxims of free Government, and as they become incorporated with the national sentiment, counteract the impulses of interest and passion." Finally, and most immediately prophetic, Madison now saw that, if ever an out-of-touch, thin-skinned, and self-interested cadre of central government officials abused power in ways that offended popular grassroots sentiment (as had happened under British rule in the 1760s and 1770s), "a bill of rights will be a good ground for an appeal to the sense of the community."

Though Madison did not use specific examples of his general idea, we can, with the benefit of hindsight, draw a direct line between this exchange of letters and the free-expression controversy that would later vault the two correspondents themselves into the presidency, seriatim. Prodded by Jefferson in 1788—and others, of course—Madison in 1789 himself began work on a bill of rights that would ultimately expressly proclaim that "Congress shall make no law . . .

abridging the freedom of speech, or of the press." Less than a decade later, under the out-of-touch, thin-skinned, and self-absorbed President John Adams, Congress made just such a law abridging the freedom of speech. Jefferson and Madison pushed back hard, rallying their troops in the name of freedom and doing so under the banner of the Bill of Rights. In precise conformity to the theories that the two correspondents had begun to develop in their important exchange of letters in 1788–1789, the Bill of Rights would indeed prove "a good ground for an appeal to the sense of the community" in a crusade that, fittingly, would be led by these two men themselves.

THE PARTISAN PARTNERSHIP

Returning to America in late 1789, Jefferson learned of his appointment as secretary of state and after some hesitation agreed to serve. The following spring, he and Madison reunited in New York, the temporary capital city, and could now converse and concert with infinitely greater ease. In Jefferson's earliest months in Manhattan, he invited Madison and Hamilton to a dinner party where, as mentioned previously, the former Publians talked turkey and traded horses. (Or at least, that is what Jefferson said later.)

Then everything changed. In the closing weeks of 1790, demagogue Patrick Henry and the Virginia legislature reacted to Hamilton's assumption bill—a bill that Jefferson and Madison had helped to broker and that Washington had signed into law—with constitutional gibberish: "We find no clause in the constitution authorizing Congress to assume the debts of the states!" In fact, assumption was deeply rooted in federal fiscal, national-security, and interstate-commerce powers, but woe unto any Virginia politician bold enough to say so publicly.

In 1791, Madison and Jefferson began to spout similar constitutional gibberish in opposition to Hamilton's bank bill. It bears repeating that their arguments repudiated what We the People had in fact agreed to ratify in 1788, garnered no real Congressional support outside the South, failed to persuade Washington, contradicted what

Jefferson and Madison themselves later did as presidents, were eventually laughed out of Court (unanimously), and have never prevailed thereafter in mainstream legal circles.

Stymied, at least for the moment, on the constitutional front, the two Virginians switched gears and hit the road. Much as John Adams and his cousin Samuel had aimed to listen, learn, and network as they headed south together in the summer of 1774, so now Jefferson and Madison headed north together in the spring of 1791. On the surface, the Virginians' multiweek sojourn through New York and parts of New England was merely recreational and scientific—a chance to relax and study local flora and fauna. But all along the way, the two statesmen met and wooed potential political allies. Quietly but consciously, Madison and Jefferson were beginning to build the foundations of an opposition party that would create powerful new conversational circles and committees of correspondence.

They paid particular attention to politicians who were starting to seethe against Hamilton for having too much power, prestige, and patronage—much as Adams and Otis had once seethed against Hutchinson for similar reasons. New York's affronted chancellor Robert R. Livingston, in particular, provided a perfect target of opportunity. Early in 1789, Hamilton's allies in New York's Albany legislature had successfully backed two Hamilton men (his father-in-law, Philip Schuyler, and his friend Rufus King) over Livingston for the US Senate. Later that year, Washington picked Hamilton himself as treasury secretary over the more senior and highborn Livingston, who had coveted the post. In early 1791, Livingston exacted some revenge, successfully backing Aaron Burr over Schuyler when the latter was up for reelection.[30]

Hamilton's former college roommate, Robert Troup, wrote his old friend (now in Philadelphia, the interim capital) in mid-1791 to alert him to the political danger brewing in New York: "There was every appearance of a passionate courtship between the Chancellor, Burr, Jefferson & Madison when the two latter were in Town. *Delenda est Carthago* [Carthage must be destroyed!] I suppose is the Maxim adopted with respect to you. They had better be quiet, for if they succeed they will tumble the fabric of the government in ruins to the ground."[31]

Troup's closing remark might seem unduly alarmist to modern eyes, accustomed as we are to political networking, ideological alliances, personal pacts, and the unquestioned legitimacy of opposition parties. But the rules of fair political engagement under a new constitutional order were still being shaped in this early era, and an astonishing letter from the following year shows that Troup was right to worry.

Led by Governor Henry "Lighthorse Harry" Lee, who would later aid Washington in suppressing the Whiskey Rebellion, some Virginians began to float the idea of creating a state bank to counter the influence of any Virginia branch of the bank of the United States. On October 1, 1792, Jefferson wrote to Madison to dismiss this compromise proposal as far too tame—"a milk & water measure, which rather recognises than prevents the planting among them [Virginians] a source of poison & corruption." What Jefferson proposed instead—coming as it did from a high-ranking federal officer who Washington supposed was entirely loyal to him and his administration—was eye-popping:

> The [Virginia] assembly should reason thus. The power of erecting banks & corporations was not given to the general government[.] It remains then with the state itself. For any person to recognise a foreign legislature [that is, Congress!] in a case belonging to the state itself, is an act of *treason* against the state [!], and whosoever shall do any act under colour of the authority of a foreign legislature whether by signing notes, issuing or passing them, acting as director, cashier or in any other office relating to it shall be adjudged guilty of high treason [!] & suffer death [!] accordingly, by the judgment of the state [!] courts. This is the only opposition worthy of our state, and the only kind which can be effectual. If N. Carolina could be brought into a like measure, it would bring the General government to respect the counter-rights of the states. The example would probably be followed by some other states.

In a short response note, Madison proclaimed Jefferson's analysis "unanswerable."[32]

The tone here was not jocular, as when Jefferson had jested that Madison should join him in praying for Patrick Henry's demise. Perhaps Jefferson was now just blowing off steam, but the multiple details—about the law, the punishment, the court, and sister states—suggest more than mere venting. If Jefferson sought merely to set up a test case in the courts, why did he suggest the death penalty and make no mention of US Supreme Court review of the envisioned state court ruling in favor of state law? Granted, Jefferson's ranting fell far short of treason itself, given that he was not organizing armed opposition to federal authority, but only contemplating things done via legal forms—state statutes and state court rulings. But it is hard to imagine that if George Washington had seen this letter he would have smiled. Indeed, he likely would have fired Jefferson on the spot and forever banished him from his sight. Jefferson was duplicitously and furtively mobilizing against a bill that Washington himself had signed into law after carefully considering and rejecting his adviser Jefferson's ideas. Though it was not treason against the United States, Jefferson was surely committing treachery against George Washington. Jefferson was becoming unglued—and this time, Madison, who himself had been publicly repudiated on the bank question, did not steady his senior partner.

Nor was this a unique act of duplicity and bad judgment. In their 1791 northern botanical tour, Madison and Jefferson met with one of Madison's Princeton chums, Philip Freneau, encouraging the New York poet to set up an anti-Hamiltonian print shop in Philadelphia.[33] Jefferson later hired Freneau as a government clerk, with a moderate salary and few demands, even though Freneau lacked the proper qualifications. Jefferson eventually admitted to intentionally subsidizing Freneau's journalism but denied controlling Freneau's actual journalistic output. Freneau's paper, the *National Gazette*, began publication in October 1791 and continued for two years. In its short life, it relentlessly attacked not only Hamilton, but also Washington and the administration's official policies. In one anonymous broadside, Freneau fantasized about the death by guillotine of Washington and Justice James Wilson.[34] Several of the *National Gazette's* most notable pieces, published pseudonymously, in fact came from the pen of Madison with the blessing of Jefferson. Jefferson was the puppet master, but in late 1792 he denied everything in a long letter to Washington: "I never did by myself, or any other, directly or indirectly, say a syllable, nor attempt any kind of influence."[35]

Jefferson was a diplomat who knew how to slice and dice words, but this was cutting things very fine. He had personally encouraged a predictably anti-administration publisher *precisely because the publisher was anti-administration,* funded the publisher (as his own clerk) with administration money, and then denied all complicity when the printer acted just as Jefferson had expected and hoped. Hamilton was not deceived by the veils. Under his own pseudonym (which he likely knew would fool no one—he was not trying to hide, only to be discreet), he pounced on his rival Jefferson in the Federalist press. The secretary of state "knows how to put a man [Freneau] in a situation calculated to produce all the effects he desires, without the gross and awkward formality of telling him—'Sir I mean to *hire* you for the purpose.'"[36]

In fact, Hamilton himself had steered government money— for example, contracts to publish government documents—to pro-administration publishers, most notably John Fenno's *Gazette of the United States.* But the situation was not entirely symmetric. Hamilton's efforts went *indirectly* (via bona fide printing contracts) to publishers *supporting* administration policy. This was standard practice for the era. Jefferson, by contrast, was *directly* (via a no-show job under Jefferson's personal supervision) funneling money to a printer *undermining* administration policy—and, critically, doing so without Washington's knowledge or consent. "No government ought to be without censors," Jefferson explained in his airy, condescending, and less than candid letter to Washington. Fair enough, but must Washington be made to subsidize his own censors? Unknowingly? By what right did Jefferson, a mere subordinate to Washington, take it upon himself to do this, without clear approval from the president himself? Hamilton understood the role of loyal aide-de-camp. Jefferson did not, or at least pretended that he did not.

Freneau did not stand alone. Other anti-administration print shops sprouted in the 1790s, none more notable than the *Aurora General Advertiser*, published by Franklin's grandson and namesake, Benjamin Franklin Bache. Perhaps Jefferson did not fully succeed, at least in the early 1790s, in establishing an entire national alliance of newspapers tightly linked to his fledgling political party, but he was, farsightedly, aiming in this direction—a proto–Fox News network.

His envisioned network involved not merely motivated printers but also motivated journalists. The Jeffersonian motivation could be pure ideology or friendly funding or both. Newspapers of earlier decades had not paid much for content, nor did these print shops boast large staffs of reporters. Much of their revenue had come from advertisers. Thus, individuals (advertisers) paid publishers to appear in print, while publishers did not generally pay individuals (writers) to produce thoughtful prose. Much political copy flowed straight from official sources—gubernatorial proclamations, legislative debates, enacted statutes, grand-jury presentments, town meeting resolutions, and so on—or from independent gentlemen (young Washington, young Otis, young Adams, Publius, etc.) seeking to see their prose in print and freely contributing their scribblings to various publications. By the 1790s, newspapers were starting to change. A cadre of professional writers began to emerge—would-be Tom Paines, not necessarily genteel, who hoped to make a living, full-time, publishing eye-catching journalistic essays and pamphlets. Perhaps inspired by his Parisian experience in which patrons and patronesses of salons sponsored promising artists, writers, and intellectuals, Jefferson saw himself as a journalistic benefactor, willing to encourage writers of the right (that is, left) sort.

The most notorious journalist on Jefferson's secret payroll was James Callender, an ambitious émigré from Britain who arrived in America in the spring of 1793. Over the course of his short and colorful life, Callender was an equal-opportunity scandalmonger. In the mid-1790s, he broke the story of Alexander Hamilton's improper behavior. Fed juicy and misleading tidbits by unprincipled allies of Madison and Jefferson, Callender publicly accused Hamilton of governmental corruption. Hamilton responded with a pamphlet of his own, proving that no public misdeed had occurred, but openly confessing to a different sort of sin: he had paid hush money to the husband of a woman, Maria Reynolds, with whom he had conducted an adulterous affair. Later in the decade, Callender blasted President Adams in print and, as we shall soon see in more detail, was prosecuted, convicted, and imprisoned for nearly a year. When Jefferson himself became president—thanks in no small measure to public backlash against Adams's imprisonment of journalists—the new chief executive pardoned Callender but did not further subsidize him, publicly or privately. Callender was no longer a political asset to Jefferson, and now that Jefferson himself sat in Washington's old chair, he began to feel that fairness did not in fact require governmental support of politically unreliable or hostile journalists. (Here, too, hypocrisy offset utopian eccentricity.) Incensed at Jefferson's lack of gratitude for his past services as a secret pet pit bull, Callender bit the hand that had once fed him. First, he made public Jefferson's past financial support of his projects. Then, in September 1802, he reported to the world that Jefferson had a slave mistress, "Sally," and that "by the wench Sally, our president has had several children," adding, "There is not an individual in Charlottesville who does not believe the story; and not a few who know it." The newspaper item first ran in the September 1, 1802, edition of the *Richmond Recorder* and was soon reprinted in most states north of Virginia.[37] Less than a year later, Callender was dead in his mid-forties, drowned drunk in three feet of water.

If Callender was an unreliable cog in the politico-journalistic machine Jefferson was quietly building, James Madison was its propeller. When Hamilton anonymously penned newspaper essays defending the constitutional propriety and policy wisdom of Washington's famous Neutrality Proclamation—announcing that America would not take sides in the latest round of warfare between England and France—Jefferson, in July 1793, urged Madison to publish newspaper essays in response: "Nobody answers him [Hamilton], and his doc-trine will therefore be taken for confessed. For god's sake, my dear Sir, take up your pen, select the most striking heresies, and cut him to pieces in the face of the public. There is nobody else who can and will enter the lists with him." Here again, we see Jefferson pulling strings, with his protégé Madison responding to the tug and doing his best (which was not very good) to counter Hamilton.[38]

And here again, we see a striking asymmetry at work. Hamilton was using a pen name in the press to *defend* Washington's character and policies. Jefferson was urging Madison to use a pen name in the press to *attack* the president and his men. Yet Jefferson at this very moment was Washington's secretary of state who had in fact acqui-esced to a neutrality proclamation of some sort when Washington had presented the matter for collective cabinet deliberation.[39]

BY THE END OF 1796, the basic wisdom and steadiness of Washing-ton's policies had begun to make themselves felt, even by many who had earlier doubted individual pieces of the larger whole. Thanks to various Hamiltonian fiscal and national-security policies—assump-tion, excise taxes, customs duties, luxury taxes, and a national bank system—the administration had staffed its professional military, made renewed peace with England and Spain, avoided major hostilities with France, opened up the Southwest and the Northwest to set-tlement, secured navigation on the Mississippi, pacified the Indians, regularized the militia, and brought order to the western backcountry. And thanks to Jefferson, Madison, freedom-lovers, and states' right-ists, a Bill of Rights was now in place, as was an Eleventh Amend-ment protecting proper states' rights and the role of state courts to decide state law. All thirteen original states were reunited, and new states had joined the fold—Vermont, Kentucky, and Tennessee. The new national capital would sit where North met South and East met West, thanks to a deal brokered by Hamilton, Madison, and Jefferson.

Much of what Madison and Jefferson understood at the outset—especially about the importance of freedom of conscience and the need for a bill of rights—was spot-on. But after 1790 these two great figures lost their bearings, in part because they (and many other financial illiterates, especially in Virginia) simply did not understand banks, which many at the time thought were inherently evil things. In 1797, Jefferson was not a good fit for the presidency.

On the other hand, Adams was untested and underqualified. He had never held ordinary executive office—such as a governorship or a cabinet post—or managed much of anything. The electoral system responded by splitting the difference in the election of 1796, awarding the presidency to Adams and the vice presidency to Jefferson.

Over the next four years, both Jeffersonians and Adamsonians misbehaved, but as we shall now see, by 1800 America rightly saw the Adamsonians as the greater threat to the American constitutional project. Hamilton and his allies had been better at building the system in its early years, but Jefferson and Madison would offer a more reassuring vision for restraining that system when true freedom—not freedom from sensible banks or from necessary taxes, but freedom of core political opinion—was genuinely at risk.

SEDITION?

One, proverbially, is a lonely number. At any given time, one and only one person shoulders the crushing burdens of the American presidency. Events combined to isolate John Adams, making his presidency a uniquely lonely one.

Adams had spent much of the decade from 1778 to 1788 far from home and friends. The next period of his life left him further isolated—a vice president without a branch, an old-fashioned statesman without a party, quite, and a politician without a partner facing emerging two-man teams (Hamilton-Washington, Jefferson-Madison).

Thanks to the Decision of 1789, incoming president Adams was entitled to cabinet officers of his own selection, but at the outset of his administration he opted simply to continue with the department heads that he inherited from Washington. Alas, he did not converse well with these men. He was never the best of listeners and did not improve with age. Also, he spent more than a quarter of his presidential tenure away from his department heads—back home in Massachusetts with his beloved, clever, nurturing, and ailing Abigail, rather than in the capital with his government.[40] President Washington, too, had spent time away from the capital, but had wisely used much of this time seeing and being seen—mingling with his fellow citizens on a celebrated New England tour in late 1789, on a quick trip to Rhode Island after it rejoined the union in 1790, and on a grand circuit of the southern states in 1791.[41]

Ultimately, Adams discovered to his horror that several of his cabinet secretaries were in tight conversation with Hamilton. Not all of this was machination on Hamilton's part. He knew how to run government; Adams did not; and it often made sense for Adams's cabinet men to receive and follow Hamilton's operational and policy advice as issues arose. In retirement, Adams colorfully complained that his initial cabinet had consisted of "Puppets danced upon the Wires of two Jugglers behind the Scene: and these Jugglers were Hamilton and Washington."[42]

Pre-inauguration, Adams made genuine efforts at outreach. Jefferson wrote Madison, "My letters inform me that Mr. A. speaks of me with great friendship, and with satisfaction in the prospect of administering the government in concurrence with me." But Adams enjoyed spirited face-to-face confrontations. Jefferson hated oral combat and thus told Madison that he would refuse any position in Adams's "executive cabinet"—a prospect that conjured up painful memories of his repeated and humiliating cabinet defeats at the hands of Hamilton: "I cannot have a wish to see the scenes of 93 [1793] revived as to myself, and to descend daily into the arena like a gladiator to suffer martyrdom in every conflict."[43]

As Adams assumed office, even those who had backed him against Jefferson harbored grave doubts. Oliver Wolcott Sr., Connecticut's Federalist governor, had served with Adams in the Continental Congress in the 1770s. In 1795, Washington chose Wolcott's son and namesake to replace Hamilton as treasury secretary. Two weeks into the Adams administration, Senior warned Junior what to expect from his new chief:

> We have done the best we could in our election. We have chosen a very honest man, a friend to order, and to our national independence and honor. But that you may know that I am not mistaken, I will for once, under a strong seal, venture to tell you that I always considered Mr. Adams a man of great vanity, pretty capricious, of a very moderate share of prudence, and of far less real abilities than he believes he possesses. I therefore sincerely wish that he may have able counsellors, in whom he will confide; though, as he will not be influenced but by an apparent compliment to his own understanding, it will require a great deal of address to render him the service which it will be essential for him to receive.[44]

Thus, Adams did not have his own Hamilton or Madison to support him, as did Washington and Jefferson, respectively. Nor did he have a political party that saw him as its founding figure and essential banner—again, unlike Washington and Jefferson. Nor did he have a handpicked cabinet to steady him. Nor did he have a vice president willing to work closely with him in a coalitional government. That left Abigail, who was generally perceptive and loyal to a fault. But Abigail was in fact too loyal to him personally and too close to him emotionally to give him detached advice on the most critical constitutional decision he confronted as president, a decision about the very structure of American constitutional conversation.

Large technological, demographic, and geopolitical forces were merging to make American public discourse far more combative in the mid-1790s than it had been only a decade earlier. Renewed warfare between Europe's two Great Powers, England and France—warfare that now had a strong ideological edge, thanks to the French Revolution—exerted a powerful gravitational pull on still-tiny America. European politics thus globalized and deepened what might otherwise have been viewed as smaller and local policy rifts between Adamsonians and Jeffersonians, or (what was almost the same thing) between Federalists and Democratic-Republicans. Heavy immigration from various Old World flashpoints—especially France and Ireland on the Jeffersonian side and England on the Adamsonian side—added still more intensity, anxiety, and emotion to the New World mix. More and more newspapers were now competing more and more fiercely than ever for eyeballs. Many new and ambitious professional writers were reacting with increasingly pointed prose.[45]

When Adams found himself insulted daily in this new and nasty newspaper environment, he chose to back a statute, the Sedition Act of 1798, that promised to put an end to the venom. His decisions first to sign and then to wildly over-enforce this law seemed plausible to many at the time, including several circuit jurists and, importantly, the usually shrewd Abigail.[46] But these fateful decisions reflected a deep misunderstanding of the American constitutional project, at whose core was the idea of a robust right of ordinary folk—even if unfair, mean-spirited, and mistaken—to criticize all manner of public servants, including the president himself.

PRESIDENT JOHN ADAMS SIGNED THE Sedition Act into law on July 14, 1798, nine years to the day after the storming of the Bastille.[47] The 1789 Parisian incident had set in motion events that ultimately toppled and killed King Louis XVI; his queen, Marie Antoinette; and their heir to the throne, the dauphin. Adams's signature likewise led to his own ouster, but the president; his lady, Abigail; and their heir, John Quincy, got to keep their heads in the transition and thereafter. On two telling dimensions—orderliness of regime change and avoidance of bloodshed—Federalist-era America showed itself vastly superior to Revolutionary France.

Under the Sedition Act, anyone who dared to criticize the federal government, the president, or Congress risked a fine of up to $2,000 and a prison term of up to two years. But venomous criticism, even if knowingly false and violence-inciting, that targeted the vice president was fair game under the law. Thus, in the impending electoral rematch between Adams and Jefferson in 1800, Adams and his allies could malign Jefferson, but Jefferson and his allies could not reciprocate with equal vigor. Congressional aspirants attacking Congressional incumbents would need to watch their words, but not vice versa. Just in case the Jeffersonians managed to win the next election, the act provided that it would poof into thin air on March 3, 1801, a day before the new presidential term would begin. (This highly partisan poofing was not quite what Jefferson had in mind back in his 1789 correspondence with Madison.)

On its surface, the act seemed modest. It criminalized only "false, scandalous, and malicious" writings or utterances that had the "intent to defame" or comparable acidic motivation. The defendant could introduce into evidence "the truth of the matter contained in the publication charged as a libel," and his jury would "have the right to determine the law and the fact, under the direction of the court, as in other cases." This was more generous than British libel law at the time. Under Charles Fox's 1792 Libel Law, a British jury could, in Zengerian fashion, decide not just whether a defendant had published a given tract but also whether the tract was libelous. However, truth was no defense at all in Britain. Indeed, truth could actually compound a British publisher's liability. "The greater the truth, the greater the libel," because the libelee would suffer a greater reputational fall if the unflattering story was in fact true.

British law was thus all about protecting His Majesty and His Lordship and His Worshipfulness from criticism; it was the product of a residually monarchial, aristocratic, and deeply deferential legal and social order. As the jurist William Blackstone explained in his magisterial *Commentaries on the Laws of England*—a runaway best seller in late eighteenth-century America—British freedom of the press meant only that the press would not be licensed or censored prepublication. Anyone could freely run a printing press, but printers might face severe punishment after the fact if they used their presses to disparage the powerful: "The liberty of the press is indeed essential to the nature of a free state: but this consists in laying no *previous* restraints upon publications, and not in freedom from censure for criminal matter when published. Every freeman has an undoubted right to lay what sentiments he pleases before the public: to forbid this, is to destroy the freedom of the press: but if he publishes what is improper, mischievous, or illegal, he must take the consequence of his own temerity."[48]

In his 1788 correspondence with Madison about the need for an American bill of rights, Jefferson himself went beyond Blackstone, but not by miles: "A declaration that the federal government will never restrain the presses from printing any thing they please, will not take away the liability of the printers for false facts printed." Jefferson envisioned liability only for "false facts printed." But what if the falsehood was a good-faith mistake, or a rhetorical overstatement in a vigorous political give-and-take? Could an honest mistake or mere exuberance ever justify serious criminal liability and extended imprisonment?[49]

Also, who would bear the burden of proof? The Sedition Act purported to criminalize only "false" statements, but in the 1790s many derogatory comments were legally presumed false. The Sedition Act said that a defendant could "give in evidence in his defence, the truth of the matter," but many edgy statements mixed truth with opinion and rhetoric. If a critic wrote that John Adams was a vain and pompous ass who did not deserve a second term, how exactly could the critic establish the courtroom "truth of the matter"?

President Adams gave insufficient attention to these issues, perhaps because he focused too much on musty English law books and not enough on what had happened in America in the transformational decade that he missed. In at least two decisive ways that had profound implications for the Sedition Act controversy, American and British constitutional law differed.

First, in America, no federal common-law crimes—that is, crimes defined solely by judicial case law and lacking statutory foundations—properly existed, and this fact undercut a key argument for the Sedition Act. Some Congressional Federalists pushing the act said that it was actually a *liberalization* of Blackstonian rules that would otherwise operate in America. These backers thus depicted the act as a blow for freedom. But as the Supreme Court would explain in a later landmark case (under Chief Justice John Marshall, an Adams appointee), the British common law of crimes had no place in the new federal government. Nor did any other kind of judge-fashioned regime of criminal liability properly operate federally. Unless and until Congress enacted a given criminal statute, with the president's signature or over his veto, the federal baseline was freedom from all federal criminal liability, period: "The legislative authority of the Union must first make an act a crime, affix a punishment to it, and declare the Court that shall have jurisdiction of the offence."[50]

Second, and far more consequentially, American constitutional law rejected British constitutional law at the most fundamental level. In England, Parliament was sovereign. In America, the people were sovereign. No mere government agent—Congress or the president— could presume to tell sovereign citizens what to think or what to say politically.

This fundamental structural point about sovereignty also translated into a clean textual argument based on "the freedom of speech." In Britain, members of the sovereign Parliament enjoyed near-absolute "freedom of speech," a right expressly affirmed in the English Bill of Rights of 1689. No one outside Parliament could punish a member of Parliament for speaking his mind on the floor of Parliament. Parliament—deriving its very name from *parler*, to speak—was a special and sovereign *speech* spot, a venue for virtually unfettered political debate, even if defamatory. But under British law, ordinary British subjects outside Parliament did not have comparably sweeping freedom of speech. Ordinary Britons were mere subjects, and Parliament had sweeping power—sovereignty—over subjects, as indeed Parliament had insisted in the 1766 Declaratory Act. (Americans had of course responded by breaking with Britain altogether.)

By contrast, as James Wilson had explained, and as the Preamble itself had made clear, in America the citizens themselves were sovereign. As such, they inherited the same (or nearly the same) sweeping power of sovereign political discourse that in Britain operated only within Parliament's walls. The First Amendment textualized this basic difference, recognizing that ordinary American citizens, unlike ordinary British subjects, enjoyed a sweeping "freedom of speech" above and beyond a British-style "freedom of the press."

Historically, the freedom of the press in the seventeenth and eighteenth centuries could sensibly be seen as meaning merely freedom from a licensing regime. When Gutenberg-style printing presses first appeared in England, they were relatively modern inventions in the world, and bulky ones at that. English laws had at one time purported to require a license to operate such machines. Eventually, Britain rejected these older laws; no license would henceforth be required to operate a press. But freedom of *speech* had entirely different historical roots and an entirely different conceptual logic. It was nonsense to think this right was merely about rejecting an earlier licensing system. Speech as such had nothing to do with the Gutenberg Revolution.

Perhaps the speech rules for ordinary citizens could not be exactly equal in every jot and tittle to the speech rules for Parliament members. Parliament members had constraints (front-end election and intra-Parliamentary punishment) that did not apply to all citizen speech everywhere. But a broad parity principle made structural sense of the Constitution read holistically. Given that, under the *Article* I Speech Clause, a member of Congress had broad immunity to criticize anyone, including his challengers, free from the threat of criminal libel law, his challengers needed to have broadly reciprocal freedom under the *Amendment* I Speech Clause to criticize him.*

---

*Compare Article I, section 6—"For any *speech* or debate in either House, they [members of Congress] shall not be questioned in any other place"—with Amendment I: "Congress shall make no law . . . abridging the freedom of *speech*, or of the press" (emphasis added). See also the Article I precursor in the Articles of Confederation (Article V, para. 5): "*Freedom of speech* and debate *in Congress* shall not be impeached or questioned in any court or place out of Congress" (emphasis added). Finally, consider the ur-text of the English Bill of Rights of 1689: "*The freedom of speech* and debates or proceedings *in Parliament* ought not to be impeached or questioned in any court or place out of Parliament" (emphasis added).

Adams did not understand this. Neither did Hamilton, quite. True, the high-strung New Yorker did not vote for the sedition law—he was now in private practice—but neither did he pen a passionate defense of free speech at this critical hour. In 1788, Hamilton had not dramatically pivoted in favor of a bill of rights, as had Madison. More recently, perhaps the abuse that Hamilton had endured in the press from penmen such as Callender tempered whatever enthusiasm the great lawyer might otherwise have felt for the broadest possible understanding of freedom to vilify public officials.

There was, however, one leading founder who understood expressive freedom deeply and viscerally—understood it the way Hamilton understood tax and trade and banks and war, the way Washington understood armies and diplomacy and national security. Whereas Alexander Hamilton and George Washington understood best of all how to create a strong government to protect against external foes, James Madison understood best of all how to protect freedom of thought and freedom of expression against internal oppression.

In 1789, at Jefferson's and Washington's prodding (but not Hamilton's), Madison had taken the lead in drafting a bill of rights promising liberty of conscience and expression. In the mid-1790s, Madison had again taken the lead, defending the rights of common citizens to criticize officialdom. "If we advert to the nature of Republican Government," explained Madison in 1794, "we shall find that the censorial power is in the people over the government and not in the government over the people." In 1798–1801, it would be Madison and his senior partner, Jefferson, who would once more take the lead in defending the freedom of the mind, and the closely related freedoms to speak one's mind and hear others speak theirs.

ADAMS ERRED NOT SIMPLY IN signing the Sedition Act but in mindlessly and mercilessly prosecuting and punishing—and never pardoning—men under it. He and his minions hounded tart but peaceful speakers and printers whose only real crime was dislike of John Adams and his policies, in cases whose facts were miles apart from treason, riot, or mayhem. Indeed, under the ridiculously strict standards of his own administration, a young John Adams himself should have been fined and imprisoned for his vigorous denunciations of Governor Thomas Hutchinson.[51]

In the first high-profile sedition case, brought in October 1798, the Adams administration targeted a sitting Republican congressman from Vermont, Matthew Lyon, for political writings and harangues, some of them at campaign rallies. Several of the allegedly criminal statements at issue had occurred before the Sedition Act's enactment, a wrinkle reflecting the government's erroneous legal theory that there existed a federal common law of criminal sedition from the moment the Constitution sprang to life. In one passage highlighted by the prosecution, Lyon had written (if we construe his text in the harshest light) that Adams had "swallowed up" every proper "consideration of the public welfare" in "a continual grasp for power, in an unbounded thirst for ridiculous pomp, foolish adulation, or selfish avarice." Adams, wrote Lyon, had "turned out of office . . . men of real merit [and] independency" in favor of "men of meanness." Lyon had also read at public meetings a communication from a French diplomat bemoaning the "extremely alarming" state of relations between France and the United States, worsened by the "bullying speech of your president and stupid answer of your senate." Congress, wrote the diplomat in words that Lyon publicly repeated, should send Adams "to a mad house."[52]

How exactly could Lyon prove in a courtroom the technical truth of these words, blending as they did fact, opinion, analysis, interpretation, and rhetoric?

Riding circuit, Justice William Paterson told the jury to pay no heed to Lyon's claim that the law was unconstitutional: "You have nothing whatever to do with the constitutionality or unconstitutionality of the sedition law. Congress has said that the author and publisher of seditious libels is to be punished; and until this law is declared null and void by a tribunal competent for the purpose, its validity cannot be disputed. Great would be the abuses were the constitutionality of every statute to be submitted to a jury, in each case where the statute is to be applied." The jury convicted and Paterson sentenced Lyon to a fine of $1,000 and a four-month imprisonment.

Dozens of newspapers across the continent brought readers detailed reports of the cause célèbre. While in prison, Lyon wrote an account of his travails that Philadelphia's *Aurora General Advertiser* published in early November, followed by newspapers in many other localities. The congressman vividly described his conditions of confinement: "I [am] locked up in [a] room . . . about 16 feet long by 12 feet wide, with a necessary in one corner, which affords a stench about equal to the Philadelphia docks, in the month of August. The cell is the common receptacle for horse-thieves, money makers [counterfeiters], runaway negroes, or any kind of felons."[53] When Lyon stood for reelection—from prison—in December, his constituents gave him a roaring vote of confidence, returning him to his House seat. Adams thus won the first courtroom battle but was beginning to lose the war of public opinion. Much as Otis had lost his case in court but won at the polls in 1761, so now Lyon was playing to the crowd to good effect. To many Americans, Adams looked like a thin-skinned bully; Lyon, a martyr to freedom.

In early 1800, America's interim capital, Philadelphia, played host to a different high-profile sedition case, this one against a colorful English émigré, Thomas Cooper, who had studied at Oxford, read law at London's Inner Temple, and dabbled in business and science. Later in life, Cooper, an intimate associate of the famed scientist Joseph Priestley, would serve as a professor at several notable colleges, including the University of Pennsylvania. Cooper had printed a handbill denouncing the president for various "political mistake[s]" including a bloated military, fiscal blundering, and improper executive interference in a notorious extradition case involving a seaman claiming to be an American, Jonathan Robbins, whom Adams had delivered up for "a mock trial of a British court-martial." (The British claimed he was an English deserter, Thomas Nash, and hanged him after a drumhead trial.)[54]

In his defense, Cooper told the jurors and the presiding judges—Justice Samuel Chase on circuit, joined by District Judge Richard Peters—that

> in the present state of affairs, the press is open to those who will praise, while the threats of the law hang over those who blame the conduct of, the men in power. . . . Nor do I see how the people can exercise on rational grounds their elective franchise, if perfect freedom of discussion of public characters is not allowed. Electors are bound in conscience to reflect and decide who best deserves their suffrage; but how can they do it, if these prosecutions in terrorem close all the avenues of information, and throw a veil over the grossest misconduct of our periodical rulers?

Justice Chase responded by vigorously defending the Sedition Act in his charge to the jury. Chase appeared to take special umbrage at Cooper's description of the Robbins affair, in which Cooper had disparaged not just Adams but also the federal judge who was involved in the extradition. (Judges have historically been hypersensitive about criticisms of the judiciary itself.) Cooper was convicted and sentenced to a $400 fine and six months' imprisonment.

The next and last big Sedition Act trial resulted in an even harsher sentence—nine months' imprisonment. The defendant was none other than the trashy yet talented journalist James Callender—the man who broke the Hamilton sex-scandal story in 1797 and would later expose the Jefferson-Hemings affair in 1802. In the run-up to the presidential election of 1800—a rematch of 1796, but this time pitting the sitting vice president against the sitting president—Callender published a campaign pamphlet, *The Prospect Before Us.*

Callender painted in bright colors and attacked Adams for just about everything: "Take your choice, then, between Adams, war and beggary, and Jefferson, peace and competency!" The "reign of Mr. Adams has been one continued tempest of malignant passions. As president, he has never opened his lips, or lifted his pen without threatening and scolding." The administration's "corruption" was "notorious." Indeed, the president had appointed his own son-in-law, William Stevens Smith, to a plum federal office, surveyor of the port of New York, thus "heap[ing] . . . myriads of dollars upon . . . a paper jobber, who, next to Hamilton and himself is, perhaps, the most detested character on the continent." Adams's "hands are reeking with the blood of the poor, friendless Connecticut sailor." (Here Callender referred, as had Cooper, to the Jonathan Robbins affair.)

Notably, Callender also blasted the Sedition Act itself, and Adams's abuse of it: "The grand object of his administration has been . . . to calumniate and destroy every man who differs from his opinions." Callender cleverly connected his advocacy of broad citizen freedom of speech to the Constitution's broad protection of Congressional freedom of speech: "If a Representative shall say in congress, that the president is a fool, the constitution secures his impunity. He has only to walk out the door, and repeat his own words, and he becomes a criminal." This was indeed a nice statement of the Adams administration's curious position in the Lyon case. "The simple act of writing a censure of government incurs the penalties, although the manuscript shall only be found locked up in your own desk," noted Callender. Here, the Sedition Act did indeed approximate mind control, yet Adams apparently never shuddered to think about his own diary diatribes against Hutchinson and other governmental figures in the 1760s and 1770s. Finally, Callender, who showed more self-awareness than Adams on this point, connected his critique of the act to the very nature of the election-year pamphlet in which his more general critiques of Adams were appearing. The act made it virtually "impossible to discuss the merit of the candidates." If a person proclaimed that he "prefer[red] Jefferson to Adams"—as Callender was of course doing in this very pamphlet—wouldn't that itself be an actionable slur on Adams? asked Callender.

The Adams administration apparently agreed, and prosecuted Callender in the spring of 1800 for what today looks like a rather typical, if overstated, campaign tract. Once again, Justice Chase presided, this time as a circuit judge in Virginia. When Callender's attorney—William Wirt, who would later become America's longest-serving attorney general—tried to appeal to the jury's sense of constitutional justice, Chase shut him down. Chase would later be impeached by the House for his overall handling of the Callender case and for refusing in a different case to allow defense counsel to argue law to the jury. (Many senators would vote to convict but not enough to clear the two-thirds bar set by the Constitution.) The transcript captures the triumph of judicial power over constitutional logic at this fraught election-year moment:

> Here CHASE, Circuit Justice—Take your seat, sir, if you please. If I understand you rightly, you offer an argument to the petit jury, to convince them that the . . . Sedition Law, is contrary to the constitution of the United States and, therefore, void. Now I tell you that this is irregular and inadmissible; it is not competent to the jury to decide this point. . . . [W]e all know that juries have the right to decide the law, as well as the fact—and the constitution is the supreme law of the land, which controls all laws repugnant to it.

> Mr. Wirt—Since then, the jury have a right to consider the law, and since the constitution is law, the conclusion is certainly syllogistic, that the jury have a right to consider the constitution.

> CHASE, Circuit Justice.—A non sequitur, sir.

> Here Mr. Wirt sat down.[55]

Callender's nine-month sentence drew the gaze of printers and readers across the continent, just as the Adams-Jefferson rematch was unfolding in a series of statewide contests for electoral votes. Alongside the convictions of Lyon and Cooper, Callender's case cast Adams in an unflattering light, as did other lower-profile cases. (One featured a Newark drunkard, Luther Baldwin, who made a crude joke about the president's rear end.)

All told, the Adams administration initiated more than a dozen—indeed, one recent historian says many dozen—prosecutions under both the Sedition Act itself and the faux federal common law of seditious libel.[56] Some cases never came to trial but still captured attention. For example, the feisty printer of Philadelphia's *Aurora General Advertiser*, Benjamin Franklin Bache, named for his famous printer-grandfather, died of yellow fever while under indictment. The *Aurora* was a high-profile anti-administration paper published in an iconic city. Going after Bache was the eighteenth-century equivalent of a Republican president today seeking to imprison the editors of the *Washington Post* or a modern Democratic president aiming to criminalize the publishers of the *National Review*.

SUPREME COURT JUSTICES ON CIRCUIT had sided with Adams, but America's ultimate supreme court consists of the sovereign American people, who express themselves most consequentially via constitutional amendments and pivotal elections. The Adams-Jefferson rematch was just such a pivotal election, and the court of public opinion ultimately sided with Jefferson and Madison, as has the court of history.[57]

True, in order to prevail politically, Jefferson did not need to prove that the Sedition Act was unconstitutional, or even unwise. His political platform (to use a modern expression) had multiple planks. But Jefferson's and Adams's radically different views about the Sedition Act did mark an especially sharp dividing line between the two men—America's two highest-ranking officials, now contesting each other directly in the rematch election of 1800—and the constitutional aspects of Jefferson's campaign did ennoble his cause.

In his musings back in 1788–1789 about the need for a bill of rights, Jefferson had emphasized to Madison the importance of judicial enforcement by independent judges: "In the arguments in favor of a declaration of rights, you omit one which has great weight with me, the legal check which it puts into the hands of the judiciary. This is a body, which if rendered independent, & kept strictly to their own department, merits great confidence for their learning & integrity."[58] In introducing various amendments "relat[ing] to what may be called a bill of rights" shortly after receiving this Jeffersonian missive, Madison said much the same thing in his Congressional speech of June 8, 1789. If a textual armful of rights "are incorporated into the constitution," he explained, "independent tribunals of justice will consider themselves in a peculiar manner the guardians of those rights. They will be an impenetrable bulwark against every assumption of power in the legislative or executive. They will be naturally led to resist every encroachment upon rights expressly stipulated for in the constitution by the declaration of rights."[59]

A decade later, Madison and Jefferson had reasons to despair at the disappointingly partisan and small-minded performance of various Federalist-appointed judges, who seemed all too willing to enforce the Sedition Act and ignore its glaring constitutional flaws—even when confronting fact patterns utterly unworthy of serious punishment in a free republic. Back in 1789, Madison and Jefferson had also hoped that juries might help enforce a proper bill of rights simply by refusing to convict; jurors, too, were part of the "independent" judicial department expected to demonstrate "integrity" and act as a "guardian" of freedom, "an impenetrable bulwark" of liberty. But Paterson, Chase, and other presiding judges had refused to allow defendants and their lawyers to make direct constitutional appeals to jurors, and in various venues, federal marshals had succeeded in packing the jury with Federalist partisans.

If judges and juries would not or could not safeguard the true meaning of the Bill of Rights, who was left? Republican congressmen? If they tried to criticize Adams at campaign rallies and in other venues outside Congress itself, Adams could prosecute them directly. That was the upshot of the Lyon case. Newspaper printers and journalists? They, too, were being targeted by the very act they themselves tried to criticize. That was the upshot of the Bache and Callender cases.

What was left, of course, was local pushback against central officialdom—a deeply rooted American practice that took Jefferson back to his early days as a leader of the American Revolution. In the 1760s and 1770s, colonial assemblies had used their own historical powers of freedom of speech and debate to denounce the central government's oppressive policies and to urge Americans everywhere to resist. In 1790, Patrick Henry had returned to this tried-and-true tactic when he spearheaded new Virginia resolutions attacking what he claimed was oppressive overreach by Congress (the assumption bill). In his half-deranged letter to Madison contemplating a Virginia death penalty for central bank clerks, Jefferson was likewise envisioning use of state legislatures to counter alleged Congressional usurpation. (The derangements were that, unlike Henry, he was contemplating vastly more than mere local denunciation and was opposing policies of his own executive-branch superior. Also, he was railing against a sensible bank law that came nowhere close to unconstitutionality or oppression.)

Remarkably, in their 1788–1789 correspondence about whether to add a federal bill of rights, both Jefferson and Madison had begun to theorize how such a bill might have special bite in a federal Constitution thanks to the existence of states and state legislatures. The theorizing began when Madison initially suggested that the need for a bill of rights was less urgent at the federal level than within any given state, because "the jealousy of the subordinate Governments afford[s] a security which has not existed in the case of the State Governments." Jefferson replied by arguing that a federal bill of rights would in fact work synergistically with state jealousy: "The jealousy of the subordinate governments is a precious reliance. But observe that those governments . . . must have principles furnished them whereon to found their opposition. The declaration of rights will be the text whereby they will try all the acts of the federal government." Days after receiving this missive from Paris, Madison publicly made this point his own in his June 8, 1789, Congressional speech calling for a bill of rights. Immediately after predicting that "independent tribunals of justice" would enforce a bill as in-court law, he further predicted that "such a declaration in the federal system would be inforced because the state legislatures will jealously and closely watch the operations of this government, and be able to resist with more effect every assumption of power than any other power on earth can do. And the greatest opponents to a federal government admit the state legislatures to be sure guardians of the people's liberty."[60]

Although not specifically addressing the yet-to-be-drafted bill of rights, both Hamilton and Madison as Publius had also highlighted the importance of state legislatures in monitoring Congress and pushing back against possible Congressional excess, much as their colonial precursors had monitored and pushed back against Parliament.

Hamilton had opened the topic in *The Federalist* No. 26: "State legislatures, who will always be not only vigilant but suspicious and jealous guardians of the rights of the citizens against encroachments from the federal government, will constantly have their attention awake to the conduct of the national rulers, and will be ready enough, if any thing improper appears, to sound the alarm to the people, and . . . be the VOICE . . . of their discontent." Hamilton returned to this theme in No. 28:

> State governments will, in all possible contingencies, afford complete security against invasions of the public liberty by the national authority. Projects of usurpation cannot be masked under pretenses so likely to escape the penetration of select bodies of men, as of the people at large. The [state] legislatures will have better means of information. They can discover the danger at a distance; and possessing all the organs of civil power, and the confidence of the people, they can at once adopt a regular plan of opposition, in which they can combine all the resources of the community. They can readily communicate with each other in the different States, and unite their common forces for the protection of their common liberty.

Summing up, Hamilton predicted that if the people's "rights are invaded by either [the state or the federal government], they can make use of the other as the instrument of redress."

Madison/Publius sang in the same key in *The Federalist* No. 46: "Ambitious encroachments of the federal government . . . would not excite the opposition of a single State, or of a few States only. They would be signals of general alarm. Every government would espouse the common cause. A correspondence would be opened. Plans of resistance would be concerted. One spirit would animate and conduct the whole. The same combinations, in short, would result from an apprehension of the federal, as was produced by the dread of a foreign, yoke."

THE NOW FAMOUS VIRGINIA AND Kentucky Resolutions of 1798 and 1799 should be seen in the light of this backdrop. The biggest problem with the Sedition Act of 1798 was its self-sealing quality. Anyone who harshly criticized this horrid law (such as Callender) risked prosecution under the law itself. But each state legislature was a special speech spot, much like Parliament and Congress. True, nothing in Article I said this, quite, even as Article I explicitly guaranteed sweeping freedom of speech in *Congress*. True, nothing in the Sedition Act itself expressly exempted speech in state legislatures from the scope of the statute. But everything in American history and tradition—and in the repeated reassurances given by Publius and others in the epic national conversation of 1787–1788—guaranteed that state legislatures would continue, as before, to operate as special speech spots. Even if newspapers risked prosecution under the Sedition Act if they initiated their own critiques of the act, or reprinted other newspapers' critiques, surely they would enjoy absolute immunity if they merely told their readers what had been said in the special speech spots in state capitals.

Thus, Madison and Jefferson quietly composed resolutions for adoption in the Virginia and Kentucky legislatures, respectively. Madison was by far the abler constitutional theorist and practitioner, and his version has aged better than Jefferson's. On Christmas Eve 1798, the Virginia General Assembly denounced the provisions of the Sedition Act as "palpable and alarming infractions of the

Constitution." The Assembly also condemned the Alien Act of 1798 giving the president broad deportation powers (aimed especially at radical French and Irish émigrés), but identified the Sedition Act as uniquely bad. That act, "*more than any other*, ought to produce universal alarm, because it is levelled against that right of freely examining public characters and measures, and of free communication among the people thereon, which has ever been justly deemed, *the only effectual guardian of every other right.*"[61] Just so.

Over the next six weeks, newspapers in most states reprinted or excerpted Virginia's protest.[62] In a follow-up report drafted by Madison in 1799, the Virginia legislature refined his structural analysis and added a powerful historical addendum. Structurally, "information and communication among the people" was "indispensable to the just exercise of their electoral rights." Free and fair elections required a level playing field; given that incumbents were allowed under the sedition law to "expose" challengers to "disrepute among the people," challengers deserved the same right to cast "animadversions" upon incumbents. Historically, the American Revolution had come about only because Americans had been able to freely criticize central officialdom. The Constitution had likewise come about thanks to vigorous criticisms of governments, both state and continental. The Sedition Act was thus un-American and unprecedented. Had sedition acts akin to the 1798 act "been uniformly enforced against the press" in previous times, "might not the United States have been languishing, at this day, under the infirmities of a sickly Confederation? Might they not, possibly, be miserable colonies, groaning under a foreign yoke?"[63] John Adams had forgotten where he came from, and where America came from.

Jefferson's performance as a ghostwriter for the Kentucky legislature in late 1798 and late 1799 was much less impressive and, at its worst moments, downright dangerous. Jefferson was a far less rigorous legal thinker and a far less precise penman than Madison (or Hamilton, for that matter). But the old revolutionary still knew how to turn a phrase. He summoned up vivid images of the "friendless alien . . . selected as the safest subject of a first experiment," of the harmless citizen assailed by a Sedition Act that "marked him as its prey," and of "those who wish it to be believed that man cannot be governed but by a rod of iron."[64]

Like Adams, Jefferson had in fact missed the constitutional revolution of 1788. He, too, was a Rip Van Winkle of sorts, stuck in 1776. His allies and acolytes in the Kentucky legislature declared "that the several states who formed" the Constitution were then and remained thereafter "sovereign and independent." These were 1776 words and 1781 words, not 1788 words. Post-ratification, states were neither fully sovereign nor independent in the strictest legal sense. (If they were, each might well retain a relatively broad right to secede, which no one thought was true in 1788—the critical year Jefferson missed, even as he tried to follow events from afar.)

The Kentucky legislature also declared that "a nullification, by [state] sovereignties, of all unauthorized acts done under colour of" the Constitution by the federal government was "the rightful remedy." (In Jefferson's draft: "A nullification of the act is the rightful remedy. . . . [E]very state has a natural right, in cases not within the compact . . . to nullify of their own authority all assumptions of power by others within their limits.")[65] This was absurd. No one had said anything of the sort in the great national conversation of 1788, even though such a statement, if true, would have boosted ratification prospects among arch states' rightists.

Jefferson and Kentucky lawmakers also took extreme positions on federal criminal law and federal immigration law. They claimed that Congress lacked power to enact criminal statutes except where the Constitution explicitly authorized *punishment*, which it did only for counterfeiters, pirates, and violators of the law of nations. On this outlandish view, Congress could not even criminalize murder in federal territories or the national capital, where no state law operated as a backstop. Rejecting the very concept of a federal Alien Act, Jefferson (via the Kentucky Resolutions) also asserted that Congress lacked power to regulate friendly foreigners within the several states.

Unlike Madison in Virginia, who correctly portrayed the Sedition Act as uniquely troubling—categorically worse than the Alien Act or

the bank law or the carriage tax or anything else—because it threatened constitutional conversation itself, Jefferson emphasized states'
rights. His (and thus Kentucky's) main criticism of the Sedition Act
was that it exceeded the enumerated powers of Congress, and that
proper regulation should be left to states. Madison and Virginia, by
contrast, grasped the nerve of the issue. No republican government—
state or federal—could properly suppress the rights of citizens to
think freely and speak freely in all matters political.

In the short run, Madison and Jefferson did not succeed in
getting other state legislatures to join the Virginia and Kentucky
bandwagon. But in the end, it did not matter whether the two
statesmen immediately convinced a majority of state lawmakers,
just as it did not matter whether they immediately convinced a majority of sitting Supreme Court justices. What mattered most in
1800–1801 was winning a majority of Electoral College votes in
the Jefferson-Adams rematch.

And that Jefferson did. When the American people, having now
seen quite clearly what freedom meant to Adams and what freedom
meant to Jefferson, again decided between these two icons of 1776,
they decided for Jefferson.

REVOLUTION?

Jefferson called his election to the presidency a "revolution"[66]—but it
wasn't, truly. (Similarly, Adams called mere opposition to his policies
"sedition," but this too was a gross misnomer.) That said, the election
of 1800 did confirm certain basic constitutional truths and prompt
important constitutional adjustments.

Most important of all, Jefferson's triumph—he won 73 electoral votes to Adams's 65 and his allies won the lion's share of the
House and Senate seats at issue—meant that the Sedition Act was
now dead and buried. The people themselves had in effect overruled

the circuit judges. Once in office, Jefferson worked to implement that informal electoral verdict.

First, Jefferson and his fellow Democratic-Republicans—who by the end of 1801 comfortably controlled the House and had roughly half the Senate—eschewed passing a new Sedition Act to replace the one that had just poofed into thin air. Rejecting tit for tat, they took no federal statutory steps to target their critics as their critics had once targeted them.

Second, Jefferson never tried to pursue anyone for sedition based on any sort of federal common-law theory.[67] In later years, a Supreme Court dominated by men that he and Madison had selected (and presided over by an Adams appointee, John Marshall) would emphatically declare that the Constitution did not contemplate federal common-law crimes of any sort. No justice openly dissented from this landmark ruling, *United States v. Hudson and Goodwin*, penned by Jefferson's first appointee, William Johnson. Johnson opened his opinion by proclaiming that the issue had "been long since settled in public opinion. In no other case for many years has this jurisdiction been asserted; and the general acquiescence of legal men shews the prevalence of opinion in favor" of Jefferson on this issue.[68]

Third, President Jefferson took no steps to prosecute anyone for any writings or utterances that had occurred late in the Adams administration, when the Sedition Act was technically still in force. The last section of that statute ended with a special proviso authorizing post-inauguration prosecutions of pre-inauguration crimes. Of course, had Jefferson accepted this proviso's invitation, he would have placed his administration in the awkward position of prosecuting his own supporters. More awkward still: he himself had likely violated the Sedition Act while serving as vice president of the United States! After all, he had secretly funded Callender's pamphlet and approved it prepublication. That alone probably made him an accomplice under the Sedition Act. If Callender could be punished under the law, as Chase had ruled, why wasn't Jefferson himself equally guilty? (Jefferson's involvement with Callender did not become public until 1802, when the colorful journalist outed him.) And of course, Jefferson had secretly drafted the Kentucky Resolutions (a fact not made public until the 1810s[69]) and had traded all sorts of related letters and other writings in connection with these Resolutions, which had denounced the government, the Congress, and the president for the Sedition Act. These actions alone were arguably enough to convict under the Sedition Act's words and glossing case law—the Lyon, Cooper, and Callender cases, most obviously. But, to repeat, no one was prosecuted under the Sedition Act on Jefferson's watch—and rightly so, given the true meaning of the Constitution as confirmed by the election of 1800. Only days after Jefferson took office, his attorney general, Levi Lincoln, informed a lower-level federal prosecutor that "the President of the United States has judged it inexpedient, that any further prosecutions should be commenced or continued under . . . the sedition law. . . . You will therefore take proper measures for staying and discharging all such [cases]."[70]

Fourth and most dramatically, in his first weeks in office Jefferson pardoned those still imprisoned under the Sedition Act and forgave their unpaid fines. Over the next several months, he also personally ordered the relevant prosecutor to drop a pending Sedition Act case inherited from the Adams administration against William Duane, the printing partner of the now dead Benjamin Franklin Bache.[71] (The Franklin, Bache, and Duane families would become tightly intertwined. In 1800, Duane married Bache's widow, Margaret. Five years later, Duane's son William John married Bache's sister—and Franklin's granddaughter—Deborah.)

Jefferson expressly defended his actions on constitutional grounds. One particularly emphatic statement appeared in the first draft of his first annual message to Congress: "I do declare that I hold that act to be in palpable & unqualified contradiction to the constitution. Considering it then as a nullity, I have relieved from oppression under it those of my fellow-citizens who were within the reach of the functions confided to me." He eventually dropped this passage at the urging of cabinet advisers but had already said much the same thing, over many months, in letters to sundry correspondents.[72]

In a truly extraordinary and tart letter to Abigail Adams herself in 1804, Jefferson minced no words:

> I discharged every person under punishment or prosecution under the Sedition law, because I considered & now consider that law to be a nullity as absolute and as palpable as if Congress had ordered us to fall down and worship a golden image; and that it was as much my duty to arrest it's execution in every stage, as it would have been to have rescued from the fiery furnace those who should have been cast into it for refusing to worship their image. It was accordingly done in every instance, without asking what the offenders had done, or against whom they had offended, but whether the pains they were suffering were inflicted under the pretended Sedition law.[73]

Later, Congress would make further amends, and would do so, symbolically, on the fourteenth anniversary of Jefferson's death. The Act of July 4, 1840, repaid Matthew Lyon's fines with accrued interest. An accompanying committee report declared that the 1798 Sedition Act was "unconstitutional, null, and void. . . . No question connected with the liberty of the press . . . was ever more generally understood, or so conclusively settled by the concurring opinions of all parties, after the heated political contests of the day had passed away."[74]

ONCE IN POWER, JEFFERSON AND his successor, Madison, quietly abandoned several other elements of their earlier oppositional politics that were constitutionally unsound. On various constitutional issues other than speech, they became Hamiltonians in practice but never admitted it.

The carriage taxes that Madison and his fellow Virginians had repeatedly denounced as unconstitutional—even as late as 1799—continued in operation during the first year of Jefferson's presidency. In marked contradistinction to his Sedition Act pardons, Jefferson issued no pardons to carriage-tax cheats. In the spring of 1802, Jeffersonians in Congress provided for the repeal of the carriage tax, but made a point to preserve liability for past taxes due, implicitly conceding the constitutionality of such taxes and the correctness of the unanimous *Hylton* case.[75] Jefferson signed this 1802 bill into law, just as Washington had signed the original carriage-tax bill into law in reliance on Hamilton. In 1813, a Congress dominated by Jeffersonians actually resurrected a carriage tax in a bill quietly signed by President Madison.[76]

A similar pattern unfolded in connection with Hamilton's bank. In 1792, Jefferson and Madison had traded unhinged letters contemplating a Virginia death penalty for central bank clerks. But once in power, Jefferson enforced the national bank law as a law of undoubted constitutional validity—as had Washington, as advised, of course, by Hamilton. On President Madison's watch, his Congressional allies allowed the bank's statutory charter to lapse in 1811.* But then, in the War of 1812, the absence of a central bank did indeed cause serious fiscal and military embarrassments, just as Hamilton had predicted.[77] In 1814, invading British forces torched parts of the White House and burned much of the Capitol to the ground. In 1816, a sheepish President Madison signed a new bank bill into law. When the constitutional issue reached the Supreme Court in the famous 1819 case of *McCulloch v. Maryland*, the Court, in a unanimous opinion by John Marshall that echoed Hamilton's 1791 opinion letter to Washington at every turn, ruled that of course Congress could create a national bank. The Court's opinion made mincemeat of Madison's and Jefferson's 1791 arguments and twice called attention to the constitutional and policy volte-face that Jeffersonians had recently executed on the

---

*George Clinton—who served as vice president under Jefferson from 1805 to 1809 and then continued as Madison's vice president—cast a crucial tie-breaking vote in the Senate against charter renewal. Clinton was an anti-Hamiltonian New Yorker. His selection as Jefferson's and then Madison's running mate flowed naturally from the New York alliances that the two future presidents began to form in their supposedly botanical expedition of 1791. Indeed, in 1792, Madison and Jefferson backed Clinton for the vice presidency; that year, he received 50 electoral votes compared to 72 for incumbent Adams. (Washington of course came in first, unanimously, with 132 electoral votes.) In 1796 and 1800, Jefferson allied with New Yorker Aaron Burr, but then (for reasons we shall explore later) switched back to Clinton in 1804.

issue.[78] Of the seven jurists who participated, two had been appointed by Adams, three by Jefferson, and two by Madison.

In short, on key issues, Jefferson, Madison, and their Virginia protégé James Monroe (who succeeded Madison) were more Hamiltonian than they cared to admit. Some artists at the time captured this truth when they placed Madison (middle) and Monroe (right) in poses that brought to mind Trumbull's famous 1792 painting of Hamilton at high tide (left).

JEFFERSON'S SELF-PROCLAIMED "REVOLUTION OF 1800" was thus, at least in some measure, a matter of style more than substance. The Federalists had too often presented themselves as haughty and aristocratic, not sufficiently in touch with common folk—especially westerners, those who lacked formal education, and those who worked with their hands.

This stylistic failure haunted Federalists even when they truly were more egalitarian than their opponents. In the carriage-tax debate, Hamilton openly favored a luxury tax that would soak, or at least splash, the rich, while in private correspondence Madison opposed the tax precisely because he saw it as a threat to wealth itself, especially landed wealth. Adams was a farmer's son, and Hamilton

had risen from the lowest rungs of the social order. Neither man was a slaveholder, and Hamilton had solid anti-slavery credentials. By contrast, Madison and Jefferson lorded over hundreds of slaves and never freed any substantial number, except for Sally Hemings and her children—a special case. Jefferson sold slaves throughout his life, both to pay debts and to punish disobedience. Madison, too, sold slaves for his own financial convenience.[79]

But in the 1790s these two brilliant Virginia bluebloods began to master the democratic art of self-presentation. Whereas Hamilton, a proud peacock, a "spirited little animal," strutted in public and flaunted his fancy clothes, silk gloves, and silver-buckled shoes— perhaps because he had so painfully lacked finery in his deprived, Dickensian, childhood—Madison almost always wore drab black. He was a master of camouflage, adept at making himself an inconspicuous target. Jefferson was a political genius, sartorially—as is evident from a simple comparison of two famous paintings of him that show not so much the "Revolution of 1800" as the stylistic redo, the fashion remake, of 1800.

Mather Brown's painting captured Jefferson in London in 1786, several years before the diplomat returned to America. Behold the true American aristocrat, powdered and wigged, bedecked in lace and frills, seated alongside elegant art, and not directly engaging the viewer. His hand is fair and elegant, even dainty. Rembrandt Peale's 1800 painting is of an older man—a man vying for America's presidency—who has cleverly learned how to present himself to an increasingly and proudly democratic society. No more wig, powder, lace, frills, or art. He fixes the viewer with his gaze, directly and democratically. There is even a faint hint of a smile as he sees us. He is one of us—plain, simple, honest, direct—and thus we can trust him. Or at least that is what he wants us to think.

Jefferson relentlessly attacked his political foes as advocates of American *monarchy* and *aristocracy*. As with much of Jefferson's writing, this charge was rhetorically brilliant but intellectually lazy. Perhaps these words fairly described some of Adams's midcareer musings and broodings, but they did not honestly describe Hamilton, who did favor elite and meritocratic government for America— but not hereditary rule, the most objectionable feature of monarchy and aristocracy. Early on at Philadelphia, Hamilton did have a kind word for the hereditary nature of the British monarchy. However, the constitutional plan that he ultimately endorsed for America had no hint of hereditary power, even as it featured long terms of office.[80]

By contrast, Jefferson was in virtually every way *himself* a true hereditary monarch ruling over others on his private mountain. He was a Virginia Randolph, his father's first son, born in wedlock and on high, destined by that high birth to eventually lord over hundreds of slaves born to serve him. None of Hamilton's sons or sons-in-law would go on to political glory (though two sons did serve as presidentially commissioned US attorneys). Jefferson conversely was two for two in transferring political power to the next (White and legitimate) generation. He sired no White sons, but one son-in-law served as Virginia governor (as had he), and the other as a US senator (in a chamber over which he had presided as vice president). Jefferson's closest friend and lifelong ally, James Madison, who likewise brilliantly railed against Hamiltonian monarchism, was himself a monarch, cut from the same cloth as Jefferson. He, too, was a firstborn Virginia lord who by dint of his high birth in-herited countless slaves, dying with more than a hundred and never freeing any of them—humans treated far worse than George III generally treated his own royal subjects.

Jefferson was comfortable playing the democrat when his social inferiors knew their place and deferred to him. Hamilton irked him in part because the brash and lowborn upstart did not yield to the Virginia grandee. Jefferson's mask slipped most tellingly when trying to hide his duplicity in the Freneau affair in the teeth of Hamilton's exposés: "I will not suffer my retirement to be clouded by the slanders of a man whose history, *from the moment at which history can stoop to notice him,* is a tissue of machinations against the liberty of *the country which has not only received and given him bread,* but heaped it's honors on his head." *Translation: The audacity of this arriviste, this lowlife—this, this, this . . . bastard—who does not know his place!*[81]

AFTER JEFFERSON'S TRIUMPHANT ELECTION IN 1800–1801, the dis-credited and dispirited Federalists seemed to many contemporary observers a spent force in America. Washington was dead; this co-lossus of the eighteenth century never lived to see the nineteenth. Adams could not be trusted to safeguard America's most basic free-dom—the freedom of expression—and in any event he was too old to vie for the presidency in any future election. Thanks to Jefferson's paid journalistic assassin James Callender, the Maria Reynolds sex scandal had badly tarnished Hamilton's political standing; and then, in 1804, Jefferson's former running mate, Aaron Burr, made any pos-sible Hamiltonian comeback impossible by killing the Federalist hero in a duel. In 1801, John Jay left the political scene altogether, declin-ing to stand for a third term as New York's governor and spurning the opportunity to return to the United States Supreme Court as chief justice. He would spend the remainder of his life in quiet retirement. Years earlier, the cerebral Federalist jurist James Wilson had died in debt and disgrace. Who then remained to hold aloft the Federalist flame—the great nationalist vision of Washington and Hamilton?

One man above all others. Although emphatically Hamiltonian and Washingtonian in his constitutional principles, he otherwise bore an astonishing resemblance to Jefferson. He, too, was a hero in the Revolutionary War, albeit with his sword and not his pen. He was also a respected Virginia blueblood; both his and Jefferson's mothers were Randolphs—first cousins once removed. Like Jefferson, he had studied at William & Mary and read law under the legendary George Wythe, and had then gone on to serve as a diplomat in France and secretary of state. He was another brilliant writer who had a great personal political touch. He knew how to lubricate serious face-to-face conversations with good wine for his guests, and he was every bit as handsome, charming, winning, and publicly unpretentious as Jefferson himself. The two men even had similar romantic tastes: the wife of this man who took up the Federalist torch was the daughter of a Virginia beauty who many years earlier had declined Jefferson's marriage proposal.

Like Jefferson—and crucially, unlike most other Federalists—this statesman had not discredited himself in the Sedition Act controversy. In fact, he had denounced the act, publicly, in a shrewd October 1798 statement published under his own name: "Had I been in congress when [the Alien and Sedition Acts] passed, I should . . . certainly have opposed them. . . . [T]hey are calculated to create, unnecessarily, discontents and jealousies at a time when our very existence, as a nation, may depend on our union." Over the next few weeks, more than twenty newspapers across the continent reprinted this passage.[82]

And, speaking of newspapers, Jefferson's Hamiltonian kinsman had a keen appreciation of printers and readers and of the importance of public opinion. Like Jefferson, he knew how to place cleverly anonymous political pieces in the press as needed. More generally, he, like Jefferson, was a popular politician who knew how to sing the people's praises to the people themselves. At critical political moments, he, too, proudly described himself as a true "democrat."

And like Jefferson, in mid-1801 he stood atop one of America's three branches of government. In fact, in that capacity he was the man who personally administered the presidential oath of office to Jefferson. Some modern scholars have speculated that this fraught moment of oath administration was supercharged by the fact that in the weeks leading up to the inauguration, the statesman administering the oath had secretly angled to grab the presidency from Jefferson and for himself in a cute legal maneuver. If so, exactly how much did Jefferson know of his rival's machinations—machinations every bit as clever as Jefferson's own political plots over the years?

In the end, Jefferson's Hamiltonian kinsman and rival would both outlive the third president and surpass him as a constitutional expounder and a keeper of the constitutional flame. In addition to this Hamiltonian's many other gifts of talent, temperament, and technique, he had one enormous epistemic advantage over the self-proclaimed author of the Declaration of Independence. John Marshall had been an integral part of the epochal constitutional conversation of 1788 and Thomas Jefferson had not.

— ten —

JEFFERSON-MARSHALL

Jᴏʜɴ Mᴀʀsʜᴀʟʟ ᴡᴀs ᴛʜᴇ ʟᴀsᴛ founder—a founder because he had prominently participated in both the Revolutionary War and the launching of the Constitution, and the last because he stayed in public life longer than anyone else in his generation. He died in office as chief justice in 1835. Although James Madison outlived Marshall by a year, the ex-president spent his last nineteen years in retirement. As he curated his papers for posterity, Madison surely had his eye on history. By contrast, Marshall continued to make history until the end.

To put the point more abstractly, Article III gave each member of Publius/Hamilton's "least dangerous branch"—a phrase immortalized in *The Federalist* No. 78—life tenure. Article II gave each president only a four-year term, which was immediately glossed by a tradition of resignation after two terms. Even if, at any given moment, a president wielded much more power than a chief justice, and even though, in the Constitution's early years, the political sprinters in Articles I and II dashed into the lead, in the long run an Article III judicial distance runner might just win the race, or at least come

close. As we shall see later in our story, John Marshall would indeed come from behind. But before pondering that episode, we must first consider how the race began.

CHIEFS

From 1801 to 1809, Thomas Jefferson and John Marshall stood atop their respective branches like sorcerers on separate mountains warily eying each other. The most famous portraits of the two statesmen presented the pair as similar in dress, gaze, and pose. These were, to be sure, mere surface resemblances, but Rembrandt Peale's 1800 painting of Jefferson and Henry Inman's 1832 depiction of Marshall hinted at the possibility of deeper parallels.

One deep parallel eludes most observers today. In his prime, John Marshall was potential presidential timber every bit as much as Jefferson. We miss this fact because of hindsight bias. Marshall never *openly* sought the presidency. (The reason for the italicized qualification will soon become clear.) Also, we forget how much the relationship between America's chief executive and America's chief justice has changed over the centuries.

Ours is a world not merely of separation of powers, but also of separation of branches, separation of career ladders, and separation of governmental personas. Early in life, a supremely ambitious prodigy nowadays must choose whether she hopes one day to be president or chief justice. The career path forks early and she must pick a branch and a persona, either political or judicial. For example, one cannot be a judge these days without going to law school, and one cannot be a Supreme Court justice or chief justice without excelling in college and law school. But presidents need not have law degrees, or college Latin Honors, for that matter. Since the end of World War II, only five out of fourteen American presidents—Nixon, Ford, Clinton, Obama, and Biden—have been lawyers.

Once our modern prodigy picks a role and career ladder, she must ascend that ladder. She can move up within the judiciary, or within politics, but cannot generally jump from one ladder to another. Presidents and presidential aspirants do not become Supreme Court justices. By contrast, Supreme Court justices and those seriously in contention for the Court do not become presidents. In the past seventy-five years, no justice has left the bench for elective politics. No current justice came from the world of elective politics, and eight of the nine current justices were sitting federal appellate judges when appointed to the Supreme Court. (The ninth held a highly judicialized position as the executive-branch lawyer most responsible for Supreme Court litigation.)[1]

Things were entirely different in the founding era. Law schools as such did not exist, and judges were sometimes legal amateurs. In colonial Massachusetts, not one of the five Superior Court judges who heard the writs-of-assistance case in 1761 was bred to the law. On the other side of the ledger, many of America's early chief executives were indeed chief magistrates of sorts—chief law officers, if you will. In the nation's first half century, every president save two had practiced law at some point in his career. One exception was James Madison, who had read a good deal about law even though he had not "read law" as a legal apprentice. The other was of course Washington, who surrounded himself with legal talent. Three of his four main advisers—Hamilton, Jefferson, and Edmund Randolph—were lawyers. (Bookseller-soldier Henry Knox was the odd man out.)

At the Founding, the positions of chief executive and chief justice were kindred offices. The presidency operated as a magistracy of sorts. In Jefferson's tart 1804 letter to Abigail Adams, he described his pardon power as quasi-judicial; he had a legal obligation as the nation's chief executive magistrate to correct the circuit judges' manifest constitutional error in the Sedition Act cases, much as if he were chief justice:

> You seem to think it devolved on the judges to decide on the validity of the sedition law. But nothing in the constitution has given them a right to decide for the executive, more than to the Executive to decide for them. Both *magistracies* are equally independant in the sphere of action assigned to them. The judges, believing the law constitutional, had a right to pass a sentence of fine and imprisonment; because that power was placed in their hands by the constitution. But the Executive, believing the law to be unconstitutional, was bound [note—not just permitted, but bound] to remit the execution of it; because that power has been confided to him by the constitution. That instrument meant that it's co-ordinate branches should be checks on each other.[2]

An earlier Thomas—the ubiquitous Hutchinson—epitomized the especially close links between the positions of chief judge and chief executive. Over the course of his career, he moved from the first chiefdom to the second. Other men who held both positions, either simultaneously or seriatim, in the late colonial or early independence period included New Hampshire's Meshech Weare, Josiah Bartlett, and Jeremiah Smith; Rhode Island's Stephen Hopkins, Samuel Ward, William Greene, James Fenner, and Isaac Wilbour; Connecticut's Jonathan Trumbull; New York's John Jay; Pennsylvania's Thomas McKean; and South Carolina's John Rutledge.

A similar pattern marked the early federal system. The two men who came in third and fourth in the first presidential election—that is, the two men right behind Washington and Adams—were Jay and Rutledge, respectively.[3] These two presidential runners-up later became America's first two chief justices, and in the same order (Jay first) as their 1789 electoral-vote finish. In the mid-1790s, Jay left the nation's chief judicial position to serve as his state's chief executive, only to be invited to serve again as US chief justice at the end of the Adams administration. (Jay declined the re-invitation in early 1801, clearing the way for John Marshall.) Like Jay, Rutledge shuttled between governments and branches—from state chief executive to the US Supreme Court (as associate justice) to state chief justice to federal chief justice. In 1796, Jay and Oliver Ellsworth—America's first ex–chief justice and its sitting chief justice, respectively—between them received 16 electoral votes. (All these votes came from New England states backing Adams; had they gone instead to Adams's South Carolina running mate, Thomas Pinckney, the popular diplomat would not only have surged past Jefferson, but would in fact have bested Adams himself, who would have become a three-term vice president.)

Over the ensuing century and a half, other US chief justices would further illuminate the tight link—a link that no longer exists—between America's top executive and judicial jobs. Salmon P. Chase, named chief justice in 1864, was a former state chief executive and presidential contender who, once on the Court, still yearned to be president.* Charles Evans Hughes, who became chief in 1930, was another former governor and presidential candidate; in 1916, he had come within a whisker of winning the presidency against Woodrow Wilson. Earl Warren, appointed chief justice in 1953, was yet another former governor and had been his party's nominee in 1948 for

---

*Before nominating Chase, President Lincoln had expressed "only one doubt" about Chase's fitness for the job: "He is a man of unbounded ambition, and has been working all his life to become President. That he can never be; and I fear that if I make him chief-justice he will simply become more restless and uneasy and neglect the place in his strife and intrigue to make himself President. If I were sure that he would go on the bench and give up his aspirations and do nothing but make himself a great judge, I would not hesitate a moment." John G. Nicolay and John Hay, *Abraham Lincoln: A History* (1890), 9:394. Lincoln knew his man; Chase never gave up his presidential dream.

the vice presidency. Most striking of all, William Howard Taft served as both president and chief justice, seriatim.

IN LIGHT OF ALL THIS, it is not outlandish to imagine an alternative universe featuring President John Marshall or presidential nominee John Marshall. Surely Marshall himself gave the idea more than a passing thought.

His impeccable credentials for the chief executive chair went beyond his status as occupant of the chief judicial chair. Like Washington, Hamilton, Burr, Clinton, and Monroe, he had served as an officer in the Continental Army. Like Washington, Jefferson, Madison, and Monroe, he was a Virginian with strong ties to the West and good friends in the North. Like most of early America's apex politicians, he was media-savvy and a gifted newspaper writer, skilled at the art of the anonymous opinion piece. Like Adams, Jefferson, Jay, Monroe, John Quincy Adams, Elbridge Gerry (Madison's vice president), and the Pinckney brothers (perennial presidential and vice-presidential candidates), he had experience as a top American diplomat in Europe. Like Jefferson, Madison, Monroe, and many presidents who would follow, he had served as secretary of state. (From 1801 to 1859, most of the men elected president—Jefferson, Madison, Monroe, John Quincy Adams, Martin Van Buren, and James Buchanan—had previously served as secretaries of state, as had two perennial contenders, Henry Clay and Daniel Webster. Of the five elected presidents in this era who were not secretaries of state, four were battlefield generals: Andrew Jackson, William Henry Harrison, Zachary Taylor, and Franklin Pierce. James Polk was the sole exception.) America was still a rising power amid larger and more established Great Powers, and the nation generally preferred candidates who had an informed vision of world affairs and/or strong military experience.

Marshall did more than just daydream about being president. In the weeks before Jefferson's inauguration, he made his move— explaining in an anonymous newspaper piece that the presidency should go to him. Or at least that is what some scholars have concluded, with considerable evidence to back them up.

THE BACKSTORY TO THIS EPISODE of palace intrigue in 1800–1801 began, fittingly enough, with the early 1790s rivalry between Jefferson and Hamilton. Who was truly Washington's *prime* minister? In particular, who should succeed to the presidency if both Washington and Adams were to die, become disabled, or resign? The Constitution's Vacancy Clause left this question for the federal legislature to decide: "Congress may by Law . . . declar[e] what Officer shall then act as President." The text authorized an *ex officio* designation—not *who* but *what*, not which person but "*what Officer*" qua officer would serve as acting president as part of his regular office. In 1791 Jefferson's partisans in Congress, led of course by Madison, proposed to designate the secretary of state as the *ex officio* next in line—a move that would simultaneously bolster Jefferson's status and deflate the pretentions of Treasury Secretary Hamilton. Hamilton's Congressional admirers balked. As a compromise, some proposed to designate the chief justice—a post then held by the Hamilton-leaning John Jay. After bouncing between House and Senate and various committees thereof, the bill as finally adopted in 1792 placed America's top senator—the Senate president pro tempore—first in line, followed by the Speaker of the House.[4]

Alas, this was unconstitutional. As Madison and others persuasively pointed out, senators and House members were not, strictly speaking, "officers" within the letter and spirit of the Constitution's Vacancy Clause. Only judges and executive officials—those who acted upon private persons, and were not mere lawmakers—were proper "officers" for succession purposes.

Textually and structurally, the distinction between executive and judicial "officers," on the one hand, and mere legislators, on the other, ran deep, ramifying throughout the Constitution. In several places, the document created a much stricter separation of powers than in England—a New World system of separation of personnel, with different persons in different branches. Under the Constitution's Incompatibility Clause, lawmakers were expressly barred from simultaneously holding "office" as executive or judicial functionaries: "No person *holding any Office* under the United States, shall be a Member of either House [of Congress] during his *Continuance in Office*" (emphasis added). In keeping with this sharp distinction, the Senate in the mid-1790s acquitted Senator William Blount in an impeachment trial. The Senate could properly expel its own miscreants, but the House had no business interfering in this internal Senate matter, and impeachment was additionally improper because only *officers* of the United States were, as a general matter, impeachable: "The President, Vice President and *all civil officers* of the United States, shall be *removed from office* on impeachment for, and conviction of," grave misconduct. Also, "Judgment in Cases of Impeachment shall not extend further than to *removal from Office*, and disqualification to hold and enjoy any [further federal] *Office*" (emphasis added). Blount was a *senator*, not an *officer*, and was thus not impeachable. But if senators were not officers under the Impeachment Clause, how could they be officers under the Succession Clause? And if in fact they were not officers under the Succession Clause, then Madison was right all along: the Succession Act of 1792 was utterly unconstitutional in trying to shoehorn mere legislators—Senate and House leaders—into a position that the Constitution reserved for true officers.

Strong structural and practical considerations tightly intertwined with the textual argument that only executive or judicial officers, and not Congress members, were proper candidates for presidential succession. The plain letter and spirit of the Incompatibility Clause forbade any member of Congress from simultaneously serving as an executive department head. Surely one man could not at the same moment be, say, a senator and the secretary of war. How, then, could he concurrently be both senator and acting president? Given that the senator would obviously need to resign his Senate seat upon assuming his position as acting president, how would this be an *ex officio* annexation of power to his Senate "office"? By resigning from the Senate, the senator would be pulling the rug out from under his own *ex officio* eligibility. Also, what would happen in the event of a temporary presidential disability of uncertain but perhaps short duration? Once the Senate's leader resigned, he would be out in the cold the instant the president recovered.

These issues would not arise for a true officer: nothing prevented a person from holding two executive offices at the same time—say, secretary of state and acting president. In the Whiskey Rebellion, Treasury Secretary Hamilton was also acting secretary of war. During the War of 1812, James Monroe was for nearly half a year both secretary of state and secretary of war. Indeed, in his last month as secretary of state—from February 4 to March 4, 1801, Marshall himself was also America's new chief justice, much as two of his predecessor chief justices, Jay and Ellsworth, had served as executive-branch diplomats while continuing to hold their judicial offices.

The executive-branch conversational circle completed by the Decision of 1789 also argued against the Succession Act of 1792. A president would often be in daily and candid communication with his trusted and handpicked secretaries, any of whom could thus catch and carry the fallen president's torch with minimal interruption or policy discontinuity. The Senate, by contrast, might not even be in session when a president fell; its president pro tempore might be far from the capital, utterly unaware of the most pressing issues confronting the nation.

ALL THIS SET THE SCENE for the post-election drama of 1800–1801. The Democratic-Republicans had won the election—with 73 electoral votes for Jefferson compared to 65 for Adams—but had blundered, slightly. They had aimed to catapult Jefferson into the presidency and his running mate, New Yorker Aaron Burr, into the vice-presidential slot, but every Jeffersonian elector had also voted for Burr. Thus there was a tie at the top. The tie would need to be untied by the lame-duck, Federalist-dominated House of Representatives.

The House could surely pick Jefferson—the only proper outcome, thought the Jeffersonians. Indeed, this is what the House ultimately did, thanks in no small measure to Hamilton's emphatic appeals to Congressional Federalists on behalf of Jefferson. Hamilton told his correspondents that despite his own fierce feuds with Jefferson and the personal dislike that each man had for the other, the former secretary of state was an honorable and capable public servant committed to his country's welfare. Once in power, Jefferson would, Hamilton hoped, eventually see the (Hamiltonian) light and govern in a way that would protect America's vital interests at home and abroad. (Hamilton guessed right on this, in general.) Hamilton told his Federalist allies that Burr, by contrast, was a charming but corrupt wild card, who might sell the nation out to the highest bidder merely to line his own pocket.[5]

Still, the Federalist-dominated Congress could lawfully pick Burr. Many Jeffersonians considered this scenario underhanded, because none of Burr's electors had truly wanted to see him president. From a legal point of view, however, Burr's votes were no different from Jefferson's. If Federalists actually preferred Burr, why shouldn't he win as the consensus candidate? After all, had Federalist electors known long in advance that Adams was a lost cause, they could have chosen to vote for Burr in the Electoral College balloting in the several states. Had even a single Federalist so voted, Burr in fact would have received more electoral votes than Jefferson, and thus would have won under the strict letter of the rules. How was the matter any different if Federalist House members opted to back Burr over Jefferson when allowed to untie the Electoral College tally? If this flipping of their ticket irked Jeffersonians, they had only themselves to blame for having picked Burr as their Second Man. Even if Burr were selected by the Federalist-dominated House, nothing would stop (President) Burr from resigning in favor of (Vice President) Jefferson. Easier still, nothing stopped Burr from publicly urging all House members to endorse Jefferson, mooting any need for post-inaugural heroics.

What if the House failed to pick either Jefferson or Burr? This sounded lawless, but it wasn't, really. The Constitution required the House to untie the election under special voting rules reminiscent of the old Articles of Confederation. Each state delegation in the House would cast one vote, and the winner would need a majority of state delegations. If a state delegation were equally divided or abstained, its vote would count for zero, not one-half for each candidate. It was thus imaginable that neither Jefferson nor Burr would have an absolute majority of state-delegation votes in the House—nine out of sixteen—when Adams's term expired at the end of March 3.

If so, could Adams simply hold over for a short period past his constitutionally allotted four years? For, say, a month? For a year? For four years? Or would the Succession Act spring to life when Adams's term expired, allowing the Senate's president pro tempore to become the president of all America? Even if that person were a Federalist? (The Federalists had a comfortable majority in the lame-duck Senate; the new Senate would be closely divided.) What about the argument that the Succession Act was in fact unconstitutional?

Enter "Horatius," stage right. In a pair of newspaper essays initially published in early January 1801 in the *Alexandria Advertiser* and widely reprinted in both the capital area and beyond, the anonymous Horatius offered a cute way of untying the "Presidential Knot."[6] Horatius argued that the Succession Act was indeed unconstitutional. The lame-duck Congress should thus enact, and the lame-duck president, Adams, should sign, a new Succession Act designating a proper "officer" to take charge after March 3 in the event of a Jefferson-Burr House deadlock. Horatius did not explicitly state what officer should now fill the blank, but the obvious choice, legally and politically, for the lame-duck Federalists was the secretary of state. After all, he was the highest-ranking officer, except for the arguable possibility of the treasury secretary and the chief justice. But the position of chief justice was vacant in early January. And although Horatius said none of this—he didn't need to—the sitting secretary of state just happened to be the Federalists' most popular and able politician, John Marshall!

It was an elegant and brilliant idea, a political and legal stroke of genius—evil genius, from a Jeffersonian perspective. But whose genius idea was it to crown John Marshall? Who was this Horatius?

The most comprehensive biographer of John Marshall, Alfred Beveridge, wrote four hefty volumes about his subject in the early twentieth century. Beveridge concluded that it was "reasonably certain" that Horatius was none other than Marshall himself. Horatius, noted Beveridge, stated his position "with great ability"—"perfectly" in line with "Marshall's method of reasoning and peculiar style of expression." In recent years, one of America's most energetic constitutional historians, Bruce Ackerman, has echoed Beveridge and adduced a wealth of additional circumstantial evidence pointing to Marshall.[7]

Even if Marshall was somehow not Horatius, Marshall surely agreed with Horatius. In mid-January, James Monroe sent Jefferson a letter bristling with concern: "It is said here that Marshall has given an opinion in conversation with Stoddard [sic; Navy Secretary Benjamin Stoddert], that in case 9 States should not unite in favor of one of the persons chosen [by the Electoral College, that is, Jefferson or Burr], the legislature may appoint a Presidt. till another election is made, & that intrigues are carrying on to place us in that situation." In an earlier letter to Jefferson, Monroe had also identified Marshall as a likely beneficiary of the Horatius gambit: "Some strange reports are circulating here of the views of the federal party in the present desperate state of its affrs. It is said they are resolved to prevent the designation by the H. of Reps. of the person to be president, and that they mean to commit the power by a legislative act to John Marshall, Saml. A. Otis or some other person till another election."[8]

Jefferson responded by treating the situation as 1776 all over again, rallying his troops and rattling his saber. In mid-February 1801, he told Monroe that he "thought it best to declare openly & firmly, one & all, that the day such [a succession] act passed, the middle states would arm, & that no such usurpation even for a single day should be submitted to." This was not casual chitchat. Perhaps Jefferson's 1792 death-penalty-for-bankers had been a mere daydream, but in 1801 Monroe was the sitting governor of Virginia, which of course bordered on the new national capital city. Jefferson was telling Monroe to ready his militia to march on Washington—with weapons—and Monroe was listening carefully.[9]

Jefferson's were the words of a sloppy, rash, and trigger-happy politico. What was his legal warrant for threatening to incite states near the national capital ("the middle states") to take up arms against the central government? The Horatius gambit was surely sharp dealing, given that it aimed to give the presidency to neither Jefferson nor Burr, but how was it illegal? The Jeffersonians themselves had created the mess that Horatius slyly offered to tidy up. Jefferson himself and his party had picked the ethically challenged Aaron Burr to be—under their own plan—a heartbeat away from the presidency.

If Burr were supremely honorable, he could simply declare, publicly and unequivocally, that he would not accept the presidency even if offered the post by the lame-duck Federalist-dominated House. Had Burr made such a clear and public declaration, it is impossible to imagine that the House could have deadlocked. Jefferson would have become president by process of elimination, much as if Burr were dead. (Imagine, say, an early 1801 duel in which Hamilton killed Burr!*) To his credit, Burr did not actively lobby in his own behalf. He did not hasten to Washington City to meet with House members, nor did he make any promises by letter or via intermediaries in exchange for House votes. But he did not, as he easily could have done, emphatically and openly disavow willingness to be selected over his senior partner.[10]

Four years earlier, Jefferson had acted with more republican modesty when he had faced a remarkably similar situation. In mid-December 1796, he wrote a letter to his campaign manager, Madison, that ended up yielding enormous political dividends. If, upon the unsealing and counting of Electoral College ballots in early 1797, he and Adams ended up tied in the contest to succeed the retiring

---

*In the preceding months, Hamilton had come close to challenging the elderly President Adams to a duel. See his letters to Adams of August 1 and October 1, 1800. With Washington in his grave, the nation had lost its polestar, and men whom Washington had held in check were at risk of spiraling out of control.

George Washington, thus obliging the House to break the tie, he wrote, "I pray you and authorize you fully to solicit on my behalf that Mr. Adams may be preferred. He has always been my senior from the commencement of our public life, and the expression of the public will being equal, this circumstance ought to give him the preference." As events unfolded, Adams ended up with an outright majority over Jefferson in the Electoral College tally, rendering Jefferson's sacrificial offer moot.[11]

Adams himself learned of the letter and was charmed. (Jefferson, who had far more self-possession and politesse, generally knew how to play Adams—via professions of friendship and fulsome praise of the senior statesman's early services to the republic.) In an exultant note to Abigail written on New Year's Day, 1797, John regaled her with (imagined and inflated) details of Jefferson's admiration and deference:

> So many Compliments, so many old Anecdotes. . . . [Dr. Benjamin Rush] met Mr. Madison in the Street and ask'd him if he thought Mr. Jefferson would accept the Vice Presidency. Mr. Madison answered there was no doubt of that. Dr. Rush replied that he had heard some of his Friends doubt it. Madison took from his Pocket a Letter from Mr. Jefferson himself and gave it to the Dr. to read. In it he tells Mr. Madison that he had been told there was a Possibility of a Tie between Mr. Adams and himself. If this should happen says he, I beg of you, to Use all your Influence to procure for me [Jefferson] the Second Place, for Mr. Adams's Services have been longer more constant and more important than mine, and Something more in the complimentary strain about Qualifications &c.

Perhaps Jefferson in late 1796 knew all along that Adams had more votes, and the letter to Madison was a brilliant ploy designed mainly to flatter Adams and put him off guard. (If so, it worked.) Or perhaps Jefferson meant everything he said (which was less than Adams recounted; the tale grew in the telling). Either way, it is notable that Aaron Burr did not follow in Jefferson's deferential footsteps, even though Burr, in 1800–1801, had infinitely more reason to yield to his senior partner and teammate Jefferson than Jefferson in 1796 had to yield to his old friend, but now rival, Adams.

In another key passage in his February 1801 message to Monroe, Jefferson was more careful and less unhinged. The Federalists in Congress, he wrote, "were completely alarmed at the resource for which we declared, to wit, a convention to reorganize the government, & to amend it. The very word Convention, gives them the horrors, as in the present democratical spirit of America, they fear they should lose some of the favorite morsels of the constitution."[12]

This was a very different idea, envisioning not a subset of states taking up arms, but rather an orderly process of constitutional revision to fix some of the flaws in the presidential selection system— and any other flaws that needed fixing, for that matter. As we shall see, a Congress filled with Jeffersonians in 1803 would indeed initiate a constitutional amendment—although not by calling a new ad hoc general constitutional convention, but by sending a congressionally drafted proposal to the states, using the same process that had resulted in eleven other amendments in the Constitution's first decade.

On Wednesday, February 11, Congress met in the new capital city of Washington in the District of Columbia to unseal the presidential ballots that had been cast by electors in the several states. Per the Constitution's explicit provisions, the Senate's presiding officer—that is, the incumbent vice president, Thomas Jefferson himself—chaired the proceedings. As expected, there was the tie at the top: 73 votes for Thomas Jefferson of Virginia and 73 votes for Aaron Burr of New York. The House immediately began balloting by state delegation. House rules said that the House "shall not adjourn until a choice be made."[13]

All through the night and the next morning, the House voted over and over, but neither Jefferson nor Burr could reach the requisite nine states (out of sixteen total). After twenty-eight continuous rounds of balloting, the exhausted legislators broke off shortly after noon on Thursday to get some sleep. Friday the 13th brought no resolution. Nor did Saturday. Still nothing when Congress reconvened on Monday the 16th. Adams's term of office was due to expire on Tuesday, March 3—a mere fortnight away.[14]

If the impasse continued, would Adams audaciously (illegally?) hold over past his allotted four years? Or would the lame-duck and electorally repudiated Federalist Congress in its final hours ram through a new Succession Act, à la Horatius, crowning Marshall *ex officio* as acting president, either in his capacity as secretary of state or in his new and additional role as America's chief justice? (He was nominated for this post by President Adams on January 20 and confirmed by the Senate on January 27; he received his judicial commission on January 31 and took his judicial oath on February 4. Thus for the last month of the Adams administration, he wore both an executive and a judicial hat.)[15] If Adams or Marshall took steps to act as president on March 4, would Jeffersonian middle-state militias in Virginia and Pennsylvania respond with force as threatened? Would the self-proclaimed acting president Adams or Marshall counter with federal military force? Whom would the federal military salute? Would Federalist New England militias mobilize and march south? Would Hamilton try to jump into the fray? (In the late 1790s, he had been commissioned as a high general, second in command to George Washington, in anticipation of possible military conflict with France.) With the irreplaceable Washington no longer alive to calm the country and rally patriots from all sides to his unionist banner, would the American constitutional project ultimately collapse in an orgy of blood and recrimination, like so many Greek republics of old and the fledgling French republic of late?

These and other dreadful questions darkened the horizon in mid-February. And then, suddenly—as if a strong blast of fresh air abruptly swept across the capital city—the impasse ended. On the thirty-sixth ballot, on the afternoon of Tuesday, February 17, enough House members changed their minds to swing the election to Jefferson, by a vote of ten states to four, with the remaining two states professing neutrality.[16] Most historians believe that Jefferson gave certain assurances to fence-sitting Federalists. Jefferson denied having made any promises, but he was a master wordsmith; his carefully crafted statements of intent (as distinct from promises) had sufficed. Much as various Anti-Federalists in 1788 had ratified the Constitution not *on the condition* that a bill of rights would follow, but merely *in the confidence* that this would happen, so now various Federalists in effect ratified Jefferson with the expectation, confirmed by winks and nods from Jefferson and his authorized intermediaries, that he would govern as a moderate.[17]

On March 4, 1801, America's new chief justice administered the oath of office to his rival and kinsman, America's new president. In light of recent events, each cousin had reason to resent and suspect the other. The various twists and turns and plots, the thrusts and parries, of 1801 set the stage for more confrontation still to come in 1803, in the now famous but widely misunderstood case of *Marbury v. Madison*.

MARBURY

High-schoolers, collegians, and law students are all taught that *Marbury* stands as perhaps the single most important constitutional decision in history. The case, they are told, invented the concept of judicial review—the power of federal courts to invalidate acts of Congress that the courts deem unconstitutional—a concept nowhere in the Constitution itself. More particularly, the standard story goes, *Marbury* made clear that the Supreme Court is the "ultimate interpreter" of the Constitution, and therein lies the epic import of the ruling.

None of this is right, and some of it is howlingly wrong. *Marbury* was not even the most important constitutional decision of 1803; at least two, and possibly three, decisions that year alone outranked *Marbury*. Two of the year's most momentous decisions came from constitutional actors other than the Supreme Court. *Marbury* itself said nothing whatsoever about the unique status of the "Supreme

Court" as the Constitution's "ultimate interpreter." (Only after World War II did the Court begin to describe itself and *Marbury* that way, never with any direct quotation.) The power and duty of courts—all courts, and not just courts—to refuse to enforce unconstitutional statutes—was deeply rooted in the Constitution and clearly established before *Marbury*. *Marbury* did not mark any decisive turning point in the actual rate of judicial invalidations of Congressional laws. Other branches and institutions wield constitutional enforcement powers not all that different from judicial review. In *Marbury* itself, although the Court purported to set aside a Congressional statute, the statute did not mean what the justices said it meant. (Concretely, the Court said that Congress could not expand the Court's jurisdiction, but Congress actually had not tried to do so.) Thus, there was no real constitutional clash between the Court and Congress in *Marbury*. There was, however, a deep rift between the branches at the heart of a companion case to *Marbury*. In that case—the now forgotten but then crucial case of *Stuart v. Laird*—the Court capitulated to a flagrantly unconstitutional Congressional statute. Most of the drama in *Marbury* involved not the Court versus the Congress, but rather the Court versus the president, Marshall versus Jefferson. Here, sparks did indeed fly, but in the end the Court retreated, unhappily but wisely. The justices in *Marbury* did next to nothing, but did so in a clever and talkative if not entirely proper way, rather like the cast in the modern sitcom *Seinfeld*.

THE CASE IS CAPTIONED *MARBURY v. Madison*, but it was in effect *Marshall, Adams, and the Federalists v. Jefferson and the Republicans*— the sequel of the furious and frantic events in the lame-duck Congress of 1801. That Federalist-dominated Congress, as has been seen, crowned Jefferson president. But not without a parting volley, the Judiciary Act of 1801.

Having lost the presidency, the House, and much of the Senate in the election of 1800, the lame-duck Federalists sought to fortify the one central garrison that would reliably remain in Federalist control at the outset of Jefferson's administration—the federal judiciary. Federalists of course already dominated this third branch, all of whose members had received their nominations and commissions from Presidents Washington and Adams. All members of this branch, both on the Supreme Court and on lower federal courts, enjoyed life tenure and salaries that could not be lawfully diminished. The lame-duck Federalists hoped to do more than merely preserve the judiciary as it had been. They aimed to expand this bastion of Federalism.

The country was large and the federal judiciary small. Its jurisdiction was just a fraction of what the Constitution permitted. The Judiciary Act of 1789 had provided that most cases arising under federal law would be tried by state courts, leaving it to the federal Supreme Court to hear an appeal from any litigant claiming that a state court had failed to properly interpret and protect his federal rights. Nationalists for years had dreamed of more—of a regime in which federal judges would have not just the last word on appeal, but also the first word at trial, in a wide swath of cases arising under federal law. Now, in early 1801, Congressional Federalists worked to make this dream a reality.

Also, the rigors of circuit riding had taken their toll. Associate Justice Rutledge and Chief Justice Jay had resigned for more comfortable jobs in their home states that would not oblige them to spend many months each year on lonely roads far from loved ones. Justice William Cushing would likely have followed suit had he been elected state governor in 1794. (He lost the race and thus stayed put.) When Justice James Iredell died in 1799, just weeks after his forty-eighth birthday, many blamed his early demise on the harshness of his circuit duty. By eliminating this burden, the lame-duck Federalist Congress hoped to entice the six existing justices—including, of course, the newly appointed chief justice, John Marshall—to stay for life and thus give incoming President Jefferson fewer chances to add his own men to the bench.

Congress passed the Judiciary Act of 1801 on February 7, and John Adams signed it into law on the ominous day of Friday the 13th. At that precise moment, John Marshall was only in his second week as chief justice (while remaining secretary of state), and the House was still wrangling over the presidency. Only in the days ahead would it become clear that Thomas Jefferson would soon take his new oath as president, and not John Marshall as acting president under the Horatius plan.

With its new Judiciary Act, Congress eliminated circuit riding, dramatically expanded the jurisdiction of lower federal courts, and created sixteen new circuit judgeships to do all the additional judicial work—judgeships that could be filled by the electorally repudiated Adams, with the advice and consent of the Federalist-dominated lame-duck Senate. As the clock ticked down to Jefferson's inauguration, Adams and the Senate did indeed fill the new slots, with notables drawn almost entirely from the Federalist ranks. In his final hours as secretary of state, John Marshall dutifully sealed the new judicial commissions and arranged for their delivery.

Although all this was strictly legal, it stank politically. Even though the act's general features—more federal judges with more jurisdiction and less circuit riding—made good sense, Adams's rush to fill all the new slots was politically piggish. A wiser and more farsighted president who understood how action begets reaction might have filled eight of the slots and left the remaining eight for the new president as a grand goodwill gesture.

Adams instead tried to pack the judiciary. Jefferson smoldered with rage at this brazen effort to entrench a constitutional vision that the voters had emphatically rejected. The Federalists, Jefferson complained to a friend, "have retired into the Judiciary as a stronghold. There the remains of federalism are to be preserved & fed from the treasury, and from that battery all the works of republicanism are to be beaten down & erased. By a fraudulent use of the Constitution which has made judges irremoveable, they have multiplied useless judges merely to strengthen their phalanx."[18]

Once in power, Jeffersonians in Congress knocked the new pieces off the chessboard in a single sweeping gesture—a one-page 1802 statute dripping with contempt. The lame-duck act "is hereby repealed," and "all the acts, and parts of acts, which were [previously] in force . . . hereby are revived . . . as if [the lame-duck act] had never been made." Action, meet reaction.[19]

Much of the 1802 repeal act was every bit as strictly legal as the 1801 lame-duck law had been. One Congress could add jurisdiction, and another Congress could subtract it. One Congress could end circuit riding for justices, and another could reinstate it. But thanks to the 1801 law, more than a dozen notables were now federal judges and were thus constitutionally entitled to salaries for life that could not be diminished. They deserved their titles and their compensation, come what may.[20]

Article III spoke plainly to this point: "The Judges . . . shall hold their Offices during good Behaviour and shall . . . receive for their Services, a Compensation, which shall not be diminished during their Continuance in Office." Jeffersonians cynically argued that no compensation was due if the underlying "Office" ceased to exist, and that Compensation was due only for "Services" rendered. Why, they asked, should the judges be paid for doing nothing once their offices had been annulled? The obvious answer was that federal judges had vested legal rights to hold their offices so long as they did not misbehave. Many of these honorable public servants had given up other positions in reliance on the promises made in Article III. The "continuance in office" language meant only that a judge should not receive a salary after resigning. Their *offices* continued to exist even if their *duties* and *jurisdiction* evaporated. The 1802 repeal law could not rewrite history. The 1801 act could not truly be annulled and treated "as if [it] had never been made." The nineteenth century's most acclaimed constitutional scholar, Associate Justice Joseph Story—whom we shall consider more carefully in our next chapter—did not hold back in his landmark 1833 treatise, *Commentaries on the Constitution of the United States*. (Judges can get quite emotional about the issue of judicial salaries.) The 1802 repeal act, he wrote, "prostrates in the dust the independence of all inferior judges, both as to the tenure of their office, and their compensation for services, and leaves the constitution a miserable and vain delusion."[21]

Alas, when litigation ensued, the Marshall Court jurists did not stand up for their ousted and unpaid brethren. In *Stuart v. Laird*, a companion case to *Marbury*, various issues raised by the Jeffersonian repeal bill came before the Court, albeit in a complex factual setting.[22] The Court issued its *Stuart* ruling less than a week after *Marbury*, in which the Court had done several notable things. First, the *Marbury* justices had declared that one technical aspect of the Judiciary Act of 1789 was unconstitutional. Second, the Court had ranged far and wide to discuss various legal issues that the case did not oblige the justices to address and in the process had scolded the Jefferson administration for various alleged illegalities. Third, the *Marbury* opinion had stressed that the very idea of the rule of law entailed legal remedies for violations of vested legal rights. The facts underlying the *Marbury* case itself were rather trivial, as we shall soon see. In *Stuart*, by contrast, core elements of judicial independence lurked in the background—the right of federal judges to hold their offices for good behavior and to be paid as promised, in keeping with the plain letter and spirit of Article III. Yet in *Stuart*, the case that truly mattered, the justices did not follow up on any of *Marbury*'s important moves. The *Stuart* justices did not use the case before them as a springboard to condemn the Jeffersonian salary grab. The ousted judges never received a proper judicial declaration that their Article III salary and tenure rights had been violated; nor did they ever receive the proper legal remedy of lifetime pay.

IN THE *MARBURY* CASE ITSELF, the underlying issues were much smaller. The case involved an obscure low-level official, a justice of the peace in Washington City, not a life-tenured Article III judge. William Marbury's commission had been signed by John Adams on the president's last day of office. In his capacity as secretary of state, John Marshall had sealed the commission before midnight. But Marshall's agent had failed to properly deliver the commission to Marbury, who now brought suit against Jefferson's secretary of state, James Madison.

Marbury commenced his lawsuit in the United States Supreme Court, sitting as a court of "original jurisdiction"—that is, a trial court as opposed to an appellate court. Marbury wanted the Court, via a writ of mandamus—a judicial order—to compel Madison to hand over the undelivered commission. There seemed to be only two paths forward for the Court, and each looked grim for the new chief justice.

One path seemed relatively safe in the short run but fraught with long-term hazards and costs. The Court could plausibly rule against Marbury on any number of technical grounds. This would be abject and inglorious surrender, both for the Federalist Party and for the judiciary. When added to the *Stuart* case also under consideration, a square ruling against Marbury might well embolden Jeffersonians to take even more aggressive actions against both Federalists and federal judges. Such a ruling would also dampen the spirit of Federalists everywhere.

The other path involved immediate risk and confrontation. The Court could order Madison to deliver the ill-fated commission to Marbury. At a minimum, this scenario would likely lead to open defiance. Madison had refused even to appear in Court to dignify the judicial proceedings. Marbury himself was not an Article III judge. He was thus a mere executive-branch official; under the Decision of 1789 the president should have broad power to control his own branch. Or at least that is what Jefferson and Madison would likely say when they simply ignored Marshall's mandamus and made the Court look impotent.

The prospect of executive defiance was only one possible response; other imaginable scenarios looked even worse. In their conversations about the draft bill of rights in 1787–1789, Jefferson and Madison had sung the praises of an independent judiciary; but once in power, Jefferson and his allies had begun to sing a different tune. (More Jeffersonian hypocrisy? Or perhaps Jefferson's disillusionment was an understandable reaction to the deeply partisan and disappointing performance of Federalist judges in the Sedition Act controversy.) Jefferson had already taken steps to encourage the impeachment of a lower court judge, John Pickering, and the following year the Jeffersonian House would impeach Supreme Court Justice Samuel Chase. If the *Marbury* Court were to rule against Madison, might Marshall himself face impeachment?[23]

Or worse? Jefferson was a known enthusiast of the French Revolution, and some of Jefferson's statements about mass executions in Paris, if read literally, were terrifying—as was his apparent willingness to contemplate the death penalty for central bankers and armed militia resistance to an entirely valid presidential succession act. The ouster of the federal circuit judges was also a direct assault on judicial independence. How far might Jefferson in fact go to smite John Marshall if the chief justice and his brethren were to rule for Marbury?

In January 1793, Jefferson had expressed himself particularly forcefully on the unfolding French Revolution:

> In the struggle which was necessary, many guilty persons fell without the forms of trial, and with them some innocent. These I deplore as much as anybody, and shall deplore some of them to the day of my death. But I deplore them as I should have done had they fallen in battle. It was necessary to use the arm of the people, a machine not quite so blind as balls and bombs, but blind to a certain degree. A few of their cordial friends met at their hands the fate of enemies. But time and truth will rescue and embalm their memories, while their posterity will be enjoying that very liberty for which they would never have hesitated to offer up their lives. The liberty of the whole earth was depending on the issue of the contest, and was ever such a prize won with so little innocent blood? My own affections have been deeply wounded by some of the martyrs to this cause, but rather than it should have failed, I would have seen half the earth desolated. Were there but an Adam and an Eve left in every country, and left free, it would be better than as it now is.[24]

As we now know—though Jefferson did not and could not know it in early 1793—more than fifteen thousand persons were officially executed during the Reign of Terror from late 1792 to mid-1794, and hundreds of thousands more perished in related violence. Also, we now know that the French Revolution failed in many ways and gave way to Napoleonic dictatorship—in part, perhaps, because of the very violence early on that Jefferson so casually approved.

Of course, we also know today that matters did not in fact spiral out of control in the early American republic as they did in the early French Republic. We now view the American lawyer and revolutionary Thomas Jefferson as quite different from the French lawyer and revolutionary Maximilien Robespierre. We can now calmly say that even the 1802 repeal law, despite its blatant assault on judicial independence, was nonviolent and, in its own way, proportionate. No judge appointed before the 1801 Federalist lame-duck session was knocked off the legal chessboard—only those whose appointments themselves were, to Jefferson's (loose but understandable) way of thinking, entirely "fraudulent."[25] But what seems clear to us today—that Jefferson was no Jacobin—may not have been obvious to John Marshall and his colleagues in 1803. Privately, Hamilton had described Jefferson to Jay in early 1800 as "a fanatic in politics."[26]

Thus, both paths ahead in *Marbury* seemed fraught with peril. So John Marshall, wily Odysseus, found a third way out.

He began by declaring that Marbury did indeed have a right to his commission. Failure of delivery was immaterial, and Jefferson had no right to remove Marbury at will. (Why not? Marshall offered little explanation.) Moreover, Marshall made clear that a court of law could ordinarily order a high-level executive official—even America's secretary of state—to do what the court determined the law required. The administration was not immune from lawsuit, and a court could indeed tell Madison (and thus, indirectly, Jefferson) what to do in the case at hand.

Thus far, it will be seen, *Marbury* was not a case about the Court versus Congress—not a case about the power of courts to set aside unconstitutional statutes. Rather, it was a case about the Court versus the president, Marshall versus Jefferson. The Marshall Court was denouncing the alleged lawlessness of Jefferson's refusal to respect Marbury's vested—and congressionally created—legal rights to his commission. In this denunciation, Marshall seemed to put himself on a direct collision course with Jefferson. The chief justice was hurtling down the second path, running directly at a charging bull.

At the last possible instant, Marshall darted aside, swiveled his hips, and avoided impact. The Court would not order Madison to issue the commission because the Court lacked proper jurisdiction. And more: the Court lacked jurisdiction because one clause of the Congressional law that purported to give the Court jurisdiction—the Judiciary Act of 1789—was unconstitutional, and the Court had the right and duty to ignore unconstitutional Congressional laws. Not only did Marshall thus avoid collision with Jefferson, but he also simultaneously asserted power vis-à-vis Congress—a power now generally known as judicial review.

Despite what high-schoolers are now taught, judicial review was not remotely a new idea or practice in 1803. Rather, it was old hat. During the Great Constitutional Conversation of 1788, Hamilton's *Federalist* No. 78 had made clear that judges would have the power to disregard unconstitutional Congressional statutes. Leading Anti-Federalists had agreed, and the Judiciary Act of 1789 had clearly presupposed that judges could rule against unconstitutional statutes. Less than three years later, multiple justices in *Hayburn's Case* pronounced a Congressional statute unconstitutional as written. (The main difference between *Hayburn's Case* and *Marbury* was that the justices in the former case acted on circuit and not en banc.) In the 1796 *Hylton* case, the Court judged the constitutionality of the carriage tax, but decided (correctly) that the tax was valid. In the Sedition Act cases—*Lyon, Cooper, Callender*, etc.—Supreme Court justices once again measured a Congressional law against the Constitution and once again decided (this time, incorrectly) that the law passed muster. Jeffersonians at the time rightly faulted the judges for *failing* to strike down the law and also for *failing* to allow juries to assess constitutionality.

The basic argument for judicial review was laughably simple: the Constitution was both higher law and ordinary law. It was higher law than a mere Congressional statute because it came directly from the people themselves, via special ratifying conventions. (Its amendments were higher law because they, too, would need to clear more elevated democratic hurdles than any mere statute.) It was ordinary law because American courts generally and federal courts in particular were authorized to hear all cases arising under the Constitution. The Philadelphia framers drafted interlocking language, using almost identical words in Articles VI and III, to drive home these two basic points. Plainly, the Constitution was higher law: "This Constitution, and the laws of the United States which shall be made in pursuance thereof; and all treaties made, or which shall be made, under the authority of the United States, shall be the supreme law of the land." Also, the Constitution was law fit for use in ordinary litigation: "The judicial power shall extend to all cases, in law and equity, arising under this Constitution, the laws of the United States, and treaties made, or which shall be made, under their authority." In both places, the legal hierarchy was clear: the Constitution, federal laws, and federal treaties—in that precise order, from the most democratic national law (the Constitution, coming from the People) to the least democratic national law (a mere treaty lacking the participation of the House of Representatives).

Marshall in *Marbury* carefully quoted the matching language of Articles VI and III and drew attention to the obvious democratic gradient. The Constitution came first because it was more democratic:

> That the people have an original right to establish, for their future government, such principles as, in their opinion, shall most conduce to their own happiness, is the basis on which the whole American fabric has been erected.* . . . The constitution is . . . a superior, paramount law, unchangeable by ordinary means. . . . [I]n declaring what shall be the supreme law of the land, the constitution itself is first mentioned; and not the laws of the United States generally, but those only which shall be made in pursuance of the constitution,

---

*Marshall's imagery—"bas[e]," "fabric," and "erect[ion]"—of course harkened back to Benjamin Russell and Hamilton/Publius's *Federalist* No. 22.

have that rank. Thus, the particular phraseology of the constitution of the United States confirms and strengthens the principle, supposed to be essential to all written constitutions, that a law repugnant to the constitution is void, and that courts, as well as other departments, are bound by that instrument.

Marshall's last phrase deserves careful attention. Courts *as well as other departments* are bound by the Constitution. Not just the Supreme Court, but all courts, and not just the judicial department, but all departments: "The framers of the constitution contemplated that instrument as a rule for the government of courts, *as well as of the legislature*" (emphasis added). Jefferson detested many things about Marshall's *Marbury* opinion but never quarreled with Marshall on the judicial review issue. Indeed, Marshall had taken care not to overclaim on this issue (unlike modern high-schoolers and today's Supreme Court justices). In his tart 1804 letter to Abigail Adams, Jefferson used language that, while loose, was actually more a paraphrase of *Marbury* than a negation of it. Any "opinion which gives to the judges the right to decide what laws are constitutional, and what not," he wrote, "not only for themselves in their own sphere of action, but for the legislature & executive also in their spheres, would make the judiciary a despotic branch."[27]

MARBURY'S MODESTY ON THIS PARTICULAR issue fit within a larger pattern. Judicial review existed alongside other mechanisms of constitutional enforcement—presidential vetoes of bills that the executive deemed unconstitutional (regardless of what judges might think); presidential pardons based on the president's independent constitutional judgment, à la Jefferson in the Sedition Act; the right and duty of criminal jurors to consider constitutionality when rendering general verdicts of guilt, despite what Chase had done to Wirt and what Paterson had said in the *Lyon* case; and more. Ordinarily, if any one branch said no in the federal criminal law context, that no would stick even if other branches said yes. Consider once again the Sedition Act as the issue arose (or, at least, should have arisen) in 1798. If either House or Senate thought the act unconstitutional, they could vote no, and their no would prevail because the correct baseline prior to their decision was freedom; no federal common law of crime properly existed. If the president found the Sedition Act unconstitutional, he could veto the bill, refuse to prosecute violators and/or pardon all those convicted, and that would be that. If grand jurors found the act unconstitutional, they could refuse to indict. Likewise, constitutionally conscientious trial jurors could simply refuse to convict. Judges, for their part, could likewise say no to the law and do so with finality in the case at bar.

Marbury's version of judicial review was also modest along another dimension: the statute that the justices set aside was a jurisdictional statute—a statute regulating the judiciary itself. The law invalidated by circuit judges in *Hayburn's Case* was likewise a law regulating the judiciary as such—unlike, say, a general carriage-tax law aimed at all citizens, or a general Sedition Act. Judicial invalidation of laws that were not *plainly* unconstitutional might be institutionally immodest in general, but in the founding era an active judicial role seemed particularly appropriate when the law in question, even if close to the line, directly and principally regulated the judiciary itself—a domain where judges had special expertise to assess the constitutional line for themselves.

BUT WHAT EXACTLY WAS THE constitutional flaw in the Judiciary Act of 1789? The *Marbury* Court said that Congress could not add cases to the original jurisdiction of the Supreme Court beyond the categories mentioned in the Constitution itself. Marshall's opinion for the Court treated the matter as if no other textual reading were syntactically possible. This overstated things. Grammatically, the Article III text could perhaps be read merely to specify the Court's initial jurisdiction subject to Congressional modification.[28]

Still, *Marbury* was right to construe Article III as it did. Expanding the Supreme Court's original jurisdiction would improperly sidestep local juries in the hinterlands. State courts and/or lower federal courts located in the countryside were the proper venues for most trials. (It might be asked why Supreme Court justices riding circuit were allowed to try cases that could not be tried in the Supreme Court itself under Article III. Precisely because they were not Supreme Court cases as such, these circuit trials satisfied the strict letter of Article III. Precisely because these cases featured proper local juries, these trials also satisfied the broader spirit of Article III.) During the ratification process, Publius and other Federalists had reassured their audience that the Supreme Court's original jurisdiction was quite limited and could not be expanded.[29]

But then why had Congress said otherwise in the Judiciary Act of 1789? In fact, *contra Marbury*, Congress had *not* said otherwise. In the key section of the Judiciary Act (section 13), the statute repeatedly spoke of the Supreme Court's "jurisdiction" and then gave the Court "power" to issue various "writs," including the writ—a writ of mandamus—that Marbury himself sought. The best reading of section 13 was that the writ-issuing power was not itself a grant of *jurisdiction*. Rather, the statute simply gave the Court remedial power to issue various writs, including writs of mandamus, only when the Court otherwise had proper jurisdiction. In every other section of the sprawling 1789 act regulating every other federal court, whenever Congress meant to confer jurisdiction, it always used the word "jurisdiction" or the word "cognizance." Where the act elsewhere used the word "power," the word never meant "jurisdiction." Rather, the act consistently used the word "power" merely to give federal courts the ability to do certain things only after they otherwise had jurisdiction.[30]

Thus, *Marbury* reached the right result, but for the wrong reason. The Court did indeed lack jurisdiction to give William Marbury the writ he wanted. But not because (as the *Marbury* Court held) Congress in 1789 had tried to expand the Court's original jurisdiction and had thereby flouted the Constitution. Rather, the Court lacked original jurisdiction simply because the Constitution did not give it to the Court in the case at hand, and neither did Congress.

Perhaps Marshall understood all this; perhaps not. The bottom-line result for William Marbury was the same either way, but the Court would look stronger, even as it was pivoting away from a violent confrontation with the executive branch, if it could flex its muscles against Congress. And if ever there were a case in which Congress would not object to judicial review, this was it—because Congress in fact never wanted the Court to hear cases like Marbury's.

ALL OF WHICH BRINGS US to Marshall's cunning in *Marbury*. The sly part of *Marbury* had nothing to do with judicial review. As we have seen, the basic concept of judicial review was easy and obvious long before *Marbury*, and *Marbury's* general version of judicial review—acknowledging the role of other branches and purporting to set aside a law regulating the judiciary itself—was rather modest. But almost everything else in *Marbury* was twisted, brilliantly, to enable wily Odysseus to transform a trap into a triumph.

The Court managed to denounce Jefferson, but made it hard for Jefferson to retaliate. There was no Court order that Madison could defy. (The Court said much but did . . . nothing.) Likewise, the Court made it hard for Jefferson to rouse popular resentment against the justices; after all, in the end they had ruled in favor of the Jefferson administration. Nor was it likely that Marshall would be impeached by an enraged Congress. It might at first seem that he had told Congress off; but not really. Nothing that Congress truly cared about had been invalidated.

Things would have been entirely different had the Court tried to use *Stuart* to demand lifetime pay for the ousted Article III midnight judges. In the 1802 debate over the repeal of the Judiciary Act of 1801, several leading Jeffersonian congressmen—for the first time and in sharp violation of what they and most others had previously agreed upon and indeed advocated—had challenged the right of courts to invalidate unconstitutional statutes.[31] *Marbury* slyly answered these revisionist Jeffersonian congressmen with an emphatic en banc precedent rebutting their denials of the judicial review power, but Marshall picked his battleground carefully. He asserted judicial review not by trying to undo the 1802 salary grab—a battle that Marshall knew he could not win, given the configuration of political forces in 1803—but by purporting to invalidate a very different Congressional bill, a bill that supposedly gave the Court *too much* power. By disclaiming judicial power (jurisdiction), Marshall in effect secured judicial power (by bolstering judicial review with a firm and unanimous en banc precedent). Gaining power by disavowing power—it was a brilliant judicial move that George Washington himself, America's original resigner in chief, would surely have admired.

While avoiding infuriating the Jeffersonians, Marshall even managed to toss a sop to his fellow Federalist William Marbury. Technically, Marbury lost. He did not get his requested mandamus; nor did he get his hoped-for commission. But he got something remarkably close—not a commission signed by John Adams and sealed by Secretary of State John Marshall proclaiming him an officer, but a judicial opinion authored by Chief Justice John Marshall filled with dicta saying that his commission was in fact valid. Unlike the commission itself, Marshall's opinion was not suitable for display above Marbury's desk. Still, it was better than nothing.

All in all, *Marbury* was a brilliant performance, but only because Marshall had engaged in "twistifications"—Jefferson's bespoke word for his cousin's great talent for legal legerdemain. "When conversing with Marshall," Jefferson once hilariously remarked, "I never admit anything. So sure as you admit any position to be good, no matter how remote from the conclusion he seeks to establish, you are gone. So great is his sophistry you must never give him an affirmative answer or you will be forced to grant his conclusion. Why, if he were to ask me if it were daylight or not, I'd reply, 'Sir, I don't know, I can't tell.'"[32]

Marbury featured multiple twistifications. If the Court truly lacked jurisdiction, the justices should not have opined on any substantive questions, such as the validity of Marbury's commission.[33] Jurisdiction should have been decided at the outset, and the Court failed to explain why it had not followed the usual rules. Even more egregiously, Marshall failed to recuse himself. As secretary of state, he was the key eyewitness to the entire transaction of Marbury's botched commissioning. Marshall, personally, had sealed the commission, and then he personally had blundered by failing to ensure its timely delivery. In any proper trial he should have played the role of a testifying witness, not a finder of fact. Another twist: Marshall had tasked his younger brother James with the chore of delivering the commission to Marbury; James had failed in his mission and later submitted a factual affidavit in the case. Here were still more reasons for the elder brother to play no role in the fact-finding that the case required, given that the Court was sitting in original jurisdiction and thus responsible for finding facts as well as pronouncing law.

But had Marshall stood aside at this critical hour, an already weak and battered judiciary might have crumbled further. The Constitution itself had placed the judiciary third out of three among the branches. Congress had the purse, the president the sword. The judiciary had only words. Congresses had broad authority to structure the judiciary, and presidents had wide power to staff it. The pre-Marshall judiciary had often stumbled and missed its best opportunities. It had not consistently spoken with one voice. It had not arranged for quick publication and broad distribution of its rulings. It had failed to persuade Congress early on—during the Washington presidency—to soften the rigors of circuit riding. Its first chiefs had jumped ship. It had overreached in *Chisholm*. Some of its members had disgraced themselves in adjudicating the Sedition Act. And now—with the repeal law of 1802, the novel and brazen denials of judicial review by leading members of Congress, the aggressive impeachment efforts in 1803, and who knows what else in the works—the Jeffersonians had the Federalist judiciary in their sights.

Borrowing a page from his mentor George Washington in the Revolutionary War, Marshall in *Marbury* and *Stuart* responded with a combination of orthodox and guerrilla tactics. He rallied his judicial troops and prevented a disorderly rout. He executed a brilliant feint and beat a hasty but disciplined retreat, because he could not hold the field that day against Jefferson's superior forces. When safely out of range, he unfurled his flags and sounded his bugles to boost his men's morale and blunt any impression of surrender. He did not fight in an entirely fair way. Metaphorically, he hid behind bushes and trees and attacked on Christmas. But thanks to his brilliant performance, his men would live to fight another day—and he would stay with them for the duration.

AMENDMENT

The text of the Constitution underwent one and only one modification after Washington and before Lincoln. Though not a full-blown Jeffersonian "revolution," the Twelfth Amendment's new rules, proposed by Congress in 1803 and ratified by states the following year, did reflect several Jeffersonian themes—popularity, partisanship, and slavery.

To appreciate the significance of the new rules, we must first recall the old rules. Article II gave each state a number of presidential electors equal to that state's total number of Congress members—or, put differently, the size of its House delegation plus two (for its two Senate seats). Via the Three-Fifths Clause, slave states thus got extra credit in presidential selection, just as in House apportionment. Members of the Electoral College would meet in their respective states, and each elector would cast two ballots for the presidency, with no formal way to designate his true first choice. Whoever came in second for the presidency would become vice president.

Under the new Twelfth Amendment, each elector would cast one ballot for president and an entirely different ballot for vice president. Political parties could now openly designate tickets that could not easily be flipped by the opposite party. If, say, Jeffersonians in the upcoming 1804 election could garner an electoral-vote majority, they would automatically win both presidency and vice presidency with no muss, no fuss, no House wrangling, and no Horatius. It would be clear from the start who was running for the top spot (Jefferson) and who would be number two (not Burr, of course; most likely, someone else quietly handpicked by Jefferson in consultation with Madison—probably a New Yorker for geographic balance).

The amendment thus cleared a path for increased involvement of political parties, which could in turn make mass appeals to the citizenry through newspapers, pamphlets, leaflets, broadsides, handbills, rallies, conventions, caucuses, parades, addresses, and other popular engines and instruments. An ordinary voter would not need to know the presidential candidates directly; he would simply need to know which national party—each a consortium of local chapters—he generally preferred.

In retirement, Jefferson recounted a revealing conversation that he had had with John Adams in late 1800, aiming to console his once and future friend by telling him that the recent election was not remotely personal: "Two systems of principles on the subject of government divide our fellow-citizens into two parties. With one of these you concur, & I with the other. As we have been longer on the public stage than most of those now living, our names happen to be more generally known. One of these parties therefore has put your name at it's head, the other mine. Were we both to die to-day, tomorrow two other names would be in the place of ours, without any change in the motion of the machine." Jefferson here was, characteristically, tactful but not entirely truthful. America in 1800 had repudiated both the Federalists in general and Adams in particular. The personal element could never be entirely eliminated from politics in general and from presidential politics in particular, given that presidential power (unlike Congressional power and judicial power) always resides at any given moment in a single person. Still, the Twelfth Amendment pushed the system away from a single-minded focus on the personality of a single presidential candidate and toward the platform of a national party.[34]

The Twelfth Amendment thus fathered a new kind of president, apt to be more popularist and partisan than America's first two chief magistrates. Whereas Washington and Adams aimed to position themselves above politics and above the national parties that were emerging, Jefferson was a more avowed man of the people and was also a party man deep down, though not always openly. The amendment crafted by Jefferson's Congressional allies reflected his essence, for it, too, was all about parties, but not openly.

The Twelfth Amendment also spawned a more brazenly slavocratic presidential-selection system than the one that America had ratified in the late 1780s. Back then, many ordinary Americans had not appreciated the full significance of the Three-Fifths Clause. Many had focused not on differences between free and slave states, but rather on possible fissures between big and small states. By 1803, the deep tension between North and South was impossible to miss.[35] Every actual combination of president and vice president (and indeed every losing ticket as well) had balanced a northerner and a southerner. Many of the major debates in Congress—over the assumption of state debt, the location of a national capital, the handling of anti-slavery petitions, the establishment of a central bank, the apportionment of representatives after the first census, the ratification and enforcement of the Jay Treaty, and much more—had either highlighted or thinly papered over obvious sectional differences. In both 1796 and 1800—the two Jefferson-Adams contests—electors had divided along sectional lines. Most of the South, twice, had backed the southerner, Jefferson, and most of the North, twice, had backed the northerner, Adams. (As Jefferson and Madison had sensed early on—hence their 1791 botanical expedition—the effective swing voters and notables were in New York, a mid-Atlantic state with a substantial slave population.) Even the final Jefferson-Burr vote in the House on February 17, 1801, had featured a north-south divide of sorts. The four states that held out to the bitter end for (northerner) Burr over (southerner) Jefferson were the four original New England states: New Hampshire, Massachusetts, Rhode Island, and Connecticut.[36]

The election of 1800–1801 had also drawn the nation's attention, in the most dramatic fashion possible, to the Philadelphia plan's pro-slavery bias. *For without the added electoral votes created by the existence of southern slaves, John Adams would have won the election of 1800—as everyone at the time plainly understood.* Jefferson's (and Burr's) electors came from states that had a smaller total free population than the states whose electors backed Adams. Had the Electoral College been apportioned on the basis of free population—with no three-fifths bonus—Jefferson would have finished with about 4 electoral votes less than Adams rather than 8 votes more. In the sharp words of several northern newspapers, Jefferson was riding "into the TEMPLE OF LIBERTY, upon the *shoulders of slaves*."[37] As at least a dozen northern publications put the point, "JOHN ADAMS has been re-elected President of the United States by a MAJORITY OF ALL THE FREE PEOPLE THEREOF."[38]

Congressional critics of Jefferson and the amendment that his political party began pushing after his election repeatedly highlighted that his supposed popular revolution had slavocratic roots. In 1802, Connecticut congressman Samuel Dana declared that any sensible amendment aiming to remedy the systemic flaws exposed by the 1800–1801 crisis should consider whether the allotment of representatives (and thus presidential electors) "should be in proportion to the whites, or in proportion to the whites compounded with slaves." In 1803, Representative Seth Hastings of Massachusetts argued that a proper Twelfth Amendment should provide for "an equal representation of free citizens, and free citizens only," thereby repairing the 1787 "compromise . . . by which one part of the Union has obtained a great, and in my opinion, unjust advantage over other parts of the Union. A compromise, sir, by which the Southern States have gained a very considerable increase of Representatives and Electors, founded solely upon their numerous black population." Massachusetts representative Samuel Thatcher likewise blasted the "peculiar inequality" between regions created by "the representation of slaves," who would add "eighteen Electors of President and Vice President at the next election."[39] In the same spirit, New Hampshire's senator William Plumer lamented the "eighteen additional Electors and Representatives" created by chattel slavery: "Will you, by this amendment, lessen the weight and influence of the Eastern states, in the elections of your first officers, and still retain this unequal article in your Constitution? Shall property in one part of the Union give an increase of Electors, and be wholly excluded in other States? Can this be right?"[40]

Alas, the Twelfth Amendment's Jeffersonian backers had no interest in remedying *this* aspect of the presidential-selection system, even as they freely revised other parts of the Article II machinery. New England states accounted for 6 of the 10 votes against the amendment in the Senate, while in the House, states north of New Jersey generated 31 of the 42 no votes.[41]

Article II originally created the presidency in the image of George Washington. Amendment XII refashioned the office in the likeness of Thomas Jefferson and in a manner that prefigured Andrew Jackson. After the adoption of this amendment, America's presidential election rules—and thus America's presidents—would generally be more democratic, more partisan, and more openly slavocratic. Prior to the amendment, America's first president had taken steps to free his slaves, and America's second president had none who needed freeing. America's third president—a transitional figure elected under Article II and reelected under Amendment XII—had passionately condemned slavery in his early years but did little to back up his youthful rhetoric after his slavery-supported triumph in 1801. The next dozen presidents—mostly southern slaveholders or northern doughfaces—likewise did little to challenge slavery.[42]

LOUISIANA

The Louisiana Purchase—America's 1803 acquisition of more than half a billion acres from Napoleonic France—nearly doubled the landmass of the United States and simultaneously eliminated any future French or Spanish threat to the ongoing existence of the American constitutional project. Compared to the judiciary's modest actions and inaction in *Marbury* and *Stuart*, and Congress's proposed revision of the Electoral College, President Jefferson's procurement of this vast territory surely ranks as the year's most notable constitutional development. Indeed, the decision to acquire and absorb this vast tract ranks as perhaps the most important constitutional event of the entire era between the ending of the Sedition Act in 1801 and the enactment of secession ordinances in 1860–1861.

It was an epic constitutional decision in at least six respects. First, the purchase all but guaranteed the survival of America, and thus America's Constitution, against potentially hostile external forces. The acquisition nudged France off the continent; pushed Spanish power far back; and gave young America firm possession of the mighty Mississippi River and its immense watershed, from its headwaters in the western wilderness to its mouth in New Orleans. Second and related, the purchase strongly tied America's backcountry region between the Appalachians and the Mississippi to its Atlantic seaboard. Even if existing and future roads and canals cutting through the Appalachians failed to fuse East and West, crops and finished goods could now float freely around the mountains to population centers along the river system and eastern coastline. Third, the purchase massively redefined the scope of the American constitutional project, both geographically and demographically, extending it west to the vast unknown and south to the Gulf coast. Fourth, the procurement prompted and framed the most important topic of constitutional debate over the next several generations, a topic and debate that would ultimately spark a civil war: Should slavery be allowed to spread to new land, and if so, under what rules? Fifth, the acquisition also intensified constitutional questions about how largely Protestant White America would absorb and assimilate—or not— new populations of Indians, Cajuns, Catholics, and others already inhabiting parts of Louisiana. Finally and most immediately, Louisiana impelled Jefferson to grow up, constitutionally—to embrace his inner Washington and Hamilton and to reject the unsound principles of ultra-strict construction, extreme Francophilia, and knee-jerk Anglophobia that the loose-minded theorist had long preached when others had been president and that he himself had generally embraced at the outset of his presidency.

JEFFERSON UNDERSTOOD THE ROUGH CONTOURS of the vast tract that America could now claim, but much of the continent's interior was *terra incognita*, especially prior to the multiyear Lewis and Clark Expedition that the ever-curious and westward-looking president would soon authorize. A state-of-the-art map from 1803 should remind us of just how much and how little was known at that date. The map's crude estimates of the shape of modern-day Michigan and the northwestern Great Lakes are particularly suggestive. These northern and western imprecisions and improvisations illustrate that in 1803 the immediate jackpot lay elsewhere: at the end of the rainbow, the great port city of New Orleans, a continental chokepoint every bit as important to America's foreseeable future as the great port city of New York was to its present. We should also recall that the entire region west of the Mississippi—all the way north to modern-day Minnesota and the Dakotas—was part of the generic territory of "Louisiana" that Napoleon was now selling to Jefferson for a mere $15 million—less than three cents an acre. (The state now named Louisiana was just a tiny, albeit crucial, piece of the larger tract.)

In mid-April 1802, Jefferson wrote a remarkable letter about New Orleans to New Yorker Robert R. Livingston. Livingston, it will be recalled, had served back in 1776 with Jefferson on the key five-man committee (later immortalized by Trumbull) that had drafted the Declaration of Independence. As chancellor of New York, Livingston had administered the presidential oath to George Washington in April 1789. In the early 1790s, the chancellor felt slighted when frozen out of the Washington administration, especially given the top judicial and diplomatic honors that had been (and would continue to be) showered upon his fellow New Yorker (and in-law) John Jay and all the power and glory given to the lowborn New York arriviste Alexander Hamilton.[43] Sensing an opportunity, Jefferson and Madison courted Livingston (along with other leading New York anti-Hamiltonians Aaron Burr and George Clinton) in their 1791 botanical expedition. In the run-up to the Revolution, the key strategic alliance had wedded Virginia and Massachusetts; but Massachusetts was Adams's backyard and increasingly anti-slavery. Thus Virginia's Jefferson and Madison hitched their political fortunes to New York, quietly supporting Clinton for the vice presidency in 1792, and more emphatically backing Burr for the second slot in 1796 and 1800. (After Burr's double-cross, the Virginians would return to Clinton, who would serve as vice president to both Jefferson and Madison from 1805 until the New Yorker's death in 1812.)

And Livingston? He, too, helped push New York into the Jeffersonian column in 1800—and New York was indeed the decisive state. Upon inauguration, Jefferson rewarded Livingston with a position of special honor and responsibility: Livingston would hold the same position that Jefferson had once held, and that Franklin had held before that—minister to France. Adams, too, had been a top American diplomat in France, in the 1780s, albeit not a formal American minister. Thus, four of the five members of the key Declaration drafting committee would eventually represent America in France—yet another reminder of how large France loomed in the early American imagination and in early American geostrategy. Marshall, it will be recalled, had also served as a key American diplomat to France in the 1790s, as had Jefferson's protégé James Monroe, another future president. (In 1803, Monroe returned to France at Jefferson's request to assist Livingston.)

In his remarkable letter of April 18, 1802, to Livingston, Jefferson opened by swooning, as he had so often in the past, about the glories of France and its natural affinities with America: "Of all nations of any consideration, France is the one which hitherto has offered the fewest points on which we could have any conflict of right, and the most points of a communion of interests. From these causes we have ever looked to her as our *natural friend*, as one with which we never could have an occasion of difference. Her growth therefore we viewed as our own, her misfortunes ours."[44]

Was this merely for French consumption—laying it on thick, much as Franklin had done in the 1780s? Washington also knew how to flatter, but deep down never saw any nation as America's "natural friend." Nations, Washington believed, pursued their respective self-interests, and it was a mistake to found diplomacy on romantic ideas about permanent friendship—or permanent enmity, for that matter.[45] "It is a maxim founded on the universal experience of Mankind," the general had admonished the Congress back in 1778 (with an opening clause that Jane Austen would doubtless have approved), "that no Nation is to be trusted farther than it is bound by its interest."[46] The gist of this Washington dictum was to warn Congress against inviting French land troops into Canada to fight the British. Once back in the middle of the New World, Washington worried, France might not want to leave. Americans might then find themselves once again bordering on and wrangling with continental Europe's mightiest power, in a repeat of the late 1750s (when Washington of course had fought against the French).

Prior to his 1802 letter to Livingston, Jefferson had seemed far more credulous. Washington loved Lafayette like a son, and Hamilton loved the Marquis like a brother, but Jefferson loved the beautiful coquette Maria Cosway in Paris in rather more erotic ways, and perhaps those tender memories warped Jefferson's response to all *choses françaises*. Or perhaps he was warped by his passionate dislike of British merchants, to whom he was deeply indebted, or of the

British government, whose soldiers had sacked and burned Richmond and despoiled Monticello, humiliating Governor Jefferson in the process. Or perhaps the utopian Virginian was simply charmed by Enlightenment-tinged revolutions anywhere, and especially revolutions that seemed inspired by the one he had helped lead in 1776.

Whatever the deep sources of his initial astigmatism, Jefferson had repeatedly failed to assess the French with a keen eye. In late 1788, he deemed it "probable" that France would "within two or three years be in the enjoyment of a tolerably free constitution, and that without it's having cost them a drop of blood"; he even mocked "the English papers" that expected mass bloodshed. As secretary of state in the early 1790s, he was initially besotted by the revolutionary French minister Edmond-Charles Genêt. "It is impossible for any thing to be more affectionate, more magnanimous than the purport of his mission," Jefferson babbled in a 1793 letter to Madison. Genêt knew how to flatter—"We see in you the only persons on earth who can love us sincerely and merit to be so loved"—and the Virginian who had left his heart in Paris was utterly enchanted. Genêt, thought Jefferson, "offers every thing and asks nothing."[47]

Events would soon show that Genêt would in fact ask and do quite a lot—much of it no good. Genêt perpetrated violations of America's express policy of neutrality, incited others to do the same, and openly sought to turn Americans against George Washington. Washington was forgiving. When it became clear that Genêt would face the guillotine if he were sent back to France, Washington allowed him asylum in America. In 1794, Genêt married the daughter of New York governor George Clinton, who would later serve as Jefferson's and Madison's vice president.

Given Jefferson's erroneous judgments about French intentions in the past, the pivot in the middle of his key 1802 letter to Livingston was particularly dramatic. Jefferson had recently learned that Napoleon had secretly taken steps to acquire New Orleans from Spain, and this changed everything. As if on a dime, Jefferson's tone switched from that of France's lovesick *amour* to something much more sober and detached, à la Washington and Hamilton:

There is on the globe one single spot, the possessor of which is our natural & habitual enemy. It is New Orleans, through which the produce of three eighths of our territory must pass to market, and from it's fertility it will ere long yield more than half of our whole produce and contain more than half our inhabitants. France placing herself in that door assumes to us the attitude of defiance. . . . The impetuosity of her temper, the energy & restlessness of her character, placed in a point of eternal friction with us . . . render it impossible that France and the US can continue long friends when they meet in so irritable a position.

Had Jefferson simply lurched from France as America's natural and eternal friend to France as America's natural and eternal enemy? No. *Any* country that controlled New Orleans held a dagger to America's throat.[48] The dagger in Spanish hands was acceptable only because Spain was weak and America could soon enough seize the dagger: "Spain might have retained it [New Orleans] quietly for years. Her pacific dispositions, her feeble state, would induce her to increase our [American] facilities there, so that her possession of the place would be hardly felt by us, and it would not perhaps be very long before some circumstance might arise which might make the cession of it to us the price of something of more worth to her." France was more formidable. France could no longer be America's best friend, even in a Jefferson administration, unless it gave up the dagger—after which, the friendship would of course resume.

Jefferson the former diplomat proceeded to instruct Livingston the current diplomat how to move forward. France should be reminded of America's deep love and special friendship—the carrot. But—the stick—France should also be told that America would really with Britain if France did not yield up the dagger. America was, Jefferson reminded Livingston, in a particularly strong position—the leverage—because open war between England and France would recommence soon enough: "The day that France takes possession of N. Orleans . . . seals the union of two nations who in conjunction can maintain exclusive possession of the ocean. From that moment we must marry ourselves to the British fleet & nation. We must turn all our attentions to a maritime force, for which our resources place us on very high ground." Such an Anglo-American maritime re-alliance and naval blockade would "render reinforcement of her [New World] settlements here impossible to France." The "first cannon which shall be fired in Europe" would be "the signal for tearing up any settlement she may have made, and for holding the two continents of America in sequestration for the common purposes of the United British & American nations."

The letter ended with a remarkable blend of carrot and stick and leverage that Livingston should deploy in conversing with France. (*We love you, but you must do what we say or we will have to join your enemy and kill you; but, to repeat, we love you.*) "This is not a state of things we seek or desire," Jefferson wrote Livingston. "It is one which this measure, if adopted by France, forces on us, as necessarily as any other cause, by the laws of nature [*sic*; and also nature's God?], brings on it's necessary effect. It is not from a fear of France that we deprecate this measure proposed by her. For however greater her force is than ours compared in the abstract, it is nothing in comparison of ours when to be exerted on our soil." (*Yes, France is much bigger, but we have massive home-field advantage.*) "But it is from a sincere love of peace, and a firm persuasion that bound to France by the interests and the strong sympathies still existing in the minds of our citizens, and holding relative positions which ensure their continuance[,] we are secure of a long course of peace. Whereas the change of friends [that is, the new projected Anglo-American alliance], which will be rendered necessary if France changes that position, embarks us necessarily as a belligerent power in the first war of Europe. In that case France will have held possession of New Orleans during the interval of a peace, long or short, at the end of which it will be wrested from her." (*One way or another, we must and will have New Orleans; don't make this hard on us.*) "Will this shortlived possession have been an equivalent to her for the transfer of such a weight into the scale of her enemy? Will not the amalgamation of a young, thriving, nation continue to that enemy the health & force which are at present so evidently on the decline?" (*Don't push us back into the arms of that decrepit and foul-smelling George III!*) "And will a few years possession of N. Orleans add equally to the strength of France? She may say she needs Louisiana for the supply of her West Indies. She does not need it in time of peace, and in war she could not depend on them because they would be so easily intercepted.

"I should suppose that all these considerations might in some proper form be brought into view of the government of France. Tho' stated by us, it ought not to give offence; because we do not bring them forward as a menace, but as consequences not controulable by us, but inevitable from the course of things." (*In the course of human events, separations are sometimes necessary; we know the drill.*) "We mention them not as things which we desire by any means, but as things we deprecate; and we beseech a friend to look forward and to prevent them for our common interests."

Jefferson ended this remarkable letter with two reminders to Livingston. First, New Orleans was the most important spot; French control over the remaining five hundred million acres of Louisiana might provoke future irritation, but the United States simply could not live with French control over the vital port, the gateway to half the continent. Second, the American people cared about the issue. Indeed, the next election could hinge on it, though Jefferson was far too polite to state the matter so crassly. Jefferson knew how to read newspapers and had his pulse on American public opinion. To Livingston, he wrote, "Every eye in the US. is now fixed on this affair of Louisiana. Perhaps nothing since the revolutionary war has produced more uneasy sensations through the body of the nation. . . . I have thought it not amiss, by way of supplement to the letters of the Secretary of state, to write you this private one to impress you with the importance we affix to this transaction."

If, in this letter, we see some of Jefferson's personal diplomatic genius—smooth talk blended with iron will—we should also appreciate the genius of the American people and their larger system of regular elections and public discourse. In 1800–1801, ordinary Americans put Jefferson in the right place at the right time. In 1802–1803, American public opinion (and the upcoming elections) fixed his gaze on the right issue.

Some of Jefferson's triumph in winning Louisiana was no thanks to him. He had inherited an ironclad position because of Washingtonian neutrality and the ensuing Jay Treaty. Though Jefferson and his surrogates had denounced Washington's approach at the time, America's first president had wisely kept the new nation out of harm's way while Britain and France resumed their ancient conflict. In 1803, Napoleon needed to abandon his New World empire for ready cash precisely because France faced immense military and financial challenges at home, much as Washington had predicted. Jefferson could credibly threaten to "marry" Britain because Washington and Hamilton had already thawed this relationship. Jefferson could also credibly threaten to deploy America's considerable "resources" on a massive naval buildup thanks to the financial structures that Hamilton had forged and Jefferson had at first opposed. America could speak powerfully with one voice, from New England to Georgia, from the Atlantic to the Mississippi, and this, too, was thanks to earlier Publian, Hamiltonian, and Washingtonian geostrategy that Jefferson had theretofore never fully appreciated or embraced.

Slave revolts in Saint-Domingue, modern-day Haiti, had also drained Napoleon's resources; but again, no thanks to Jefferson. Adams had backed Haitian rebels, whereas Jefferson, like most southerners, was horrified by the prospect of slaves killing masters, and as president, he cut off all assistance.[49]

But Jefferson had also made his own luck. Perhaps Napoleon would never have parted with Louisiana had he been obliged to sell it to John Adams, who never loved the French, who was never loved by them, and who would likely never have sent a negotiator such as Monroe, himself a Francophile and French favorite. Perhaps, had Adams won reelection in 1800 and continued to help Haitian slaves and ex-slaves, this stance would have induced Napoleon to retaliate against, rather than reward, America. If so—if Thomas Jefferson was the only man who could have played the French so perfectly—then the American system at the turn of the century had indeed achieved a double triumph when it selected Jefferson as the man of the hour, a man who brilliantly thwarted both Adams's authoritarianism domestically and Napoleon's imperialism diplomatically. Also, Jefferson had far more credibility with western Americans than did Adams, and this credibility would help him seal the deal on the American side.[50]

By mid-1803, Jefferson had triumphed in Paris; it remained for him to win in Washington City. As a professed strict constructionist, he faced a nice set of constitutional questions. Of course, the land transfer from France to America via treaty would require the approval of two-thirds of the Senate, and payment to France would require a proper law, which the House would also need to approve. But would a constitutional amendment also be required?[51]

In mid-August, Jefferson explained his preliminary thinking to fellow strict constructionist John Breckinridge, who had been his key ally in crafting the Kentucky Resolutions in 1798 and 1799: "The Constitution has made no provision for our holding foreign territory, still less for incorporating foreign nations into our union." In having seized the once-in-a-lifetime opportunity to double America's landmass, he as president had thus "done an act beyond the Constitution." His motives were pure—he had "advanced the good of their country"—but an amendment was still necessary to legalize, *ex post facto*, *nunc pro tunc*, his extraconstitutional (unconstitutional?) improvisation.[52]

On second thought . . . an amendment would surely be time-consuming. What if Napoleon in the meantime changed his mind and yanked the deal off the table? This was a realistic concern.[53] By early September, writing to another ally, Wilson Cary Nicholas (whose daughter would later marry Jefferson's oldest grandson), the president thus seemed to narrow the question considerably. Perhaps he could make the deal with Napoleon now and lawfully hold and annex the new tract without an amendment. But surely he would need an amendment to carve new states out of the new lands. He worried about loose construction: "Our peculiar security is in the possession of a written constitution. Let us not make it a blank paper by construction."[54]

It was a noble and beautifully expressed sentiment, but by the end of the letter, he abandoned it: "I think it important in the present case to set an example against broad construction by appealing for new power to the people. If however our friends shall think differently, certainly I shall acquiesce with satisfaction."[55] *It's important to set a proper constitutional example; let's not make the Constitution a blank paper! Oh, unless our friends want to, and if so I'm totally fine with that.*

Here again we see Jefferson's brilliantly offsetting vices—his seeming hypocrisy exquisitely counterbalanced his muddled thinking: many of the grand principles he was so willing to abandon were in fact half baked and entirely worthy of abandonment.[56]

Why, after all, had he ever thought that an amendment was necessary? In the letter to Nicholas, he wrote, "The limits of the US are precisely fixed by the treaty of 1783. . . . The Constitution expressly declares itself to be made for the US. I cannot help believing the intention was to permit Congress to admit into the union new states which should be formed out of the territory for which & under whose authority alone they were then acting."[57]

This was absurd. The Constitution gave the federal government plenary power to make treaties—just as the Articles of Confederation had vested plenary treaty-making power in the old Congress. Land and sovereignty transfers were the basic stuff of treaty-making, time out of mind. Indeed, an agreement to alter legal borders lay at the center of the most notable American treaty already on the books—the 1783 Treaty of Paris, in which both France and England abandoned prior claims to the trans-Appalachian West. True, the Constitution did not expressly say "treaties of land transfer." But of course it did not say "treaties of war" or "treaties of peace" or "treaties of trade" or "treaties of amity," either. It just said "treaties" generically—treaties of all sorts. It was silly to think that the treaty-making

power under the Constitution was more limited than it had been under the Articles, under which America had acquired a clear right to
land, ceded by France, that would later become states. The Louisiana
Purchase was no different.

Jefferson in 1803 said that he "cannot help believing the intention" in 1787–1788 was only to allow new states in then existing
union land. But he provided absolutely no evidence for this odd belief. Nothing in the Constitution's text limited new states to areas
claimed by the United States circa 1787. Such language had indeed
been considered and rejected behind closed doors at Philadelphia.[58]
The 1783 Articles of Confederation had expressly guaranteed that
Canada—which of course lay outside America—could automatically
join the old Confederacy. The proposed Constitution drafted at Philadelphia did not repeat this guarantee, but simply gave unqualified
authority to the new federal government to wage wars of all kinds,
make treaties of every type, and admit new states as appropriate.

So the Constitution's text gave no support whatsoever to Jefferson. Neither did the document's enactment history. Jefferson was
not even in the country when the Great Conversation of 1788 had
unfolded; but virtually everyone in America that year wanted navigation down the Mississippi all the way to and through the mouth.
The widely reprinted *Federalist* No. 2 emphatically focused on the
Mississippi, as did much of the conversation in the Virginia Ratifying Convention. As many Americans from Washington, Hamilton,
Jay, and Madison on down surely understood that year, the best way
to secure free transit along the Mississippi was not a treaty of *navigation permission* with Spain, but a treaty of *acquisition* from Spain,
or whoever else might hold New Orleans at any moment.

Everyone in the ratification conversation thus understood that
New Orleans was not within America's existing borders, but many
Americans nevertheless openly dreamed of buying this spot or taking it by force. *Indeed, the whole geostrategic point of the Constitution
was to create a stronger union that would be in a better position to do
just that, and other things like that.* As Hamilton told Washington
in mid-1790, in a communication also shared with then secretary

of state Jefferson, "when we are able to make good our pretensions, we ought not to leave in the possession of any foreign power, the territories at the mouth of the Mississippi, which are to be regarded as the key to it."[59]

So no amendment was needed—and no amendment ever ensued—in 1803 to buy and annex Louisiana. The relevant Congressional votes were overwhelming. The Senate approved the treaty by a vote of 24 to 7; a bill establishing an Article IV provisional territorial government passed 89 to 23 in the House and 26 to 6 in the Senate; and the accompanying appropriation bill sailed through by a similar vote of 90 to 25 in the House and 26 to 5 in the Senate.[60] The entire transaction thus prevailed based on an emphatically Hamiltonian understanding of the relevant principles of constitutional interpretation. As president, Jefferson embraced all this without openly acknowledging that the New York continentalist had been right all along.[61]

In 1828, Chief Justice John Marshall, writing for a unanimous Court, briskly affirmed the obvious propriety of these principles in a case arising from Florida territory acquired by an 1819 treaty negotiated by John Quincy Adams and endorsed by President James Monroe, a Jefferson protégé. In Marshall's words, "The Constitution confers absolutely on the government of the Union, the powers of making war, and of making treaties; consequently, that government possesses the power of acquiring territory, either by conquest or by treaty. . . . If it be ceded by the treaty, the acquisition is confirmed, and the ceded territory becomes a part of the nation to which it is annexed." (The case was argued and won by Daniel Webster. Interestingly enough, all five of the main characters—Jefferson, Monroe, Adams, Marshall, and Webster—had served or would serve as secretary of state.)[62]

But what about Jefferson's narrower claim that an amendment was needed to carve one or more new states out of freshly annexed land? The obvious answer is that the text of the Article IV New State Clause said no such thing, and the Constitution's general spirit was in fact strongly anti-colonial. Americans in 1788 generally wanted new lands to be on an equal footing with old lands. That was the basic promise of the Northwest Ordinance, adopted by the old Confederation Congress even before the Constitution was ratified. Jefferson in 1803 was in fact contradicting his earlier self. The grand vision of the Ordinance—equal treatment of westerners, whose states would enter the union on equal footing—was a principle that Jefferson himself had helped shape as one of the initial architects of the Northwest Ordinance back in early 1784, before he headed off to France and apparently contracted a case of amnesia.

Jefferson's 1803 letter to Nicholas featured one other notable argument: "I do not believe it was meant that [the United States] might receive England, Ireland, Holland &c into it, which would be the case on your construction. When an instrument admits two constructions[,] the one safe, the other dangerous, the one precise the other indefinite, I prefer that which is safe & precise." But no one was arguing that America was *required* to annex Louisiana, only that the federal government could *choose* to do so. If annexing, say, Ireland, or admitting Ireland as a state, would be dangerous, then the Senate could simply say no to any treaty adding Ireland; and the House could say no to any bill making Ireland a state; and the president could say no using his foreign affairs powers and veto pen. (A later generation of constitutional conversationalists would make one more textual argument relevant to Jefferson's hypothetical: the Constitution in its Preamble and Executive Power Clause spoke of a "United States of America." Louisiana was surely within *the Americas*, but Ireland, England, and Holland were not.)

THE LOUISIANA PURCHASE CREATED VAST possibilities but also vast problems. Should slavery be allowed to spread to new parts of the territory, beyond its existing footprint in places such as New Orleans? How should the United States deal with Native tribes in this immense region?

A truly farsighted president might have seen that the possibilities could themselves be the answer to the problems. Indians had never posed an existential threat to America, but Indians allied to France or Britain were a very different story. Now that France was off the continent for good, perhaps America could create large homelands for Indians; surely there was now enough land for all, no? And perhaps America could also now open large tracts to free Blacks (and perhaps also intrepid White volunteers). Such a policy might enable states with large numbers of slaves to adopt gradual emancipation plans, à la Pennsylvania, without fear of explosive racial mixing. Under such long-range schemes, slavery would end without the immediate freeing of slaves. Rather, the unborn children of current slaves could walk free after, say, age twenty-five, and could be given homesteads (either separate from or alongside White homesteads) in some dedicated part of the Louisiana Territory—say, modern-day Nebraska or Colorado.

But Jefferson, for all his savvy, was not particularly farsighted, especially on the slavery issue. He obsessed about self-government in the present. The earth belonged to the living. Jefferson did not understand long-term borrowing and long-range capital budgeting. He himself died in debt and never freed his slaves. Franklin, Washington, and Hamilton all saw further into the future and in many ways predicted it better. Not coincidentally, all three of these more farsighted statesmen were more emphatically and honestly anti-slavery, especially late in life, than was Jefferson, who talked a good game but never did much once he rose to power. Indeed, Jefferson did less and less as time passed and as he increasingly tied himself to a pro-slavery party that he himself had created, with his eyes open (except to the extent that he managed to fool himself).

Jefferson's greatest failure in this regard came in the immediate aftermath of his greatest triumph. For all its enormity, the failure is easy to miss, because it involves something that did not happen, but that could and should have happened. Jefferson never proposed a federal statute excluding slavery from the northern part of the Louisiana lands—areas that would eventually become all or part of Oklahoma, Missouri, Kansas, Colorado, Iowa, Nebraska, Wyoming, Minnesota, the Dakotas, and Montana. Such a territorial free-soil law might have abstractly offended some elements of Jefferson's southern base but would not have threatened any entrenched practices or deeply established property rights. The South would not have been obliged to give up anything it already had. (Indeed, such a law might well have allowed slavery not just in the vicinity immediately around New Orleans, where the practice already had deep roots, but also in closely adjoining Deep South areas—say, most of modern-day Louisiana and Arkansas.) A northern Louisiana free-soil law gesturing toward a free-soil future for America as a whole would have been an entirely fitting continuation of the Northwest Ordinance, which had prohibited new slavery in federal territories north of the Ohio River acquired from France (and Britain) in America's first great diplomatic coup—the Treaty of Paris of 1783.

An imaginable 1804 law extending the Northwest Ordinance to America's new Northwest in the wake of America's latest diplomatic triumph in Paris would have been all the more fitting coming from Thomas Jefferson. For Jefferson himself, as a young dreamer, had sired the free-soil principles of the Northwest Ordinance back in the early 1780s. If anyone had the muscle, the mandate, and the moment to pull off another sweeping free-soil law, it was Thomas Jefferson in the wake of his spectacular triumph over Napoleon and over a clump of small-minded New Englanders who had opposed the Louisiana Purchase. Given that most of the immediate benefits of the purchase accrued to the South, this was Jefferson's best chance, à la Washington, to extend an olive branch to his domestic skeptics and to teach the world yet another stunning lesson about American freedom and American greatness. But Jefferson's vision and nerve failed him at this critical hour. He neglected to seize the moment, doing nothing when he could and should have done something grand.[63]

In later years, he moved off the fence—in the wrong direction. During the Missouri Compromise conversation of 1819–1820, ex-president Jefferson expressed deep anxiety about efforts to prohibit the spread of slavery into northern parts of the Louisiana Territory— efforts to do precisely what he had failed to do in 1803–1804, when doing it would have been infinitely easier. As an elder statesman,

Jefferson instead endorsed the diffusion idea—the precise opposite of the more admirable views that he had championed for the old Northwest in the 1780s. If slaves could spread west, the diffusion argument ran, then this dispersion would lower the slave density in eastern states, to the benefit of all. But only a three-year-old thinks that spreading peas around on a plate somehow lessens the overall number of peas. And surely Jefferson, of all people, knew deep down that slave masters in both the East and the West would breed more slaves—for he himself was a slave breeder, as were many of those around him. Sending slaves to the West would just spread the virus with no ultimate diminution in density—just more slaves in more places.

Freeing Blacks and then sending these *free* Blacks out west to special homesteads in special homelands would have been something quite different—yet Jefferson, tellingly, never envisioned a plan along those lines. (To extend the virus metaphor, this alternative strategy would have created large pockets of herd immunity to slavery and truly flattened the curve.) Nor did Jefferson take the much easier step of simply proposing a westward extension of the Northwest Ordinance. As president and later in retirement, he turned his active and playful mind to many problems, but not to this one.

The northern newspapers in 1801 were right. Jefferson had ridden into the Executive Mansion on the backs of slaves. He and Madison had founded a party of (White) freedom and republicanism that had slavery at its rotten core. In opposing the Sedition Act—which of course needed opposing—the two Virginians had created a coalition with a strong southern base, a base solidified by the Twelfth Amendment, which consecrated the Three-Fifths Clause. Strong actions against slavery's expansion might have risked shattering the political machine that had been built so carefully. Jefferson and Madison, consummate politicos, hesitated to do this. They had chosen their political bedfellows and made their political bed, and they would lie in it and lie on it and lie pure and simple—lie to themselves and to others about slavery. As we shall see later, Franklin and Washington—untied to any political party—had improved with age on the slavery issue.

Jefferson and Madison soured with age, betraying their own youthful anti-slavery ideals as they grew more powerful and successful. Theirs was a downward arc on slavery, an arc that most of their prominent biographers have failed to carefully trace and highlight.

THE AGED JEFFERSON'S HOSTILITY TO various efforts to limit slavery in the West also sounded in states' rights. Why, he asked, should the new state of Missouri have fewer self-determination rights on the slavery issue than any older state? Here again, Jefferson revealed himself as a man of 1776. At his worst moments, he focused more on states' rights than on human rights. Thus, he never opposed moderate sedition laws in states, even as he objected to any federal sedition law.

Indeed, deep down, Jefferson was a proto-secessionist, or at least a secession-sympathizer.[64] Each state was sovereign, free, and independent. That is what he had written in 1776 and what Americans had agreed to in 1783 before he left for Paris. But in 1788 Americans had emphatically rejected that vision. Alas, Jefferson, off in France, never got the memo. Jefferson Davis was aptly named.

Thomas Jefferson's 1803 remarks to Breckinridge—his literal partner in crime from 1798 and 1799, given that their collaboration on the Kentucky Resolutions had been technically criminal under the Sedition Act itself—reflected this strong states' rights vision. Jefferson seemed utterly nonchalant about the possibility of a future secession of western states: "The future inhabitants of the Atlantic & Mispi states will be our sons. We leave them in distinct but bordering establishments. We think we see their happiness in their union, & we wish it. Events may prove it otherwise; and if they see their interest in separation, why should we take side with our Atlantic rather than our Mispi descendants? It is the elder & the younger son differing. God bless them both, & keep them in union if it be for their good, but separate them if it be better." In early 1804, Jefferson wrote much the same thing to the famed scientist and political theorist Joseph Priestley: "Whether we remain in one confederacy, or form into Atlantic and Mississippi confederacies, I believe not very important to the happiness of either part."[65]

No one who truly understood the opening essays of Publius or Washington's Farewell Messages of 1783 and 1796 could have written anything quite so airy and insouciant. If present-minded Americans in different regions chose to separate, then future Americans on one side of the separation line might choose to "marry themselves" to, say, Prussia, while future Americans on the other side might "marry themselves" to, say, France. And then, sucked into the vortex of future European wars, Americans might find themselves on American soil fighting other Americans with no naturally defensible borders between them—with the result that Americans in general would enjoy none of the liberty benefits that Britain enjoyed thanks to her island status.

JEFFERSON'S LEAD, MARSHALL'S COMEBACK

In the fierce contest between the Virginia cousins, the early race went to Jefferson.

In 1801, he won the presidential scepter, leaving Marshall with the irksome duty of administering the official oath. Had the Horatius gambit worked, Marshall himself would have taken the presidential oath. (If our minds run to whimsy, we might even imagine an alternate universe in which Marshall, in his capacity as chief justice, administered the oath to himself. Surely if anyone knew how to wear multiple hats simultaneously—secretary of state and chief justice, fact-witness and fact-finder—it was John Marshall. Across the water, Napoleon in 1804 placed the crown on his own head rather than allowing the pope to do the honors.)

In Jefferson's first term in office, the man from Monticello triumphed, with a strong hand and a friendly smile, over continental Europe's mightiest power in a land transfer of epic proportion. The president then steered his diplomatic triumph through Congress by mere treaty and statute. Jefferson also watched with satisfaction as the Congress proposed and the states ratified a Twelfth Amendment that revised the Constitution in his own image and virtually guaranteed his reelection with the running mate of his choice. Marshall, meanwhile, was obliged to hold his fire, and indeed retreat, in *Marbury* and *Stuart*.

In the years that followed, it seemed that the future would belong to Jefferson. He named new justices to the Court. After his Washington-inspired eight years in office, his protégé James Madison replenished the federal judiciary for eight more years. After Madison, yet another Jefferson protégé, James Monroe (who, with his Virginia militia at the ready, had helped Jefferson prevail in 1801, and had then helped negotiate the Louisiana Purchase in 1803), continued to restock the judiciary for yet another eight years. With all these new Jeffersonians, Madisonians, and Monrovians on the bench, Marshall was surrounded and outnumbered in his own department. Jefferson's triumph seemed complete.

Yet things did not turn out that way. Marshall found his own younger partner and protégé—a judicial version of Jefferson's Madison—and together the two Supreme Court jurists in the main enshrined Hamilton's constitutional vision and not Jefferson's into the law books. Amazingly enough, the protégé who brilliantly teamed up with Marshall in case after case and year after year—indeed, decade after decade—was a former Jeffersonian congressman named to the Court by none other than Jefferson's own protégé, James Madison. It was an astonishing turn of events, a remarkable story.

Or perhaps we should say, a remarkable Story.

eleven

MARSHALL-STORY

I F THE REAL FATHER OF the Constitution was George Washington, and not, as modern Americans have been taught, James
Madison, then we must adjust our national narrative, our cultural
rankings, and our legal schema. Within the American pantheon,
Madison must slide down a few notches. So must Jefferson. After working closely with both men, Washington eventually and
emphatically cut them off. He did so not because he had changed
or grown senile, but because Secretary Jefferson rejected his vision
of strong unionism and robust executive power—which was the vision of the Constitution itself—and because Congressman Madison sided with Secretary Jefferson, an intimate friend and political
partner since the 1770s. Also, both Jefferson and Madison were at
times dishonest and disloyal in their dealings with Washington. In
the 1790s, Madison recanted much of what he had said and written
in the Great Debate of 1788.[1] His volte-face did, however, play well
with his Anti-Federalist Virginia base. (Madison was nothing if not
a nimble politician.) Madison's and Jefferson's generally fawning biographers—the admirable exception here being Madison's clear-eyed

profiler Richard Brookhiser[2]—often play a distraction game by try-ing to heap the blame on Hamilton, whom they paint in dark tones.[3] But on issues such as assumption, federal debt policy, the bank, the carriage tax, Freneau, the Neutrality Proclamation, Genêt, the French Revolution, Jay's Treaty, the Whiskey Rebellion, military policy, and much else, the Jefferson-Madison team was not merely at odds with Hamilton but with Washington himself.

When Jefferson and Madison eventually landed seriatim in Washington's chair, the two men came to behave more like Wash-ington himself, who on many previously contested issues—backed and advised by Hamilton—had been right all along. A national bank was constitutionally valid, as was a carriage tax. America needed to play the British card against the French (and vice versa, of course). Federal powers—tax powers, treaty powers, and so on—had to be construed sensibly and purposively, not hyper-strictly, not with a jaundiced eye, especially where the proposed exercise of such powers plausibly promoted national security. The nation needed a moderate peacetime army to supplement the militia. Deep down, President and ex-president Jefferson remained a proto-Confederate who flirted, preposterously, with the right of each state to engage in nullification and secession. Madison never followed Jefferson down these twisted disunionist rabbit holes, and did his best, after Jef-ferson's death, to hide these embarrassing parts of his friend's un-even life and legacy. (And also other embarrassing parts? The Sally Hemings part?)

In this revised saga and schema, Washington moves up not just as a towering, if taciturn, constitutionalist, but also as a gifted judge of men, spotting greatness in the likes of Hamilton, Madison, and Jefferson, and ultimately discarding the latter two for reasons that reflect well on him and reflect ill on them. Hamilton also moves up, especially during the years when he was tightly connected to Wash-ington. When Washington was not there to guide and calm his high-strung protégé and surrogate son, Hamilton's performance was far more erratic. (One general exception: Hamilton's anti-slavery ideas and actions were not always guided by Washington; in this domain, Washington was not the guider but the guided.)

How, then, does John Marshall fit into this new picture?

MARSHALL RISES. HE WAS A Washington man—first, last, always— and Washington was a Marshall man. Marshall served under Washington (though not up close) in the Revolutionary War. Later, like Washington, Marshall rose to the military rank of general, albeit within the Virginia militia and not the Continental Army. In 1788, Marshall acted as a Washington surrogate in the ratification process in their home state of Virginia. In 1798, Marshall ran for Congress at Washington's personal urging. Just as the old general was exiting public life, he encouraged the young general to enter—a metaphoric passing of the baton. (Here again, Washington showed a great eye for fresh talent.) Like Washington, Marshall was in awe of Hamilton's many gifts, shared Hamilton's national vision, and often heeded (but did not slavishly follow) Hamilton's opinions. All three—Washington, Hamilton, and Marshall—saw the French Revolution with clear eyes, unlike Jefferson, Madison, and Monroe, who wore rose-tinted glasses. In his major extrajudicial writing, Marshall was Washington's first biographer, publishing a five-volume series, *The Life of George Washington*, between 1804 and 1807. At the outset of Marshall's greatest judicial opinion, upholding a Hamiltonian national bank, the acclaimed chief justice took care to remind readers that Washington himself—a "mind[] as pure and as intelligent as this country can boast"—had emphatically backed Hamilton over Madison and Jefferson on this issue in 1791.

Reminders such as this surely did not endear Marshall to Jefferson and Madison, but they should endear him to us. More than anyone, he carried Washington's flag—the Constitution's flag—deep into the nineteenth century.

And he did so, in true Washingtonian fashion, by finding his own gifted protégé. Just as President Washington skillfully guided and deployed Treasury Secretary Alexander Hamilton, so Chief Justice Marshall guided and deployed Associate Justice Joseph Story. Both partnerships between mentor and protégé worked especially well because they combined the strengths of North and South. The Jefferson-Madison partnership (or, if we prefer to extend the comparison further, the Jefferson-Madison-Monroe partnership) was ultimately weaker because it was too narrowly Virginian: too inbred, too reactionary, too attentive to the plantations of the past and inattentive to the corporations and the factories of the future, too agrarian and insufficiently commercial and proto-industrial, ultimately more dynastic than dynamic. Also, the Marshall-Story partnership succeeded in impressive fashion because Story was himself a tireless and forceful legal thinker and doer. He was for Article III what Hamilton was for Article II.

Madison and Jefferson were politicos who always had their fingers in the wind and their eyes on the next election. Often this concentrated their minds wonderfully, as when they focused on the national need and channeled the national mood in 1800 and 1803, occasioning the death of the Sedition Act and the doubling of the national domain. But sometimes Jefferson's and Madison's political instincts led them into embarrassing parochialism, as when they pandered to economically and constitutionally illiterate Virginia extremists in the early 1790s. The Virginia duo mastered the local politics but misunderstood the national policies. (In modern jargon: Jefferson and Madison were better pols, but Hamilton was a superior wonk.) Much of Hamilton's best work arose when he aimed to please Washington alone and (what was virtually the same thing) serve the nation as a whole.

Likewise, Story's best work arose when he saw the national picture—especially the indivisible nature of the American union. Article III life tenure, which he defended passionately in his greatest constitutional opinion and in his greatest slice of constitutional scholarship, freed him from the need to placate a local base and enabled him to devote years of careful study to the Constitution itself. His ambitious three-volume exposition of the document—*Commentaries on the Constitution*, mapping and analyzing the terse text's animating purposes and overarching structures—was especially essential after living memories faded and flickered out, as members of the founding generation aged and died.

WHY MARSHALL?

John Marshall understood and expounded the Constitution better than did his main rivals—Thomas Jefferson and other self-described strict constructionists, who in fact were often remarkably loose and willful.

By the time Marshall reached the Court, America's constitutional conversation had sped along for a full forty years, but had now reached a critical juncture. The conversation that had begun in the 1760s and ripened in the 1770s had culminated in a concrete text in the late 1780s. A series of amendments had then followed in the 1790s. The task after 1800 was no longer to ponder what the text *should* say and should mean, but rather to discern what the terse text, including amendments, truly *did* say and mean, and to explain that meaning to ordinary Americans, many of whom had no firsthand knowledge of earlier epic events or had begun to forget. Of course, if what the terse text said and meant no longer made sense, America as a whole could amend the document yet again.

Amendment aside—only one amendment occurred in the first sixty years of the nineteenth century—the requisite attribute was no longer the audacity of the dreamer (Jefferson) or the acumen of the draftsman (Madison) aiming to create a new legal order. Rather, the necessary talent was the skill of the interpreter and expositor, the sober jurist who could carefully read the rules previously agreed upon and then persuasively explain their meaning and implications to others. The key questions for truly faithful constitutional interpreters in the early nineteenth century were questions such as these: What words did the document in fact use and not use? Why had the document used certain words and rejected other words? What were the overarching purposes that animated the document? What had the

American people in fact agreed to, and why had they done so when they said "yes, We do," in the pivotal year of 1788? How should the words of 1788 be read in light of the amendments of the 1790s and vice versa? To the extent that the document contained ambiguities, should the early precedents and practices that emerged in the First Congress and the Washington administration carry any weight, and if so, how much weight and what kind of weight?

In pondering these questions, John Marshall began with a huge advantage over Thomas Jefferson and many Jefferson acolytes. Marshall had played a leading role in the ratification process itself and thus had deep firsthand knowledge of the momentous constitutional conversation of 1788. The same was true of Madison, but Madison at many a turn needed to placate parochial voters and fellow politicos hungry for patronage and power. Marshall did not. As chief justice, he needed in the moment to persuade earnest and honest life-tenured associate justices—some quite dazzling, others rather dim-witted—appointed by different presidents at different times. More generally, he needed to build an enduring structure of constitutional interpretations that would stand the test of time, a matrix of expositions whose ultimate strength would derive not from any power of purse or patronage—Marshall had no such power—but wholly from historical truth and legal logic. Often the specific facts of the cases that bubbled up to Marshall's Court did not much matter. The particular disputes were merely excuses and opportunities for Marshall to pronounce sweeping constitutional principles that would govern many other situations not strictly before the Court.

By the 1810s, a pattern had emerged that offered a powerful template for subsequent constitutional interpretation. The most successful expositions and analyses of the 1780s, 1790s, and early 1800s blended big and small. They linked the panoramic and the particular; they showed how the Constitution's specific words fit into its larger structures and grand purposes. On the Decision of 1789: Madison showed the Congress how the very nature of the president's job required that he retain control over men within his own branch, how the Constitution's words "executive power" plausibly encompassed the power to fire underlings, and how its words about Senate "advice and consent" applied to appointments but not removals. On the bank: Hamilton in 1791 showed Washington how this proposed institution would serve the Constitution's overarching purposes of national security and national stability, and how the constitutional word "necessary" in context meant *conducive* or *useful* as distinct from *mathematically indispensable*. On carriage taxes: Hamilton in 1795 showed the Court how a regime of efficient taxes was absolutely crucial to the entire constitutional project, and then offered nice ways to construe the Constitution's technical word "direct" so that it would not swallow up the document's general command that "Duties, Imposts, and Excises" must be "uniform" across states. On free expression: Madison in 1798–1799 showed America how the very nature of republican government and fair elections required broad freedom to criticize incumbents, and how the First Amendment's specific words about "speech" and "press" freedom operated within the context of the American Revolution and the Great Debate of 1788, as distinct from English common law à la Blackstone. On treaties: Jefferson's 1803 allies in Congress defended what he publicly did, and thus repudiated what he privately said, by appealing to the Constitution's broad aims of national security and anti-colonialism and its specific words that sweepingly and unqualifiedly authorized "treaties" of every sort and invited "new states" from every region. The words emphatically did not say that land-acquisition treaties were off-limits or that new states had to arise within America's 1787 footprint, and attempted interpolations to that effect disserved the Constitution's overall design. (Self-described "strict constructionist" critics were simply concocting, *ex post facto*, interpretive rules and restrictions of their own invention.) On judicial review: Marshall in *Marbury* explained how a central purpose of the written Constitution was to use law and courts to limit government, and how "the peculiar expressions of the constitution"—extending "judicial power" to "all cases . . . arising under this Constitution" and affirming supremacy only of Congressional laws "in pursuance of" the Constitution—confirmed this panoramic purpose.

Early expositions had also supplemented textual and structural claims with appeals to common sense and actual practice. On the bank issue, Hamilton reminded Washington that the new Congress in its very first year of operation had already authorized a territorial corporation and had already enacted countless laws that were not mathematically indispensable. On press freedom, Madison appealed to the actual "practice in America" of broad free expression "in every state, probably," pre–Sedition Act. In the 1792 debate over presidential succession, Madison might have enjoyed more success in persuading his audience that the words "what officer" contemplated an *ex officio* ("what") annexation of power to a true "officer" (such as a cabinet officer) had he stressed the practical implications and logical entailments of the conversational circle already created by the Decision of 1789. That Decision had encouraged presidents to confide in their department secretaries; in the event of presidential death or disability it would make more sense to transfer presidential power—perhaps only briefly in the event of a temporary disability—to persons in daily communication with the president. In 1801, Horatius added an additional twist based on actual practice: the 1798 impeachment acquittal of Senator William Blount strongly reinforced the textual argument that senators were not "officers," as a rule.

MARSHALL'S MASTERPIECE WAS *McCULLOCH V. Maryland*. In legal circles, Marshall's unanimous 1819 opinion for the Court upholding the constitutionality of a national bank is generally reckoned one of the Court's three greatest moments, alongside *Marbury v. Madison* and *Brown v. Board of Education*.

But why? *McCulloch* did not (as some think *Marbury* did) invent judicial review or establish the Supreme Court as the "ultimate interpreter of the Constitution." Nor did *McCulloch* (as *Marbury* in fact did) mark a brilliant tactical pivot that helped save the Court from an impending Jeffersonian onslaught. Nor did *McCulloch* mark the end of a great moral and constitutional evil, as *Brown* did when it doomed American apartheid.

By 1819, the main constitutional controversy over the bank was effectively over. Jefferson and Madison had quietly abandoned their prior constitutional objections and now backed the bank. Thus, the substantive stakes in *McCulloch* were exceedingly small, and the ultimate judicial outcome—a victory for federal power to create a central bank—was virtually foreordained, when extremists in Maryland brought suit arguing that Madison and Jefferson had actually been right the first time around, back in 1791.

McCulloch's fame rests on Marshall's genius as a reader and writer. He used the case to do much more than uphold the bank. By example, he showed his audience—all Americans, both in the moment and for all time—how to read the Constitution both closely and holistically. In his hands, the words and music of We the People came to life. His genius as a writer was not the genius of a constitutional draftsman or dreamer—of a framer or amender. It was the genius of a democratic legal expositor carefully engaging a text written by the people and offering a compelling interpretation of that text to and for the people—an interpretation accessible to all literate Americans, both at that moment and forevermore.

Marshall thus used the case to teach Constitutional Law 101. He began the lesson by recurring to first principles: We the People— and not ordinary state governments—had ordained and established the Constitution in 1788. The document "was submitted to the people . . . assembling in convention. . . . From these conventions, the constitution derives its whole authority. . . . The government of the Union, then (whatever may be the influence of this fact on the case), is, emphatically and truly, a government of the people. In form, and in substance, it emanates from them. Its powers are granted by them, and are to be exercised directly on them, and for their benefit."

Of the people, from the people, by the people, for the people. These were words and ideas that would resonate in American history, as young Americans like Daniel Webster (one of several oral advocates who argued the bank's case in *McCulloch*) and even younger Americans like Abraham Lincoln (still a boy in 1819) would later carry the Washington-Hamilton-Marshall flag deeper into the century.

But what did any of this have to do with the case at hand and the specific issue of the bank? Marshall himself teed up this question in his nice parenthetical—"whatever may be the influence of this fact on the case." Readers did not have long to wait for Marshall's answer, which he delivered over the next few paragraphs while admitting, forthrightly, that the Constitution did not *expressly* provide for a bank or a corporation.

He opened with a fine-grained point about text and history: "There is no phrase in the instrument which, like the articles of confederation, excludes incidental or implied powers; and which requires that everything granted shall be expressly and minutely described." The Articles of Confederation had *expressly* said that Congress had no powers except those *expressly* granted. The Constitution purposefully and pointedly omitted that key word. Everyone who took part in the Great Ratification Debate of 1788 and who paid close attention—including Marshall himself, of course—had noticed this pointed omission. Indeed, Madison/Publius in *The Federalist* No. 44 had taken great pains to contrast the Articles' inclusion of the word *expressly* with the Constitution's pregnant omission of this word. Jefferson, off in France, had missed the debate.

Marshall then added another fine-grained point about text and original intent, this time about the Bill of Rights: "Even the 10th amendment, which was framed for the purpose of quieting the excessive jealousies which had been excited, omits the word 'expressly.'" In fact, Madison had himself proposed an early version of the Tenth Amendment in the First Congress. Strict states' rightists in Congress had then tried to add the word *expressly*. Their proposal was emphatically rejected by Congress, led by none other than Madison, back when he was still working closely with George Washington. As Madison had explained on the House floor in August 1789, "it was impossible to confine a Government to the exercise of express powers; there must necessarily be admitted powers by implication, unless the Constitution descended to recount every minutia."[4] Jefferson had also missed all this; he was still in France at the time.

Marshall did not quote Madison's 1789 remarks, but he did elaborate the 1789 context, reminding readers of large issues that had loomed in the background: "The men who drew and adopted this [tenth] amendment had experienced the embarrassments resulting from the insertion of this word ["expressly"] in the articles of confederation, and probably omitted it, to avoid those embarrassments." Marshall here was a smooth and understated southern gentleman. Here is what he meant by "embarrassments": *Thanks to the Articles of Confederation's inadequate authorization of Congressional power, America almost lost its War of Independence, and countless heroes died needlessly at Valley Forge and elsewhere. I would know; unlike my kinsman Jefferson, I was there. And so was Washington and so was Hamilton and so were many others who somehow survived and who later pointedly omitted the word "expressly" from the original Constitution and successfully opposed all efforts to insert it into the Bill of Rights.*

What, then, was the proper approach to constitutional interpretation, according to Marshall? "A fair construction of the whole instrument"—that is, an evenhanded interpretation of the Constitution as a whole in light of its overarching purposes. Not a *strict* construction, with an artificial thumb on the scale against federal power, but a *fair* construction—and not of just one word, but of the entire document and its overarching themes, its driving purposes, its deep structures. Why was this the right approach? Because of the very nature of the Constitution as a popular and parsimonious document—as a document that had been designed to come before the people, and that had in fact been ordained by the people, in a special way.

Here, crucially, Marshall looped back to his opening reminder that the Constitution had come before the people themselves for special ratification. A proper *People's* Constitution necessarily had to be a *short* Constitution, a document suitable for printing in full in a newspaper. Not every niggling power and application—"bank," "corporation," "carriage," and so on—could be spelled out in a popular Constitution the way it might be itemized in a certain kind of detailed and comprehensive tax code or bill of lading. A *Constitution* needed to be understood by *the people*, and proper interpretation needed to be holistic, connecting interpretive results to the big picture that the people had in fact endorsed in 1788. In Marshall's now famous formulation, "A constitution, to contain an accurate detail of all the subdivisions of which its great powers will admit, and of all the means by which they may be carried into execution, would partake of the prolixity of a legal code, and could scarcely be embraced by the human mind. *It would, probably, never be understood by the public.* Its nature [as a popular document—the people's document], therefore, requires, that only its great outlines should be marked, its important objects designated, and the minor ingredients which compose those objects, be deduced from the nature of the objects themselves."[5]

After having explained the nature of the Constitution as a popular and public document, and the kind of interpretation it therefore required—fair, holistic, practical, and logical—Marshall proceeded to explain in three simple steps what all this meant for the bank in particular. First, Americans had adopted the Constitution for national security above all else. Second, a bank was genuinely conducive to national security. Third, genuine conduciveness was the right test; the people were getting what they had in fact agreed to. Next case.

As had Hamilton back in his 1791 report to Washington, so now Marshall made the case for the bank, first and foremost, as a national security tool:

> Although, among the enumerated powers of government, we do not find the word "bank" or "incorporation," we find the great powers, to lay and collect taxes; to borrow money; to regulate commerce; to declare and conduct a war; and to raise and support armies and navies. The sword and the purse, all the external relations, and no inconsiderable portion of the industry of the nation, are intrusted to its government. . . . Throughout this vast republic, from the St. Croix to the Gulf of Mexico, from the Atlantic to the Pacific, revenue is to be collected and expended, armies are to be marched and supported. The exigencies of the nation may require, that the treasure raised in

the north should be transported to the south, that raised in the east, conveyed to the west, or that this order should be reversed.

A bank with branches and affiliates across the nation and capable of borrowing money anywhere would be useful to shuttle funds quickly to armies in the field and to suppliers of matériel, wherever on the vast continent these soldiers and suppliers might be. To be sure, a bank was only one tool that might be useful, but Congress had a choice of tools among "any appropriate means" to accomplish the main purposes for which the people had ordained the Constitution.

Modern students have been taught that Marshall rested his argument on the Constitution's Necessary and Proper Clause, but in fact he clinched the basic case for the bank before saying even a single word about that clause. He did not need the clause to add one iota to federal power. The bank would win as long as the clause did not subtract federal power already in place under the various great powers to tax, spend, regulate interstate commerce, conduct foreign affairs, wage war, and raise armies and navies.

And surely, the clause did not subtract federal power, as Marshall proceeded to demonstrate in a flurry of arguments exhibiting textual virtuosity of the highest order. Toggling now from the panoramic whole to the technical and textual nitty-gritty, Marshall showed himself a close reader, and showed others how to play the game of constitutional interpretation the right way. The Necessary and Proper Clause, he noted, appeared in a section of the Constitution *granting* Congressional power (Article I, section 8) and not a section *limiting* Congressional power (Article I, section 9). It was syntactically styled as an *affirmative* authorization rather than a *negative* prohibition: "Congress *shall have power*" to pass necessary and proper laws of a certain sort, as distinct from "Congress *shall have no power* to pass laws except those that are necessary and proper." The word "necessary" when used without qualification did not sensibly mean "absolutely necessary." Elsewhere the Constitution did use the phrase "absolutely necessary," and this pointed contrast proved that the document meant something different in the two different clauses.

Hamilton had made many but not all of these points in 1791, and Marshall did not hesitate to borrow liberally from the maestro himself. (Good lawyers and judges need not reinvent wheels; they merely need to spot them and use them. Marshall had likewise borrowed from Hamilton's *Federalist* No. 78 in explicating the judiciary's power of constitutional interpretation and enforcement in *Marbury v. Madison*.) Like Hamilton, Marshall showed that Congress had already passed countless laws that flunked the super-strict test of absolute mathematical necessity that Jefferson had tried to peddle in 1791. (Jefferson's test, Marshall proved beyond cavil, was unworkable in practice; it would render almost all federal action unconstitutional.)

Marshall also nicely turned the tables on an argument that Madison had made against the bank on the House floor and that Hamilton had not addressed in detail in 1791. Why, Madison had asked, did the Constitution explicitly authorize Congress to pass laws prohibiting counterfeiting, given that Congress already had power to coin money? Wasn't the Counterfeiting Clause proof that the Constitution frowned on broad implied powers? If a power to punish counterfeiters needed to be specifically mentioned above and beyond a power to coin money, surely the same should be true of a power to incorporate a central bank. It, too, needed to be specifically mentioned. But it was not, and so no such federal power existed, proclaimed Madison.[6]

Madison's was a stunningly clever argument—until, that is, one gave the matter a minute's thought. The argument was too clever by half. It proved too much. For if Madison was right back in 1791, Marshall in *McCulloch* showed, then virtually all federal criminal laws other than counterfeiting laws were unconstitutional. Oops. (Why then *had* the framers inserted the Counterfeiting Clause? Perhaps the clause was in fact duplicative and declaratory, in the belt-and-suspenders tradition. Or perhaps it clarified that in America, Congress, and not the president, would regulate counterfeiting. In England, anti-counterfeiting policy fell within the royal prerogative. Thus, perhaps the clause had more to do with separation of powers than federalism; it was about the line between Congress and the federal executive, not between Congress and the states.)

Marshall's masterpiece dazzled not just for its substance but for its style. Like the Constitution it expounded, Marshall's opinion was written for ordinary folk, couching Hamiltonian ideas in Jeffersonian prose. *McCulloch* was short and accessible. It contained no footnotes, no arcane legal citations. It avoided legal jargon. It used vivid and practical examples. Like the Constitution itself and like Washington's best writings—his 1783 Circular Letter, his 1789 First Inaugural, his 1796 Farewell Address—*McCulloch* was written to be published in full in newspapers. Within weeks of its release in March 1819, more than a dozen print shops in at least eight states did in fact publish the decision in its entirety.[7] Responding quickly to Virginia extremists who blasted the ruling in the *Richmond Enquirer*, Marshall himself—the former Horatius?—dashed off a remarkable series of eleven op-eds that appeared in the *Philadelphia Union* and the *Enquirer* under the pen names "A Friend to the Union" and "A Friend of the Constitution."[8] As with all the other major founding figures, Marshall was a newspaperman.

MARSHALL'S MEDIA SAVVY ALSO DROVE his major administrative reforms as chief justice. In *McCulloch*, the Court spoke with one voice—a unanimous opinion, announced by Marshall himself. This was the trademark of the Court under his judicial administration—a revolution in American judicial communication that he engineered at the outset of his tenure.

Prior to 1801, the justices had often delivered their rulings in disorganized, desultory fashion. Individual justices often spoke impromptu from the bench, or produced seriatim written opinions that were not immediately published. Lawyers and the general public had to puzzle out for themselves which legal propositions in fact commanded the support of a Court majority and why. Marshall immediately changed that. Virtually all the Court's important rulings were distilled into a collective written statement, often a unanimous opinion delivered by Marshall himself. Only seven times between 1801 and 1815 did the Court revert to the old seriatim model.[9]

In the eight years that Jefferson occupied the Executive Mansion, Marshall spoke for the Court in about a hundred cases while all associate justices combined took the lead in no more than a dozen lawsuits. (The most important in this latter group was the 1803 companion case to *Marbury v. Madison*, *Stuart v. Laird*, in which Senior Associate Justice William Paterson announced the Court's opinion.) By 1815, of the roughly three hundred occasions on which the Marshall Court had issued a collective ruling on an important matter, Marshall had announced the Court's decision over two hundred times.[10] Perhaps he did not always write these opinions himself from start to finish. Some pronouncements may have been collectively crafted and others may have been primarily drafted by specific junior colleagues. But Chief Justice John Marshall spoke for the Court, first among equals, and he managed to keep announced dissents down to a minimum.[11]

The framers and ratifiers of the Constitution had structured a system in which many voices would speak in a largish legislature, and the executive would speak with one voice—the president's. Prior to Marshall, the Supreme Court was more akin to Congress in this regard. After Marshall, the Court was more presidential. It, too, would henceforth often speak with one voice. From 1801 to 1835, that voice belonged to John Marshall, who openly dissented only once in a constitutional case (*Ogden v. Saunders* in 1827).

THIS TACTICAL ACHIEVEMENT—MARSHALL'S UNCANNY ABILITY to keep his troops together, to avoid breaking ranks—was all the more impressive given that his colleagues over time were increasingly Jeffersonian appointees of various sorts. In *Marbury* itself, Marshall had acted the role of a partisan. But that was when all his judicial colleagues were fellow Federalists appointed by George Washington and John Adams. Part of Marshall's juridical genius was his ability to execute a sweeping pivot in the ensuing years—to depoliticize, legalize, and juridify the Court by working with and winning the assent of justices appointed by emphatically non-Federalist presidents: Thomas Jefferson, James Madison, and James Monroe.

The 1812 case of *United States v. Hudson and Goodwin* provides one of the two best examples of Marshall's grand pivot. The anti-Jeffersonian chief justice silently acquiesced in a decision announced by Jefferson's first appointee, William Johnson, proclaiming that no federal common law of crimes properly existed. This was a principle dear to the heart of every Jeffersonian, a principle electrified by the Sedition Act controversy of 1798–1801. Back then, leading Federalist jurists on circuit—William Paterson most visibly—had repudiated this cherished Jeffersonian principle. On this issue, most Federalists were wrong, the Jeffersonians were right, and Chief Justice Marshall wisely cast his lot with the Jeffersonians. We should recall that, in 1798, Marshall, while running for Congress as a pro–George Washington Virginian, had been a leading Federalist who had spoken out against the Alien and Sedition Acts. Put differently, John Adams's future secretary of state—who would later become Adams's pick for the chief justice slot—had been an open critic of the ill-starred statutes that in no small measure defined Adams's own presidential tenure and legacy.

Although the Court's *Hudson and Goodwin* opinion did not carefully and compellingly elaborate the ruling's deep foundations—William Johnson was no John Marshall—several constitutional factors strongly supported the justices' bottom line. Textually, the Constitution emphatically did not give federal courts unlimited power to criminalize at will any and all conduct occurring far outside the courtroom itself. Of course, as *McCulloch* would later make clear, not everything in the Constitution was expressly itemized. But implied federal judicial power to criminalize infinitely would have warped rather than served the document's basic structure. Strangely, unelected federal courts would have had vastly more power to deprive citizens of basic liberty than did elected federal lawmakers. (Congress generally enjoyed power to regulate and criminalize conduct only if the conduct implicated some identifiable pocket of federal concern, such as national security, foreign affairs, interstate commerce, territorial governance, or federal spending.) Unlike a national bank system or a federal tax code, an unlimited federal-common-law-of-crimes regime would bear no close connection to the core issues of national security and national solvency that had driven the 1788 ratification process. Also—and crucially—a regime in which unelected judges could throw ordinary Americans in prison (or pronounce death sentences upon them? what were the limits?) without any vote whatsoever by the House or Senate would surely have threatened individual and collective liberty drastically more than, say, a bank law or a tax law duly enacted by Congress. Open-ended federal criminalization based on conduct that Congress had never targeted, backed by penalties that Congress had never authorized and capped, would have improperly sidestepped both the people, as represented in the House, and the states, as represented in the Senate. In cases where, as in the sedition controversy, the criminalized conduct might lie perilously close to the boundaries of individual constitutional rights, the sidestepping of Congress would be especially problematic, even if federal judges convinced themselves that their judicially crafted sedition code did not actually cross the boundary. After all, Congress, in theory, might have a more libertarian view of the boundary's true location. In the domain of federal criminal law, the Constitution's structure generally promised that Americans would enjoy the benefit of the most libertarian branch of the federal government, whichever branch that might be on a given issue.[12]

Johnson's opinion for the Court said only some of this, but it did get the bottom line right. Federal judges had no proper business punishing Americans without Congressional authorization. Along the way, Johnson said one thing that was plainly wrong: "The powers of the general Government are made up of concessions from the several states—whatever is not *expressly* given to the former, the latter *expressly* reserve" (emphasis added). As we have seen, the twice-mentioned "expressly" was precisely the wrong word—a word that the Constitution emphatically and pointedly omitted, twice:

first in Article I in 1787–1788 and again in the Tenth Amendment in 1789–1791. It was a South Carolinian—Thomas Tudor Tucker—who tried, unsuccessfully, to add this word to the Tenth Amendment back in 1789. Johnson, too, was a South Carolinian.[13] Unduly strong states' rights rhetoric was dear to many South Carolinians long before that state's challenges to federal authority in the Nullification Crisis of 1832–1833 and the Secession Winter of 1860–1861.

Marshall, of course, emphatically rejected the idea that the federal government had only express power and thus lacked fairly implied powers. But he wisely kept mum in *Hudson and Goodwin* and let Jefferson's South Carolinian have his moment in the sun. Seven years later, when the time was right, Marshall's *McCulloch* opinion smoothly corrected Johnson's slip-up but did not embarrass Johnson by openly citing and disavowing the awkwardly worded 1812 sentence. Marshall executed his maneuver so gracefully that Johnson himself, and every other justice, agreed to join the chief's *McCulloch* ruling. Marshall's opinion thus stressed that the *McCulloch* Court was "unanimous"—a word that notably had not appeared in *Hudson*[14]—in upholding Congress's power to create a "bank" and a "corporation," words that he also stressed did not expressly appear in the Constitution.

The second great example of Marshall's pivot—transcending partisan division and uniting justices of all sorts—came at the end of his tenure and from his own pen. In 1833, a case captioned *Barron v. Baltimore* reached the Court. John Barron, a wharf owner, argued that the City of Baltimore had violated the federal Constitution by swallowing up some of his real estate without compensating him for his loss. Narrowly framed, the issue involved the Fifth Amendment's rule that "private property shall [not] be taken for public use without just compensation." Did this clause, couched as it was in the passive voice, limit state and local governments, or only federal officialdom?

As was his style, Marshall saw and explained the universe in this grain of sand. The issue, he understood, ranged far beyond the Takings Clause. Apart from the First Amendment, which referred explicitly to the federal government—"*Congress* shall make no law" of a certain sort—the Constitution's early amendments generally used the passive voice. So the question at hand involved virtually the entirety of the Bill of Rights. Did the various rights in the Second through Eighth Amendments—rights to bear arms, to be free from unreasonable searches, to be criminally tried in public and by an impartial jury, to be immune from double jeopardy and unusually cruel punishment, and so on—apply only against federal officials, or against all governments? If the Court sided with Barron and against Baltimore, federal courts could presumably invalidate state and local laws and practices across a wide range of matters not otherwise implicating national security or the interests of sister states.

In *Hudson and Goodwin*, individual rights and states' rights had worked together to defeat federal power. Now, individual rights and states' rights tugged in different directions. Speaking for a unanimous Court, Marshall in *Barron* chose states' rights. He was right to do so, and once again, he offered a compelling constitutional exposition.

As in *McCulloch*, he began with constitutional first principles, as trumpeted in the Constitution's opening words, reflecting the epic events of 1788 in which young Marshall himself had played a notable role: "The constitution was ordained and established by the people of the United States." In *McCulloch*, Marshall had used this fact to explain proper rules of constitutional interpretation, rules that in that case resulted in a victory for federal authority. But now, Marshall elaborated the other side of the coin.

The people of America in 1788 had ordained the Constitution of the United States

> for themselves, for their own government, and not for the government of the individual states. Each state established a constitution for itself, and in that constitution, provided such limitations and restrictions on the powers of its particular government, as its judgment dictated. The people of the United States framed such a government for the United States as they supposed best adapted to their situation and best calculated to promote their interests. The powers they conferred on this government were to be exercised by itself; and the

limitations on power, if expressed in general terms, are naturally, and, we think, necessarily, applicable to the government created by the instrument. They are limitations of power granted in the instrument itself; not of distinct governments, framed by different persons and for different purposes.

Having begun panoramically (as in *McCulloch*), Marshall quickly switched (as in *McCulloch*) to a close textual analysis that confirmed his panorama. Like Amendments II through VIII, Article I, section 9 used the passive voice: "No Bill of Attainder or ex post facto law shall be passed." This section 9 rule limited only the federal government, which is why, Marshall explained, a *separate* section—Article I, section 10—expressly provided that "No State shall . . . pass any Bill of Attainder [or] ex post facto law." When the Constitution meant to regulate states, Marshall explained, the document generally said so quite plainly, by using words such as "No State shall."

Most of the time, the *federal* Constitution focused on empowering, structuring, and limiting the *federal* government. Unless otherwise specified, the Constitution was a document of federal governance addressing federal concerns such as foreign affairs, national security, national solvency, interstate commerce, and territorial governance, as distinct from internal state matters. Had the framers of the Bill of Rights meant to apply their rules about fair trials, government snooping, and so on, against states, the document would not have spoken, as it did, in the passive voice à la Article I, section 9, but in the same affirmative language as Article I, section 10. The early amendments would have said, "No state shall . . ." (When, in the 1860s, Americans did decide that states should henceforth abide by the principles of the first eight amendments, they did indeed use the words "No state shall" in section 1 of the Fourteenth Amendment. And they did so in express reliance upon Marshall's opinion in *Barron*, which was repeatedly invoked by the amendment's leading sponsor, Congressman John A. Bingham of Ohio.)[15]

Marshall closed his short opinion by returning to his panoramic picture. Recalling his own first moments on history's center stage, he linked the amendments of 1789–1791 to the Great Ratification Debate of 1788, when he and Madison had worked together as Washington's men. The amendments, he reminded readers, had emerged as an olive branch to Anti-Federalists who in 1788 had expressed anxiety about the federal Leviathan being conjured into existence. The amendments thus aimed to limit federal and only federal officialdom. (Congressman Madison had wanted to go further, but he had lost; his proposed amendment limiting states—an amendment that had indeed featured the words "no state shall"—had failed to pass the Senate, which had acted to safeguard state governments and states' rights in the new federal system.)[16] Were the Court now to use these amendments to assert power over states, this new power grab by federal judges would be a perfidious bait-and-switch in violation of the deep principles of the Tenth Amendment that had also been part of this early amendment package.

"It is universally understood, it is a part of the history of the day," Marshall reminded his audience—many of whom had not been eyewitnesses or participants at the Founding, now more than forty years in the past—

> that the great revolution which established the constitution of the United States, was not effected without immense opposition. Serious fears were extensively entertained, that those powers which the patriot statesmen, who then watched over the interests of our country, deemed essential to union, and to the attainment of those invaluable objects for which union was sought, might be exercised in a manner dangerous to liberty. In almost every convention by which the constitution was adopted, amendments to guard against the abuse of power were recommended. [The Massachusetts "yes, but" compromise.] These amendments demanded security against the apprehended encroachments of the general government—not against those of the local governments. In compliance with a sentiment thus generally expressed, to quiet fears thus extensively entertained, amendments were proposed by the required majority

in congress, and adopted by the states. These amendments contain no expression indicating an intention to apply them to the state governments. This court cannot so apply them.

In *McCulloch*, Marshall sided with federal power; in *Barron*, with states' rights. Both times, he reached the right answer. Both times, he spoke for a unanimous Court. Both times he spoke clearly and compellingly to his fellow citizens in a brisk opinion suitable for a newspaper audience. Unlike Thomas Jefferson, John Marshall was not a narrow ideologue. He was a close reader and a grand expositor of the Constitution, able to both unify the Court and edify the country.

AMONG THE BRETHREN, MARSHALL METAPHORICALLY took lemons and made lemonade—and did so, literally, by serving Madeira. The justices had to sit en banc in the national capital city, but only for a few weeks a year. The rural capital site of Washington offered few amenities. Marshall thus encouraged his colleagues to live together in a single boardinghouse and to socialize with one another. Every bit as cordial and hospitable as his presidential cousin, he presided over meals and conversations with charm and grace and good wine. He created a tight conversational circle among the justices, much as Washington had tried to do among his department heads.

Given the strong personal and political clash between Hamilton and Jefferson, Washington had only mixed success in the early 1790s cabinet. Washington's successor—Adams—enjoyed far less cabinet success, and Adams himself deserved much of the blame. He spent too much time away from the national seat, rusticating on his Massachusetts farm, and when back in the capital he did not always behave well. Jefferson once regaled a friend with the gossipy tidbit that Adams "sometimes decided things against his [cabinet] council by dashing & trampling his wig on the floor. This only proves . . . that he had a better heart than head."[17]

Jefferson boasted that he himself had developed an excellent conversational circle at the top of his own administration:

> All matters of importance or difficulty are submitted to all the heads of departments composing the cabinet; sometimes by the President's consulting them separately & successively as they happen to call on him; but in the gravest cases by calling them together, discussing the subject maturely, and finally taking the vote, on which the President counts himself but as one. So that in all important cases the Executive is, in fact, a Directory, which certainly the President might controul, but of this there was never an example [in my] administration.[18]

Marshall's conversational style resembled his cousin Jefferson's. The Court's small size and its members' life tenure also worked to the chief's advantage. The House was far too large for a true conversation among all its members, on or off the floor, and the rapid turnover among its members made it hard to establish enduring conversational connections. Less than a fifth of the members of the inaugural House in 1789 remained in the House a decade later.[19] The Senate was smaller and its members served for six years, but the Court was even smaller, tighter, and more enduring.

Marshall himself encouraged this endurance both by his own example—staying in office for more than thirty-four years—and by his good grace and good wine. He made service on the Court more joyous and enjoyable. (John Adams was not always fun to be around. John Marshall was.) Shortly after joining the Court, young Joseph Story, who sorely missed his bride, wrote her to describe life with and under Marshall: "The Judges live here with perfect harmony, and as agreeably as absence from friends and from families could make our residence. Our intercourse is perfectly familiar and unconstrained, and our social hours when undisturbed by the labors of law, are passed in gay and frank conversation, which at once enlivens and instructs."[20] Prior to Marshall's ascension, no chief justice had served for more than six years. Of the twelve men who reached the Court before Marshall, five left early, despite their entitlement to serve for life. By contrast, only one of the eleven justices named to the Court on John Marshall's watch would opt to leave.[21]

The slow trickle at which new members arrived on the Court further solidified the strength of the conversational circle that Marshall built. Each new man, one at a time, joined a conversation already in progress, and Marshall could devote his attention to the proper socialization of each newcomer as he arrived.[22] There was never a mass turnover on the Court, as had happened in the House in 1801, with Jefferson's self-proclaimed revolution of 1800.

And it was Marshall's circle. He was the chief justice. He did not owe his position to any majority vote of his colleagues. He could never be displaced by a rival jurist the way any House leader or Senate leader might at any moment be ousted from the chair, at least in theory. He presided over his circle every bit as much as Thomas Jefferson presided over his executive-branch cabinet circle. To be sure, he had not picked the men on the Court; nor could he fire them at will. But in general he made them his own,[23] with wit, logic, charm . . . and time. Unlike Jefferson and all the presidents who followed—and who also followed Washington's two-term template—John Marshall had decades in the presiding chair of his branch.

BEYOND THE BOARDINGHOUSE, MARSHALL ALSO presided over a revolution in the conversational relationship between the Court and the country. *McCulloch*—a major opinion on a topic of broad public interest designed for immediate newspaper publication and followed by Marshall's own anonymous op-eds—was part of that revolution, but only part.

Another part was purely stylistic and sartorial. (Thomas Jefferson had no monopoly on the politics of style in the early nineteenth century.) Pre-Marshall, judges at both the state and federal levels often wore grand garb to signal their elevated status. Back in 1761, Thomas

Hutchinson and his colleagues on the provincial Superior Court had bedecked themselves in "new fresh Robes of Scarlet English

cloth" and "immense Judicial Wigs."[24] America's first chief justice, John Jay, wore no wig but nonetheless favored fancy judicial apparel, as nicely captured by the acclaimed artist Gilbert Stuart in 1794.

Famed for his easygoing manner and unpretentious demeanor, Marshall wore a simple black robe—small-r republican outerwear less apt to provoke envy or ridicule in a culture that was increasingly egalitarian (among Whites). Here, too, Marshall showed himself as a keen match for his kinsman, offering his fellow Americans Hamiltonian substance with Jeffersonian style.

Yet another part of the conversational revolution in the Age of Marshall involved a subtle shift away from casual judicial commentary on contemporary political issues. Pre-Marshall justices had routinely aimed to engage citizens while riding circuit, especially via remarks to federal grand juries convened by the circuit jurists, remarks often reprinted in local newspapers. These secular sermons had tried to provide broad civics lessons to the citizenry, as part of the federal judiciary's outreach into the hinterlands,[25] but the justices had at times strayed into partisan and political thickets. The early justices were all Federalists, and they routinely failed to appreciate that many Americans did not share their affiliations and assumptions, some of which came to be seen as unduly partisan.

In 1804–1805, one of the impeachment charges brought against Associate Justice Samuel Chase grew out of a hot-blooded grand-jury address that he had delivered in Baltimore in 1803, which

House impeachers condemned as "an intemperate and inflammatory political harangue."[26] Still reeling from the assault on judicial independence inherent in the 1802 repeal of sixteen federal circuit judgeships, Chase had railed against a recent "change of the state constitution . . . allowing universal suffrage." Chase thundered that this change would "certainly and rapidly destroy all protection to property, and all security to personal liberty; and our republican constitution will sink into a mobocracy, the worst of all possible governments."[27] The Senate acquitted Chase, but Marshall wisely redirected his colleagues' sermonizing into opinions of the Court, which avoided some of the vices of the earlier grand-jury "harangues." The opinions emerged from the Court collectively—a Court that reflected both parties, as time passed—and these opinions centered more on the deep legal issues on the docket than on the hot political issues of the moment.[28]

Most important of all, Marshall's tenure in office witnessed dramatic improvements in official Supreme Court reporting practices. Inadequate judicial reports had long bedeviled the fledgling American constitutional project at both the local and continental levels. How could ordinary folk even begin to understand what their judges were doing in the name of constitutions and constitutionalism if the citizenry had no handy, timely, comprehensive, and permanent access to the relevant legal advocacy and judicial pronouncements?

Back in the winter of 1760–1761, no official Court reporter had existed to transcribe the oral arguments of James Otis, Jeremiah Gridley, and Oxenbridge Thacher, or to publish whatever the five Superior Court judges might issue in writing or pronounce orally. Young Adams had scribbled and then polished an account of the oral argument, but apparently decided not to publish this abstract. (In 1773, a rogue apprentice, acting without Adams's authorization, leaked it to a local newspaper, *The Massachusetts Spy*.) Adams never even attended the Court's second and critical hearing in November 1761. Happily for history, young Josiah Quincy Jr. did witness this event and took notes. But Quincy's write-up remained unpublished until the mid-1860s—more than a century after the event.

By the early 1810s, fully fifty years after the writs case, Americans still lacked timely and complete access to most state and federal judicial rulings. Massachusetts and New York had official Court reporters, but the United States did not. Beginning in 1804, a system of informal reports began to issue compiling US Supreme Court decisions. The event met with public approval, but the private reporting system was slow and erratic.[29]

Things finally changed in the spring of 1817, almost precisely the midpoint of Marshall's judicial tenure. Prodded by both Chief Justice Marshall and Associate Justice Story, Congress enacted a bill to regularize the reporting of Supreme Court decisions.[30] The statute provided for a salaried official reporter, to be appointed by the Court itself. The law directed the reporter to publish Court decisions within six months of their release and to furnish multiple permanent copies to various government officials and the Library of Congress. Other hardbound copies, of course, would be available for purchase by private persons and public organizations. Americans could now begin to read and respond to contemporaneous and accessible compilations of the pronouncements of John Marshall and his colleagues. More than ever before, the Court en banc was beginning to converse with the citizenry.

FOUNDING SON

America's last founding father forged a particularly close bond with one of America's first founding sons.

In his own words, Joseph Story was the son of "a sturdy Whig [who] took an early part in all the revolutionary movements." Joseph's father, Elisha, "was one of the Indians who helped to destroy the tea in the famous Boston exploit." Later, Elisha "fought at Concord and Lexington, pursuing the British troops at every step during their retreat . . . and was in the trenches as a volunteer at the battle of Bunker Hill." He "was with General Washington during the campaign of 1777 in the Jerseys." Elisha "entertained the highest admiration of General Washington, and of John Adams, though in the political controversies between the latter and Mr. Jefferson, he took side with Mr. Jefferson."[31]

Unlike every major character in our constitutional drama thus far, Joseph Story was born after 1776. (His precise date of birth was September 18, 1779.) He never lived as a British subject; nor could he rely on personal memory when pondering the significance of the Revolution and the Constitution. In these respects, he is the first character in our narrative who was like us.

But not fully—and not just because he lived and died in an America where women rarely succeeded in making their voices heard in political discourse, where no women voted (apart from a brief blip in New Jersey), where millions of Blacks groaned in bondage, and where many tribal Indians were not citizens but enemies. These enormous exclusions—for so they seem in retrospect—surely constrained what Story was easily able to read and hear and thus think. Still, in one key respect, Story enjoyed a huge advantage over our generation, enabling him to espy things that are harder for us to see. He had intimate and extended access to the last leading character of 1788 still in office, John Marshall, who in turn was Washington's protégé, Jefferson's cousin, Hamilton's friend, Madison's ratification partner, and Adams's main man.

With this access, combined with his own native intelligence and astonishing drive, Story as a young man could hope to become, and in middle age in fact did become, a great chronicler—his generation's greatest chronicler—of the American Constitution. Above and beyond his work on the Court, he could hope to write, and in fact did write, the most ambitious and intelligent general exposition of the Constitution post-Publius and pre-Reconstruction.[32] He could and did use his inimitable access to Marshall's stories, Marshall's wisdom, Marshall's papers, and Marshall's network to record and recount for founding sons and daughters everywhere what in fact had been said and done, and why, in the Great Debate of the 1780s and the great consolidation thereafter.

Marshall had every incentive, in turn, to deputize Story. When Story joined the Court in November 1811 to fill its seventh seat—a seat that had been added in 1807—he was barely thirty-two years old, the youngest justice ever, and a great bet to outlast Marshall himself and everyone else on the bench.

But was Story open to being Marshall's deputy? On the one hand, Story had been a Jeffersonian congressman, and was named to the Court by Jefferson's junior partner, James Madison. On the other hand, he hailed from Adams's home state of Massachusetts, the heartland of the once dominant Federalist Party. His father, Elisha, had been a proud Son of Liberty alongside Samuel and John Adams. Marshall himself had worked well with President Adams, and young Story was in many ways a superior version of Adams—Harvard trained, scholarly, indefatigable, ambitious, public-minded, much like Adams, but with more acumen and less attitude. (Duties of public service obliged Adams to spend many years of his life far from Abigail, and these long bouts of separation surely did not improve his disposition.) The only other Federalist appointee on the Court when Story joined was Bushrod Washington, tapped by Adams in 1798. Counting Story, Washington was the Court's third youngest member. If Marshall could somehow cultivate and convert Story, the Marshall-Washington-Story axis would have a good chance of dominating the Court for years, perhaps decades.

How could Story be cultivated and converted? Not with patronage. Once on the Court, he already had his dream job, and the appointment power generally resided in the president and not the chief justice. Rather, Marshall could and did use the tools and the resources within his own personal and professional arsenal—grace, charm, facts, and logic—to win Story over.

Young Story was a skilled politician who had risen meteorically. While still in his twenties he had served in Congress, and in early 1811 he became Speaker of the Massachusetts Assembly. This was a position of great prestige in early nineteenth-century New England—the very seat that Colonel James Otis Sr. had once held, and that James Otis Jr. had coveted. Other Bay State notables who had held this high seat included James Warren, John Hancock, Nathaniel Gorham, Samuel Allyne Otis, Artemis Ward, Theodore Sedgwick, and Harrison Gray

Otis. (Several of these predecessors were members of the Otis dynasty. Warren was the Colonel's son-in-law; Samuel was the Colonel's son—that is, James Jr.'s younger brother; and Harrison was Samuel's son.)

Leaving his Speakership for the bench, Story opted for a life of the mind—a life of reading and writing over politicking and electioneering. Like Alexander Hamilton before him, Story was an intellectual powerhouse and prodigy. Whereas Hamilton was a frenetic doer and builder, perfectly suited for Article II, the Constitution's branch of action and administration (and armies!), Story was a doer and builder in a different way, far better suited to Article III. Somehow, the American system had yet again managed to place true talent on just the right governmental pedestal.

Concretely, Joseph Story sought to build an enduring legal and scholarly edifice as a scholar-judge in the tradition of Britain's William Blackstone, America's James Wilson, and New York's James Kent. Once he had life tenure, Story never again needed to pander to the crowd, any crowd. Rather, he aimed to state correctly the factual and legal truth of every matter that came before him as a judge and that crossed his mind as a scholar. Like Hamilton, he craved fame above all—not the celebrity or popular adulation of the moment, à la James Otis or Patrick Henry, but the enduring acclaim that could only be bestowed by history. To win that acclaim, he did his best to get his law and history straight.

He often failed—trying to do too much, too fast. But he had the right attitude as an open-minded and humble seeker of truth. In 1818, he sent a charming unsolicited letter to Harrison Gray Otis, a former political rival, confessing that some of his own earlier views had been wrong: "Many opinions are taken up & supported at the moment, which at a distance of time, when the passions of the day have subsided, no longer meet our approbation. He who lives a long life & never changes his opinions may value himself upon his consistency; but rarely can be complimented for his wisdom. Experience cures us of many of our theories; & the results of measure often convince us against our will that we have seen them erroneously in the beginning."[33]

Despite his various missteps and mistakes, Joseph Story as both a judge and a legal scholar laid a strong foundation for later generations to improve and build upon.

JOSEPH STORY WAS NOT, TO put it mildly, President James Madison's first choice to fill the Court vacancy created by the death of William Cushing in mid-September 1810. In his two terms in office, President Jefferson had placed three men on the seven-member Court. Now, at long last, his junior partner had the chance to give the Jeffersonians a decisive majority at the apex of the federal judicial pyramid. Although formally retired, Jefferson followed the matter from Monticello with an intensity that belied his public image of detachment. (In this, ex-president Jefferson behaved more like ex-secretary Hamilton in quasi-retirement than ex-president Washington in true retirement.)

Within days of hearing the news of Cushing's demise, Jefferson dashed off a pair of letters to men in his and Madison's inner circle. First, he penned a note to Caesar Augustus Rodney, whom he had named attorney general and who still held that post under President Madison: "The death of Cushing is therefore opportune as it gives an opening for at length getting a Republican majority on the supreme bench. Ten years has the Anti-civism of that body been bidding defiance to the spirit of the whole nation, after they had manifested their will by reforming every other branch of the government." Next, Jefferson wrote to another acolyte and holdover cabinet member, Treasury Secretary Albert Gallatin: "I observe old Cushing is dead. At length then we have a chance of getting a republican majority in the supreme judiciary. For ten years has that branch braved the spirit & will of the nation, after the nation had manifested it's will by a compleat reform in every branch depending on them. The event is a fortunate one, and so timed as to be a godsend to me." As this last line betrayed, Jefferson was taking all this quite personally. (His cousin had definitely gotten under his skin; he was particularly incensed by Marshall's pro-defendant rulings in 1807, when Jefferson's minions unsuccessfully prosecuted Aaron Burr for treason in connection with Burr's shady behavior in America's western backcountry.)[34]

Jefferson's cruelest and coldest letter went to his best friend, who, he knew, would forgive the cold cruelty, as this friend had always forgiven Jefferson's other imperfections. "Another circumstance of congratulation is the death of Cushing," Jefferson wrote Madison.[35]

It was understood that the Bay Stater Cushing would need to be replaced by another New Englander, especially given the importance of circuit riding; much of a justice's duties required intimate familiarity with the law of his home circuit. There were not many qualified northeastern Republicans to pick from, but Jefferson warned Madison in particular about a former Massachusetts congressman who in 1808–1809 had gone wobbly on Jefferson's embargo policies, which had strangled New England shipping and proved hugely unpopular in and around Boston: "Story . . . deserted us on that measure & carried off the majority. . . . [He] is unquestionably a tory & . . . too young."[36]

It has been said that Americans can usually be relied on to do the right thing—after trying everything else. This was Madison's experience in filling the Cushing seat. First, he named Jefferson's former attorney general, Levi Lincoln, who won Senate confirmation but declined the post for health reasons. Madison then tried Connecticut's Alexander Wolcott. A legal mediocrity, Wolcott was best known for having strictly enforced economically devastating embargo laws, provoking nearly as much resentment in New England as had Charles Paxton back in the 1760s. Although Madison's party dominated the Senate by a four-to-one ratio, Wolcott lost his Senate confirmation vote in a landslide, 24 to 9. Back in Boston, the hub of the circuit at issue, Benjamin Russell's *Columbian Centinel* spoke for many: "Even those most acquainted with modern degeneracy were astonished at this abominable nomination."[37]

Madison then turned to a name likely to prove more popular in Boston: Adams. The former president's son, John Quincy Adams, won easy confirmation, but turned down the job. This was a

fortunate development. JQA was law trained, but not a gifted constitutional thinker. (For example, in the Louisiana Purchase episode, he
had embraced the dubious strict-constructionist position that a constitutional amendment was somehow necessary. In 1820, long after
Hudson, he clung to the propriety of a federal common law of crimes.
Both instincts were wrong, but in opposite directions—the first in
ignoring what the Constitution did say about treaties; the second
in ignoring what the Constitution did not say about judicial power
and criminal law. On Louisiana, he read federal power too strictly
when national security was at stake and personal liberty was not at
risk; on *Hudson*, he read federal power too broadly when national
security was not at stake and personal liberty was at risk.[38]) He would
have brought a lot of family baggage to the Court, which already had
Washington's nephew as its second most senior member.

Finally, in desperation, Madison did the right thing, ignored Jefferson, and named the best man for the job. Modern scholars have
often overrated Madison and his contributions to American constitutionalism, but on this specific point, history has not done Madison
justice. When out of power, Jefferson talked about judicial independence, but when in power, he never named a great and independent
jurist to the bench because he was not, in truth, looking for judicial
independence and excellence. He sought party loyalism. Madison,
on the other hand, was more genuinely committed to the idea of
impartial experts trying to govern impartially. In *The Federalist* Nos.
10 and 43, he had dreamed of "judges" able to overcome "bias" and
had celebrated "the impartiality of judges." In the person of Joseph
Story, Madison (albeit in desperation) truly found a judge who aimed
for impartiality—an early Jeffersonian open to hearing what John
Adams's appointees John Marshall and Bushrod Washington had to
say. Just as Adams had admirably picked a chief justice who had previously crossed party lines and criticized the Sedition Act, so now
Madison picked a young justice unafraid to question partisan dogma.*

---

*The insularity of the pool from which Madison was picking—genteel New England
Jeffersonians—is reflected in the interesting fact that all of Madison's picks were
in-laws of various sorts. Story's wife, née Sarah Waldo Wetmore, was the niece of

MASSACHUSETTS MEETS VIRGINIA (AGAIN)

Marshall and Story made a great judicial team—a Virginia Federalist paired with a Massachusetts Republican.

Virginia and Massachusetts, Massachusetts and Virginia: much of America's constitutional history from the 1760s through the 1830s can be seen as a story of various partnerships—some smashingly successful, others less so—between men from America's two oldest and proudest states.

In the 1760s, firebrands James Otis and Patrick Henry worked in tandem, even though they never met, to rouse America to resist British oppression. In 1774 and again in 1787, Samuel Adams notably reached out to his Virginian kindred spirit Richard Henry Lee. In 1776 and for most of the ensuing decade, John Adams famously collaborated with Thomas Jefferson at Philadelphia and in Europe. From 1797 to 1801, the American system once again paired these two, this time with much less success. At the end of their lives, these two frenemies reunited in epistolary conversation and somehow managed to die in their separate states on the fiftieth anniversary of the Declaration of Independence—making it impossible for posterity to think deeply about the one without pondering the other. Back in 1775, Adams had also worked well with the greatest Virginian of all—His Excellency—and the two men again paired up between 1789 and 1797. Both times, the relationship worked well enough, if at a distance. In his second presidential term, Virginia's Madison chose as his vice president Massachusetts's Elbridge Gerry. In four

---

Wolcott's wife, née Lucy Waldo. Levi Lincoln's wife was the former Martha Waldo, Lucy's and Sarah's third cousin (once removed, in Sarah's case). All three women directly descended from Deacon Cornelius Waldo Sr., who died in 1701. John Quincy Adams's ties to this clan were more tenuous, but there were Waldos in his family tree, although not in his direct lineage. Note that Madison's other appointee to the Court, Gabriel Duvall, is today sometimes seen as "the most insignificant justice in history." The other contender for this title, Thomas Todd, was a Jefferson appointee. See David P. Currie, "The Most Insignificant Justice: A Preliminary Inquiry," *University of Chicago Law Review* 50 (1983): 466; Frank Easterbrook, "The Most Insignificant Justice: Further Evidence," ibid., 481.

of America's first seven presidential elections, the system produced a Virginia president and a Massachusetts vice president, or vice versa. (In the other three elections, a Virginian won the presidency and the second slot went to a New Yorker—Aaron Burr once and George Clinton twice.) In addition, Adams made Marshall his protégé, and Monroe later tapped John Quincy Adams as his chief minister.

Virginia's Marshall and Massachusetts's Story were not the only men on the Court, of course, but they were the intellectual leaders and most powerful penmen on and off the bench. Between them, they sat for more than sixty-eight years. No chief justice in history has exceeded Marshall's tenure in office, and only a few justices have served longer than Story, barely.

WHAT MADE MARSHALL AND STORY—WHAT made the Marshall Court—great? Some revisionist scholars have sought to topple them from their pedestals, challenging the generally accepted narrative that has placed them high in the legal pantheon.[39]

The constitutional significance of the Marshall Court cannot be fully measured simply by tallying the number of statutes, federal and state, that the Court invalidated in the name of the terse text of the US Constitution. Only once did Marshall's Court purport to invalidate a significant Congressional statute, and that purported invalidation, in *Marbury*, was a mirage. It was also pre-Story.

True, the Court did strike down state statutes in various landmark cases. In *McCulloch*, the Court not only unanimously upheld the national bank, but unanimously struck down Maryland's clumsy effort to destroy the bank. In a later case, *Osborn v. Bank of the United States*, the Court reiterated *McCulloch* when the state of Ohio tried to emulate Maryland. In the 1810 case of *Fletcher v. Peck*, in which Story came before the Court as a lawyer for the winning side, the Marshall Court notably read the Article I, section 10 Contract Clause broadly to protect private property rights. Even though shady Georgia lawmakers had corruptly sold state land to insider investors at sweetheart prices, a deal was a deal. The state had no right to renege and snatch the land from innocent third parties who had bought their lots at fair value from the original investors. In 1819, the same year as *McCulloch*, Marshall and Story teamed up to lead the Court in striking down another high-profile state legislative assault on private property. Like *Fletcher*, *Dartmouth College v. Woodward* pivoted on the Contract Clause, which the Court once again read broadly. Before the Revolution, Dartmouth College had received a charter to operate a nonprofit educational institution, and the independent state of New Hampshire thereafter confirmed this charter. The charter was a valid contract, and thus, the Court ruled, New Hampshire lawmakers could not, decades later, simply revoke the charter and grab the school for their own purposes.

To dwell on these invalidations, important as they were, would be to miss the true significance of the Marshall Court. *McCulloch* did not *invalidate* any Congressional law, but it surely did *legitimize* what Congress had done by emphatically and unanimously ruling that the bank was proper and that constitutional objections (such as Jefferson's and Madison's in 1791) were poppycock—and it did all this in a carefully reasoned opinion that could be understood by ordinary citizens. The decision to validate what Congress and the president had enacted into law came from a branch formally independent of both Congress and the president, and from a Court with jurists from across the political spectrum. After *McCulloch*, although the bank continued to provoke fierce political controversy, fewer opponents continued claiming that the bank was generically unconstitutional, as opposed to unwise or imperfect in this respect or that. So, too, the justices upheld most of the state laws that came before the Court, and in the process legitimized them. The Court had the power to strike these laws down, and when it decided not to do so, it explained to America why the laws were in fact valid.

Although President Madison had signed into law the very bank bill upheld in *McCulloch*, he had failed to offer his fellow citizens any satisfactory account of the relevant constitutional principles. He did not want to publicly confess error on the merits. The bank, he quickly said, could be upheld simply because it had operated for many years.[40] *McCulloch* went much further and deeper and surely annoyed the president whose bill it upheld: the bank should be upheld, said the Marshall Court—unanimously—because James Madison and Thomas Jefferson were wrong in 1791 and George Washington and Alexander Hamilton were right. Because of, well, the Constitution, and what it truly did and did not say.[41]

The key to the Marshall Court, then, is that it tried to explain—in clear written opinions, accessible to all—what the Constitution did and did not mean and why. In the process, the Court tried to exemplify proper rules for constitutional interpretation. In short, the Marshall Court deserves its place in the pantheon because it helped create and solidify an institutionalized constitutional culture—a general framework for constitutional interpretation above and beyond a calculus of immediate political or partisan preferences. Put differently, the Marshall Court aimed to study, preserve, and explain what We the People had in fact agreed to in the Constitution, and why. In landmark cases such as *Marbury*, *McCulloch*, *Martin v. Hunter's Lessee* (which we shall examine shortly), and *Barron v. Baltimore*, the Court laid the foundations for what later generations of Americans would call *originalism*—fidelity to the Constitution's original meaning and purpose.

The Marshall Court had no strict monopoly on the power of constitutional exposition. *Marbury* never claimed that it did, though one sentence, quoted in isolation and ripped from the rest of the opinion, has often been misread as claiming monopoly power: "It is emphatically the duty and province of the judicial department to say what the law is." (Note that even this sentence does not say that *only* judges declare law.) Monopoly or no monopoly, the Marshall Court was often simply better at interpretation and exposition than were other contemporary actors.

The Marshall Court had several advantages above and beyond its greatest advantage, Marshall himself. Life tenure enabled justices to rise above popular or parochial opinion. Politicians were, quite immediately, failures if they lost. Judges, by contrast, would ultimately be failures if they erred. The Court also was small, with six members when Marshall joined and seven when he left. Its leadership circle—Marshall and Story—was even smaller. It made sense for each justice—and especially for each leading justice—to spend time carefully studying the Constitution. This would be a lifetime investment and might well determine the justice's ultimate historical reputation. In the short run, the need to generate cogent written opinions helped concentrate the judicial mind. By contrast, there was little incentive for any one of two hundred House members—focused on immediate reelection and highly unlikely to be in Congress ten years later—to become a true constitutional expert, especially if the right answer constitutionally turned out to be the wrong answer politically in his district in the here and now.[42]

In many of the most important cases, the Marshall Court could also count on a talented bar of lawyers, some of whom were themselves long-term repeat players able to research various issues and edify the bench. For example, oral argument in *McCulloch* lasted six days, featuring several of the nation's best lawyers, including Daniel Webster, William Wirt, William Pinkney, Luther Martin, and Walter Jones. The ever-courteous Marshall took care to praise their performance in the course of his opinion: "A splendor of eloquence, and strength of argument, seldom, if ever, surpassed, have been displayed."

TODAY, LIFE TENURE IS A defining feature not merely of federal judgeships but also of university professorships in general and law school professorships in particular. Not so in the early nineteenth century, when most academics had less formal job security. Still, it is apt that the Supreme Court justice who emphasized the issue of Article III life tenure more strenuously than did anyone else in the early nineteenth century was also the most literally professorial.

When he took the bench in 1811, Story also took a pay cut. His rising law practice yielded about twice as much as would a Court seat, which came with a guaranteed annual salary of $3,500.[43] He explained his reasoning to a friend in language that could just as well describe a modern litigator's decision to give up practice to become a law professor. He was drawn to "the permanence of the tenure, the respectability, if I may so say, of the salary, and the opportunity it will allow me to pursue, what of all things I admire, juridical studies." The bench would offer him a perch "to look out upon the political world without being engaged in it."[44]

It is one thing to give up a probable but uncertain $6,000 or $7,000 a year for a guaranteed $3,500. It is another to forgo an eye-popping likely salary of $15,000 or perhaps $20,000. But that, too, Story did when in 1816 he declined an offer to take over William Pinkney's law practice at a moment when Pinkney's income approximated that of the president (who received $25,000 per annum). As Story's son would later explain, his father preferred "the functions of a Judge to those of an advocate. His ambition reached after the solid fame resting upon judicial exposition, rather than the mere brilliant and ephemeral reputation to be won by contests at the Bar, and for this he was willing to sacrifice affluence."[45]

Thus, young Joseph Story was already a remarkably successful politico and could have been an astronomically wealthy lawyer, but preferred a life of "juridical studies" with time to devote to the enduring "exposition" of law. This ambition and aptitude for study and exposition led him not merely to America's highest Court but also to America's oldest school. As he added luster to the Marshall Court, so he brought glory to the Harvard Law School as the Dane Professor of Law, a post he accepted in 1828.

Today's Harvard Law School houses a charming sculpture of Joseph Story. The statue presents Story with book in hand. It is not a stretch to imagine that in the moment captured by the statue he is making a profound point about the book, index finger extending out to engage us. Crafted by the justice's doting son, William Wetmore Story, himself a talented lawyer and an acclaimed sculptor, the statue resides, fittingly, at the entrance of the Harvard Law School Library.

Joseph Story was to the Harvard Law School what John Marshall was to the Supreme Court—not its first man, chronologically, but its greatest early leader. Before Story, law was at best an undergraduate area of study. Most would-be lawyers did not learn law in college, but simply "read law" as apprentices and clerks to local

attorneys. The few law schools that existed were not grand centers of scholarship. In the main, they were for-profit operations run by practicing lawyers. Story aimed to create a more scholarly law school, in which professors would be more than mere practitioners and graduates would become genuine jurists and not mere pettifoggers.

As Marshall bent the arc of the Supreme Court, so Story bent the arc of Harvard Law School. Before 1828, no member of the Supreme Court was a graduate of Harvard Law School (as distinct from Harvard College—Story's own alma mater). But Benjamin Curtis—a graduate of the HLS class of 1832, an early beneficiary of the Story revolution—would join the Court in the early 1850s. Many more alumni would follow. Seventeen justices in history have reached the Court after studying at Harvard Law School. After Story's remodel of legal studies, many other university-based American law schools eventually sprouted up in imitation of the academic template that he embodied and established in Cambridge, Massachusetts. Story's remarkable influence on the Court and American law more generally can be seen, even today, in the striking fact that, for every year between 1993 and 2019, one school—Story's school—held at least as many seats on the Court as all other schools combined.*

---

*Some observers have claimed that a small law school in New Haven, Connecticut, has also done rather well in this category. Note that Justice Ruth Bader Ginsburg started her law studies at Harvard and finished them at Columbia. Both schools proudly claimed her, and in this tally she is counted as a product of each.

BACK IN THE 1760s, HARVARD graduates such as James Otis Jr. and John Adams had seethed at the contempt that arrogant English overlords in London harbored for mere colonists. Revolutionary and post-Revolutionary Americans had something to prove. *We are as good as the Brits—actually better!* Defeating the British in the War of Independence was a first step in proving America's equality, nay, superiority; creating a series of state and continental constitutions to rival or excel the British system of government was a second step; generating great jurists on the bench and in the academy was a third step. John Marshall was America's counterpart to Lord Mansfield, and Joseph Story was its answer to William Blackstone.

Blackstone was not merely a judge but also a scholar. His four-volume *Commentaries on the Laws of England*, published in the 1760s, emerged from his Viner Lectures at Oxford. The treatise was a best seller on both sides of the Atlantic. Supreme Court associate justice James Wilson had tried to offer an early American answer in his Philadelphia Lectures on Law in 1790 and thereafter, but had not quite succeeded. Wilson never managed to publish the lecture series in his lifetime. Several years after he died in debt and disgrace in 1798, the lectures eventually came before the public but failed to capture the American imagination. Thus, when Story decided to join the Court, America had yet to find its Blackstone.

Story aimed high. He sought to marry his judicial authority with his academic ability, build up Harvard as America's Oxford, and offer a set of commentaries on America's Constitution every bit as power-ful and ambitious as Blackstone's English *Commentaries*.

Story's three-volume *Commentaries on the Constitution of the United States*, published in 1833, were dedicated to John Marshall. They took the reader through all the great historical events that had led to the American Revolution, the Articles of Confederation, and the culminating Constitution of the United States. They then walked the reader through the Constitution's text, article by article and amendment by amendment, exploring both the purposes behind each provision and the ensuing implementations and interpretations, especially by the Marshall Court. They explained proper methods of constitutional interpretation and explored the larger spirit of the document alongside its strict letter. They blended big and small, offering both grand panoramic vision and exquisite technical detail. Their main aim was to refute, utterly, Jeffersonian extremism of the sort that South Carolina had recently embraced in the Nullification Crisis of 1832. The Constitution, Story's *Commentaries* proved, was just what Washington, Hamilton, and Marshall had said it was—not a mere compact among enduringly sovereign states, but higher law that had come from the American People themselves and that created an indivisible nation endowing its central government with broad powers.

This magisterial work opened with a crisp preface locating the project within the larger worlds of law, history, and political science. Story introduced himself to his readers not as a judge, but as a scholar discharging the "duties" attending "the Dane Professorship of Law in Harvard University." The biggest scholarly challenge he had faced, he explained, was to gather up all the relevant constitutional and conversational materials from the previous seventy-plus years, materials that lay "loose and scattered . . . among pamphlets and discussions of a temporary character" and "among obscure private and public documents." How could Americans in the 1830s and beyond remain faithful to the Constitution if they had no reliable record of the conversations that had birthed it? And not just a reliable record, but an intelligent constitutional analysis of those conversations that would "bring together," as Story hoped to do, "the irregular fragments, and . . . form them into groups, in which they might illustrate and support each other."

"Two great sources," Story reported, soared above all others: "*The Federalist*, an incomparable commentary of three of the greatest statesmen of their age; and the extraordinary Judgments of Mr. Chief Justice Marshall upon constitutional law." Great as these precursors were, their ideas and insights had not been fully systematized and synthesized. Publius had written for the moment, even if many of his ideas were timeless. Marshall's opinions were scattered essays responsive to specific issues that had arisen haphazardly in various litigated cases over the course of three decades. In fact, Marshall had tried to do more than that, using his cases as springboards for more general discussions of constitutional method and substance. But Marshall's project would become clear only when his various opinions were assembled, tweaked, and properly folded into a more comprehensive account of constitutional law of the sort that Story was now trying to offer.

Story ended his preface by defining his mission more precisely:

> The reader must not expect to find in these pages any novel views, and novel constructions of the Constitution. . . . My object [is rather to bring] before the reader the true view of its powers maintained by its founders and friends, and confirmed and illustrated by the actual practice of the government. The expositions to be found in the work are less to be regarded, as my own opinions, than as those of the great minds, which framed the Constitution, or which have been from time to time called upon to administer it. . . . [I hope] it may not be wholly useless, as means of stimulating abler minds to a more thorough review of the whole subject; and of impressing upon Americans a reverential attachment to the Constitution, as in the highest sense the palladium of American liberty.

This passage nicely captured both the opportunities and the constraints that confronted the most determined and faithful founding son of the 1830s. Story's treatise was remarkable for its blend of modesty (purporting to offer America a work "not . . . wholly useless" as a prompt to "abler minds"), ambition (aiming to present "the true view" of "the great minds" on "the whole subject"), and reverence (envisioning the Constitution as "the palladium of American liberty").

BIG IDEAS AND "ALL CASES"

Early in life, almost every one of the men who would go on to become America's greatest founding fathers and sons did something quite extraordinary, something that would imprint each man, define his animating constitutional vision, and underlie his biggest idea or ideas.

Washington, Hamilton, and Marshall were shaped by war— Washington by the French and Indian War, Hamilton and Marshall by their service under Washington in the War of Independence. These searing and death-drenched experiences made these men ardent nationalists, ever attentive to external threats posed by the Old Powers of Europe. War brought them together with men from across the continent and helped them see with blinding clarity that Americans' best hope against much larger powers lay in a strongly united continental nation-state.

Adams, Jefferson, and Madison were all men of 1776, but not military men. The year 1776 meant something different to each of these three statesmen, thanks to their three very different sets of experiences and achievements that fateful year, each set exceptional in its own way. For Jefferson, 1776 meant state sovereignty in general and Virginia sovereignty in particular. His was a case of arrested intellectual and constitutional development; he never moved entirely beyond this vision, which was indeed at the heart of the Declaration of Independence, over which he later claimed authorship. Unfortunately for him, the Constitution of 1788 emphatically repudiated this aspect of 1776 and the Declaration. Jefferson never grasped this most essential of all constitutional points, perhaps because he was an ocean away during the middle and late 1780s—almost the entire "Critical Period" of American history. Jefferson never stopped thinking about 1776 and saw all later events through the prism of that year. Hence his undue enthusiasm for Shays' Rebellion, the French Revolution, and the Whiskey Rebellion; his troubling daydreams about death to central bankers in 1791; his extremist call for local nullification in Kentucky in 1799; his enthusiasm for hyperaggressive state militia action in 1801; his unduly grandiose vision of his own presidential election as "the Revolution of 1800"; and his professed nonchalance about future western secessions.

For Adams, who likewise missed the great events of the Critical Period, 1776 meant the centrality of . . . Adams. To be more charitable, 1776 meant independence—both collective and individual. Adams himself was a fiercely independent man—so independent he was never able to partner up politically with anyone other than Abigail. (In early adulthood, he had flashed this fiercely independent streak by refusing to enter the ministry as his father had wanted.[46] Much as he had then and there declared his independence from his biological father, John Adams Sr., so in 1776 he joined others in declaring his independence from his political father, George III.) For Adams, 1776 was also memorable as the year in which American state constitutions sprang to life, many of them in line with his widely published *Thoughts on Government*, which had championed bicameral legislatures and independent executives and judiciaries. These would be Adams's lifelong constitutional watchwords. Perhaps his greatest contribution to the American constitutional project— greater than anything he himself did post-1776—was his selection of Marshall as chief justice, a man who had not parroted the party line on the Sedition Act and who had intelligently and honorably shown his independence even from Adams himself.[47]

Young James Madison had not been in Congress in 1776 alongside Adams and Jefferson. Rather, he had been in Williamsburg alongside Mason. Then and there, barely twenty-five years old, he had championed freedom—religious freedom in particular, freedom of the mind as he later called it. Freedom would indeed become his credo (though we must always remember that this was, for him, only freedom for Whites). His most important intellectual contributions at Philadelphia in 1787 involved efforts to structure the federal government so that it would respect the freedom of various minorities. Similar ideas would shape his most original, though at the time unnoticed, contribution to the ratification process—*The Federalist* No. 10, where he abruptly tried to change the Hamiltonian conversation of the earlier *Federalist* essays, which had focused on armies, navies, warfare, national security, international affairs, and geostrategy. Madison's later advocacy of the Bill of Rights powerfully extended his early ideas about freedom. In 1798–1799, he brilliantly championed freedom of expression, which intertwined with freedom of thought—freedom of the mind. Political minorities needed to be free to think and speak, as did religious minorities. Indeed, the boundary between religious thought and political thought might sometimes blur, a point he had noticed years before in *The Federalist* No. 10. His presidential tenure was less than glorious—waging a war against Britain in 1812 that did not need to be waged; doing so when America was, thanks to his own lapses, unprepared; allowing America's capital city to be sacked and torched; and failing to see the military value of a bank early on. For all that, President Madison—in sharp contrast to President Adams and unusually for a war president—did not seek to silence critics.

Washington, Hamilton, Madison, and Marshall had also played particularly notable roles in 1788. For the three older men, this experience tended to confirm their preexisting big ideas—national-security unionism for Washington and Hamilton, freedom for vulnerable White minorities for Madison. For Marshall, 1788 was different. This was his first appearance on a grand political stage.

In that debut, Marshall stressed the Constitution's democratic bona fides. In the process, he helped sway the people of Virginia, specially embodied in an ad hoc ratifying convention, to throw their weight behind the Constitution at a pivotal moment in American and world history. The special nature of this democratic moment and this populist process became a profound theme for Marshall, with variations on the theme prominent in many of his most notable judicial statements.

In *Marbury*, he stressed how this moment and this special process meant that the Constitution was *higher* law than any mere federal statute: "That the people have an original right to establish, for their future government, such principles as, in their opinion, shall most conduce to their own happiness, is the basis on which the whole American fabric has been erected. The exercise of this original right is a very great exertion; nor can it nor ought it to be frequently repeated. . . . The constitution is . . . a superior, paramount law, unchangeable by ordinary means, [and not merely] on a level with ordinary legislative acts." In *McCulloch*, the special nature of popular ratification meant that the Constitution was *simple* law that perforce omitted many details. "A constitution" designed to be "understood by the public" that was asked to ratify it had to be a text whose "nature requires, that only its great outlines should be marked." In *Barron*, the document's origin in a multistate and multiconvention process meant that the Constitution was presumptively *federal* law regulating only *federal* officials: "The constitution was ordained and established by the people of the United States for themselves, for their own government, and not for the government of the individual states." In two other Marshall classics, his 1821 opinion *Cohens v. Virginia* and his 1824 opinion in *Gibbons v. Ogden*, the 1788 ordainment meant that the Constitution was *continentally binding* law that state governments could not ignore or nullify: "The people made the constitution, and the people can unmake it. . . . But this supreme and irresistible power to make or to unmake, resides only in the whole body of the people; not in any sub-division of them. The attempt of any of the parts to exercise it is usurpation, and ought to be repelled by those to whom the people have delegated their power of repelling it." Although states "were sovereign, were completely independent, and were connected with each other only by a league" prior to 1788, everything "underwent a change" when Americans "converted their league into a government, when they converted their Congress of Ambassadors, deputed to deliberate on their common concerns, and to recommend measures of general utility, into a Legislature, empowered to enact laws on the most interesting subjects."

What was Joseph Story's early defining moment? Did it shape any of his big ideas?

THE MOMENT, OF COURSE, WAS his appointment to the Court itself—for life—at an astonishingly young age, younger than any other justice, before or after. Of the seventeen men to precede him on the Court, only two had joined the bench in their thirties, and one, Bushrod Washington, had the considerable advantage of being childless George Washington's favorite nephew. Story was entirely self-made—his father's eighth child, who graduated from Harvard in 1798 with "a high rank . . . for scholarship."[48] (Harvard stopped ranking its graduates by family social standing in 1773.)

Even before he joined the Court, Story had highlighted the significance of life tenure for his own life and life choices. Fittingly, his most notable judicial opinion likewise highlighted the themes of life tenure, nondiminishable salary, and judicial independence.

The case of *Martin v. Hunter's Lessee* came to the Court in 1816. The suit involved a large land dispute in Virginia. Because the Marshall family claimed some of the land in dispute and other similarly situated property, the chief justice recused himself—thus enabling Story to take the lead in crafting and announcing the Court's ruling. Marshall drafted various pleadings himself, and Story surely recognized his mentor's handwriting and expositional style. Case-related conversations between Marshall and Story may well have occurred in the boardinghouse before the case reached the Court or even as the case was pending. Story proudly told a friend that his opinion "contains a full survey of the Judicial powers of the General Government and Chief Justice Marshall concurred in every word of it." Story's son also took note of the similarities of tone and theme between his father's masterpiece and the greatest opinions of his father's mentor. The *Martin* opinion, declared William Wetmore Story, with filial pride, was "one of the most prominent constitutional opinions ever delivered by the Court" and had "all the peculiar merits of the best judgments of Marshall—compactness of fibre and closeness of logic."[49]

The biggest Article III issue in the case was in fact laughably easy, but arose in a complicated context. Virginia was trying to manipulate state law to cheat Revolution-era British loyalist landowners, in violation of the letter and spirit of America's 1783 peace treaty with Britain. In 1813, the Supreme Court, per Justice Story, rejected the Virginia ruse and sent the case back to Virginia's state court system for proper proceedings. Indignant, Virginia's highest court, led by Spencer Roane, denied that the United States Supreme Court had any appellate authority over state courts. Roane was a son-in-law of Patrick Henry, a close confidant of Thomas Jefferson, and an archrival of John Marshall.

Roane's claim was preposterous. No significant scholar in the past century has ever endorsed it, nor has any Supreme Court justice in history. The Constitution explicitly confers appellate jurisdiction on the Supreme Court "in all Cases, in Law and Equity, arising under this Constitution, the Law of the United States, and Treaties made, or which shall be made, under their Authority." Roane claimed that this meant appellate jurisdiction only over inferior federal courts, not over wholly independent state courts. But when the Constitution was drafted and ratified, there was no guarantee that any lower federal courts would exist. The Article III text spoke of "such inferior courts as the Congress *may* from time to time ordain and establish" (emphasis added). Had the first Congress opted not to create lower federal courts, state courts would have been the only trial courts in America outside the very strictly limited (per *Marbury*) original jurisdiction of the United States Supreme Court itself. In this scenario—the scenario many early Anti-Federalists in fact favored back in 1788–1789—the *only* courts over which the Supreme Court's appellate jurisdiction would have operated would have been state courts.

Anyone who paid even the slightest attention in 1788 understood that the Supreme Court would have appellate authority over state courts. The Philadelphia plan sought to prevent states from defying the Constitution in the same way that they had routinely ignored the Articles of Confederation. In particular, the system aimed to ensure that no state could flout a federal treaty in ways that might be popular locally but would ire a foreign government that might then wreak revenge on the United States as a whole—precisely the facts of *Martin* itself.

The Federalists made all this emphatically clear when urging the American people to say "yes, We do," in the ratification process. Hamilton/Publius addressed the issue at length in *The Federalist* No. 82:

What relation would subsist between the national and State courts
. . . ? I answer, that an appeal would certainly lie from the latter, to

the Supreme Court of the United States. The Constitution in direct terms gives an appellate jurisdiction to the Supreme Court in all the enumerated cases of federal cognizance in which it is not to have an original one, without a single expression to confine its operation to the inferior federal courts. The objects of appeal, not the tribunals from which it is to be made, are alone contemplated. From this circumstance, and from the reason of the thing, it ought to be construed to extend to the State tribunals . . . , else the judiciary authority of the Union may be eluded at the pleasure of every plaintiff or prosecutor.

The proto-Roane view, Hamilton/Publius proceeded to explain,

would defeat some of the most important and avowed purposes of the proposed government, and would essentially embarrass its measures. . . . [T]he national and State systems are to be regarded as ONE WHOLE. The courts of the latter will of course be natural auxiliaries to the execution of the laws of the Union, and an appeal from them will as naturally lie to that tribunal which is destined to unite and assimilate the principles of national justice and the rules of national decisions. The evident aim of the plan of the convention is, that all the causes of the specified classes [that is, all cases arising under the federal Constitution, laws, and treaties] shall, for weighty public reasons, receive their original or final determination in the courts of the Union. To confine, therefore, the general expressions giving appellate jurisdiction to the Supreme Court, to appeals from the subordinate federal courts, instead of allowing their extension to the State courts, would be to abridge the latitude of the terms, in subversion of the intent, contrary to every sound rule of interpretation.

When the issue reached the First Congress in 1789, not a single member claimed that state courts were constitutionally exempt from Supreme Court review. On the contrary, section 25 of the landmark Judiciary Act of 1789 gave the Supreme Court appellate review over every single case, civil or criminal, in which an appellant claimed that the state court system had deprived him of a federal right. Washington unhesitatingly signed the act into law, and by the mid-1810s, at least sixteen cases had reached the Supreme Court under section 25. Prior to Roane's ruling, almost no one had the audacity to claim that section 25 was unconstitutional.[50]*

That was the easy part of *Martin*, and Story could have left it at that. But like Marshall, Story used the case as a platform to teach Americans much bigger lessons about the Constitution, and also to highlight key technical issues that most others had likely missed. Like Marshall, Story blended panorama with precision.

Not only was section 25 constitutionally permissible; it was also, in some form, constitutionally required, Story explained. Just as Marshall in *Marbury* had taken a case about Jefferson's actions and used it to assert power against Congress, so now Story took a case about Roane's antics and used it to give a lecture to America more generally. He did not invalidate any Congressional law; but he told Congress that if it ever tried to repeal section 25, the Court would invalidate such an attempt. *Martin* was a preemptive shot across Congress's bow at a moment when Congress was unlikely to take umbrage—since

---

*Pre-Roane, anti-unionist audacity of a different sort had twice briefly surfaced and quickly receded in New England. In 1804, some of Jefferson's Boston-centered adversaries muttered about seceding from the union. When Hamilton got wind of such talk, he moved vigorously to quash it. See pages 659–660. Similar northeastern mutterings occurred during Madison's presidency, leading to an informal meeting of disaffected partisans—the so-called Hartford Convention of 1814–1815. No secession proposal emerged from this gathering of grumblers. Indeed, the claim that the convention was in fact secessionist was mainly used by Madison's allies, now in control of the federal government, as a rhetorical club to bludgeon the grumblers.

In neither episode were the key constitutional issues crisply framed. Did any grumblers somehow think that each state had a constitutional right to unilaterally secede? If so, this idea was flatly unconstitutional, though it would be revived by John C. Calhoun and his southern disciples in the next generation, as we shall see in the next chapter. Or did grumblers instead envision a national plan of peaceful partition, via an Article V amendment or a federal statute or some other legal mechanism in which all states and regions would be involved in deciding whether and how the split would occur? This variant would have been deeply unwise, for reasons that geostrategic continentalists such as Washington and Hamilton had repeatedly explained, but it would not necessarily have been unconstitutional.

Congress had done nothing yet to touch section 25, which had of course issued from Congress itself back in 1789. (And here again, we see that a mere tally of actual judicial invalidations misses the point. *Martin* was a preemptive and conditional invalidation: if Congress ever did *x*, we the Court would undo it.)

Many years after *Martin*, when Congress did indeed seriously consider restricting section 25, Story wrote a friend that "if the twenty-fifth section is repealed the Constitution is practically gone."[51] For Story, federal judicial authority was central to the entire constitutional project.

But why couldn't state courts substitute for the Supreme Court, à la Roane? Because state courts lacked true judicial independence. For himself and his *Martin* brethren, Story was willing to "very cheerfully admit" that "the judges of the state courts are, and always will be, of as much learning, integrity, and wisdom, as those of the courts of the United States." (Like Marshall, Story was gracious to fault.) But, Story hastened to add, "the constitution has proceeded upon a theory of its own, and given or withheld powers according to a the judgment of the American people, by whom it was adopted. . . . The constitution has presumed (whether rightly or wrongly we do not inquire) that state attachments, state prejudices, state jealousies, and state interests, might some times obstruct, or control, or be supposed to obstruct or control, the regular administration of justice."

As Story reminded his readers in *Martin*, the Constitution provided that all federal judges "both of the supreme and inferior courts, shall hold their offices during good behaviour, and shall, at stated times, receive, for their services, a compensation which shall not be diminished during their continuance in office." Thus Congress could never "create or limit any other tenure of the judicial office" or "refuse to pay, at stated times, the stipulated salary, or diminish it during the continuance in office." All federal judges were suitably independent. *But none of the essential aspects of Article III judicial independence directly applied to state courts.*

Story thus offered his readers a structural and panoramic argument about the nature of judicial power in America. All federal judges were essentially equal. All federal judges, whether on the Supreme Court or an inferior court, had the requisite Article III independence. But no state judge could say the same. Consequently, Story explained, Congress could indeed allow lower federal courts but not state courts to act as the last word in various cases involving federal law. If some future Congress wanted to limit Supreme Court review of state courts in cases involving federal rights, perhaps it could do so, but only by switching appellate review to some other federal court (say, a circuit court) staffed by judges with Article III judicial independence—the same life tenure that had induced Story himself to join the bench in 1811.

STORY ADDED SEVERAL ADDITIONAL RAMPARTS to his grand castle. To appreciate his interpretive and expositional artistry, we must first examine with extreme care the relevant technical language of Articles II and III, which contains several features that only legal eagles might spot, but that are worth spotting, as Story would prove in *Martin* and prove again in his *Commentaries*.

Article II

Section 1. The executive power shall be vested in a President of the United States of America . . .

Article III

Section 1. The judicial power of the United States, shall be vested in one Supreme Court, and in such inferior courts as the Congress may from time to time ordain and establish. . . .

Section 2. The judicial power shall extend to all cases, in law and equity, arising under this Constitution, the laws of the United States, and treaties made, or which shall be made, under their authority;—to all cases affecting ambassadors, other public ministers and consuls;—to all cases of admiralty and maritime jurisdiction;— to controversies to which the United States shall be a party;—to controversies between two or more states;—between a state and citizens of another state;—between citizens of different states;—between citizens of the same state claiming lands under grants of different states, and between a state, or the citizens thereof, and foreign states, citizens or subjects.

First, the vesting clauses of Articles II and III obviously interlocked. They used the same words—"the _____ power shall be vested"—and in precisely parallel places, as the gateposts of Articles II and III, respectively. The two clauses thus needed to be read together, holistically. Issues of judicial power could profitably be analyzed alongside issues of executive power.

Second and related, the opening sentences of Article III, section 1, and Article III, section 2—each beginning with the words "The judicial power . . ."—also operated as interlocking mandates. The judicial power of the United States *shall* be vested in federal courts *and shall* extend to various cases and controversies. (The obvious contrast here is that inferior federal courts are optional—the document speaks of "such inferior courts as the Congress *may* from time to time ordain and establish.")

Mortaring these textual bricks together, Story explained that the judicial power of the United States was the power to pronounce the last judicial word in any given case. The American people vested this power in *federal courts* and not in Congress, and this power *must* extend over *all* cases involving federal law. Just as the powers vested in the president were his, not Congress's—recall the Decision of 1789 about the president's removal powers over his cabinet—so the powers vested in the federal judiciary belonged to the third branch, not the first. Congress had no right to snatch the president's removal-power pen or veto pen or pardon pen and hand it to state governors; nor could Congress transfer the final word in federal-law cases from federal courts to state judges.

Story's next point was his most brilliant and subtle. Article III, he explained, contained two different tiers—two distinct classes—of lawsuits:

The first class includes cases arising under the constitution, laws, and treaties of the United States; cases affecting ambassadors, other public ministers and consuls, and cases of admiralty and maritime jurisdiction. In this class, the expression is . . . that the judicial power shall extend to *all cases*; but in the subsequent part of the clause which embraces all the other cases of national cognizance, and forms the second class, the word "all" is dropped seemingly *ex industria* [on purpose]. Here the judicial authority is to extend to controversies (not to *all* controversies) to which the United States shall be a party, &c.

What precise meaning should be attributed to the two-tiered language of Article III, to the intriguingly selective use of the word "all"—a word used not once, not twice, but three times in the key sentence, and then pointedly omitted? "In respect to the first class," Story wrote, "it may well have been the intention of the framers of the constitution imperatively to extend the judicial power either in an original or appellate form to all cases; and in the latter class to leave it to congress to qualify the jurisdiction, original or appellate, in such manner as public policy might dictate."

Spotting with his legal-eagle eye this tiny textual pinhead, Story showed how this pinhead fit into a grand panoramic picture: "The vital importance of all the cases enumerated in the first class to the national sovereignty, might warrant such a distinction." This "first class" of cases turned on federal law, law that inherently implicated "national policy," "national rights," and "national sovereignty." By contrast, cases in the second tier of controversies involved only matters of state law that could, if Congress thought proper, be left to state courts for final decision.

Then came one last and elegant touch. In 1816, Story had no access to as-yet-unpublished Philadelphia Convention committee records, which confirm that the framers did indeed aim to create two tiers of jurisdiction, one mandatory and one permissive, via the selective use of the word "all."[52] But Story—himself a former congressman—did know what Congress had done in its landmark 1789

Judiciary Act. That act had allowed state courts to be the last word in various second-tier lawsuits involving mere state-law disputes, but had carefully provided that all first-tier cases, involving claims of federal right under federal law, would be finally resolved by federal courts—some by inferior federal courts, others by the US Supreme Court. "It is also worthy of remark," he wrote, "that congress seem, in a good degree, in the establishment of the present judicial system, to have adopted this distinction." Even when telling Congress what it could and could not do—on an issue, we must remember, involving core issues of judicial power—Story smoothly presented himself as deferential to Congress.

Story's tight logic and good manners paid off. In several of his own landmark opinions for the Court, Marshall endorsed *Martin*'s two-tiered thesis—first in *Cohens v. Virginia*, in 1821, then in *Osborn v. Bank of the United States*, three years later, and finally in *American Insurance Company v. Canter*, in 1828.[53] In 1831, arch states' rightists in Congress pushed back. Inspired by Vice President John C. Calhoun and Senator Robert Hayne—both South Carolinians—ultras led by yet another South Carolinian, Warren R. Davis, drafted a bill to repeal section 25 and steered it through the House Judiciary Committee. Constitutionalists repelled the attack. A blistering House committee minority report insisted that the bill was flatly unconstitutional, repeatedly stressing the words "all cases"—four times in italics—and explicitly invoking "the very able and conclusive argument of the Supreme Court" in *Martin* and *Cohens*. No other cases were cited. When the bill reached the House floor, it went down to a crushing defeat, 138 to 51. (The three authors of the forceful minority report were an interesting trio: James Buchanan, a Jacksonian Democrat and future US president from Pennsylvania; William W. Ellsworth, an Anti-Jacksonian from Connecticut and a son of a past US chief justice; and Edward D. White, an Anti-Jacksonian from Louisiana and father of a future US chief justice.)[54]

In his 1833 *Commentaries*, Story devoted more than 225 pages to the issues at the heart of *Martin*, *Cohens*, and the closely related *Federalist* essays by Hamilton/Publius discussing judicial power and judicial independence. Article III was quite obviously central to Story's vision of the Constitution, and section 25 was in turn central to Article III. The scholarly judge summarized his big idea in a key sentence: "It is clear, from the language of the constitution, that in one form or the other [that is, either original or appellate jurisdiction], it is absolutely obligatory upon congress, to vest all the jurisdiction in the national courts, in that class of cases at least, where it has declared, that it shall extend to '*all cases*.'"[55]

THE PUBLICATION OF STORY'S *COMMENTARIES* in 1833 marked a critical moment in the maturation of the founding project, enabling a rising generation of men—and, as time passed, women—who had not witnessed the Great Constitutional Conversation of 1788 to assess what had and had not been agreed to by the American people that fateful year. As Story himself admitted with admirable modesty, the *Commentaries* were not the last word on all things constitutional. Rather, they were the first full draft penned by a powerful interpreter and analyst who was not himself a founder—an interpreter and analyst who was thus rather like us, the Constitution's "posterity," so pointedly invoked at the end of its grand Preamble.

Other key elements of intergenerational infrastructure also clicked into place as the last of the founders exited the stage in the 1830s. In 1834, government-sponsored printers Joseph Gales Jr. and William Winston Seaton finally published the *Annals of Congress*, compiling and reprinting many of the great debates of the House and Senate stretching back to the Washington administration. In 1836, political journalist Jonathan Elliot likewise published, with Congressional blessing, a revised four-volume compilation of *The Debates in the Several State Conventions on the Adoption of the Federal Constitution as Recommended by the General Convention at Philadelphia in 1787*. Elliot supplemented this ratification-centered compilation with a pair of firsthand accounts of the once secret Philadelphia conclave from two disgruntled Anti-Federalist delegates, Luther Martin and Robert Yates, and various materials from the Virginia and Kentucky

Resolutions of 1798–1799. Elliot linked himself financially to South Carolina's John C. Calhoun, who took a special interest in the project. The 1836 edition opened with polite testimonials—nineteenth-century blurbs—from Madison and Story and a rather more enthusiastic endorsement from Calhoun. Elliot's *Debates* were incomplete and imperfect—slanted to advance Calhoun's political fortunes and arch states' rights theories[56]—but like Story's *Commentaries*, Elliot's volumes laid a foundation for future scholarship and analysis. In 1840, Congress posthumously published Madison's *Notes of Debates in the Federal Convention of 1787*—by far the most extensive, albeit a selective and self-serving, account of the initially secret meeting. In 1845, Elliot added a fifth volume featuring Madison's material.

One phase of America's constitutional conversation—the consolidation phase—was thus coming to an end. New actors would soon leap onto center stage.

— twelve —

JACKSON

O N BOTH AN INDIVIDUAL AND a collective level, the 1830s
marked an important inflection point in America's constitutional conversation. If, in the tradition of Thomas Carlyle, we focus
on history's "great men," we should note that the last of the towering Revolutionaries, John Marshall and James Madison, died in this
decade. If, instead or in addition, we attend to larger demographic,
legal, political, social, intellectual, technological, and cultural forces,
we should observe that by the end of the decade, America had begun
to approach parity with Britain.

When America's constitutional conversation began in the early
1760s, Britain overshadowed America in almost every way, to the
chagrin of ambitious young colonists such as John Adams and James
Otis. By 1840, young America was as populous and muscular as old
Britain, much as Benjamin Franklin had predicted in a pamphlet
published back in 1755, and as Thomas Paine had forecast in *Common Sense*.[1] America's five largest cities—New York, Philadelphia,
Baltimore, New Orleans, and Boston—and their environs boasted a
combined population of more than three-quarters of a million souls.

America now had more newspapers and newspaper readers than did Britain, thanks to robust literacy rates for both men and women, and astonishing improvements in transportation and postal delivery that made it easier than ever for Americans to converse with each other. Nearly three thousand miles of railroad track crisscrossed the nation; for the first time in world history, humans could traverse land faster than could horses. One enormously consequential and complementary infrastructural improvement—the Erie Canal, completed in 1825—made it possible to circle the main body of America by water, much as the British isle itself could be circumnavigated. Newspapers and letters could now float from Chicago to Buffalo on the Great Lakes, then over to Albany on the Erie Canal, then down to Manhattan on the Hudson, from there to New Orleans by ship, and up the Mississippi back to Chicago—or vice versa.

In 1828, Noah Webster produced a dictionary of American English rivaling Samuel Johnson's English lexicon. Four majestic oils by John Trumbull depicting the great moments of the American Revolution—America's answer to the grand English political paintings of Benjamin West and John Singleton Copley (both American-born)—now graced the Capitol Rotunda. In 1833, Story matched Blackstone. Indeed, Story's treatise arguably surpassed Blackstone's, because the ambitious Harvard jurist elaborated an American constitutional project that, except for slavery—a huge exception, to be sure—excelled the creaky, semi-feudal British system that Blackstone had summarized in the 1760s.

Story was not the only figure of his generation contributing mightily to the maturation of America's constitutional conversation. The northeastern jurist's most significant constitutional contemporary was a southwestern general—Andrew Jackson, a founding son who won the presidency twice, first in 1828 and again in 1832.

WHY JACKSON?

Born in 1767, Andrew Jackson was a child of the Revolution. Over the course of his public life, he offered his fellow Americans a synthesis of Washington and Jefferson. He was a triumphant general (like Washington) and a rural lawyer (like Jefferson), a staunch unionist (Washington) and a friend of legitimate states' rights (Jefferson), a commanding personality (Washington) and a man of the people (Jefferson), a scourge of the British (Washington) and a champion of New Orleans (Jefferson). And, like both Washington and Jefferson, he was a southern planter who owned hundreds of slaves.

These parallels were not happenstance. The Constitution had created a fixed script, with defined rules and roles for different actors. The most difficult role of all to enact was the American presidency. In the Constitution's first half century, only three men—Washington, Jefferson, and Jackson—won the role and then played it well enough to satisfy both the high demands of their contemporaries and the harsh judgment of history. It is thus not utterly coincidental that the three had certain things in common.

What was so great about these three? What are we to make of the fact that the five other presidents in the first half century fell short by comparison?

LET'S BEGIN BY DEFINING SOUND criteria of presidential success and presidential greatness. First, to even have a shot at being a great president, one of course has to win the presidency. Marshall and Story were lofty judicial figures, but obviously not great presidents. Likewise, John Jay and Alexander Hamilton might well have made great presidents, but we will never know. Ditto for later perennial presidential aspirants such as Daniel Webster and Henry Clay. As shall soon become clear, we can nonetheless say with complete confidence that John C. Calhoun could never have made a great president. Though he stood a heartbeat away from the office for nearly eight years, his profound contempt for constitutional first principles made him utterly unfit for an office uniquely designed to "preserve, protect, and defend the Constitution of the United States."

Second, seconds. It's hard to be reckoned a great president without a second term. Presidential success generally involves not just winning the office, but keeping it—winning a second term after proving one's fitness in the first term. John Adams cannot be deemed a great president because his countrymen threw him out of office (the judgment of his era) and rightly so (the judgment of history). No one eager to imprison peaceful and patriotic political critics can be deemed a great or even a very good president.[2] Later one-term presidents in the first half century—John Quincy Adams (1825–1829) and Martin Van Buren (1837–1841)—did not disgrace themselves in office, as did old Adams. But these presidents, too, failed to persuade their contemporaries to renew their four-year Executive Mansion leases. In the ultra-competitive presidential-greatness derby, the fact that these one-termers left office as losers places them in a category distinctly below Washington and Jefferson.

A third point implicates war and national security. James Madison (1809–1817) was not an appalling president. He did not imprison his critics before, during, or after the War of 1812, which he commenced, with Congressional approval, late in his first term. He won a second term, left office with popular support, and handed off power to a protégé (James Monroe). But on his watch, British troops sacked the national capital city and torched its iconic buildings in a war that Madison had elected to start without dire need or strong preparation, and that he ended without achieving any of his professed war aims. These facts make Madison inapt for Mount Rushmore. Madison's last years in office would likely have been far worse had it not been for General Jackson's emotionally satisfying but diplomatically moot victory over the British at New Orleans at war's end. (The battle occurred on January 8, 1815—a fortnight after the belligerents signed a Christmas Eve peace at Ghent, but before word had reached America.) Perhaps not every great president must understand war—why wage war, when to wage war, how to wage war, how to win war—but surely a great *wartime* president must understand war, and Madison did not.

Finally, presidential greatness requires some exceptional talent, some extraordinary strength of character, and/or some grand achievement. Though James Monroe (1817–1825) was reelected resoundingly, he was no great thinker and no great doer. Meh. Even the less-than-great Adams and Madison placed titans on the Supreme Court, Marshall and Story. Monroe named Smith Thompson. More meh.[3]

By contrast, each of America's three greatest early presidents performed heroic deeds even before taking office, and then did additionally impressive things in office.

CONSIDER FIRST EACH PRESIDENTIAL TITAN'S pre-presidential triumphs. In America's War of Independence, Washington not only bested the world's most overwhelming military, but then dissolved his army and walked away from the absolute power that could have been his. Later, when summoned back into service by the urgent pleas of his countrymen, he quietly induced America's leading statesmen to craft an ambitious new Constitution in his image and then quietly induced an entire continent of common voters to say "yes, We do"—twice. First, America ratified Washington's audacious Constitution in a continental act of ordainment unprecedented in the annals of world history. Never had so many ordinary persons across so vast a land been invited to decide how they and their posterity would be governed. Never had so many been able to speak so freely—both pro and con—on a decision of such significance. And then, America said "yes, We do," to Washington himself, by *unanimously* selecting him to lead the new nation. These were all astonishing achievements that would have immortalized Washington even had he died before inauguration.

Next, consider Thomas Jefferson's pre-presidential accomplishments. True, the Virginia redhead did not single-handedly author the Declaration of Independence. Jefferson had not dined alone in 1776. But by 1800, even before winning the presidency, Jefferson had won credit in the American popular mind and popular press as *the* author of the Declaration, and the July 4 text had come to be seen as *the* great event of July 1776, as distinct from the mere act of declaring independence on July 2. In 1776, John Adams had loomed large on July 2, even larger than Jefferson, as Adams himself never forgot.

But in the ensuing decades, Adams lost the credit-claiming contest, thanks mainly to Jefferson's first epic achievement: the creation of America's first national popular party, combining slick electioneering tactics with an affiliated newspaper network.

In 1800–1801, Jefferson used the political machine that he had built to accomplish his second epic pre-presidential achievement: wresting the presidency away from an incumbent, and doing so by standing on a constitutional platform that would give him a principled presidential mandate. Jefferson's partisans insisted, correctly, that the Sedition Act was unconstitutional and that the American people themselves could adjudge the constitutional matter in the 1800 election.

All this was far more significant than anything that Adams had done in 1796 to win America's first contested presidential election. Adams had not done much because he was trapped in Old World thinking. He believed himself entitled to the presidency simply by dint of seniority and past public service. Adams disdained electioneering, sloganeering, partisanship, coalition-building, and logrolling.[4] Jefferson may not have loved all these things, but he and Madison did what they had to do to win. Call it hypocrisy, call it flexibility, or call it vision. Jefferson better foresaw and more easily embraced America's democratic future.

And Jackson? Though not of the same magnitude, his most notable pre-presidential accomplishments echoed Washington's and Jefferson's.

First, like Washington, he bested the British on the battlefield, in a conflict seen by both contemporaries and historians as a Second American War of Independence, a continuation of the contest that had begun in the 1760s and 1770s. In one purely symbolic way, Jackson's triumph at New Orleans was greater than any single military event in the Revolutionary War. Lexington and Concord were merely preliminary skirmishes. At Bunker Hill and Breed's Hill, the British drove Americans from the field (though at a fierce cost). Washington's tactics at Dorchester Heights dislodged but did not damage the British fleet, which promptly sailed to other points of attack. In

Brooklyn and Manhattan, Washington's troops did not prevail but merely survived, barely. The clashes at Trenton and Princeton boosted American morale, but they did not dramatically tip the scales from a strictly military point of view. Saratoga was a triumph, but the commanding American general there, Horatio Gates, was not a home-grown republican American hero, and the other hero there was the future turncoat Benedict Arnold. Monmouth was a tactical draw and the southern theater a mixed bag. At Yorktown, Americans finally won decisively, but only thanks to the French all around on both land and sea. At New Orleans, by contrast, America alone, led by an authentic homegrown American hero, Andrew Jackson, humiliated the British army in a major European-style pitched battle. Britain suffered nearly 2,500 casualties and losses (killed, wounded, missing, or captured) compared to some 300 on the American side. America had decisively beaten Britain at its own game, and every American could henceforth hold his head high.

True, weeks earlier the war had formally ended in a draw at the Ghent peace talks, with each belligerent agreeing to return to the status quo ante bellum. At Ghent, Madison had failed to achieve any of his initial war aims. Britain continued to assert a right to search American ships on the high seas and to seize—impress—alleged British deserters. America pried no Canadian land loose from Britain, as Madison had all but promised at the outset. Nothing that happened at New Orleans altered the formal terms of peace, which the president and the Senate blessed in February 1815.

Even so, New Orleans mattered, hugely. The War of 1812 was driven by American honor and American emotion.[5] The passions on display in the 1761 Boston Court House continued to throb a half century later: in countless ways, Americans felt demeaned by Britain. The British were arrogant, insolent bullies who treated their transatlantic cousins with contempt. At New Orleans, a homegrown republican American general and a homegrown republican American army at long last punished the British snobs and put them in their place. If Washington was America's answer to George III, if Marshall was Mansfield's equal, and if Story would become the

new nation's Blackstone, so Jackson was the New World's Wellington. (The defeated general at New Orleans, who lost both the battle
and his life, was in fact Wellington's highborn brother-in-law, Major
General Sir Edward Pakenham.)

Several of Jackson's other notable pre-presidential achievements
synthesized the best of Washington and Jefferson, as he used his
military prowess and backcountry experience (Washington) to add
new lands to America's domain (Jefferson). In 1814, Jackson's forces
smashed a band of Red Stick Creek Indians at the Battle of Horse-
shoe Bend in modern-day Alabama. Later that year, in the Treaty of
Fort Jackson (named for the general himself), the Creeks ceded more
than twenty million acres in central Alabama and southern Georgia
to the victorious Americans. In 1817–1818, Jackson's troops chased
nettlesome Seminole and Creek warriors into West and East Florida, territory then claimed by Spain, and managed to grab control of
the region. With American boots now on the ground and in charge,
Spain eventually ceded the entire gulf and peninsula region to America—a huge acquisition of more than forty million acres attributable
to Jackson's muscular patriotism. Meanwhile, Jackson in late 1818
also negotiated the acquisition of some seven million acres of fertile
Chickasaw land between the Mississippi and Tennessee Rivers in
western Kentucky and western Tennessee. The "Jackson Purchase," as
it was called, cost America $300,000, less than five cents an acre, and
won quick approval from the Congress and the president—James
Monroe, who himself had helped negotiate the Louisiana Purchase
back in 1803.

Jackson's final impressive pre-presidential achievement recalled
Jefferson more than Washington, and indeed echoed Jefferson with
startling precision. Like Jefferson, Jackson lost a close presidential
contest to a Harvard-trained lawyer from Massachusetts named
John _____ Adams and then beat him in the rematch. Ousting an
incumbent president was no small feat—the only person to do it
before Jackson had been Jefferson—and both challengers succeeded
via mass popular appeals, strong electioneering, newspaper networks,
and a national party machine. Jackson reinvented, renamed ("Dem-

ocrats"), and made permanent the national Democratic-Republican Party apparatus that Jefferson had previously created. Jackson was not merely a victorious general in the Washington tradition, but an ardent small-d democrat, a champion of the working White man, in the Jefferson tradition. Whereas Washington transcended party and region, Jefferson and Jackson first won as regional partisans— spokesmen for southern and western democrats arrayed against New England pride and pretension. Compared to the cosmopolitan and genteel Jefferson, Jackson was, however, more western and roughhewn, himself an embodiment of America's restless westward migration and raucous frontier culture.

ONCE IN OFFICE, EACH OF America's three most successful early presidents continued to achieve. In the process, these three proved that in the right hands, the presidency as created by the Constitution could work rather well. President Washington launched and stabilized the union; President Jefferson doubled its landmass; and President Jackson preserved, protected, and defended the Constitution against nullifying extremists led by his own vice president, John C. Calhoun.

Each of the three thus helped the Constitution pass a critical test early in the document's life cycle. Although the framers at Philadelphia had tried to learn from the past, they had also chosen to break with all previous historical experience. The Constitution and the presidency were truly novel. No prior democracy in history had ever aimed to span nearly so large a land, over quite so heterogeneous a population. Various ancient republics and Britain had blended democratic ideas and institutions with major elements of hereditary political power. America aimed to repudiate hereditary rule entirely in all three branches of government. (Hereditary slavery, which factored into apportionment rules, was the enormous exception.)

Could the Philadelphia blueprint actually work in practice as its friends had hoped and predicted it would? President Washington proved that it could. But that was only the first great test. After all, the document—and the presidency—had been designed by and for Washington himself. After Adams's failed efforts to fill his predecessor's shoes, President Jefferson proved that the system could work for someone *other than George Washington*. That was the second great test.

Then came the third great test: Could the system work *for the next generation*? Could America first produce and then identify new figures large enough to fill the enormous shoes of Article II? Once in office, could presidents who were merely founding sons, and not founding fathers, do the job? Unlike Britain's monarchs, American presidents would not be trained from birth to head the nation. Unlike British prime ministers after 1832—a year that saw major Parliamentary reform—American presidents would not necessarily command the ongoing support of the national legislature; nor could they hide behind a collective and coalitional cabinet. Rather, Article II vested massive power in one man, alone, electable and reelectable independently of the Congress. Post-founding America would need to consistently produce, and then consistently select, presidents big enough to hold their own against possible assaults from powerful states and from Congresses perhaps controlled by captious critics and rivals. The Jackson presidency proved that the Constitution was indeed robust enough to work not merely for the founding generation but for posterity.

SLAVERY

Alas, the Philadelphia Constitution also had a fatal flaw, an Achilles' heel. Slavery was not merely tolerated but privileged. Slave states would have extra electoral clout by dint of the slaves in their midst. Unlike the Constitution's rule that Congress could halt the importation of slaves from abroad in 1808—an option that Congress exercised at the end of the Jefferson era—the document made no provision for phasing out the Three-Fifths Clause. That clause formed the foundation not just of House apportionment but also of Electoral College apportionment. Slave states would have extra seats in the Electoral College because of their slaves. The more slaves, the more seats.

After the Three-Fifths Clause notoriously provided Jefferson's margin of victory, leading New Englanders urged that any potential Twelfth Amendment revising the rules of presidential and vice-presidential election should also eliminate or phase out this mathematically unrepublican clause. Jeffersonians ignored these pleas and America continued to give an inside track to its slavocracy in its presidential election system. Until Lincoln, America's presidents were all southern slave owners or northern appeasers (including both Adamses while in office). Prior to 1861, no sitting president—indeed, not a single incumbent cabinet officer—ever called for slavery's eventual abolition, even gradually with full compensation to slave masters.[6]

In 1803–1804, President Jefferson, a Virginian, acquired vast new lands for America, but he took no steps at that magic moment to prevent slavery's spread. In 1820, President Monroe, another Virginian, signed a bill—the Missouri Compromise—excluding slavery from some western lands while allowing slavery in other large tracts. Both of Virginia's senators opposed the slavery restriction—the so-called Thomas Amendment, named for Illinois senator Jesse B. Thomas, excluding slavery from Louisiana Purchase territory (apart from Missouri) north of the latitude line 36°30'. In the House, nearly half the no votes came from eighteen Virginia members. In private correspondence, ex-presidents Jefferson and Madison sided with these Virginia reactionaries; Madison even questioned the constitutionality of the prohibition. Centuries earlier, Virginia had lost her own virginity, and now many leading Virginians stopped insisting, as they once had, on preserving the virginity of America's West to the maximum extent possible.[7]

Old Madison's new position was particularly disappointing and outlandish (and has been ignored or minimized by most of his admiring modern biographers).[8] His new notion that Congress lacked authority to prohibit slavery in federal territory was utterly inconsistent with the Constitution's text, enactment history, and early implementation under President Washington and his then prime minister—Madison himself. The document unequivocally gave Congress plenary power to regulate territories, where no competing state law existed and thus federalism concerns were minimal: "Congress shall have Power to . . . make all needful Rules and Regulations respecting the Territory . . . belonging to the United States." Even before the Philadelphia Convention ended, the Confederation Congress, building on ideas initially proposed by none other than Thomas Jefferson, had prohibited slavery in the Northwest Territory. In the ratification process, leading anti-slavery Federalists such as James Wilson had publicly reassured anti-slavery northerners that Congress under the Constitution would follow this template.[9]

True, nothing in the Constitution guaranteed federal free soil, but surely nothing in it prohibited federal free soil. In 1788, no leading Federalist, north or south, publicly contradicted Wilson's claim that the new Congress could and would follow in the free-soil footsteps of the old Congress. The following year, Washington, backed by House leader Madison, proudly added his name to a Congressional statute—one of the first ten laws adopted under the new Constitution—reaffirming the Northwest Ordinance's free-soil rules. In 1820, when President Monroe signed on to a statute that included the Thomas Amendment, none of his cabinet members—not even South Carolina's John C. Calhoun—claimed that the free-soil provisions were unconstitutional.[10]

Later, the Supreme Court, in its most infamous decision of all time—*Dred Scott v. Sanford*—would assert, preposterously, just that: the Thomas Amendment provisions and various other post-1789 efforts to exclude slavery from various federal territories were unconstitutional, said the 1857 Court. A brilliant constitutional lawyer in Illinois, Abraham Lincoln, would rightly label this claim an "astonisher." Lincoln would eventually win the presidency, in Jeffersonian fashion, on a platform condemning *Dred Scott* as every bit as constitutionally outrageous as the Sedition Act of 1798. Still later, Lincoln would become the first president since Jackson to win a second term.[11]

But Lincoln would come to power by running, in effect, against Jackson. The author of the infamous *Dred Scott* opinion, Roger

Taney, was a former Jackson cabinet member placed on the Court by Jackson himself. Two other members of the *Dred* majority were also Jackson men.

Jackson's election and reelection marked an important turning point in America's constitutional conversation on slavery. America's earlier presidents were deeply embarrassed by human bondage. Jackson was not. The early presidents hoped that the slavery issue might largely solve itself. If Congress halted the international slave trade, slavery would, they prayed, gradually wither away.[12] But in fact national policymakers could not solve the problem simply by looking east and south—simply by halting slave importation from Africa and the Caribbean after 1808. The West, too, was key. To end American slavery, the federal government would likely need to prevent the peculiar institution from spreading to virgin soil and thus taking root in lands that would later join the system as slave states. Washington and Jefferson had often looked west, but Jackson was America's first truly western president. If anyone understood the West personally and viscerally it was Andrew Jackson. Yet he took no steps to stop slavery's western spread. On the contrary, he himself embodied slavery's western spread, both personally and politically.

Decennial census data available to Jackson conclusively proved that slavery was not withering away as initially hoped. Even after the formal end of slave importation from Africa and the Caribbean in 1808, America's slave population continued to mushroom because of "natural increase"—homegrown American slaves, many of whom were born in, or taken to, America's western lands. In 1810, America had 1.2 million slaves; in 1820, 1.5 million; in 1830, 2 million; in 1840, 2.5 million. True, the percentage of Americans in bondage was trending downward, but at a snail's pace, from 16.4 percent in 1810 to 14.6 percent in 1840.

On the key question of slavery, Jackson was not a great or even a good president. Born in South Carolina,[13] America's most aggressively and shamelessly pro-slavery state, he eventually set up a cotton plantation, the Hermitage, in his adopted state of Tennessee. He came to own hundreds of slaves, and he did so by choice. Unlike his highborn Virginia predecessors—Washington, Jefferson, and Madison—Jackson did not inherit his slaves or marry into them. He bought Black humans unashamedly as a self-made man on the rise and never freed any significant number in life or at death. His most important public choices mirrored his private ones. President Washington gave America Chief Justice John Jay; President Adams gave America Chief Justice John Marshall; and President Jackson gave America Chief Justice Roger Taney.

The arc traced by America's three most successful early presidents thus evidenced a troubling trajectory that rather predictably ensued from the powerful gravitational pull of the Three-Fifths Clause created at Philadelphia and consecrated by the Twelfth Amendment. All three of America's great early presidents were slaveholders. The first two came from Virginia, and the third was more unequivocally southern and western—born in South Carolina, and politically re-born in Tennessee. The negative trajectory of these three notable presidents spelled trouble for the fast-maturing nation. Washington was an increasingly embarrassed slaveholder; Jefferson was an increasingly unembarrassed slaveholder; and Jackson was a proud slaveholder. On this most critical issue, Andrew Jackson was no George Washington.

ABOMINATION AND NULLIFICATION

On other issues, however, Jackson was ardently and self-consciously Washingtonian. His inner Washington emerged most dramatically in opposition to various forms of disunionism preached by John C. Calhoun.

Calhoun's core constitutional claims were absurd—phantasmagorical creatures conjured from the spirit world of his overactive imagination, hallucinations that flatly contradicted what the Constitution's text actually said, what its structure plainly meant, and what the American people did in fact quite deliberately agree to in 1788 when they said "yes, We do." Jackson—also a South Carolinian by birth, and not one to back away from a fight—called Calhoun's bluff and stared him down in some of the most dramatic moments of American constitutional history.

The drama began in 1828, when Congress passed a protective tariff bill. The Constitution plainly gave Congress sweeping power to tax imports, and to do so not just to raise revenue but also to promote national security: "Congress shall have Power to lay and Collect Taxes, Duties, Imposts, and Excises, to Pay the Debts and provide for the common Defence and General Welfare of the United States." Unbroken Congressional practice tracing back to the earliest days of the constitutional republic confirmed that the text meant what it said,[14] as did common sense. Protecting America's burgeoning industrial base would render the nation less dependent on European manufacturers, less vulnerable to possible future British naval blockades and depredations, and better able to supply itself with necessaries in any war yet to come. The 1828 tariff was thus the very sort of law that a young Calhoun, an ardent "war hawk" and nationalist back in the 1810s, had himself routinely supported in Congress.

But Calhoun changed his stripes in the 1820s. Protective tariffs helped northeastern manufacturers at the expense of South Carolinian consumers. Many South Carolinians hated the 1828 law, which critics labeled "a Bill of Abominations." Some also worried that notions of broad federal power might one day lead Congress to think it could abolish slavery, not just in territories but also in slave states. Given these home-state sentiments, Calhoun needed to secure his political base. Over the course of a decade he careened from extreme nationalism to its polar opposite. This was akin to Madison's shift in the early 1790s, but Calhoun's volte-face was far more vivid and violent. Even if there was nothing insincere in this reversal, it was inane.

In 1828, Calhoun was vice president of the United States under President John Quincy Adams, who signed the high-tariff bill into law. A decade earlier, Calhoun and Adams had been warm friends in President Monroe's cabinet—much as Thomas Jefferson and John Adams had been close colleagues in the 1770s and 1780s. But the signing of the 1828 Tariff Act split John Q. and John C. every bit as dramatically as the signing of the 1798 Sedition Act had split

John and Thomas. Vice President Calhoun responded just as Vice President Jefferson had—secretly authoring a tract championing state sovereignty and nullification as the proper response to federal unconstitutionality. This time, the tract was composed not for Kentucky but for South Carolina. Although the state legislature declined to enact the vice president's clandestine handiwork, the lawmakers did order the printing and distribution of five thousand copies of the document.

The South Carolina Exposition and Protest of 1828 was a conscious echo of and homage to Jefferson's Kentucky Resolutions of 1798 and 1799. "To the States respectively *each in its sovereign capacity* [emphasis added] is reserved the power, by its veto, or right of interposition, to arrest the encroachment," asserted the closeted Calhoun. Each state could thus nullify—undo for its own citizens—any federal law that it and it alone deemed unconstitutional. Even if the rest of the union strongly disagreed and responded with a formal constitutional amendment endorsed by two-thirds of each Congressional house and three-quarters of the states, this would not end the matter. Here, Calhoun followed Jefferson's logic to its bitter end, though Jefferson himself had not explicitly done so. If each state was indeed sovereign, Calhoun reasoned, it retained a right to exit—to trigger "a dissolution of the political association, as far as it is concerned."

Calhoun also went further than Jefferson in one other regard. He was threatening immediate nullification (and perhaps ultimate secession) in response to an utterly anodyne and clearly constitutional statute. By contrast, Jefferson (and Madison) had rallied to resist a Sedition Act that was in fact unconstitutional and that threatened to shut down proper constitutional conversation itself—the very essence of the American constitutional project, the entire system's sine qua non.

Over the next several years, the tariff law remained on the books. Jackson wrested the presidency from Adams in the election of 1828, while Calhoun won reelection as vice president separately and independently (per the Twelfth Amendment).

Jackson believed in limited federal power and legitimate states' rights. He, too, was a proud Jeffersonian. But nullification and secession were to him, as they had been to Washington, anathema. The strong unionism of both Washington and Jackson had common roots. Both battlefield generals understood that an indivisible union was essential to America's ability to repel Britain (or France) if necessary. Also, although the national-security aspects of the 1828 Tariff Act may have failed to move most South Carolinians, they struck a chord with Jackson.

Jackson and Calhoun thus had entirely different understandings of the founders' legacy. In 1830, at a Democratic Party Jefferson Day dinner—a partisan event in honor of the party's recently deceased founding father—Jackson rose to propose a toast. Fixing Calhoun with a steely gaze (as if in a duel), he raised his glass to "Our federal Union—it must be preserved." This was pure Washington. Calhoun coolly countered with a Jeffersonian toast of his own: "The Union— next to our liberty, the most dear. May we all remember that it can only be preserved by respecting the rights of the states, and distributing equally the benefit and burden of the Union."

Over the next three years, the confrontation between the two native South Carolinians—both Scotch-Irish and both fierce— widened and burst into full view. In mid-1831, Calhoun issued public remarks from his Fort Hill home, proclaiming "nullification" as "the fundamental principle of our system." In mid-1832, Jackson signed into law a revised tariff bill with gentler rates to placate South Carolina, but the state refused to back down. In late 1832, the state legislature called an ad hoc state convention that in turn purported to nullify both the 1828 and 1832 laws, declaring them unenforceable in South Carolina. Siding with his home state and home base, Calhoun promptly resigned from the vice presidency so that he could represent South Carolina as a US senator.[15]

In his Nullification Proclamation of December 10, 1832—a declaration that deserves to be remembered today alongside other landmark presidential pronouncements, such as Washington's 1793 Neutrality Proclamation and Lincoln's 1863 Emancipation Proclamation—Jackson responded with a forceful statement of first principles:

Our social compact in express terms declares, that the laws of the United States, its Constitution, and treaties made under it, are the supreme law of the land; and for greater caution adds, "that the judges in every State shall be bound thereby, anything in the Constitution or laws of any State to the contrary notwithstanding." . . . If this [nullification] doctrine had been established at an earlier day, the Union would have been dissolved in its infancy. . . . [T]he doctrine of a State veto upon the laws of the Union carries with it internal evidence of its impracticable absurdity, [and] our constitutional history will also afford abundant proof that it would have been repudiated with indignation had it been proposed to form a feature in our Government. . . . I consider, then, the power to annul a law of the United States, assumed by one State, *incompatible with the existence of the Union, contradicted expressly by the letter of the Constitution, unauthorized by its spirit, inconsistent with every principle on which it was founded, and destructive of the great object for which it was formed.*

The emphatic italics were Jackson's. He went on to wrap himself in the mantle of George Washington and to make a classic and compelling *originalist* argument, that is, an argument based on the Constitution's text and structure and the original understanding of the American people in 1788 when they had agreed to the document:

Did the name of Washington sanction, did the States deliberately ratify, such an anomaly [nullification] in the history of fundamental legislation? No. We were not mistaken. The letter of this great instrument is free from this radical fault; its language directly contradicts the imputation, its spirit, its evident intent, contradicts it. No, we did not err. Our Constitution does not contain the absurdity of giving power to make laws, and another power to resist them. The sages, whose memory will always be reverenced, have given us a practical, and, as they hoped, a permanent constitutional compact. The Father of his Country did not affix his revered name to so palpable an absurdity. Nor did the States, when they severally ratified it, do so under the impression that a veto on the laws of the United

States was reserved to them, or that they could exercise it by application. Search the debates in all their conventions—examine the speeches of the most zealous opposers of federal authority—look at the amendments that were proposed. They are all silent—not a syllable uttered, not a vote given, not a motion made, to correct the explicit supremacy given to the laws of the Union over those of the States, or to show that implication, as is now contended, could defeat it. No, we have not erred! The Constitution is still the object of our reverence, the bond of our Union, our defense in danger, the source of our prosperity in peace. It shall descend, as we have received it, uncorrupted by sophistical construction to our posterity.

Jackson also responded with military and legal force. He sent naval warships into Charleston Harbor and threatened to prosecute and hang Calhoun—or anyone else resisting proper federal authority—for treason. In February 1833, Congress passed, over Senator Calhoun's vociferous objections, a Force Bill expanding federal court jurisdiction in revenue cases and authorizing broad use of federal military power to overcome local efforts to obstruct federal law or federal officers.[16]

Like 1800, 1832 was a presidential election year. In 1800, Americans had sided with the *opponents* of the recent Sedition Act. In 1832, the nation overwhelmingly backed the *supporters* of the recent tariff act. Jackson won reelection by a wide margin, with 55 percent of the popular vote and 76 percent of the electoral vote. Roughly 37 percent of the popular vote and 17 percent of the electoral vote went to another nationalist candidate, Henry Clay. John Floyd, a Calhoun ally, got no popular votes at all and won a paltry 4 percent of the total electoral vote, all of which came from South Carolina (where the legislature directly picked the electors and did not allow common voters to weigh in). Meanwhile, Calhoun himself was dumped from the national Democratic Party ticket in favor of Martin Van Buren, who became Jackson's new vice president in 1833. Van Buren went on to win the presidency in his own right in 1836 as Jackson's handpicked successor.

In all of this, America in effect once again voted for George Washington.

IN OR AROUND 1833, JUST as Jackson was winning reelection, painter Ralph Earl depicted the general in the tradition of Washington—a tall, erect, uniformed horseman astride a magnificent steed, firm in the saddle, controlled and self-possessed, embodying American strength, pride, resolve, and martial dignity.

Jackson's strong anti-nullification stand at the end of his first term casts light backward on a closely related but lesser-known consti-

tutional skirmish that had broken out in 1831. The most extreme form of Calhoun-ism asserted that each sovereign state could veto any federal law it chose. A subtle variant conceded that the Constitution's Supremacy Clause generally obliged a state to obey a duly enacted Congressional statute, but only if the statute was in fact constitutional—a determination that each state must make for itself, claimed Calhoun. On this view, a nullifying state had to do more than call a Congressional statute an abomination. The state had to call the statute an *unconstitutional* abomination. Jackson's proclamation declared that this was largely a distinction without a difference. An "uncontrolled right" of each state "to decide what laws deserve" to be called unconstitutional would "give the power of resisting all laws."

A precursor of the Calhoun-Jackson debate had arisen in *Martin v. Hunter's Lessee* in the mid-1810s. Virginia's Spencer Roane had ridiculously claimed that the Supreme Court lacked authority to reverse state courts on issues of federal statutory and constitutional law.[17] Story and his *Martin* colleagues emphatically smacked Roane down. Section 25 of the Judiciary Act of 1789 quite explicitly gave the US Supreme Court authority to review any state court ruling that threatened federal rights—including any ruling setting aside a Congressional statute on alleged constitutional grounds. If on the merits the Supreme Court justices agreed with the state court below, they could of course say so and the Congressional statute would indeed be set aside: that was standard judicial review. But if the Supreme Court determined that Congress had in fact acted within its constitutional bounds, the justices could, thanks to section 25, reverse the state court below—nullifying the attempted nullification.

The Judiciary Act that *Martin* relied upon was a landmark law passed by the First Congress, a body filled with Philadelphia framers. In the House, Madison had enthusiastically supported the 1789 act in general and section 25 in particular, which squarely built on his own ideas at Philadelphia, especially the idea that states needed to be monitored from above by an American Privy Council of sorts. Washington had signed the 1789 bill into law without hesitation. Although ex-president Jefferson in 1815 had privately encouraged Roane's silly claims[18]—if then president Madison knew this, he surely cringed—*Martin* seemed to end the matter the following year.

Or did it? In the middle of Jackson's first term, Calhoun's South Carolinian allies in Congress tried to repeal section 25. The Court in *Martin*, and in several subsequent cases, however, had insisted that section 25 in some form or other was not merely constitutionally permissible, but constitutionally obligatory. Story once confided to a friend that if the twenty-fifth section were ever repealed, the Constitution would be "practically gone."[19] As noted earlier, Congress in 1831 overwhelmingly sided with Story and against Calhoun.

Many Jackson allies in Congress voted against repeal—against Calhoun, against state nullification via state courts—but Jackson himself had not played a high-profile role in this mid-1831 Congressional conversation. Via his emphatic 1832 proclamation, Jackson now made clear to all exactly where he stood—squarely opposed to any form of Calhoun-ism in which each state claimed to be the final arbiter of federal power for its own citizens, whether in a state convention, a state legislature, or a state court.[20]

EXECUTIVE POWER

Several of the most notable constitutional conversations in the Jackson era had a touch of déjà vu—Calhoun's failed efforts to revive Jefferson's and Roane's worst ideas, and Jackson's successful repetition of Washington's and Story's best ideas. Happily for the American constitutional project, stronger constitutional arguments generally continued to prevail against weaker ones: founding sons in the 1830s generally sought to follow, and generally succeeded in following, the Constitution as ordained, established, and understood by their founding fathers.

The Age of Jackson was thus not a scene of open and avowed constitutional infidelity run amok, even as outlandish claims surfaced prominently—as they do in every era, including our own. Calhoun claimed that his peculiar ideas had strong roots in the Constitution's text, history, and structure, much as willful politicians today claim that black is white. But as Jackson made clear, Calhoun was wrong on the facts: black was not white, and words actually meant what they said. Thanks in no small part to Jackson's stern fidelity and plain-spoken clarity, Calhoun lost deservedly and decisively.

The Calhoun-Jackson jousts largely involved issues of federalism—national power versus states' rights. A similar dynamic of originalism and déjà vu played out in a different arena, the separation of powers between Congress and the president. Here, the chief offender trying to revive old discredited ideas was not John C. Calhoun but Henry Clay.

Both Clay and Calhoun dreamed of displacing Jackson, and both failed. Because America by the 1830s had developed sound rules, principles, and practices for proper constitutional interpretation, it was not a coincidence that in Jackson's key contests with these men, the views that were in fact more faithful to those of the founding fathers—Jackson's views—won out. Nor was it unsurprising that

Calhoun and Clay, who hitched their political wagons to flawed constitutional claims, never reached their desired destination, the Executive Mansion, a mere sixteen blocks from the Capitol. So close yet so far.

THE CONSTITUTIONAL CLASH BETWEEN JACKSON and Clay was triggered in late 1833 when Jackson fired his treasury secretary, William John Duane, who had defied presidential directives concerning the Bank of the United States.* Led by Clay, whom Jackson had trounced in the preceding presidential election, various senators blasted Jackson and urged Congress to repudiate the Decision of 1789.

In early March 1834, Clay introduced a series of resolutions. The first asserted that "the constitution of the United States does not vest in the President power to remove at his pleasure" executive officers, even department heads such as Duane. The second said that Congress was "authorized by the constitution" to prescribe by law what tenure was appropriate for executive subordinates. A third urged the Senate Judiciary Committee to consider legislation generally requiring Senate approval of all high-level firings except for ambassadors and except during Senate recesses (during which temporary firings would be allowed). This third resolution was the most aggressive of the lot, contemplating as it did direct Senate involvement in executive-branch removals—a species of "legislative veto" that today would be unanimously laughed out of Court.[21]

No legislation along the lines of Clay's resolutions ensued—a sign of the constitutional system's health and strength. Even so, in late March 1834 the Senate passed a resolution censuring Jackson for his general conduct vis-à-vis the national bank, without specific mention of his removal of Duane.[22] Jackson countered in mid-April with

---

*Duane hailed from a family of Jeffersonian journalists who took over the edgy *Aurora General Advertiser* after the death of Benjamin Franklin Bache. Duane's wife, Deborah Franklin Bache, was Benjamin Franklin Bache's sister and Benjamin Franklin's granddaughter.

a blistering protest message insisting, among other things, that the Decision of 1789 had settled the removal question. Jackson described the Decision of 1789 as "a full expression of the sense of the Legislature" supported by "the concurrent authority of President Washington, of the Senate, and the House of Representatives, numbers of whom had taken an active part in the convention which framed the Constitution and in the State conventions which adopted it." Jackson also invoked the "numerous removals made by" his predecessors in pursuance of the Decision of 1789.[23]

In 1836, Clay's party—the newly named Whigs—did not renominate him for the presidency, and Jackson's protégé, Martin Van Buren, coasted to a comfortable victory. In the ensuing lame-duck session, the Senate expunged its earlier censure resolution, much to the satisfaction of soon-to-be-ex-president Jackson.[24] When close to death, Jackson reportedly said that the two biggest things he had left undone were that "I didn't shoot Henry Clay and I didn't hang John C. Calhoun."[25]

JACKSON'S VETO PRACTICES HARKENED BACK to Washington's sound examples and Jefferson's sensible elaborations. Washington had used his veto pen twice—once against an apportionment bill that he deemed unconstitutional and again to thwart an army-regulation bill that he considered unwise. Jefferson never had need to veto a bill but had thoughtfully outlined a "departmentalist" approach to constitutionally based vetoes. Jackson did not hesitate to use his veto pen for both constitutional and policy purposes.

Jackson's most famous veto, withholding his assent from a July 1832 bill to renew the Bank of the United States yet again, has been widely misunderstood by modern students and scholars. The bank of course had been upheld against constitutional attack by a unanimous Supreme Court in the 1819 *McCulloch* case. Jackson nevertheless vetoed the bank renewal bill largely on constitutional grounds. Contrary to popular belief today, Jackson did not say that an incorporated national bank was inherently unconstitutional and beyond

Congress's enumerated power—the extremist position staked out by Congressman Madison and Secretary of State Jefferson back in 1791, and later quietly abandoned by President Madison in 1816. Rather, Jackson identified certain specific details about the bank bill that he found objectionable on both constitutional and policy grounds. Aliens, he thought, should not be allowed to hold shares in a proper American central bank. Jackson's additional stated objection was narrow and fine-grained: given that state-chartered banks had to pay various state taxes, the national bank should have to pay state taxes at the same rates. Anything less, he declared, was unequal and disrespectful of states.[26]

Jackson also scolded Congress for not having solicited his views earlier in the legislative process and stressed that a sound bank bill could easily be crafted within Congress's enumerated powers, properly construed:

> *That a bank of the United States, competent to all the duties which may be required by the Government, might be so organized as not to infringe on . . . the reserved rights of the States I do not entertain a doubt.* Had the Executive been called upon to furnish the project of such an institution, the duty would have been cheerfully performed. In the absence of such a call it was obviously proper that he should confine himself to pointing out those prominent features in the act presented which in his opinion make it incompatible with the Constitution and sound policy.[27]

In sound Jeffersonian fashion—echoing the Virginian's explanation of his presidential actions in connection with the Sedition Act—Jackson also offered a classic defense of constitutional departmentalism, the view that each of the Constitution's three main departments—legislative, executive, and judicial—may properly determine constitutional law for itself in certain situations. Jackson did not claim (nor did Jefferson before him) a general right as an executive to refuse to enforce court orders. Jackson surely did not say (nor did Jefferson) that a president could defy a Supreme Court judgment holding federal action to be illegal or unconstitutional. Rather, Jackson made clear, à la Jefferson, that even after a court declared that a given federal action was constitutionally *permissible* (say, the Sedition Act or a bank bill), a president was free to think and act otherwise—to say no when the court had said yes—when wielding his veto pen or pardon pen. Thus, Jefferson had repeatedly and correctly insisted that as president he was permitted (indeed, he thought obliged) to pardon anyone convicted under the Sedition Act because he deemed the act unconstitutional, regardless of what Justice Chase and Justice Paterson thought. He was likewise permitted (and perhaps obliged) to veto any legislative effort to revive the Sedition Act.[28]

What was true of the Sedition Act was also true of the bank bill, Jackson explained. As a lawmaker, via the veto power, he was surely free to take a stricter view of federal power than the Court had taken in *McCulloch*. (To repeat: he did not take the ultra-strict view, à la Jefferson and Madison in 1791, that Congress simply lacked power to create a national bank corporation.)

"The Congress, the Executive, and the Court," he explained in his famous bank veto,

> must each for itself be guided by its own opinion of the Constitution. Each public officer who takes an oath to support the Constitution swears that he will support it as he understands it, and not as it is understood by others. It is as much the duty of the House of Representatives, of the Senate, and of the President to decide upon the constitutionality of any bill or resolution which may be presented to them for passage or approval as it is of the supreme judges when it may be brought before them for judicial decision. The opinion of the judges has no more authority over Congress than the opinion of Congress has over the judges, and on that point the President is independent of both. The authority of the Supreme Court must not, therefore, be permitted to control the Congress or the Executive *when acting in their legislative capacities*, but to have only such influence as the force of their reasoning may deserve.[29]

None of this was inconsistent with what John Marshall had said in *Marbury*, or in *McCulloch*, for that matter. Jackson had a robust view of executive power, but not a lawless view. Indeed, Jackson's view of executive power aligned him with Washington and Jefferson at their best.

SPEECH

Alas, Jackson's pro-slavery worldview squinted against free speech—an ironic twist for a man who presented himself as a neo-Jeffersonian. Jefferson, of course, had swept to power by championing free expression against Adams and the Sedition Act.

ACTUALLY, JEFFERSON'S POSITION, ON CLOSE inspection, was more mixed and more troubling. Emphasizing states' rights above all—even above expressive rights—Jefferson, in his Kentucky Resolution drafts and in private correspondence, had embraced the right of states to suppress speech as they chose. *Congress* had no Article I enumerated power to abridge free expression to begin with, and the prohibitory language of the First Amendment underscored this absence of power: "Congress shall make no law . . . abridging the freedom of speech or of the press." But states, thought Jefferson, were surely not bound by limited enumerations of Congressional power in Article I, or the express language of Amendment I limiting Congress and only Congress.

So far, so good, as even Jefferson's "twistifying" cousin John Marshall would have agreed, and did in fact expressly agree in his Jeffersonian opinion in the 1833 case of *Barron v. Baltimore*. However, *Barron* on its facts was a dispute about just compensation for an alleged taking of private property. The case had not directly involved speech, much less political speech.

A strong argument could in fact be made that, above and beyond the First Amendment, the very nature of democratic government entailed a right of citizens to criticize government officials—state as well as federal. Such a right was a logically necessary ingredient of a truly republican government—a government of the people, a government in which, as Madison had declared in 1794, "the censorial power is in the people over the government and not in the government over the people."[30] Structurally, the people in America, not state governments, were sovereign. State officials were mere servants who at all times were indeed subject to proper political reproach and chastisement by their true legal masters, the sovereign citizens. Textually, the Constitution in Article IV demanded that each state government maintain a proper "Republican Form." A state that punished political dissent was not truly republican in nature. Or so one might think.

Indeed, in the years between 1789 and 1800, James Madison began to think in just these ways. Young Madison believed and said that state governments should abide by proper principles of freedom, and the federal government should safeguard these freedom principles from above.

Despite their impressive Madisonian pedigree and their powerful structural foundation, these ideas faced strong opposition in the 1830s, because they construed federal power—power to enforce the Republican Government Clause—broadly. A related argument also interpreted federal power broadly: many political issues were in fact issues of national import. If states could not properly shut down a national bank (as *McCulloch* had held), surely states could not properly shut down a national debate about the need for a national bank. Or even a national debate about, say, the need to abolish slavery, everywhere, not just in federal territories but within the several states, via a constitutional amendment, if necessary.

In the 1830s, many who worshipped at the altar of states' rights and strict construction of federal power refused to follow young Madison's approach to various issues of free expression that exploded all around them. Instead, Jackson and many Jacksonians followed Jefferson, and did so with anxieties about slavery and abolition very much in mind.

THE INTERTWINED ISSUES OF SLAVERY and speech arose in several settings. First, slave states criminalized anti-slavery and abolitionist discourse, and did so with increasing aggressiveness. In 1819, Maryland unsuccessfully prosecuted a Methodist minister, the Reverend Jacob Gruber, for preaching a relatively tame sermon that condemned the institution of slavery while exhorting slaves in Pauline fashion to obey their masters.[31] In 1830, with Jackson in the White House, Louisiana passed a law saying that any person—even a preacher or stage actor or someone in private conversation—could be put to death if he used language "having a tendency to produce discontent among the free colored population of this State or to excite insubordination among the slaves." Ditto for anyone who brought into the state "any paper, pamphlet, or book having such tendency."[32] Merely bringing in a copy of, say, an anti-slavery Quaker sermon for one's personal edification thus exposed the would-be reader to the risk of capital punishment.

On Madisonian grounds, such a law seemed nightmarish, a direct threat to freedom of the mind and freedom of religion as well as freedom of expression. Louisiana criminalized written words, oral expression, and literature importation even in the absence of any *intent* to foment rebellion; even if the words at issue did not risk any *imminent* harm; and even if these words simply had a *tendency* to provoke mere *insubordination* or *abstract intellectual discontent* as opposed to *active* and *violent insurrection*. Truth was no defense; on this count, the Louisiana law was much worse than Adams's hated Sedition Act. If read at face value, the Louisiana law would make it felonious to run for Congress on an avowedly anti-slavery platform. Even if the law might not be read so strictly in an actual trial, who would be willing to risk his life on the mere hope that judges would soften the statute's scary words? Yet to a strict Jeffersonian, the Constitution imposed no limits on a state law like this.

In 1831, a Virginia-born slave preacher named Nat Turner led a slave revolt near the state's North Carolina border. Officials eventually restored order, but not before some fifty Whites died at the hands of desperate Blacks seeking the same freedom that the Whites claimed as their birthright. Some Jacksonians blamed a rising abolitionist movement led by Whites and free Blacks, male and female. If only these troublemakers would stop agitating!

In 1833, Britain outlawed slavery within its empire. The pride that Americans had felt from 1776 to 1815 now mixed with feelings of shame. America was generally more democratic than Britain (where only a tiny fraction of the adult male population could vote), and equally muscular (as New Orleans had proved). But Britain was now surging ahead along one critical dimension of human civilization— the pursuit of liberty and justice for all.

IT WAS AGAINST THIS IDEOLOGICALLY charged backdrop that the next great free-speech debate began to unfold, a debate implicating federal rules alongside state laws.

In mid-1835, South Carolina postmasters sought guidance from Jackson's newly appointed postmaster general, Amos Kendall. Kendall had been a prominent Kentucky newspaperman in the mid-1810s and the 1820s, editor and part owner of a highly influential backcountry publication, the Frankfort-based *Argus*. Along with his friend Francis P. Blair, a newspaperman who eventually came to run the *Washington Globe*, the house organ of the Jackson wing of the Democratic Party, Kendall had helped Jackson build and maintain fame and popularity across America. The tight links between these two key newspapermen; the publications they ran; the Democratic Party; the emerging party boss, Martin Van Buren; and the party's ultimate chieftain, Andrew Jackson—now president of the United States—were the sinews of Jackson's system. Media mastery, political networking, electioneering, patronage, and legal authority were now all working together in ways that Jefferson and Madison had begun to foresee and forge decades earlier.

Before assuming official power as postmaster general, Kendall had been a critical adviser to Jackson, as was Blair—key members of Jackson's informal "Kitchen Cabinet," which was an even more powerful conversational circle for the president than were his official department heads. In 1835, Kendall moved inside the formal system, into the very cockpit of power. As postmaster general, he had vast control over local mail deliverers—a huge network of potential patronage. Even more critically, the postal service was the backbone of America's communication infrastructure. Postmen delivered newspapers and other printed material that shaped public opinion, which in turn determined public elections and public policy. Now, Kendall, himself an old newspaperman, was being asked by men in South Carolina about the government's newspaper-delivery policy.

As in Louisiana, distribution of "incendiary" publications was a felony in South Carolina,[33] but federal law seemed to require delivery of all mailed materials to willing recipients. Kendall initially inclined toward a position that federal law could not properly override the criminal laws of sovereign states within their own borders. But this position seemed perilously close to the notion that states could nullify federal law on their own soil, a position that Jackson had emphatically rejected as a general matter in 1832, and indeed had rejected in a high-profile showdown with none other than South Carolina.

Even if South Carolina could not dictate unilaterally to the union, surely Congress itself could decide, within proper limits, how to run the federal post office, pursuant to its explicit Article I power to "establish Post Offices and post Roads." But what exactly were the proper limits?

There ensued a fascinating constitutional conversation about constitutional conversation itself—perhaps the most important reflexive conversation of this sort since the Sedition Act controversy. The conversation also featured a captivating cast of characters. Several of America's leading founding sons played their parts with gusto as the nation watched with rapt attention. This was a debate about newspapers—and newspapers, in both the capital and the hinterlands, covered it with special interest.

JACKSON MADE THE OPENING MOVE. In his Seventh Annual Message to Congress, dated December 7, 1835, he proposed a new federal statute that would, in his broad outline, "prohibit, under severe penalties, the circulation in the southern states, through the mail, of incendiary publications intended to instigate the slaves to insurrection."[34]

Bad as Jackson's proposed law was, it was infinitely better than Louisiana's approach. It proposed "severe penalties," but not death. It applied only to items sent through the mail. It thus left untouched private circulation of printed matter and oral communication. It said nothing about writings for or about free Blacks as such. It targeted only publications *intended* to provoke actual *insurrection*.

Still, it leaned toward slavery and pro-slavery partisans. Though not so slanted as the Sedition Act, which had criminalized challengers who criticized incumbents but not vice versa, Jackson's proposed bill was not truly evenhanded in purpose and effect. It did not propose severe penalties for the circulation in the southern states, through the mail, of incendiary publications intended to instigate *violence against persons who peacefully advocated for the abolition or amelioration of slavery*. (As we shall see, such abolitionists were in fact genuinely at risk.) Nor did Jackson propose severe penalties for the circulation in the *northern states*, through the mail, of incendiary publications intended to instigate *insurrection against anti-slavery state officials urging the abolition or amelioration of slavery*. If slavery were indeed a matter for each state to decide for itself, as a pure states' rights theory might hold, why was Jackson inviting the federal post office to take sides?

Also, Jackson's formulation had no limiting language that insurrection must be both likely and imminent. Without such limits, his proposal threatened to criminalize postal circulation of abstract political, philosophical, and religious discourse. Would it be a crime to mail a treatise on the right of revolution? What about a treatise on the Declaration of Independence itself and its claim that in situations of "absolute despotism," a people has a "right," and indeed a "duty," to "throw off . . . government"? Suppose that William Lloyd Garrison's fledgling abolitionist weekly, *The Liberator*, merely published the text of the Declaration itself with the avowed intent to encourage slave rebellions. Would postal circulation of this, too, be criminal?

In the Senate, Calhoun—the man whom Jackson had recently threatened to hang—opposed Jackson's bill on states' rights grounds. He worried that if Congress today could prohibit anti-slavery (and only anti-slavery) mail, then Congress at some later date could prohibit pro-slavery (and only pro-slavery) mail. The underlying logic of Jackson's bill, claimed Calhoun, would "clothe Congress with the power to abolish slavery." (This was the eternal South Carolinian anxiety and dog whistle against all manner of federal legislation.) As a substitute for Jackson's bill, Calhoun proposed that Congress borrow state laws for its federal standard. Wherever a state made it criminal to circulate a certain publication "touching the subject of slavery," the federal mails should be closed to that publication.[35]

But this, too, posed a Jeffersonian problem, because, on the strictest Jeffersonian view, the First Amendment counseled against any federal intervention whatsoever. Even if Congress merely incorporated state rules, wouldn't this still be a violation of the rule that "*Congress shall make no law* . . . abridging freedom of speech or of the press"?[36]

Massachusetts senator Daniel Webster opposed Calhoun's substitute bill as akin to prepublication censorship in violation of Blackstonian principles of press freedom. Punishing writings after the fact was very different from preventing their publication and circulation. Liberty of the press, Webster declared, was "the liberty of printing as well as the liberty of publishing in all the ordinary modes of publication; and was not the circulation of papers through the mails an ordinary mode of publication?"[37]

Not really, countered Pennsylvania senator and future pro-slavery president James Buchanan: "Every person may print, publish, and circulate whatever he pleases; but are we therefore compelled to become his agents, and to circulate for him everything he may choose to publish? . . . It was one thing not to restrain or punish publications;

and it was another and an entirely different thing to carry and circulate them after they have been published."[38]

At this point, Senator Henry Clay of Kentucky jumped into the fray, relishing the opportunity to blast two of his least favorite people, Jackson and Calhoun (who at this point cordially detested each other and, of course, Clay). Both Jackson and Calhoun, Clay needled, were violating their professed Jeffersonian principles of strict construction, states' rights, and limited federal power. Why shouldn't the entire matter be left to states? While in the federal mail system, the publications were harmless enough, and the instant they left the mail system and were delivered, "it was perfectly competent to the State authorities" to regulate the matter: "He wanted to know whence Congress derived the power to pass this law." Rebutting Jackson's ally Buchanan, Clay denied that "the post office power" gave Congress "the right to regulate what should be carried in the mails." He finished with a classic slippery-slope argument: "Why, if such a doctrine prevailed, the Government might designate the persons, or parties, or classes who should have the benefit of the mails, excluding all others." If Buchanan and Jackson were right, could Congress limit the mails to members of the Democratic Party, or to strictly pro-incumbent publications?[39]

At the end of this fascinating debate, Calhoun's bill failed. For the moment, freedom of expression had prevailed—at least in Washington City.

REPRESSIVE STATE LAWS, ESPECIALLY IN the South, still operated in full force, and elsewhere anti-abolition rioters took matters into their own hands, going far beyond what crowds had done back in colonial Boston.

In 1836, Jackson's last full year in office, anti-abolitionist thugs in Cincinnati twice demolished the printing press that James G. Birney used to produce his abolitionist weekly, *The Philanthropist*. The *New York Evening-Post* grimly predicted that "probably . . . nothing short of murder [would] effect" the mob's evident aim to silence Birney.[40]

Birney somehow managed to save his skin, and indeed, he later ran for president. Others were not so lucky. On November 7, 1837, pro-slavery rioters in Alton, Illinois, murdered Presbyterian minister Elijah Lovejoy two days shy of his thirty-fifth birthday. Lovejoy had used his weekly church circular to condemn slavery. Gangs had repeatedly destroyed his printing machinery—the Birney treatment, farther west—but the preacher had persisted, and indeed intensified, eventually urging immediate abolition of slavery. His death shocked decent Americans everywhere, from Abraham Lincoln in nearby Springfield to John Quincy Adams in far-off Washington, DC. But many pro-slavery extremists thought the uppity minister had gotten what he deserved, reaping what he had sown.

Meanwhile, Philadelphia abolitionists were completing work on a grand edifice only steps from the spot where both the Declaration of Independence and the Constitution were drafted. The abolitionists' new building, christened Pennsylvania Hall, aimed to provide a special speech spot to house meetings and lectures. At the building's dedication ceremony on May 14, 1838, organizers read aloud a congratulatory letter from former president and then congressman John Quincy Adams, who exulted in the opening of a "large building in your city, wherein liberty and equality of civil rights can be freely discussed, and the evils of slavery fearlessly portrayed. . . . I rejoice that, in the city of Philadelphia, the friends of free discussion have erected a Hall for its unrestrained exercise."[41] Before the week was out, the new building lay in ruins, burned to the ground by anti-abolitionist mobbers in the worst act of arson in America to that date, apart from what the British had done to Washington City in the War of 1812.

The American dilemma—the basic contradiction between American slavery and American freedom, and the myriad ways in which unfreedom for Black slaves eventually came to threaten freedom for White citizens—did not begin in the 1820s and 1830s. But it did become much worse on President Andrew Jackson's watch and with his encouragement.

KINGS AND WHIGS

In trying to make their case to the American public, Jackson's leading critics unsurprisingly used the memes and tropes, the images and templates, of the opening stages of America's constitutional conversation. These stylistic and political choices evidenced the enduring grip of the Revolution and Constitution on the minds of founding sons more than a half century after the Declaration.

Jackson's allies and admirers, such as the painter Ralph Earl and various sponsors of the Jefferson Day dinner, aimed to present the stern yet unpretentious lawyer-general as a faithful heir of Washington and Jefferson, heroes of 1776. Jackson's foes depicted him as a replica of the tyrannical George III and the tyrant's domineering New World minions, villains of 1776.

IN THE WIDE-OPEN AND INCREASINGLY inclusive elections of the Age of Jackson, presidential candidates openly vied for power with catchy slogans, symbols, and simplifications aimed at the common (White) man. The winning jingle in 1840 was "Tippecanoe and Tyler, too," flanked by campaign symbols of log cabins and hard cider. As the nineteenth century unfolded, property qualifications for Whites dropped away in many places and the Electoral College system dramatically democratized. In 1800—the election that had brought Jefferson to power over John Adams—only one-third of the states let voters pick electors directly. In 1828—the election that swept Jefferson's (political) heir to power over Adams's (literal) heir—voters directly decided in twenty-one of the twenty-four states.[42]

Politics, it would later be said, ain't beanbag. In the first presidential election tapping a man whose inner circle routinely used backcountry words like "ain't," political discourse was indeed rough-and-tumble, and in revealing ways. To his admirers, Jackson was both a war hero and a self-made Everyman. His critics responded by taking direct aim at his popular image in an effort to blunt his greatest political assets.

Jackson's detractors took their boldest shot in a series of "Coffin Handbills," such as the one published in 1828 by Philadelphia printer John Binns. The six named coffins arrayed along the top of this handbill—one of several versions that circulated that election year—dramatized allegations that Jackson had at one point rashly and wrongly ordered the execution of six militiamen. The handbill's other coffins denoted other men dead at Jackson's hand or on his orders. The six grouped coffins in 1828 aimed to grab viewers by the throat, as had the four arrayed coffins in Paul Revere's 1770 Boston Massacre cartoons. The allusion seems quite direct: *Jackson is a killer, a bloodthirsty military man reminiscent of British military brutes of yore.*

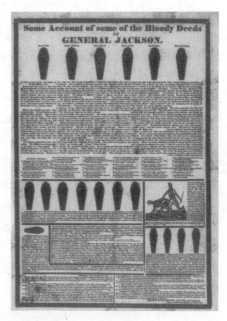

Another of Jackson's political assets was his life story as a self-made man in the tradition of Franklin and Hamilton. None of his presidential predecessors had climbed so steep a path to America's apex. Washington, Jefferson, and Madison were Virginia grandees, born to elite families and tied by marriage to other notable families.

Monroe was the son of a moderately prosperous planter. The Adamses were Harvard men connected to the high-status Quincy family, and JQA was of course a president's heir and namesake. Except for Washington, who had excellent home tutors, each of America's first presidents had attended college at a time when only a handful of their countrymen did so. Each, including Washington, had strong familial and communal support in his tender years. (Washington lost his father at age eleven but came under the wing of his affectionate and well-connected older half brother, Lawrence. After Jefferson's father died when was he was fourteen, he received strong tutoring and entered college at sixteen. Orphaned at age sixteen, Monroe came under the care of a childless uncle who was a member of the House of Burgesses.) Jackson, by contrast, was born fatherless. His family was rather common. By age fifteen he was alone in the world—with no parent, no sibling, and no fairy-tale guardian. His early education was scantier than that of any predecessor. In his late teens and early twenties, he managed to read law under the eye of a local attorney and then began to practice law and to buy land and slaves.

Critics tried to invert this remarkable tale of early adversity and self-improvement, presenting Jackson as a playing-card incarnation of George III: King Andrew the First.

There were traces of truth in this cutesy cartoon, composed circa 1833. Jackson had a harsh, domineering personality. As president, he wielded executive power with astonishing assertiveness. (Washington had vetoed two bills, Jefferson none. By the end of 1833, Jackson had already vetoed eight bills and would go on to veto four more.) As evidenced by his brusque removal of Duane, Jackson demanded unblinking obedience and loyalty from his executive-branch subordinates. Earlier in life, he had been an intimidating general and imperious military governor wielding peremptory power over the countless soldiers, civilians, and captives under his control. On his plantation, he ruled despotically over hundreds of slaves.

Yet the portrayal of Jackson as a robed, crowned, sceptered, begowned king was also faintly ludicrous. European kingly power was

BORN TO COMMAND.

OF VETO MEMORY.

HAD I BEEN CONSULTED.

KING ANDREW THE FIRST.

hereditary. It was particularly inapt—absurd—to depict America's lowest-born and sharpest-rising president as "*Born* to Command." Jackson's 1824 and 1828 adversary, John Quincy Adams, might indeed have been fairly described as "King John II, born to rule." Andrew Jackson had started out life with nothing but wit and drive. He was in this respect much closer to Emperor Napoleon I than to King George III. But the core memes of the American Revolution continued to exert a strong gravitational pull over the American imagination throughout the antebellum era.

Contrary to the thrust of the cartoon, the veto power that Jackson wielded was not some absolute English royal prerogative claimed by divine right. Rather, the veto was a defeasible and deliberation-promoting American instrument placed in Jackson's hand by a written Constitution that the people had ordained and by a presidential election (actually two elections) in which the people had spoken. The phrase "Had I Been Consulted" alongside Jackson's veto-clenching fist aimed to be a cutting reference to Jackson's most famous veto message. But what exactly was wrong with Jackson's public statement that Congress had not crafted its bank bill in close collaboration with him?

THE VERY NAME THAT JACKSON'S main opponents eventually took for themselves also recalled the American Revolution. If Jackson was a replica of King George III, then the virtuous patriots opposing him were of course "Whigs"—a label directly borrowed from the old Revolutionaries. (Recall that Joseph Story described his own father—a Massachusetts Son of Liberty present at the Tea Party, Concord, Lexington, and Bunker Hill—as "a sturdy Whig.")

The three most prominent Whigs of the Age of Jackson all sought the presidency repeatedly—one from the Northwest (William Henry Harrison, top left), one from the Northeast (Daniel Webster, top right), and one from the Southwest (Henry Clay, bottom left). The leading Anti-Jacksonian presidential aspirant from the fourth geographic quadrant, the Southeast, was a Democrat, John C. Calhoun (bottom right).

The only one to win the presidential brass ring (which he did not hold for long) was Harrison, whose résumé most resembled Jackson's. Indeed, just as Jackson was a synthesis of Washington and Jefferson, so Harrison was a synthesis of Washington, Jefferson, and Jackson himself (with a dash of John Quincy Adams thrown in for good measure).

Like Washington and Jefferson, Harrison was a Virginia blueblood. As a member of the Continental Congress in the mid-1770s, his father, Benjamin Harrison V, voted for and signed the Declaration of Independence alongside Jefferson and Adams. In the early 1780s, Harrison père served as a governor of Virginia for three years. As signers' scions, William Henry and John Quincy were thus constitutional cousins of sorts—founding sons, indeed.

But John Quincy went east, to Europe, where he served America in several key diplomatic posts. William Henry, like Jackson (and a young Washington in the 1750s), went west, where he served America in arms and in territorial administration.

Harrison's major accomplishments were closely akin to Washington's and Jackson's: he knew how to treat with friendly Indians, kill hostile Indians, charm backcountry White Americans, secure large chunks of western land for the United States, and defeat British troops. As a young soldier, Harrison had been part of President Washington's pivotal (and not particularly bloody) victory over northwestern Indians at the 1794 Battle of Fallen Timbers. In 1795, he witnessed and attested to the ensuing 1795 Treaty of Greenville, in which the defeated Indians agreed to sell most of modern-day Ohio, opening the northwestern floodgates to American settlement. (Fallen Timbers, in turn, led to Jay's Treaty, the evacuation of British northwestern forts, Pinckney's Treaty, the opening of the Mississippi, and eventually the Louisiana Purchase.)

What Jackson was to the Southwest, Harrison was to the Northwest. Wielding both carrots and sticks as the presidentially appointed governor of the Indiana Territory from 1801 to 1812, Harrison negotiated nearly a dozen Indian treaties collectively resulting in the transfer to the United States of sixty million acres in modern-day

Illinois and Indiana. At the 1811 Battle of Tippecanoe in northern Indiana, his troops clashed with Shawnee warriors encouraged and supplied by British Canada. Dozens died on both sides, and Harrison claimed victory in official dispatches and in the American press. In 1813, Harrison's troops killed the charismatic Shawnee leader Tecumseh at the Battle of the Thames, not far from Detroit. Thus ended the war chief's energetic but doomed effort to forge a grand tribal confederacy capable of thwarting America's inexorable push for more farmland. Tecumseh fell alongside his British allies—the War of 1812 was by then in full swing—and Major General Harrison's victory over the British in this northern theater was America's best showing against the British until Major General Jackson's victory over the British in the southern theater.

WHAT ABOUT THE ALSO-RANS IN the Age of Jackson—Webster, Clay, and Calhoun? High school civics students are often taught that these were the towering intellects of their era and that they lit up the Senate—the world's greatest deliberative chamber—like never before and never since.

As with old Adams in his nineteenth-century accounts of young Otis, there is some truth here, as evidenced in the intricate abolitionist mail debate. But as with old Adams and young Otis, there is also some mythmaking at work.[43] Webster, Clay, and Calhoun were surely great orators and witty wordsmiths in an era when Americans especially admired soaring oratory and clever repartee, and a maturing national press corps was well positioned to publicize great speechifying and cutting commentary. Great senators in the middle third of the nineteenth century also loomed large because of the large issues that lay before them—slavery, secession, Civil War. But Webster, Clay, Calhoun, and the lesser senatorial lights of their era labored under large structural disadvantages—at least if measured by the standards of constitutional acumen and accuracy. Alas, Clay and Webster were quite erratic, and Calhoun was consistently erroneous.

These founding sons were not themselves founders, so they brought less firsthand understanding of the issues than had, say, members of the First Congress in the great debates over the Decision of 1789, the Judiciary Act of 1789, and so on. Nor were Jackson-era senators true scholars able to devote themselves in disinterested and systematic fashion to constitutional issues, à la Justice and Professor Joseph Story. As is true today, so it was true in the Age of Jackson: the right political answer is not always the right legal answer, and senators are ultimately politicos. Even great senators must spend much of their time and mental energy doing things far removed from serious constitutional thought—rolling logs, barreling pork, raising money, grabbing attention, charming journalists, coining slogans, mending fences, serving constituents, kissing babies, and so on. Then as now, serious issues would often arise faster than well-intentioned senators could master them. Nor could any given senator rely on a strong staff of professional legal advisers as could every president. Also, executive-branch bureaucrats often had superior access to various documents and to the analyses of their predecessors.

In sum, there were structural reasons that President Jackson's official statements and Joseph Story's books and opinions often compared rather well to the once famous but now fading speeches of Webster, Clay, and Calhoun.

OUTSIDERS

Beyond the political insiders in Washington, DC, lay outsiders of various sorts. Some joined America's constitutional conversation in notable ways in the 1830s; others would soon do so; and still others would for many decades to come remain largely outside the conversational circles that determined the major political and legal outcomes in America.

EUROPEAN INTELLECTUALS FORMED ONE KEY cohort. In the founding era, Americans were net importers of ambitious tomes on constitutionalism. William Blackstone's four-volume *Commentaries on the Laws of England* sold more copies per capita in America than in Britain. Federalists and Anti-Federalists in the late 1780s cited "the celebrated Montesquieu" even more than they did Blackstone.[44] In that era, before a mature discourse of homegrown constitutionalism had become dominant, *American republicans* were thus seeking essential guidance from a *French nobleman* discoursing on the *English mixed monarchy*!

The tables turned in the Jackson era. European intellectuals now began studying America for its strength and vitality. The French Revolution had tried to imitate the American Revolution, and Americans loved the attention.[45] They were flattered, at least at first, by the likes of the French Revolutionary diplomat Edmond-Charles Genêt. Their lingering sense of inferiority vis-à-vis the British underlay their initial attachment to the Parisians who were claiming to look for constitutional guidance from Philadelphia, New York, and Boston, not London. But the French Revolution failed, yielding to a Reign of Terror, then Napoleonic despotism, and then another Old World monarchy of sorts. America's relationship to France became more complex. In the 1830s, many Americans fell in love with France yet again, thanks to Alexis de Tocqueville and his two-volume masterpiece, *Democracy in America*, an extraordinary study of American law, politics, economy, culture, and society.

Tocqueville held up a mirror in which Americans could see themselves in comparative perspective. They had managed to create a dynamic and democratic culture unique in the world—a culture that might well sweep the planet in the decades to come, thought Tocqueville.

Tocqueville's portrait was neither dismissive nor fawning. American culture was coarse, materialistic, utilitarian, entrepreneurial, open, scrambling, footloose, energetic, upwardly mobile, literate, and religious. Common folk mattered enormously in politics, which was often raucously democratic and egalitarian, among Whites at least. White men without property voted and served regularly on juries, which wielded real power. Newspapers, journals, and publications of every sort abounded, bristling with barbed opinions and assertions. Voluntary associations of all types dotted the landscape. The West, especially, lacked refinement. Northern culture and southern culture diverged sharply, thanks to slavery. Many political disputes eventually ripened into legal disputes, and lawyers were emerging as an American aristocracy of sorts—an aristocracy of habit and manner, but not of hereditary entitlement. The three main races on the continent— Whites, Blacks, and Indians—did not live in harmony, and America had yet to develop a sensible plan for handling this racial tinderbox. American women were particularly respected in their own sphere of family and church.

WOMEN IN JACKSONIAN AMERICA WERE indeed beginning to play particularly important roles in churches and reform societies across a wide range of issues, including, critically, issues of race and slavery.

A small but growing abolitionist movement opened itself to women, who used these openings to write, travel, teach, and speak in bold new ways. No woman, speaking or writing openly as a woman, had played a large public role in the imperial debates of the 1760s and early 1770s or in the constitutional debates, state and federal, between 1776 and 1788. Nor had many women weighed in, openly as women, on the big constitutional issues of the next forty years—the Decision of 1789, the Bill of Rights, the Sedition Act, the Virginia and Kentucky Resolutions, the Jeffersonian repeal of the Judiciary Act of 1801, the Louisiana Purchase, the Twelfth Amendment, the Missouri Compromise, the "Bill of Abominations," and so on. But in the 1830s, women of different races and regions occasionally popped up in public venues and influential newspapers.

In early December 1833, Lucretia Mott and several other women attended the founding convention of William Lloyd Garrison's American Anti-Slavery Society. The fledgling society allowed only men to sign the meeting's Declaration of Sentiments, but Mott boldly addressed the mixed audience, many of whom had likely never heard a woman speak in a public setting. Such oratory, however, was nothing new for Mott, a Quaker minister who had for years been preaching and proclaiming at Quaker events far and wide. Later in December, Mott helped found a racially inclusive women's organization, the Philadelphia Female Anti-Slavery Society.

Farther north, another Quaker woman, Prudence Crandall, was also gaining attention for expressive activity. Crandall ran a girls' boarding school in Canterbury, Connecticut, that she opened up to Blacks and Whites, local or otherwise. She ran a series of 1833 advertisements in Garrison's *Liberator* publicizing her willingness to accept "young Ladies and little Misses of color." The state prosecuted her for violating a state law restricting "any school . . . for the instruction and education of coloured persons, who are not inhabitants of this state." Crandall won her state court case on a pleading technicality. She did not win any sweeping judicial affirmation of her own rights to teach Blacks, or the rights of her nonresident Black students to learn and receive fair treatment in sister states. But Crandall did win wide newspaper coverage of her case. Local ruffians responded by trying to set her school ablaze, and when that failed, smashing its windows, obliging Crandall to close the school and leave the state.

Women born and raised in the South were also beginning to speak and write in brave new ways. Most prominent were Sarah and Angelina Grimké, South Carolina sisters who moved to Philadelphia and became Quaker activists. Angelina, the younger sister, joined Mott's Philadelphia Female Anti-Slavery Society and traveled throughout the Northeast, as did Sarah, offering firsthand accounts of the evils of slavery to anyone, male or female, willing to listen. In 1838 one Salem newspaper declared, "We had rather hear Angelina Grimke preach (whether truth or error), than half the men in the world."[46] In 1836, the American Anti-Slavery Society published Angelina's *Appeal to the Christian Women of the South*—a religiously infused tract by a religious southern woman explicitly aimed at other religious southern women. In 1837, Sarah wrote *Letters on the Equality of Sexes and the Condition of Women*, which first appeared in serial form in newspapers, including Garrison's *Liberator*, and then as a book in 1838.

In all this, women were talking publicly about women and to women, and men were beginning to listen. In 1839 the sisters joined Angelina's husband, Theodore Dwight Weld, in authoring *American Slavery As It Is*—compiling the "Testimony of a Thousand Witnesses" to present a scathing picture of the barbarism and savagery of American slavery.

But women's participation in serious constitutional conversation was still in its infancy in this era—limited in scope and controversial among both men and women. When Mott attended the World's Anti-Slavery Convention in London in 1840, the male delegates voted to exclude her and several other women seeking to participate, obliging them to sit as spectators in the gallery. In protest, Garrison and others refused to sit as delegates and joined the women. The Salem newspaper squib praising preacher Grimké appeared in apology for a mocking ditty on "Female Preaching" that the paper ran on the previous page, which opened as follows: "How pleasing the sight, how imposing and grand / When Reverends in *petticoats* traverse the land / When the office that *honored* old Paul is brought down / To the grasp of the sex that is clad in a gown!" Angelina's *Appeal* met with strong criticism from Catharine Beecher, the daughter and sister of several notable preachers and also the sister of the not-yet-famous Harriet Beecher Stowe. Catharine Beecher wrote that women should refrain from direct political advocacy. Because "heaven has appointed to one sex the superior, and to the other the subordinate station," she stood "entirely opposed to the plan of arraying females in any Abolition movement."[47]

Beecher notwithstanding, the tiny saplings sprouting in the 1830s would grow into giant oaks over the next quarter century. Between 1840 and 1870, women would come to play roles in America's constitutional conversation that would have astonished the founding generation. At the 1840 London Convention, Philadelphia's Mott met another extraordinary woman, a New Yorker named Elizabeth Cady Stanton. It was a meeting as fateful, perhaps, as the day Jefferson met Madison, or the moment Washington hired Hamilton. Though both Mott and Stanton were shunted aside at the London Convention, the two women would later organize a conclave of their own, this one devoted to the topic of women's rights—primarily by women, for women. For many women in generations to come, this 1848 conclave in Seneca Falls, New York, would become (with the benefit of hindsight and perhaps a touch of mythmaking[48]) as renowned as the grand federal convention of 1787. In the 1850s, Catharine Beecher's sister Harriet would write an anti-slavery book, *Uncle Tom's Cabin*, that would outsell everything except the Bible and electrify Americans more than any tract since Paine's *Common Sense*. No previous American woman had ever written anything with remotely comparable political impact. Stowe identified *American Slavery As It Is* as her major inspiration. She said she had slept with it under her pillow every night.[49]

WHAT ABOUT THE BLACK AND Indian races that Tocqueville worried about?

In the aftermath of the American Revolution, abolitionist efforts bore significant if sometimes slow-ripening fruit in the northeastern, northwestern, and mid-Atlantic states. Well before 1800, Massachusetts (including its northern Maine district), New Hampshire, and Vermont effectively ended human bondage on their soil. In the 1780s and 1790s, Pennsylvania, Connecticut, Rhode Island, and New York enacted laws guaranteeing gradual abolition. In 1804 New Jersey followed suit, and in 1817 New York accelerated abolition by providing that all remaining Empire State slaves would walk free on July 4, 1827. The Northwest Ordinance helped prevent slavery from putting down deep roots in Ohio, Indiana, Illinois, Michigan, Wisconsin, and Minnesota, all of which eventually entered Congress as free states prior to the Civil War, as did several states even farther west—Iowa, California, Oregon, and Kansas—thanks in part to the spirit of the Missouri Compromise.

Even as slavery dried up in the North, it mushroomed in the South, nourished by the profits to be made in slave-tended cotton plantations. By 1840, South Carolina had more than three hundred thousand slaves who constituted over 55 percent of the state's population—a sharp increase in the half century since America's first census, when a hundred thousand slaves made up 43 percent of the state's humanity. Census figures from Georgia told a similar story; there, the slave population skyrocketed tenfold in the same years, rising from less than thirty thousand to nearly three hundred thousand—and thus from roughly 35 percent to more than 40 percent of the state's population as a whole. Census data west of the Mississippi likewise chronicled a widening chasm between Americans North and South, portending serious tension between the regions in the years ahead.

Gradual abolition in the North did not always spell broader voting rights for free Blacks. On the contrary, even as property qualifications for voting generally fell away for White men in the Age of Jackson, state after state began to add racial qualifications. At the Founding, only three states—Virginia, South Carolina, and Georgia—barred free Blacks from voting. Colored persons suffered significant disfranchisement in the Jefferson era and even more in the Age of Jackson. Delaware, Kentucky, Maryland, Ohio, and New Jersey began the exclusionary trend in the 1790s and early 1800s; after 1835, no southern state allowed Blacks to vote. Also, no new state entering the union after 1819 extended the franchise to African Americans. By the early 1860s, only five states—all in New England, and together encompassing less than one-half of 1 percent of the nation's Blacks—allowed free men of color to vote on equal terms. A sixth state, New York, permitted some Blacks to vote, but only if they met a special property qualification not imposed on Whites.[50]

Exclusion from the franchise, however, did not invariably mean exclusion from America's constitutional conversation. Free Blacks would in fact move quickly toward the center of that conversation in the years following 1840. The most dramatic Black conversationalist, Frederick Douglass, would write multiple books, publish his own newspaper, articulate sophisticated theories of constitutional interpretation and meaning, and win acclaim as a spellbinding constitutional orator in the tradition of James Otis and Patrick Henry.

By contrast, American Indians largely remained, and in future decades would continue to remain, outside the conversational circle. The most famous Indian of the early nineteenth century, Tecumseh (left), was a British-backed warrior who spoke little English; he did not publish any books or essays aimed at American voters. Even Indians who tried to join the American conversation fared poorly in the Age of Jackson. The great Cherokee leader Sequoyah (middle) developed a syllabary in 1821, and between 1828 and 1834 the tribe had its own newspaper, the *Cherokee Phoenix* (right), which was printed in both English and Cherokee using Sequoyah's syllabary. In 1827, the Cherokee crafted a written constitution for their tribe, broadly modeled on the US Constitution.[51]

But by then the die was cast. White Americans often failed to distinguish between the difficult tribes that had often warred against the United States and the dependable tribes that had usually backed the nation in war and diplomacy. The tribes themselves had neither an indivisible continental union on the model of Washington and Hamilton nor a precise intertribal written confederacy on the model of Jefferson. Lacking clear lines of authority, allegiance, and jurisdiction, and also lacking diplomatic and military heft—lacking, among other things, full Westphalian sovereignty—tribes continued to lose ground, literally.

Tecumseh's life and death illustrated some of the larger forces at work. The Shawnee warriors he grew up around fought on the British side in both the American War of Independence and the Northwest

Indian War of the 1790s. In 1794, Tecumseh himself fought against the United States at Fallen Timbers, where one of his brothers died. After that battle, most of the tribal chieftains in the region explicitly made peace with America in the Treaty of Greenville; Tecumseh, however, refused to consider himself bound by the treaty, or by a related treaty negotiated by William Henry Harrison in Fort Wayne in 1809. Backed by the British, Tecumseh and his expanding band of warriors fought Americans yet again in a bloody armed conflict in the 1810s known as Tecuhmseh's War. In 1812, this conflict merged into the larger war between Britain and America, a war in which the chief lost his life in 1813 at the Battle of the Thames.

Tecumseh was a brave and charismatic warrior, but what was his grand strategy? Time and again he fought on the British side. His epaulettes came from London, and the British-minted medal he wore around his neck featured the likeness of George III. That British monarch did not heed American newspapers and public opinion in the 1760s and 1770s; neither did Tecumseh in subsequent decades; and both lost, in part, because they did not understand what they were up against. Washington and Franklin better understood the strategic context in which they were enmeshed. Washington understood when to flee fights he could not win, and Franklin was a master diplomat in Paris who played the French and the British brilliantly.

The United States treated Native American tribes poorly, but so did the British, cynically and repeatedly goading tribes to war against America, and then at war's end abandoning their Indian allies—at Paris in 1783, again at Fallen Timbers and in Jay's Treaty in the mid-1790s, and yet again in the War of 1812. In 1783, a Creek chief poignantly asked whether George III aimed "to sell his friends as slaves, or only give our lands to his and our enemies."[52]

But to blame only the cynical British and the land-greedy White Americans would be to deny agency to Native Americans themselves, who made fateful and not always farsighted choices when confronting hard realities. In the rough-and-tumble world of high-stakes international diplomacy, countries on occasion ruthlessly pursue their self-interest. The indivisible American union created in 1788 was designed in large part so that European powers could not play divide-and-conquer among Americans the way they did among New World Indian tribes (and in Old World India itself, for that matter). The Native tribes did not have anything like an indivisible continental union. Tribal Indians were vastly outnumbered by Americans, by a ratio of more than twenty to one. Indians were at a massive technological and military disadvantage. They also generally lacked America's communications infrastructure of newspapers and public opinion, and its interrelated system of elections and constitutional law. The Cherokee were the leading exception to this generalization. In the 1820s and 1830s, many Cherokee were in fact moving toward the dominant American model of newspapers and constitutional law.

In modern circles, Andrew Jackson is sometimes seen as uniquely blameworthy in his violent vision of Indian tribes, whom he ruthlessly pushed out of their ancestral homelands into the trans-Mississippi West—even tribes that had not always fought against the United States. Arguably, Jefferson's philosophy of Indian affairs in the early 1800s was more generous and respectful, as was Washington's in the 1790s.[53]

But as Tecumseh's life and death itself showed, allegiances among tribal Americans were complex and fluid. This year's peaceful tribe or band or clan, many White Americans worried, might not be so peaceful next year. Jackson himself was hardly the only American of his era who thought in crude and racially insensitive terms. William Henry Harrison won the White House precisely because he, too, knew how to beat both the Indians and the British—Tippecanoe and the Thames, too. Consider also Colonel Richard Mentor Johnson, who claimed to have personally felled Tecumseh in battle. In 1836–1837, Johnson's friends used the boast to lift this otherwise unremarkable man into the vice presidency with a coarse slogan: "Rumpsey Dumpsey, Rumpsey Dumpsey, Colonel Johnson killed Tecumseh."

The Lockean ideas of land use prevalent among White Americans in the colonial and founding periods continued to resound in the Age of Jackson. In 1823, lawyers in the Supreme Court explicitly cited Locke for the proposition that most American Indians prior to the arrival of Englishmen in the New World "had not acquired a fixed property capable of being transferred." On this view, "the North American Indians could have acquired no proprietary interest in the vast tracts of territory which they wandered over; and their right to the lands on which they hunted, could not be considered as superior to that which is acquired to the sea by fishing in it. The use in the one case, as well as the other, is not exclusive."[54] In his Second Annual Message to Congress in 1830, Jackson spoke less abstractly and more bluntly: "Philanthropy could not wish to see this continent restored to the condition in which it was found by our forefathers. What good man would prefer a country covered with forests and ranged by a few thousand savages to our extensive Republic, studded with cities, towns, and prosperous farms, embellished with all the improvements which art can devise or industry execute, occupied by more than 12,000,000 happy people, and filled with all the blessings of liberty, civilization, and religion?" Jackson's pointed use of the word "savages" doubtless reflected ethnocentric bias and bigotry, but it also linked Jackson to Washington and Jefferson, who both used this word routinely—Jefferson in the Declaration of Independence itself.[55]

In the 1830 Indian Removal Act enacted several months before Jackson's message, Congress authorized the president to push various Indian tribes out of the organized states east of the Mississippi and into federal territory west of the river. In theory, these relocations would occur pursuant to agreements with tribal leaders. In practice, Jackson chose to recognize the authority of compliant chieftains, whether or not they truly spoke for their supposed followers. Here, too, Jackson emulated Washington and Jefferson, but with more iron fist and less velvet glove. Brutal relocations ensued along an infamous "Trail of Tears" stretching from Georgia to modern-day Oklahoma. Thousands died en route, many of them members of tribes such as the Cherokee closer in sentiment to Sequoyah than to Tecumseh.

The most famous Indian-law case of the Jackson era, *Worcester v. Georgia*, encapsulated several of the themes of its period. Samuel Austin Worcester was a Christian missionary and printer who befriended (and was befriended by) many Cherokee, who called him *A-tse-nu-tsi*—"the Messenger." Hoping one day to translate the Bible into Cherokee, Worcester also cast the type for the pathbreaking Cherokee newspaper, the *Cherokee Phoenix*. His federally authorized work among the Cherokee earned him the enmity of Georgia officials, who prosecuted and convicted him for violating a state law prohibiting White persons from living on tribal lands without state approval. Other sections of the Georgia law took aim at persons on tribal lands who tried to "assembl[e] . . . any council or other pretended legislative body of the said Indians or others living among them, for the purpose of legislating (or for any other purpose whatever)." Yet another part of the Georgia law purported to shrink the boundaries of tribal land.[56]

In early 1832, the Marshall Court reversed Worcester's conviction. Georgia had no right to "interfere forcibly with the relations established between the United States and the Cherokee nation, the regulation of which, according to the settled principles of our constitution, are committed exclusively to the government of the union." Georgia's rules, the Court said, were "in direct hostility with treaties, repeated in a succession of years, which mark out the boundary that separates the Cherokee country from Georgia; guaranty to them all the land within their boundary; solemnly pledge the faith of the United States to restrain their citizens from trespassing on it; and recognize the pre-existing power of the [Cherokee] nation to govern itself. They are in equal hostility with the acts of congress for regulating this intercourse, and giving effect to the treaties."

In the course of his decision, Marshall, as was his wont, ranged far beyond the facts at hand. Seizing the chance to elaborate the broader constitutional framework applicable to Native Americans, Marshall took care not to proclaim the full-blown Westphalian sovereignty of any tribe. As he had already made clear in a related 1831 case, *Cherokee Nation v. Georgia*, no tribe was remotely the equivalent of, say, France, Britain, or Russia. Still, Marshall in *Worcester* ruled that tribes were constitutionally special; they were more than mere Tocquevillian clubs or voluntary associations. Federal treaties and statutes recognized special rights of the Cherokee tribe, rights that Georgia had to respect.

In an earlier Cherokee-related case that unfolded in 1830–1831, Georgia had dared to defy the Supreme Court, placing the state alongside nullifiers like Virginia's Spencer Roane and South Carolina's Robert Hayne, Warren R. Davis, and John C. Calhoun.[57] But in *Worcester*, Georgia ultimately yielded to Marshall by freeing the Messenger and setting aside his conviction via a gubernatorial pardon. Contrary to lurid claims in the opposition press that have congealed into modern folklore (in the apocryphal sentence attributed to Jackson, "Marshall has made his decision; now let him enforce it!"), the president did not withhold federal executive support from the Court, which had not sought aid from federal marshals or any other arm of the federal executive.[58] But even after Worcester went free, Georgia continued to improperly pressure the Cherokee Nation more generally as Jackson looked on, winking.

Jackson's later actions in connection with the Indian Removal Act and the Trail of Tears, heartbreaking as they were, did not violate the strict letter of Marshall's ruling. Indeed, much of Marshall's underlying logic actually provided constitutional support for the Removal Act and for Jackson's implementation of it. American policy concerning the tribes, Marshall held, was to be set by the federal government, not the states. Put differently, Marshall in *Worcester* sided less with the tribe than with the federal government—with the Congress that was expressly empowered by Article I to "regulate" Indian policy and foreign policy, and with the president who was implicitly empowered by Article II to choose which Indian leaders to recognize, much as he was empowered to choose which European leaders to recognize. In the 1790s, President Washington had made the key decision to treat the French Revolutionaries, rather than the imprisoned Louis XVI, as the legitimate government of France, and had also determined for himself which Native American leaders he would parley with and which leaders he would ignore. Now, in the 1830s, President Jackson wielded similar sweeping power over Indian treaty-making. Even formally recognized tribes labored at an enormous disadvantage. No tribe in the nineteenth century was ever accorded, either by the United States or by the great Old Powers of Europe, the full Westphalian status of, say, France, Britain, or Russia.

Nor would the situation of tribal Indians improve in the next generation. The first Abraham Lincoln—the future president's grandfather—was a Kentucky farmer who was ambushed and slain by Indians in 1786 while working in his fields. His grandson and namesake served as a militia captain in the 1832 Black Hawk War. In the Civil War, several leading tribes would yet again unwisely side against the United States in a continental conflagration that the United States would win. After the war—a war in which 180,000 Blacks fought for the Union—slavery would end for America's Black population, thanks to a Thirteenth Amendment ratified in 1865. Two additional amendments would quickly ensue, offering Blacks equal civil and political rights. But the Fourteenth Amendment would pointedly exclude "Indians not taxed" and Indians not "subject to the jurisdiction" of states—tribal Indians—from the protections extended to all other Americans, including White Americans, Black Americans, and assimilated Native Americans.

With the prospects for true tribal independence and complete tribal sovereignty thus severely limited, one pathway into the American constitutional conversation nevertheless remained open for some Native Americans: full assimilation. For all his harshness toward many organized tribes in both war and peace, Andrew Jackson— himself an orphan of war—adopted an infant Red Stick Creek orphan of war and raised him in his own household, Lyncoya Jackson.

IN HIS LAST MONTHS IN office, Andrew Jackson found himself in an unprecedented situation. With Madison's death in mid-1836, Jackson became the first American president unable to seek direct advice from any of the great men most responsible for launching the Constitution. We today are in the same position.

One way for modern Americans to ponder the founders' complex constitutional legacy is to think hard about the text that these statesmen jointly created and the early glosses that they jointly applied to that text. That, of course, has been the project of the preceding pages.

We should also heed how America's greatest founders lived and died. Let us then, in conclusion, reconsider these great actors one last time and pay particular attention to how they left history's grand stage. Studying how they died will yield insights into how they lived, which in turn will help us better see what they did and what they left undone.

— thirteen —

ADIEUS

N ONE OF AMERICA'S GREATEST FOUNDERS composed a grand letter to his countrymen on his deathbed. Still, Americans searching for implicit farewell messages did not have far to look.

FRANKLIN AND WASHINGTON

Franklin went first. He died as he had lived, trying to better himself and the world.[1] He was always tinkering, always inventing, always self-improving. He believed in progress and he saw both himself and his country as works in progress. Some of his progressive ideas involved science and technology—the lightning rod, bifocals, the Franklin stove. Other progressive ideas were more social and political—a lending library, a volunteer fire company, a philosophical society, a nonsectarian university, the intercolonial Albany Plan.

In 1787, just days before the start of the grand federal convention, Franklin accepted the presidency of the world's first notable abolition society. He had bought and owned slaves earlier in his life. Doubtless influenced by his Quaker surroundings, but also moved by Enlightenment philosophy, common sense, and grand strategy, he eventually came to see that slavery was wrong, that it should end, and that America should lead the way.

Knowing that death was near, he decided that within America, he himself should lead the way and make abolition his last great cause, his last gift to America and the world. As president of the Pennsylvania Abolition Society, Franklin signed a petition in early 1790 that reached Congress on February 12. Exactly nineteen years later (a magic number for Thomas Jefferson), Abraham Lincoln and Charles Darwin would be born on this day—a multiple coincidence about moral and scientific progress that surely would have delighted Franklin.

Franklin's petition was direct and earnest. (This was one side of Franklin.) Paraphrasing the Declaration, on whose drafting committee Franklin had served, the petition proclaimed that "mankind are all formed by the same Almighty Being, . . . and equally designed for the Enjoyment of Happiness. . . . Equal liberty was originally the portion, and is still the birth-right of all men." From these basic premises flowed the petition's conclusion and prayer for relief. Congress should "remov[e] this inconsistency from the character of the American people" and "step to the very verge of the power vested in you for discouraging every species of traffic in the persons of our fellow-men."[2]

Congressmen from the Deep South raged at the very idea of discussing slavery. A couple of Quaker anti-slave-trade petitions had reached Congress on February 11; now that Franklin's great name was directly involved, and American slavery itself, as distinct from the African slave trade, was apparently being drawn into question, the stakes shot up. Seconds after Franklin's petition was read aloud on the House floor, South Carolina representative Thomas Tudor Tucker leaped to his feet: "Do these men expect a general emancipation of slaves by law? This would never be submitted to by the Southern States without a civil war." (In July 1776, it will be recalled, South Carolina's continental congressman Thomas Lynch Jr. had made a similar statement: "If it is debated, whether . . . slaves are [our] property, there is an end of the confederation.") Tucker displayed remarkable confidence in his own superiority as a constitutionalist, compared to the mere likes of Benjamin Franklin. The condescending South Carolinian "was surprised to see [a] memorial on the . . . subject [of slavery and abolition] signed by a man who ought to have known the Constitution better."[3]

Other representatives joined the fray. Georgia's James Jackson and Abraham Baldwin and South Carolina's Aedanus Burke and William Loughton Smith proclaimed the petition's substance anticonstitutional because Congress had no power to do anything whatsoever until 1808.[4] Even to seriously consider the petition would be "unconstitutional."[5] Many other House members countered, correctly, that the 1808 clause governed only the early abolition of the international slave trade, and that Congress surely had power to consider a wide range of other measures that might tend to lessen or ameliorate slavery.[6] In 1789, Congress had briefly considered imposing a ten-dollar head tax on each imported slave, as pointedly allowed by the 1808 clause itself,[7] and had in fact prohibited slavery in the Northwest Territory.

Even more fundamentally, many on the floor and in the galley were disturbed to hear some members insist that mere discussion of an important issue was itself unconstitutional. Even if Congress lacked power to act immediately (which was not true), surely Congress could also consider amending the Constitution to give itself the power. But how could it do this without discussing the matter? Also, what were anti-slavery folk to make of Jackson's claim that locals would likely kill any future Georgia federal judge who tried to promote emancipation?[8]

As we look back at this debate, a great deal is blindingly clear in hindsight. Unfreedom for southern Black slaves threatened freedom of speech for White citizens everywhere, from the very beginning, and South Carolina and Georgia, in particular, were always dangerously extreme.

As debate continued on February 12, 1790, growing ever angrier, Madison became alarmed that things had taken "a serious turn."[9] The very debate about the debate was ill-serving the Deep South's cause, but the South Carolinians had no sense of prudence or of their audience. In the process of repeatedly insisting, with much fist pounding, that the issue could not be discussed, they were . . . discussing the issue, openly and with the Manhattan press watching from the galleries, agog. The southern extremists, some of whom had never been up north before 1789, were also precipitating strong and polarizing pushback, as action prompted reaction. The open debate was discomfiting men such as Madison—Upper South slaveholders who, unlike the South Carolinians, were ashamed of slavery, and agreed in principle with Franklin, but hesitated to do much about it. So Madison, the master legislative tactician, the de facto prime minister, urged the House to refer the petition to a special committee so that things could calm down.[10]

They didn't. When the committee rendered its report in mid-March trying to delineate what Congress could and could not do, several days of open floor debate ensued. Georgians and South Carolinians once again insisted that even consideration and discussion of the report was "unconstitutional and tending to injure some of the states in the union."[11] When this extremist gambit failed, Georgia's Jackson returned to center stage to defend American slavery with a flurry of arguments. America's economic development required slave labor, he said, and Blacks were suited for the work that needed doing in "climates" that were "unhealthy" for White "constitutions." If America refrained from using slaves in such lands, Spain would fill the vacuum and "in a short period" dominate various lucrative markets. It was "immensely preferable" to be a slave in America than to remain in Africa. Once freed, Blacks would be unable to intermingle and intermarry with most Whites, who would not want to associate with them or help to create a "motley breed" of mixed-race offspring. Sending Blacks to Africa was impracticable. "Custom" and "habit" deserved respect. The Bible blessed slavery.[12]

Franklin countered with a lovely satire in the press. (This was another side of Franklin.) This would turn out to be his very last journalistic piece, and it poetically recalled his very first journalistic hoax, when, as a teenage lad, he had puckishly posed as a middle-aged matron, Silence Dogood. Franklin likewise published his 1790 parody under a pen name, but no one who knew him could miss his signature style and sly wit. The piece pretended to be an earnest letter to the editor, telling readers about a 1687 debate among Algerian Muslims concerning their customary practice of enslaving European Christians:

Reading last night in your excellent Paper the speech of Mr. Jackson in Congress against their meddling with the Affair of Slavery, or attempting to mend the Condition of the Slaves, it put me in mind of a similar One made about 100 Years since by Sidi Mehemet Ibrahim, a member of the Divan of Algiers. . . . It was against granting the Petition of the Sect called *Erika*, or Purists who pray'd for the Abolition of Piracy and Slavery as being unjust. Mr. Jackson does not quote it . . . in his eloquent Speech, [despite its] surprising similarity. . . . The African's Speech, as translated, is as follows. . . .

"Have these *Erika* considered the Consequences of granting their Petition? If we cease our [Piratic] Cruises against the Christians, how shall we be furnished with the Commodities . . . which are so necessary for us? If we forbear to make Slaves of their People, who in this hot Climate are to cultivate our Lands? . . . Must we not then be our own Slaves? And is there not more Compassion and more Favour due to us as Mussulmen [Muslims], than to these Christian Dogs? . . .

"And if we set our Slaves free, what is to be done with them? Few of them will return to their Countries; they know too well the great Hardships they must there be subject to; they will not embrace our holy Religion; they will not adopt our Manners; our People will not pollute themselves by intermarrying with them. . . . And what is there so pitiable in their present Condition? Were they not Slaves in their own Countries?

". . . Is their Condition then made worse by their falling into our Hands? No. . . . Here they are brought into a land where the Sun of Islamism gives forth its Light, and shines in full Splendor, and they have an Opportunity of making themselves acquainted with the true Doctrine, and thereby saving their immortal Souls.

". . . How grossly are they [the petitioners] mistaken in imagining Slavery to be disallow'd by the Alcoran [Koran]? Are not the two Precepts, to quote no more, '*Masters, treat your Slaves with kindness; Slaves, serve your Masters with Cheerfulness and Fidelity,*' clear Proofs to the contrary?"

Of course, Franklin's tongue-in-cheek topsy-turvy reversed everything—a classic satirical move. In his alternate universe, dark-skinned Africans who deemed themselves racially and culturally superior were enslaving light-skinned European folk. Christians were the slaves, not the masters. The *Erika* (the phonetic ending syllables of America) were an almost-anagram of the Quakers. The scriptural passages came not, as claimed, from the Koran; rather, they were the very biblical texts that Jackson had himself quoted.

Franklin's spoof ran in the March 25, 1790, issue of Philadelphia's *Federal Gazette*. Less than a month later, he was dead at age eighty-four, and his countrymen began to see, with hindsight, the special significance of the words that he likely knew were his last. His playful piece was also deadly serious. They were his dying words to America.

By pretending to excavate the past, Franklin's farewell message was in fact inviting his fellow Americans to envision the future. How would the Constitution's project appear to posterity in 1887, a hundred years after the grand Philadelphia Convention? If America as a whole did not change course and move toward abolition—as his own Pennsylvania had already done in 1780—would the nation's continuing embrace of slavery, and its hodgepodge of Jacksonian rationalizations, one day come to seem every bit as twisted and despotic as Franklin's fictional Algerians of 1687?

FRANKLIN AND WASHINGTON WERE AMERICA's two greatest founding figures, and it is remarkable that Washington's de facto farewell message, when he passed away in 1799 at his Mount Vernon home, was so similar in substance—though not at all in tone—to Franklin's parting soliloquy. Metaphorically, both men died with abolition and emancipation on their lips. *Rosebud*.

Franklin envisioned virtuous public action: Congress should pass laws freeing all slaves. Washington embodied virtuous private action: slaveholders should take actions freeing their own slaves, just as he was doing on his deathbed. Franklin championed abolition as a public petitioner and journalist. Washington effected manumission as a private manager and planter. Franklin was hoping for a complete official end of slavery—abolition, something like the later Thirteenth Amendment. Washington offered freedom for individual existing slaves and hoped that others would follow suit—manumission, his own miniature Emancipation Proclamation.

Washington was not garrulous in life; nor was he so in death. He did not compose another elaborate formal Farewell Message to his countrymen. (Had he done so, it would have been his third.) Rather, this most private of public men sent a public message via his private choices in his last will and testament. His favorite slave and companion, William Lee, won instant emancipation, and the more than one hundred other slaves that Washington owned would soon walk free: "It is my Will & desire that all the Slaves which I hold in my own right, shall receive their freedom."

Through no fault of Washington's, hundreds of other Mount Vernon slaves lay beyond his testamentary decree. He had no legal authority to free the Mount Vernon slaves whom Martha had inherited from her first husband, Daniel Parke Custis. By law, these "dower slaves" did not fully belong to George; nor did they even fully belong to Martha. They had to go to Martha's Custis heirs—who had no blood relation to George—after her death.

Actions proverbially speak louder than words, and in life Washington had been a man of action. So in death. As in much of his life—as an entrepreneur, as a general, as a president—Washington in his testamentary actions was a model of careful preparation, sacrifice, and even secrecy. In his will, he made substantial financial provision for his freed slaves, as required by both prudence and Virginia law.

He had scraped together enough to do this thanks to years of careful financial planning and penny-pinching. He had kept his manumission plan quiet, not even telling Martha, much as, years earlier, he had kept his Yorktown plan quiet until the last push. Success sometimes required stealth.

Washington's characteristic firmness and seriousness of purpose shone through in the stern prose of his last will and testament: "And I do moreover most pointedly, and most solemnly enjoin it upon my Executors . . . to see that this clause respecting Slaves, and every part thereof be religiously fulfilled at the Epoch at which it is directed to take place; without evasion, neglect or delay, after the Crops which may then be on the ground are harvested, particularly as it respects the aged and infirm."

The greatest political figure of the eighteenth century died as the century died, in December 1799. He was only sixty-seven, but he was painfully aware that he did not come from a long-lived male line. Neither his father nor his two older half brothers had reached fifty; all three of his younger brothers predeceased him. Thus, death did not ambush this military man; he was ready for it, and he knew that all the world would be watching his final act closely. He had lived in the public eye for a quarter century.

As his fame had grown, he, too, had grown. As he became more and more extraordinary in the eyes of the world, he came to demand more of himself. (Unlike, say, Jefferson.) In his early years, Washington had not been an exceptionally thoughtful or self-critical slave owner. He took slavery for granted—it was the way of the world, the way things had always been. He was not gratuitously cruel, but he was stern and cold and he worked his slaves hard.[13] If they shirked, he had them flogged. If they fled, he had them caught and sold.[14] As time passed, he became increasingly uncomfortable with slavery. He vowed to stop buying slaves and resolved not to break apart slave families on auction blocks.[15] He told his private correspondents that he hoped slavery might somehow end, and that he was open to ideas about how to do this.[16]

Over many years, Washington bonded in particular with his man-servant William Lee. In his will, Washington spoke rather tenderly (for Washington, that is) of Lee's "attachment to me" and of Lee's "faithful services during the Revolutionary War." The genuine if painfully asymmetric relationship between the general and his valet was poignantly captured by John Trumbull circa 1780. In this painting, Lee's garb in the background is every bit as fancy as that of his famous master, who is utterly comfortable turning away from Lee. Lee has his back.

Revolutionary talk in the 1770s obliged Washington to rethink the premises of his upbringing. If all men truly were created equal, with unalienable rights of life, liberty, and happiness, then . . . ? In the end, the Revolution became more than talk. In light of all the other revolutionary changes that he himself had sparked as much as anyone, why shouldn't he spark additional revolutionary changes by repudiating the most obvious form of tyranny still left? Between 1775 and 1797, Washington spent more than a dozen years living in the North as general and president, with anti-slavery Whites and free Blacks all around him, both in his army and in his wider conversational circle. Inwardly, he yearned to be a great man. The world increasingly thought of him as a great man. After 1783, many openly called him the greatest man in the world. How, he came to think, quietly, could such a man as himself die without making some sort of anti-slavery statement? What would Lafayette think? What would the French think? What would his fellow countrymen think? And what would posterity think?

For if he was indeed the father of his country, then all future Americans were his children, his progeny, his posterity. What would they think of him? Much as the Philadelphia drafters—led, of course, by Washington himself—had laced the document with democratic sweeteners in anticipation of the democratic ratification process that lay ahead, so now Washington self-consciously thought about the future democratic ratification process that would determine his own enduring reputation and fame. Would future Americans continue to say, "yes, We do," when asked to honor him, and his memory, if he did nothing to reduce the large remaining stain on his good name?

Thus, we today should think especially carefully about Washington's death and his personal Emancipation Proclamation, because in all this he was surely thinking of us.

HAMILTON

Alexander Hamilton, so polarizing in life, polarized also in death—and polarizes even today. Unsurprisingly, different interpretations of his death among contemporaries and modern historians reflect different takes about his life more generally.

HERE IS ONE TAKE ON Hamilton's death: *Hamilton died as he lived.* He was false, disloyal, selfish, partisan, and scheming. He could have easily declined to duel Aaron Burr in their infamous July 1804 "interview" at Weehawken, where Burr fatally shot him. After all, he claimed to be a Christian. But (some say) this was a pose, as was his claim to be in love with his rich and wellborn wife, and his claim to love Washington, who, like his wife, was useful to him but nothing more. His whoring proved his true character, as did his dueling. He reaped as he sowed and got his comeuppance—an extreme partisan done in by his own disloyal, scheming, and self-promoting hyperactivity in 1800–1801.

This was the rancid view that filled the writings of John Adams for years—decades—after Hamilton's death. Adams thought that Hamilton had been duplicitous to . . . Adams. (For Adams, it was usually about Adams.) As Adams saw it, Hamilton had pretended to be Adams's admirer, but had schemed against him in 1789 (encouraging Adams men in the Electoral College to cast dishonest votes by balloting for persons whom they in fact dispreferred to Adams), and again in 1796 (ditto).[17] And then, Hamilton betrayed Adams with a defamatory pamphlet in 1800, after which Adams lost to Jefferson and Burr. When Hamilton found himself in 1801 obliged to undo the Electoral College tie by backing Jefferson and denouncing Burr, resulting in bad blood between the two New Yorkers that ultimately led to the duel—well, wrote old Adams, perhaps there was a touch of cosmic justice in all that.[18] Burr and Hamilton were electioneers and schemers, and the duel happily ended both their political careers. Adams also claimed that Hamilton had never truly loved Washington—had in fact tried to blackmail Washington at Yorktown[19]—and that Washington had thereafter backed Hamilton out of fear that Hamilton might publish something damaging to Washington's reputation.

Even after death, Hamilton's ghost was false and partisan, wrote old Adams. In July 1804, Federalists cynically used Hamilton's slaying to rally their party, and they continued to use Hamilton's death in later years for dishonest and partisan purposes—often polluting the Fourth of July in the process (a day that in Adams's mind should have been all about Adams). An 1808 letter to his close friend and fellow Declaration signer Benjamin Rush nicely captured Adams's take: "On the fourth of July, Washington's Picture is placed behind the Table of the Principal Magistrates, Hamilton's opposite to him in the most conspicuous Spot in the whole Hall, while the Pictures of Samuel Adams and John Hancock are crowded away in two obscure Corners. Thus is Fanuel [*sic*] Hall which ought to be as Sacred in Boston, as the Temple of Jupiter was on the Capitol Hill in Rome, made the Head Quarters of Fornication, Adultery, Incest, Libelling and Electioneering Intrigue."[20]

The sins listed at the end of this gripe were of course not Washington's but Hamilton's, and Adams did not hesitate to include incest—a reference to Hamilton's suspiciously close relationship to his wife Eliza's beloved sister Angelica. Adams's indignation at Boston's failure to lavish honor on Samuel Adams and John Hancock was pure projection—these were placeholders for John Adams himself (as was young Otis, in a way, in old Adams's memories of 1761). In Adams's mind, Hamilton had absolutely no place in a proper July 4 event, and even Washington, technically, had not signed the Declaration as had Adams; his correspondent, Rush; his cousin Samuel; and Hancock.

This first take on Hamilton's life and death has had influence in American history because old Adams has had influence. He outlived Hamilton for more than two decades, wrote prodigiously and colorfully, and filled his writings with anti-Hamilton bile that affected contemporaries and later generations. Adams's son John Quincy went on to become president, and John Quincy's grandson Henry Adams wrote a hugely influential nine-volume history of the United States in its early years.[21]

The evidence does not support most of the Adams charges. Hamilton did not misbehave in the 1789, 1796, or 1800–1801 elections. He actually respected Adams but thought that Washington was infinitely better in 1789 and that the Pinckney brothers—Adams's running mates in 1796 and 1800—were more temperamentally suited for the presidency. Hamilton was surely right in 1789 and 1800 and perhaps right in 1796. His 1800 pamphlet did not likely tip the election, which Adams had already lost thanks in no small part to the

Sedition Act and to Burr's out-politicking of Hamilton in New York City. (And the Three-Fifths Clause didn't help.)

More generally, Hamilton's "scheming" in presidential elections was a by-product of the systematic flaws in the original Electoral College, and also a result of Hamilton's astute grasp of emerging forms of American democracy, which required political coordination and strategic (and at times insincere) voting. "Electioneering" and "intrigue" were necessary and legitimate parts of the new electoral game, a game that an old-fashioned man like Adams never mastered, but that was in fact the future of America. Ultimately, Adams's frenemy Jefferson proved even better at these political arts than Hamilton—and Jefferson is on Mount Rushmore.

Adams notwithstanding, Hamilton was not a backstabber. He was a front-stabber, open and honest in his confrontations.[22] (Jefferson, on the other hand . . .) There is no evidence—nor is it credible— that Hamilton blackmailed Washington. Washington came to love Hamilton, and Washington did not love easily. Hamilton, in turn, was fiercely loyal to Washington, even as their relationship was at times intense, as are many father-son and mentor-mentee relationships. The blackmail accusation, too, was more projection on the part of Adams. (He thought Hamilton betrayed him, so he thought Hamilton must have also betrayed Washington.) Washington generally backed Hamilton after 1789 because Hamilton understood many things that Adams did not—banks, commerce, armies, taxes, administration, and more. Hamilton grasped the Constitution better than Adams did because he had helped craft it, and then had helped explain and justify it to the American people in 1787–1788, and then had helped run it. Adams had not done these things, but found it hard to admit the truth: Washington followed a whippersnapper such as Hamilton because Hamilton was far superior to Adams on the things that mattered between 1787 and 1797.

What of Adams's fixation on Hamilton's admitted adultery, and his more general view that Hamilton was false and used others for his own purposes? "Hamilton had no more gratitude than a Cat," wrote Adams. "If you give a hungry famished Cat, a Slice of meat,

She will not accept it as a Gift: She will snatch it by Force, and express in her Countenance and Air, that She is under no obligation to you; that She has got it by her own Cunning and Activity, and that you are a fool for giving it to her."[23]

True, Hamilton was weak in the flesh; he was not sexually faithful to Eliza, as Adams was to Abigail. (Hamilton himself admired this aspect of Adams, as he philosophically admired many of Adams's genuine virtues.) But Hamilton loved his wife deeply and she loved him back—theirs was as powerful and emotional a bond as John and Abigail's. Hamilton at the end of his life was indeed religious—more so than Adams, probably.[24] He did not himself initiate the duel; nor did he shoot to kill or maim Burr. Alas, he feared, with good reason, that if he refused the duel he might lose political credibility in a culture that still took gentlemanly honor seriously.[25]

Adams was also far too quick to see in Hamilton a general and overarching tendency of disloyalty simply because Hamilton was not born in the mainland colonies. In this, there was more than a whiff of bigotry on Adams's part. Adams consistently called Hamilton a foreigner and doubted that Hamilton truly loved America.[26] Hamilton in fact loved America with the same ferocity as did Adams. Adams and Hamilton both dreamed of American glory and wanted to be part of it—they both blended their own large egos into the larger project of American greatness. They both yearned for personal glory and national glory, and saw personal glory and national glory as intertwined. It was a tragedy that the two never fully appreciated how much they had in common in their love of America—Adams's native land and Hamilton's chosen homeland.

HERE IS A SECOND TAKE on Hamilton's death. *Hamilton died as he lived.* He was reckless, impetuous, honor-driven, hot-blooded, high-strung, and Napoleonic. His needless death at Burr's hand was entirely in character, because Hamilton, for all his talent, often lacked good judgment and evenness of temperament. He picked too many fights, made too many enemies, and took too many risks. He romanticized violence and manly confrontation, and he tended to veer off course when Washington was not there to steady him.

This take captures a good deal about Hamilton and his world, and the interaction between them. The earliest extant scrap of paper in Hamilton's hand is a startlingly prophetic letter to a childhood friend, written before he turned fifteen: "I shall Conclude saying I wish there was a War." This line captures his personality, but also his predicament. As a lowborn lad, he needed something like a war to launch his rise. A revolution, quite literally, is a turning of the wheel of fate, enabling those at the bottom, perhaps, to rotate to the top. The first letter is quite explicit on this point, as Hamilton reflects with astonishing self-awareness on his own driving impulse, hard but pure: "My Ambition is prevalent that I contemn the grov'ling and condition of a Clerk or the like, to which my Fortune &c. condemns me and would willingly risk my life tho' not my Character to exalt my Station." Someone at the bottom of the social order has less to lose than someone already at the top and sensibly leans into risk. Hamilton's was indeed a world in which military valor could catapult careers—Hamilton's, Napoleon's, and Jackson's, for example.[27]

Hamilton was always prickly about his honor—"my Character," as he put it at age fourteen—because his low birth status had indeed "condemn[ed]" him, initially, to the "grov'ling" status of a "Clerk." All this made it difficult for Hamilton to walk away from a duel when Burr assailed his honor. In his world, the duel was a way for him to display his honor. That is precisely why duels were called "affairs of honor," and dueling grounds were known as "fields of honor."[28]

The prejudice that Hamilton encountered because of his technical bastardy was real. Adams, in particular, seemed to believe that bastards were inherently base,[29] and that the fornication involved in Hamilton's biological conception intrinsically tainted the love child himself. Hamilton's origins, Adams told a friend, were "infamous."[30]

Though this second take captures real truths about Hamilton's life and death, and about the larger social, political, and cultural context at work, it misses certain key elements about both Hamilton and his constitutional vision—the deepest meaning and noblest aspects of his death and his implicit farewell message.

HERE, THEN, IS A THIRD and final take on Hamilton's death. *Hamilton died as he lived.* Hamilton loved the union, and he was willing to sacrifice his life for it. In earlier years, he had risked his life repeatedly for America and had sacrificed his talents again and again for it. His death was a hero's death because he perceived Aaron Burr as a mortal threat to the American union. He thwarted that threat not by taking Burr's life, but, once again, by risking his own for his country.

This is the story that the great historian Ron Chernow tells in his magnificent modern biography of Hamilton.[31] Hamilton yearned to be great and saw American greatness as an extension of himself. Not tied to any individual state—neither Adams's Massachusetts nor Jefferson's Virginia—he embraced continentalism as the key to America's greatness. One of his earliest pen names was "The Continentalist," and his brilliant 1781–1782 essays under that nom de plume powerfully foreshadowed his early essays as Publius in late 1787—essays that were far more influential in the ratification process than anything Madison ever wrote. American greatness—and thus, for Hamilton, his own greatness, for the two were tightly fused in his mind—required a strong indivisible union able to repel Britain, France, and Spain, and then conquer the continent. (Hamilton always dreamed big.)

It is one of history's larger ironies that Hamilton, who had risked his life fighting the British, was often accused, after the war, of being suspiciously pro-British. Hamilton sought to mimic British ideas— an indivisible union, a strong tax system, a national bank, a funded debt, a powerful army and navy, a robust executive branch—*precisely to defeat the British again, if need be.* If you can't (or won't) join 'em, beat 'em.

Jefferson—who never risked his life in battle and had far less understanding of military matters than did Hamilton—never fully grasped the enormous significance of continental indivisibility. And Burr—Jefferson's carelessly chosen running mate—cared only about his own interests, not America's. That was why Burr was so dangerous. In 1804, Hamilton began to worry that Burr might be plotting to ally with secessionist elements in New England. Burr thus had to be stopped, and Hamilton had to stop him. Franklin was dead, Washington was dead, Adams was old and discredited, and Jefferson was the feckless man who had picked Burr to begin with, and who had never fully understood that secession would be America's undoing. That left Hamilton as the man to do the job.

Stopping Burr entailed censuring Burr, and when Burr demanded that Hamilton forswear any future criticism of him, and renounce all past criticism of his shady character and ideas, Hamilton could not honorably yield to this demand. He did not relish the prospect of dueling, but he worried that his viability as an American leader would have been weakened had he cravenly refused the "interview." To bow to Burr would have been to concede that—quite literally—he did not stand by the strong and true words that he had uttered and would continue to utter if necessary.[32]

Just as Franklin knew that his final spoof might be his parting soliloquy, and Washington surely knew that his last will and testament would function as his truly final Farewell Address, so Hamilton chose his words in the days before the duel with special care, because he knew that they might carry extra weight. Four days before the duel, he and Eliza threw a lavish ball at which he pointedly took aside one of their guests, the great artist Colonel John Trumbull, who had, like Hamilton, served as an aide-de-camp to His Excellency in the War of Independence. "You are going to Boston. You will see the principal men there," he said. "Tell them from ME, at MY request, for God's sake, to cease these conversations and threatenings about a separation of the Union. It must hang together as long as it can be made to."[33] In the last letter he ever penned, the day before the duel, he wrote to another friend to express his anxiety about secessionist talk: "I will here express but one sentiment, which is, that Dismemberment of our Empire will be a clear sacrifice of great positive advantages, without any counter-balancing good."[34]

At the Weehawken duel itself, Alexander Hamilton knowingly risked his life by exposing himself to Burr's fire and fury, shrewdly betting, it is fair to infer, that if Burr did kill him, Burr would also be killing his own political future. And the union would live. On his deathbed, he forgave Burr, confessed his sins, and received Communion.

Near the end, he said, "If they [secessionists] break this union, they will break my heart."[35] Alexander Hamilton thus truly died as he lived—exposing his body to mortal risk for his adopted homeland, America, just as he had when leading a bayonet charge at Yorktown in 1781.

JEFFERSON AND ADAMS

What should we make of the most famous dual (not duel) death in American history—the passing away of frenemies John Adams and Thomas Jefferson on the same day, within hours of each other, in their homes far apart?

The most important facts that require analysis hide in plain view. It at first seems preposterously improbable that these two men would die as they did. Not just on the same day; not just with one mentioning the other in his dying breath (even though, of course, they were not in instantaneous contact); not just on the anniversary of their most famous joint venture, the Declaration of Independence; but on precisely the silver anniversary, the fiftieth birthday of the United States of America, over which they had both presided—at first together (almost). If this were a novel, it would be ridiculed as infinitely too pat. The odds against such a confluence of coincidence seem a million to one.

But this confluence was not freakish in the way, say, that a previously unknown geyser briefly and harmlessly erupting on the outskirts of Philadelphia, beginning precisely at high noon, July 4, 1826, would be virtually impossible to explain except as a sign from

God. The Adams and Jefferson deaths involved human agency—human willpower.

The "coincidence" wore two faces, private and public. On the private side, taking each man separately, we can only marvel at the strength of will involved. Each man died knowing the date—waiting for it, and then expiring precisely on cue, like a great stage actor. Jefferson famously said, "This is the Fourth," or words to that effect. There is no record of his saying on each of the preceding days, "This is the Thirtieth," or "This is the First," or "This is the Second," or "This is the Third." Each man willed himself to make it to the Fourth. And then, each sought natural release on that day, and indeed willed it. No hemlock was involved; this was not the death of Socrates. Rather, each man let go and desperately wanted to end on the Fourth and not, say, on the Fifth or the Sixth. There would be far less glory on any other day, earlier or later. (Jefferson had taken the opiate laudanum in the preceding days, and he refused any more drugs once he thought he had made it to the Fourth. In fact, his last recorded words were "No doctor, nothing more.")[36]

Jefferson's protégé James Monroe also managed to die on July 4—exactly five years later, 1831. Nearly five years after that, in 1836, Madison found himself on death's door in late June, but he refused the drugs that might have gotten him to the Fourth, dying instead on June 28.[37] Of course, July 4 was a less meaningful date for Madison. He had not been in Philadelphia in 1776.

What kind of person is able to die on cue? Only a person of extraordinary will, with an eye on history and an astonishing drive to be remembered and celebrated in a certain way. The leading founders sought acclaim above all. The love of fame was, in the words of Hamilton's *Federalist* No. 72, "the ruling passion of the noblest minds." If America's great founders died on cue like actors, that is precisely because they were actors of a certain sort, intensely aware of their public audience.[38]

Thus, Adams and Jefferson each aimed to die on a key American date, not a personal one—not a special birthday or wedding anniversary, not the death date of a beloved soulmate or a favorite parent or child. Each privately aimed for an American date connected to his greatest public moment—his involvement in midwifing the birth of America itself.

Recall that President Washington carefully chose a different date for his formal Farewell Address in his last season in office in 1796—September 17. That was the anniversary of the Constitution itself—or, to be more precise, the anniversary of the date on which the grand federal convention over which he had presided had made public its proposed Constitution and his famous accompanying letter. The Constitution was his creation, his baby. He had not voted for or signed the Declaration. By contrast, Adams and Jefferson were no part of the Constitution-making process. They were Declaration men, men of 1776, and in ways that later prompted each to misunderstand the Constitution—Jefferson by thinking that it, too, was animated by state sovereignty (it wasn't) and Adams by thinking that a younger man like Hamilton, who was offstage in 1776, was a mere bit player (he wasn't).

FOR JEFFERSON, THE DECLARATION WAS all about its soaring words—words that he, as a proud wordsmith, had largely composed—and its grand ideas about revolution and about free and independent states. In fact, the Constitution had repudiated this last idea. Jefferson never understood this. He was, as has now just been seen, an intensely willful man, and he could not see what he would not see, just as, in the end, he could not die on any day other than the day of his choice.

Jefferson's attachment to the Declaration—his sense of special authorship of it—is the unmistakable message of his gravesite inscription, instructions for which he had composed well before July 1826:

> *On the faces of the Obelisk the following inscription, &*
> * not a word more*
> *"Here was buried*
> *Thomas Jefferson*

Author of the Declaration of American Independence
Of the Statute of Virginia for religious freedom
& Father of the University of Virginia."
because by these, as testimonials that I have lived, I wish
  most to be remembered.

Note that there is not a word in these instructions (or on the final obelisk) about the Constitution or about Jefferson's service under the Constitution as the first secretary of state, the second vice president, or the third president. Jefferson wanted to be remembered because of the Declaration and wanted the Declaration itself remembered above all else. How perfect would it be if he could make it to the silver Fourth! How imperfect would it be if he lasted past that day! His death plan was thus set long before the silver Fourth, as was his gravestone inscription. To be sure, the gravestone was not yet inscribed. But the *plan* to carve in stone his reference to the Declaration was indeed already metaphorically carved in stone.

ADAMS'S DEATH ON JULY 4, 1826, shows that he, too, was a man of truly extraordinary will and inner strength—every bit as able as Jefferson to live as long he had to and then die on a dime for fame. Indeed, Adams had to make it past his ninetieth birthday, whereas Jefferson perished at age eighty-three. For many years, perhaps, John Adams was living just to die in just the right way.

But there were obvious differences between the two men who seemed to die in perfect harmony. Adams was obsessed by Jefferson, but not vice versa. Jefferson made no recorded mention of Adams at or near the end, whereas Adams's last words were "Thomas Jefferson still survives." In fact, Jefferson had predeceased Adams by a matter of hours, though there was, of course, no way that Adams could possibly have known this fact, given the time it took news to travel.

There is something oddly apt in old Adams's last words, and one aspect of the aptness is that old Adams was in fact wrong. As was seen in our microscopic examination of the writs-of-assistance episode, old Adams in his declining years often got key things wrong, but wrong in ways that nonetheless were then and remain today deeply revealing.

What, then, was so significant about the false line about Jefferson? First, with this reference, Adams wanted his collaboration with Jefferson remembered. Adams had once been a team player. He lost that skill as he aged, but his partnership with Jefferson in 1776 was indeed among his greatest moments.

Second, even as Adams died with a revealing "Rosebud" on his lips—"Jefferson"—the error in his reference should remind us that he and Jefferson were not quite in sync. There was friendship in Adams's dying breath but also rivalry. The two men were emphatically not peas in a pod, even though they were together in 1776 and died together (and apart) exactly fifty years later. They were not best friends, even if Adams said so and believed it so. They were, at best, intensely rivalrous friends—frenemies, we would say today.

The two in death wanted America to remember entirely different things. Jefferson wanted the *words and the state sovereignty principles of the Declaration of Independence* remembered. Adams wanted *Adams* remembered—the fact that he and Jefferson had been in the room where it happened, when even Washington was not in the room, and when no one had yet heard of a "boy"—old Adams's word, oft-repeated—named Hamilton.[39]

Old Adams's compulsive need to see himself as, and to be remembered as, Jefferson's friend began long before 1826. In late 1809, Adams wrote a jaw-dropping letter to Benjamin Rush, himself a Declaration signer and a friend of both Adams and Jefferson—indeed, the man who brokered the famous epistolary rapprochement between the two ex-presidents in their final years. According to Adams's 1809 missive, "There has never been the smallest Interruption of the Personal Friendship between me and Mr. Jefferson that I know of. You should remember that Jefferson was but a Boy to me. I was at least ten years older than him in age and more than twenty years older than him in Politicks. I am bold to say I was his Preceptor in

Politicks and taught him every Thing that has been good and solid in his whole Political Conduct."[40]

The inaccuracies and self-delusions of this passage are mind-boggling. Never the smallest interruption of friendship? *Adams boycotted Jefferson's presidential inauguration. Before that, Adams signed into law a Sedition Act that criminalized Jefferson's subsequent collusion with James Callender and clandestine authorship of the Kentucky Resolutions.* More than twenty years older, politically? *Adams scribbled his first private notes on the writs-of-assistance episode in 1761 and anonymously published his first notable writings on the imperial crisis in late 1765; Jefferson won election to the House of Burgesses in 1769 and published his famous pamphlet,* A Summary View, *in 1774. Jefferson was thus a prominent lawmaker before he had even heard of Adams, who first openly set foot on a continental stage in the Boston Massacre trial in late 1770—defending the British soldiers!* Taught him everything? *Funny that Jefferson never said anything like that.*

In 1822, in response to a Fourth of July address by an earnest youngster, Adams went even further: "Jefferson and Adams were never rivals; it was Hamilton that was the rival of Jefferson."[41] Never even rivals? *What an odd view of the election of 1800. In the end, it was Hamilton who pushed the Federalist House to pick Jefferson, while Adams sulked in his tent.*

Old Adams felt humiliated by his 1800 loss to Jefferson, and these deep feelings of humiliation generated a complex psychic response. If Jefferson really was always his friend and indeed pupil, he really hadn't entirely lost, quite. He had simply passed the baton. By late 1809, Jefferson himself had passed the baton to Madison, and old Adams was beginning to think about what might happen next. Unlike other leading founding fathers, old Adams had a son and namesake, John Quincy. Perhaps John Quincy could himself become president, but only if old Adams made lasting peace with the Virginia dynasty[42]—and with Jefferson, in particular, who himself had been a father figure and mentor to the "Boy," John Quincy, back in Paris in the 1780s. Maybe John Adams could indeed win a second—even a third!—term, vicariously through John Quincy. He whose son wins last, laughs best. When old Adams died, his son was indeed in the Executive Mansion. If Jefferson still lived—in fact he did not— perhaps (old Adams dreamed) the great Virginian could help John Quincy in 1828 against the military madman Andrew Jackson.*

For all of the unreliability of old Adams's claims, there is still a deep truth lurking in all the falsity—just as there was in old Adams's tales about young Otis. Adams and Jefferson had not dined alone in 1776. They had dined together, and worked together—along with others, of course. And amazingly, they died just as they had lived— together, in a way, but also apart.

MADISON

If Adams was thinking about Jefferson when he died, Jefferson was thinking about Madison. "Take care of me when dead, and be as- sured that I shall leave with you my last affections," wrote Jefferson to Madison in early 1826.[43]

Jefferson did not care about his corpse. Rather, he wanted Madi- son to protect his reputation, his fame—his "sacred honor," to borrow a phrase—and also his many secrets. For example, Jefferson wanted his obelisk inscription to mention that he was the "father" of the

---

*The correspondence late in life between Adams and Jefferson must thus be treated with caution by anyone seeking to use these missives to illuminate prior events. Ad- ams's memory was erratic and self-serving. His logorrheic letters—more than two for every one of Jefferson's and often much longer—reflected a jumble of emotions and stratagems. Jefferson, always secretive, was especially careful (and often not candid) in this freighted correspondence, knowing that the letters would eventually become public. One example may suffice. Many historians have erroneously treated at face value the closing words of Adams's February 2, 1817, letter: "Notwithstanding a thousand Faults and blunders, his [Madison's] Administration has acquired more glory, and es- tablished more Union, than all his three Predecessors Washington Adams and Jefferson put together." Old Adams's claim here is outlandish—Rushmore features Washington and not Madison for good reason. Adams found it hard to admit just how much Wash- ington had soared over all others (including Adams himself). Adams was also prone to wild rhetorical overstatement. Moreover, flattering Madison in a letter to Jefferson in early 1817 would likely boost JQA's prospects. Indeed, just as Jefferson had picked Madison as his secretary of state and presumptive successor, so Madison had picked Monroe, and so Monroe was in early 1817 in the process of picking JQA.

University of Virginia. But what about other ways in which he was a father, including his fatherhood of Sally Hemings's children? As with all other leading framers, Jefferson was acutely aware of history looking over his shoulder. He showed what he wanted to show; he hid a great deal; and he wanted Madison to help him, even after his death, both in the showing and in the hiding.

MADISON DID AS REQUESTED, MOST importantly concerning Jefferson's words and deeds in connection with the Kentucky Resolutions of 1799.

In the Nullification Crisis of the late 1820s and early 1830s, Madison emphatically sided with Andrew Jackson and against South Carolina. In both private correspondence and public newspapers, the old man insisted that the Virginia Resolutions, which he himself had drafted, provided absolutely no support for Calhounism. Having left office as winners, most ex-presidents had generally tried to keep a low profile in public discourse. (Old Adams was an exception, battling publicly as well as privately to regain his lost reputation.) When Calhoun and other ultras in the late 1820s contended that the Virginia Resolutions backed their outlandish claims, Madison felt compelled to set the record straight.

A lifelong journalist of sorts, Madison published his last important journalistic piece under his own name in the October 1830 issue of the *North American Review*. Styled as a letter to the *Review*'s editor, Edward Everett, the essay made clear that Madison had never—in the Virginia Resolutions or elsewhere—supported nullification. "It appears, that the proceedings of Virginia have been misconceived by those who have appealed to them," he wrote. Though the *Review* essay did not discuss secession, as distinct from nullification, in detail, Madison emphatically repudiated secession in a letter to a friend, complaining, "I know not whence the idea could proceed that I concurred in the doctrine, that altho' a State could not nullify a law of the Union, it had a right to secede from the Union. Both spring from the same poisonous root."[44] Writing to President

Jackson's personal secretary, Nicholas P. Trist, Madison insisted that the argument for unilateral secession rested upon a logical "fallacy."[45]

Unfortunately for Madison, Jefferson's Kentucky Resolution drafts were expressly supportive of nullification and, arguably, implicitly supportive of secession. Madison tried to cover up for his mentor on these points in the 1830s because he believed, rightly, that these Jeffersonian writings were embarrassing.[46] And Jefferson in 1826 had told Madison to protect the Jefferson trademark above all.

At first, Madison claimed, incorrectly, that Jefferson had absolutely nothing to do with the specific nullification language of the Kentucky Resolutions of 1799. But as drafts from Jefferson's own pen surfaced, Madison shifted ground.[47] Nullification à la Jefferson, claimed old Madison, could not be resorted to at will, but could properly occur only in situations of extreme tyranny and utter breakdown of constitutional order—conditions akin to those of 1776.

Alas, Jefferson had not said that. His careless nullifcation language in his private correspondence in the 1790s had not spoken of "a long train of abuses and usurpations" portending "absolute Despotism." Rather, he had said that any state could nullify unilaterally whenever that state believed that Congress had exceeded its powers in any respect—whenever Congress's pinkie toe had crossed the constitutional line, however trivially and inadvertently. Jefferson, in other words, had in effect said that each state had a power like the modern Supreme Court power of judicial review, a power that each state could exercise unreviewably. This was closely akin to the power that Spencer Roane tried to claim for the Virginia state judiciary in the 1810s, only to be laughed out of Court by Joseph Story and his unanimous colleagues in *Martin v. Hunter's Lessee*.

Although Jefferson in the moment had in fact encouraged Roane, Madison thought Roane's ideas not merely wrong but ludicrous: "I hope that all who now see the absurdity of nullification, will see also the necessity of rejecting the claim to effect it, thro' the State Judiciaries; which can only be kept in their Constitutional career, by the controul of the Federal Jurisdiction. Take the linchpins from a carriage, and how soon would a wheel be off its axle; an emblem of the speedy fate of the Federal system, were the parties to it loosened from the authority which confines them to their spheres."[48] On this issue, Madison thus stood squarely with the likes of Marshall, Story, and the unanimous *Martin* Court.

How then, to handle the awkward facts that Jefferson had in life not always seen this issue with Madisonian clarity? With Jefferson now in his grave in the 1830s and unable to say or write anything additionally embarrasing, Madison ultimately defended his friend by suggesting that Jefferson was prone to exaggeration and should not be read literally: "Allowances also ought to be made for a habit in Mr J. as in others of great genius, of expressing in strong and round terms impressions of the moment."[49]

What about secession as distinct from nullification? Although Jefferson had not in life explicitly endorsed a state's right to unilaterally secede from the union, his view that each state in the union, even after 1788, continued to be free, fully sovereign, and independent, à la 1776, logically pushed in the direction of a right of secession. This, too, was anathema to old Madison, who worked hard after death had silenced Jefferson to protect Jefferson's legacy by blurring the exuberant Virginian's most troublesome assertions: "It is remarkable how closely the nullifiers, who make the name of Mr. Jefferson the pedestal for their colossal heresy, shut their eyes & lips, whenever his authority is ever so clearly & emphatically agst. them. . . . It is high time that the claim to secede at will should be put down by the public opinion; and I shall be glad to see the task commenced by one who understands the subject."[50]

At some point in the early 1830s—the best estimate is 1834—Madison also penned a brief memo that was found among his papers and published posthumously in 1839. In its entirety, it read as follows:

As this advice, if it ever see the light will not do it till I am no more it may be considered as issuing from the tomb where truth alone can be respected, and the happiness of man alone consulted. It will be entitled therefore to whatever weight can be derived from good intentions, and from the experience of one, who has served his Country in various stations through a period of forty years, who espoused in his youth and adhered through his life to the cause of its liberty, and who has borne a part in most of the great transactions which will constitute epochs of its destiny. *The advice nearest to my heart and deepest in my convictions is that the Union of the States be cherished & perpetuated.* Let the open enemy to it be regarded as a Pandora with her box opened; and the disguised one, as the Serpent creeping with his deadly wills into Paradise.[51]

Publicly and privately until the end of his days, Madison thus always adhered to the view that he had communicated to Hamilton in July 1788 and that Hamilton had read aloud to the New York Ratifying Convention. Ratification needed to be in toto and forever.

WHEN MADISON DIED IN 1836—THE last of the great founders to go*—he left America an additional and more elaborate adieu with deep portent: the notes he had taken at the grand Convention of 1787. His distinctive, albeit implicit, farewell message was thus that posterity should carefully study the Constitution's history. Like every other leading founder, he yearned to be remembered as *a*, if not *the*, hero of the founding story.[52] He wanted posterity to see the constitu-

---

*John Marshall outlived Adams and Jefferson but predeceased Madison. Although the great chief justice does not generally rank among the six most notable founders—the six whose deaths form the spine of this concluding chapter—it is worth noting that Marshall's passing, too, came with an important, albeit implicit, constitutional message. Unlike the big six, Marshall died in office—died, indeed, nearly halfway into his fourth decade on the Court. The obvious message of his death in 1835 was that Article III life tenure surely mattered, offering federal judges dramatic opportunities to find, refine, and elaborate their constitutional visions over the course of decades of continuous service. Prior to 1835, no president had served continuously more than eight years; no senator had served continuously more than twenty-two years; and no House member had served continuously more than thirty years. (This tally does not count those who hopped from post to post—for example, North Carolina's Nathaniel Macon did serve continuously in Congress for more than three and a half decades, but only by hopping midcareer from the House to the Senate.)

tional story from his angle, and in death he made it easy for posterity to do just that.

In the fateful summer of 1787, the bookish Virginian had taken more detailed notes than had anyone else in attendance. Much of his own agenda had not prevailed—Washington's Constitution won out, not Madison's. Still, as he left Philadelphia in 1787, Madison resolved to work for ratification of the plan that had emerged. In the ensuing years, and especially in his post-presidential retirement years, Madison revised and polished his notes. Some of these revisions were likely consciously designed to vindicate his own later views, but old Madison was in general a more scrupulous historian—a truer American Thucydides—than was old Adams.[53]

Approaching death, Madison at last took steps to provide for the publication of his trove of historical material. Because he outlived everyone else at Philadelphia, he knew that none of the other participants could directly contradict his account. (He, too, willed himself to live as long as he needed to.) In his last act, he tried to give himself the last word.

Madison could not afford to simply donate his papers to the public. Financially, his estate was in shambles, and he worried about his surviving wife, Dolley. He bequeathed her his papers so that she could quickly sell them for publication. He also left her his slaves.

Like Jefferson, and unlike Washington, Madison on his deathbed thus failed to free any substantial number of slaves, as he had been counseled to do by some of those close to him. Dolley's cousin, Edward Coles, was a Virginia planter who freed his own slaves in the late 1810s after serving as Madison's private secretary. In 1832, Coles wrote a blunt and confidential letter to Madison urging his friend, mentor, and in-law to follow Washington's noble example: "You should make provision in your Will for the emancipation of your Slaves. . . . [Y]ou should turn your attention to this subject, and digest a plan and pursue a course that will redound to your fame, and may be calculated to induce others to follow your example."[54] Instead, most of Madison's slaves—more than a hundred in all—eventually stood on auction blocks to pay off their master's accumulated debts.[55]

In this, as in so many other things, Madison unfortunately followed Jefferson rather than Washington. Thus, the two younger Virginians who had once been intimates and allies of George Wasington disappointed His Excelllency in death, as they had often done late in life.

Pursuant to an act of Congress signed by Jackson on his last day in office, Madison's widow sold her husband's papers to the federal government for $30,000—roughly $1 million in today's currency.[56] This was a pretty penny for Dolley, but the American people surely got their money's worth. The government arranged for the prompt publication of Madison's Convention notes in 1840. Thanks to this farsighted purchase and quick publication, Americans in the 1840s and thereafter have had an extraordinary, though not entirely unbiased, window into the founding moment, the hinge of human history, when a grand Convention drafted an epic document and Americans said "yes, We do."

The broad public dissemination of Madison's notes in 1840–1841 marked a milestone in the maturation of constitutional discourse, all the more so because it coincided felicitously with a notable anniversary. A full eighty years had now elapsed since the events in colonial Boston that could sensibly be seen, with the benefit of hindsight, as the commencement of America's constitutional conversation.

FOURSCORE YEARS AFTER THAT CONVERSATION began in a Boston Court House, the nation had yet to redeem the loftiest aspects of James Otis's speech, which condemned "slavery" even though Otis likely did not advocate abolition then and there, as old Adams later claimed. Otis's ambitious sister, Mercy Otis Warren, who would eventually chronicle some of the great events of the American Revolution, did not witness her brother's Court House oration in 1761.[57] Nor did any other woman attend the oral argument that day. Fourscore years later, most women remained on the periphery of the great American constitutional conversation.

More promisingly, on July 4, 1840, Congress formally apologized for the 1798 Sedition Act by repaying from the federal treasury fines that had been imposed on Matthew Lyon in 1799 and by proclaiming, in an accompanying report, that it was now "conclusively settled" that this early effort to stifle the American constitutional conversation was flatly unconstitutional. The repeal date marked the sixty-fourth anniversary of the Declaration of Independence and the fourteenth anniversary of Jefferson's and Adams's deaths. On this issue, old Adams was right, at least metaphorically. Thomas Jefferson still survived.

Postscript

Why This Book?

W HAT'S NEW IN THE PRECEDING pages? What's missing? What's next? If my tale is anywhere close to correct, what tales told by other narrators must be rejected or revised?

THE BIGGEST NEWS IS THAT a book such as this now exists, as it did not before—a book that brings together between a single set of covers the main constitutional episodes of the fateful era in which America became America.

As I write the words of this postscript, in the late summer of 2020, I am frankly worried about the widespread constitutional illiteracy that surrounds me, illiteracy of young and old, left and right. A nation that does not understand its history is like a person who suffers amnesia. Without a strong memory of one's own past, how can a person live a meaningful life? Without a deep understanding of our collective constitutional past, how can Americans live together? In 1860–1861, South Carolinians forgot what South Carolinians had in fact plainly agreed to in 1787–1788: an indissoluble union. And the war came.

This historical point can be recast as a legal one. Without a shared understanding of the basic rules of constitutional interpretation, how can Americans live free and thrive? Return once again to the secession question. The Constitution's terse text and overarching structure really do prohibit unilateral secession. But to see this with crystal clarity, we need to read the document through a proper legal prism, with attention to both letter and spirit, noting how the text's precise syntax and panoramic structure reinforce each other.

We Americans are a famously diverse and contentious lot. Today's citizens bear myriad ethnic backgrounds and skin colors. We profess a multitude of faiths, and some profess agnosticism or atheism. We speak countless different languages. Our forebears came to this land at wildly different times and in profoundly different ways, some with bullwhips, some in chains. Some of us are male, others female, still others neither or both; some are gay, others straight, still others in between or beyond. We passionately embrace a wide range of ideologies and viewpoints.

But despite—or rather precisely because of—all these differences, there must be a common core. *E Pluribus Unum*. The United States Constitution and its history are what We (with a capital W) have in common, and if We don't like the document as is, We can amend it, as indeed, previous generations of Americans have made amends and amendments. This terse text and the saga that underlies it are what make us Americans. Without broad agreement on the constitutional basics—not on every detail, but on the big picture, the main narrative—we are lost. We are Babel. We are not a We. And if so, We may ultimately lose the Republic that Franklin hoped we could keep. Hence my title, *The Words That Made Us*, which can also be understood as *The Words That Made [the] US*.

Every four years, We must pick a president. *This is a constitutional decision*. We cannot make this decision well without an understanding of the presidency as an office structured by the Constitution, which both empowers and limits the person who holds this unique and uniquely dangerous post. The first thing that a president must do in office is swear an oath to "preserve, protect, and defend the Constitution of the United States." For this system to work, an oath-taking president—and We Americans who pick that oath-taking president—must understand the basic outlines of our Constitution. What does it say and why does it say that? How has it been implemented over the years by prior presidents and other leading government actors? Which of our past presidents did this job well, and which did not? Why and how? These and related civics questions form the spine of this book. Thus, this is a book for my fellow citizens.

This is also a book for my fellow scholars. Too few law professors know history, and too few history professors know law. (Even historians familiar with the legal issues of their own main period of study often know little about the legal issues of earlier or later eras.) Every week this summer, as I sat in my family room, I saw scholars and pundits on cable TV saying silly things. On C-SPAN, distinguished Civil War historians airily opined that the Constitution of 1787–1788 was indeterminate on the secession question. *Nonsense.* On MSNBC, radical-chic intellectuals proclaimed, with barely suppressed smirks, that Americans revolted in 1776 mainly to protect slavery, which the British government was seeking to abolish. *Ridiculous.* On Fox News, pundits told viewers that the founders loathed "democracy" as a word and as a concept, and embraced only "republics," which were always and everywhere sharply contradistinguished from "democracies." *Baloney.*

Today's Hillsdale graduates say that America's founders never did anything wrong, and today's Harvard graduates say that America's founders never did anything right. (Okay, okay—that's a gross oversimplification, but it felt good to blow off some steam.) We need facts and analysis, not reflexive right-wing boosterism or knee-jerk leftist hooting. Of course, the truth is not always and necessarily in the middle. On some issues, today's conservatives are absolutely right on the law and the facts; on other issues, today's liberals are 100 percent correct. But we can only decide which is which, and see when the truth is instead somewhere in between or something entirely different, once we know the key historical facts of America's constitutional conversation and the basic legal rules for assessing those facts. Enter this book, which tries to offer readers the essential facts and figures, the notable quips and quotes, the relevant legal rules and principles, both substantively and methodologically—all in support of a coherent national narrative.

The claims made in this book may well elicit sharp responses and rejoinders from other scholars. I hope so! As I shall explain below, the preceding chapters tell a fresh story of America—a story that, in ways both large and small, breaks with reigning academic orthodoxies. If, as I believe, some of the greatest scholars of my youth—scholars for whom I have enormous respect, and who have inspired me to do what I do—have missed or misstated key points, then there is every reason to think that I too have erred in various ways that, alas, I cannot now see. Just as I seek to correct my predecessors, mentors, and role models, so I expect that scholars of the next generation will push back against some of what I say here.

In other words, dear reader, the book that you have just read is nothing if not ambitious. I have aimed to offer you the most penetrating and wide-ranging book about America's Constitution and America's founders now available, a book that seeks to take its place alongside, and indeed to synthesize and (dare I say it?) succeed, George Bancroft's *History of the Formation of the Constitution of the United States of America* (1882), Charles Beard's *An Economic Interpretation of the Constitution of the United States* (1913), Andrew C. McLaughlin's *A Constitutional History of the United States* (1935), and Gordon S. Wood's *The Creation of the American Republic, 1776–1787* (1969) and *Revolutionary Characters: What Made the Founders Different* (2006).

ALLOW ME, THEN, TO SUMMARIZE my most notable points in each chapter, and in the process to connect these dots, bringing into sharper focus the new narrative that I offer.

The first thing to note about Chapter One—and about this book—is my start date, 1760. Not 1763—the opening year of just about every book on the American Revolution now in print. For all his craziness, old Adams was right, and old Hutchinson was even more right. It all started with imperial geopolitics, the death of the old king, and the fall of Montreal in 1760, even before the 1763 Treaty of Paris, the 1764 Sugar Act, and the 1765 Stamp Act. Ultimately, Americans revolted because they could. This was not a sufficient condition for revolution, but it was a necessary one.[1] *After the fall of Montreal, colonists began to imagine life without the British shield, and it did not take long after Montreal's fall for this imagination to reveal itself.* Even before the British started seriously misbehaving—indeed, even before the Treaty of Paris formally confirmed the new facts on the ground in Montreal—some Americans (at least in Boston, where it all began) were beginning to itch and agitate. True, the Brits were negligent and inattentive. They never even bothered to send timely proclamation instructions! But they were not tyrannical—not yet. On the law, Hutchinson was actually on solid ground, and the great Pitt backed him to the hilt, but that hardly mattered to young Otis or old Adams.

No leading American scholar nowadays begins the story of the American Revolution quite this way, with detailed attention lavished upon the events in the Boston Court House in 1761.[2] In fact, in recent decades almost no general textbook or trade book about the Revolution—almost no broad-gauge historian of the Revolution—has offered more than a fleeting mention of *Paxton's Case*, perhaps because this lawsuit about writs of assistance teemed with legal technicalities, and perhaps also because old Adams muddied the waters.[3] (The Supreme Court has routinely mentioned the case, but has bungled the technicalities, and never come close to seeing what the episode was *really* all about.) Despite all this (and with thanks to Billy Crystal, Meg Ryan, Rob Reiner, and the late Nora Ephron), I have chosen to begin my movie—Act I, scene 1—with the *first time* Harry Met Sally. The bad blood between Otis and Adams on the one side and Hutchinson on the other began in 1760–1761 and proved quite significant over the next fifteen years.

Chapter One also features important cameo appearances. Benjamin Franklin, George Washington, and William Pitt quickly stride across our stage, because in the backdrop of *Paxton's Case*, there was a world at war. All three of these great men had played key roles in that world war before Otis ever opened his mouth.

Chapters Two and Three tell the story of 1763 to 1776—from the Treaty of Paris to the Declaration of Independence—in a broadly conventional way. These chapters owe an enormous debt (duly acknowledged in the endnotes, I hope) to three towering scholars, now deceased, whom I first met in my course books as a Yale College freshman: Edmund Morgan, Bernard Bailyn, and Pauline Maier. Morgan later became my teacher and senior colleague; Maier, my dear friend. I never met Bailyn in the flesh, alas.

Three-quarters of a century after his first writings in the field, Morgan's work remains definitive: In the great imperial debate, the patriots had the more astute and farsighted arguments. George III was a blockhead who surrounded himself with other blockheads. Americans' top patriots were an impressive bunch, but few of America's best (other than Hutchinson) became leading loyalists. Bailyn and his star student Gordon Wood also helped me see the light: The great imperial debate revolved tightly around the key legal concept of indivisible Parliamentary sovereignty. And Maier's work is pitch-perfect: Colonists paid close attention to English libertarians and friends of America like Wilkes, Camden, Pitt, and Barré. Colonists also carefully distinguished riotous looting and rampaging from mob actions that were more controlled and socially acceptable—proportionate and poetically just, even if not law-abiding in the strictest sense. In 1776, Jefferson was not a creative genius, but a good scribe, distilling the common sense of Americans evident in countless precursors to the Declaration that dotted the land. Then Congress edited him good and hard.

My most original touches in Chapters Two and Three involve a pair of notable native Bostonians, Thomas Hutchinson and Benjamin Franklin, who were strikingly akin to each other prior to 1765[4] but chose divergent paths thereafter. History has treated these two titans utterly differently. Benjamin Franklin is nowadays a proverbial rock star. His first name has become a generic noun, as in the hip-hop song "It's All About the Benjamins." (In total dollars, more American currency in circulation bears his likeness than anyone else's, and indeed Benjamins outrank all other denominations combined.) By contrast, Thomas Hutchinson is almost unknown, even among well-educated Americans passionate about history. *How can this be?* After all, Hutchinson was America's most distinguished and discerning loyalist and was ubiquitous in the run-up to the American Revolution. To overlook him is to miss central aspects of the imperial crisis—the best voice on the other side.

True, Bernard Bailyn wrote a penetrating book on Hutchinson a half century ago, but Bailyn's subtle style, intricate analysis, and myriad detours have made this academic classic, *The Ordeal of Thomas Hutchinson*, a challenge for general readers who do not already know the basic story and cast of characters. Only a handful of more recent books have quoted Hutchinson's affecting courtroom speech the morning after his home was destroyed. Surely this extraordinary, if uncomfortable, episode deserves a prominent place in the standard story of the American Revolution—as does the colony's subsequent decision to indemnify Hutchinson (a point that I stress and that most other narratives omit). Chapter Two also highlights the specific ways in which Samuel Adams avoided anything like the Hutchinson mansion riot when patriots dumped some 340 tea chests into Boston Harbor eight years later. (Readers should recall that I write this postscript at a moment when Americans are once again trying to draw lines between abominable mass lootings and acceptable—many would say admirable—mass protests.)

The story of the Hutchinson Letters Affair gets more attention in my narrative than in most standard accounts of the Revolution. The story casts light on the complex interpersonal relationships among several leading protagonists: Whately, Hutchinson, Franklin, and the Adams cousins. More abstractly, I see the Hutchinson Letters Affair as pivotal to my larger story, and not just because the episode seems so strikingly modern, featuring as it does leaked emails—er, letters—and proto-muckraking publishers. Hutchinson's letters generated colonial outrage that drove the Boston Tea Party, which in turn precipitated the Coercive Acts and thus the Revolution. On the other side of the Atlantic, the purloined (?) letters led to the January 1774 Cockpit incident—Franklin's Rubicon, when he ceased being the loyal British subject he had long been (rather like Hutchinson himself) and became forevermore a committed American Revolutionary.

As for Franklin more generally, I hope that readers now have even more reason to marvel at the man's genius—not just as a world-class scientist and inventor, but as a great democratic communicator, the father of the modern political cartoon, and the originator of the world's first truly global proto-meme, *Join or Die*. I confess, I personally don't much like snakes. In fact, they terrify me. But I find the story of Franklin's inky serpent—its early appearances, its hibernations, its revivals at key moments, and its evolution—compelling. Yet few historians over the past century have told this ophidian story in any detail. In future work, I hope to show that cartoonists in the Civil War era revived Franklin's reptile in revealing ways.

Franklin was a newspaperman extraordinaire, and Chapters Two and Three stress the strong links between American newspapers and the American Revolution. In the years after *Paxton's Case*, newspapers were circulating faster and more widely, across both land and sea, than ever before, enabling colonists to begin to read and write and think continentally. Given this fact, Britain's decision to tax all sorts of colonial paper products, including newspapers, was especially obtuse. Arthur Schlesinger Sr. made this point nearly a century ago,[5] but most recent historians have failed to reiterate and build on this theme. Deep in the endnotes of Chapter 2, interested readers will find exciting new data, based on a fresh analysis of the newspapers themselves, detailing how different print shops in different ways mocked the Stamp Act by refusing to print on stamped paper.[6]

Chapter Four marks a fork in my narrative road, and a complicated fork at that. At least five divergent paths branched off from the Declaration of Independence, but I narrate only three stories. The military story, especially the story of Washington's army, was of course critical to the American Revolution, but I do not recount this saga in any detail. Long Island, Kip's Bay, Fort Washington, Fort Lee, Trenton, Princeton, Brandywine, Germantown, Saratoga, Valley Forge, Monmouth, Morristown, Camden, Cowpens, Guilford Courthouse, Yorktown—all of these episodes occur offstage in my narrative, but my onstage protagonists were powerfully affected by the carnage and hardship all around. The careful reader must thus keep the war and its implications constantly in mind. So, too, with a second critical offstage story: the diplomatic drama in Paris, London, and Amsterdam starring (on the American side) Adams, Jay, and, most of all, Franklin.

The three narrative paths that I do tread in Chapter Four involve the West, the states, and the Confederation. On the West, I am broadly in agreement with the influential historian Alan Taylor: Although Revolutionary unrest first began on the coast (a Massachusetts story), many colonists lusted for land in the backcountry (a Virginia story). British taxation without representation outraged colonials; so did a British proclamation that generally barred colonists from settling beyond the Appalachian crest. Americans seethed at the tyrannical 1774 Coercive Acts targeting Massachusetts; Americans also smoldered in response to that year's Quebec Act, which snatched away from British Virginians western lands that they had won in the French and Indian War, but that the empire awarded instead to British Canadians.[7]

My version of the western story, however, is rather more Whiggish than Taylor's. Chapter Four celebrates the strong anti-imperialist thrust of the Northwest Ordinance, which promised that western Americans could join the American constitutional project on an equal republican footing. I also highlight and praise the free-soil, rights-protecting, education-promoting, pro-republican, egalitarian, and tribe-sensitive aspects of the Ordinance. My most original thought is that the Ordinance was a powerful counterpart of and precedent for the US Constitution itself. In effect, the drafters of both the Ordinance and the Constitution sidestepped the Articles of Confederation, but each time, the states in the room acted *unitedly*, with a strong supermajority of states going beyond the Articles and simply doing what needed to be done in the summer of 1787. In New York, the Confederation Congress passed the Ordinance 8–0. In Philadelphia, the grand Convention drafted the Constitution, 11–0, in contemplation of ratification by 9 or more states.

As for the state constitutions that sprang to life in and shortly after 1776, there was little new work that I needed to do, given that this ground has been so well plowed by Gordon Wood in *The Creation of the American Republic* and Willi Paul Adams in *The First American Constitutions*. Is there anything original left to say? Perhaps this: Newspapers! I stress that Americans' first constitutions emerged alongside an extraordinary and fast-rising newspaper culture. Revolution-style written constitutions were truly terse texts designed to appear in full in newspapers, and newspapers did in fact dramatically disseminate constitutions and constitutional ideas across the continent for easy replication.

My account of the many weaknesses of the Articles of Confederation is quite conventional. But here's the odd twist: the most influential scholars over the past century have often conceded the utter unworkability of the Articles and then proceeded to ignore that elephant in the room in their accounts of the ensuing Constitution. My view, by contrast, is simple and straightforward: *The Constitution of 1787 was a direct, logical, and proportionate response to the basic failures of the Articles. Period.*

Indeed, that is one of my key claims in Chapter Five. In order to explain the emergence of the United States Constitution, we need not posit self-interested moneymen aiming to enrich themselves, à la Charles Beard. Nor was the Constitution a Madisonian project centrally addressed to solving the perceived internal governance flaws of individual state constitutions, as Gordon Wood has cleverly—too cleverly—argued in a truly brilliant lifetime body of work.

To drive home my key point, Chapter Five narrates the drafting of the Constitution in a distinctive manner. There are now in print dozens of books that take the reader deep into the bowels of the Philadelphia delegates' deliberations, week by week, debate by debate. This standard approach is an obvious way to tell the tale, given the chronological structure of Madison's notes and of the official Convention journal. But neither Madison's notebook nor the official journal was contemporaneously available to the Americans who were asked to say yes or no in 1787–1788. True, the secrecy ban lapsed at Convention's end—a key point that I am at pains to prove (with extensive endnote details and documentation),[8] because so many today wrongly think otherwise. But almost no one in 1787–1788 sought or got a week-by-week, vote-by-vote, issue-by-issue, blow-by-blow account, à la modern Philadelphia stories in the tradition of Andrew McLaughlin, Catherine Drinker Bowen, Clinton Rossiter, Jack Rakove, Richard Beeman, and Michael Klarman (to name only the most notable authors—there are, to repeat, countless others in this genre).[9] Rather, Americans in late 1787 began—just as I begin—by confronting the Constitution's text as a whole. They began—as I begin—by trying to understand the final Philadelphia plan (and not some intermediate set of rejected drafts) as a comprehensible and comprehensive solution to the problems that expressly triggered the Convention. Those problems involved the failures of the continental government—not, as Wood and his neo-Madisonian followers would have it, the internal republican failures of individual states.

The standard chronological-narrative approach to the grand Convention has serious drawbacks. First, in showcasing individual delegates and their speeches, this approach tends to miss America in the room. Delegates came to Philadelphia bearing constitutional ideas from all across the land, especially ideas embodied in their respective home-state constitutions. Delegates also understood that newspaper publication and popular debate would begin immediately after the Convention adjourned; America's likely reactions in the ratification process to come thus hovered over the Philadelphia conclave from start to finish. Second, the standard approach typically slights the basic *structural* features that powerfully shaped the Convention's big state–small state showdown: the recapitulation phenomenon, with the Convention itself voting state by state, rather than proportionately; the infinite-regress, no-census, and slave-apportionment issues that doomed any other internal voting rule at Philadelphia; and the counterbalancing fact that big states enjoyed an enhanced threat advantage once immediate ratification unanimity was abandoned. Put differently, the standard accounts typically feature too much colorful storytelling and too little hardheaded rational-choice analysis. Third, the standard approach gives far too much weight to Madison's notes, often treating them as if they were objective and complete verbatim transcripts. Far from it—and even scholars who in principle understand this methodological problem end up, in practice, for reasons of research ease and narrative convenience, overrelying on Madison's undeniably selective, perhaps self-serving, and sometimes non-contemporaneous paraphrases. Fourth, and related, the standard approach pays far too little attention to the man who almost never spoke, because he did not need to speak, but who was far more important than any who did speak.

George Washington presided, literally and figuratively. He got what he wanted—a strikingly strong presidency (by American Revolutionary standards) and a robust central government able to cure the union's problems (though not the internal problems of individual states). At Convention's end, he spoke officially for his colleagues in an accompanying letter that virtually every American read alongside the Constitution itself—a letter stressing the Constitution's solution to the Confederation's flaws, not those of individual states. Thereafter, he was *unanimously* elected president, twice. *The Constitution of 1787 was emphatically Washington's Constitution, not Madison's.*

In insisting on this absolutely crucial point, I stand on the shoulders of the great historian Edward Larson and stand squarely opposed to a cadre of influential Madison boosters. This distinguished group is led by the incomparable Gordon Wood, who is by acclamation America's greatest living scholar of the founding era. The neo-Madisonian cadre also includes the estimable Jack Rakove and his fellow Madison biographers Lynne Cheney and Noah Feldman.

Wood, Rakove, Cheney, Feldman, and many other modern schol-ars—even Bailyn[10]—have also stumbled in their accounts of the ratification process by paying far too much attention to Madison's *Federalist* No. 10. This lavish emphasis would be perfectly acceptable if their project were pure intellectual history and/or political theory. Madison's provocative opening contribution to *The Federalist* bubbles over with interesting and subtle ideas worthy of careful exposition and analysis. But for anyone purporting to explicate America's Constitution as understood by actual Americans when enacted in 1787–1788, it simply will not do to dwell on No. 10.

As I stress in Chapter Six, *almost no one paid any attention to Federalist No. 10 in the ratification process*—or for the next century, for that matter. The eagle-eyed historian Douglass Adair first flagged this issue in the early 1950s. The more recent and massive twenty-nine-volume *Documentary History of the Ratification of the Constitution* corroborates Adair, as does the careful empirical work of the political scientist William Riker. Indeed, after painstaking investigation of the matter, law professor Larry Kramer has reported that Madison's distinctive ideas in No. 10 were "virtually absent from the contest to secure the Constitution's adoption."

The key to ratification was a *Federalist* No. 8 argument, a Washingtonian-Hamiltonian argument, an England-Scotland-Act-of-Union argument, a "Join or Die" argument. This argument addressed the basic failures of the Confederacy to achieve the central purpose of common defense and had almost nothing to say about Madison's aim of reforming state governments to effect a kinder, gentler, worthier, and more elitist republicanism state by state.

Fence-sitting ratifiers everywhere said yes for common-defense, collective-action reasons. For example, Edmund Randolph, Virginia's flip-floppy governor—a pivotal man in a pivotal state—changed his mind for common-defense, collective-action, English-Scottish-Act-of-Union, *Federalist* No. 8 reasons and said so openly and repeatedly. The argument of *Federalist* No. 10 did not become more compelling as the months passed, but the Washingtonian and Hamiltonian *Federalist* No. 8 argument did become stronger—a classic bandwagon, gaining velocity over time—as more states said yes. Once most states were in, their bordering states had to join—or die. (Franklin in 1754 was truly farsighted, as were those who revived his snake in 1765 and 1774.) Momentum became self-fulfilling; new states had to say yes because other states had already done so, as newspaper publisher Benjamin Russell brilliantly understood and underscored with his deceptively simple pillar cartoons.

This common-defense, collective-action, Federalist *No. 8 argument was utterly inconsistent with a state's alleged right to unilaterally secede post-ratification.* At every turn in Chapter Six, I am at pains to stress this point—a point, astonishingly, either ignored altogether or barely mentioned in passing by most standard founding narratives. (Founding historians' widespread inattention to the secession issue is astonishing because this issue was central to the Constitution of 1787–1788 and turned out to be, well, rather important later in American constitutional history.) I cap off my anti-secession argument with compelling newspaper evidence from venues far and wide, even Charleston, South Carolina—evidence that has never before been presented in any previous work of constitutional scholarship, including my own.[11] (I have been writing about secession for more than thirty years, ever since my first article as a law professor in 1987.) As Washington stressed in his accompanying official letter, the nation's *existence* required an indissoluble *consolidation* of states and the transcendence of individual state *sovereignty.* Washington later reiterated this point in his 1797 Farewell Address. Alas, scholars have often ignored this essential part of the address in their rush to analyze more peripheral aspects of this parting pronouncement.

Standing alone, Madison's *Federalist* No. 10 was rather agnostic on the crucial question of secession. If the chief reason for a state to join was that the central government would stabilize it from above for its own *internal* benefit, well and good; but if that state later decided it did not really want or need that stabilization, thank you, why shouldn't it be allowed to leave? To repeat: *The Federalist* No. 10 is not the key to understanding what the Constitution was all about, or what ratification was all about, in the fateful year when America became *indivisibly* America.

Indeed, if Madison's essay was convincing, why didn't the subsequent Bill of Rights limit state governments? After all, on Madison's view, each state government posed a greater threat to liberty than did the federal government. In late 1789, Madison in fact desperately wanted a "No state shall" amendment, but he lost on this issue in the First Congress because his *Federalist* No. 10–ish arguments did not persuade his contemporaries. *The Bill of Rights that emerged was Washington's Bill of Rights even more than Madison's—and one of its main purposes was to woo North Carolina and Rhode Island back into the fold for* Federalist *No. 8 reasons.*

Readers seeking more specifics on the central topic of Chapter Six—the state-by-state ratification process in the fateful year when Americans said "yes, We do"—should consult Pauline Maier's splendid 2010 book, *Ratification*. Yet for all its virtues, her marvelously detailed book sometimes misses the larger pattern that unfolded.

Because Chapter Six is so much shorter than Maier's book, it perforce emphasizes the big picture. Ultimately, the ratification decision did not turn on this fine point or that one. The key question was simply this: Union or no union? And if no union, what was the Anti-Federalists' workable alternative? *They had none.* The debate was thus best framed by the opening *Federalist* essays of Hamilton and Jay. The two biggest and best critiques of the Constitution deplored its unduly small House and its omission of a Bill of Rights. On both issues, Federalists sensibly pivoted during and immediately after the ratification, thanks to the crowd-sourcing that ratification conventions facilitated.

More generally, Maier is too kind to neo-Beardian critics of the Constitution. She was an exceedingly gracious and gentle person. I am more blunt and sharp-elbowed—a product of law-school culture, perhaps—and here is my bottom line: *Almost everything that Charles Beard and his modern-day debunking followers have said about the Constitution's launch is either dead wrong or more wrong than right.*

The Constitution's ratification was remarkably democratic, legal, and legitimate—a truly stunning achievement for its time and place.

Concretely: Beard argued that the document was basically undemocratic. But unlike the Declaration of Independence, the Articles of Confederation, and every early (that is, pre-1778) revolutionary state constitution, the Constitution was put to a vote. And what a vote it was! Ordinary property qualifications were lowered or eliminated in most states, and nowhere raised. (Beard evidently knew these key facts but withheld them from his readers. The truth on all this did not generally come to light until 2005, in the opening pages and endnotes of my book, *America's Constitution: A Biography*.) Beardians have argued that the Constitution was illegal, breaking as it did with the unanimity requirement of the Articles of Confederation. Wrong again. Then sovereign states had a legal right to secede from a widely breached and failing treaty, especially when mass secession and reunion might secure their very existence and vindicate the core common-defense purposes of the initial treaty. Neo-Beardians also fault the Philadelphia delegates for breaching their state-issued instructions. But delegates led by George Washington went beyond the *letter* of their instructions to fulfill the *spirit* of their instructions—please fix the union's problems!—and nothing in their plan was binding. Rather, it was a mere proposal for their legal masters, the American people, to consider and then say yea or nay. Without a syllable of criticism, the Confederation Congress promptly *and unanimously* forwarded the Philadelphia plan to states for proper consideration under the special ratification process envisioned by the grand Convention.[12] Neo-Beardians routinely fault Philadelphia delegates for their secrecy. But this secrecy facilitated thoughtful early deliberation and then lapsed—a point neo-Beardians either do not know or do not tell their readers. Neo-Beardians try to make hay of the few and paltry episodes of mild political violence that occasionally flared up in the year of ratification. But the big news was precisely the opposite: virtually no one died or was maimed. (Relatedly, neo-Beardians confuse political hardball with legal impropriety, as when they fail to recognize that early Pennsylvania Federalists were entirely within their rights to forcibly compel the attendance of Anti-Federalists who attempted to break a legislative quorum.) Neo-Beardians bellyache that the ratification game was rigged. On the contrary, the press was free; pamphlets and essays of every sort proliferated; political discourse was robust, uninhibited, and wide open. Anti-Federalists in Massachusetts and elsewhere spoke their piece in convention, in full view and with their words often reprinted, even by Federalist publishers. Many thoughtful men in fact changed their minds, and many Anti-Federalists graciously acquiesced precisely because they deemed the process fair. Neo-Beardians present the basic contest as rich against poor. Actually, various prominent rich men opposed the Constitution (for example, George Mason, Elbridge Gerry, and notable Virginia Lees). By contrast, working folk in cities generally favored the Constitution, as did veterans high and low, who, along with countless others, combined to stage massive and dazzling pro-Constitution parades in Philadelphia and New York City that bespoke the terse text's genuine popularity. We should also note that convention apportionment rules in Massachusetts, and perhaps elsewhere, gave rural Anti-Federalists more than their fair share of seats. *If the system was rigged, why did voters overwhelmingly reward Federalists in the first set of federal elections?* (Of course, direct House elections took place that year thanks to the Constitution itself, which mandated popular involvement in selecting the members of Congress—in dramatic contrast to the Articles of Confederation, which failed to do anything of the sort.)[13]

Most damning of all to the neo-Beardian school is that the great mass of Americans at the time (unlike many scholars today) understood that the Constitution was designed by and for George Washington. *If the system was truly bad, unfair, illegitimate, illegal, rigged—blah, blah, blah—why did Americans unanimously elect George Washington, twice, and in the process, in effect, re-ratify and re-re-ratify the Constitution that was his two-dimensional counterpart?*

Which brings us to Part III of this book, beginning with Chapter Seven—"Washington." The chapters in Part III seek to blend biographical narrative with constitutional analysis in distinctive ways. For example, if the Constitution truly was designed by and for Washington, surely Washington's views about the Constitution in general and particularly about his own constitutional article—Article II—deserve special attention, even special weight, I would argue. (Chief Justice John Marshall thought so, too.) In the Decision of 1789, Madison and Hamilton were acting as Washington's lieutenants, much as they had acted as his aides, in the main, both at Philadelphia and in the ratification process. On most issues that arose in the Washington administration, I'm a Hamilton man, because Hamilton, on most issues, was a Washington man, and Washington, in turn, on most issues, was the Constitution's man. To repeat, the document was in large part designed by and for George Washington, and was ratified with Washington constantly in the minds of Americans, especially those who voted yes. Then, everyone agreed that he was the man to make the Constitution real, effective, operational, three-dimensional. These key *historical* facts, in my view, have *legal* significance.

When Madison and Jefferson opposed Hamilton, they also opposed Washington, who generally sided with Hamilton, and whom Hamilton served loyally. This is one factor that should weigh against Madison's and Jefferson's constitutional claims circa 1791–1797. Several other factors also weigh against Madison's and Jefferson's views in this time period. The duo themselves in later years quietly slinked away from some of their most outlandish claims; judges of all stripes, including men they themselves placed on the Court, repeatedly rejected many of their views; and later generations of judges have generally followed suit. Most decisive of all, what Madison and Jefferson said between 1791 and 1797 was often inconsistent with what the Constitution itself said, when rightly read and judged against the backdrop of the Great Ratification Debate of 1787–1788.

In researching and writing my opening chapters, I paid painstaking attention to America's best historians. In Part III, I frankly felt less diffident, because in the time period covered in these chapters there was now—at last!—a written and ratified Constitution I could expound. This written Constitution (flanked of course by unwritten legal rules and principles) is something that I have thought about and written about and lectured about and testified about for more than three decades. It is a legal document that invites proper use of the legal tools of analysis that I wear on my daily tool belt as a law professor.

Many of the topics that I highlight in Part III have rarely received careful attention from generalist historians. Examples include *Chisholm v. Georgia* (on state sovereign immunity), *Hayburn's Case* (on the proper role of judges), the justices' 1793 letter to President Washington (on judicial advisory opinions), *Hylton v. United States* (on taxes—the biggest issue to reach the Court in the 1790s), the Presidential Succession Act (lurking in the backdrop of the Jefferson-Burr-Marshall election crisis), *Marbury v. Madison* (on the technical question of Supreme Court original jurisdiction above and beyond the broader question of judicial review), *Stuart v. Laird* (on judicial independence and the validity of the 1802 repeal act—an enormous issue at the time), *Hudson and Goodwin* (on the absence of a federal common law of crimes), *Martin v. Hunter's Lessee* (on the Supreme Court's appellate jurisdiction), and *Barron v. Baltimore* (on the scope of the Bill of Rights). Other passages in Part III address legal topics that have often found their way into general textbooks and trade books by mainstream historians. Examples include the Alien and Sedition Acts, the Virginia and Kentucky Resolutions, the Louisiana Purchase, *Marbury v. Madison* (on the topic of judicial review itself), *McCulloch v. Maryland*, the Missouri Compromise, *Worcester v. Georgia*, the Nullification Crisis, and the Jackson-era controversies over presidential removal power and abolitionist mail.

On both sets of issues—those usually ignored by historians and those routinely discussed by historians—I have generally followed my own lights as a constitutional-law scholar. Many of my passages summarize positions that I have explicated elsewhere in law journals aimed at judges, lawyers, and other legal specialists. On many of the biggest issues in Part III, I side with the Hamiltonian nationalists. Prominent examples include *Hylton*, the Louisiana Purchase, *Martin*, *McCulloch*, the Missouri Compromise, *Worcester*, and the Nullification Crisis. On other important topics, I ally with Madison, Jefferson, and/or states' rightists. Prominent examples include *Chisholm*, the Sedition Act, *Hudson and Goodwin*, and *Barron v. Baltimore*. In all this, I have not aimed merely to split the difference between the broad camps that emerged in the 1790s, and that endured thereafter in various incarnations. Rather, I have tried to get each issue right on its own legal merits, using proper methods of constitutional analysis. In every case, I have tried to tell the reader not just which side was right but why. In the process, I have tried to explain and exemplify the proper way to do constitutional interpretation, and thus the proper way to discover the meaning of America.

So much for the constitutional aspects of Part III. What about the biographical aspects? Readers will surely have noticed that each of the first six chapters in Part III bears the name of a leading statesman (or the names of an ensemble of leading statesmen) in the Constitution's first half century. A few themes are worth highlighting.

First, I try to attend to key relationships among my protagonists. Washington and Hamilton teamed up. So did Jefferson and Madison. Marshall and Story also made a great duo. Adams, by contrast, was a political loner, but at least he had Abigail. Adams hated Hamilton, unfairly, much as Adams had earlier hated Hutchinson, unfairly. There was bad blood between Jefferson and Hamilton. Madison started out as Hamilton's friend and Washington's acolyte and later betrayed them both, partly to save his own political skin back in Virginia, partly because he was a policy lightweight on certain big issues (including banks, trade, and national defense), and partly because he was smitten by Jefferson. Jefferson and Marshall were always rivals. Andrew Jackson came to loathe Henry Clay and John C. Calhoun. Adams had a quirky frenemy relationship with Jefferson, who thought about Adams late in life much less than Adams thought about him.

It might seem that all these observations are merely gossip, but if researching and writing Chapter One has taught me anything, it is that personal dynamics, like the strong antipathy that Otis and Adams came to have for Hutchinson, can often have enormous political repercussions. Old Hutchinson characteristically understated the matter when he looked back on the events of 1760–1761: "From so small a spark" as the Otis family resentment, he wrote, "a great fire [the Revolution] seems to have been kindled." Sometimes the personal is indeed the political.

Nothing is more personal than fatherhood and spousal fidelity, which brings me to a second point. While mine is in general an account of the public lives of public figures, I have at the margins alluded to certain arguably private matters. Thus I discuss in passing Franklin's estrangement from his loyalist son William, Washington's childlessness, Hamilton's philandering, Adams's special bond with Abigail and his high hopes for their son John Quincy, Jefferson's secret relationship with Sally Hemings and their children, Story's tight bonds with his wife and son, Jackson and his wife's informal adoption of an orphan Native American, and Madison's deathbed need to provide financially for Dolley. All these matters became topics of public, political conversation in the lifetimes of these public figures, and thus seemed fair game for a book such as this.

A third, related point: I have tried where possible to analyze even personal and private matters using standard empirical techniques. Perhaps the best example is the detailed addendum to Chapter Seven. In that compendium, I trace the bloodlines of early prominent American politicians in order to measure the strength of dynastic forces, state by state, in an idealistic republic that proudly renounced titles of nobility, but where in fact blood still mattered, often immensely.

Fourth, I am particularly interested in how my main protagonists' memories sometimes failed and did so self-servingly. Old Adams routinely misstated matters and in the process inflated his own role and deflated others' contributions. Old Jefferson claimed, misleadingly, that he was *the* author of the Declaration as opposed to being merely the chief composer of a rough draft that underwent substantial and salutary editing. Old Madison initially forgot some of the worst things about Jefferson's proto-secessionist rantings in the late 1790s and later tried to wish everything away. Prominent scholars— led most notably by Mary Sarah Bilder—have raised serious questions about the accuracy and integrity of old Madison's Philadelphia Convention notes.[14]

Finally, I aim to pay particular attention to the main arc of my protagonists' lives. Indeed, I have openly criticized various leading biographers who have failed in their obligation to trace these arcs, be they soaring, sagging, or sideways. This theme is particularly pronounced in my final chapter, "Adieus." As they aged and approached the end, Franklin and Washington got better on the slavery question. Jefferson and Madison got worse. They started out as youthful antislavery idealists but ended up creating an emphatically pro-slavery party that would in time become the enabler of Andrew Jackson. Neither in life nor in death did Jefferson or Madison ever liberate any substantial number of slaves, many of whom eventually stood on auction blocks, ripped apart from their loved ones to pay for their masters' sins and selfishness.

Jefferson's and Madison's disappointing life vectors are particularly notable on the specific topic that would ultimately precipitate Civil War in America: slavery in America's virgin West. As young dreamers and reformers, Thomas Jefferson and James Madison, respectively, drafted (in 1784) and enacted into federal law (in 1789) a clause of the Northwest Ordinance banning slavery in western land. As old men, this very same slaveholding duo opposed the Missouri Compromise provision banning slavery in additional western land. Both sagging statesmen eventually and self-servingly managed to convince themselves that spreading the virus of slavery would somehow help cure the disease of slavery. Madison even wrote that the 1819 slavery ban was unconstitutional, a truly outrageous assertion, albeit one that the Supreme Court would later endorse, to its everlasting shame, in the 1857 *Dred Scott* decision. The ablest constitutional lawyer of the *Dred Scott* era, a rising politician named Lincoln, would famously denounce that ruling as an "astonisher" in legal history. Lincoln was right to be incredulous.

Alas, many of Jefferson's and Madison's most distinguished biographers—including Dumas Malone, Jack Rakove, Lynne Cheney, and Noah Feldman—have either minimized or ignored their protagonists' troubling downward trajectory on slavery, with little or no analysis of the Virginians' regression on western free soil. Future biographers need to do better on this score.

AND WHERE, THE READER MAY fairly ask at this point, should I my-self have done better in this book? I wish I knew for sure. Despite my best efforts, there are doubtless many flaws in the preceding pages. Future scholars will, I hope, expose and correct them, much as I in this postscript have bluntly exposed and corrected what I believe to be the flaws of earlier scholarly works.

My biggest present regret is also my greatest source of excite-ment. My story, at least for now, has ended too soon—before Amer-ica's most notable crusading women and most influential African Americans have had a proper chance to stride onto center stage. Frederick Douglass, Elizabeth Cady Stanton, Sojourner Truth, Har-riet Beecher Stowe, Lucy Stone, Susan B. Anthony, Hiram Revels, Alice Stone Blackwell, Ida B. Wells, W. E. B. Du Bois, Carrie Chap-man Catt, Alice Paul—none of these individuals appear, except per-haps in passing, in the preceding pages. Prior to 1840, White men overwhelmingly dominated America's constitutional conversation. White men were the ones whose voices and votes most counted, whose political preferences invariably prevailed.

But all that would soon change. This is a story I can't wait to tell in my next book, *The Words That Made Us Equal: America's Consti-tutional Conversation, 1840–1920*. This sequel will begin with the world's first anti-slavery conference, a conference attended by both Blacks and Whites, women and men—though the women's atten-dance was not without complexity and controversy. The story will travel through the Reconstruction Amendments, which promised freedom and equal civil rights for all—Black and White, male and female—and equal political rights (voting, jury service, officehold-ing, and the like) for men of all races. By the end of this sequel, the election of 1920, America's women will have won the right to vote equally with men at all levels of government. So, dear reader, if you want to learn more about the era in which non-Whites and women transformed America's constitutional conversation and won astonishing constitutional victories, I hope to have something ready for your consideration in the years to come. (After that, I hope to add a third volume, *The Words That Made Us Modern: America's*

Constitutional Conversation, 1920 to 2000, to complete my projected trilogy by chronicling the hot and cold world wars against totalitarianism, the civil rights movement, the Warren Court revolution, second-wave feminism, and the resurgence of originalism.)

Chapter One of the current volume began with the story of the *Racehorse*, a transatlantic ship that in 1760 brought important tidings to the New World, the biggest news since word of the fall of Montreal. Chapter One of the next volume will begin with an 1840 transatlantic ship that went in the other direction, a ship bearing an improbably coincidental name, the *Montreal*. Aboard that ship, Elizabeth Cady Stanton, a twenty-four-year-old bride on her honeymoon, began conversing seriously about abolition and related topics with two of America's leading activists, all three on their way to the world's first anti-slavery convention in London. Upon arrival in the grand imperial city, Stanton, a New Yorker, met Philadelphia's anti-slavery crusader Lucretia Mott, then in her mid-forties. As the convention opened on June 12, a majority of the world's most utopian, philanthropic, liberal, and racially egalitarian men voted to exclude women from formal participation. That evening, Stanton and Mott strolled through London "arm in arm" and "resolved to hold a convention as soon as we returned home, and form a society to advocate the rights of women." Or at least that is how Stanton remembered it much later. (Mott had a different recollection. Perhaps old Stanton's story was not entirely accurate. Shades of John Adams!)[15]

THE OPENING SCENE OF *The Words That Made Us Equal* is not yet cast in concrete. So if any earnest reader of this postscript has suggestions, I'm all ears. But however this sequel begins, a more demographically diverse cast of characters will be stepping onto center stage. As will Lincoln. I hope you will come to love him as much as I do.

Acknowledgments

THE OLDER I GET, THE more I owe. Mind you, I'm not complaining. My accrued debts, personal and intellectual, are the most wonderful obligations imaginable, running to family members, friends, and scholars who have made me who I am and have made this book what it is.

Many of my deepest debts to my most special friends and family members are described in detail in my previous works, and here I shall simply incorporate by reference all that I have said before with one additional global thank-you: Bless you, my darlings! As for my myriad and profound debts to the various scholars who lit the path under my feet, readers should consult this book's postscript and notes.

Three former deans of the Yale Law School merit special mention here. On his first day as dean in 1985, Guido Calabresi hired me to join the Yale faculty, and for that I will be forever grateful. Four years earlier, Guido had been my torts professor. (Indeed, his was my very first class as a 1L student.) What I learned from Guido back in 1981 came in remarkably handy as I pondered the legal issues at the heart of this book's opening chapter. Although James Otis missed the key point in his fiery oral argument, the 1761 writs of assistance were not as bad as they seemed: they offered no tort immunity to a Customs House officer unless the officer *actually found* smuggled goods when searching a colonist's home or warehouse. Like Otis, later commentators have generally overlooked this crucial fact, but Guido taught me long ago to keep my eye on tort law's fine points. Guido's successor as dean, Tony Kronman, likewise nurtured me in my student days. More recently, Tony encouraged me to pay close attention to Thomas Hutchinson and to Bernard Bailyn's extraordinary scholarship on this ubiquitous yet understudied loyalist. In 2008, Tony's successor, Harold Koh, arranged for me to receive a Sterling Professorship at Yale University, a chair once held by my mentor Edmund Morgan. Ever since receiving this high honor—thanks to Harold's generosity—I have longed to write something in the Morgan tradition. I hope this book comes close.

Two other mentors have also inspired me from my earliest days at Yale Law School. Owen Fiss taught me how to read a case and love the law, and Bruce Ackerman taught me how to combine law with history and political science.

Several friends read all or parts of this book in draft. My brilliant student Ben Daus-Haberle reviewed every word and offered surefooted advice about both style and substance. So did Andy Lipka and Steve Calabresi. Indeed, Andy pored over every word several times and discussed each paragraph with me in exquisite detail, because my bosom buddy and *consiglieri* (who is also my ophthalmologist) never does anything halfway. Vikram David Amar (my kid brother), Vikram Paul Amar (my son), Jack Balkin, Jon Blue, Vernon Bogdanor, Rick Brookhiser, Rebecca Brooks, Chris Duggan, Al Hirsch, Duncan Hosie, Rem Katyal (Neal's son), Ed Larson, Kelly McClure, Travis Pantin, Sai Prakash, Kim Roosevelt, and Daria Rose also offered helpful comments on various parts of this manuscript.

At every step of research and writing, I have kept in mind my co-teacher Philip Bobbitt's ideas about the geostrategic context that gave birth to the Constitution and shaped its early development. My other long-standing co-teacher and conversation partner, Steve Calabresi, has likewise had a pervasive influence on me, especially regarding presidential power, originalism, and departmentalism. Ed Larson will soon become my next co-teacher. We are hoping to explore with students the central role that George Washington above all others played in the American constitutional project—a key theme of this book, building on what Ed saw first.

The preceding chapters were completed during a pandemic. In this final stage, I had only limited access to traditional libraries and archives housing physical books, pamphlets, old newspapers, private paper collections, and the like. I am thus grateful beyond words to those who have created and who continue to curate various Internet sites that made it easy for me to locate and/or relocate letters to and from leading founders; complete editions of early American newspapers; ratification-era pamphlets, essays, speeches, and cartoons; and key early American governmental documents, state and federal. Five Internet portals in particular have been godsends: the Library of Congress's "A Century of Lawmaking" collection, the National Archives Founders Online website, the Digital Documentary History of the Ratification of the Constitution, Yale's Avalon documentary history compilation, and the Readex-sponsored "America's Historical Newspapers" website. I urge interested readers to explore these electronic venues and experience for themselves the richness and user-friendliness of these extraordinary digital resources.

Readers seeking still more information and links are warmly invited to visit a website that I have recently created with Andy Lipka's help. (Where would I be without him?) This recent creation is designated in the notes section as *AW*—a shorthand for Author's Website. My home page URL is akhilamar.com.

In the publishing world, I am as always indebted to my literary agents, Glen Hartley and Lynn Chu. Special thanks are once again due to Brian Distelberg and Lara Heimert at Basic Books and to their entire editorial team, including Katie Lambright, Abby Mohr, Kathy Streckfus, Michelle Welsh-Horst, and Liz Wetzel. This is the second book that I have written with Brian's able assistance, my third working with Kathy and Michelle, and my fourth under Lara's superintending eye. I would like to think that this is the best one yet, but of course readers must judge for themselves.

A few final words about this book's dedication page. Two years ago, my former student Neal Katyal, whom I have come to love as a brother, invited me to fly to Puerto Rico to meet Lin-Manuel Miranda, Vanessa Nadal, and Ron Chernow and to watch Lin reprise (for charity) his iconic role as Alexander Hamilton. I thought the trip would be great fun, but I had no idea this lark would also change my life. It did. So did meeting Khizr Khan on a separate occasion, also thanks to Neal.

This book is a love letter to America. Neal, Lin, Vanessa, Ron, and Khizr have helped me to better understand why I so adore this land, its people, and its history.

Illustration Credits

291   Painting by Edward Savage, 1790s, National Gallery of Art. Courtesy Wikimedia Commons.

384   Painting by Frederick Kemmelmeyer (?), circa 1795, Metropolitan Museum of Art. Courtesy Wikimedia Commons.

389   Painting by John Trumbull, 1792, Crystal Bridges Museum of American Art and Metropolitan Museum of Art. Courtesy Wikimedia Commons.

461   Painting by John Trumbull, 1792, Crystal Bridges Museum of American Art and Metropolitan Museum of Art. Courtesy Wikimedia Commons.

461   Engraving and painting by David Edwin and Thomas Sully, between 1809 and 1817. Courtesy Library of Congress.

461   Painting by John Vanderlyn, 1822, New York City Hall Portrait Collection. Courtesy NYC Public Design Commission.

462   Painting by Mather Brown, 1786, National Portrait Gallery. Courtesy Wikimedia Commons.

462   Painting by Rembrandt Peale, 1800, White House. Courtesy Wikimedia Commons.

468   Painting by Rembrandt Peale, 1800, White House. Courtesy Wikimedia Commons.

468   Painting by Henry Inman, 1832, Library of Virginia. Courtesy Wikimedia Commons.

506   Map by Benjamin Davies, 1805. Courtesy Library of Congress.

550   Painting by Gilbert Stuart, 1794, National Gallery of Art. Courtesy Wikimedia Commons.

565   Statue by William Wetmore Story, Harvard Law School. Courtesy Wikimedia Commons.

604   Painting by Ralph Earl, circa 1833, The Hermitage. Courtesy The Hermitage.

621   Drawing by Paul Revere, first published in the *Boston Gazette*, 3-12-1770. Courtesy Library of Congress.

621   Handbill by John Binns, 1828. Courtesy Library of Congress.

623   Anonymous drawing, 1833. Courtesy Library of Congress.

624   Photo by Albert Sands Southworth and Josiah Johnson Hawes, 1841, Metropolitan Museum of Art. Courtesy Wikimedia Commons.

624   Painting by Francis Alexander, 1835, National Portrait Gallery. Courtesy Smithsonian.

624   Painting by Henry F. Darby, circa 1858, US Senate. Courtesy Wikimedia Commons.

Notes

WORKS FREQUENTLY CITED

Annals   Joseph Gales Sr., compiler, *The Debates and Proceedings in the Congress of the United States*, 24 vols. (1834–1856) (*Annals of the Congress of the United States*).

AW   akhilamar.com.

CG   *Congressional Globe.*

DHRC Digital   Merrill Jensen, John P. Kaminski, and Gaspare J. Saladino, eds., *The Documentary History of the Ratification of the Constitution* (1976–), 29 vols. Available online and word-searchable at University of Virginia, Documentary History of the Ratification of the Constitution, Digital Edition, https://rotunda.upress.virginia.edu/founders/RNCN.

Elliot's Debates   Jonathan Elliot, ed., *The Debates in the Several State Conventions on the Adoption of the Federal Constitution as Recommended by the General Convention at Philadelphia in 1787*, 5 vols. (1888).

Farrand's Records   Max Farrand, ed., *The Records of the Federal Convention of 1787*, 4 vols., rev. ed. (1966).

JCC   *Journals of the Continental Congress.*

Maclay's Journal	Edgar S. Maclay, ed., *Journal of William Maclay* (1890).
NEQ	*New England Quarterly.*
Quincy's Reports	Josiah Quincy Jr., *Reports of Cases Argued and Adjudged in the Superior Court of Judicature in the Province of Massachusetts Bay Between 1761 and 1772, with an Appendix Upon the Writs of Assistance* (1865).
Reg Deb	*Register of Debates.*
Stat.	*Statutes at Large.*
WMQ	*William and Mary Quarterly.*

The Words That Made Us reflects many years of extensive original research into founding-era materials, especially newspapers. The most important newspaper citations appear in full in the endnotes that follow. Other more mundane (and sometimes long) newspaper citation lists are housed on the author's website, which also includes a wide range of additional elaboration on various endnote materials—notes on notes, so to speak.

Readers will also find a wealth of information, including many of the sources listed above, at the Library of Congress website "A Century of Lawmaking for a New Nation." Many LOC databases are word-searchable. Letters to and from leading founders are online and word-searchable at the National Archives' Founders Online (NAFO) website. Interested readers are encouraged to consult these sources directly. Frequently used abbreviations for the founders' letters are as follows: AA (Abigail Adams), AH (Alexander Hamilton), BF (Benjamin Franklin), GW (George Washington), JA (John Adams), JM (James Madison), and TJ (Thomas Jefferson). Many historical newspapers are now available online at the subscription-based website "America's Historical Newspapers," sponsored by Readex. Detailed citations are generally omitted for other easily web- and word-searchable materials such as *The Federalist* essays and US Supreme Court opinions.

CHAPTER ONE: "SEEDS"

1. An unconfirmed report of the death had reached Boston on Christmas Day. See *Boston News-Letter*, 1-1-1761. On Partridge's relationship with Boston's newspaper publishers, see ibid.; *Boston Post-Boy*, 12-29-1760 (receiving from Partridge British newspapers dated Nov. 8 and 10); *Boston Gazette*, 12-29-1760; *Boston Evening-Post*, 12-29-1760. See also Thomas Hutchinson, *History of the Province of Massachusetts Bay from 1749 to 1774* (1828), 88 (news confirmed by "the people on board" who "all agreed").

2. For more on America's fledgling cities, see the 1790 US Census and the US Census document "Population in the Colonial and Continental Periods," United States Census Bureau, www.census.gov/history/pdf/colonialbostonpops.pdf.

3. Richard Hofstadter, *America at 1750: A Social Portrait* (1973 Vintage ed.), 3 (sextupling); Hutchinson, *History*, 85 ("Men whose minds were turned to calculation found that the colonies increased so rapidly . . . [they] would soon exceed the parent state"). Hutchinson was likely referring to a 1755 tract by Benjamin Franklin, *Observations Concerning the Increase of Mankind, Peopling of Countries, etc.* On this essay's far-reaching implications for Franklin's evolving vision of the British Empire, see Edmund S. Morgan, *Benjamin Franklin* (2002).

4. *Boston Gazette*, 12-29-1760; *Boston Evening-Post*, 12-29-1760; *Boston Post-Boy*, 12-29-1760; *Boston News-Letter*, 1-1-1761; *Boston Gazette*, 1-5-1761; *Boston Evening-Post*, 1-5-1761; *Boston Post-Boy*, 1-5-1761.

5. See *Boston Evening-Post*, 12-29-1760 (twenty guns—other newspapers from the era sometimes report twenty-four or twenty-eight guns); *New-York Gazette*, 1-19-1761 (NYC arrival on Jan. 15; proclamation orders); Thomas M. Truxes, *Defying Empire: Trading with the Enemy in Colonial New York* (2008), 122–24 (similar—but describing NYC arrival on Jan. 16). This was not the *Fowey*'s last brush with history. On its adventures in 1775 (when it loomed large in confrontation between Virginia patriots and the colony's royal governor, Lord Dunmore) and 1781 (when it saw action at Yorktown), see *AW*.

6. 6 Anne c. 41, sec. 10.

7. Hutchinson, *History*, 88–89.

8. *Boston News-Letter*, 1-1-1761.

9. Ibid. For similar accounts, see *Boston Gazette*, 1-5-1761; *Boston Evening-Post*, 1-5-1761; *Boston Post-Boy*, 1-5-1761.

10. For an early example of the widening rift, see the *Gazette*, 11-23-1761. Also compare the *Gazette*, 4-4-1763, with the *News-Letter*, 4-7-1763; see also the *Gazette*, 4-11-1763. In the 1770s, the *Gazette*'s masthead was a woodcut designed by Paul Revere, and the *Gazette*'s supporters included Otis, Samuel Adams, John Adams, and John Hancock. As the conflict with Britain heated up, all these men, including Edes, supported the Sons of Liberty, which likely used Edes's house and the *Gazette*'s print shop to plan and carry out the 1773 Boston Tea Party.

11. Demise of the Crown Act, 1 Anne c. 2 (1702), esp. sec. 5.

12. On "Jangle Bluster," see M. H. Smith, *The Writs of Assistance Case* (1978), 161n, 314, 327, 474, 484, 502.

13. Hutchinson, *History*, 148.

14. Peter Oliver's *Origin and Progress of the American Revolution*, quoted in Smith, *Writs*, 206.

15. Hutchinson, *History*, 86; Smith, *Writs*, 211. On Hutchinson's family tree, see James K. Hosmer, *The Life of Thomas Hutchinson* (1896), 1–4.

16. Customs Act of 1660, 12 Car. II, c. 19, sec. 1; Customs Act of 1662, 14 Car. II, c. 11, sec. 4; Navigation Act of 1696, 7 & 8 Wm. III, c. 22, sec. 5 (1696); Demise of the Crown Act, 1 Anne c. 2 (1702), esp. sec. 5.

17. For more details and wrinkles of the forfeiture system, see generally Smith, *Writs*.

18. Ibid., 95–125; Hutchinson, *History*, 92–93.

19. Hutchinson, *History*, 93–94 & n*; Smith, *Writs*, 132–34. The London essay was eventually published in the *Boston Evening-Post* on Jan. 19, 1761.

20. Smith, *Writs*, 202–30.

21. JA to William Tudor Sr., March 29, 1817. For a similar statement, see JA to AA, July 3, 1776—the very week America declared independence.

22. JA to William Tudor Sr., March 29, 1817.

23. Ibid. Adams's reference to a portrait of "King Charles the second" was a lapse on Adams's part—one of many. The portrait was of King Charles I. See Bernard Bailyn, *The Ordeal of Thomas Hutchinson* (1974), 138. The lapse is revealing; see infra pp. 713–14n55.

24. Adams's "Abstract of the Argument," ca. April 1761, National Archives' Founders Online (NAFO hereinafter). On the 1690s provincial law, see Josiah Quincy Jr., *Reports of Cases Argued and Adjudged in the Superior Court of Judicature in the Province of Massachusetts Bay Between 1761 and 1772, with an Appendix Upon the Writs of Assistance* (1865), 420 [*Quincy's Reports* hereinafter].

25. Adams, "Abstract."

26. Hutchinson, *History*, 94. In the mid-1760s, eyewitnesses willing to report on smuggling put their persons at risk, at least in some times and places. See "Letters of Governor Francis Fauquier," *William and Mary Quarterly* (*WMQ* hereinafter) 21 (1913): 163–68 (describing in detail the 1766 stoning, maiming, mocking, tarring, feathering, tethering, parading, near-blinding, and near-drowning of a suspected informing witness, Captain William Smith, near Norfolk, Virginia); Pauline Maier, *From Resistance to Revolution* (1972), 6–16 (placing this incident into the broader category of mob resistance to customs enforcement); ibid., 127 (describing the 1769 tarring and feathering of a "suspected customs informer" in Boston).

27. Adams, "Abstract."

28. Ibid.; JA to William Tudor Sr., June 1, 1818.

29. Adams, "Abstract."

30. Ibid. (emphasis in original); cf. *Semayne's Case*, 5 Co. Rep. 91a, 91b (K.B. 1604), 77 Eng. Rep. 194, 195 ("The house of every one is to him as his castle and fortress, as well for his defence against injury and violence, as for his repose").

31. Adams, Minutes of the Argument: Suffolk Superior Court, Feb. 24, 1761, NAFO; cf. *Bonham's Case*, 8 Co. Rep. 113b, 118a (C.P. 1610), 77 Eng. Rep. 646, 652 ("The common law will controul Acts of Parliament").

32. Adams, "Abstract" (punctuation altered).

33. Hutchinson, *History*, 94; *Quincy's Reports*, 414–18; Smith, *Writs*, 388.

34. Hutchinson, *History*, 94; *Quincy's Reports*, 57, 414–34; Smith, *Writs*, 387–413.

35. For more details and citations, see Akhil Reed Amar, *The Law of the Land* (2015), 244–49, 341–42; *Quincy's Reports*, 533n41. In a piece that appeared in the Jan. 4, 1762, *Boston Gazette*, the anonymous author (probably Otis) attempted to tame the Superior Court's ruling by noting the possibility of an ex post damage suit, without acknowledging that this possibility powerfully undercut Otis's extravagant claims at oral argument. On Otis as the likely (sheepish) author attempting anonymous damage control, see Smith, *Writs*, 424, 562.

36. For the best reasons to believe that the writs were deeply problematic, despite their special safeguards, see Amar, *Law of the Land*, 246–48.

37. In later months, the *Gazette* published additional pieces discussing various aspects of writs of assistance. Otis likely wrote or inspired these follow-ups. See the *Gazette* issues of Dec. 7, 1761; Jan. 4, 1762; Feb. 22, 1762.

38. JA to William Tudor Sr., March 29, 1817; JA to same, Dec. 18, 1816. In addition to the contemporaneous *Boston Gazette* report, there exist several other confirmatory firsthand accounts of the November 1761 hearing published after Adams's death. See, e.g., Hutchinson, *History*, 94; *Quincy's Reports*, 51–57.

39. Cf. *Quincy's Reports*, 417n2 (Horace Gray noting his "unpleasant duty" of "point[ing] out the [obvious] inaccuracies in [old Adams's] spirited account"); ibid., 469n1 (similar).

40. Smith, *Writs*, 231–68, 286–92, 319, 379, 477; JA to William Tudor Sr., March 29, 1817 ("notes . . . stole[n] from my desk and printed in the *Massachusetts Spy*" on April 19, 1773).

41. BF to Robert Livingston, July 22, 1783.

42. For a particularly revealing (and absurd) statement bristling with envy of Washington, see JA to François Adriaan Van Der Kemp, Aug. 23, 1806 ("Hancock, Samuel Adams, John Jay, and several others have been much more essential Characters to America than Washington—Another character almost forgotten, of more importance than any one of them all was James Otis").

43. JA to William Tudor Sr., June 1, 1818. Legislation championed by Otis in the 1762 Massachusetts Assembly also conceded the basic propriety of English trade law, even as it aimed to codify strict search rules. See infra p. 717n33.

44. JA to William Tudor Sr., June 1, 1818.

45. JA to William Tudor Sr., April 15, 1817. See also JA to Hezekiah Niles, Jan. 14, 1818 ("Some of the Heads [i.e., the main topics of Otis's oral argument] are remembered [by old Adams, fifty-seven years after the fact] out of which Livy or Sallust would not Scruple to Compose an Oration for History"); JA to Jedidiah Morse, March 4, 1815 ("I have little Faith in History. I read it as I do Romance; believing what is probable and rejecting what I must. Thucidides [*sic*] Tacitus, Livy, Hume Robertson Gibbon, Raynal and Voltaire are all alike."). For a similar reading of old Adams's method and model, see Smith, *Writs*, 252. In fairness to Thucydides, by his own account he would appear to have been a far more scrupulous, self-critical, and impartial historian than was old Adams, who (true to form) did not fairly characterize—and surely did not closely emulate—Thucydides's practice and method. See *The History of the Peloponnesian War*, Book 1, Chapter One (quoted and discussed in more detail in *AW*). As a historian attempting to offer an impartial narrative of epic events in which he himself had played a part, Hutchinson, not Adams, was far truer to the rigorous method described by Thucydides. Despite many important disagreements with Adams's narrative, Hutchinson's history does agree with Adams on the biggest historical point of all: the opening scene of the American Revolution truly did unfold in Boston in 1760–1761 thanks largely to Otis. See supra pp. 35–36.

46. JA to William Tudor Sr., March 29, 1817. For more correspondence in this vein, see infra p. 713nn51–52.

47. If, alternatively, this grand artwork were thought to depict the actual *adoption* and/or the actual *signing* of the Declaration of Independence (as many casual observers assume), then Trumbull's allegorical elements and artistic license would loom even larger. The Declaration parchment was not ready for signing until August 1776, and delegates trickled in over the course of several weeks to add their names. They were never all together for any signing ceremony remotely resembling the painting. Also, after June 28, the five-man committee no longer stood separate from the Congress as a whole, which significantly edited the committee's draft before voting to adopt a final text on July 4. (Independence itself, as distinct from the text of the Declaration, was formally agreed to on July 2.) For more on the painting and the signing, see *AW*.

48. Richard Stockton (the younger—son of the signer) to JA, Sept. 12, 1821. Signer Stockton himself was a relative latecomer to the Second Continental Congress.

49. This was a theme not just for old Adams, but also for middle-aged Adams. See JA to AA, July 3, 1776—just hours after America declared independence by adopting a resolution that he himself had seconded and strongly championed.

50. JA to William Tudor Sr., March 29, 1817.

51. JA to John Trumbull, March 18, 1817. The following day, Adams wrote in the same vein to Benjamin Waterhouse. See also JA to same, March 25, 1817.

52. For more on Boston and 1761 as the place and time where the Revolution began, as Adams looked back, see JA to Jedidiah Morse, Nov. 29, 1815. See also JA to Benjamin Waterhouse, Aug. 14, 1817 ("American History; whether in Fable, Allegory, Painting, Sculpture Architecture, Statuary, Poetry, Oratory or Romance: which forgets to acknowledge James Otis to have been the Father of the American Revolution; will be nothing but *a Lie*"). Several months later, Adams was particularly provoked by a flattering biography of Patrick Henry authored by William Wirt, a native Marylander who made his career in Virginia. On Jan. 5, 1818, Adams wrote Wirt that "I am jealous, very jealous of the honour of Massachusetts. The Resistance to the British System for Subjugating the Colonies began in 1760 and in 1761 in the Month of February when James Otis electrified the Town of Boston[,] the Province of Massachusetts Bay and the whole Continent more than Patrick Henry ever did in the whole Course of his life."

53. For the fascinating story of how Harvard-trained jurists in the late nineteenth and twentieth centuries came to stress Boston, Adams, and the writs of assistance, see *AW*. Although the Supreme Court has rightly identified the 1761 writs controversy as the opening scene of the American Revolution, virtually all the justices have erred in their understanding of the specific search-and-seizure issues underlying that case and underlying the Fourth Amendment more generally. Despite what the Court has said and implied, Otis and Adams were embarrassingly wrong on certain central issues; the great Parliamentary leader William Pitt and the great English jurist Lord Camden, whose speeches and rulings did indeed inspire the Fourth Amendment, were never on Otis's and Adams's side of the writs issue. That said, the 1761 writs were deeply problematic, and the post-1764 writs even more so, but not quite for the reasons Otis identified or that modern justices have articulated. For the real reasons, see Amar, *Law of the Land*, 246–49; see also infra p. 721n65. For more on what the Fourth Amendment truly was and was not originally about, see Akhil Reed Amar, *The Constitution and Criminal Procedure: First Principles* (1996), 1–45; Akhil Reed Amar, "Fourth Amendment First Principles," *Harvard Law Review* 107 (1994): 757.

54. David McCullough, *John Adams* (2002), 49; Bernard Bailyn, "Butterfield's Adams: Notes for a Sketch," *WMQ* 19 (1962): 238; Bailyn, *Ordeal*, 15.

55. On the political significance of the art: Adams repeatedly described the senior portrait in the chamber as that of Charles II when it was in fact a painting of Charles I; see supra p.710n23. Adams's lapse was a Freudian slip of sorts: brothers Charles II and James II had together abrogated the Massachusetts charter in the 1680s and thus formed a particularly unpopular duo in colonial Boston. As for

Charles I, the elder Stuart monarch was himself infamous for trying to impose unilateral taxes and for disrespecting duly elected legislators. His ham-fisted rule triggered the English Civil War. A High Anglican wed to a Catholic, Charles I was also mistrusted by Puritan dissenters. Thus, the Stuart sire of Charles II and James II was himself not loved by the residents of 1760s Boston, many of whose ancestors were dissenters and roundheads; old Adams's larger political point about this painting holds true even if he bungled the details.

On the origins of the art: Anthony van Dyck died in 1641, when the future Charles II and James II were both boys—eleven and eight years old, respectively. The paintings that Adams described were of two men—indeed, robed royals. The best-known van Dyck painting of Charles I as a robed royal, done in 1736, now hangs in Windsor Castle. This was likely the model for the copy that came to Boston, but surely the much-copied van Dyck original stayed put. The council chamber painting of the adult James II was also probably a copy, but not of van Dyck.

56. JA to William Tudor Sr., March 29, 1817. See also JA to Benjamin Waterhouse, March 19, 1817 ("Bernard and Hutchison had produced this Scenery").

57. On the emotional, psychological, and passionate dimensions of Revolutionary thought, see, e.g., Gordon S. Wood, "Rhetoric and Reality in the American Revolution," in *The Idea of America: Reflections on the Birth of the United States* (2011), 25–55; Pauline Maier, *American Scripture: Making the Declaration of Independence* (1998), 139–42.

58. Hutchinson, *History*, 86–88 (emphasis added).

59. On "shoelickers," see JA to Hezekiah Niles, Feb. 13, 1818. For young Adams's own emotional resentment, see his anonymous essay in the Oct. 21, 1765, edition of the *Boston Gazette*: "Have we not been treated formerly, with abominable insolence, by officers of the navy? . . . Have not some generals, from England, treated us like servants, nay more like slaves than like Britons? Have we not been under the most ignominious contribution, the most abject submission, the most supercilious insults of some custom house officers? Have we not been trifled with, browbeaten, and trampled on, by former governors, in a manner which no king of England since James the second has dared to indulge towards his subjects?"

For Adams's particularly sulfurous resentments against what he perceived as the Hutchinson machine, see Gordon S. Wood, *The Creation of the American Republic* (1969), 79–82. For more discussion, see *AW*.

60. William Pitt to Francis Bernard, Aug. 23, 1760, reprinted in *Quincy's Reports*, 407–8.

61. Hutchinson, *History*, 83–84.

62. Ibid., 85–86 (emphasis added).

63. JA to Benjamin Waterhouse, March 25, 1817. In his *Autobiography*, Adams also erroneously referred to the "memorable Year [!?] 1759" in linking the fall of Montreal to the writs issue [Braintree Lawyer, 1759–1761], NAFO. Adams here apparently conflated the fall of Quebec to General Wolfe in late 1759 and the fall of Montreal to General Amherst a year later. After Quebec, Montreal's fate was indeed foreseeable even if not inevitable. Cf. JA to Hendrik Calkoen, Oct. 4, 1780; JA to Jedidiah Morse, March 9, 1809.

64. William Blackstone, *Commentaries on the Laws of England*, 1st ed. (1765), 1:156.

65. See O. M. Dickerson, "Writs of Assistance as a Cause of the Revolution," in *The Era of the American Revolution*, ed. Richard B. Morris (1939), 40, 43.

CHAPTER TWO: RESISTANCE

1. On the social, cultural, and political significance of Dickinson's pose here, see *AW*.

2. On "Sophia Thrifty" herself, see *New-York Mercury*, 12-24-1764; *Boston Evening-Post*, 2-4-1765. Some forty years earlier, another Boston publisher had been fooled by his own teenage brother, Benjamin Franklin, who had published a charming series of letters that claimed to be from a matronly widow, Mrs. Silence Dogood.

3. *Boston Evening-Post*, 1-19-1761.

4. Sugar Act, 4 Geo. III, c. 15 (1764) (emphasis added); M. H. Smith, *The Writs of Assistance Case* (1978), 164–76.

5. Bernard Bailyn, *The Ideological Origins of the American Revolution* (1967), 100–1.

6. Edmund S. Morgan and Helen M. Morgan, *The Stamp Act Crisis*, rev. ed. (1995), 26–27.

7. 5 Geo. III, c. 12 (1765).

8. For a detailed list of newspaper editions, see *AW*.

9. For a detailed list of representative publications, see *AW*.

10. *Boston News-Letter*, 5-31-1764. On Samuel Adams as the likely penman or one of the leading penmen, see James K. Hosmer, *The Life of Thomas Hutchinson* (1896), 82–83; JA to William Wirt, March 7, 1818. On Otis, see Andrew C. Mc-Laughlin, *A Constitutional History of the United States* (1935), 43n21.

11. *Boston News-Letter*, 5-31-1764.

12. Circular Letter of June 25, 1764, reprinted in *Proceedings of a Special Meeting of the Massachusetts Historical Society* (1874), 43–44; Morgan and Morgan, *Stamp Act Crisis*, 34–35.

13. Reprinted in Edmund S. Morgan, ed., *Prologue to Revolution: Sources and Documents on the Stamp Act Crisis, 1764–1766* (1959), 8–14.

14. Morgan and Morgan, *Stamp Act Crisis*, 36.

15. Reprinted in Morgan, *Prologue*, 16–17.

16. Morgan, *Prologue*, 3; Morgan and Morgan, *Stamp Act Crisis*, 37–40.

17. William Blackstone, *Commentaries on the Law of England*, 1st ed. (1765), 1:163–64; Morgan and Morgan, *Stamp Act Crisis*, 86–87.

18. See Pauline Maier, *From Resistance to Revolution* (1972), 43.

19. Reprinted in Morgan, *Prologue*, 17–23 (emphasis altered).

20. Reprinted in Morgan, *Prologue*, 77–88 (emphasis altered).

21. Morgan and Morgan, *Stamp Act Crisis*, 40, 89–90, 113; Maier, *From Resistance*, 43.

22. "Novanglus X," April 3, 1775. On American awareness that Ireland was not in fact taxed by Parliament, see infra p. 721n63. See also Edmund S. Morgan, "Colonial Ideas of Parliamentary Power, 1764–1766," in *The Challenge of the American Revolution* (1976), 28; Morgan and Morgan, *Stamp Act Crisis*, 297.

23. See Morgan and Morgan, *Stamp Act Crisis*, 54–74; Edmund S. Morgan, "The Postponement of the Stamp Act," *WMQ* 7 (1950): 353.

24. See generally Bailyn, *Ideological Origins*, 198–229; Gordon S. Wood, *The Creation of the American Republic* (1969), 344–54; Gordon S. Wood, "The Problem of Sovereignty," *WMQ* 68 (2011): 573.

25. Cf. Adams's Minutes of the Argument: Suffolk Superior Court, Feb. 24, 1761, NAFO ("As to Acts of Parliament. An Act against the Constitution is void: an Act against natural Equity is void."); Adams's "Abstract of the Argument," ca. April 1761, NAFO ("AN ACT AGAINST THE CONSTITUTION IS VOID"). For one attempted harmonization, see McLaughlin, *A Constitutional History*, 26–27 & nn1–2, 32. On "executive courts"—ordinary judicial tribunals as distinct from the provincial legislature, aka its "General Court"— see ibid., 26n1.

26. 5 Geo. III, c. 12 (1765).

27. On notification neglect and negligence, see Morgan and Morgan, *Stamp Act Crisis*, 105, 140–41; Edmund S. Morgan, *The Birth of the Republic, 1763–1789*, rev. ed. (1977), 19.

28. See Morgan and Morgan, *Stamp Act Crisis*, 33, 91, 274; Maier, *From Resistance*, 71–76.

29. Morgan and Morgan, *Stamp Act Crisis*, 129–32; Maier, *From Resistance*, 53–54.

30. See generally Maier, *From Resistance*; Gordon S. Wood, "A Note on Mobs in the American Revolution," *WMQ* 23 (1966): 635.

31. On proportionality, "moderation and purposefulness," see Maier, *From Resistance*, 24. On conspiracy-law issues implicated by boycott agreements, see ibid., 131–33.

32. Bernard Bailyn, *The Ordeal of Thomas Hutchinson* (1974), 35.

33. Ibid., 56n30; *Quincy's Reports*, 414–16n2; Joseph R. Frese, "James Otis and Writs of Assistance," *New England Quarterly (NEQ* hereinafter*)* 30 (1957): 496, 502; Smith, *Writs*, 436–37. Even after his defeat in the Superior Court, Otis had continued to agitate within the Assembly, pushing through a rabble-rousing and merchant-pleasing anti-writs bill that Bernard was obliged to veto in 1762. Frese, "James Otis," 499–501; John J. Waters and John A. Schutz, "Patterns of Massachusetts Colonial Politics: The Writs of Assistance and the Rivalry Between the Otis and Hutchinson Families," *WMQ* 24 (1967): 543, 562–63; Smith, *Writs*, 424–37.

34. Hosmer, *Hutchinson*, 90–98; Edmund S. Morgan, "Thomas Hutchinson and the Stamp Act," *NEQ* 21 (1948): 459; Morgan and Morgan, *Stamp Act Crisis*, 220–29; Bailyn, *Ordeal*, 36.

35. Thomas Hutchinson, *History of the Province of Massachusetts Bay from 1749 to 1774* (1828), 148–49; Bailyn, *Ordeal*, 112–13.

36. *Quincy's Reports*, 171–73; Hosmer, *Hutchinson*, 95–96.

37. The victim-relief issue engendered considerable political maneuvering and posturing—Hutchinson had many enemies and detractors. Still, the money was paid by the province. Hutchinson, *History*, 124–25, 157–60; Hosmer, *Hutchinson*, 122–23, 351–62; Bailyn, *Ordeal*, 113–14. For further evidence that leading patriots sharply distinguished between the Oliver incident and the Hutchinson mansion riot, applauding the first while condemning the second, see Maier, *From Resistance*, 51–66; Pauline Maier, *The Old Revolutionaries: Political Lives in the Age of Samuel Adams* (1980), 27; Morgan and Morgan, *Stamp Act Crisis*, 138.

38. Reprinted in Morgan, *Prologue*, 43–62 (protests from Virginia, Rhode Island, Pennsylvania, Maryland, Connecticut, Massachusetts, South Carolina, New Jersey, and New York—the first two omitted explicit challenge to admiralty's invasion of ancient jury rights).

39. See McLaughlin, *A Constitutional History*, 20–24.

40. Circular Letter of June 25, 1764; Circular Letter of June 8, 1765, reprinted in *Annals of the American Revolution*, ed. Jedidiah Morse (1828), 113–14. See generally Morgan and Morgan, *Stamp Act Crisis*, 107–10.

41. Message to King, Oct. 1, 1765, in *Debates and Proceedings of the British House of Commons, from 1765 to 1768* (1772), 89–91.

42. The list of 1776 loyalists or neutralists should include Ruggles, William Bayard, John Cruger Jr., William Samuel Johnson, and Oliver Partridge. On the first

four, see Morgan and Morgan, *Stamp Act Crisis*, 304. Johnson eventually embraced the patriot cause; see Akhil Reed Amar, *America's Constitution: A Biography* (2005), 506n9. Partridge was a trimmer in the mid-1770s but in the end joined the patriot cause. Delegate Metcalf Bowler professed patriotism in 1776 but apparently collaborated with the British. Philip Livingston, John Morton, and Caesar Rodney all signed the Declaration in 1776; John Dickinson, William Samuel Johnson, and John Rutledge all helped draft the Constitution in 1787.

43. Livingston should not be confused with his son and namesake, the future New York chancellor who would administer the oath of office to George Washington in 1789 in the very same New York City Hall building where his father had helped host the Stamp Act Congress.

44. Morgan, *Birth*, 4.

45. Only two of the twenty-seven delegates, Ruggles and New Jersey's Robert Ogden, refused to endorse the Congressional Declaration. Both were denounced for their defections by their home assemblies. Morgan and Morgan, *Stamp Act Crisis*, 114–15 & n54.

46. Reprinted in Morgan, *Prologue*, 62–63.

47. Emphasis added. See generally Morgan and Morgan, *Stamp Act Crisis*, 103 & n26.

48. Caesar Rodney to Thomas Rodney, Oct. 20, 1765, reprinted in Burton Alva Kondle, *George Bryan and the Constitution of Pennsylvania, 1731–1791* (1922), 70–71.

49. For old Adams's recognition of the significance of the Stamp Act Congress and Otis's catalytic role, see JA to Jedidiah Morse, Nov. 29, 1815.

50. See Morgan and Morgan, *Stamp Act Crisis*, 150–64, for the remarkably similar colony-by-colony stories, quite obviously and consciously following the pattern set by Bostonians and Oliver in mid-August. In "the colonies which later participated in the American Revolution there was no one able or willing on November first to put the Act into execution." Ibid., 163. By contrast, "Quebec, Nova Scotia, Florida, Barbados, Grenada, and Jamaica consistently made use of the stamps—to the great disgust of the other colonies." Ibid., 174. For a slightly different tally, see Alan Taylor, *American Revolutions: A Continental History, 1750–1804* (2016), 102. See also Maier, *From Resistance*, 53–55.

51. Morgan and Morgan, *Stamp Act Crisis*, 139–49, 165–86; Hutchinson, *History*, 141.

52. In Portsmouth, the *New-Hampshire Gazette* published a day early, on Oct. 31, 1765, with a special explanatory masthead announcement: "This is the Day before the never-to-be-forgotten STAMP-ACT was to take Place in *America*." The following week and thereafter, the *Gazette* came out on time and unstamped, but did omit its customary colophon identifying printers Daniel and Robert Fowle. Their names returned only mid-May 1766, post-repeal. In Boston, Benjamin

Edes and John Gill's *Boston Gazette*, closely affiliated with the emerging Sons of Liberty, defiantly cranked out editions without pause, without modification, and without stamps (but with the customary colophon), beginning, as scheduled, on Nov. 4. By contrast, Richard Draper's Crown-supported *Boston News-Letter* ("Printer to the Governor and Council") changed its masthead after Nov. 1, 1765, dropped its Draper-identifying nameplate, and operated as the *Massachusetts Gazette*, officially returning as the *News-Letter* on May 22, 1766, post-repeal. The *Boston Post-Boy* published weekly without interruption but omitted from its Nov. 4 and 11 nameplate the usual "Published by Green & Russell, Printers to the Honourable House of Representatives." From Nov. 18, 1765, through April 14, 1766, the following truculent words appeared in their place: "The united Voice of all His Majesty's *free* and *loyal* Subjects in **AMERICA,**—*LIBERTY* and *PROPERTY* and *NO STAMPS.*" The *Boston Evening-Post* did much the same thing—publishing as usual on Nov. 4 and 11, 1765, and then adding the same new truculent words beneath the masthead beginning November 18, but only for three editions, through Dec. 2, then back to the pre–Stamp Act format. The colophon identifying publishers Thomas and John Fleet disappeared in Nov. and reappeared post-repeal. Also, on Nov. 18, the *Evening-Post*'s truculent addition expressly credited the *New-York Gazette* for the inspirational slogan—compelling evidence of thickening inter-colonial conversation among printers. In Newport, the *Newport Mercury* carried on without stamps or interruption, but its first two post–Stamp Act editions, on Nov. 4 and 11, omitted printer Samuel Hall's colophon. In New London, Timothy Green's *New-London Gazette* bravely published unstamped beginning on D-Day itself, Nov. 1. On Nov. 15, the *Gazette* dropped its old masthead featuring the British lion and unicorn. That day's masthead in its entirety read: "Liberty and Property, and **NO STAMPS**"—an abridged version of the truculent slogan that had already appeared in Manhattan to the South and would soon appear in Boston to the North. After an apparent monthlong pause, December editions returned to the old masthead label, *New-London Gazette*, but the lion and unicorn were gone for good. In Hartford, Timothy's brother Thomas Green suspended publication of the *Connecticut Courant* in November, but resumed, unstamped, in December with a different look. In New York, the newspaper that had originated the truculent slogan, John Holt's *New-York Gazette or Weekly Post-Boy*, printed without interruption and without stamps. The *New-York Mercury* ran three disguised early and mid-November editions that hedgingly replaced the usual masthead with "No *Stamped Paper* to be had," and returned to the old masthead when the coast seemed clear on Nov. 25. *Mercury* printer Hugh Gaine's name reappeared on Dec. 2, and his proud nameplate returned to its usual place below the masthead on Dec. 9. William Weyman's *New-York Gazette* (not to be confused with Holt's similarly named publication) had closed down for much of the fall; in December, it resumed operation, unstamped. In Philadelphia, *Pennsylvania Gazette* printer David Hall mournfully told readers on Oct. 31, in a third-page paragraph framed by thick black obituary bars, that "the most UNCONSTITUTIONAL ACT that ever these Colonies could have imagined . . . is feared to be obligatory upon us after . . . the FATAL TOMOR-ROW." The newspaper would thus "stop a While, in order to deliberate whether any Methods can be found to elude the Chains . . . and escape the insupportable Slavery." After a week off, Hall (who had taken over from *Gazette* founder Frank-lin) issued an irregular mid-November edition with a hedged "No *Stamped Paper* to be had" masthead exactly mirroring (including the selective italics) the *New-York Mercury*—additional compelling evidence of close journalistic conversation across colonies. On Nov. 21, the *Gazette* resumed publishing openly as before, unstamped; Hall at first dropped his identifying colophon, and then restored it in February. William Bradford's *Pennsylvania Journal* also came out unstamped in November and thereafter, after warning readers on Oct. 31 of a suspension in wording almost identical to Hall's ("the Fatal *To morrow* . . . STOP awhile . . . deliberate . . . Methods . . . elude . . . Chains . . . Slavery"). That day's mast-head mocked the act with a fake skull-and-crossbones stamp (following a similar mock-up at the bottom of the front page the previous week) and proclaimed that the paper was "EXPIRING: in Hopes of a Resurrection to LIFE again." In Wil-liamsburg, Alex Purdie's *Virginia Gazette*, after a long pause, resumed publication (stampless, of course) on March 7, and a new publication—*Rind's Virginia Ga-zette*, named for its printer, William Rind—commenced stampless publication on May 16. In Savannah, the *Georgia Gazette* published three unstamped editions, on Nov. 7, 14, and 21. On the 14th, proto-loyalist printer James Johnston announced that he "was under the necessity of putting a stop to the publication." The follow-ing week came this update: "NOTWITHSTANDING our advertising last week that a stop was put to the publication of this Gazette, we shall continue printing the same as long as we are allowed to make use of unstampt paper." But no further editions issued until the repeal of the Stamp Act.

Except for editions issued by Holt, the foregoing information and analysis are based entirely on my personal examination of originals and facsimile images of the newspapers themselves. See also Arthur M. Schlesinger, "The Colonial Newspapers and the Stamp Act," *NEQ* 8 (1935): 63; S. F. Roach Jr., "The *Georgia Gazette* and the Stamp Act: A Reconsideration," *Georgia Historical Quarterly* 55 (1971): 471.

53. On the Connecticut newspaper—New Haven's *Connecticut Gazette*—see Schlesinger, "The Colonial Newspapers and the Stamp Act," 75. On the conspir-atorial ideology that abounded in this era, see Bailyn, *Ideological Origins*, 144–59; Gordon S. Wood, "Rhetoric and Reality in the American Revolution," in *The Idea of America: Reflections on the Birth of the United States* (2011), 25–55; "Conspiracy

and the Paranoid Style: Causality and Deceit in the Eighteenth Century," in ibid., 81–123.

54. Declaratory Act, 6 Geo. III, c. 12 (1766).

55. Revenue Act, 7 Geo. III, c. 46 (1767); Indemnity Act, ibid. c. 56.

56. Edmond Fitzmaurice, *Life of William, Earl of Shelburne* (1876), 2:38; Morgan, "Colonial Ideas of Parliamentary Power," 5.

57. Franklin's Examination Before the Committee of the Whole of the House of Commons, Feb. 13, 1766, NAFO.

58. See generally Morgan and Morgan, *Stamp Act Crisis*, 112–21, 282–87; Morgan, "Colonial Ideas of Parliamentary Power."

59. McLaughlin, *A Constitutional History*, 55 & n6.

60. Morgan and Morgan, *Stamp Act Crisis*, 36.

61. Ibid., 288–303.

62. Ibid., 288–89. On the other hand, the preamble of the 1766 Declaratory Act expressly said that the colonial assemblies' claim to enjoy "the sole and exclusive right of imposing duties and taxes" on their respective constituents was "against law." Here, Parliament did use the magic T-word. It was possible to explain away this language; maybe Parliament merely meant to assert power to impose "duties" for trade-regulation purposes. But such narrow readings were arguably just wishful thinking. As with many London ministers, many colonial patriots were hearing what they wanted to hear. Cf. ibid., 299.

63. See generally ibid., 288–303, esp. 297. See also Franklin's Examination Before the Committee of the Whole of the House of Commons, Feb. 13, 1766 ("I think the resolutions of right will give them [colonists] very little concern, if they are never attempted to be carried into practice. The Colonies will probably consider themselves in the same situation, in that respect, with Ireland; they know you claim the same right with regard to Ireland, but you never exercise it. And they may believe you never will exercise it in the Colonies, any more than in Ireland, unless on some very extraordinary occasion.").

64. Morgan, *Birth*, 33–41; Taylor, *American Revolutions*, 107–8.

65. Sugar Act, 4 Geo. III, c. 15, sec. XLVI (1764). See also Morgan, *Birth*, 37. The Boston town meeting in the autumn of 1772 blasted the laxness of this probable-cause standard in practice, complaining of "frequent[]" and "flagrant instances" of "wanton exercise" of Customs House power to intrude into "our houses and even our bed-chambers" whenever officials "are pleased to say they *suspect* there are in the house" uncustomed wares. *Pennsylvania Journal*, 3-3-1773.

66. See O. M. Dickerson, "Writs of Assistance as a Cause of the Revolution," in *The Era of the American Revolution*, ed. Richard B. Morris (1939); Frese, "James Otis," 506–8; Smith, *Writs*, 1–5.

67. See especially *Wilkes v. Wood*, 19 Howell's State Trials 1153 (C.P., 1763), 98 Eng. Rep. 489. Note that Parliament itself had never explicitly authorized general warrants, and indeed expressly repudiated certain kinds of general warrants in the aftermath of Camden's rulings. By contrast, Parliament had indeed authorized general writs of assistance. For details, see Akhil Reed Amar, *The Law of the Land: A Grand Tour of Our Constitutional Republic* (2015), 246–49.

68. On "Wilkes and Liberty," see Hutchinson, *History*, 103; Allan Nevins, *The American States During and After the Revolution, 1775–1789* (1924), 18–19; Pauline Maier, "John Wilkes and American Disillusionment with Britain," *WMQ* 20 (1963): 373; Bailyn, *Ideological Origins*, 110–31; Maier, *From Resistance*, 162–89.

69. For a smattering of press pieces on Pitt, Wilkes, and Camden as a heroic trio, see *AW*.

70. Speech of Jan. 14, 1766, reprinted in *Morgan, Prologue*, 134–41. On Camden, see Morgan and Morgan, *Stamp Act Crisis*, 290. On Dulany as a possible source for Pitt, see McLaughlin, *A Constitutional History*, 38n2, 42–43 & n20.

71. *Boston Post-Boy*, 5-27-1765; *New Hampshire Gazette*, 5-31-1765 (emphasis altered).

72. The township of Wilkes-Barre, Pennsylvania, was named in 1769. In November 1776, a Massachusetts district that had been named Hutchinson (in honor of the ubiquitous Thomas) renamed itself Barre. In the 1780s, Vermont also named a city and town after Colonel Barré.

73. Taylor, *American Revolutions*, 107–9. See also supra p. 710n26.

74. Adams's Argument for the Defense, Dec. 3–4, 1770, NAFO. For other commentaries by Adams tinged or tainted by bigotry, see JA to AA, April 14, 1776 (referring mockingly to "Canadians, Indians, Negroes, Hanoverians, Hessians, Russians, Irish Roman Catholicks, [and] Scotch Renegadoes"); James McHenry to JA, May 31, 1800 (quoting Adams calling Hamilton a "man devoid of every moral principle—a Bastard, and as much a foreigner as Gallatin"); JA to Benjamin Rush, Jan. 25, 1806 (referring to Hamilton as "a bastard brat of a Scotch Pedler"); JA to TJ, July 12, 1813 (similar); JA to John Taylor, Jan. 9, 1815 (similar); JA to John Quincy Adams, May 20, 1816 (similar); JA to James Warren, April 13, 1783 (attacking Franklin's open and unembarrassed acknowledgment of his illegitimate son and grandson as an "Insult to good Manners and to Decency" and "Outrages to Morality & Decorum"). For similarly bigoted bile spewing from Adams's ally and idol Otis, see Morgan and Morgan, *Stamp Act Crisis*, 53 (quoting pseudonymous 1765 Otis pamphlet blasting Rhode Island conservatives as a "little dirty, drinking, drabbing contaminated knot of thieves, beggars, and transports [i.e., convicts], or other worthy descendants of such, collected from the four winds of the earth, and made up of Turks, Jews and other Infidels, with a few renegade Christians

and Catholics"). Note that Thomas Hutchinson, a descendant of the famous free-thinker Anne Hutchinson, was rather free from religious bigotry, as was another famous native Bostonian, Benjamin Franklin.

75. Bailyn, *Ordeal*, 157–58; Hosmer, *Hutchinson*, 159–63. Cf. Maier, *From Resistance*, 18 ("Troops could be used against British subjects, as in the suppression of civil disorder, only upon the request of local magistrates"); Hosmer, *Hutchinson*, 152–53 (similar).

76. On Hogarth and the Hutchinson mansion, see Bailyn, *Ordeal*, 20–21 & n33.

77. For a detailed list of newspapers and broadsides featuring the coffins, see *AW*.

78. Morgan, *Birth*, 49.

79. Ibid., 49–50.

80. Maier, *From Resistance*, 43.

81. Bailyn, *Ordeal*, 259; Gordon S. Wood, *The American Revolution: A History* (2002), 37.

82. For more details, see *AW*.

83. *Boston Gazette*, 12-20-1773.

84. On the general importance of proportionality, see Maier, *From Resistance*, 24. On the Tea Party and tea tax opposition elsewhere as a "model of justified forceful resistance upon traditional criteria," see ibid., 275–78.

85. *Boston Gazette*, 12-20-1773. Some participants doubtless stuffed their pockets with loose tea as souvenirs, but in general the chests and their contents went into the water, not into a thieves' den. On the key distinction between public purpose and redress of mere private grudge or grievance, see Maier, *From Resistance*, 33–34.

86. For earlier occasions on which colonial vigilantes had used blackface or redface of various sorts, see Morgan and Morgan, *Stamp Act Crisis*, 42, 46, 127, 152, 188; Maier, *From Resistance*, 7; Taylor, *American Revolutions*, 74; Philip J. Deloria, *Playing Indian* (1998), 10–12. For a general critique of the racial and cultural dimensions of the Tea Party, see ibid., 1–37.

87. Morgan and Morgan, *Stamp Act Crisis*, 218.

88. Years after the mansion riot, Hutchinson vented to a friend about "all the inferior people" not legally qualified to vote who nonetheless did so in town meetings: "This has given the lower part of the people such a sense of their own importance that a gentleman does not meet with what used to be common civility." Hosmer, *Hutchinson*, 189. For similar statements, see ibid., 206–7, 231. See also Bernard Bailyn, *The Origins of American Politics* (1965), 87 (quoting Hutchinson's complaint that "anything with the appearance of a man" could vote).

89. See Hosmer, *Hutchinson*, 87; Bailyn, *Ordeal*, 24.

90. For a somewhat similar, and characteristically clever, gesture by Benjamin Franklin, see Edmund S. Morgan, *Benjamin Franklin* (2002), 213. Hutchinson secretly owned about 4,000 pounds of stock in the East India company itself—nearly half the total loss suffered by the company. His annual gubernatorial salary was 1,500 pounds sterling. Bailyn, *Ordeal*, 259. On the heated 1772 debate over the proper source of this salary—whether it should come directly from London or instead come as a free gift of the Massachusetts Assembly (a gift properly withheld if the Assembly ever found him undeserving)—see ibid., 202–6.

91. Hosmer, *Hutchinson*, 324n1, 442–43; Bailyn, *Ordeal*, 372–73. For Hutchinson's poignant—already homesick—description of the charms of his Milton estate in his first audience with King George, see Thomas Hutchinson, *Diary and Letters of His Excellency Thomas Hutchinson*, ed. Peter Orlando Hutchinson (1883), 1:165. See also supra p. 147.

92. Boston Port Act, 14 Geo. III, c. 19 (1774); Massachusetts Government Act, ibid., c. 45 (1774); Administration of Justice Act, ibid., c. 39 (1774); Quartering Act, ibid., c. 54 (1774).

93. Morgan, *Birth*, 55–56; Wood, *American Revolution*, 36–37.

94. Virginia Resolutions Establishing a Committee of Correspondence, March 12, 1773; E. I. Miller, "The Virginia Committee of Correspondence of 1773–1775," *WMQ* 22 (1913): 99.

95. Hillsborough's Circular Letter, April 1768; Morgan, *Birth*, 41. In response to the Massachusetts dissolution, Boston successfully urged other towns to send delegates to an informal statewide convention, which met in September 1768 and largely echoed the sentiments that the Assembly had previously articulated. Along with the Stamp Act Congress of 1765 and the Continental Congresses that would follow in the mid-1770s, this 1768 convention would be an important precursor to other extralegal conventions that would play key roles later in American history. Ibid., 44–45.

96. Ibid., 47–48.

97. On the close ties between the Sons of Liberty and printers in many colonies, see Schlesinger, "The Colonial Newspapers and the Stamp Act," 73 (describing an "interlocking directorate"); Morgan and Morgan, *Stamp Act Crisis*, 194–98; Maier, *From Resistance*, 91. On links between Sons and towns, see ibid., 98–99. On links between towns and boycotters, and between the Sons and boycotters, see ibid., 117; Taylor, *American Revolutions*, 107–8. On the links between boycotters and printers (who published lists of boycott violators), see ibid. On links between towns and printers, see supra pp. 84–85; on the increasing conversation among newspapers themselves, see Schlesinger, "The Colonial Newspapers and the Stamp Act," 74 & n22; Morgan and Morgan, *Stamp Act Crisis*, 163 ("The printers of colonial newspapers sent exchange copies to one another").

98. For a list of reprintings, see *AW*.

99. Reprinted in Morgan, *Prologue*, 48.

100. Speech of April 19, 1774.

101. Randolph Greenfield Adams, *Political Ideas of the American Revolution: Britannic-American Contributions to the Problem of Imperial Organization, 1765–1775* (1922); Wood, "The Problem of Sovereignty"; Bailyn, *Ordeal*, 94.

102. In 1714, George I became the first of five British monarchs to rule both Hanover and Great Britain, an arrangement that lasted until 1837.

103. For Hutchinson's remarks, see supra pp. 87, 724n98, and *AW*. See also Hutchinson to Lord Hillsborough, March 9, 1771, quoted in Hosmer, *Hutchinson*, 204 (dominion model would "destroy[]" the "connexion" of the King's subjects in Massachusetts "with Great Britain, and leave[] them no better claim to protection than the King's subjects have in the electorate of Hanover"). Note that when Prussia acquired Hanover, the tiny electorate no longer had a British monarch on its throne; but this fact itself illustrates one weakness of purely personal unions (a weakness also on display in the English Civil War). Even when the personal union did exist between Britain and Hanover, British law and custom sharply limited the ability of British monarchs to use British forces to defend Hanover. See, e.g., the Act of Settlement, 12 and 13 Will. 2, c. 2, sec. 3 (1701). For more, see *AW*.

104. On the significance of this high-level and widely reprinted constitutional debate between the most impressive American-born loyalist (who was also a provincial governor) and one of America's leading patriot theorists (backed by a provincial assembly), see Morgan, *Birth*, 63; Bailyn, *Ideological Origins*, 219–22; Wood, *Creation*, 345–50.

105. Reply of the House to Hutchinson's First Message, Jan. 26, 1773 (Adams Papers), NAFO. On Adams's role in composing the main constitutional arguments, see Editorial Note, NAFO ("While John Adams was concluding . . ."). Note Adams's and the Assembly's key word "Connection"—a word along with its cognate, "connected," later featured in three key clauses of the Declaration of Independence; see infra p. 730n48.

106. James Wilson, "Considerations on the Nature and Extent of the Legislative Authority of the British Parliament" (1774); John Adams, "Novanglus VII," *Boston Gazette*, 3-6-1775; Thomas Jefferson, "Summary View of the Rights of British America" (1774); Alexander Hamilton, "The Farmer Refuted" (Feb. 1775). Wilson apparently composed his pamphlet in 1768 but waited several years to go public. Similar ideas had occasionally surfaced even earlier in American newspapers. See Morgan and Morgan, *Stamp Act Crisis*, 86–87. On Franklin, see Morgan, *Birth*, 64 ("Franklin got there as early as 1766 and waited for his countrymen to catch up."); BF to William Franklin, March 13, 1768; BF to Samuel Cooper, June 8, 1770.

107. For an emphatic admission by the Massachusetts Assembly of sweeping Parliamentary authority over Massachusetts as late as 1757, see Hutchinson, *History*,

63–66n* ("The authority of all acts of parliament which concern the colonies, and extend to them, is ever acknowledged"—a statement drafted by the ubiquitous Hutchinson himself). In 1761, that same Assembly declared that "every act of the province, repugnant to an act of parliament extending to the plantations, is *ipso facto* void." Ibid., 92. In 1765 the Stamp Act Congress's opening resolution expressly proclaimed that "His Majesty's subjects in these colonies, owe . . . all due subordination to that august body the Parliament of Great Britain." And in its Circular Letter of Feb. 11, 1768, the Massachusetts Assembly conceded that, generally speaking—putting aside, for example, special rules about taxation power and various fundamental rights fixed by the British Constitution and nature itself—"his Majesty's high court of Parliament is the supreme legislative power over the whole empire."

108. See Edmund S. Morgan, "The Revolution Considered as an Intellectual Movement," in *The Challenge of the American Revolution*, 81; Gordon S. Wood, *The Purpose of the Past: Reflections on the Uses of History* (2008), 183.

109. Frank Warren Coburn, *The Battle on Lexington Common* (1921), 28; ibid., 70 (rev. 2nd ed., 1922); Morgan, *Birth*, 2. In this book, "British-born" refers broadly to natives of any of the British Isles, including Ireland.

110. On the inattentiveness of George, his minions, and British political leaders more generally to American newspapers and pamphlets, see Morgan, *Benjamin Franklin*, 120. Lord Dartmouth, secretary of state for the colonies from 1772 to 1775, was probably better intentioned and better informed than most other insiders, but ultimately feckless. See ibid., 158, 217–18.

111. Including Scotland's estimated population of 1.5 million, but not counting Ireland with an additional estimated 3 million to 4 million inhabitants.

CHAPTER THREE: INDEPENDENCE

1. *Boston News-Letter*, 5-31-1764.

2. British settlements far north of New Hampshire (St. John's, Nova Scotia, and Newfoundland) and far south of Georgia (East Florida, West Florida, and the British West Indies) were literally or functionally noncontiguous, requiring oceanic travel to and from the middle thirteen. British Quebec, which bordered America's northwestern backcountry, was likewise unable to threaten the populous parts of the middle thirteen via well-worn coastal roads or year-round interior waterways. Nonsupport from these peripheral provinces would be a pain in the neck, but not a dagger to the throat.

3. On the same day, the *New-York Gazette* also printed the essays and a woodcut; I have been unable to locate a copy. For the classic study, see Albert Matthews, "The Snake Devices, 1754–1776, and the Constitutional Courant, 1765," *Publications of the Colonial Society of Massachusetts* 11 (1906–1907): 409.

4. New England was not only farther north but also farther east of its neighbors—that is, to their right on a conventional map, a geographic feature captured by Franklin and by all the major colonial cartoonists who emulated his template, despite other variations.

5. Thomas Hutchinson to BF, Nov. 18, 1765.

6. For a thoughtful contemporaneous meditation on the meaning of this running masthead, which ran from June 23, 1774, through Dec. 8, 1774 (after which it was replaced by a different image, also featuring a snake), see the *New-York Journal*, 9-1-1774. On the 1764 circular letter, see supra p. 59.

7. This masthead ran from July 7, 1774, through April 6, 1775, after which the print shop was interrupted by the run-up to the Battles of Lexington and Concord. Escaping Boston on the fateful day of April 19, patriot printer Isaiah Thomas relocated to Worcester, where he recommenced operation in May with a different headpiece.

8. This masthead ran from July 27, 1774, through Oct. 18, 1775. On Dec. 27, 1775, the *Journal* ran a playful meditation on the snake's biblical, biological, and heraldic significance. Was Franklin himself the essay's pseudonymous author, "An American Guesser"?

9. On delegate selection procedures, see Andrew C. McLaughlin, *A Constitutional History of the United States* (1935), 83 & n3.

10. Virginia Resolutions Establishing a Committee of Correspondence, March 12, 1773; E. I. Miller, "The Virginia Committee of Correspondence of 1773–1775," *WMQ* 22 (1913): 99.

11. Edward J. Larson, *Franklin & Washington: The Founding Partnership* (2020), 42–48, 53–54.

12. John Dickinson, Eliphalet Dyer, Christopher Gadsen, Philip Livingston, Thomas Lynch Jr., Thomas McKean, John Morton, Caesar Rodney, and John Rutledge had all attended the 1765 Congress; Livingston and Stephen Hopkins had both served in the Albany Congress. Future state governors included Samuel Adams, Richard Caswell, Thomas Cushing (acting), John Dickinson, Patrick Henry, John Jay, Thomas Johnson, William Livingston, Thomas McKean, Thomas Mifflin, William Paca, George Read, Caesar Rodney, Edward Rutledge, John Rutledge, and John Sullivan. John Dickinson, William Livingston, Thomas Mifflin, George Read, John Rutledge, Roger Sherman, and George Washington would all return to Philadelphia in 1787 to draft the Constitution.

13. Adams Diary, June 20, 1774, NAFO.

14. On Hutchinson's experience of oceanic travel as alternatingly uneventful and nauseating, see Thomas Hutchinson, *Diary and Letters of His Excellency Thomas Hutchinson*, ed. Peter Orlando Hutchinson (1883) 1:152–54; James K. Hosmer, *The Life of Thomas Hutchinson* (1896), 17, 325; Bernard Bailyn, *The Ordeal of Thomas Hutchinson* (1974), 274.

15. Hosmer, *Hutchinson*, 37, 129, 265; Thomas Hutchinson, *History of the Province of Massachusetts Bay from 1749 to 1774* (1828), 6–8.

16. Adams Diary, June 28, 1776, NAFO; ibid., July 1, 1776.

17. *Journals of the Continental Congress* (*JCC* hereinafter), 1:71–73 (Oct. 14); ibid., 73–80 (Oct. 14–20), 102 (Oct. 22).

18. Ibid., 101–13 (Oct. 21–26).

19. Ibid., 43–51 (Sept. 28); 102n1 (Oct. 21); Notes in the Debates of the Continental Congress, Sept. 28, 1774 (Adams Papers, from John Adams's Diary, quoting Virginia's Richard Henry Lee ["This [Galloway] Plan would make such Changes in the Legislatures of the Colonies that I could not agree to it, without consulting my Constituents"] and Patrick Henry ["We shall liberate our Constituents from a corrupt House of Commons, but thro them into the Arms of an American Legislature that may be bribed"]), NAFO.

20. *JCC*, 1:115–21 (Oct. 26) (capitalization and style altered).

21. In one particularly notable passage, Hutchinson had written that "there must be an abridgment of what are called English liberties. . . . [I]n a remove from the state of nature to the most perfect state of government there must be a great restraint of natural liberty. I doubt whether it is possible to project a system of government in which a colony 3000 miles distant from the parent state shall enjoy all the liberty of the parent state. . . . I wish the good of the colony when I wish to see some further restraint of liberty rather than the connexion with the parent state should be broken; for I am sure such a breach must prove the ruin of the colony." Thomas Hutchinson to _____, Jan. 20, 1769 (Franklin Papers), NAFO. For more on the Hutchinson Letters Affair, see Bailyn, *Ordeal*, 221–57; Edmund S. Morgan, *Benjamin Franklin* (2002), 185–205; Gordon S. Wood, *The Americanization of Benjamin Franklin* (2004), 139–47; Gordon S. Wood, *Revolutionary Characters: What Made the Founders Different* (2006), 83–85.

22. For an earlier and remarkably similar incident also involving the unauthorized diversion and republication of controversial transatlantic letters addressing the imperial constitutional crisis in Massachusetts—this time starring not Hutchinson but his predecessor Bernard, leading to provincial calls for Bernard's ouster—see Bailyn, *Ordeal*, 131–32, 222; Morgan, *Benjamin Franklin*, 179–80; Hosmer, *Hutchinson*, 147–48.

23. "The Pennsylvania Assembly: Instructions to Its Delegates in Congress," May 9, 1775 (Franklin Papers), NAFO; BF to Jonathan Shipley, July 7, 1775.

24. JA to AA, June 11, 1775 (June 17 addendum).

25. Adams Diary, June and July 1775, NAFO; JA to AA, June 11, 1775 (June 17 addendum). According to Adams's "Diary" entry, revised (if not composed) decades after the fact, Adams proposed Washington's name informally in a mo-

tion seconded by his cousin Samuel: "I had but one Gentleman in my Mind for that important command." Later, a formal motion naming Washington came from another delegate and passed unanimously. This account should be treated with appropriate caution given that (1) it is not contemporaneous; (2) it is not fully confirmed by any other contemporaneous account (including John's letter to Abigail); (3) the after-the-fact account makes midcareer Adams look very good; and (4) old John's memory was, as we have seen and will continue to see, unreliable and self-serving. Also, would it have made sense for a motion of great consequence to be moved and seconded solely by delegates from a single state? The letter to Abigail does, however, confirm that, details aside, Adams was a strong backer of Washington in June 1775.

26. *JCC*, 2:158–62 (July 8); Edmund S. Morgan, *The Birth of the Republic, 1763–1789*, rev. ed. (1977), 69–71.

27. Proclamation of Aug. 23, 1775 (emphasis added).

28. *JCC*, 2:193 (July 20), 240 (Sept. 13).

29. *JCC*, 3:293–94 (Oct. 13); ibid., 392 (Nov. 29).

30. Speech from the Throne, Oct. 27, 1775; 16 Geo. III, c. 5, sec. 1 (Dec. 22, 1775).

31. *JCC*, 4:342, 357–58.

32. *JCC*, 5:425–26 (June 7 motion), 506–7 (July 2 approval) (emphasis added). Note the key word "connection"; see infra p. 730n48. New York's delegation abstained, having not received sufficient authorization from its home Assembly. On July 9, New York's Assembly voted its approval. Although the July 2 vote was not immediately made public, informal word leaked out in the Philadelphia area. *Pennsylvania Evening Post*, 7-2-1776; *Pennsylvania Gazette*, 7-3-1776.

33. For a detailed list of publications, see *AW*.

34. Pauline Maier, *American Scripture: Making the Declaration of Independence* (1998), 159. For a detailed list of July 1776 newspaper editions reprinting the Declaration, see *AW*.

35. Maier, *American Scripture*, 156–58.

36. The immediate goals of printing and public proclamation to American citizens and soldiers are visible on the surface of the Congressional journal. On July 4, moments after approving the Declaration, the delegates ordered: "That the declaration be authenticated and printed"; that "copies of the declaration be sent" to each state and to "the several commanding officers of the continental troops"; and that "it be proclaimed in each of the United States, and at the head of the army." *JCC*, 5:516.

37. See generally Maier, *American Scripture*.

38. "Westphalia" here refers to the 1648 Peace of Westphalia following Central Europe's Thirty Years' War, a settlement giving rise to modern international-law notions of national sovereignty.

39. The June 7 Lee-Adams motion for independence was accompanied by the following additional and related proposed resolutions: "That it is expedient forthwith to take the most effectual measures for forming foreign Alliances. That a plan of confederation be prepared and transmitted to the respective Colonies for their consideration and approbation." *JCC*, 5:425.

40. Emphasis added.

41. Examination Before the Committee of the Whole of the House of Commons, Feb. 13, 1766 (Franklin Papers), NAFO.

42. See generally Maier, *American Scripture*, 47–96 (chapter aptly titled "The 'Other' Declarations of Independence").

43. For detailed analysis and appreciation of Congress as editor, see ibid., 143–53 (subsection aptly titled "Congress's Declaration").

44. On the committee's role, see ibid., 99–105 (subsection aptly titled "The Drafting Committee").

45. For a brilliant albeit controversial analysis of Jefferson's vision, with sustained attention to his original draft, see Garry Wills, *Inventing America: Jefferson's Declaration of Independence* (1978). Cf. Maier, *American Scripture*, 105–43 (subsections on "Jefferson's Draft").

46. JA to Timothy Pickering, Aug. 6, 1822. As with all recollections long after the fact—and especially old Adams's—these remembrances should not be treated as gospel.

47. TJ to Henry Lee, Aug. 20, 1825.

48. Emphasis added. On the key word *connected* and its cognate *connection* in American dominion theory, see supra pp. 91, 725n105, 729n32.

49. John Locke, *Two Treatises of Government* (1689), chap. 19, sec. 225.

50. On the Whig idea that a monarch "unkinged" himself and forfeited his right to rule by his own acts of tyranny, see McLaughlin, *A Constitutional History*, 96–97; Pauline Maier, *From Resistance to Revolution* (1972), 40. On the complexities behind James II's abdication, see Maier, *American Scripture*, 51–53.

51. On the crucial idea that proper revolutionaries had to seek a legal and peaceful redress of grievances before resorting to arms, see Maier, *From Resistance*, 32, 48, 64–65.

52. Parliament encompassed more than the House of Commons. It also included the House of Lords and for certain purposes the king himself, who summoned Parliament into existence and could prorogue or dissolve it at will. Parliamentary bills were generally submitted to the monarch for signature or absolute veto, but the veto fell into disuse in the early eighteenth century. Combin-

ing the One, the Few, and the Many—King, Lords, and Commons—"Parliament" was for certain purposes technically understood and described by jurists as "King-in-Parliament."

53. Maier, *From Resistance*, 286; Paul H. Smith, "The American Loyalists: Notes on Their Organization and Numerical Strength," *WMQ* 25 (1968): 259. Cf. Gordon S. Wood, *The American Revolution: A History* (2002), 113 ("20 percent of white Americans"); Alan Taylor, *American Revolutions: A Continental History, 1750–1804* (2016), 141 ("a fifth"), 212 ("peaked early at a fifth"). In 1780, John Adams claimed (caveat: in a letter seeking foreign aid and thus presenting an optimistic assessment of American odds of ultimate military triumph) that among Americans willing to choose sides by taking up arms, patriots enjoyed a massive advantage over loyalists. JA to Hendrik Calkoen, Oct. 5, 1780. In 1813, Adams estimated (another caveat: in letters late in life magnifying the heroism of patriots such as Adams himself by puffing up the strength of their loyalist opponents) that "two thirds" of Americans supported the patriots and "one third" the loyalists. JA to Thomas McKean, Aug. 30 and Nov. 26, 1813.

54. On the impressive nature of patriot leaders and their ideas, see generally Edmund S. Morgan, "Challenge and Response," in *The Challenge of the American Revolution* (1976).

55. For more on the Arnold effigy, see *Pennsylvania Packet*, 10-3-1780; *Pennsylvania Journal*, 10-4-1780; Benjamin Huntington to Oliver Ellsworth, Oct. 2, 1780, reprinted in Paul H. Smith, ed., *Letters of Delegates to Congress, 1774–1789* (1976), 16:129; Benjamin H. Irvin, "The Streets of Philadelphia: Crowds, Congress, and the Political Culture of Revolution, 1774–1783," *Pennsylvania Magazine of History and Biography* 129 (2005): 7.

56. For more on the emotions underlying this passage, see Maier, *American Scripture*, 139–42. Note also the key word "connections"; see supra pp. 91, 725n105, 729n32, 730n48.

57. On Americans' attempts to converse with potentially like-minded allies in Ireland, see Maier, *From Resistance*, 161–63, 178–80, 199, 208.

58. On the failure of George III and his minions as readers, see supra p. 726n110. On the king's two-hour audience with Hutchinson within hours of Hutchinson's arrival in London, see Hutchinson, *Diary and Letters of Hutchinson*, 1:157–75. (George, however, was not a great listener; he heard what he wanted to hear; see ibid., 158n*.) For a valiant, if ultimately unpersuasive, effort to rehabilitate the British political leadership that massively misjudged America, see Andrew Jackson O'Shaughnessy, *The Men Who Lost America: British Leadership, the American Revolution, and the Fate of the Empire* (2013).

59. See infra pp. 632, 698. Akhil Reed Amar, *The Bill of Rights: Creation and Reconstruction* (1998), 236–41, 245–46, 260–61n*.

60. See generally Linda K. Kerber, *Women of the Republic: Intellect and Ideology in Revolutionary America* (1980). See also Wood, *American Revolution*, 33; Taylor, *American Revolutions*, 199–203.

61. See Ron Chernow, *Alexander Hamilton* (2004), 140–42; Taylor, *American Revolutions*, 205–6.

62. See William Blackstone, *Commentaries on the Laws of England*, 1st ed. (1765), 1:432. For a powerful analysis, see Reva Siegel, "'The Rule of Love': Wife Beating as Prerogative and Privacy," *Yale Law Journal* 105 (1996): 2117.

63. John's initial April 14 reply to Abigail made light of her concerns. Abigail responded sharply on May 7: "Whilst you are proclaiming peace and good will to Men, Emancipating all Nations, you insist upon retaining an absolute power over Wives." See also Abigail's related April 27 letter to Mercy Otis Warren blasting the "unlimited power to the Husband to use his wife Ill."

64. See generally Taylor, *American Revolutions*, esp. 6–9, 57–62, 72–77, 251–63.

65. See ibid., 72 (estimating Native population of this region as "approximately 150,000"); Wood, *American Revolution*, 9–10 (same); Gordon S. Wood, *Empire of Liberty: A History of the Early Republic, 1789–1815* (2009), 123 & n56 ("nearly one hundred thousand").

66. See generally Wood, *Revolutionary Characters*, 13; Wood, *Empire*, 42, 122–27.

67. *JCC*, 6:1080 (July 30).

68. Taylor, *American Revolutions*, 228 ("While enticing slaves away from Patriot owners, the British forced runaways to return to Loyalist masters. British officers even sent troops to suppress slave strikes on Loyalist-owned plantations by whipping the leaders. Some officers also sold blacks taken as plunder from Patriot plantations. Rather than destroy plantation slavery, the British sought to capture it."). But cf. Jill Lepore, *These Truths: A History of the United States* (2018), 94 ("Not the taxes and the tea, not the shots at Lexington and Concord, not the siege of Boston; rather it was this act, Dunmore's offer of freedom to slaves, that tipped the scales in favor of American independence"). This provocative claim fails to survive close scrutiny; see *AW*.

69. See *Pennsylvania Packet*, 5-23-1787; Edward Needles, *A Historical Memoir of the Pennsylvania Society for Promoting the Abolition of Slavery . . .* (1848); Edward Raymond Turner, "The First Abolition Society in the United States," *Pennsylvania Magazine of History and Biography* 36 (1912): 92. See also Bernard Bailyn, *The Ideological Origins of the American Revolution* (1967), 245 ("first antislavery society in the Western world"); Gordon S. Wood, *The Radicalism of the American Revolution* (1991), 186 (similar); Wood, *Revolutionary Characters*, 38 (similar); Gordon S. Wood, *The Purpose of the Past: Reflections on the Uses of History* (2008), 177 (similar); Wood, *Empire of Liberty*, 518 (similar).

70. See *Re-dedication of the Old State House, Boston, July 11, 1882*, 4th ed. (1887), 90–94. On the paintings, see Bailyn, *Ordeal*, 138.

71. *American Gazette*, 7-23-1776; *New-England Chronicle*, 7-25-1776; *Continental Journal* (Boston), 7-25-1776; *New-Hampshire Gazette*, 7-27-1776; AA to JA, July 21, 1776.

72. Hutchinson, *Diary and Letters of Hutchinson*, 1:356.

CHAPTER FOUR: WE

1. John Adams, *Thoughts on Government*, April 1776, NAFO.

2. For two brilliant treatments, see Gordon S. Wood, *The Creation of the American Republic, 1776–1787* (1969), and Willi Paul Adams, *The First American Constitutions*, expanded ed. (2001).

3. See infra p. 228.

4. Precisely because of that general amendability, modern state constitutions do indeed differ in many ways from their 1776 forebears, particularly on issues such as electoral timing, executive power, executive selection, and religious equality. These modern constitutions are nonetheless lineal descendants of the revolutionary documents of 1776, for they continue to share most of the same fundamental features, including, of course, amendability.

5. *Virginia Gazette* (Dixon and Hunter), 6-1-1776.

6. *Pennsylvania Evening Post*, 6-6-1776; *Pennsylvania Ledger*, 6-8-1776; *Pennsylvania Journal*, 6-8-1776; *Pennsylvania Gazette*, 6-12-1776; Pauline Maier, *American Scripture: Making the Declaration of Independence* (1998), 126, 268n59.

7. *Essex Journal* (Newburyport), 7-5-1776.

8. *Pennsylvania Ledger*, 8-24-1776; *Norwich Packet*, 8-26-1776 to 9-2-1776; *Independent Chronicle* (Boston), 11-7-1776.

9. *Independent Chronicle*, 1-9-1777.

10. *Virginia Gazette* (Dixon and Hunter), 7-6-1776; *Dunlap's Maryland Gazette*, 7-12-1776; *Pennsylvania Gazette*, 7-17-1776; *New-York Journal*, 7-25-1776; *Continental Journal* (Boston), 8-2-1776.

11. Andrew C. McLaughlin, *A Constitutional History of the United States* (1935), 108–13; Wood, *Creation*, 307. See also ibid., 275, 287; Gordon S. Wood, *The American Revolution: A History* (2002), 144–45; Gordon S. Wood, "The Origins of American Constitutionalism," in *The Idea of America: Reflections on the Birth of the United States* (2011), 177–78.

12. Adams, *First American Constitutions*, 83–90.

13. Ibid.

14. There were, however, some serious voting-tabulation wrinkles that were ironed over by the Assembly, which announced that the proposal had passed. Ibid.

15. Some have suggested that Otis here was a hypocrite who failed to free his own slave. See, e.g., A. J. Langguth, *Patriots: The Men Who Started the American Revolution* (1988), 73. J. L. Bell's more recent scholarship has aimed to acquit Otis of this charge. See J. L. Bell, "Boston 1775," http://boston1775.blogspot .com/2017/06/james-otis-jr-and-slavery-revisited.html ("I've seen no evidence that as an adult he owned slaves, and in 1771 he definitely didn't").

16. Adams, *First American Constitutions*, 88; Oscar and Mary Handlin, eds., *The Popular Sources of Political Authority: Documents on the Massachusetts Constitution of 1780* (1966), 277. See also ibid., 192, 202, 217, 231–32, 248–49, 263, 282, 302, 312.

17. *JCC*, 5:431–33 (June 11–12, 1776).

18. See Alan Taylor, *American Revolutions: A Continental History, 1750–1804* (2016), 187–91, 291–93; Wood, *American Revolution*, 75–76, 82; Edward J. Larson, *Franklin & Washington: The Founding Partnership* (2020), 152–53.

19. Akhil Reed Amar, *America's Constitution: A Biography* (2005), 26. Note that the key resolution of June 11, 1776, spoke of "enter[ing] into" a confederation that did not yet formally exist. *JCC*, 5:431.

20. On this key point, see Amar, *America's Constitution*, 21–33.

21. *JCC*, 11:652 (June 25, 1778).

22. GW to John Hancock, Dec. 31, 1775; *JCC*, 4:60 (Jan. 16, 1776). The following month, Washington sent a pair of notable letters expressing his admiration of the "great poetical Genius" of a recently freed New England Negress, Phillis Wheatley. See GW to Joseph Reed, Feb. 10, 1776; GW to Phillis Wheatley, Feb. 28, 1776.

23. *Essex Gazette*, 4-26-1775 (listing "Prince Easterbrooks (a negro man) of Lexington" among the wounded in the Battles of Lexington and Concord [actually Estabrook]); *New Hampshire Gazette*, 4-28-1775 (similar); *Massachusetts Spy*, 5-3-1775 (similar); *Connecticut Courant*, 5-8-1775 (similar); *Newport Mercury*, 5-8-1775 (similar); *Norwich Packet*, 5-11-1775 (similar); *Providence Gazette*, 5-13-1775 (similar); *Virginia Gazette*, 5-27-1775 (similar). None of these reports described Estabrook as a "slave." In fact, he was a slave in 1775 who later won his freedom after serving in the Continental Army. At Bunker Hill, notable Blacks included Salem Poor and Peter Salem.

24. Larson, *Franklin & Washington*, 113; Taylor, *American Revolution*, 231.

25. Amar, *America's Constitution*, 57; Gordon S. Wood, *The Purpose of the Past: Reflections on the Uses of History* (2008), 183; Gordon S. Wood, "Monarchism and Republicanism in Early America," in *The Idea of America*, 234.

26. JM to TJ, Oct. 24, 1787.

27. See infra p. 763n67.

28. See Taylor, *American Revolutions*, 6–7, 61–62.

29. Ibid., 339.

30. Amar, *America's Constitution*, 207, 569n2. Rhode Island and Connecticut chose their own judicial officers, just as these colonies chose their own governors.

31. See generally Bernard Bailyn, *Ideological Origins of the American Revolution* (1967), 198–229; Wood, *Creation*, 344–54; Gordon S. Wood, "The Problem of Sovereignty," *WMQ* 68 (2011): 573.

32. Cf. Jack N. Rakove, *Original Meanings: Politics and Ideas in the Making of the Constitution* (1996), 206–7.

33. The Articles thus created a system rather akin to today's North Atlantic Treaty Organization (NATO) and European Union (EU). Another analogy: In version 1.0 of the "United States of America," the states were not much more "united" than the nations of the world are now in the "United Nations"—which is to say, not strongly united. Today, America is sovereign but not the United Nations. Each nation in the United Nations has one vote, regardless of size. Each is supposed to follow UN orders and pay UN dues and abide by UN edicts, but nations today do not always do as told. USA version 1.0, after the French and Indian War and the Revolutionary War, was thus not so different from UN version 1.0 after World War I and World War II.

34. These two conclaves, meeting many miles (and thus several days) apart, are curiously conflated in a misleading passage of Jill Lepore's ambitious new book, *These Truths: A History of the United States* (2018), 124–25.

CHAPTER FIVE: AMERICA

1. As Professor Morgan pointed out, "France and Spain might have helped England suppress the American rebellion in exchange for the restoration of Canada to France and of the Floridas to Spain. That alternative had been seriously considered." Edmund S. Morgan, *Benjamin Franklin* (2002), 260–61. In negotiations culminating in the 1783 Treaty of Paris, France did not initially support America's land claims west of the Appalachians. Americans won this vital region at the bargaining table only by clever dealing—first negotiating directly with Britain and then presenting the French with a diplomatic fait accompli, sugarcoated with Franklin's charm.

2. See Frederick W. Marks III, *Independence on Trial: Foreign Affairs and the Making of the Constitution* (1973); Gordon S. Wood, *The American Revolution: A History* (2002), 148–50; Akhil Reed Amar, *America's Constitution: A Biography* (2005), 141; Gordon S. Wood, *Revolutionary Characters: What Made the Founders Different* (2006), 146–47; Gordon S. Wood, *Empire of Liberty: A History of the Early Republic, 1789–1815* (2011), 15; Alan Taylor, *American Revolutions: A Continental History, 1750–1804* (2016), 348–51.

3. On this functional and structural approach, the key limit on federal power would not be insistence that a given matter be narrowly economic in nature, but rather insistence that the matter be truly interstate, international, or tribal in nature—spilling across state boundaries or truly affecting US relations with foreign nations or domestic tribes. The Articles of Confederation gave Congress plenary power to "manag[e] all affairs with the Indians, not members of any of the States." The Constitution conferred the same broad power, substituting the word "commerce" for the word "affairs" when empowering the new constitutional Congress to handle Indian matters. The word "commerce" can indeed mean "affairs" more generally, and it would be odd to read the Constitution as giving the new Congress less power in any respect over Indian matters than the old Congress had in the Articles. Chief Justice John Marshall recognized as much in his most important pronouncement on Indian law: "The *whole intercourse* between the United States and this [Indian] nation, is, by our constitution and laws, vested in the government of the United States" (emphasis added). *Worcester v. Georgia*, 31 U.S. (6 Pet.) 515, 561 (1832). Ten times in *Worcester*, Marshall spoke of Congress's power to "*regulate . . . intercourse*" (emphasis added)—whether or not narrowly economic—with Indians. These repeated references obviously glossed the Article I clause giving Congress power to "*regulate Commerce*" (emphasis added) with Indians—a clause also glossed by Congress in a slew of early statutes (several signed by Washington and cited by Marshall) expressly entitled Acts "to *Regulate Trade and Intercourse*" (emphasis added) with Indians. See, e.g., 1 Stat. 137 (1790); 1 Stat. 329 (1793); 1 Stat. 469 (1796); 1 Stat. 743 (1799); 2 Stat. 139 (1802); 3 Stat. 332 (1816). These statutes ranged beyond economic regulation and squarely applied to tribes that were not treaty partners of the federal government. As self-evident in the very titles of these statutes, the early Congress plainly read Indian "commerce" as synonymous with Indian "affairs" and Indian "trade and intercourse" more generally. The same broad reading of "commerce" likewise applies to Congressional power to handle international and interstate spillovers; the word "commerce" appears once, and it sensibly means the same thing in all three contexts, giving Congress broad power over truly Indian affairs, over truly foreign affairs, and over truly interstate affairs, whether or not narrowly economic in nature. See Amar, *America's Constitution*, 107–08 & n*, 542nn18–19.

4. In the months prior to the Philadelphia Convention, Jay, Knox, and Madison, acting separately, had each sent Washington a brief sketch of a new constitution. All three advocated "replacing a toothless unicameral congress composed of delegates from sovereign states with a [muscular] national government [with sweeping national power] comprised of a bicameral legislature, independent executive, and separate judiciary." Edward J. Larson, *Franklin & Washington: The Founding Part-*

nership (2020), 187. John Jay to GW, Jan. 7, 1787; Henry Knox to GW, Jan. 14, 1787; JM to GW, April 16, 1787.

5. On the significance of this key language, from Queen Anne's July 1, 1706, letter to the Scotch Parliament, see the opening passage of Jay/Publius's *Federalist* No. 5.

6. In 1776, Adams had argued for a bicameral legislature with independent executive and judicial branches, but these ideas were old hat, describing the basic structure of the British Constitution and most colonial constitutions. This essay said almost nothing about the process of constitution-making itself and absolutely nothing about the need for an ad hoc convention distinct from an ordinary assembly to draft the Constitution itself. (Indeed, the word "convention" nowhere appeared.) In suggesting in passing that a future "legislature at its leisure" could change the rules of executive selection and tenure—say, by providing for a popularly elected governor for life—*Thoughts* in fact seemed miles away from more mature American ideas about a constitutional convention or some other special institution or protocol being needed to ordain or alter a constitution. For discussion of a June 2, 1775, autobiographical passage in which Adams did ruminate about conventions, see *AW*.

7. JM to GW, April 16, 1787.

8. See Wood, *Revolutionary Characters*, 156–64; Gordon S. Wood, "Interests and Disinterestedness in the Making of the Constitution," in *The Idea of America: Reflections on the Birth of the United States* (2011), 149–50.

9. Adams Diary, Sept. 5–6, 1774, NAFO.

10. *JCC*, 1:25 (Sept. 6, 1774).

11. Max Farrand, ed., *The Records of the Federal Convention of 1787*, 4 vols., rev. ed. (1966) (*Farrand's Records* hereinafter), 1:10–11n* (May 28).

12. Ibid., 1:510 (July 2). Cf. ibid., 250 (June 16) ("If a proportional representation be right, why do we not vote so here?") (Paterson); ibid., 515 (July 2) ("Mr. Wilson objected to the Committee, because it would decide according to that very rule of voting which was opposed on one side").

13. Ibid., 255 (June 16).

14. For the most fair-minded assessment of Madison in general and as a constitutionalist in particular, see Richard Brookhiser, *James Madison* (2011), esp. 6–13. Cf. Noah Feldman, *The Three Lives of James Madison: Genius, Partisan, President* (2017). Feldman offers a detailed portrait of Madison that glitters with local insights. Alas, Feldman wildly overstates the case for Madison as the Constitution's creator and guardian and routinely fails to present contrary evidence or analysis. Feldman's shabby treatment of Hamilton is particularly disappointing, as is his failure to appreciate the full magnitude of George Washington. Brookhiser's

account is more balanced, perhaps because he is also a distinguished biographer of (among others) Washington and Hamilton. Feldman is not and falls victim to "biographer's disease"—a tendency to exaggerate the contributions and the virtues of the biographer's protagonist, to minimize the protagonist's weaknesses and failures, and to diminish the achievements and virtues of the protagonist's contemporaries (and especially rivals).

15. On the Knox and Jay letters, see supra p. 736n67. On Washington's circular letter, see supra pp. 391–93; on Adams, see supra p. 408. On Washington's early call for a convention, see GW to William Gordon, July 8, 1783.

16. For a different view, see Gordon S. Wood, "Interests and Disinterestedness," 131 ("Madison [was] the father of the Constitution if ever there was one"); Wood, "Monarchism and Republicanism in Early America," in *The Idea of America*, 236 ("Madison . . . more than anyone was responsible for the new Constitution"); Gordon S. Wood, *The Purpose of the Past: Reflections on the Uses of History* (2008), 146 (Madison was "the major architect of the Constitution"); Wood, *Revolutionary Characters*, 143 (same). But see ibid., 156 ("We have to soften, if not discard, the traditional idea that [Madison] was the father of the Constitution"). This last-quoted aperçu is Wood's best. In the course of a magnificent lifetime body of work on the Founding, Wood has repeatedly placed too much weight on Article I, section 10—which itemized, à la Madison, things that a state would not be allowed to do internally—and not enough weight on the rest of the Constitution as a whole. As a brilliant intellectual and cultural historian, Wood naturally enough has gravitated to Madison, himself a fascinating cultural analyst, but Wood has thereby slighted the less intellectual and less talkative but far more consequential Washington—the true indispensable man. Perhaps because Wood's first and pathbreaking book, *The Creation of the American Republic*, focused on state constitutions, he has often exaggerated (as did Madison himself) the internal failures of state constitutions as the main engine driving the drafting and ratification of the federal Constitution. Correspondingly, Wood has failed to explain persuasively why the federal Constitution (or at least 95 percent of it) cannot be understood as fitting snugly within the simple Euclidian solution to the genuinely existential geostrategic threats that loomed (or at least were plausibly seen to loom) on the horizon at the Confederation level. Cf. Wood, *Empire of Liberty*, 15 ("The deficiencies of the Confederation . . . cannot account for the unprecedented nature of the Constitution created in 1787"). My analysis in this chapter of the geostrategic problem and the necessarily complex solution to that problem (in which x entailed y and z, requiring changes far beyond the deeply unserious New Jersey plan) accounts for far more of the Constitution than does Wood's emphasis on Article I, section 10, as a response to internal state constitutional failures. This chapter's focus on the national-security crisis as the key to the Constitution also better

accounts for both the specific mandate of the Convention (to fix the Confederation, not the states internally) and what the Federalists themselves emphasized in the ratification period. Historiographically, my national-security story harkens back to the mainstream of historical scholarship prior to Charles Beard (much of whose work has now been discredited, as Wood himself acknowledges). For examples of this earlier orthodoxy, see George Bancroft, *History of the Formation of the Constitution of the United States of America*, 2 vols. (1882); John Fiske, *The Critical Period of American History, 1783–1789* (1888). For a powerful update, see Marks, *Independence on Trial*.

On my view, the Constitution aimed primarily to solve national-security problems that obsessed leading military men such as Washington and Hamilton. It also, but more incidentally and incompletely, addressed cultural and state-level issues that preoccupied Madison. Throughout his writings, Wood has returned repeatedly to a passage in an Oct. 24, 1787, letter from Madison to Jefferson as the key to the Constitution: "The evils issuing from these sources [the 'mutability' and internal injustice of state laws] contributed more to that uneasiness which produced the Convention, and prepared the public mind for a general reform, than those which accrued to our national character and interest from the inadequacy of the Confederation to its immediate objects." But this private letter is not the key to the Constitution—and indeed, Madison's letter went on to lament that the Philadelphia plan *failed* to solve the state-level problem that he saw as critical. The real key to the Constitution may be found not in Madison's private musings, but in Washington's most public pronouncement of all. Writing to Congress on behalf of the entire Convention in a letter accompanying the proposed Constitution itself—a letter reprinted everywhere in 1787–1788, most often adjoining the text of the proposed Constitution—Washington explained to all Americans (not merely one overseas friend, as with Madison's letter to Jefferson) the essence of the plan, the true key: "The friends of our country have long seen and desired, that *the power of making war, peace and treaties, that of levying money and regulating commerce, and the correspondent executive and judicial authorities should be fully and effectually vested in the general government of the Union*: but the impropriety of delegating such extensive trust to one body of men is evident—*Hence results the necessity of a different organization.* It is obviously impracticable in the fœderal government of these States, to secure all rights of independent sovereignty to each, and yet provide for the interest and safety of all. . . . In all our deliberations on this subject we kept steadily in our view, that which appears to us the greatest interest of every true American, *the consolidation of our Union*, in which is involved our prosperity, felicity, safety, *perhaps our national existence.*" *Farrand's Records*, 2:666–67 (emphasis added). For more elaboration on how and why I break with Wood on this important set of issues, see Amar, *America's Constitution*, 141–42, 549n31.

17. See Mary Sarah Bilder, *Madison's Hand: Revising the Constitutional Convention* (2015).

18. On Madison's slave-selling and failure to free his own slaves, see Amar, *America's Constitution*, 627n3; see also supra pp. 671–72.

19. For more on Madison's disappointing track record on slavery, see Brookhiser, *James Madison*, esp. 9 ("His solutions to the problem of slavery were worthless, a pathetic case of intellectual and moral failure"); Feldman, *Three Lives*, 52, 69, 121, 164, 205, 214–15, 235–36, 301–2, 354, 466–68, 617–21. On Hamilton, by contrast, see *AW*.

20. Here, too, Madison/Publius cheated, misleadingly emphasizing the tax issue alongside representation. He surely knew that taxes would come mainly from duties, imposts, excises, and the like. The Three-Fifths Clause applied only to "direct taxes" on heads and land, and such taxes were unlikely to be particularly important. See Amar, *America's Constitution*, 93–94.

21. James Wilson, "Considerations on the Nature and Extent of the Legislative Authority of the British Parliament" (1774).

22. See generally Bernard Bailyn, *Ideological Origins of the American Revolution* (1967), 198–229; Gordon S. Wood, *The Creation of the American Republic* (1969), 344–54; Gordon S. Wood, "The Problem of Sovereignty," *WMQ* 68 (2011): 573. On "imperium in imperio," see also Thomas Hutchinson to BF, Jan. 1, 1766.

23. On Wilson's popular sovereignty ideas in the ratification process, see Wood, *Creation*, 530–31; James Wilson, *The Works of James Wilson*, ed. Robert Green McCloskey (1967), 2:770–71. For Wilson's later public lectures on this topic, see ibid., 1:77, 304, 405.

24. For examples, see, e.g., *Farrand's Records*, 1:49–50 (May 31, popular election of House), 60 (May 31, scope of legislative powers), 67, 70 (June 1, executive power), 86 (June 2, proportional representation in presidential removal), 104, 138 (June 4, June 6, Council of Revision), 125 (June 5, inferior courts), 126–27 (June 5, popular ratification), 164–66 (June 8, Congressional negative over state laws), 252–55, 314–22 (June 16–19, objections of New Jersey plan), 373 (June 22, national legislative salary), 386–89 (June 23, scope of Congressional incompatibility to appointive office), 488–90 (June 30, Senate apportionment compromise proposal); 584, 605 (July 11, July 13, fair rules of apportionment for western Americans), 2:268 (Aug. 13, liberal eligibility rules for immigrants to serve in public positions).

25. *Farrand's Records*, 2:56–57 (July 19); ibid., 111 (July 25).

26. Ibid., 1:252–55, 260–61, 265–67, 269–80 (June 16).

27. On the lectures, see Wilson, *Works of James Wilson*, 1:69–2:707. On Wilson's state-sovereignty opinion, see supra pp. 336–39.

28. For a thoughtful appreciation of Wilson, see Nicholas Pederson, "The Lost Founder: James Wilson in American Memory," *Yale Journal of Law and the Humanities* 22 (2010): 257.

29. For a similar assessment that helped me see the light, see Edward J. Larson, *The Return of George Washington: Uniting the States, 1783–1789* (2015), esp. 135–65 (chapter aptly titled "In His Image").

30. See Charles C. Thach Jr., *The Creation of the Presidency, 1775–1789*, rev. ed. (1969).

31. Richard Beeman, *Plain, Honest Men: The Making of the American Constitution* (2009), 163–64; Clinton Rossiter, *1787: The Grand Convention* (1968), 145; Wood, *Empire of Liberty*, 111.

32. See Akhil Reed Amar, *America's Unwritten Constitution: The Precedents and Principles We Live By* (2012), 66, 73.

33. See generally Larson, *Return of George Washington*; Stanley Elkins and Eric McKitrick, *The Age of Federalism* (1993), 34–46.

34. Jonathan Elliot, ed., *The Debates in the Several State Conventions on the Adoption of the Federal Constitution as Recommended by the General Convention at Philadelphia in 1787*, 5 vols. (1888) (*Elliot's Debates* hereinafter), 3:453–54 (Madison, June 17, 1788); *Farrand's Records*, 2:375 (Ellsworth, Aug. 22, 1787). See also ibid., 364–65, 371–74, 559 (remarks of three South Carolina delegates—Charles Pinckney, Charles Cotesworth Pinckney, and John Rutledge—and Connecticut's Roger Sherman, Aug. 21–22 and Sept. 10, 1787).

35. *Elliot's Debates*, 1:132–33 (Virginia's initiatives on Oct. 16 and Dec. 4, 1786); ibid., 119–20 (Congress's blessing on Feb. 21, 1787). See also *JCC*, 32:71–74 (similar, Feb. 21, 1787).

36. *Farrand's Records*, 1:15.

37. Ibid., 3:478–79.

38. For prominent works misconstruing the secrecy command as strongly operative post-adjournment, see, e.g., Feldman, *Three Lives*, 402; Jill Lepore, *These Truths: A History of the United States* (2018), 121. These mistaken assertions blur the Convention rule's letter and spirit and garble the actual practice that ensued. The rule in fact authorized disclosures with the permission of the Convention. Once the Convention dissolved, no permission could issue. Thus, if the blanket ban had aimed to extend for even an instant after adjournment, it would have preposterously extended forever. *In fact, delegate James McHenry's notes expressly record that the "Injunction of secrecy [was] taken off" on the Convention's final day* (emphasis added). See *Farrand's Records*, 2:650 (Sept. 17). (At the conclave's close, delegates also authorized Washington to retain the Convention's official records, subject to whatever rules might one day emerge from Congress under the new

Constitution. Ibid., 641, 648 (Sept. 17). The initial May 29 secrecy rule, however, involved far more than official records.)

In mid-October 1787, delegate Charles Pinckney published a pamphlet under his own name titled "Observations on the Plan of Government Submitted to the Federal Convention," compiling ideas that he had floated at Philadelphia. Ibid., 3:106–23. In a letter to Madison, Washington tartly observed that young Pinckney was "unwilling . . . to lose any fame that can be acquired by the publication of his sentiments." Ibid., 131 (Oct. 22). But nowhere did Washington suggest that the publicity-hungry South Carolinian had breached any secrecy rule.

Beginning in late November 1787, Wilson, in the Pennsylvania Ratifying Convention, publicly described various summer drafting discussions and motions (for example, about whether to include a bill of rights). See ibid., 143 (Nov. 28), 161 (Dec. 4). Disaffected delegate Luther Martin simultaneously offered his own harsher and more detailed account of the summer discussions in a report to the Maryland legislature, naming names (including Randolph, Paterson, Washington, and Franklin) and specifying votes (for example, on Senate apportionment). Ibid., 151–59 (Nov. 29). Delegate McHenry also unreservedly briefed the Maryland lawmakers about drafting deliberations. Ibid., 144–50 (Nov. 29). For Martin's much longer and juicier tirade, published in *Dunlap's Maryland Gazette* between Dec. 28, 1787, and Feb. 8, 1788, see ibid., 172–232.

Meanwhile, newspapers in at least eight states published Benjamin Franklin's grand conciliatory closed-door speech of Sept. 17, which the good doctor had sent to multiple friends doubtless expecting broad public dissemination. See ibid., 2:641n1. For a detailed list of these publications, see *AW*.

In pseudonymous essays published in late 1787 and early 1788, yea-saying Connecticut delegate Oliver Ellsworth attacked various naysaying delegates by name (Virginia's George Mason, Massachusetts's Elbridge Gerry, and Maryland's Martin) while offering his own spicy recollections of who said what, when, why, and how. Gerry and Martin quickly and openly responded in print. For Ellsworth's initial attacks, see *Farrand's Records*, 3:164–65 ("The Landholder VI," critiquing Mason, printed in the *Connecticut Courant* on Dec. 10), 170–72 ("The Landholder VIII," blasting Gerry, which ran in the *Courant* on Dec. 24). For Gerry's response in the Jan. 5, 1788, issue of the *Massachusetts Centinel*, see ibid., 239–40; and for Martin's defense of Gerry in the Jan. 18 *Maryland Journal*, see ibid., 259–60. For the Landholder's reply, see ibid., 271–75 ("The Landholder X," which ran in the Feb. 29 issue of the *Maryland Journal*). Naturally, Martin responded in detail. Ibid., 276–95. These essays appeared in the *Maryland Journal* on March 7, 18, and 21. Gerry also jumped back in the fray, in a piece that ran in the *New-York Journal* on April 30. Ibid., 298–300.

When the Massachusetts Ratifying Convention met in mid-January, Philadelphia delegates Caleb Strong, Nathaniel Gorham, and Gerry all publicly discussed specifics of summer horse-trading and mutual accommodation. Ibid., 247, 260–62. In a detailed letter to Lafayette composed between April 28 and May 1, Washington himself shared tidbits about the general views of Convention members, without mentioning specific names or votes.

Philadelphia alumni in later conventions continued the tradition of openness, as when Madison explained in Richmond that the Constitution's rules prohibiting Congress from ending slave importation prior to 1808 had been drafted to mollify Deep Southern delegations. See supra pp. 215–16. In Poughkeepsie, Philadelphia alums John Lansing, Robert Yates, and Hamilton sharply debated exactly what the latter had said and meant in his lengthy closed-door speech of June 18, 1787. *Elliot's Debates*, 2:376 (June 28, 1788) (describing a "warm personal altercation" between Lansing and Hamilton); *Daily Advertiser* (New York), 7-4-1788 (describing in more detail the June 28, 1788, flap and the follow-up on June 30, in which Yates as a witness relied openly and extensively on his Philadelphia notes). According to New York Convention secretary John McKesson, Lansing expressly declared in the June 28 altercation that "the Matters of that [Philadelphia] Convention were no longer Secrete when their proceedings were published." Fourth Speech of June 28, 1788 (John McKesson's version, Hamilton Papers), NAFO.

Post-ratification, Georgia's Abraham Baldwin in House debates in 1789 paraphrased and parried Gerry's comments at the Convention and in subsequent "newspaper declamation"; Madison discussed Philadelphia drafts and votes in the 1791 debate over Hamilton's bank bill; and Washington went even further, invoking the official Convention journal, in a 1796 debate about the role of the House in implementing treaties. Joseph Gales Sr., compiler, *The Debates and Proceedings in the Congress of the United States*, 24 vols. (1834–1856) (known as *Annals of the Congress of the United States*; *Annals* hereinafter), 1:578–79 (June 19, 1789); ibid., 2:1945 (Feb. 2, 1791); Message of Washington to House of Representatives, March 30, 1796. In open Court, Paterson likewise discussed the role that slavery had played in drafting rules about taxes. See *Hylton v. United States*, 3 U.S. (3 Dall.) 171, 177 (1796). In 1818–1819, various Philadelphia delegates and their heirs shared their papers with Secretary of State John Quincy Adams, who published a treasure trove of material in 1819. *Farrand's Records*, 1:xi–xiv; 3:425–35. Versions of Lansing's and Yates's Philadelphia notes were published in 1821, and Madison arranged for posthumous publication of his own copious notes, which came to print in 1840.

Hamilton himself believed that he should not name names and disclose details of individual speeches made—especially trial balloons floated—by others behind closed doors. Ibid., 3:368–69. Even while taking this position, he disclosed information about closed-door votes and positions in broad, impersonal terms. Hamilton also thought post-Convention disclosures casting disrepute upon individual delegates—especially upon himself (he was always prickly about his honor)—were "highly improper and uncandid." This was the nub of his dispute with Lansing in late June 1788; see Hamilton's Fourth Speech of June 28, 1788, NAFO. Some of Hamilton's concerns may have stemmed not from the specific rules promulgated at Philadelphia but rather from more general norms of conduct among gentlemen—norms not unrelated to the code duello.

A few delegates privately (and improperly) leaked tidbits to friends during the Convention. (For details, see John P. Kaminski's brisk 2005 pamphlet "Secrecy and the Constitutional Convention.") Other delegates kept their lips sealed long after adjournment, beyond what the rules required. But most delegates clearly understood throughout the Convention that the strict secrecy ban would lapse at adjournment. *Farrand's Records*, 3:64 (Alexander Martin to Governor Caswell, July 27, 1787); JM to TJ, June 6, July 18, and Sept. 6, 1787. *And in actual fact, when the final draft went public, so did a great many delegates.*

39. See *Farrand's Records*, 1:125 (Pierce Butler, June 5: "We must follow the example of Solon who gave the Athenians not the best Govt. he could devise; but the best they wd. receive").

40. Ibid., 1:22 (emphasis added; punctuation altered).

41. On the slippages and distortions in the process, see Bilder, *Madison's Hand*; James H. Hutson, "The Creation of the Constitution: The Integrity of the Documentary Record," *Texas Law Review* 65 (1986): 1; James H. Hutson, "Riddles of the Federal Constitutional Convention," *WMQ* 44 (1987): 411.

42. *Farrand's Records*, 2:201–10.

43. See generally Douglass Adair, *Fame and the Founding Fathers: Essays by Douglass Adair*, ed. Trevor Colbourn (1974); Garry Wills, *Explaining America: The Federalist* (1982), 83–86; Garry Wills, *Cincinnatus: George Washington and the Enlightenment* (1984), 99–132; Wood, *Revolutionary Characters*, 23, 43, 137–38.

44. *Farrand's Records*, 2:644. Technically, Washington was merely commenting on a last-minute motion that had been made by Nathaniel Gorham, and duly seconded, but it seems highly likely that Gorham introduced this motion by prearrangement with the Convention's presiding officer.

CHAPTER SIX: PEOPLE

1. For details, see Akhil Reed Amar, *America's Constitution: A Biography* (2005), 7–10, 503–7.

2. For a detailed list of leading newspaper printings, see *AW*.

3. The list of Anti-Federalists who went on to high office under the Constitution includes President James Monroe, Vice Presidents George Clinton and Elbridge Gerry, and Supreme Court Justice Samuel Chase. The biggest blemish in the ratification process, involving a Manhattan Anti-Federalist printer, Thomas Greenleaf, who fell victim to illegal violence, occurred late in the game, after eleven states had agreed to the Constitution. See Pauline Maier, *Ratification: The People Debate the Constitution, 1787–1788* (2010), 398. Also, after ten states had already ratified, July 4 paraders and revelers became brawlers and rioters in Albany; Federalists and Anti-Federalists clashed in the streets, causing more than a dozen casualties. *Daily Advertiser* (New York), 7-10-1788; *Massachusetts Spy*, 7-24-1788. Months earlier and miles away, a Federalist crowd in Philadelphia had banged on the doors and broken the windows of an Anti-Federalist boardinghouse. Richard Beeman, *Plain, Honest Men: The Making of the American Constitution* (2009), 326. Given the temporal duration, the geographic sweep, the political intensity, and the gigantic stakes of the ratification debate, the wonder is not that the pot sometimes boiled over, but rather how rarely it did so and how little damage actually occurred.

4. For Hamilton's early musings on this topic, see *The Continentalist* No. III, which appeared in the *New-York Packet* on Aug. 9, 1781: "Political societies, in close neighbourhood, must either be strongly united under one government, or there will infallibly exist emulations and quarrels. . . . Though it will ever be their [the states'] true interest to preserve the union, their vanity and self importance, will be very likely to overpower that motive, and make them seek to place themselves at the head of particular confederacies independent of the general one. A schism once introduced, competitions of boundary and rivalships of commerce will easily afford pretexts for war. European powers may have inducements for fomenting these divisions and playing us off against each other. But without such a disposition in them, if separations once take place, we shall, of course, embrace different interests and connections. The particular confederacies, leaguing themselves with rival nations, will naturally be involved in their disputes; into which they will be the more readily tempted by the hope of making acquisitions upon each other, and upon the colonies of the powers with whom they are respectively at enmity."

Several other *Continentalist* essays foreshadowed other *Federalist* themes. For example, *The Continentalist* No. II, which appeared in the *Packet*'s July 19 edition, strongly prefigured Hamilton's later *Federalist* No. 28.

5. See Douglass Adair, *Fame and the Founding Fathers: Essays by Douglass Adair*, ed. Trevor Colbourn (1974), 75–76 (reprinting "The Tenth Federalist Revisited," *WMQ* 8 [1951]: 48); Larry D. Kramer, "Madison's Audience," *Harvard Law Review* 112 (1999): 611, 664 (Madison's distinctive arguments in No. 10 were "virtually

absent from the contest to secure the Constitution's adoption"). The reprinting data on *The Federalist* essays more generally confirm the lack of impact of No. 10. See Merrill Jensen, John P. Kaminski, and Gaspare J. Saladino, eds., *The Documentary History of the Ratification of the Constitution*, 29 vols. (1976–), available online and word-searchable at University of Virginia, Documentary History of the Ratification of the Constitution, Digital Edition, https://rotunda.upress.virginia.edu/founders /RNCN (*DHRC Digital* hereinafter), 19:540–49, App. IV ("Printings and Reprintings of *The Federalist*"). For still further confirmation of the limited contemporaneous impact of No. 10's most distinctive ideas, see William H. Riker, *The Strategy of Rhetoric: Campaigning for the American Constitution* (1996). See also Amar, *America's Constitution*, 43–44.

6. For specific examples of Publius's rapid response, see *AW*.

7. For a detailed list of newspaper editions featuring Russell's motifs and metaphors, see *AW*. See also Robert L. Alexander, "The Grand Federal Edifice," *Documentary Editing* 9 (June 1987): 13.

8. *Farrand's Records*, 1:49–50 (May 31). Here and elsewhere, I have substituted "base" for "basis" to highlight the underlying construction metaphor.

9. In his famous June 8, 1783, Circular Letter to States—his first Farewell Address, in retrospect—General Washington had labeled "an indissoluble Union of the States under one federal Head," as the first of four "pillars on which the glorious fabrick of our Independancy and National Character must be supported—Liberty is the basis."

10. Russell's cartoon omitted Article VII language that the Constitution would take effect after nine or more ratifications only in "the States so ratifying the same." A Russell-inspired cartoon that appeared the following day in another Boston paper, the *Independent Chronicle*, helpfully included this key language, see supra p. 235.

11. A modern exhibit in the Maryland State House refers to a revival of the cartoon in the April 25, 1788, issue of the *Maryland Journal*, but the copy of that issue that I have examined does not include any such cartoon.

12. In late 1789, Russell marked North Carolina's ratification with a final cartoon in the pillars series, but offered his readers no picture when Rhode Island said yes to the Constitution in mid-1791. See *Massachusetts Centinel*, 12-16-1790; ibid., 6-2-1791.

13. *Elliot's Debates*, 2:432, 458 (Nov. 26–27, Dec. 4–6; emphasis and punctuation altered).

14. On the hard-hitting but legal tactics in the Keystone State, see Akhil Reed Amar, *America's Unwritten Constitution: The Precedents and Principles We Live By* (2012), 530–31n10.

15. See Maier, *Ratification*, 166 ("A stunning fifty-one [newspapers] in other states reprinted accounts of the debates, sometimes almost in their entirety"). On the Boston Convention more generally, see ibid., 154–213.

16. *Elliot's Debates*, 2:3.

17. Ibid., 6 ("the inquiry of the Hon. Mr. Adams").

18. Ibid., 6–11.

19. Ibid., 11. For a contemporaneous account, see *Massachusetts Centinel*, 1-19-1788.

20. For a detailed list of newspapers reprinting this particular Convention conversation, see *AW*.

21. *Elliot's Debates*, 2:160–61 (Feb. 5, emphasis altered). For a contemporaneous account, see *Massachusetts Centinel*, 3-5-1788.

22. *Elliot's Debates*, 182–83 (Feb. 7). For a contemporaneous account, see *Massachusetts Centinel*, 2-9-1788.

23. *Elliot's Debates*, 181–83 (Feb. 6–7). For a contemporaneous account, see *Massachusetts Centinel*, 2-9-1788.

24. On the printing details, see Amar, *America's Unwritten Constitution*, 66, 73.

25. *Farrand's Records*, 2:666–67.

26. See generally Edward J. Larson, *The Return of George Washington: Uniting the States, 1783–1789* (2015), 197–233.

27. Emphasis altered. See Washington's stern follow-up letter to Carter on Jan. 12, 1788.

28. On the handbook, see infra p. 751n49; see also George Nicholas to JM, April 5, 1788; JM to Nicholas, April 8, 1788. On the Richmond Convention more generally, see Maier, *Ratification*, 254–319.

29. *Elliot's Debates*, 3:222 (June 10) (emphasis added). Marshall's repeated and celebratory use of the word "democracy" suggests that many modern commentators—see, e.g., Jill Lepore, *These Truths: A History of the United States* (2018), 12–13—have erred in asserting that this word had universally and unequivocally negative connotations at the time of the Founding and/or that the word was generally sharply contradistinguished from "republic." For additional positive invocations of "democracy" and "democratic" ideals, and/or general equations of the words "republic" and "democracy," see Amar, *America's Constitution*, 16–17, 276–79; Gordon S. Wood, *Empire of Liberty: A History of the Early Republic, 1789–1815* (2011), 220, 223, 285, 288, 331, 350, 429, 718.

30. *Elliot's Debates*, 3:75 (June 6).

31. Ibid., 123 (June 7).

32. Ibid., 197 (June 10) (emphasis added).

33. Ibid., 603 (June 24).

34. "Be assured," Richmond's Anti-Federalist delegate James Monroe wrote Jefferson on July 12, Washington's "influence carried this government." See generally Larson, *Return of George Washington*, 179–233 (including chapter aptly titled "Ratifying Washington").

35. On the New York ratification contest more generally, see Maier, *Ratification*, 320–400.

36. On the parades, see Amar, *America's Constitution*, 10; Maier, *Ratification*, 393–95.

37. *Elliot's Debates*, 2:412 (July 23–24).

38. Alexander Hamilton, "First Speech of July 24," NAFO.

39. *Daily Advertiser* (New York), 7-28-1788; *New-York Packet*, 7-29-1788; *Pennsylvania Packet*, 7-30-1788; *Independent Gazetteer* (Philadelphia, with circulation in New Jersey and Delaware), 7-31-1788; *New-York Journal*, 7-31-1788; *Pennsylvania Mercury*, 7-31-1788; *Massachusetts Gazette*, 8-5-1788; *Essex Journal* (Newburyport, with circulation in New Hampshire), 8-6-1788; *New-Haven Gazette*, 8-7-1788; *Newport Herald*, 8-7-1788; *United States Chronicle* (Providence), 8-7-1788; *Connecticut Gazette*, 8-8-1788; *City Gazette* (Charleston, South Carolina), 8-11-1788; *Norfolk and Portsmouth Journal* (Virginia, with circulation in North Carolina), 8-13-1788; *Cumberland Gazette* (Portland), 8-14-1788. For coverage of earlier speeches by Jay and Hamilton to the same effect, see *Daily Advertiser* (New York), 7-16-1788; *New-York Journal*, 7-17-1788; *New-York Morning-Post*, 7-17-1788; *Albany Journal*, 7-21-1788; *Massachusetts Centinel*, 7-23-1788; *Massachusetts Gazette*, 7-25-1788; *Independent Chronicle* (Boston), 7-24-1788; *New Hampshire Gazette*, 7-24-1788; *Massachusetts Spy*, 7-24-1788; Maryland *Journal*, 7-25-1788; *Salem Mercury*, 7-29-1788; *Essex Journal*, 7-30-1788; *United States Chronicle*, 7-31-1788; *Freeman's Oracle* (Exeter), 8-2-1788.

40. The final count was 30–27. *Elliot's Debates*, 2:413 (July 26). Had any yes voter switched to a no, the tally would have been 29–28; the chair could then have cast a tie-making (not tie-breaking) vote. Had the chair, Anti-Federalist governor George Clinton, voted no, the motion to ratify the Constitution would have failed by a tie vote, 29–29.

41. See generally Akhil Reed Amar, *The Law of the Land* (2015), 3–28.

42. In Massachusetts: Samuel Nasson pointed to the Preamble as proof that the Constitution would effect a "perfect consolidation of the whole Union" that would "destroy" the Bay State's status as "a sovereign and independent" entity. *Elliot's Debates*, 2:134 (Feb. 1). Samuel Adams likewise got the message: "I meet with a National Government instead of a Federal Union of Sovereign States." Letter to R. H. Lee, Dec. 3, 1787. Pseudonymous Anti-Federalist essayist "John De Witt" made the same point by stressing Article V, whose rules for amendment

obviously precluded unilateral change by the people of any given state. "John De Witt (II)," reprinted in *DHRC Digital*, 4:156.

In Virginia: Patrick Henry clearly understood the stakes and explained them in vivid detail: "The fate . . . of America may depend on this. . . . Have they made a proposal of a compact between the states? If they had, this would be a confederation. It is otherwise most clearly a consolidated government. The question turns, sir, on that poor little thing—the expression, We, the *people*, instead of the *states*, of America." If "the states be not the agents of this compact, it must be one great, consolidated, national government, of the people of all the states." This difference, Henry warned, would severely limit the rights of future Virginians to act on their own: "Suppose the people of Virginia should wish to alter their government; can a majority of them do it? No; because they are connected with other men, or, in other words, consolidated with other states. . . . This government is not a Virginian, but an American government." Because the Revolution had made Virginia free and independent, the proposed Constitution was "a resolution as radical as that which separated us from Great Britain." *Elliot's Debates*, 3:44, 22, 55 (June 4–5).

In New York: The influential "Federal Farmer" warned that when a state populace "shall adopt the proposed constitution, it will be their *last* and supreme act" qua sovereign. "Letters of a Federal Farmer (IV)," reprinted in *DHRC Digital*, 19:232. New York's "Brutus" complained that the Constitution would not be "a compact" among states but rather would create a "union of the people of the United States considered" as "one great body politic." "Essays of Brutus (XII)," reprinted in *DHRC Digital*, 20:758–59. A similar view was expressed by another New York Anti-Federalist (perhaps Governor George Clinton) in "Letters of Cato (II)," reprinted in *DHRC Digital*, 19:82.

In Maryland: Luther Martin advised his audience of the strongly nationalist logic of the Constitution's Treason Clause, which made allegiance to the United States paramount over allegiance to a single state in the event of armed conflict between the two. *Farrand's Records*, 3:158–59, 223 (Nov. 29, 1787, reprinted in multiple publications in multiple states in early 1788; see *DHRC Digital*, 11:270).

In Pennsylvania: See *DHRC Digital*, 2:630 ("The Address and Reasons of Dissent of the Minority of the Convention of the State of Pennsylvania to Their Constituents"); ibid., 393, 407–8, 447–48 (Whitehill, Smilie, Findley).

43. Of course, the union as a whole could choose to dismember itself using Article V or some other proper procedure that involved all the states—a Congressional statute or a treaty, perhaps. The claim here is that no single state may *unilaterally* secede at will. Analogously, Scotland and England enacted a perfect union in 1707, but in 2014 the British government—the government of the union as a whole—opted to allow a Scottish referendum on secession. For more discussion, including pointed refutation of a 2020 book that preposterously claims that

"no state would have joined the Union had its citizens not believed that such a [unilateral secession] right was necessarily implied," see *AW*.

44. Beyond the items quoted or paraphrased earlier in this chapter, a few other important statements on this issue deserve special mention.

In New York: Hamilton/Publius in *The Federalist* No. 11 explicitly spoke of the need for a "strict and indissoluble" union.

In Pennsylvania: Wilson contradistinguished traditional "confederacies," which he said historically "have all fallen to pieces," with the proposed Constitution, in which "the bonds of our union" would be "indissolubly strong." *Elliot's Debates*, 2:463 (Dec. 4–6). (Wilson was an émigré from Scotland.) Thomas McKean declared that the Philadelphia plan "unites the several states, and makes them like one, in particular instances and for particular purposes—which is what is ardently desired by most of the sensible men in this country." Ibid., 2:540.

In North Carolina: Governor Samuel Johnston declared that "the Constitution must be the supreme law of the land; otherwise, it would be in the power of any one state to counteract the other states, and withdraw itself from the Union." Ibid., 4:187 (July 29). (Johnston, too, was an émigré from Scotland.)

In Virginia: The eminent legal scholar George Wythe explained the stakes by blending language from the Declaration (which he had signed in 1776) and the Preamble: "To perpetuate the blessings of freedom, happiness, and independence," he said, Americans must form "a firm, indissoluble union of the states" and thereby avoid "the extreme danger of dissolving the Union." Ibid., 3:586–87 (June 24).

45. *Farrand's Records*, 2:666–67 (Sept. 17) (emphasis added).

46. On the increased size of the newly independent state assemblies compared to colonial assemblies, and the democratic significance of these increases, see Jackson Turner Main, "Government by the People: The American Revolution and the Democratization of the Legislatures," *WMQ* 23 (1966): 391; Gordon S. Wood, *The Creation of the American Republic* (1969), 167; Amar, *America's Constitution*, 59, 77 & n*; Wood, *Empire of Liberty*, 16, 34; Alan Taylor, *American Revolutions: A Continental History, 1750–1804* (2016), 355, 357–58.

In 1791, Parliament for the first time authorized elected assemblies in Canadian provinces, but sharply limited their size—guaranteeing only sixteen members for all of Upper Canada and fifty members for all of Lower Canada. Constitutional Act, 31 George III, c. 31, sec. XVII (1791). Each province was also saddled with a royally appointed governor and a life-tenured appointed council that doubled as the legislative upper house—all subject, of course, to a hereditary British monarch and British Parliamentary sovereignty.

47. See *Farrand's Records*, 1:568–69 (Madison, July 10), 2:553–54 (Madison and Hamilton, Sept. 8).

48. See Amar, *America's Constitution*, 76–84; Akhil Reed Amar, *The Bill of Rights: Creation and Reconstruction* (1998), 10–14.

49. *Farrand's Records*, 3:260 (Strong, Jan. 18, 1788); *Elliot's Debates*, 3:11–12 (Nicholas, June 4, 1788, borrowing "take it for granted" phraseology directly from Madison/Publius); ibid., 2:238–39, 251–53 (Hamilton, June 20–21, 1788). See also supra p. 747n28 (citing letters arranging for Madison to furnish Nicholas and other Richmond Federalist delegates multiple copies of *The Federalist* as a debaters' handbook).

50. Ibid., 3:46 (June 5, 1788).

51. *Farrand's Records*, 2: 587–88 (Sept. 12).

52. See especially James Wilson, "Speech in State House Yard," Oct. 6, 1788.

53. For the best discussion of this deep theoretical problem, see Gary Rosen, *American Compact: James Madison and the Problem of the Founding* (1999).

54. *Elliot's Debates*, 2:102 (Jan. 25) (emphasis added).

55. For a detailed list of newspaper editions reprinting Singletary's comments, see *AW*.

CHAPTER SEVEN: WASHINGTON

1. The opening reference here is to a famous anecdote involving Benjamin Franklin at the end of the Philadelphia Convention. A lady—likely the prominent socialite Elizabeth Powel—asked Dr. Franklin, "Well, Doctor what have we got, a republic or a monarchy?" "A republic," replied Franklin, "if you can keep it." *Farrand's Records*, 3:85.

2. The eight Philadelphia Convention alumni present at the outset of the first House were Georgia's Abraham Baldwin, Maryland's Daniel Carroll, Pennsylvania's George Clymer and Thomas Fitzsimons, Massachusetts's Elbridge Gerry (who had refused to sign the Constitution on the Convention's last day), New Hampshire's Nicholas Gilman, Virginia's James Madison, and Connecticut's Roger Sherman. When North Carolina rejoined the union, Philadelphia delegate Hugh Williamson joined the first House. In the first Senate, the eleven Philadelphia alumni were Delaware's Richard Bassett, South Carolina's Pierce Butler, Connecticut's Oliver Ellsworth, Georgia's William Few, Connecticut's William Samuel Johnson, New Hampshire's John Langdon, New York's Rufus King (who had represented Massachusetts in Philadelphia), Pennsylvania's Robert Morris, New Jersey's William Paterson, Delaware's George Read, and Massachusetts's Caleb Strong. On the overall balance between Federalists and Antis, see Stanley Elkins and Eric McKitrick, *The Age of Federalism* (1993), 33; Gordon S. Wood, *Empire of Liberty: A History of the Early Republic, 1789–1815* (2011), 53; Fergus M.

Bordewich, *The First Congress: How James Madison, George Washington, and a Group of Extraordinary Men Invented the Government* (2016), 11.

3. The Constitution had itemized, in north-south order, the number of House seats each state could initially claim until a proper census could take place. New Hampshire got three seats; Massachusetts, eight; Rhode Island, one; Connecticut, five; New York, six; New Jersey, four; Pennsylvania, eight; Delaware, one; Maryland, six; Virginia, ten; North Carolina, five; South Carolina, five; and Georgia, three—sixty-five seats in all. Because Rhode Island and North Carolina had yet to join the new Constitution, the House began with fifty-nine authorized seats, and the Senate with twenty-two—two for each state in the new union. The Electoral College system created by Article II entitled each state to select a number of presidential electors equal to its House plus Senate apportionment. Thus, New Hampshire could choose five electors; Massachusetts, ten; and so on. The fifty-nine House seats plus twenty-two Senate seats added up to eighty-one Electoral College seats. Only sixty-nine presidential electors participated in the first presidential selection because New York failed to select its allotted electors in timely fashion and Virginia and Maryland submitted fewer ballots than allotted.

4. For details, see Akhil Reed Amar, *America's Constitution: A Biography* (2005), 219 & n*, 574n27. Note that one (rather obscure) Supreme Court confirmee, Maryland's Robert Harrison, declined to serve and was quickly replaced by a prominent North Carolina Federalist, James Iredell. In addition to Jay and Wilson, the other members of the Supreme Court at the launch were South Carolina's John Rutledge, Massachusetts's William Cushing, and Virginia's John Blair. Each of the first six justices on the Court had played a key role in the ratification process, voting yes as a delegate in his respective state convention. Additionally, Wilson, Rutledge, and Blair had helped draft the Constitution and had signed it at Philadelphia.

5. Address by Charles Thompson, April 14, 1789 (Washington Papers, presumably delivered verbally to George Washington at Mount Vernon), NAFO.

6. *New-York Daily Gazette*, 4-7-1789; *New-York Weekly Museum*, 4-11-1789; *Massachusetts Centinel*, 4-11-1789.

7. GW to JM, March 30, 1789. On the draft inaugural address, see "Editorial Note," NAFO ("By early 1789 . . .").

8. In a candid letter of Oct. 3, 1788, to his once and future aide Alexander Hamilton, Washington asked, "If the friends to the Constitution conceive that my administering the government will be a means of its acceleration and strength, is it not probable that the adversaries of it may entertain the same ideas? and of course make it an object of opposition?"

9. Diary entry, April 16, 1789, NAFO; Address to the Mayor, Corporation, and Citizens of Alexandria, April 16, 1789.

10. Address to the Citizens of Baltimore, April 17, 1789, NAFO; Address to the President and Faculty of Princeton College and the Inhabitants of Princeton, April 21–22, 1789, NAFO.

11. On Washington's extraordinary diplomatic vision and skill, see Edmund S. Morgan, *The Meaning of Independence* (1976), 46–52; Edmund S. Morgan, *The Genius of George Washington* (1980), 14–15; Garry Wills, *Cincinnatus: George Washington and the Enlightenment* (1984), 93–94. This geostrategic acumen was particularly on display in a highly confidential letter the general sent to Congress president Henry Laurens, on Nov. 14, 1778, explaining why it would be folly to invite French ground troops into Canada in support of Americans, as some short-sighted men in Congress seemed inclined to do.

12. TJ to JM, Feb. 14, 1783.

13. Thomas Hobbes, *Leviathan* (1651), chap. 13.

14. For representative examples, see Amar, *America's Constitution*, 162–63.

15. *JCC*, 2:92 (June 16, 1775).

16. For crisp summaries, see Edward J. Larson, *The Return of George Washington: Uniting the States, 1783–1789* (2015), 3–24; Edward J. Larson, *Franklin & Washington: The Founding Partnership* (2020), 136–62.

17. See generally Wills, *Cincinnatus*.

18. Undelivered First Inaugural Address: Fragments, April 30, 1789, NAFO.

19. "Federal Farmer XIV," reprinted in *DHRC Digital*, 20:325, 330 (May 2, 1788).

20. *Independent Gazetteer*, 9-26-1787 (Philadelphia), reprinted in *DHRC Digital*, 2:138, 140 (Tench Coxe, "An American Citizen I").

21. Elkins and McKitrick, *The Age of Federalism*, 45; Richard Brookhiser, *Founding Father: Rediscovering George Washington* (1996), 111–12.

22. On Sharp's honorary degree, see Gordon S. Wood, *The Purpose of the Past: Reflections on the Uses of History* (2008), 299–300; Wood, *Empire of Liberty*, 521; Terry L. Meyers, "Thinking About Slavery at the College of William and Mary," *William & Mary Bill of Rights Journal* 21 (2013): 1215. On Virginia's slave policies more generally, see William M. Wiecek, *The Sources of Antislavery Constitutionalism in America, 1760–1848* (1977), 60–61, 90–91.

23. Wiecek, *Sources*, 144–48.

24. A computer word search of the comprehensive materials compiled by the Documentary History of the Ratification project generates 109 distinct references to "eastern states" compared to 66 mentions of "northern states." A similar global word search of the nearly 200,000 items in the NAFO database identifies 876 items discussing "eastern states" and only 393 using the phrase "northern states."

25. Rosemarie Zagarri, *The Politics of Size* (1987), 8–60, 151; Gordon S. Wood, *The American Revolution: A History* (2002), 140–41; Wood, *Empire of Liberty*, 16.

26. Adams Diary, Sept. 1774, NAFO.

27. See supra p. 749n42.

28. On Washington's western lands and canal plans, see generally Larson, *Return of George Washington*, 32–65. On Jefferson and the Shenandoah, see Dumas Malone, *Jefferson the President: First Term, 1801–1805* (1970), 241; Wood, *Empire of Liberty*, 357.

29. GW to Lund Washington, Aug. 20, 1775.

30. He had spent several weeks traveling through and attempting to learn about the Northeast in June 1784, prior to his voyage to France.

31. Wood, *Empire of Liberty*, 165.

32. See generally Edward E. Baptist, *The Half Has Never Been Told: Slavery and the Making of American Capitalism* (2016); Wood, *Empire*, 508–14.

33. See supra pp. 215–16.

34. On Yorktown, see letter to Brigadier General Thomas Nelson Jr., Sept. 2, 1777.

35. Wood, *Empire of Liberty*, 472.

36. On pumping, see, e.g., GW to Henry Knox, Dec. 26, 1786: "I am exceedingly obliged to you for [your information and assessments]; & pray you, most ardently, to continue [them]."

37. Edmund S. Morgan, *Benjamin Franklin* (2002), 120.

38. See Amar, *America's Constitution*, 312n*; Robert A. Feer, "Shays's Rebellion and the Constitution," *NEQ* 42 (1969): 388, 390, 397–98, 401–2, 409–10; Forrest McDonald, *E Pluribus Unum: The Formation of the American Republic*, 2nd ed. (1979), 243, 256; Forrest McDonald, *States' Rights and the Union: Imperium in Imperio, 1776–1876* (2000), 15.

39. Pauline Maier, *The Old Revolutionaries: Political Lives in the Age of Samuel Adams* (1980), 31.

40. GW to JM, Nov. 5, 1786. On the deep social and cultural issues of honor, rectitude, and status implicated by certain types of debtor relief, as Washington and like-minded gentlemen saw things, see Gordon S. Wood, "Interests and Disinterestedness in the Making of the Constitution," in *The Idea of America: Reflections on the Birth of the United States* (2011), 164–67; "Illusions of Power in the Awkward Era of Federalism," in ibid., 264–65.

41. GW to JM, Nov. 5, 1786.

42. Ibid.

43. GW to Knox, Dec. 26, 1786. The June 9, 1787, issue of the *New-Hampshire Spy* told readers that Shays had recently visited British Montreal and had returned with a "considerable quantity" of gunpowder, and that British officials there were strengthening and preparing their military for possible action. For extensive documentation of the widespread view in the late 1780s that Canada and Britain

were backing Shays, or at least hoping that he would succeed and preparing to take advantage of the ensuing disruption, see *DHRC Digital*, 13:71 (Headnote on "American Fear of British Domination, New York Journal 15 March [1787]"). For more general discussion of the British-Canadian and geostrategic aspects of Shays' Rebellion, see Frederick W. Marks III, *Independence on Trial: Foreign Affairs and the Making of the Constitution* (1975), xi–xiv, 102–5. Cf. Alan Taylor, *American Revolutions: A Continental History, 1750–1804* (2016), 336 ("By keeping the [northwestern military] posts and cultivating Indian allies, the British also wanted to be in a strong position for the anticipated collapse of the American union").

44. On Washington as the great listener at Philadelphia, see Elkins and McKitrick, *The Age of Federalism*, 44–45.

45. For a long list of newspaper editions mentioning Washington in 1754, see *AW*.

46. JA to John Taylor of Caroline, June 9, 1814. For a similar counterfactual dripping with envy and delusional egotism, see JA to John Randolph Jr., circa 1815 or 1816 ("The Name of John Adams was so much respected in Virginia, that had John Adams lived in Virginia, and George Washington in Massachusetts, the former would have had the unanimous Votes of Virginia to be President of the United States").

47. To be sure, he was a Fairfax in-law.

48. Larson, *Franklin & Washington*, 10.

49. On Hamilton's first big break, see Ron Chernow, *Alexander Hamilton* (2004), 36–38. On his brilliant collegiate journalism, see ibid., 58–72, esp. at 70. On the intertwined threads that eventually made him Washington's de facto chief of staff and literary alter ego, see ibid., 72–92.

50. See the *National Gazette* entries in the Madison Papers, available on the NAFO website, for Nov. 19, 1791; Dec. 3, 12, 19, 31, 1791; Jan. 18, 23, 28, 31, 1792; Feb. 4, 18, 1792; March 3, 20, 27, 31, 1792.

51. See Noah Feldman, *The Three Lives of James Madison: Genius, Partisan, President* (2017), 62–67.

52. Adams began publishing anonymous pieces in the *Boston Gazette* no later than 1765. See his series "A Dissertation on the Canon and Feudal Law," which appeared in the *Gazette* issues of Aug. 12 and 19, Sept. 20, and Oct. 21.

53. See *DHRC Digital*, 13:337–38 (editorial note on Wilson's Pennsylvania State House Yard speech of Oct. 6, 1787); ibid., 14:206–7 (editorial note on Wilson's ratification convention speech of Nov. 24, 1787).

54. On Washington's encouragement and assistance, see Larson, *Return of George Washington*, 191, 207; GW to David Stuart, Oct. 17, 1787; AH to GW, Oct. 20, 1787; GW to AH, Nov. 10, 1787; JM to GW, Nov. 18, 1787; JM to GW, Nov. 30, 1787; GW to David Stuart, Nov. 30, 1787; GW to JM, Dec. 7, 1787.

55. *The American Minerva*, 12-9-1793 (maiden edition). The Philadelphia-based *Pennsylvania Packet*, founded as a weekly in 1771, became America's first viable daily in 1784, proudly adding the words *Daily Advertiser* to its masthead on Sept. 21, the precise moment of transition. In later incarnations, the *Packet* became *Dunlap's American Daily Advertiser* (1791), *Dunlap and Claypoole's American Daily Advertiser* (1793), and *Claypoole's American Daily Advertiser* (1796). Several other fledgling dailies also flaunted their astonishing publication frequency in their very names, including the Manhattan-based *Daily Advertiser*, founded in 1785; the affiliated *New-York Morning Post and Daily Advertiser*, founded as a semiweekly in 1782 and rebranding itself as a daily in 1785; and the *New-York Daily Gazette*, founded in 1788.

56. Undelivered First Inaugural Address, April 30, 1789, NAFO; GW to AH, Aug. 28, 1788.

57. The First Congress would reject this self-sacrificing offer, insisting on a proper presidential salary, so that the office would remain realistically open to men of moderate means who could otherwise not afford to serve. For details, see Amar, *America's Constitution*, 181.

58. A key passage of Washington's first draft strongly foreshadowed his final version: "Certain propositions for taking measures to obtain explanations & amendments on some articles of the Constitution, with the obvious intention of quieting the minds of the good people of these United States, will come before you & claim a dispassionate consideration. Whatever may not be deemed incompatible with the fundamental principles of a <free> & efficient government ought to be done for the accomplishment of so desirable an object. . . . I will barely suggest, whether it would not be the part of prudent men to observe it [the Constitution] fully in movement, before they undertook to make such alterations, as might prevent a fair experiment of its effects?—and whether, in the meantime, it may not be practicable for this Congress (if their proceedings shall meet with the approbation of three fourths of the Legislatures) in such manner to secure to the people all their justly-esteemed priviledges as shall produce extensive satisfaction?" Undelivered First Inaugural Address, NAFO.

According to the editors of Washington's papers (see supra p. 752n7), this draft was evidently composed "sometime before" January 2—that is, *before* Madison publicly came out in favor of a bill of rights. See infra p. 757n59. Here, too, the conventional view pushed by modern Madisonians (see, e.g., Feldman, *Three Lives*, 263) needs revising: the Bill of Rights was Washington's idea as much as it was Madison's.

59. JM to George Eve, Jan. 2, 1789; JM to Thomas Mann Randolph, Jan. 13, 1789, reprinted in *Virginia Independent Chronicle*, 1-28-1789; JM to a Resident of

Spotsylvania County, Jan. 27, 1789, reprinted in *Virginia Herald*, 1-29-1789. See Pauline Maier, *Ratification: The People Debate the Constitution, 1787–1788* (2010), 440–64.

60. For more discussion and analysis, see Amar, *America's Constitution*, 315–19 and accompanying endnotes.

61. See Donald S. Lutz, "The States and the U.S. Bill of Rights," *Southern Illinois University Law Journal* 16 (1992): 251; Steven G. Calabresi, Sarah E. Agudo, and Kathryn L. Dore, "State Bills of Rights in 1787 and 1791: What Individual Rights Are Really Deeply Rooted in American History and Tradition?," *Southern California Law Review* 85 (2012): 1451. Some of these state constitutional and ratifying convention provisions had roots in older texts, such as the English Bill of Rights of 1689 and interpretations (not always historically accurate) of Magna Carta.

62. *Annals*, 1:784 (Aug. 17, 1789).

63. For more on the bill's textual sequence, see Akhil Reed Amar, *The Bill of Rights: Creation and Reconstruction* (1998), 36–37.

64. James K. Hosmer, *The Life of Thomas Hutchinson* (1896), 132–33; Bernard Bailyn, *The Ordeal of Thomas Hutchinson* (1974), 197–99; Neil L. York, "Tag Team Polemics: The 'Centinel' and His Allies in the 'Massachusetts Spy,'" *Proceedings of the Massachusetts Historical Society* 107 (1995): 85.

65. Act of April 14, 1792, 1 Stat. 253. Why, we might wonder, did Congress's first amendment fail? Ten states said yes—one state shy of the eleven that were needed and that did say yes to the amendments that became America's Bill of Rights. The difference was Delaware, which said yes to the rest of the Bill of Rights but no to the House-size amendment. As the least populous state in the union, perhaps Delaware did not mind a small House. Given that each state would always get at least one representative, Delaware might have preferred Patrick Henry's nightmare hypothetical of a House in which each state had one member—a hypothetical making tiny Delaware and mighty Virginia equal in both Congressional chambers! Congress's original first amendment also had a technical glitch that may have discouraged other states from saying yes. Rushing to get an amendment package out the door before its first major adjournment, Congress in its haste had not noticed that the amendment's rules for early House growth clashed with its final clause (added at the eleventh hour) governing mature House size. For details of the proposed amendment's odd math, See Akhil Reed Amar, *The Bill of Rights: Creation and Reconstruction* (1998), 15–16.

66. Act of Jan. 14, 1802, 2 Stat. 128; Act of Dec. 21, 1811, 2 Stat. 669.

CHAPTER EIGHT: HAMILTON

1. Jack N. Rakove, *Original Meanings: Politics and Ideas in the Making of the Constitution* (1996), 297–302.

2. *Georgia v. Brailsford*, 3 U.S. (3 Dall.) 1, 4 (1794) (punctuation modernized; emphasis altered).

3. Act of March 23, 1792, 1 Stat. 243.

4. See the circuit judges' pronouncements as reported in *Hayburn's Case*, 2 U.S. (2 Dall.) 409, 410–14 (1792).

5. Act of Feb. 28, 1793, 1 Stat. 324.

6. *Farrand's Records*, 2:150, 152 (Committee of Detail drafts V and VI); Akhil Reed Amar, *America's Constitution: A Biography* (2005), 505n3.

7. Charles Warren, *The Supreme Court in United States History*, rev. ed. (1926), 1:100–101.

8. In full the amendment read as follows: "The judicial power of the United States shall not be construed to extend to any suit in law or equity, commenced or prosecuted against one of the United States by citizens of another state, or by citizens or subjects of any foreign state." For analysis of how and why this amendment left federal jurisdiction wholly intact in cases arising under substantive federal law—say, a federal statute or treaty, or the federal Constitution itself—see Amar, *America's Constitution*, 597–98n29.

9. In *Erie*, the Court said that unless substantive federal law applied, substantive state law, whether statutory or judge-fashioned, should apply in full force in federal courts, and that federal courts should follow state-law principles (such as ordinary contract law) *as state judges routinely apply those principles*. The *Chisholm* justices had not done this; the Eleventh Amendment solved the problem by returning certain state-law cases back to state courts, thus cutting the officious federal justices out of the loop.

10. Congress's Carriage Tax Law of 1794 built upon a recommendation made by Hamilton in his Nov. 30, 1792, Report on the Redemption of Public Debt. See generally Julius Goebel Jr. and William H. Smith, eds., *The Law Practice of Alexander Hamilton: Documents and Commentaries* (1980), 4:300.

11. 1 Stat. 373, 374 (June 4, 1794).

12. William Bradford to AH, July 2, 1795. On Hamilton as the inspiration for the law, see ibid.; see also supra p. 758n10. On Madison, see *Annals*, 4:730 (May 29, 1794) ("Mr MADISON objected to this tax on carriages as an unconstitutional tax; and as an unconstitutional measure, he would vote against it").

13. John Griffith McRee, *Life and Correspondence of James Iredell* (1857–1858), 2:461–62.

14. Alexander Hamilton, *Works of Alexander Hamilton*, ed. Henry Cabot Lodge (1904), 8:378–83.

15. *Farrand's Records*, 2:350 (Aug. 20).

16. Amar, *America's Constitution*, 93–95.

17. *Annals*, 1:1243 (remarks of Abraham Baldwin, Feb. 12, 1790).

18. Amar, *America's Constitution*, 95, 613–14n6.

19. McRee, *James Iredell*, 2:461–62.

20. *Farrand's Records*, 3:628.

21. The Court was short-staffed—only four justices sat on the case. Justice Wilson, who had heard the case below, simply announced that "my sentiments, in favor of the constitutionality of the tax in question, have not been changed."

22. On Madison as the "first man" of the first House, see Gordon S. Wood, *Empire of Liberty: A History of the Early Republic, 1789–1815* (2011), 61–62; Noah Feldman, *The Three Lives of James Madison: Genius, Partisan, President* (2017), 259.

23. Wood, *Empire of Liberty*, 92, 108; Ron Chernow, *Alexander Hamilton* (2004), 339.

24. Act of Sept. 2, 1789, 1 Stat. 65–66, sec. 2.

25. Gordon S. Wood, *Revolutionary Characters: What Made the Founders Different* (2006), 128–29; Wood, *Empire of Liberty*, 91–92. See also ibid., 91 ("Hamilton saw himself as a kind of prime minister to Washington's monarchical presidency").

26. *Annals*, 1:387 (May 19).

27. Indeed, in 1790, Congress provided by statute that even federal judges would automatically lose their seats in a bribery-conviction scenario. Strictly speaking, Article III gave judges tenure not for "life" but rather, technically, "during good behavior"; taking bribes feloniously was surely bad behavior; and ordinary criminal courtrooms provided more than sufficient due process for any accused bribe-taker. See Amar, *America's Constitution*, 222–23.

28. Akhil Reed Amar, *America's Unwritten Constitution: The Precedents and Principles We Live By* (2012), 567n13; Rakove, *Original Meanings*, 350.

29. *Annals*, 1:389 (May 19).

30. Ibid. (Jackson), 391 (White, May 19).

31. Ibid., 395–96 (May 19).

32. Similarly, even after the Senate has given its advice and consent to a proposed treaty, the president and the president alone decides whether to formally "ratify" the treaty on behalf of the United States. Washington himself waited several weeks after the Senate said yes to the Jay Treaty before formally activating the treaty. By symmetry with the Decision of 1789, presidents may in certain situations abrogate treaties without any Senate involvement. Presidents over the years have

indeed done just this—as when Jimmy Carter unilaterally decided to cease formal diplomatic recognition of Taiwan and thereby abrogated a US-Taiwan treaty. In both situations, even though the Senate participates in making (an appointment or a treaty), the president alone may unmake (an appointment or a treaty). See Amar, *America's Constitution*, 561–63n33.

33. *Annals*, 1:390 (Madison, May 19) ("He begged his colleague (Mr. BLAND) to consider the inconvenience his doctrine would occasion, by keeping the Senate constantly sitting, in order to give their assent to the removal of an officer; they might see there would be a constant probability of the Senate being called upon to exercise this power, consequently they could not be a moment absent").

34. It might be argued that the Article II Clause authorizing the president alone to *appoint* temporary officers during a Senate recess implicitly and by symmetry authorized the president alone to *suspend* officers during a Senate recess. But symmetry could instead be read merely to authorize a president to unilaterally fire *a recess appointee* who had been unilaterally hired, but no other appointee. These wrinkles illustrate that the principle of implied symmetry alone does not clearly resolve all issues of appointment and dis-appointment. Often, competing visions of symmetry are at play—for example, should firing be symmetric to the advice-and-consent process (the Bland position) or to the commission process (the ultimate 1789 Decision and the modern-day position)?

35. *Annals*, 1:392 (May 19).

36. GW to Elénor-François-Elie, Comte de Moustier, May 25, 1789 (emphasis added).

37. Cf. GW to James Anderson, May 22, 1798 ("I shall never relinquish the right of judging, in my own concerns").

38. *Annals*, 1:480–81. See also ibid., 514–21 (Madison remarks of June 17); JM to Edmund Randolph, May 31, 1789.

39. Edgar S. Maclay, ed., *Journal of William Maclay* (1890) (*Maclay's Journal* hereinafter), 111–17 (July 14–16).

40. Act of July 27, 1789, 1 Stat. 28, 29 (Secretary of Foreign Affairs—later renamed Secretary of State); Act of Aug. 7, 1789, 1 Stat. 49, 50 (Secretary of War); Act of Sept. 2, 1789, 1 Stat. 65, 67 (Secretary of Treasury); see also Act of Aug. 7, 1789, 1 Stat. 50, 53 (recognizing presidential removal power over territorial officers). See Saikrishna Prakash, "New Light on the Decision of 1789," *Cornell Law Review* 91 (2006): 1021; Amar, *America's Unwritten Constitution*, 320–21.

41. On the special precedential significance that early glosses were expected to have and have indeed had over the centuries, see *Annals*, 1:514 ("The decision that is at this time made, will become the permanent exposition of the constitution") (Madison, June 17, 1789). See generally Amar, *America's Unwritten Constitution*,

309–32. On Adams's role, see *Maclay's Journal*, 116 (July 16); Stanley Elkins and Eric McKitrick, *The Age of Federalism* (1993), 51–52.

42. Elkins and McKitrick, *The Age of Federalism*, 114–23.

43. JM to TJ, May 11, 1794 ("By breaking down the barriers of the constitution and giving sanction to the idea of sumptuary regulations, wealth may find a precarious defence in the shield of justice. If luxury, *as such*, is to be taxed, the greatest of all luxuries, says Payne [Paine], is a great estate."). See also JM to TJ, April 14, 1794; June 1, 1794.

44. See Feb. 9, 1787 Draft Tax Act, NAFO (proposing annual state taxes on "Every coach . . . Every Chariot . . . Phaetons & other 4 Wheeled Carriages . . . two Wheeled Carriages . . . [and] Pleasure slays"); Report of March 4, 1790, NAFO ("Carriages, such as Coaches, Chariots &c."); Draft of an Act Making Further Provision for the Payments of Debts of the United States, 1790, NAFO (proposing a 15 percent ad valorum tax on "coaches Chariots Phaetons Chaises chairs solos or other Carriages or parts of Carriages"). See also supra p. 758n10.

45. Wood, *Revolutionary Characters*, 130; Wood, *Empire of Liberty*, 152–53, 232–33.

46. Elkins and McKitrick, *The Age of Federalism*, 147.

47. Jefferson's Account of the Bargain on the Assumption and Residence Bills (1792?) ("The assumption of the state debts in 1790 . . ."), NAFO; Jefferson's Explanation of Three Volumes Bound in Marbled Paper (the so-called "Anas"), Feb. 4, 1818 ("Hamilton was in despair . . ."), NAFO. See also Fergus M. Bordewich, *The First Congress: How James Madison, George Washington, and a Group of Extraordinary Men Invented the Government* (2016), 243–48.

48. Cf. Richard Brookhiser, *James Madison* (2011), 16 (Madison named a nominal militia colonel in 1775, but he never fought). On Madison's misunderstandings of trade realities and related issues of public finance, fiscal policy, and capital markets, see Elkins and McKitrick, *The Age of Federalism*, 65–74, 138–45, 243, 376–77. In Hamilton's words, "Although [Madison] is a clever man, he is very little Acquainted with the world." Conversation with George Beckwith, Oct. 1789, NAFO. On Jefferson, too, as a financial illiterate, see Elkins and McKitrick, 243–44; for Adams, see supra p. 410. For more on Madison's unimpressiveness on issues of public finance and the like, see Bordewich, *First Congress*, 193.

49. Elkins and McKitrick, *The Age of Federalism*, 229.

50. Benjamin B. Klubes, "The First Federal Congress and the First National Bank: A Case Study in Constitutional Interpretation," *Journal of the Early Republic* 10 (1990): 19, 26–27.

51. *Annals*, 2:1791 (Jan. 20, 1791) (Hawkins, Izard, Butler, Few, Gunn).

52. The no votes were cast by Ashe (NC), Baldwin (GA), Bloodworth (NC), Brown (VA), Burke (SC), Carroll (MD), Contee (MD), Gale (MD), Giles (VA), Grout (MA), Jackson (GA), Lee (VA), Madison (VA), Mathews (GA), Moore (VA), Parker (VA), Stone (MD), Tucker (SC), White (VA), and Williamson (NC). *Annals*, 2:2012 (Feb. 9, 1791).

53. See Elkins and McKitrick, *The Age of Federalism*, 137.

54. *Annals*, 2:1944–52.

55. Elkins and McKitrick, *The Age of Federalism*, 226.

56. Spelling and punctuation altered.

57. In an anonymous 1795 pamphlet that showed that Madison had drifted from reality into his own constitutional fantasy world, he objected to the carriage tax as a "breach of the constitution; an objection insuperable in its nature, and which there is reason to believe, will be established by the judicial authority, if ever brought to that test." Political Observations, April 20, 1795, NAFO. See also JM to Edmund Pendleton, Feb. 7, 1796. As has been seen, in March 1796 the Supreme Court unanimously treated this constitutional claim as rubbish. Alas, the leading biography of Madison as a constitutionalist—Feldman, *Three Lives*—makes no mention of, and thus provides no analysis of, Madison's outlandish carriage-tax ideas, which Madison first expressed in Congress in 1794, reiterated repeatedly pre-*Hylton*, repeated again and prominently post-*Hylton* in 1798 (see infra p. 770n63), and then quietly abandoned in 1813 (see infra p. 772n76). Given Feldman's claim that Madison was America's greatest constitutionalist and given Feldman's own status as a constitutional scholar, the failure of *Three Lives* to even notice the carriage-tax issue is disappointing.

Additionally disappointing is Feldman's failure to even mention two other egregious constitutional lapses on Madison's part: Madison's disgraceful free-soil flip-flop in 1819–1820, and his quiet backing of his fellow Jeffersonians' repeal act of 1802, which purported to defrock and defund more than a dozen federal judges—a shocking violation of Article III judicial independence. See infra pp. 595–96, 774n25.

Feldman does not duck the issue of Madison's volte-face on the national bank. (The wily Virginian opposed it on constitutional grounds in 1791 and then signed it into law in 1816.) But Feldman does fail to present the reader with the best reasons for believing that Madison's initial constitutional position in 1791 was lame and that Madison's eventual reversal was self-serving and uncandid. Less significant, but still worth noting (as Feldman does not), is that in 1783 Madison favored continental assumption of state public debt and nondiscrimination among public creditors, but in 1790 he took the opposite stance. See Elkins and McKitrick, *The Age of Federalism*, 104, 137; Bordewich, *First Congress*, 191–92.

Feldman is right to see that Madison was a partisan as well as a genius, but wrong in the ratio between these two personae.

58. Elkins and McKitrick, *The Age of Federalism*, 90.

59. On increasing public attendance at and newspaper coverage of legislative debates, see Amar, *America's Constitution*, 82–83; Wood, *Empire of Liberty*, 17, 58–60.

60. *Maclay's Journal*, 129–31 (Aug. 22, 1789); John Quincy Adams, *Memoirs of John Quincy Adams*, ed. Charles Francis Adams (1875), 6:427 (diary entry of Nov. 10, 1824). See Amar, *America's Unwritten Constitution*, 329–30, 571n28.

61. On Virginia, see Elkins and McKitrick, *The Age of Federalism*, 26–27.

62. John Jay, James Wilson, John Blair, James Iredell, and William Paterson to GW, Aug. 8, 1793. On individual communication, see Wood, *Empire of Liberty*, 414.

63. GW to Samuel Huntington, Aug. 20, 1780; GW to Joseph Reed, May 28, 1780. See also GW to Joseph Jones, July 22, 1780.

64. GW to Joseph Reed, May 28, 1780.

65. Edmund S. Morgan, *The Genius of George Washington* (1980), 12. See GW to John Hancock, Feb. 18–21, 1776 ("The means used to conceal my Weakness from the Enemy conceals it also from our friends, and adds to their Wonder").

66. Wood, *Empire of Liberty*, 129–30.

67. According to Chief Mash-i-pi-nash-i-wish (Match-E-Be-Nash-She-Wish), "It was our father, the British, who urged us to bad deeds, and reduced us to our present state of misery. He persuaded us to shed all the blood we have spilled." Treaty of Greenville Minutes (July 22, 1795).

68. Cf. Elkins and McKitrick, *The Age of Federalism*, 126 (noting Washington's grasp of the "interconnectedness" of various factors).

69. GW to Edmund Pendleton, Jan. 22, 1795.

70. Garry Wills, *Cincinnatus: George Washington and the Enlightenment* (1984), 106.

71. GW to AH, July 10, 1787.

72. JA to Benjamin Rush, Nov. 11, 1806 ("Hamilton's project of raising an Army of fifty thousand Men, ten thousand of them to be Cavalry and his projects of Sedition Laws and Alien Laws and of new Taxes to Support his army, all arose from a superabundance of secretions which he could not find Whores enough to draw off. . . . [T]he Same Vapours produced his Lies and Slanders by which he totally destroyed his party forever and finally lost his Life in the field of honor."). Thus the 1798 Sedition Act—which Adams alone signed into law and then mindlessly overenforced—retroactively became in his mind Hamilton's project. Here

as elsewhere, old Adams lacked balance and self-awareness, rewriting history in a self-serving way.

73. JA to John Trumbull (the poet, not the artist), Nov. 18, 1805.

74. Hamilton's most celebrated reports were "Treasury papers on public credit, taxation, a national bank, and a program of government-encouraged manufactures." Elkins and McKitrick, *The Age of Federalism*, 23.

75. AH to Tobias Lear, Jan. 2, 1800. On Hamilton's pride, see Garry Wills, *Explaining America: The Federalist* (1982), 83–86.

76. In a stern letter of July 6, 1796, to Jefferson—the last letter he ever sent his former secretary of state, save a perfunctory note the following month—the president recalled that "there were as many instances within [your] *own* knowledge of my having decided *against,* as in *favor of* the opinions of the person evidently alluded to [Hamilton, Washington inferred]. . . . I was no believer in the infallibility of the politics, or measures of *any man living.*"

77. Morgan, *The Genius of George Washington*, 11–12; GW to Samuel Huntington, President of Congress, Aug. 20, 1780 ("For want of a force which the Country was completely able to afford," Washington's troops were "at Valley forge with less than half the force of the enemy—destitute of every thing," and "The Country ravaged—our Towns burnt—The Inhabitants plundered—abused—Murdered with impunity, from the same cause").

78. Gordon S. Wood, *The American Revolution: A History* (2002), 86–87.

79. GW to AH, March 31, 1783.

80. *The Continentalist* Nos. I, III (July 12 and Aug. 9, 1781).

81. GW to Edmund Randolph, April 9, 1787.

82. GW to AH, Oct. 3, 1788.

83. John Avlon, *Washington's Farewell: The Founding Father's Warning to Future Generations* (2017), 89–90.

CHAPTER NINE: ADAMS-JEFFERSON-MADISON

1. Friction with France in the late 1790s did force Adams—at Washington's insistence—to promote Hamilton into high military command. But no large army actually mobilized under Commander Washington or second-in-command Hamilton. In fact, Adams wisely eased military tensions, in part because he worried that Hamilton might become a dangerous wild card. On perceptions of Hamilton as Napoleonic, see Edward J. Larson, *A Magnificent Catastrophe: The Tumultuous Election of 1800, America's First Presidential Campaign* (2007), 71.

2. JA to AA, April 19, 1794. See also Madison's conversations with Washington ("Substance of a Conversation with the President," May 5–25, 1792, Washington Papers, NAFO).

3. On Jefferson and the Declaration, see, e.g., *Aurora General Advertiser*, 11-11-1795. For more on Jay and Hamilton, see *AW*.

4. "Novanglus VII," March 6, 1775, NAFO. On Greece and Rome, see also Allan Nevins, *The American States During and After the Revolution, 1775–1789* (1924), 26; Edmund S. Morgan, *The Meaning of Independence* (1976), 3; Jack P. Greene, *Peripheries and Center* (1986), 7–9.

5. Adams Diary, Oct. 18, 1775, NAFO.

6. In an addendum to his diary entry of Nov. 4, 1775, Adams wrote that his "Researches . . . undoubtedly contributed to produce the . . . Constitution of the United States. . . . They undoubtedly also contributed to the Writings of Publius, called the Federalist." In a July 20, 1807, missive to Mercy Otis Warren, Adams boasted that his 1787 book, *A Defence of the Constitutions of the United States of America*, "had such an Effect upon the [Philadelphia framers] that it united them in the System they adopted. . . . [M]y 'Defence' had produced the Constitution of the United States. . . . The general Principles and System of that Book were adopted by the Writers of Publius, or the Federalist."

But, to repeat, Publius never cited Adams. Most of Publius's best ideas—the geostrategic arguments of the early essays, Madison's provocative musings in *The Federalist* No. 10, Hamilton's analysis of taxation, the detailed meditations on specific patches of text drafted at Philadelphia, and much, much more—had nothing to do with Adams. As for Philadelphia, Adams's name appears only once in the most comprehensive modern compilation of the delegates' conversations: on June 27, Luther Martin noted that Adams had advocated a bicameral and tripartite system only for state governments, not the federal government. *Farrand's Records*, 1:439. Indeed, Adams had explicitly written that "a single assembly was every way adequate to the management of all their [Americans'] fœderal concerns; and with very good reason, because congress is not a legislative assembly, nor a representative assembly, but only a diplomatic assembly. A single council has been found to answer the purposes of confederacies very well." *Defence*, Letter LIII. This Adamsonian idea was emphatically repudiated at Philadelphia. In fact, Knox, Jay, and Madison had all recommended to Washington a bicameral and tripartite federal constitution in early 1787, before Adams's book reached America. Adams ultimately came to agree with Knox, Jay, Madison, Washington, Hamilton, and others about the basic system crafted at Philadelphia, but he was surely not its father. No major element of the Constitution was uniquely Adamsonian, and many major elements (e.g., biannual, quadrennial, and sextennial elections; perpetual reeligibility; a qualified veto; popular ratification) deviated from Adams's *Thoughts* and *Defence*. Madison contemporaneously told Jefferson that many of the "political principles avowed in" Adams's book were widely viewed as "obnoxious." JM to TJ, Oct. 17, 1788; see also JM to TJ, June 6, 1787 ("Men of learning find nothing

new in it. Men of taste many things to criticize."). Although the eminent historians Stanley Elkins and Eric McKitrick passingly credited Adams with "great
influence" at the grand Convention, *The Age of Federalism* (1993), 862n9, they
adduced no evidence from the Convention itself or its delegates. In the ratification essays and debates they cited, the sporadic invocations of Adams came from
opponents of the Constitution. Standing upon his father's writings, young John
Quincy Adams leaned Anti-Federalist. See his letter to William Cranch, Dec. 8,
1787, *DHRC Digital*, 14:226–28.

7. See JA to John Trumbull (the poet, not the artist), Nov. 18, 1805; JA to Benjamin Rush, Aug. 23, 1805 ("You rank Colonel Hamilton among the Revolutionary Characters. But why? The Revolution had its beginning its middle and its End
before he had any thing to do in public affairs. . . . I never knew that Such a Man
or Boy was in [General Washington's] Suite. . . . The Parts We acted from 1761
to 1776 were more difficult more dangerous and more disagreeable than all that
happened afterwards till the peace of 1783. I know therefore of no fair title that
Hamilton has to a revolutionary Character."). It is remarkable that Adams could
think it self-evident that his and Rush's roles were "more difficult and dangerous"
than that of a "Boy" soldier who endured winters at Valley Forge and Morristown
and led a bayonet charge at Yorktown. Cf. JA to Benjamin Rush, Dec. 4, 1805
("The Storming of a Redoubt by a Boy was to be the Coup de Theatre . . . to make
him afterwards Commander in Chief of the Army and President of Congress,
though there is no more qualification for either, in Storming a redoubt, than there
would have been in killing a Deer in the Woods"). See also JA to *Boston Patriot*,
1809 ("And pray what could this West India Boy just from Scotland . . . have known
any Thing of the first Stages of the Revolution? . . . The Revolution began before he
was born, and was compleated before he knew any Thing about it. It began in 1759
and was finished in 1774. Hamilton it is believed was not born in 1759 and was not
out of Colledge in 1774."). In fact, Hamilton was likely born in 1755, and the odd
claim that the Revolution was finished in 1774 seems designed merely to diminish
the "Boy" Hamilton, who was indeed a young prodigy in the 1770s and was in the
thick of Revolutionary resistance from 1774 on, even while still in college. And for
the record, Hamilton never set foot in Scotland; this, too, was one of Adams's recurrent tropes to belittle Hamilton and portray him as un-American. See, e.g., JA
to Henry Guest, Sept. 5, 1809 ("a West India Boy" and a "Scotch Boy"). For more
dismissive letters in this genre, see supra p. 722n74, infra p. 787n26.

8. AH to James Wilson, Jan. 25, 1789; Ron Chernow, *Alexander Hamilton*
(2004), 271–73; Fergus M. Bordewich, *The First Congress: How James Madison,
George Washington, and a Group of Extraordinary Men Invented the Government*
(2016), 33.

9. Gordon S. Wood, *Revolutionary Characters: What Made the Founders Different* (2006), 112–13, 135. See also JA to TJ, Nov. 15, 1813.

10. *Maclay's Journal*, 3 (April 25, 1789); JA to AA, Dec. 19, 1793.

11. David McCullough, *John Adams* (2001), 460.

12. Adams was occasionally consulted, sometimes individually, sometimes as part of a cabinet; see Andrew C. McLaughlin, *A Constitutional History of the United States* (1935), 245–46.

13. *Farrand's Records*, 2:536–37 (Sept. 7).

14. JM to TJ, Dec. 19, 1796; TJ to JM, Jan. 22, 1797.

15. TJ to JA, Dec. 28, 1796 (never delivered to Adams).

16. JM to TJ, Jan. 15, 1797. See also Chernow, *Alexander Hamilton* (2004), 509–11.

17. John Quincy Adams, *Memoirs of John Quincy Adams*, ed. Charles Francis Adams (1876), 8:272 (Jan. 12, 1831) (Jefferson had "a memory so pandering to the will, that in deceiving others he seems to have begun by deceiving himself").

18. Wood, *Revolutionary Characters*, 100–107.

19. Gordon S. Wood, *Empire of Liberty: A History of the Early Republic, 1789–1815* (2011), 277.

20. See generally Annette Gordon-Reed, *Thomas Jefferson and Sally Hemings: An American Controversy* (1997); Annette Gordon-Reed, *The Hemingses of Monticello: An American Family* (2008).

21. TJ to JM, Dec. 8, 1784.

22. JM to TJ, Jan. 22, 1786.

23. TJ to JA, Aug. 30, 1787.

24. TJ to John Wayles Eppes, June 24, 1813.

25. Wood, *Revolutionary Characters*, 100; Wood, *Empire of Liberty*, 278. See also Stanley Elkins and Eric McKitrick, *The Age of Federalism* (1993), 92 (Jefferson was "never able to live within his means").

26. Morgan, *The Meaning of Independence*, at 60: "He placed a higher value on collecting books and drinking good wine than he did on freeing his slaves."

27. JM to TJ, Oct. 24, 1787; TJ to JM, Dec. 20, 1787.

28. TJ to JM, Feb. 6, 1788.

29. TJ to JM, July 31, 1788.

30. Elkins and McKitrick, *The Age of Federalism*, 241–42; Chernow, *Alexander Hamilton*, 285–88; Richard Brookhiser, *James Madison* (2011), 99; Wood, *Empire of Liberty*, 109. In order to phase in properly staggered Senate terms, one-third of the senators in the First Congress initially served two-year terms, and one-third served four-year terms. Thereafter, the usual six-year cycle went into effect. In 1789, Schuyler had drawn the short term.

31. Robert Troup to AH, June 15, 1791.

32. JM to TJ, Oct. 9, 1792.

33. TJ to Thomas Mann Randolph Jr., May 15, 1791; TJ to JM, July 21, 1791; Philip Freneau to TJ, Aug. 4, 1791.

34. Notes of Cabinet Meeting on Edmond-Charles Genêt, Aug. 2, 1793 (Jefferson Papers, quoting Washington's outburst about "that rascal Freneau . . ."), NAFO; cf. Cabinet Meetings: Proposals Concerning the Conduct of the French Minister [Aug. 1–23, 1793] (Hamilton Papers editorial note referring to Freneau's broadside, "The Funeral Dirge of George Washington and James Wilson, King and Judge"), NAFO.

35. TJ to GW, Sept. 9, 1792.

36. "An American No. II," *Gazette of the United States*, 8-11-1792, also available in NAFO. See generally Elkins and McKitrick, *The Age of Federalism*, 285–86.

37. For a detailed list, see *AW*.

38. Writing as "Helvidius," in response to Hamilton's "Pacificus," Madison argued for a narrow interpretation of executive power. But Washington in fact had done precisely . . . nothing. He had simply publicly announced that under his reading of existing treaties, America need not and should not fight on France's side in a war that France had started. This was a sound legal position and an intelligent policy stance. Surely the executive had the power to construe treaties in the first instance. Surely the executive also acted properly in announcing its stance to the world and in admonishing individual Americans that any active effort on their part to aid either belligerent would lack the support of the American government and might place them in legal peril. Madison ended up twisting himself into knots to please Jefferson and assail Hamilton. If, as Madison himself said in the Decision of 1789 debate, the executive power vested in the president encompassed the power to oversee subordinate executive officials, it also sensibly encompassed the power to declare neutrality to the world. Madison/Helvidius stressed that a president could not unilaterally take the country into war, but Washington was doing no such thing. He was keeping the country at peace. (Hence Hamilton's nom de plume: *Pacificus*.) Just as the Senate had a role in appointing but not firing—as Madison had himself said in 1789—so, too, Congress might be needed to declare war, but not to declare peace.

Still bleeding from the drubbing that he had suffered in the Pacificus-Helvidius debate in 1793, Madison found himself unable to charge as instructed by his political field marshal in late 1795. Notably, Jefferson used almost identical language in seeking to enlist Madison in another journalistic joust: "For god's sake take up your pen, and give a fundamental reply to [Hamilton]." This time, the issue was the Jay Treaty, which Washington, encouraged by Hamilton, sensibly accepted, and which Hamilton, aided by Rufus King under the joint pen name

"Camillus," publicly championed in a detailed series of newspaper essays, "The Defence." As Hamilton understood and as Camillus helped his readers understand, Washington needed to play the long game as a prudent warrior and statesman. Time was on America's side. Every year that America avoided a fight was a year that America grew stronger. Increased trade with the British Empire would enrich American citizens and fatten the federal treasury (thanks to imposts). See especially *The Defence* No. II, July 25, 1795. (Seen in this light, Washington's patient peacetime strategy was an extension of his wartime Fabian strategy of avoiding battles that might destroy his army.) Jefferson was cockeyed, partly because of his hatred of the British, and partly because of his animus toward Hamilton, who had consistently bested him in cabinet debate and who was indeed a journalistic dynamo. As Jefferson noted ruefully elsewhere in his unavailing Sept. 21, 1795, missive to Madison, "Hamilton is really a colossus to the antirepublican party. . . . In truth, when he comes forward, there is nobody but yourself who can meet him." Actually, Madison was no match for Hamilton on national-security, international-law, diplomatic, military, executive-power, or tax-and-trade issues, and deep down he knew it. But later in the decade, Madison would be more than a match on an issue that he instinctively grasped far, far better than Hamilton: freedom of speech.

Note that the Neutrality Proclamation, standing alone, did not provide a sufficient basis for federal criminal prosecution. Congress later enacted a proper criminal statute to implement Washington's stance.

39. Elkins and McKitrick, *The Age of Federalism*, 336–41.

40. *House Executive Document* No. 162, 44th Cong., 1st Sess., p. 4 (May 4, 1876) (reckoning that President Adams was absent from the capital for "three hundred and eighty-five days").

41. See Elkins and McKitrick, *The Age of Federalism*, 74–75.

42. JA to TJ, June 30, 1813.

43. TJ to JM, Jan. 22, 1797.

44. Oliver Wolcott Sr. to Oliver Wolcott Jr., March 20, 1797.

45. Wood, *Empire of Liberty*, 238, 250–58.

46. Writing to her sister Mary on April 26, Abigail railed against "vile incendiaries" and fretted that "nothing will have a [salutary] effect until Congress pass a Sedition Bill." She thought "the wrath of public ought to fall upon [the] Heads" of opposition speakers and writers who by attacking her husband were "insult[ing] the Majesty of the Sovereign People" who had chosen John Adams. This was indeed one common view in the 1790s—but the wrong view, it is now clear—of popular sovereignty. John was a mere servant of the people, who at all times retained a broad right to chasten their servants, scold them, and indeed send them packing via elections and impeachments. In a follow-up on May 25, Abigail

confessed, "I wish the laws of our country were competent to punish the stirrer up of sedition." On Abigail's influence on John on the sedition issue, see McCullough, *John Adams*, 506–7.

47. Act of July 14, 1798, 1 Stat. 596.

48. William Blackstone, *Commentaries on the Laws of England*, 1st ed. (1769), 4:151–52.

49. TJ to JM, July 31, 1788.

50. *United Sates v. Hudson and Goodwin*, 11 U.S. (7 Cranch) 32, 34 (1812). The Judiciary Act of 1789 had not specified any elements of criminal misconduct or delimited the extent of permissible criminal punishment in its bland section 11, which merely conferred jurisdiction over crimes defined elsewhere in the federal criminal code. 1 Stat. 73, 78–79.

51. On Adams's personal involvement in Sedition Act prosecutions, see Saikrishna Prakash, "The Chief Prosecutor," *George Washington Law Review* 73 (2005): 521.

52. *Lyon's Case*, 15 F. Cas. 1183 (C.C.D. Vt. 1798) (No. 8,646); *Spooner's Vermont Journal*, 7-21-1798.

53. *Aurora General Advertiser*, 11-9-1798. For more newspapers, see *AW*.

54. *U.S. v. Cooper*, 25 F. Cas. 631 (C.C.D. Pa. 1800) (No. 14,865).

55. *U.S. v. Callender*, 25 F. Cas. 239 (C.C.D. Va. 1800) (No. 14,709).

56. James Morton Smith, *Freedom's Fetters: The Alien and Sedition Laws and American Civil Liberties* (1956); Geoffrey R. Stone, *Perilous Times: Free Speech in Wartime, from the Sedition Act of 1798 to the War on Terrorism* (2004), 33–78; Wood, *Empire of Liberty*, 260–61. For the most recent and eye-popping tally, see Wendell Bird, *Criminal Dissent: Prosecutions Under the Alien and Sedition Acts of 1798* (2020).

57. Granted, the judgment of the court of public opinion in 1800–1801 was skewed by the Three-Fifths Clause. For discussion of this important twist, see supra pp. 502–504, infra p. 781n2.

58. TJ to JM, March 15, 1789 (punctuation altered).

59. *Annals*, 1:457 (punctuation altered).

60. JM to TJ, Oct. 17, 1788; TJ to JM, March 15, 1789.

61. *Elliot's Debates*, 4:528–29 (emphasis added).

62. For a detailed list, see *AW*.

63. *Elliot's Debates*, 4:570–74. In passing, Madison could not resist doubling down on his earlier claims—that "the bank law" and "the carriage tax" exceeded Congress's proper enumerated powers. Ibid., 550. Analytically, these implausible claims did not improve with unelaborated repetition. In modern lingo, they were merely red meat for the base.

64. TJ to JM, Nov. 17, 1788.

65. Ibid.

66. TJ to Spencer Roane, Sept. 6, 1819 ("The revolution of 1800 . . . was as real a revolution in the principles of our government as that of 76").

67. When, late in his second term, Jefferson learned of efforts by federal officials in Connecticut to initiate federal common-law prosecutions for seditious libel against Federalists, he ordered dismissal of the charges. Charles Warren, *The Supreme Court in United States History*, rev. ed. (1926), 1:435–37; Charles Grove Haines, *The Role of the Supreme Court in American Government and Politics, 1789–1835* (1944), 306–7.

68. *United States v. Hudson and Goodwin*, 11 U.S. (7 Cranch) 32 (1812). Alas, in keeping with his states' rights approach, Jefferson encouraged Democratic-Republican state officials to initiate state prosecutions. But state sedition prosecutions contradicted Madison's arguments that the nature of republican government at both the federal and state levels required the broadest imaginable freedom of speech when citizens aimed to criticize public servants and "canvass[] the merits and measures of public men." Virginia Report of 1799–1800. In the 1780s, Jefferson had seemed to say similar things: "The people are the only censors of their governors. . . . The basis of our governments being the opinion of the people, . . . were it left to me to decide whether we should have a government without newspapers or newspapers without a government, I should not hesitate a moment to prefer the latter." TJ to Edward Carrington, Jan. 16, 1787. As president, he chose to side with newspapers. But he didn't mind when friendly governors did the dirty work of press suppression, so long as printers could introduce evidence of the truth of the underlying derogatory statements. As we have seen, this was not sufficient to protect a robust press. See also TJ to AA, July 22, 1804.

69. Dumas Malone, *Jefferson and the Ordeal of Liberty* (1962), 399–400 & n14.

70. Levi Lincoln to A. J. Dallas, March 25, 1801, cited in George Lee Haskins and Herbert A. Johnson, *Foundations of Power: John Marshall, 1801–15* (1981), 148–49.

71. Draft of Message to the Senate [Before Nov. 12., 1801], NAFO ("I caused it to be discontinued").

72. Fair Copy, First Annual Message, Nov. 27, 1801, NAFO. On Jefferson's eventual decision to omit this passage at the urging of advisers, see "Editorial Note, Drafting the Annual Message to Congress," NAFO; Noble E. Cunningham, *The Process of Government Under Jefferson* (1978), 75–76. For earlier statements, see TJ to William Duane, May 23, 1801; TJ to JM, July 19, 1801; TJ to Edward Livingston, Nov. 1, 1801; TJ to Albert Gallatin, Nov. 12, 1801.

73. TJ to AA, July 22, 1804.

74. Act of July 4, 1840, c. 45, 6 Stat. 802, accompanied by H.R. Rep. No. 86, 26th Cong., 1st sess. (March 5,1840); see also *Congressional Globe* (*CG* hereinafter),

26th Cong., 1st sess., 411 (May 23, 1840). For an earlier House report with similar language, see H.R. Rep. No. 491, 23rd Cong., 1st sess. (May 28, 1834), 2–3.

75. Act of April 6, 1802, 2 Stat. 148.

76. Act of July 24, 1813, 3 Stat. 40. The carriage-tax episode goes unmentioned in Noah Feldman, *The Three Lives of James Madison: Genius, President, Partisan* (2017), an important but, alas, imbalanced account of Madison as a constitutionalist.

77. Brookhiser, *James Madison*, 191–93, 212.

78. *McCulloch v. Maryland*, 17 U.S. 316, 402, 422–23 (1819).

79. On Jefferson, see Wood, *Empire of Liberty*, 514–15. On Madison, see Akhil Reed Amar, *America's Constitution: A Biography* (2005), 627n3.

80. See *Farrand's Records*, 1:289, 310 (June 18); ibid., 3:395–96, 617–30.

81. See TJ to GW, Sept. 9, 1792 (emphasis added).

82. For a detailed list, see *AW*.

CHAPTER TEN: JEFFERSON-MARSHALL

1. The last justice to depart for politics was James F. Byrnes in 1942. Justice Arthur Goldberg's decision to leave in 1965 was in contemplation of future judicial reappointment. On the ladder to today's Court, see Akhil Reed Amar, *The Law of the Land* (2015), 58–70.

2. TJ to AA, Sept. 11, 1804 (emphasis added).

3. Technically, Rutledge tied for fourth.

4. Act of March 1, 1792, sec. 9, 1 Stat. 239, 240. For the backstory, see John Feerick, *The Twenty-Fifth Amendment: Its Complete History and Applications*, rev. ed. (1992), 37–40. See also JA to John Quincy Adams, Dec. 24, 1804; JA to John Trumbull (the poet, not the artist), Nov. 18, 1805; JA, Review of James Hillhouse Propositions, April 12, 1808, NAFO.

5. See, e.g., AH to Oliver Wolcott Jr., Dec. (undated) and Dec. 16, 1800; AH to Theodore Sedgwick, Dec. 22, 1800; AH to Harrison Gray Otis, Dec. 23, 1800; AH to Gouverneur Morris, Dec. 24 and 26, 1800; AH to James A. Bayard, Dec. 27, 1800; AH to James Ross, Dec. 29, 1800; AH to James McHenry, Jan. 4, 1801; AH to John Rutledge Jr., Jan. 4, 1801; John Marshall to AH, Jan. 1, 1801. Cf. JA to William Tudor Sr., Dec. 13, 1800 ("Mr Hamilton has carried his Eggs to a fine Markett. The very Man the very two Men, of all the World, that he was most jealous of, are now placed over him.").

6. For a detailed list of newspapers printing and reprinting this essay, see *AW*.

7. Albert J. Beveridge, *The Life of John Marshall* (1916), 2:541–42 & n2; Bruce A. Ackerman, *The Failure of the Founding Fathers: Jefferson, Marshall, and the Rise of Presidential Democracy* (2005), 45–54.

8. James Monroe to TJ, Jan. 6 and 18, 1801. See also TJ to JM, Dec. 26, 1800.

9. TJ to James Monroe, Feb. 15, 1801; Dumas Malone, *Jefferson the President: First Term, 1801–1805* (1970), 7–11. See also TJ to Thomas McKean, March 9, 1801.

10. Long before the state ballots were unsealed, Burr wrote a Dec. 16 letter that seemed to say that he would "utterly disclaim all competition" with Jefferson in the "highly improbable" situation of a tie. The recipient, Maryland representative Samuel Smith, a Jefferson supporter, released the letter to newspapers, which widely reprinted it in early winter. *Federal Gazette* (Baltimore), 12-27-1800; *New-York Gazette*, 1-2-1801; *The Bee* (New London), 1-7-1801; *New Brunswick Advertiser*, 1-8-1801. But by then Burr had already begun to backtrack, and when the ballots were unsealed and Burr did indeed find himself in a tie with Jefferson, he pointedly refused to publicly or privately renounce his claim to be chosen over Jefferson, despite being encouraged to do so. Edward J. Larson, *A Magnificent Catastrophe: The Tumultuous Election of 1800, America's First Presidential Campaign* (2007), 246–47, 260–61; Gordon S. Wood, *Empire of Liberty: A History of the Early Republic, 1789–1815* (2009).

11. TJ to JM, Dec. 17, 1796.

12. TJ to James Monroe, Feb. 15, 1801.

13. *Annals*, 10:1010 (Feb. 9, 1801).

14. Ibid., 1023–28 (Feb. 11–16).

15. Beveridge, *Life of John Marshall*, 2:557; George L. Haskins and Herbert A. Johnson, *Foundations of Power: John Marshall, 1801–15* (1981), 82. Trivia buffs may wonder who processed Marshall's commission as chief justice—a task that would ordinarily have been performed by the secretary of state, John Marshall! Adams gave this pleasant duty to Treasury Secretary Samuel Dexter, authorizing him in this special case to act as secretary of state—yet another illustration of the propriety of multiple officeholding and *ex officio* designations within the executive branch itself. See JA to Samuel Dexter, Jan. 31, 1801.

16. *Annals*, 10:1028 (Feb. 17, 1801).

17. Thomas Jefferson, Notes on Aaron Burr, April 15, 1806 (Anas) ("Certain I am that neither [Smith], nor any other republican ever uttered the most distant hint to me about submitting to any conditions or giving any assurances to any body"), NAFO; Joanne B. Freeman, *Affairs of Honor: National Politics in the New Republic* (2001), 250–53; Wood, *Empire of Liberty*, 285.

18. TJ to John Dickinson, Dec. 19, 1801. See also TJ to Thomas Mann Randolph, Jan. 9, 1802 (repeating the argument that the lame-duck Congress had engaged in "a fraudulent use of the constitution"); TJ to Joseph H. Nicholson, May 13, 1803 ("The midnight appointments . . . were a mere fraud not suffered to go into effect").

19. Act of March 8, 1802, 2 Stat. 132.

20. According to Hamilton, this was Marshall's view. Charles Warren, *The Supreme Court in the United States*, rev. ed. (1926), 1:224–25n1.

21. Joseph Story, *Commentaries on the Constitution of the United States* (1833), 3:494–95 (section 1627). As had Marshall, Story conceded Congress's power to rearrange judicial duties but denied that Congress could repeal judicial offices or refuse judicial pay. Ibid., 495n2.

22. The *Stuart* case did not involve a direct lawsuit by the ousted Article III judges to receive the life pay to which they were constitutionally entitled. But it did involve other aspects of the repeal law of 1802—in particular, the restoration of circuit-riding. An aggressive Court could have used *Stuart* as a vehicle to treat the entire repeal law as one nonseverable package, and thus to opine on the ouster and pay issues alongside the circuit-riding issues.

23. TJ to the House of Representatives, Feb. 3, 1803; Beveridge, *Life of John Marshall*, 3:111–12; Haskins and Johnson, *Foundations of Power*, 185 & n16; Warren, *Supreme Court*, 1:228–30; Charles Grove Haines, *The Role of the Supreme Court in American Government and Politics, 1789–1835* (1944), 260–65; Wood, *Empire of Liberty*, 422–23.

24. TJ to William Short, Jan. 3, 1793. For Jefferson's broadly similar thoughts about Shays' Rebellion, see TJ to AA, Feb. 22, 1787; TJ to William Stevens Smith, Nov. 13, 1787.

25. In a letter to Benjamin Rush, Jefferson on Dec. 20, 1801, referred to the upcoming repeal as merely "lopping off the parasitical plant engrafted at the last session of the judiciary body." Formally, of course, there was nothing legally improper or fraudulent about the late-term Adams appointments. If, as many have claimed, James Madison was a truly great champion of constitutionalism, why did he stand mute at this pivotal moment when his political partner trampled basic constitutional principles of judicial independence? The leading biographers of Madison have simply ignored this episode and this key question. The omission is most glaring in Noah Feldman, *The Three Lives of James Madison: Genius, Partisan, President* (2017), which presses the case for Madison as America's greatest constitutionalist.

26. AH to John Jay, May 7, 1800.

27. TJ to AA, July 22, 1804. See also TJ to Spencer Roane, Sept. 6, 1819 ("Each department is truly independant of the others, and has an equal right to decide for itself what is the meaning of the constitution in the cases submitted to it's action; and especially where it is to act ultimately and without appeal. . . . A legislature had passed the sedition law. The federal courts had subjected certain individuals to it's penalties, of fine and imprisonment. On coming into office I released these individuals by the power of pardon committed to Executive discretion, which could never be more properly exercised than where citizens were suffering without the authority of law, or, which was equivalent under a law unauthorised by the

constitution, & therefore null. . . . These are examples of my position that each of the three departments has equally the right to decide for itself what is it's duty under the constitution, without any regard to what the others may have decided for themselves under a similar question.").

28. See generally Akhil Reed Amar, "*Marbury*, Section 13, and the Original Jurisdiction of the Supreme Court," *University of Chicago Law Review* 56 (1989): 443, 463–78.

29. Ibid.

30. Ibid., 453–63.

31. Warren, *Supreme Court*, 1:215–17, 224–25.

32. On "twistifications," see TJ to JM, May 25, 1810. Elsewhere in this letter, Jefferson railed against "the rancorous hatred which Marshall bears to the government of his country, & from the cunning & sophistry within which he is able to enshroud himself." The following day, Jefferson vented to John Tyler, accusing Marshall of engaging in a "prostitution of law to party passions"—a cynical game in which "the law is nothing more than an ambiguous text to be explained by his sophistry into any meaning which may subserve his personal malices." On Jefferson's hilarious take on "conversing with Marshall," see Warren, *Supreme Court*, 1:182n1.

33. Years and even decades later, this aspect of *Marbury* still rankled Jefferson. See TJ to George Hay, June 2, 1807; TJ to William Johnson, June 12, 1823.

34. TJ to Benjamin Rush, Jan. 16, 1811.

35. See, e.g., *Annals*, 13:157 (Jackson, Dec. 2, 1803), 704–5, 722–23 (Gregg, Campbell, Dec. 8, 1803).

36. Until 1820, Maine was part of Massachusetts; Vermont formally won independence from New York in the early 1790s.

37. For a detailed list of newspapers, see *AW*. For more on theme, see generally Garry Wills, *"Negro President": Jefferson and the Slave Power* (2003).

38. For a detailed list of the newspapers, see *AW*.

39. *Annals*, 11:1290 (Dana, May 1, 1802), 13:536–38 (Hastings and Thatcher, Oct. 28, 1803).

40. Ibid., 155 (Dec. 2, 1803). For an extended version of Plumer's speech, taken from his own papers, see William Plumer, *William Plumer's Memorandum of Proceedings in the United States Senate, 1803–1807*, ed. Everett S. Brown (1923), 46–73. See especially ibid., 67: "Why should the four states of Maryland, Virginia, North & South Carolina be entitled for their slaves to more than thirteen Electors & Representatives, while all the wealth of New England does not give them a single vote, even for the choice of one of those officers?"

41. Alan P. Grimes, *Democracy and the Amendments to the Constitution* (1978; reprint, 1987), 25.

42. The language and analysis here borrow from Akhil Reed Amar, *America's Constitution: A Biography* (2005), 346–47.

43. John's wife, Sarah Livingston Jay, was the chancellor's second cousin. On Livingston's ambitions and resentments, see Ron Chernow, *Alexander Hamilton* (2004), 285–88; Richard Brookhiser, *James Madison* (2011), 99; Wood, *Empire of Liberty*, 109.

44. TJ to Robert R. Livingston, April 18, 1802.

45. See generally Edmund S. Morgan, *The Meaning of Independence* (1976), 46–52; Edmund S. Morgan, *The Genius of George Washington* (1980), 14–25.

46. Cf. Jane Austen, *Pride and Prejudice* (1813) ("It is a truth universally acknowledged, that a single man in possession of a good fortune, must be in want of a wife").

47. TJ to James Monroe, Aug. 9, 1788; TJ to JM, May 19, 1793.

48. "Whatever power, other than ourselves, holds the country East of the Mississippi becomes our natural enemy." TJ to Pierre Samuel du Pont de Nemours, Feb. 1, 1803.

49. Malone, *Jefferson the President*, 251–253; Wood, *Empire of Liberty*, 537.

50. Malone, *Jefferson the President*, 240.

51. For a crisp summary with helpful references to the primary texts, see Eberhard P. Deutsch, "The Constitutional Controversy over the Louisiana Purchase," *American Bar Association Journal* 53 (Jan. 1967): 50.

52. TJ to John Breckinridge, Aug. 12, 1803. For similar views, see Jefferson's letters to John Dickinson and Thomas Paine on Aug. 9 and 10, respectively.

53. See Robert R. Livingston to TJ, June 2, 1803 (received Aug. 17); Robert R. Livingston to JM, June 3, 1803 (received Aug. 22); Robert R. Livingston and James Monroe to JM, June 7, 1803 (received Aug. 14). See also TJ to Thomas Paine, Aug. 18, 1803; TJ to Wilson Cary Nicholas, Sept. 7, 1803.

54. TJ to Nicholas, Sept. 7, 1803.

55. Ibid.

56. For classic contrasting treatments of this Jeffersonian hairpin turn, compare Henry Adams, *History of the United States of America During the First Administration of Thomas Jefferson* (1909), 2:78–134, esp. at 90–92, with Malone, *Jefferson the President*, 318–19. My stance is closer to Adams's, but Adams (and Malone, for that matter) lacked sufficient legal training, legal skill, and legal judgment to properly analyze the underlying constitutional issues. This left Adams with attitude, and lots of it. I myself plead guilty to attitude, but I aim here to offer a superior legal analysis that supports and justifies the attitude. Adams repeatedly conflated at least three distinct sets of issues, and garbled each set: the outer limits of the treaty power (Which treaties cannot be achieved absent amendment?—the Louisiana puzzle); the self-execution conundrum (Which treaties

require statutory support, and under what circumstances may the House refuse such support?—a set of issues raised by certain aspects of the Jay Treaty); and 1798 Sedition Act issues (implicating the propriety of a federal common law of crimes and the scope and nature of citizen speech rights above and beyond Tenth Amendment issues). On self-execution, see Akhil Reed Amar, *America's Constitution: A Biography* (2005), 302–7.

57. TJ to Nicholas, Sept. 7, 1803.

58. *Farrand's Records*, 2:147, 173 (Committee of Details drafts IV and IX).

59. "Answers to Questions Propounded by the President of the United States to the Secretary of the Treasury," Sept. 15, 1790, NAFO (emphasis deleted).

60. *Sen. Exec. J*, 1:450 (treaty vote, 24–7, Oct. 20); *Annals*, 13:26 (Senate territorial governance vote, 26–6, Oct. 26); ibid., 546 (House territorial governance vote, 89–23, Oct. 28); ibid., 488 (House appropriation vote, 90–25, Oct. 25); ibid., 73 (Senate appropriation vote, 26–5, Nov. 3, 1803); Deutsch, "Constitutional Controversy," 56.

61. Wood, *Empire of Liberty*, 371.

62. *American Insurance Company v. 356 Bales of Cotton*, 26 U.S. (1 Pet.) 511, 542 (1828).

63. Cf. Don E. Fehrenbacher, *The Dred Scott Case* (1978), 96 (finding it "incredible" that America failed in 1804 to seriously consider extending the Northwest Ordinance to northern Louisiana lands).

64. See, e.g., TJ to JM, Aug. 23, 1799 (suggesting that Virginia and Kentucky should declare themselves "determined, were we to be disappointed in [appeals to sister states and federal authorities], to sever ourselves from that union we so much value, rather than give up the rights of self government which we have reserved, & in which alone we see liberty, safety, & happiness").

65. TJ to Breckinridge, Aug. 12, 1803; TJ to Joseph Priestley, Jan. 29, 1804.

CHAPTER ELEVEN: MARSHALL-STORY

1. Stanley Elkins and Eric McKitrick, *The Age of Federalism* (1993), 224, 231–34, 263–70. For a valiant effort to rehabilitate Madison, see Gordon S. Wood, *Revolutionary Characters: What Made the Founders Different* (2006), 141–72. Wood denies that there is an enormous "James Madison Problem," but he is too gentle. In dealing with Madison's multiple flip-flops, Wood tends to boost the level of generality, to downplay Madison's double flips (going from a 1780s nationalist to a 1790s states' rightist and then back to a nationalist in the 1800s), and to be insufficiently skeptical of Madison's own self-serving rationalizations. Also, although Wood's account does not ignore slavery, my narrative places more emphasis on the corrupting influence of slavery on both Madison and Jefferson.

2. Richard Brookhiser, *James Madison* (2011).

3. See, e.g., Noah Feldman, *The Three Lives of James Madison: Genius, Partisan, President* (2017), esp. at xii, xiv, 337–409, 626–27. Feldman's depiction of Hamilton as an American Rasputin and his portrayal of Washington as a mere dupe of Hamilton are unpersuasive. More generally, Feldman overstates Madison's constitutional contributions and understates his recurrent duplicity, his myriad and large lapses of constitutional and political judgment, and his inferior policy-analytic competence, compared to Hamilton, in many key areas of statecraft. For similarly imbalanced—conclusory and misleading—attacks on Hamilton in the service of bolstering Madison, see Lynne Cheney, *James Madison: A Life Reconsidered* (2014), 257 ("many times worse" than Randolph), 266 (a "threat to the Republic" circa 1796), 279 ("stark mad," credulously quoting and implicitly seconding Adams), 289 ("deranged").

4. *Annals*, 1:790 (Aug. 18, 1789). See also Fergus M. Bordewich, *The First Congress: How James Madison, George Washington, and a Group of Extraordinary Men Invented the Government* (2016), 129–30.

5. Emphasis added.

6. *Annals*, 1:1949 (Feb. 2, 1791).

7. For a detailed list, see *AW*.

8. John Marshall, *John Marshall's Defense of* McCulloch v. Maryland, ed. Gerald Gunther (1969).

9. George L. Haskins and Herbert A. Johnson, *Foundations of Power: John Marshall, 1801–15* (1981), 382.

10. Ibid., 652.

11. William Johnson to TJ, Dec. 10, 1822 ("Our Chief Justice in the Supreme Court deliver[s] all the Opinions in Cases in which he sat, even, in some Instances when contrary to his own Judgment & vote").

12. See supra pp. 494–95; Akhil Reed Amar, *America's Constitution: A Biography* (2005), 60–63; Akhil Reed Amar, *America's Unwritten Constitution: The Precedents and Principles We Live By* (2016), 426–32.

13. As with other leading South Carolinians, Johnson was confused and inconsistent. Despite his use of the word "expressly," twice, in his mistaken sentence, his opinion went on to repeatedly acknowledge the permissibility of "implied" federal powers in certain situations. The word "implied" in fact appeared four times in an opinion of fewer than eight hundred words.

14. Johnson purported to offer "the opinion of the *majority* of this Court" (emphasis added).

15. See Akhil Reed Amar, *The Bill of Rights: Creation and Reconstruction* (1998).

16. Ibid., 22–23; see also supra p. 316.

17. TJ to William Short, June 12, 1807.

18. Ibid.

19. Amar, *America's Constitution*, 316, 594n1.

20. Joseph Story to Sarah Wetmore Story, March 5, 1812, reprinted in Joseph Story, *Life and Letters of Joseph Story*, ed. William W. Story (1851), 1:217.

21. This tally includes Marshall himself among the eleven. A sixth pre-Marshall justice left the Court early on Marshall's watch.

22. For a frank account of the strategic disadvantage of the newcomer in this situation, see William Johnson to TJ, Dec. 10, 1822.

23. William Johnson was the hardest nut to crack (ibid.). Johnson hailed from South Carolina, which produced many of America's fiercest states' rightists.

24. See supra p. 15.

25. See Ralph Lerner, "The Supreme Court as Republican Schoolmasters," *Supreme Court Review* (1967): 127; Gordon S. Wood, *Empire of Liberty: A History of the Early Republic, 1789–1815* (2009), 412–13.

26. US Congress, *Journal of the House of Representatives of the United States*, 8th Cong., 2nd sess., December 4, 1804, 5:33 (Article VIII).

27. *Annals*, 14:674–75 (Senate Trial Appendix).

28. Wood, *Empire of Liberty*, 424, 452–53.

29. Charles Warren, *The Supreme Court in United States History*, rev. ed. (1926), 1:288, 454–55.

30. Act of March 3, 1817, 3 Stat. 376. On Story's prodding, see G. Edward White, *The Marshall Court and Cultural Change, 1815–35* (1988), 387–89. On Marshall's support, see Warren, *Supreme Court*, 1:455n1.

31. Story, *Life and Letters*, 1:2–4, 12.

32. Two earlier efforts pale in comparison—St. George Tucker's 1803 edition of Blackstone's *Commentaries* and a treatise by William Rawle published in 1825 and revised in 1829, *A View of the Constitution of the United States*.

33. Samuel Eliot Morison, ed., *Life of Harrison Gray Otis* (1913), 1:122–23 (Letter of Dec. 27, 1818). On some of this letter's interesting wrinkles, see *AW*.

34. TJ to Augustus Rodney, Sept. 25, 1810; TJ to Albert Gallatin, Sept. 27, 1810; Warren, *Supreme Court*, 1:400–402.

35. TJ to JM, Oct. 15, 1810.

36. Ibid.

37. *Columbian Centinel*, 2-13-1811. See generally Warren, *Supreme Court*, 1:410–13.

38. On Louisiana, see John Quincy Adams, *Writings of John Quincy Adams*, ed. Worthington Chauncy Ford (1914), 3:19–22; *Annals*, 13:67 (Nov. 3, 1803); Dumas Malone, *Jefferson the President: First Term, 1801–1805* (1970), 330–32; Henry Adams, *History of the United States of America During the First Administration of Thomas Jefferson* (1909), 2:111. On federal common law of crimes, see John Quincy

Adams, *Memoirs of John Quincy Adams*, ed. Charles Francis Adams (1875), 5:213–14 (Diary entry of Dec. 18, 1820).

39. See, e.g., Michael J. Klarman, "How Great Were the 'Great' Marshall Court Decisions?," *Virginia Law Review* 87 (2001): 1111.

40. In early 1815, Madison vetoed an early version of the bank bill, but he did so purely on policy grounds concerning certain specifics in the bill. His Jan. 30 veto message declared that general constitutional objections to the bank were now "precluded . . . by repeated recognitions, under varied circumstances, of the validity of such an Institution, in acts of the Legislative, Executive, and Judicial branches of the Government, accompanied by indications, in different modes, of a concurrence of the general will of the nation." NAFO.

41. On Madison's annoyance, see JM to Spencer Roane, Sept. 2, 1819.

42. In a letter to an unknown correspondent in December 1834, James Madison elaborated some of the reasons why Supreme Court opinions were especially worthy of respect. True, Madison was a classic "departmentalist." In *Federalist* No. 49, he had opined that "the several departments being perfectly co-ordinate by the terms of their common commission, none of them, it is evident, can pretend to an exclusive or superior right of settling the boundaries between their respective powers." Jefferson and Jackson would later say similar things, and in 1834 Madison continued to stand his departmentalist ground: "As the Legislative, Executive & Judicial Departments of the U.S. are co-ordinate, and each equally bound to support the Constitution, it follows that each must in the exercise of its functions, be guided by the text of the Constitution according to its own interpretation of it; and consequently, that in the event of irreconcileable interpretations, the prevalence of the one or the other Departmt. must depend on the nature of the case, as receiving its final decision from the one or the other, and passing from that decision into effect, without involving the functions of any other." But old Madison went on to add that the Supreme Court generally warranted "the public deference to & confidence, in the Judgments of the Body" as "the surest Expositor of the Constitution," thanks to "the gravity and deliberations of their proceedings, and by the advantage their plurality gives them over the unity of the Executive Dept. and their fewness over the multitudinous composition of the Legisl: Departmt."

43. Gerald T. Dunne, *Joseph Story and the Rise of the Supreme Court* (1971), 81, 151.

44. Story, *Life and Letters*, 1:200–201.

45. Ibid., 279; Warren, *Supreme Court*, 1:416n1.

46. Elkins and McKitrick, *The Age of Federalism*, 531; Wood, *Revolutionary Characters*, 176.

47. In a candid conversation about judicial appointments, Adams told Benjamin Rush, "I am not obliged to vote for a man because he voted for me." Rather,

a candidate's "Services[,] Hazards, Abilities and Popularity" were the key considerations for Adams. JA to Rush, May 17, 1789.

48. Story, *Life and Letters*, 1:60–61.

49. Ibid., 276; ibid., 2:49 (letter of Jan. 22, 1831, to Professor George Ticknor).

50. Warren, *Supreme Court*, 1:443–44.

51. Story, *Life and Letters*, 2:49 (letter to Ticknor).

52. The details are presented in Amar, *America's Constitution*, 579n50.

53. *Cohens v. Virginia*, 19 U.S. (6 Wheat.) 264, 378 (1821); *Osborn v. Bank*, 22 U.S. (9 Wheat.) 738, 819–22 (1824); *American Insurance Company v. Canter*, 26 U.S. (1 Pet.) 511, 545 (1828).

54. H. Rep. 43, 21st Cong., 2nd sess., 11–20 (Jan. 24, 1831) (also mentioning in passing *Martin*'s prequel case, *Hunter v. Fairfax*); *Register of Debates (Reg Deb* hereinafter), 21st Cong., 2nd sess., 542 (Jan. 29, 1831).

55. Joseph Story, *Commentaries on the Constitution of the United States* (1833), 3:572–73 & n2, sec. 1696.

56. James H. Hutson, "The Creation of the Constitution: The Integrity of the Documentary Record," *Texas Law Review* 65 (1986): 1, 13–19. In 1832, Elliot published a collection titled *The Virginia and Kentucky Resolutions of 1798 and '99 with Jefferson's Original Draught Thereof. Also, Madison's Report, Calhoun's Address, Resolutions of the Several States in Relation to State Rights. With Other Documents in Support of the Jeffersonian Doctrines of '98*. For more on Elliot's connections to Calhoun and states' rights extremism, see H. Jefferson Powell, "The Principles of '98: An Essay in Historical Retrieval," *Virginia Law Review* 80 (1994): 689.

CHAPTER TWELVE: JACKSON

1. America's population was roughly seventeen million, as was Britain's (not counting Ireland).

2. True, Adams lost his bid for reelection by a close vote; Jefferson won thanks in no small part to the infamous Three-Fifths Clause and to clever New York City electioneering by Aaron Burr. But most incumbent presidents in the republic's early years won reelection resoundingly or at least comfortably. Had Adams governed sensibly, his reelection should have been a shoo-in. Instead, the Sedition Act was a political albatross around his neck and around the necks of Federalists everywhere, who suffered a sweeping defeat in House and Senate elections in 1800.

3. On Monroe's diplomatic gaffes and blunders, bordering on incompetence and insubordination as minister to France in the Washington administration and culminating in his unceremonious recall, see Stanley Elkins and Eric McKitrick, *The Age of Federalism* (1993), 498–513.

4. See ibid., 515, 533.

5. Gordon S. Wood, *Empire of Liberty: A History of the Early Republic, 1789–1815* (2009), 629–30, 659.

6. Don E. Ferhrenbacher, *Constitutions and Constitutionalism in the Slaveholding South* (1989), 54.

7. TJ to John Holmes, April 22, 1820 (promoting "diffusion"); JM to Robert Walsh, Nov. 27, 1819 (implausibly claiming that the Territories Clause was ambiguous—"ductile"; casting doubt on whether a free-soil law was "really needful or necessary"; and distinguishing away the Northwest Ordinance ban as pre-constitutional—in fact, Congress under the Constitution expressly reauthorized the Ordinance's free-soil rules while tweaking other provisions to conform to the new Constitution); JM to James Monroe, Feb. 23, 1820 (asserting that a free-soil territorial law was not "within the true scope of the constitution," and further claiming, in the self-serving and implausible diffusionist tradition, that "an uncontrouled dispersion of the slaves, now within the U.S., was not only best for the nation, but most favorable for the slaves also"). See generally Akhil Reed Amar, *America's Constitution: A Biography* (2005), 584–85n34.

8. Madison's Ohio-Missouri U-turn goes entirely unmentioned in Noah Feldman, *The Three Lives of James Madison: Genius, Partisan, President* (2017). Jack N. Rakove, *James Madison and the Creation of the American Republic*, 2nd ed. (2002), 211–13, briefly touches on the Missouri question but does not carefully juxtapose Madison's 1819–1820 position with his earlier stance on the Northwest Ordinance. Nor does Rakove even mention Madison's lame efforts to construe away the sweeping federal free-soil power conferred by the Constitution's Article IV Territories Clause. (For a pointed corrective, see Amar, *America's Constitution*, 264–66, 584–85n34.) Lynne Cheney, *James Madison: A Life Reconsidered* (2014), 431–33, also disappoints on the momentous Missouri issue. In her detailed and at times delightful book, she touts Madison as a great constitutionalist and statesman. Yet she devotes more careful attention to Dolley Madison's breasts than to slavery in America's West—the issue that would eventually trigger the Civil War, thanks largely to the political party that Madison himself cofounded. On the aforementioned bosom, see ibid., 248, 314, 322–23, 354–55, 358.

9. *Elliot's Debates*, 2:452 (Dec. 3, 1787).

10. Don E. Fehrenbacher, *The Dred Scott Case: Its Significance in American Law and Politics* (1978), 109.

11. Abraham Lincoln, Speech of July 10, 1858 (Chicago).

12. Wood, *Empire of Liberty*, 523.

13. Jackson himself in 1824 claimed the state as his birthplace. Some scholars have suggested that perhaps he was born on the North Carolina side of the border, but found it politically convenient to claim South Carolina as his native land.

Or perhaps he was mistaken. Records back then were murky and land surveys imperfect.

14. See JM to Joseph C. Cabell, Sept. 18, 1828.

15. South Carolina Ordinance to Nullify Certain Acts of the Congress, Nov. 24, 1832.

16. Act of March 2, 1833, 4 Stat. 632.

17. *Hunter v. Martin*, 18 Va. 1, 12 (1816) ("The Courts of the United States, therefore, belonging to one sovereignty, cannot be appellate Courts in relation to the State Courts, which belong to a different sovereignty—and of course, their commands or instructions impose no obligation").

18. TJ to Spencer Roane, Oct. 12, 1815.

19. Quoted supra p. 577.

20. See JM to Joseph C. Cabell, Sept. 16, 1831, quoted supra p. 667 (linking nullification and section 25 issue).

21. See, e.g., *Reg Deb*, 23rd Cong., 1st sess., 834–36 (March 7, 1834, statements and proposed resolutions of Sen. Henry Clay). On today's unanimity on this issue, see Akhil Reed Amar, *America's Unwritten Constitution: The Precedents and Principles We Live By* (2012), 568–69n18, 584n48; *Free Enterprise Fund v. Public Company Accounting Oversight Board*, 561 U.S. 477 (2010) (citing the "landmark case" of *Myers* early and often in both majority and dissenting opinions); ibid., 494n3 (opinion of the Court, per Chief Justice John Roberts, declaring that any Senate veto on presidential removal is today "universally regarded" as unconstitutional); *Morrison v. Olson*, 487 U.S. 654, 685–86 (1988) ("Congress' attempt to involve itself in the removal of an executive official [is] sufficient grounds to render [a] statute invalid").

22. *Reg Deb*, 23rd Cong., 1st sess., 1187 (March 28, 1834).

23. Protest Message of April 15.

24. See *Reg Deb*, 24th Cong., 2nd sess., 504–5 (Jan. 16, 1837).

25. Robert V. Remeni, *Henry Clay: Statesman for the Union* (1991) 1n1.

26. Veto Message of July 10, 1832.

27. Ibid. (emphasis added).

28. See supra pp. 459, 774n27.

29. Emphasis added. For more elaboration on Jackson's key distinction between a president's role as legislator/vetoer (hence my added emphasis) and his role as a strictly executive officer, see Charles Warren, *The Supreme Court in United States History*, rev. ed. (1926), 1:762–64.

30. *Annals*, 4:934 (Nov. 27, 1794).

31. Akhil Reed Amar, *The Bill of Rights: Creation and Reconstruction* (1998), 238. Cf. Ephesians 6:5, Colossians 3:22. The lawyer who won Gruber's acquittal was none other than Roger Taney.

32. *State v. Read*, 6 La. Ann. 227 (1851) (quoting statute of March 16, 1830).

33. William Wiecek, *The Sources of Antislavery Constitutionalism in America, 1760–1848* (1977), 132 & n18.

34. Seventh Annual Message, December 7, 1835.

35. *Elliot's Debates*, 4:593 (Calhoun's Report, Feb. 4, 1836); S. Doc. 118, 24th Cong., 1st sess. (Feb. 4, 1836), 11 (SB 122); *Reg Deb*, 24th Cong., 1st sess., 1146 (April 12, 1836).

36. Emphasis added.

37. *CG*, 24th Cong., 1st sess., 453 App. (June 8, 1836).

38. Ibid., 454 App. (June 8, 1836).

39. Ibid., 455–56 App. (June 8, 1836).

40. *New York Evening-Post*, 8-9-1836.

41. Reprinted in *History of Pennsylvania Hall, Which Was Destroyed by a Mob* (1838), 11.

42. Amar, *America's Constitution*, 342.

43. Some of the leading mythmakers have been unduly generous biographers, especially of Calhoun. Other mythmakers include countless later senators in the tradition of John F. Kennedy and Robert Byrd, glorifying their chamber. JFK of course was aiming to win for himself the very prize that had eluded many of the senators he lionized in his 1956 panegyric, *Profiles in Courage*.

44. Donald S. Lutz, *A Preface to American Political Theory* (1992), 134–40.

45. TJ to JM, Aug. 28, 1789; Elkins and McKitrick, *The Age of Federalism*, 308–11.

46. *Salem Gazette*, 2-20-1838.

47. Catharine E. Beecher, *Essay on Slavery and Abolitionism* (1837).

48. On hindsight and mythmaking, see Lisa Tetrault, *The Myth of Seneca Falls: Memory and the Women's Suffrage Movement, 1848–1898* (2014).

49. Gilbert Hobbs Barnes, *The Anti-Slavery Impulse, 1810–1844* (1977), 231.

50. Wood, *Empire of Liberty*, 302; Don E. Fehrenbacher, *The Dred Scott Case: Its Significance in American Law and Politics* (1978), 62; Amar, *America's Constitution*, 393–96; Alexander Keyssar, *The Right to Vote: The Contested History of Democracy in the United States* (2000), 54–60, 87–88, 349–54.

51. See H.R. Doc. 91, 23rd Cong., 2nd sess. (1827), 10.

52. Alan Taylor, *American Revolutions: A Continental History, 1750–1804* (2016), 334. See also supra p. 763n67; Daniel Walker Howe, *What Hath God Wrought: The Transformation of America, 1815–1848* (2007), 74–76.

53. On Washington, see supra pp. 385–87. On Jefferson, see, for example, his January 7, 1802, Message to his Brothers & Friends of the Miamis, Poutewatamies

& Weeuahs, NAFO; see also TJ to Henry Dearborn, Dec. 29, 1802; TJ to William Henry Harrison, Feb. 27, 1803.

54. *Johnson v. M'Intosh*, 21 U.S. (8 Wheat.) 543, 569–70 (1823).

55. In correspondence, Adams routinely described Indians as "savages," as did Madison. For uses of this word by Boston Tea Party leaders and Benjamin Franklin, see supra pp. 79, 142–43n.* For Hamilton/Publius's usage, see *The Federalist* No. 24 ("The savage tribes on our Western frontier ought to be regarded as our natural enemies, [Britain's and Spain's] natural allies, because they have most to fear from us, and most to hope from them"). Hamilton/Publius also argued that "small garrisons on our Western frontier . . . will continue to be indispensable, if it should only be against the ravages and depredations of the Indians." Ibid. See also *The Federalist* No. 25 (Hamilton: "The territories of Britain, Spain, and of the Indian nations in our neighborhood do not border on particular States, but encircle the Union from Maine to Georgia. . . . Indian hostilities, instigated by Spain or Britain, would always be at hand.").

56. Cited in *Worcester v. Georgia*, 31 U.S. (6 Pet.) 515, 521–28 (1832).

57. See Warren, *Supreme Court*, 1:731–36 (discussing the case of George "Corn" Tassel, in which Georgia defiantly executed a Cherokee tribe member convicted of murder after the Supreme Court had accepted his case for appellate review).

58. See Joseph C. Burke, "The Cherokee Cases: A Study in Law, Politics, and Morality," *Stanford Law Review* 21 (1969): 500, 524–31; Warren, *Supreme Court*, 1:755–79.

CHAPTER THIRTEEN: ADIEUS

1. For an outstanding analysis from which I have greatly profited, see Edward J. Larson, *Franklin & Washington: The Founding Partnership* (2020).

2. *Annals*, 1:1239–40.

3. Ibid., 1240–41.

4. Ibid., 1241–46.

5. Ibid., 1241 (Burke, "unconstitutional"), 1243 (Smith, "unconstitutional").

6. Ibid., 1241–46 (Maryland's Joshua Seney, Pennsylvania's Thomas Scott, Connecticut's Roger Sherman, New York's John Laurance, Virginia's John Page, Massachusetts's Elbridge Gerry, New Jersey's Elias Boudinot).

7. *Annals*, 1:349–56 (May 13).

8. Ibid., 1242.

9. Ibid., 1246. For Madison's expressions of concern on the previous day, see ibid., 1231.

10. See JM to Edmund Randolph, March 21, 1790 ("The true policy of the Southn. members was to have let the affair proceed with as little noise as possible"); Fergus M. Bordewich, *The First Congress: How James Madison, George Washington, and a Group of Extraordinary Men Invented the Government* (2016), 205–7, 217–18; Noah Feldman, *The Three Lives of James Madison: Genius, Partisan, President* (2017), 300–302.

11. *New-York Gazette*, 3-17-1790. See also *Daily Advertiser* (New York), 3-18-1790 (Tucker, objecting to "even its [the House's] deliberations" on the report).

12. *Daily Advertiser* (New York), 3-18-1790.

13. Edmund S. Morgan, *The Meaning of Independence* (1976), 30–33; Jack N. Rakove, *Revolutionaries: A New History of the Invention of America* (2010), 118; Edward J. Larson, *The Return of George Washington: Uniting the States, 1783–1789* (2015), 36–37; Larson, *Franklin & Washington*, 248–50.

14. See, e.g., Anthony Whitting to GW, Jan. 16, 1793; GW to Whitting, Jan. 20, 1793.

15. See GW to Lund Washington, Feb. 24–26, 1779; GW to John Francis Mercer, Sept. 9, 1786.

16. GW to Lafayette, May 10, 1786; GW to Lawrence Lewis, Aug. 4, 1797.

17. JA to John Trumbull (the poet, not the artist), Nov. 18, 1805; JA to Benjamin Rush, June 23, 1807; JA, Review of James Hillhouse Propositions, April 12, 1808; JA to *Boston Patriot*, 1809.

18. JA to John Trumbull (the poet, not the artist), July 27, 1805; JA to *Boston Patriot*, 1809; cf. JA to Benjamin Rush, June 23, 1807.

19. JA to John Trumbull (the poet, not the artist), July 27, 1805; JA to Benjamin Rush, Sept. 30, 1805; JA to Benjamin Rush, Dec. 4, 1805; JA to *Boston Patriot*, 1809 (Hamilton "calumniated Burr, with a cool deliberate, insidious, persevereing malice, the parallel of which I never knew, and which finally cost him his life").

20. JA to Rush, Feb. 25, 1808. See also JA to Rush, July 25, 1808; JA to Rush, March 14, 1809; JA to TJ, Sept. 3, 1816 (similar).

21. To be sure, Henry Adams was not merely a mouthpiece for his great-grandfather; the relationship between the two Adamses—both historians and memorialists of sorts, both full of attitude—was complex, to put it mildly.

22. Stanley Elkins and Eric McKitrick, *The Age of Federalism* (1993), 93.

23. JA to *Boston Patriot*, 1809. On sexual misconduct, see JA to Benjamin Rush, Sept. 1807. On using others more generally, see John Trumbull (the poet, not the artist) to JA, Oct. 19, 1805; JA to John Trumbull (the poet, not the artist), Nov. 18, 1805.

24. Cf. JA to John Quincy Adams, December 24, 1813. See also Douglass Adair and Martin Harvey, "Was Alexander Hamilton a Christian Statesman?," *WMQ* 12 (1955): 308.

25. For the complex cultural and political background of founding-era dueling, see Joanne B. Freeman's *Affairs of Honor: National Politics in the New Republic* (2001).

26. See supra pp. 722n74, 766n7. See also JA to Oliver Wolcott Jr., Sept. 24, 1798 (probably unsent); JA to Benjamin Rush, June 23, 1807 (referring to Callender's "CoPatriot, his Brother Scotchman Alexander Hamilton"); JA to *Boston Patriot*, 1809 (suggesting that Hamilton "might have returned to Scotland" and also that Hamilton, "Born among Slaves in Nevis and educated among Oatmeal Earter's [*sic*] in Scotland, . . . had no Idea of the Character of Beef Eating Freemen"). Contra old Adams, Hamilton was never in Scotland; he was born in North America under the British Crown (as was Adams himself) and came to the mainland pre-independence.

27. AH to Edward Stevens, Nov. 11, 1769. Historians have suggested that Stevens may in fact have been Hamilton's biological half brother. Ron Chernow, *Alexander Hamilton* (2004), 27–28.

28. See generally Freeman, *Affairs of Honor*; Gordon S. Wood, *Revolutionary Characters: What Made the Founders Different* (2006), 137–38.

29. See supra p. 722n74; Chernow, *Alexander Hamilton*, 612–16; Gordon S. Wood, *Empire of Liberty: A History of the Early Republic, 1789–1815* (2009), 273–74. Cf. William Shakespeare, *King Lear*, 1.2.339–43 ("Why bastard? wherefore base? / When my dimensions are as well compact, / My mind as generous, and my shape as true, / As honest madam's issue? Why brand they us / With base? with baseness? bastardy? base, base?").

30. JA to Benjamin Rush, Sept. 1807.

31. Chernow, *Alexander Hamilton*, 665–709. For a brisker biography of Hamilton in the same appreciative spirit, see Richard Brookhiser, *Alexander Hamilton, American* (1999).

32. See generally Freeman, *Affairs of Honor*, 159–98.

33. John C. Hamilton, *History of the Republic of the United States as Traced in the Writings of Alexander Hamilton and His Contemporaries* (1865), 7:822–23; Chernow, *Alexander Hamilton*, 665–709.

34. Chernow, *Alexander Hamilton*, 697; AH to Theodore Sedgwick, July 10, 1804.

35. Chernow, *Alexander Hamilton*, 708. Chernow describes this as a literal deathbed statement. Hamilton's son, John, omits this claim, but reports that, shortly before his father's conversation with Trumbull at the lavish party on July 7, his father solemnly told a friend that "if this Union were to be broken, it would break my heart." Hamilton, *History of the Republic*, 7:822.

36. Henry S. Randall, *The Life of Thomas Jefferson* (1858), 3:544; Dumas Malone, *The Sage of Monticello* (1981), 497; David McCullough, *John Adams* (2001), 646.

37. Richard Brookhiser, *James Madison* (2011), 245; Feldman, *Three Lives*, 624.

38. See generally Douglass Adair, *Fame and the Founding Fathers: Essays by Douglass Adair*, ed. Trevor Colbourn (1974); Elkins and McKitrick, *The Age of Federalism*, 78; Wood, *Revolutionary Characters*, 43, 70, 229–30; Wood, *Empire of Liberty*, 77.

39. See supra p. 766n7.

40. JA to Benjamin Rush, Oct. 25, 1809.

41. JA to Andrew Dunlap, July 13, 1822.

42. See, e.g., JA to John Quincy Adams, Jan. 8, 1808.

43. TJ to JM, Feb. 17, 1826.

44. JM to Joseph C. Cabell, Sept. 16, 1831. See also JM to Alexander Rives, Jan. 1, 1833 ("I do not consider the proceedings of Virginia in 98–99 as countenancing the doctrine that a State may at will secede from its constitutional compact with the other States") (emphasis deleted).

45. JM to Nicholas P. Trist, Dec. 23, 1832. See also JM to Trist, Feb. 15, 1830 (rejecting the idea that either the Constitution or the Virginia Resolutions of 1798 [which he himself had drafted] allowed "the parties to the Constitution of the U.S. *individually* to annul within themselves acts of the Federal Government, or to withdraw from the Union. . . . [A key decision such as secession] must necessarily derive its authority from the whole not from the parts, from the States in some collective not individual capacity."). In this 1830 letter, Madison also touched on the geographic incongruities that would flow from partial secession—leaving behind a patchwork of loyal states that might not be contiguous with each other or viable commercially or militarily. For related geographic and geostrategic discussions in the Hamilton-Jay tradition of *The Federalist* Nos. 2–8, see JM to Charles Eaton Hayne, Aug. 27, 1832; JM to Andrew Stevenson, Feb. 10, 1833.

46. Feldman, *Three Lives*, 418–21, 430n*.

47. JM to Edward Everett, Sept. 10, 1830.

48. JM to Joseph C. Cabell, Sept. 16, 1831.

49. JM to Nicholas P. Trist, May 15, 1832.

50. JM to Nicholas P. Trist, Dec. 23, 1832. See also JM to Joseph C. Cabell, April 1, 1833.

51. Emphasis added.

52. For a recent, important, at times brilliant, but wildly overstated book that presents Madison in just this light, see Feldman, *Three Lives*. For my critiques, see supra pp. 196–206, 737–38n14, 756n58, 762–63n57, 772n76, 774n25, 778n3, 782n8. For another recent engaging but imbalanced biography in the same spirit, see Lynne Cheney, *James Madison: A Life Reconsidered* (2014), 5 (claiming that between 1787 and 1792, Madison "more than any other individual, would be responsible for creating the United States of America in the form we know it today"—no,

that would be Washington; also, Hamilton, on balance, did more than Madison did in these years to create today's United States, with its strong central government and its extraordinary military and fiscal sweep); ibid., 61 (asserting that "Madison drafted a Constitution for the nation"—no, not really; he was not the sole nor even the predominant actor at Philadelphia); ibid., 71 (asserting that Jefferson and Madison "each was probably the brightest person the other ever knew"—actually, probably not, given that they both knew Franklin and Hamilton); ibid., 180 (referring even more outlandishly to Jefferson and Madison as "the two greatest minds of the eighteenth century"—so much for Isaac Newton and countless other contenders, including Franklin; and if the two Virginians were such geniuses, why did they both die so deeply in debt?); ibid., 72 (asserting that Madison and Jefferson "both hated slavery"—well, not nearly enough, if actions in fact speak louder than words, and if the sad downward trajectory of their positions on slavery is clearly traced for the reader, which Cheney fails to do, offering instead puffery on the elder Jefferson's and the elder Madison's stance on the Missouri Compromise; ibid., 431–33). An earlier and briefer work in the same tradition as Feldman and Cheney is Jack N. Rakove, *James Madison and the Creation of the American Republic*, 2nd ed. (2002). In his thoughtful and notable book *Original Meanings: Politics and the Ideas in the Making of the Constitution* (1996), Rakove begins by declaring that "we simply cannot understand how or why the Constitution took the form it did unless we make sense of Madison." Ibid., xvi. Fair enough, but we must also make sense of Washington and Hamilton (and Wilson, for that matter), and if we must pick one of these, we must pick Washington. Only a Madison biographer of a certain sort could think otherwise. Readers seeking a more balanced treatment of Madison should start with Brookhiser, *James Madison*.

53. On Madison's revisions, see generally Mary Sarah Bilder, *Madison's Hand: Revising the Constitutional Convention* (2015); James H. Hutson, "The Creation of the Constitution: The *Integrity* of the *Documentary Record*," *Texas Law Review* 65 (1986): 1; James H. Hutson, "Riddles of the Federal Constitutional Convention," *WMQ* 44 (1987): 411; Christopher Collier, "The Historians Versus the Lawyers: James Madison, James Hutson, and the Doctrine of Original Intent," *Pennsylvania Magazine of History and Biography* 112 (1988): 137. For smoking-gun evidence of Madison's willingness to tamper with the historical record on at least one occasion—an effort that we might today term "attempted obstruction of history," see infra p. 791n14.

54. Edward Coles to JM, Oct. 8, 1832. On certain details, Coles advised Madison to deviate from Washington's last will and testament, even while following His Excellency on the biggest issue—deathbed manumission.

55. Feldman, *Three Lives*, 621, 716n28.

56. 5 Stat. 171. Congress later paid Dolley $25,000 for a second batch of papers. Cheney, *James Madison*, 457; Feldman, *Three Lives*, 623.

57. This book has not attempted to highlight the writings of Mercy Otis Warren because they did not significantly influence America's constitutional conversation when first published; nor did they generate large reverberations later. In sharp contrast, the speeches and writings of leading women in the next generation—for example, Lucretia Mott, the Grimké sisters, and Harriet Beecher Stowe—did command significant attention both in the moment and in ensuing decades.

POSTSCRIPT

1. On this crucial point—but not on others later in my story—I build on Lawrence Henry Gipson, "The American Revolution as an Aftermath of the Great War for Empire, 1754–1763," *Political Science Quarterly* 65 (1950): 86.

2. Ray Raphael comes closest and offers several insightful gems in his brisk discussion of *Paxton's Case* in *Founders: The People Who Brought You a Nation* (2009), 13–17. For an earlier account of the Revolution that also opens with Otis, see A. J. Langguth, *Patriots: The Men Who Started the American Revolution* (1988), 13–27.

3. The most comprehensive treatment of the matter is M. H. Smith, *The Writs of Assistance Case* (1978), a dense monograph filled with interesting details but not designed for a general audience. Some of the biggest points of all—young Otis's large errors, old Adams's huge misstatements, and the key background fact of the fall of Montreal (a fact later emphasized by both Hutchinson and Adams)—do not come across with clarity.

4. See Gordon S. Wood, *The Americanization of Benjamin Franklin* (2004), 10–11.

5. Arthur M. Schlesinger, "The Colonial Newspapers and the Stamp Act," *NEQ* 8 (1935): 63.

6. See supra pp. 718–20n52.

7. See generally Alan Taylor, *American Revolutions: A Continental History, 1750–1804* (2016), esp. at 6–7, 61–62.

8. See supra pp. 741–44n38.

9. See Andrew C. McLaughlin, *A Constitutional History of the United States* (1935); Catherine Drinker Bowen, *Miracle at Philadelphia: The Story of the Constitutional Convention, May to September 1787* (1966); Clinton Rossiter, *1787: The Grand Convention* (1966); Jack N. Rakove, *Original Meanings: Politics and the Ideas in the Making of the Constitution* (1996); Richard Beeman, *Plain, Honest Men: The Making of the American Constitution* (2009); Michael J. Klarman, *The Framers' Coup* (2016).

10. See Bernard Bailyn, *To Begin the World Anew: The Genius and Ambiguities of the American Founders* (2008), 100–30, esp. at 118, 121–23.

11. See supra pp. 260–65, 748–50nn39–44.

12. *JCC*, 33:549 (Sept. 29, 1787).

13. For my critique of the best neo-Beardian account, Klarman's *The Framers' Coup*, see *AW*.

14. See Mary Sarah Bilder, *Madison's Hand: Revising the Constitutional Convention* (2015). For an example of old Madison's elaborate efforts to rewrite history and cover his tracks—unsuccessfully, thanks to the outstanding detective work of modern scholars—see JM to TJ, Oct. 17, 1784. The original letter contained an unkind remark about Lafayette that old Madison later took great pains to hide by forging Jefferson's handwriting and doctoring the cipher. For details, interested readers should consult the editorial notes to this letter in both the Jefferson Papers project and the Madison Papers project, available at NAFO. If old Madison was so calculatingly and intricately dishonest in this small item, what other larger frauds and fudges that have thus far escaped detection might he have attempted elsewhere while massaging his papers over the years? Future historians should be on notice: Perhaps because of the pervasiveness of slavery in their lives, both Madison and Jefferson were accomplished liars when they needed to be and even when they did not. The potential link between personal slaveholding and personal deceptiveness will be explored in more detail in my future work. Cf. GW to Tobias Lear, April 12, 1791 (rotating slaves out of free-soil Pennsylvania in a way that would "deceive both them and the Public").

15. Elizabeth Cady Stanton, *Eighty Years and More* (1898), 83. On Mott, see Lisa Tetrault, *The Myth of Seneca Falls: Memory and the Women's Suffrage Movement, 1848–1898* (2014), 12, 16.

Index

AKHIL REED AMAR is the Sterling Professor of Law and Political Science at Yale University and the author of several books on constitutional law and history, including *America's Constitution: A Biography* and *America's Unwritten Constitution*. He lives in Woodbridge, Connecticut.